# Golf

## HISTORY & TRADITION

### 1500–1945

# Golf

## HISTORY & TRADITION

## 1500–1945

*David Stirk*

EXCELLENT PRESS
LUDLOW

First published in 1998 by Excellent Press
Palmers' House, 7 Corve Street, Ludlow
Shropshire sy8 1DB

Standard edition ISBN 1 900318 07 5
Limited edition ISBN 1 900318 08 3

British Library Cataloguing in Publication Data
A catalogue record for this book is available from the British Library

*Both the Author and the Publishers are very much indebted to Bill Waugh, the well-known golf artist, who kindly agreed to prepare four original paintings especially for this book (one of which is also used on the jacket). Bill retired from a career as a mechanical design engineer at the age of 52 in order to concentrate on painting. He has been highly successful and has produced an acclaimed series of paintings of golfing subjects in association with Severiano Ballesteros. He has also been commissioned by Robert Trent Jones to paint his favourite golf holes.*

*Bill has had a number of very successful one-man exhibitions of his paintings at the Burlington Gallery in London. In 1992 he started to produce ceramic ware of golf-related items and formed his own company; in 1993 he was commissioned by Garrards Ltd of London to produce the Ryder Cup decanter, the Open decanter and plaque, and the US Open decanter and plaque.*

*Bill has continued to develop his art in both painting and ceramics and has become highly regarded on the international golfing scene.*

Produced for the publishers by
John Taylor Book Ventures
Hatfield, Hertfordshire

Designed by Malcolm Preskett Associates

Made and printed in Great Britain by
BAS Printers Ltd, Over Wallop, Stockbridge, Hampshire

# Contents

**Acknowledgments 8**

① **The History of Early Golf 9**
Holland 11; Flanders 13; France 16
The Court Game of Paille Maille 21
Summary 21

② **Ancient Families and the Origins of Golf 23**
The Stewarts 23; The Silver Club of the Society of Golfers at St Andrews 24
The Silver Club of the Gentlemen Golfers at Edinburgh 28; The London Connection 31
Other Families of Flemish origin connected with Early Golf 32; Summary 34

③ **The Formation of Golf Clubs 35**
Early Golf Societies in Scotland and England 37; The Grail Romances 40
The Royal Blackheath Golf Club 40; The Royal Burgess Golfing Society 43
The Honourable Company of Edinburgh Golfers 44; Bruntsfield Links Golf Club 46
The Royal Aberdeen Golf Club 47; The Royal Musselburgh Golf Club 47
The Royal and Ancient Golf Club of St Andrews 47; The Effect of the 1745 Uprising 50
The Society of Golfers at St Andrews 52; Historical Connections between Golf and Archery 52
Archery at St Andrews 53

④ **Wooden Clubs and their Makers 1790–1930 57**
Forms of Wooden Clubs 57; Change in the Shape of Wooden Clubheads 58
Wood used for Clubheads 59; Golf club Shafts, 1600–1900 59
Horn 60; Lead 61; The Grip 61; The Joining of the Shaft to the Head 62
The Bulger 64; The Clubmakers 65; Types of Wooden Club 75

⑤ **Iron Clubs 1750–1910 77**
Some Notable Cleekmakers 83; Some General Comments 87

**COLOUR PLATES 89**

⑥ **Putters: The Special Clubs** 97

The Robertson Collection, Royal Sydney Golf Club 105

⑦ **The Golf Ball 1800–1910** 107

The Golf Ball 107; The Feather Ball 107; The Making of a Feather Ball 108; Value and Size of Feather Balls 110
Size of Golf Balls 110; Musselburgh as a Golf Centre 111; Life Expectancy of Feather Ballmakers 112
The Gutta Percha Golf Ball 112; The Effects of the Arrival of the Gutta Percha Golf Ball 114
The Making of Gutta Golf Balls 115

⑧ **The Golfing Scene in the 18th Century** 119

The Upkeep of Golf Links in the Eighteenth Century 120; Golf Trades 120; Caddies 121
Golfing Traditions 121; Development of Organised Golf 122; Clubhouses and Club Entertainment 123
Golf Club staffing 125; Keepers of the Green as Club servants 127; Keepers of the Green as Golfers 128
The Caddies and Professionals 130; The Club Secretary 135

**COLOUR PLATES 137**

⑨ **Notable Golfers in the 18th and 19th Centuries** 145

Some Notable Golfers in the Eighteenth Century 145
Notable Amateur Golfers of the first part of the Nineteenth Century 147
Clubhouses and Trophies 148; Silver Clubs 149; Medals 150; Trophies 152
Notable Secretaries of the second half of the Nineteenth Century 153
Some Notable Golfers in the second half of the Nineteenth Century 157
Further Developments of Golf Clubs 166
Notable Men and Families in Golf in the Nineteenth Century 169

⑩ **The Spread of Golf outside Britain** 179

The Start of Golf in the United States 179; The Start of Golf in India and the Far East 184
Golf in the British Empire in Africa 189; Australia 190; The Beginnings of Golf in New Zealand 191
The Beginnings of Golf in Europe and around the Mediterranean in the Nineteenth Century 193
The Start of Golf in the Mediterranean Region 196; The Start of Golf in Canada 197
Argentina 198; Japan 199

**COLOUR PLATES 201**

⑪ **Championships and Challenges** 209

Allan Robertson (1815–59) 210
Willie Dunn Senior (1821–78) & Jamie Dunn (1821–71), Musselburgh 211
Thomas Morris Senior 212; William Park Senior 215; The Great Foursome 216
The Championship Belt 218; The Professionals in the second half of the Nineteenth Century 219
Golf clubs and Balls at the end of the Nineteenth Century 231

## ⑫ Golf at the start of the 20th Century 233

Harry Vardon (1870–1936) 236; J.H. Taylor in the Twentieth Century 243
James Braid in the Twentieth Century 245; Alexander ('Sandy') Herd (1868–1944) 248
Edward Ray (1877–1943) 248; Jack White (1873–1949) 250; Arnaud Massy (1877–1958) 251
Men Amateurs between 1900 and 1920 251; The Open Championship 1920–30 254; The Old Guard 258
Steel Shafts 262; Changes in the Playing of Golf 263; The Amateurs (1920–32) 263
The British Golf Scene 1932–39 267; The Amateurs (1931–39) 271

## ⑬ The Ladies and their Game 273

The Ladies' Championship 277
Dress for Lady Golfers 281; The Ladies' Open Championship (continued) 284
Miss Joyce Wethered and Foursome Play 289; Origins of Ladies' Golf in other countries 291
Notable American Lady Golfers 294; The Curtis Cup 295
Lady Professionals 296

## ⑭ Getting to the Golf Course 297

The Coming of the Railways 297

## ⑮ Golf in Time of War 303

The South African War (1899–1902) 303
The First World War (1914–18) 303; Golf in the Second World War (1939–45) 310

## ⑯ Patents and Inventions 315

1. The Rubbercore Golf Ball 316
2. The Centre-Shafted Putter 317; 3. Steel-shafted Clubs 319

## ⑰ Some Comments on the Rules of Golf 323

The Stymie or Stimie 326; Golf Course Design and Upkeep 329
The Size of a Golf Hole 335

## Bibliography 340

## Index of Names 341

# Acknowledgments

Bотн the Author and the Publishers are deeply grateful to the many Publications, Publishers, Golf Clubs and individuals who have contributed to the information which has been used in compiling this book. We would like to thank the Presidents, Captains and Committees of the following Golf Clubs for, at different times, allowing access to Club Archives and Club Histories and allowing us to obtain illustrations for the book from the materials that they own, and all the Secretaries of these Clubs for their help in the research:

The Royal and Ancient Golf Club of St Andrews
The Royal Blackheath Golf Club, London
The Royal Calcutta Golf Club, Calcutta, India
The Royal Colombo Golf Club, Colombo, Sri Lanka
The Kobe Golf Club, Japan
The Royal North Devon Golf Club, Westward Ho!,
    North Devon
The Royal Perth Golf Club, Western Australia
The Royal Perth Golfing Society, Perth
Prestwick Golf Club, Prestwick, Ayrshire
The Royal Selangor Golf Club, Kuala Lumpur, Malaysia
The Royal Sydney Golf Club, Sydney, Australia
The Royal Wimbledon Golf Club, London

The Author and Publishers also gratefully acknowledge the use of the wealth of first-hand material that has been obtained from the back numbers of *Golf Monthly* and *Golf Illustrated*.

We are indebted to the Tim Smartt Collection for allowing us to reproduce the picture of Biarritz Golf course and to Mr Peter A. Harding for allowing us to reproduce the picture of the Golf Links Station from his publication *The Rye and Camber Tramway*. We thank the Manchester City Art Galleries for allowing us to reproduce the picture of Mr George Fraser and we thank Davies Clubs Westward Ho! Ltd for permission to reproduce pictures from their archives of Harry Vardon's father playing golf, Miss E. A. Neville 1900 and Golf in the Channel Islands 1905.

The portrait of John Whyte Melville is reproduced by kind permission of the Sanyo Golf Club Golf Museum, Japan, who own the original.

Cassells of London have kindly allowed us to reproduce pictures from *The Great Clubmakers* and from *Carry Your Bag, Sir?*

We are grateful to Phaidon Press of London for permission to reproduce some pictures from *Golf: The History of an Obsession*.

We are most grateful to *Golf Monthly* and its Editor, Mr Colin Callander, for permission to reproduce pictures from that magazine.

Lastly, and by no means least, we thank Mr John Taylor for his expertise, invaluable help and considerable patience in his capacity as consultant publisher and Mr Malcolm Preskett for his ingenious book design.

Every effort has been made to locate and credit copyright holders of material reproduced in this book; the Author and the Publishers apologise for any omissions.

# The History of Early Golf

For a game that is played by more people than any other sport it is remarkable that there are so few facts available concerning the origins of golf. Because so few facts exist, those enthusiasts who, in past years, were determined to weave a history of golf, used their imagination to a point where they lost touch with reality. The result has been that some delightful fairy tales, with no foundation in fact, have been repeated so often that they have become hallowed myths which many find difficult to discard.

They have not been helped by those in authority; it is interesting that, although many learned men have spent many years considering the rules of the game of golf and deciding what is, and what is not, a golf club and which balls are suitable and legal, there is not, as a preamble to the Rules of Golf, a definition of golf itself.

Because there were many games played with a stick and a ball which were not golf, one must start with an exact definition of golf, and adhere to that, so that no game that is not within that definition is considered as golf.

Golf is a game in which a stationary ball is hit with a club into a hole in the ground. Each golfer plays his, or her, own ball, or shares alternate shots with a partner and is unimpeded by the opponent(s). This is the fundamental essence of the game; of what the ball is made, what sort of club is used, the type of swing, and the size of the hole are irrelevant.

In assessing the meagre facts, prejudice must not be allowed to enter into consideration; it is of no value to start with a premise that golf started in Scotland, or Holland, and then seek to prove the case by emphasising the points that support the premise while glossing over, or ignoring, those facts which do not support it.

On this basis, it is necessary to face the fact, seldom considered, that until 1687, when Kincaid's diary mentions 'holling the ball', there is no evidence that 'golve', 'gowf' of 'goff' in Scotland involved striking the ball into a hole in the ground; the game does not come within the definition of golf and one cannot call it that. All historians agree that the terms golf, goff, gowf, golve, colf, kolf, colven, etc, all stem from the German word 'Kolbe' meaning a club. All that these names tell us is that the game was played with a club.

We know that the game was so popular in 1457 that there was a Royal Edict to forbid the playing of it, as it interfered with the practice of archery. The exact nature of the game is not known; indeed, David Hamilton, in his book *Early Aberdeen Golf*, points out that the three Acts forbidding golf of 1457, 1471, and 1491, hint that golf was then 'a confined, churchyard game possibly played at the Kirk door as a target, and early Scottish golf may have resembled "colf" more closely than has been thought'. The reader could be forgiven for believing that this was what golve, gowf or goff was all about, but this is not the case.

**Arcuanian Indian boy from South America, striking a ball. From Darwin's *The Zoology of the Voyage of HMS Beagle***

Apart from games that have names that indicate that a club was used, there are club and ball games which either have no names, or have names peculiar to their own country and language. In Charles Darwin's *The Zoology of the Voyage of HMS Beagle*, written in about 1835, there is a picture of an Arcuanian boy, in South America, hitting a ball with a curved stick. The style and method are very like a golf swing but, as one knows no more than this, calling the game golf is not justified.

In *Golf Monthly* (June 1911), Lewis Spence describes a game played by the Mayans and the Aztecs. The game was called 'tlachtli' and was played in a court, using a club quite like a golf club, and a ball of about golf-ball size. The object of the game was to strike the ball through the stone ring. The game had a religious basis and the movements of the ball were said to imitate the movements of the heavenly bodies. The same author describes another game played by the Cherokee Indians in which the ball was hit on the move and which appears to have been like a rather violent game of hockey; again, the game had a religious connotation. As we know no more than this,

these games cannot be called golf. There are also reports of a game in ancient China in which a ball was hit with a club, but there are no really accurate records. None of these games are entitled to be called golf: they serve only to show that the hitting of a ball using a club has a universal appeal, whether as a religious ceremony or as a game, and that many 'golf-like' games existed in the past.

It is known that the Romans played a game called 'paganica' in which a ball, consisting of a leather casing stuffed with feathers, was struck with a crooked stick or club. The game was played by peasants and country folk. Nothing more of it is known than this. In about 1500, Hieronymus Mercurialis wrote a treatise *De Arte Gymnastica*, in which he described a game played with a stick and ball, which had to be hit through an iron hoop. He called the game 'pila malleus', the hammer ball game, and wrote of it contemptuously, calling it 'an old man's game'. We know no more of it than this – though the phrase 'old man's game' carries overtones of some of the contemptuous descriptions of golf! That Hieronymus Mercurialis described the game at all must mean that it was a popular and well-known game at the time. Was this the game of paganica played by Roman peasants many years before? We do not know.

There is general agreement that the Romans, when they embarked on their Imperial expansion, took their stick and ball game with them and introduced it to those whom they had conquered. One of their early conquests was France, beginning in the South. When this game arrived in France it was called by the French 'paille maille'; the similar sound of paille maille and pila malleus cannot have been a coincidence and suggests that the game was paganica, or a variation of it.

In the South of France two variations developed of the game that the Romans had introduced. One was paille maille, which was played in a large court with well-defined sides and ends. The court was roughly rectangular in shape and 300–600 yards in length. The object of the game was to hit a stationary ball, using a club, from one end of the court, through a hoop or gate in the centre, to a stake at the other end. There is no evidence that the opponent was allowed to interfere with the shot in any way.

The other form of the game was called 'Jeu de mail à la chicane'. This was not played in a court but along roads or paths, or cross country, from a starting point to a 'mark', which would be a barn door, a tree, a stake, or a church door. The ball was stationary when hit and the opponents do not appear to have been allowed to interfere, in any way, with the play. This is close to golf but it is not golf, since the ball was not played into a hole in the ground. Another variation from paganica was that both games were played with a wooden ball; as we shall see later in the history of golf, feather balls were difficult to make and required much skill. Perhaps it was difficult to get balls from Rome and, rather than try to teach the locals the art of feather-ball making, the soldiers settled for playing with wooden balls. These two games travelled, with the Roman armies, across Europe to Northern France and the Low Countries. As they arrived in different countries they underwent changes according to the ideas of the local people and the dictates of the local terrain and climate. Although the descriptions of the two games makes them sound completely different, there were a number of 'in-between games'. Although a paille maille court was artificially prepared, it was not always level, often having a pronounced slope. Jeu de mail à la chicane was frequently played in towns and villages where the street served as a sort of curved paille maille court, having definite sides and walls but no central gate or hoop. The length of the court depended on the length of the street and there were plenty of doors to be used as marks.

This must have been rather like playing in a maille court – one which was not rectangular, and not level, but which had well defined edges. The game was not always played with the traditional mallet.

## Holland

THERE are few descriptions of the early game in Holland. One, however, is of great importance in defining at least one of the forms of jeu de mail played in Holland in 1297. It has been most ably described by the late Steven van Hengel in his beautifully researched book *Early Golf*, which contains the most detailed and accurately recorded facts about the Dutch form of 'colf'.

The initial game took place at the Castle of Kronenberg in 1297, close to the town of Loenen aan de Vecht. There were apparently four players on each side who struck a wooden ball in turn, the winners being those who hit the targets in the fewest number of strokes. The targets were: the kitchen door, the door of a mill, the front door of a nearby castle, and the door of a courthouse, etc. The stretch to the courthouse is described as a long highway and it is probable that the other targets also lay along roads or paths.

The game is described by van Hengel as 'colf'; as the description is clearly one of jeu de mail, then Dutch colf was jeu de mail. If this game reached Holland by 1297 (and it may have reached it before) then paille maille reached southern France long before that.

We hear no more of this form of colf, though it was probably played even if not described, but we do hear a

**Stone with a hole, as used in the wall of a Mayan 'tlachtli' court (*Golf Monthly*, June 1911)**

lot about colf played on open ground. This evidence is in the form of ordinances to prevent the playing of the game in towns and villages; clearly, playing colf in the streets was both tiresome, noisy and damaging to houses, as well as, on occasions, being downright dangerous. The town and village councils of the day introduced the severest penalties to try to stop it, but even these were not always successful and one town in particular, Haarlem, went a step further, when the Count of Holland gave the citizens of the town a course/court in perpetuity.

A map showing the course/court shows it to be roughly rectangular in shape and having well-defined edges. The court was kept mown by the archers, who also used it. The impression is of a paille maille type of game on a well-mown court with the game being played to a tree at either end. Van Hengel says that by the seventeenth century there were mail courses at The Hague, Leyden, Utrecht and Amsterdam.

Although they were supposed to be strictly for mail, and colf was forbidden, this did not work and colf was frequently played on them. The paille maille type of court was very suitable for colf, clearly showing that the two games were almost the same. This implied, however, that the longer, chicane type of mail was disappearing. The vigorous, rough game through the streets had been killed by legislation, and a tamer, quieter, and altogether more sedate and refined game had taken its place.

In the absence of written evidence about colf, there is not much more that can be said; if there were a large number of pictures, this would be a clear measure of its continuing popularity – there are, at the most, two and neither of them shows the ball being played into a hole in the ground, so there is no question of colf being converted to golf by the Dutch.

## The Ice Game

Perhaps because van Hengel was so keen to associate Dutch colf with golf, he does not, in his book, make much of the Dutch game played in the winter on the ice, and yet over 400 pictures were painted of such games between 1500 and 1746. There is a certain similarity about them, although, admittedly, there are plenty of differences in the fine detail. One point of interest in all the pictures of colf, whether on land or on ice, is that all the players played with only one club. Depicting the game of colf on dry land rather than ice would, one would think, be more attractive to the artist since there would be more variety in the settings of the game. The fact that there are so few paintings of the game on dry land and so many of the game on ice suggests that the ice game was painted because it was popular and common. Further evidence that it was popular comes from an unusual source; Gerrit de Veer wrote an account of the voyages of William Barentz to the Arctic, in 1597. On 3 April 1597 he wrote: 'The 3 of Aprill it was faire cleer weather, with a north east wind and very calme; then we made a staffe to play at colfe, thereby to stetch our jointes, which we sought by all meanes we could to doe'. Keen colfers indeed!

The Dutch canal system, when frozen in winter, would have provided a large number of ready-made frozen mail courts, all long, narrow and rectangular, with

**Club and ball as used in 'kolf' courts in Holland after 1700**

**Seventeenth-century tile from Suffolk**

well-defined edges, but, if the mail game was to be played on ice, it would have needed modification, for the following reasons:

1. The distance that a ball could be hit on ice. Browning, in his *History of Golf*, observes that, on one occasion at Wimbledon, when the pond was frozen over, a golfer hooked his drive on to it. The ball is said to have travelled 600 yards and hit the far bank at a good speed, the bank stopping it. When one sees the crowds on the ice in the Dutch paintings it is impossible to believe that anybody could have taken a full stroke without the greatest danger to others; furthermore, there are no records of any legislation to prevent the playing of the ice game, which certainly would have been the case if bystanders had complained that they had been injured by a colf ball, as happened in the colf game on land.

2. The impossibility of making a body turn, in the manner of jeu de mail, in spite of the use of special skates. In essence, the game on ice must have been in the nature of a series of long putts. The game must have required a great delicacy of touch – if the present-day professionals complain of the speed of the greens

**A modern 'kolf' court**

in some of the major tournaments they should try putting on ice!

This Dutch variation of jeu de mail, or paille maille, was a long way from jeu de mail à la chicane. A form of jeu de mail was certainly played on land and van Hengel's book reproduces 74 Dutch tiles as evidence of this. Twenty-one of the tiles show the game being played at a stake and none show play at a hole in the ground. The finding of clubheads in the wrecks of Dutch East Indiamen suggest a game played on land in the Dutch East Indies.

*Kolf*

As the chicane form of the game had given way, in Holland, to a form of paille maille played in a well-mown court, the general run of the game there suggests a much tamer and quieter game. This paved the way for the game which took over completely in the eighteenth century and which van Hengel calls 'kolf'. This was played in a small enclosed court, or yard, which had a roof, walls and a smooth floor.

In van Hengel's book there is only one illustration of a ball being holed out – and more of that anon. Kolf is

still played in Holland, in an indoor court with a very smooth floor. The balls are large and the single club is long, stiff and has a head rather like a hockey stick but covered in brass. There is a stake at each end of the court and these stakes are the targets to be hit; the game requires an extreme nicety of touch. In the 'backswing' the club is not lifted from the ground. An excellent description of it is given in van Hengel's *Early Golf*.

## Flanders

The game in Flanders was a variation on the form of jeu de mail as played in Holland. The early form of the game was called 'chole' and the same game in Northeast France was called 'soule'. In chole the ball was called a 'chouette' and in soule a 'souette'. In this game a wooden ball, stationary when hit, was played cross-country using a club of unique and unusual shape, the club-head having a flat side and a curious, spoon-shaped facet at the toe. When the game was called chole, the head was of wood.

The game in Flanders was later called 'croisse' or 'la croisse' (not to be confused with the game of lacrosse). It

A croisse swing, with hands widely separated

Left-handed player playing to the mark in croisse,
Belgium 1989

is reported that the first recorded game of croisse was in 1262. It is obvious, therefore, that chole was a game of very great antiquity and that jeu de mail, of which chole was a variation, could well have been introduced to Southern France at the time when the Romans were conquering Europe. Steven van Hengel was of the opinion that Dutch colf originated from chole, which, he accepted, was an older game.

The game was not played on any defined 'course' but was simply played cross-country to a mark, or series of marks. It was, clearly, a form of jeu de mail à la chicane and very like the game played at Kronenberg. It differed from it in that the single implement was a club and not a mallet, and that the game, apparently, did not necessarily follow roads or paths. But there was another, even greater difference; the game was played by teams and after 'Team A' had struck the ball three times toward the mark the opposing 'Team B' were entitled to strike the ball in the opposite direction, or into any difficult spot that they might choose; this stroke was known as the 'dechole'. Play was then continued, with Team A again having three shots toward the mark. Team A had a bet with Team B as to how many shots they would need to reach the mark. When the game came to be called croisse, the heads of the clubs, while retaining the same shape, were made of wrought iron.

The game was, and still is, popular in Belgium, in the vicinity of Mons, and in Northeast France. The two areas play joint tournaments together at various local sites. The author made a trip to the Mons area and, with the help of some good Belgian friends, was able to see the game being played. Introduced to keen croisse enthusiasts, all anxious to promote the idea of the game and explain the finer points to a visiting foreigner whose French is somewhat rudimentary, the author had a splendid visit and returned across the Channel with a quantity of literature on the game.

The game of croisse as witnessed by the author in 1989 was played across three large fields which were entirely in their natural state, except for a very small area where the grass had been cut and which was marked by a flag – this was the starting-point. Not only was the field untouched but cows were grazing there, apparently unmoved by the activity around them. Three white boards, about four feet high and twelve inches across, had been stuck into the ground by a single spike attached to the lower end; the first board was about 350 yards from the starting-point and the other two were at roughly the same distance from each other. The shape of the course was triangular, so that the last board was adjacent to the starting-point. The players had a wide variety of clothing, berets, sweaters, gumboots and old trousers being

**Scene at croisse: not actually as disordered as the English phrase 'pell mell' might suggest**

much in evidence. All carried one club, some two; each had a net bag of balls carried on a shoulder strap. There were probably 10 to 16 balls in each bag, most made of wood and oval in shape rather than round. They were all of different sizes, the smallest being about golf-ball size and the largest about the size of a cricket ball. The tournament was 'matchplay, knockout' and there were approximately 120 competitors. The game was played in pairs and each player played alternate shots with his partner. There were no women players. At the start of each 'hole' there was bidding, each pair nominating how many shots they would take to reach the mark; the lowest bid had the honour. The ball was struck from the starting ground using a golf swing, the only difference being that several players played with the left hand below the right (not unknown on a golf course!) and the grip was crude and two-handed, the hands being quite widely separated. The ball flew in the same trajectory as a golf shot and a good shot was about 150 yards.

The author attempted to follow a local champion in his game and, although able to do this, found that the going was difficult since, by the time the game was in full swing, there were some 60 couples playing, each, after three shots, playing the 'dechole', when the ball could be hit in any direction in order to make it difficult for the opposition to get back to the mark. The gallery was

**A left-handed croisse player drives off, his net of balls on the ground beside him**

constantly assailed with cheerful shouts of 'Garde!' 'Au derrière!' 'Prenez garde!', as balls whizzed by in all directions. It is a game better viewed from the sidelines! In all, the game was played with vigorous cheerfulness and Gallic panache and was clearly a game requiring both skill and tactical ability; the most talented players were going to win. The tournament took about two days to complete and the author gathered that on the evening in between, good food, good wine and a good time was enjoyed by all! With the form of the present game kept in mind, it is now time to return to the past.

The Flanders form of jeu de mail was quite different from the Dutch form. How did the men of Flanders come to play with clubs instead of mallets? We have no direct knowledge but there is a pointer; Nithard, writing of the year AD845, remarks that, at that time, among the Saxons and Franks, the only weapon that slaves were allowed to carry was a club. Lambert of Ardres, in Flanders, writing about the years 1091–1137 concerning the area of Guines (now part of the Pas de Calais region) observes that there were, in that area, men called 'Colverli' who carried clubs – the only weapon that they were allowed; at a later date they were released from slavery and became free men. Dr Ernest Warlop, author of *The Flemish Nobility before 1300*, to whom I am indebted for this information, suggests that colf with clubs may have originated with them, but one feels this is unlikely because playing games implies that there is leisure to do it and it seems unlikely that slaves would have had much time to disport themselves. It is more likely that the nobles of Flanders, rich landowners (with slaves), who had some leisure and would have been well aware of the clubs owned by these men, found them handier for playing jeu de mail than the original mallets.

Although van Hengel treats Holland and the Low Countries together in his account of colf, they should be separated because colf was played in Holland and croisse in Flanders.

Early legislation against the playing of colf is recorded by van Hengel in Holland, Brussels (1360), Brugge (Bruges) (1477), Antwerp (1553) and Malines. The latter are now in Belgium and were then in Flanders.

Having seen croisse played in its present form the author feels that any form of croisse played in the street would have been dangerous to passers-by and potentially damaging to houses; it is probable that the game of colf banned in the towns in Belgium/Flanders was the same sort of game that was banned in Holland. When the citizens of towns in Flanders were driven outside by punitive legislation they took to the more vigorous and combative form of jeu de maile-chole, later to become croisse. The croisse club was originally made of wood but in 1420 it

became the practice to make the head of iron; the blacksmiths of the Borinage area became famous for making the best heads. This iron-tipped club was a most fearsome weapon and it is recorded that, during a battle at Quevy in 1570, one combatant killed his adversary using a 'crosse ferrée'.

A report of a croisse tournament in 1552 at Gouberville on the left bank of the river Orne in the Cotentin Peninsula in Normandy describes the game as brutal and, occasionally, lethal. It is no accident that the dictionary definition of the English phrase 'pell-mell' is 'In disorder, promiscuously, headlong, recklessly'.

The noble knights of Flanders who, we are told, played croisse and gave prizes to be competed for, were accustomed to robust pastimes such as jousting, and played a violent and combative form of croisse.

That the game was played in 1552 in the Cotentin Peninsula in Normandy, a long way from Flanders, is due to the fact that, for reasons ably expounded by Mrs Beryl Platts in *Scottish Hazard* (Volume Two), from 1027 onwards the title of Comte de Mortain in that area of Normandy was held by a Flemish family. Not only did the Flemings play croisse in Flanders but they took the game with them when they moved to Normandy.

## France

J EU DE MAIL remained in southern France from the time that the game was introduced until the Second World War. The last remaining area in which the game was played was in the region of Montpelier. They continued to use the wooden balls and mallets – or what appears to be a form of club. Both forms – paille maille form and chicane – were played. An account of the chicane version appears in *Historical Gossip about Golf and Golfers* (Edinburgh 1863). The description is of a game played along byways and roads. The 'goals' were not very far away – about half a mile – and there was a touchstone which had to be hit at the end.

Various types of stick and ball game have been identified in Holland, Flanders and France. Each has some characteristic suggestive of golf, but none can be termed golf because none conform totally to the definition of the game which was out set at the beginning and to which we must adhere. These games may be first cousins to golf, they may be ghosts of golf to come, but they are not the real thing and cannot be recognised as the real thing.

Before leaving this attempt at deduction from relatively few facts, one must consider three pictures which offer startling and factual evidence of yet another game played in Flanders, certainly in the sixteenth century, if not before. The pictures are to be found in three Flemish

Books of Hours dated between 1500 and 1560. It was the custom to decorate the margins of religious books with secular pictures of everyday scenes and events; it follows that particular representations of such scenes and events must have been commonplace and familiar to everyone.

The first of these pictures is well known and has been reproduced many times. It shows four men playing with clubs (not mallets), apparently not interfering with one another's play, hitting a stationary ball into a hole in the ground. The picture appears in *Early Golf* – the only illustration in the book which shows a ball being hit into a hole in the ground. Yet van Hengel treats this lightly, saying that the men are playing colf, and concerns himself with the clubs and balls that they are using. The picture fulfils all the criteria that have been laid down for golf and is clear evidence that golf was played in Flanders nearly 150 years before we have evidence of the game in Scotland.

Two other pictures have been found, not so elaborate, being simple line drawings and showing only two players but, in each case, the ball is being struck into a hole in the ground without there being any interference from the opponent. One of these pictures is reproduced; the other, unfortunately is not available for reproduction. They were seen by the author in catalogues of sales of illuminated manuscripts; that these particular pages were depicted in the catalogues was pure chance and the catalogues make no mention of the startling facts that they reveal. It is very probable that further examination of the margins of illuminated manuscripts from Flanders at about this date could yield yet more pictures but three pictures must surely establish that a game which we can call golf was played in Flanders in the sixteenth century. The reader may wonder that this pictorial evidence has not been remarked on before, but research has shown that it was noted, almost one hundred years ago. Writing to the journal *Golf* on 6 July 1894, Henry J. Hillène, in one of a series of articles on Continental and British games, made a number of interesting points. The French and Latin names 'croisse' and 'cambuca' mean the same thing – an ecclesiastical staff (or, perhaps, a bishop's crozier. *Author*). Hillène noted that a Mr Andrew Lang had stated that there was nothing to show, as far as he was aware, that the early Flemish players putted at holes. Hillène then referred to the 'recent discovery' of a quaint picture in a Flemish Book of Hours of

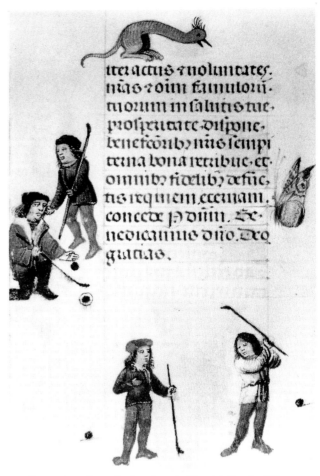

Illustrations from the border of a Flemish Book of Hours, *c.*1530. On the left, a ball is being hit into a hole in the ground; at the foot, a club is being used to hit a ball

the early sixteenth century. The picture included in the article is reproduced as a colour illustration in this book. From this picture Hillène deduces, accurately, that, in the early sixteenth century the Flemish players were:

1. Putting at holes.
2. Using one club each.
3. Using clubs similar in size and shape to golf clubs.
4. Using a ball larger than a golf ball.
5. Awaiting turns to play.
6. Using clubs with steel faces.

All these observations are accurate except, possibly, that the faces are steel, which is not easy to see. In subsequent issues of the journal there are no 'Letters to the Editor', although there are columns in the magazine for this purpose, nor is there any comment by the Editor. It seems as if the golfers of Britain were so sure that golf originated in Scotland that they chose to ignore the evidence presented to them.

Having traced variations of jeu de maille across Europe to the coasts of Holland, Flanders and France one must now consider how these games might have crossed the Channel or the North Sea to reach, ultimately, Scotland.

In a most interesting account of the history of croisse written by M. André Auquier in 1983 he quotes Robert Hervet, writing of 'Sports et Jeux de weekend' as saying that mail/crosse was taken across the Channel by William the Conqueror. Hervet makes a strong assertion of this opinion but does not offer any supporting evidence. The author has found, if not supporting factual evidence, at least strong pointers that this may be true.

One must go back in history to at least 1066 to examine the evidence; here it is important to acknowledge that what follows is largely extracted from books written by Mrs Beryl Platts, *Scottish Hazard* (Volumes One and Two).

Mrs Platts is an expert on heraldry and has written extensively on the subject. The précis that follows is but a small part of a very interesting and detailed account of the subject, as it applies to the origins of the Scottish nobility. The author must bear the blame for any inaccuracies which may occur in the extraction of information from these books in pursuing their relevance to the history of golf.

One important point concerning heraldry is that it was not solely concerned with decorative banners to identify knights in battle. Heraldic patterns and designs, especially in the Court of Charlemagne, became a means of identifying families and the complicated inter-marriages between families, so that any knowledgeable member of the noble families in Flanders could easily recognise a family and its antecedents from the arms that it bore.

A second point made by Platts is the importance, in medieval Flanders, of the maternal blood connection, the so-called *noblesse uterine* in which the blood of the mother was of greater importance than in any other society of the time.

When the Romans left Britain and Europe, these areas entered into what is popularly referred to as the Dark Ages; such civilisation as the Romans had brought to the lands that they conquered, disappeared. In this dark and bloody time one kingdom stood out as a shining beacon, a kingdom which fought off the Norse invaders, defended the Christian faith and maintained a level of discipline and culture not seen in the rest of Europe; this was the kingdom of Charlemagne. Charlemagne was born in Flanders and his Kingdom had as its capital, Aix-

la-Chapelle, in eastern Flanders, now known as Aachen, in western Germany. Charlemagne was appointed 'Defender of the Faith' by the then Pope; his capital city was a nucleus of culture and elegance but his nobles and knights were not ornaments, but efficient and excellent administrators, as well as experienced and brave soldiers. They were, in fact the most able and experienced soldiers on the Continent of Europe; the Romans respected the 'Belgae' as the most brave and tenacious fighters that they had encountered in Europe.

Charlemagne laid down certain rules and precepts for his knights and nobles; for our purposes, of great importance was the obligation to defend widows and orphans.

In order to preserve the class distinction between landed gentry and peasants there were strict rules of marriage, so that those of noble birth could only marry others of equal distinction. However, in the time of Charlemagne it was the bride's bloodline which was important – the *noblesse uterine*. The most important bloodline was that of Charlemagne himself; to be a blood relative of Charlemagne was to attain the highest rank.

In this close and well-ordered society, with its strict rules about marriage, a Norman such as William the First, Duke of Normandy, was beyond the pale. Under these circumstances he would have been ignored by Flemish society. William the First had, however, one important factor in his favour; when he conquered the Cotentin Peninsula he sacked the town of Bayeux and defeated the Count Berengar. He took the Count's daughter, Popa, forcibly, as his mistress. He was a huge and violent man of forty and she was fourteen; surprisingly, he fell in love with her and she bore him a son, whom he made his sole heir, despite the fact that, it seems, they were never married. He later married the daughter of the King of France, but Popa remained his consort and was recognised as the mother of his son and heir. This liaison was of the greatest important to William the First because Popa was a de Senlis and descended from Charlemagne's second son, Pepin de Senlis.

Although William the First may not have gained greatly from this circumstance, his son, William, although illegitimate, was accepted by the Flemish because his mother had Carolingian blood in her veins.

For other, and more complicated reasons, for an understanding of which the reader is referred to Mrs Platts' excellent books on the subject, when William the Conqueror decided, in 1066, to attack Britain, he had help and support from the highly professional and experienced soldiers of Flanders, who were his blood relatives. They included the very powerful Duc de Boulogne who was in a position to offer crucial help since he controlled the only professional navy in Europe; without the help of this navy to transport his army William could not have made a successful attack.

In William the Conqueror's army there was a numerical majority of Normans, but the east wing of the army was composed of the men of Flanders and Boulogne; although numerically inferior, they were the cream of the whole army because they were a highly disciplined professional force. Accounts of the Battle of Hastings suggest that it was the discipline and tactical skill of the knights of Flanders that had much to do with the victory.

Perhaps because William was a Norman and most of his army were Normans, contemporary accounts of the battle give most of the credit for the victory to the Normans, and certainly the Bayeux Tapestry gives considerable prominence to their part in the battle. It is when the rewards to those who helped, as shown in the Doomsday Book, are examined that the important part played by the men of Flanders is fully revealed.

The Duc de Boulogne was given Manors in Kent, Surrey, Hampshire, Somerset, Hertfordshire, Bedfordshire, Oxfordshire, Cambridgeshire, Huntingdon, Essex, Norfolk and Suffolk. Arnulf of Hesdin (brother of the Duc) was given Manors in Hampshire, Berkshire, Bedfordshire, Wiltshire, Dorset, Somerset, Middlesex, Oxfordshire. Gilbert of Ghent was given Manors in fourteen counties. The Anglo-Saxon owners of all these Manors – and many more – were dispossessed and their lands given to men from Flanders. The list is considerably greater, in all, than that given here: those interested should consult Mrs Platts' account.

Not only were the areas handed out to the Flemings of considerable extent but they were also some of the best agricultural land in Britain. Although these Manors were scattered through many parts of England, by far the greatest concentration was in the East Midlands and Lincolnshire; in these areas Flemish landowners lived close together and were situated close to navigable rivers which ran into the North Sea and thus allowed good communications with their Flanders homeland.

They seem to have settled well into their new lands and it is surely likely that these rich landowners, with plenty of slave labour and accustomed to recreations such as jeu de mail and croisse (and, perhaps, even golf?) would have lost no time in continuing these games in those parts of Britain which they now inhabited.

While there is no direct indication of these games being played shortly after the Conquest, there are records of a game being played in England in 1363 – less than 200 years after the Battle of Hastings. This game was called 'cambuca' and is mentioned in Rymer's *Foedora* in 1363, in which he states that he firmly believes that

cambuca, known to all, is the game of crooked stick or curved club or playing mallet with which a small wooden ball is propelled forward. This is a most interesting statement: first he states that the game is 'known to all' which suggests that it was generally popular and a commonplace sight in England; second, he remarks that the game can be played with a crooked stick, curved club or a mallet. At first this might suggest that he was not familiar with the game and was not sure with what implement the game was played but we have seen that the game of jeu de mail was played with a mallet or a curved club and that croisse was played with a crooked stick. It is likely therefore that he meant exactly what he said and that croisse and jeu de mail were both played and were known, in England, under the general heading cambuca; whether the game that was golf was also included under cambuca one does not know.

That the game was very popular is shown by a Royal Edict of 1363 which forbade the playing of it (and other games) for the same reasons that golfe or gowf was forbidden in 1457 by Royal Edict in Scotland, namely that it interfered with the practice of archery, a form of sport that was also necessary for the better defence of the Realm.

Further evidence of the playing of cambuca is to be found in the 'Crecy window' of Gloucester Cathedral; this window is dated 1350 and shows a man hitting a ball with a curved stick – and hitting it, moreover, in a distinctly 'golf-like' manner; as it is not known whether he is hitting it into a hole in the ground, however, it is not proper to call it golf.

Thus there was a game, involving both a club or mallet and a wooden ball, that had become so popular by 1363 that a Royal Edict was necessary to forbid the playing of it. The implication is that it was being played long before 1363 and that it could have been played soon after 1066. The general description suggests that it was a form of jeu de mail; whether that form was the original jeu de mail, croisse, or golf we do not know.

In that excellent and readable book *A History of Golf in Britain*, Sir Guy Campbell, to whom the author is indebted for the translation of Rymer's *Foedora*, points out that cambuca was not written about before 1363 and that, after that date, it disappeared from English history and the next reference is to 'Golfe' 150 years later, in the reign of Henry VIII. Campbell wonders why this should be so and what had happened to the game in that period in England.

An explanation is available but requires a further dip into the researches of the indefatigable Mrs Platts.

After his victory at Hastings, William continued to extend his conquest northward, taking over all the territories and disowning the local landowners as he moved north. When he came to the kingdom of Northumbria he called a halt. Siward, King of Northumbria, was a well-loved monarch and a great hero. He was a Dane and had all the Viking belligerence and willingness to fight. Siward had taken no part in the Battle of Hastings because he was dying of dysentery. He had two sons, one who was killed in a battle in Scotland and the other, Waltheof, who, at the time of Hastings, was only about ten years old and thus played no part in the battle. When his father died he had an unassailable right to the title of King of Northumbria. Northumbria was an extensive kingdom and included Cumbria and, at one time, Lothian, in southeast Scotland.

What William's motives were in not attacking Northumbria are not known. It may have been that such a large and united Kingdom would have provided stiff resistance to a Norman army which had, by now, very long lines of communication, or it may have been that William, always a cool and calculating man, felt that such a strong Kingdom was a useful buffer between him and the Scots and was best left alone. Whatever the reason, he made no serious attack and subsequently went out of his way to befriend the young Waltheof, entertaining him at his court in Rouen. Having made friends with him, he then married him to his niece, Judith, daughter of his sister Adèle. The marriage was a disaster and Judith eventually got rid of Waltheof by telling William (probably falsely) that Waltheof was guilty of treachery towards him. William had Waltheof removed to Winchester, where, after a hurried and secret trial, he was beheaded. This left Judith a rich widow with all Northumbria in her possession and large tracts of land in the East Midlands.

Judith, who remained a widow, had three daughters by Waltheof. The one that we are particularly concerned with is Maud, a wealthy young heiress living in the East Midlands and surrounded by relations from Flanders. She was married to Simon de Senlis, a marriage which was arranged by William and which would have met with the complete approval of her Flemish relations. After what seems to have been a happy marriage, during which Maud presented Simon de Senlis with two sons and a daughter, Maud was widowed in 1111.

Once again, the Flemings in the East Midlands were called upon to look after and succour a young widow, a task which, true to their tradition, they gladly undertook. The choice of a second husband was David, King of Cumbria.

Although not equal, in terms of lineage, to his wife, he was related to four successive kings of Scotland, and his wife's paternal grandfather had helped to put his father on the throne of Scotland. Although he was the eleventh, and youngest, son of the king, and therefore seemed an unlikely successor, he nevertheless became King of Scotland in 1126.

He and his Queen, Maud, moved to Scotland and most of Maud's Flemish relations moved with her. Platts is of the opinion that the Flemings moved north because tradition demanded that they should support her but this seems rather unlikely; after all, she was no longer a young widow, so that their protection was no longer required. The Flemish families had been given extensive areas of the best land in England, and it seems odd to have given all this up in order to move to Scotland. There were a number of reasons for the move, however; although the Flemings held extensive lands in England, they held them as a gift from William, whereas in Flanders they held lands as of right; the rest of England had been divided up between the Normans, and the Normans, in the eyes of the Flemings, were nouveau riche of no education, little taste and no coats of arms. The Flemings may have felt uncomfortable in such circumstances and were not too happy that their liege lord, the King, was, basically, a Norman who favoured his race in England. Because he had Carolingian blood in his veins they would not have considered any sort of insurrection but the tenure of their lands depended on his goodwill. For William's part, he must have seen the well-organised and competent Flemings making the most of their lands and getting richer and more influential. Perhaps he feared that with their skill at making marriages to promote their ambitions they might make themselves even more influential. It is possible that the Flemings felt that, with the goodwill of their brother-in-law in Scotland, they might make a new start in a country which was independent of William and where their lands would be secure. William, for his part, would have been happy that such a dominant minority would leave his kingdom and transfer their power to Scotland, knowing that, because their code would never allow them to take up arms against him, he need not fear their military skills. David must have welcomed his wife's relatives, as they brought with them a wealth of administrative skills, a small, but very significant, military strength (which would always support Maud's husband), considerable wealth and a cultured and sophisticated way of life.

The Flemings, once settled in Scotland, became readily integrated into the life of Scotland and became the true foundation of much of the Scottish nobility of today. Platts, using her expert knowledge of heraldry, has been able to identify the following Scottish families as having direct links with noble, landowning families in Flanders at, or before 1066: Abernethy, Auchinleck,

Anstruther, Baird, Balliol, Brodie, Bruce, Cameron, Campbell, Comyn, Crawford, Douglas, Erskine, Fraser, Graham, Hamilton, Hay, Innes, Leith, Lindsay, Leslie, Lochore, Montgomerie, Murray, Oliphant, Seton, Stewart (including the Royal House), Sinclair (originally St Clair) and Stirling.

It is interesting, but too much significance should not be read into the fact, that the first magistrate of St Andrews was from Flanders. He was appointed in 1120 by David I.

The Flemings must have taken their favourite games with them and one game would have been one of the Flemish versions of jeu de mail; we do not know which but, just as variations of jeu de mail were to be found in Europe, so variations in its form in Scotland may have occurred and it could well have been that the variation most suitable to Scotland was a game involving 'holling the ball'. It will be seen, as the tale progresses, how many of the names of Scottish families originating from Flanders appear in the early annals of the game of golf.

**A paille-maille player, an illustration copied from Lautier's *Treatise*, 1717**

This account, somewhat sketchy perhaps, offers a plausible way in which the Flemish versions of jeu de mail might have reached Scotland early in the twelfth century.

In his *Early Golf*, Steven van Hengel points out that there was a constant passage of fishing boats from Holland up the northeast coast of England and the east coast of Scotland, in search of shoals of herring. If, or when, these boats could not return because of adverse winds and put into harbour in Scotland, might have been the time when the Dutch fishermen could have gone ashore with clubs and balls and introduced the Scots to golf. This might be true but it is surely doubtful if hardworking fishermen, crowded into a small boat which was cluttered up with fishing gear, catches of fish, and food and water for the voyage, would have bothered to carry clubs and balls because of the possibility that they might be delayed by adverse winds!

Mrs Platts points out that Flanders fishing boats undertook the same voyage as the Dutch, for the same reasons; the Flemish name for such boats was 'hareng buss' and the Scottish name for a similar fishing boat was (and is) 'herring buss'; the men of Flanders may have

done the same thing but the amount of traffic to carry these clubs and balls could never have equalled the volume of traffic between Boulogne, the East Midlands and Scotland; nor could it have equalled the volume of trade that went from the Port of Leith and back, in somewhat larger boats, carrying wool from Scotland to both Holland and Flanders. The Cloth Hall at Ypres bears witness to the considerable trade between Scotland and Flanders in wool.

The Port of Leith was named after a Flemish family who owned it. Not much is known of the family except that the family held lands in the Boulogne area. The Arms of Boulogne and the Arms of Leith are identical – which cannot be coincidence.

## The Court Game of Paille Maille

THERE is evidence of the playing of the game in the Paris area in about 1700. That the game crossed the Channel to England is clear, for the largest mail court in Europe, and therefore in the world, was in London. The court was 1000 yards long. We do not know when it was made but Charles I certainly played on it in 1629. It may have been the place where the Court of Henry VIII played at golfe in 1513 – one simply does not know. The court was situated on land between St James's Palace and Trafalgar Square. In 1660 this area was made into a road, still known as Pall Mall, and a new court was made running from what is now Buckingham Palace to Trafalgar Square, the site of which is now known as the Mall. The use of the paille maille court appears to have been discontinued early in the nineteenth century.

## Summary

A Roman game, paganica, or pila malleus, was taken by the Roman armies into France. In France it was called paille maille. This game was played in a court but a variation of paille maille, called jeu de mail à la chicane was played along roads and paths to the goal of a door or tree.

When the game moved to Flanders and Holland further changes took place; jeu de mail was played in

Holland, but because of damage in the town streets, it was the subject of penal legislation. As a result, a variation of jeu de mail was played on ice in the winter and a paille maille form of the game was played in the summer. The 'ice game' is not named, but in Holland the paille maille form was called 'colf'. In the eighteenth century neither game is recorded and a form of 'mini-colf' called 'kolf' appeared. It was played in an indoor court with a roof and was part of pub life.

In Flanders, jeu de mail took a different course. Jeu de mail, as in Holland, was played in the street and did so much damage that penal legislation drove it out. Paille maille in a court never became popular and there was no 'ice' game. Instead, a cross-country form of jeu de mail developed. The early form was called chole which later became a game called croisse. This was a combative type of game in which the parties, playing with special iron-headed clubs, played the 'dechole' and, generally, tried to put their opponents into difficulties. It became so violent and dangerous that new nineteenth-century rules were made governing play, which cooled things down, while still allowing the dechole. Between 1500 and 1560 there

**Playing jeu de mail: although there is a hoop, the implement is a 'golf club' not a mallet**

are pictures from Flanders which show golf 150 years before there is evidence of golf in Scotland.

In 1066, the nobles of Flanders supported William the Conqueror in his victory at Hastings; as a result they were given very extensive lands in Britain, particularly in the East Midlands and Lincolnshire. When Maud, an important Flemish relation and a widow, was married to David I of Scotland, the Flemings moved north to Scotland and came to form a very important and influential part of the Court. Their descendants form a large portion of the noble families of Scotland.

The Flemings took their game of chole or croisse across the Channel to England and the English game of cambuca was probably the English version of croisse. When the game arrived in Scotland it was probably not golf but some variation of jeu de mail or croisse (David Hamilton points out that it was likely to be a game played in a churchyard, or some such defined space, to a barn door or a church door). When the game, first seen in Flanders in 1500–1560, became Scottish golf is not known but, in 1687, Thomas Kincaid is 'holling the ball', so it had certainly arrived by that date.

## 2

# Ancient Families and the Origins of Golf

**Antecedents of some Families and Individuals associated with
the foundation of the Society of Golfers at St Andrews, the Gentlemen Golfers
at Edinburgh and the Society of Goffers at Blackheath**

BEFORE considering the people connected with the beginning of these institutions, one should give pride of place to a family who were not associated with any one institution but who were keen and determined golfers and had a great influence on the development of golf for the best part of 250 years – the Royal House of Stewart.

## The Stewarts

ALAN Fitz Flaald was the original ancestor of the House of Stewart. He was Steward to the Count of Pol in Brittany. The Counts of Pol originated in Flanders. 'Noblesse uterine', the Flemish concept that the mother's bloodline is the important factor in the lineage of a family, gave significance to the fact that Fitz Flaald was a descendant, through his mother, of the Counts of Hesdin, an ancient and venerated Flemish family.

There is no definite evidence that he fought at Hastings nor that he was given lands in England, but he arrived in Scotland at the time of David I, who made him his Steward or Stewart; Fitz Flaald's knowledge of court procedure and of the codes of behaviour of the Flemish aristocracy was of great value to David, whose wife was a

Fleming and who was not, himself, well versed in such matters. Fitz Flaald would have been very acceptable to the Flemish nobles at court because he was of good Flemish stock on his mother's side, which was their only concern. A later Fitz Flaald, Walter, married the daughter of King Robert the Bruce, and their son, Robert, became Robert II, when David II died without issue.

When Robert became King he became the first monarch of the House of Stewart. With his Flemish lineage he might have been expected to have some knowledge of the game of golf but there is no evidence of this. Instead, the early Stuarts, as they came to be called, made pronouncements against golf, but this was only because it was decided that any sport which interfered with the practice of archery (with its military implications) must be stopped.

James I, in 1424, banned the playing of 'fute-bal' for this reason, and James II, in 1457, again banned football and added 'Gouff' for good measure. James III and James IV followed suit. In 1501, the Treaty of Glasgow was signed, giving lasting peace between Scotland and England; the practice of archery thus became less important, the ban on golf was not enforced and the Stuart King,

James IV, almost as if he had been waiting impatiently for it to end, took up golf.

The King's Lord High Treasurer, in 1503, was called upon to pay for 'clubbs' for his Master, bought of a bow-maker at Perth. Not much is heard of Royal golf after that until James VI of Scotland (James I of England) ascended the throne of both countries, in 1603. He appointed William Mayne of Edinburgh to be a Royal clubmaker. Apart from this move, we hear nothing more of James I as a golfer, but his sons were certainly golfers. Golf was now a Royal game and the court took it up with enthusiasm, not only in Scotland but, when the King went south, in England too. The only snag to the court's enthusiasm for golf was that it became expensive and beyond the means of ordinary people. When James I moved the Royal Court to Greenwich he took with him a large retinue of followers, each accompanied by many servants.

The King's eldest son, Henry Frederick, Prince of Wales, was a lively young man who was fond of sport. The French Ambassador, writing to a friend in France in a letter dated 13 October 1606, says of him: 'He plays willingly at tennis and another Scots diversion, not unlike paille maille, but this always with persons older than himself, as if he despised those of his own age.' (Drake's edition of Halstead, *History of Kent*, 'Hundreds of Blackheath', p.120). On another occasion, when playing golf, he was warned that his tutor was standing nearby and to beware of hitting him.

The letter to France has interesting implications. It tells us that, in 1606, in England, golf and pall mall coexisted, were quite alike, but were still separate entities. The Ambassador is writing to a Frenchman; he clearly expects his friend to know what mall is, but not what golf is; the former was commonplace in France in 1606 but the latter did not exist.

By the age of seventeen, the Prince of Wales was dead. James's second son, James, Duke of York (later to become James II), at the time when he was Duke of York is reputed to have played in a match in which, for a large bet, he joined with Paterson, a shoemaker in Edinburgh, to play a foursome against two English noblemen. He and Paterson won the match, and Paterson built a house in Edinburgh out of his share of the wager. It is not possible to find any documentary evidence of this match: the tale is probably apocryphal and was meant to illustrate the equality which prevailed on the golf links and the pleasurable indication that two Scotsmen could always beat two Englishmen!

Long before this time, there is evidence that, between 1513 and 1542, James IV of Scotland visited Gosford to play at golf; as also visited a number of ladies in the district, it is not possible to say whether he actually played golf at Gosford, or whether the golf was used as an excuse to visit Gosford for other purposes: perhaps both?

One of the charges against Mary Stuart, Mary Queen of Scots, at her trial in 1586, was that she played golf and paille maille 'in the fields beside Seton' a few days after the murder of Darnley, her husband. This statement has interesting implications, as in the report of the Prince of Wales playing golf in 1606. It suggests that golf and pall mall were co-existent in 1586 but were different games. This account also suggests that both golf and pall mall could be played over the same 'course'. It is likely, in fact, that at this time the only difference between the two was that, after a similar cross-country journey, one game was finished by hitting the ball into a hole in the ground and the other by hitting a stake, a tree, or a barn door.

It is recorded that Mary Queen of Scots was in the habit of playing golf with Mary Seton at Seton Palace, and that Mary Seton was the better golfer. Perhaps because Mary Stuart lost to Mary Seton, she gave her a necklace and a Holbein picture. Both picture and necklace came into the possession of the Eglinton family when a Montgomery married a Seton girl at a later date.

In 1642, Charles I was playing golf at Leith when the news of the Irish Rebellion was brought to him.

Finally, when Charles Edward Stuart, 'Bonnie Prince Charlie', fled the country into exile after his defeat at Culloden in 1745 he went to Rome and is reported to have played golf in the Borghese Gardens. It is fitting that the last of the Stuarts should have brought back to Rome a variation of a game which started there 700 years before. The Stuarts were gone but golf, which they did so much to support, continued; nevertheless, it continued as a game for the rich and it was not until 1848, when the gutta ball came into being, that ordinary folk were again able to enjoy it.

# The Silver Club of the Society of Golfers at St Andrews

IN 1754, twenty-two Gentlemen signed the petition for the right to play for the Silver Club. Those who signed the petition were:

1.  The Right Honourable Charles, Fifth Earl of Elgin and Ninth Earl of Kincardine.
2.  David, Fourth Earl of Wemyss.
3 & 4. The Honourable Thomas and The Honourable James Leslie, sons of John, the Ninth Earl of Rothes.
5.  The Honourable Francis Charteris, son of the Fourth Earl of Wemyss.
6.  Sir James Wemyss, Bart.
7.  Lieutenant-General James St Clair.

**This etching purports to show Charles I receiving news of the Irish Rebellion on the links at Leith**

8.   James Oswald of Dunnekier.
9.   Sir Robert Henderson.
10 & 11.  Professor David Young and Professor James Young, brothers and Professors at the University of St Andrews.
12.   James Lumsdain. Provost of St Andrews.
13.   David Scot.
14.   Thomas Spens.
15.   Maurice Trent of Pitcullo, whose forebears were merchants at Leith.
16.   James Wemyss.
17.   Walter Wemyss.
18.   John Bethune.
19.   Henry Bethune.
20.   James Cheape.
21.   Arthur Martin of Milston, a Fifeshire laird.
22.   Robert Douglas. Solicitor of Edinburgh.

None of these Gentlemen claimed to be members of, or to represent, any Club or Society: they were simply admirers of the ancient and healthful exercise of golf and interested in the prosperity of the ancient City of St Andrews, etc.

## The Bethune Family

John Bethune of Blebo and Henry Bethune of Clatto were signatories. A town of that name still exists in France, in the Pas de Calais area; in the eleventh century, Bethune was in the Comté de Boulogne, an independent kingdom under the total control of the Duc de Boulogne, who had close blood ties with Flanders and the heirs of Charlemagne.

The family of Bethune was Flemish and the name appears in many charters in Flanders in the eleventh and twelfth centuries. Seven Bethunes are named as advocates in Boulogne and the Bethunes were called upon to represent Eustace, the Duc de Boulogne, when he was away. They had a private army and were named as defenders and advocates of St Vaast, in Flanders, in the year 1000.

They do not seem to be specifically recorded as being at Hastings, but this may have been because they were part of the entourage of Eustace, Duc de Boulogne, who was definitely there. In Domesday, they received lands in England but the Bethunes found that owning land in England and in Flanders tended to split up the family; thus, Robert de Bethune, the father, decided to return to Flanders and continue to look after the Bethune lands there, while his son and heir remained in England. In due course, the 'English' Bethunes went north to Scotland, when Maud became David I's Queen, and a Bethune was witnessing charters in the time of

King William the Lion, in Lothian and, at about the same time, at Leuchars.

Mrs Platts is of the opinion that the first man to use Leith as a surname was a younger son of the Seton family married to a daughter of Bethune. The arms of Leith are the same as those of the Cathedral at Boulogne and the arms of the family of Leith show that they were Bethunes from the Comté de Boulogne. The Bethunes, or Beatons, were well placed when the time came, 600 years later, to support golfing societies in both St Andrews and Leith and thus to promote the continuance of a game which, with some variations, their forebears had brought from Flanders.

Fittingly, in 1770, John Bethune of Nydie was Captain of the R&A and, in 1869, Alexander Bethune of Blebo held the same appointment. It seems entirely fitting, too, that it was Admiral Bethune who, in 1864, suggested to the R&A that they should start a Museum of old golf clubs and balls in the R&A Clubhouse.

James Sharp, Archbishop of St Andrews, 1662, was the Laird of Strathtyrum, having bought the property in 1669. Strathtyrum, just across the road from the Old Course at St Andrews, has close links with golf there. Sharp was the great-great-great-great grandson of Robert Bethune. Bethune of Blebo became a member of the Royal Company of Archers in 1720. Bethune of Kilconguhair became a member in 1726. Bethune of Balfour became a member in 1730.

## The Wemyss Family

The name of Wemyss is prominent among the signatories of the petition for the Silver Club at St Andrews:

> David, Fourth Earl of Wemyss;
> Sir James Wemyss, Bart, of Logie;
> James Wemyss of Wemysshall;
> Walter Wemyss of Lothacar.

The Wemyss family name was Erskine. Mrs Platts has established, from the arms that they bear, that they were descendants of the Lords of Alost, one of the most ancient families of Flanders, so ancient, in fact, that they could trace a direct bloodline to the Emperor Charlemagne. There is a lack of information about this family at the time of the Battle of Hastings, nor does one know if they were granted lands in England.

The first Wemyss reported in Scotland was between 1165 and 1214. He is described as of Methil, a town on the north shore of the Firth of Forth, between Leven and Kirkaldy, in Fife. In 1392, the Wemyss family had a partial holding in the Barony of Leuchars.

The first earldom of Wemyss was created in 1625. The fifth Earl bought Gosford from Sir Peter Wedder-

**The Honourable Francis Charteris, later Fifth Earl of Wemyss, elected to the Royal Company of Archers 1747, Captain of the R&A 1765**

burn in 1769. The house at Gosford had been held, before the Wedderburns, by a St Clair, and Gosford has been associated with golf for over 400 years. This house became the family home of the Earls of Wemyss and has been so ever since.

The eldest sons of the family took the title Elcho. David, the fourth Earl, was Captain-General of the Royal Company of Archers and some Masonic regalia is on show at Gosford House. Wemyss, as Lord Elcho, won the Silver Arrow of the University of St Andrews, when he was a student there, in 1716.

Although the name of Wemyss does not appear as Captain of the R&A until 1854, when Erskine Wemyss held that office, another member of the family, the Honourable Francis Charteris of Amisfield, was Captain in 1765. (He was elected to the Royal Company of Archers in 1747.) In 1787 and 1788, Lord Elcho was Captain of the Honourable Company of Edinburgh Golfers.

That so many Wemyss names appear in the R&A lists is because they were originally a Fifeshire family and only became closely associated with Lothian when they went to live at Gosford.

Once at Gosford, they were very active in golf. They were much in evidence in the early days of the North Berwick Golf Club and founded the Luffness Golf Club. More will be said of this golfing family when golf in the nineteenth century is considered.

## The Leslie Family

The arms that the family bear show, according to Mrs Platts, that they were descendants of the Flemish family of Bartolf. The Bartolf arms suggest a close connection with the family of Malet, who fought well at Hastings. The Bartolfs held lands in the Ypres area and it is likely that they fought under the banner of Malet at Hastings, which is why there is no specific record of their exploits, nor evidence that they were granted lands in England under their own name.

They appear in Scotland as the Earls of Rothes, and the Honourable Thomas and James Leslie, who both signed the petition for the Silver Club at St Andrews, were the sons of the ninth Earl of Rothes. Thomas Rothes, brother to the Earl, was elected a member of the Royal Company of Archers in 1725.

In 1715, John Leslie won the Silver Arrow of the University of St Andrews as a student – he later became the Earl of Rothes. Thomas Rothes, John's brother, also won the Arrow as did James Leslie in 1720.

## Lieutenant-General James St Clair

He signed the petition in 1754. He was the nephew of William St Clair of Roslyn and succeeded to the family estates on William's death – but not to his hereditary title of Grand Master Mason of Scotland, his uncle having voluntarily given up that title. More will be said of the St Clairs later.

## The Spens Family

The Spens were an old Scottish family of Lathallan. The roll of members of the Royal Company of Archers, from the earliest times recorded, has a large number of entries bearing the name. Dr Nathaniel Spens was a very senior member of the Company and was so highly thought of that the Company had his portrait painted by Raeburn.

**David, Fourth Earl of Wemyss, Captain-General of the Royal Company of Archers 1715–1720**

His son, Dr Thomas Spens, who signed the St Andrews petition, was Treasurer to the Royal Company.

## The Bruce Family

The first signature on the petition for the St Andrews Silver Club is that of 'Rt Hon. Charles, 5th Earl of Elgin and 9th of Kincardine'; their family name was Bruce.

The Bruce family's origins lie in Flanders. Their arms, according to Mrs Platts, are derived from the House of Louvain and are connected with the De Lens family. It is possible that they did not take part in the Battle of Hastings but their name appears in charters relating to Annandale in southwest Scotland as early as 1124.

The family was represented in Scotland, in 1360, by Sir William Bruce of Clackmannan. A later Sir William Bruce, Bart, is mentioned, as of Kinross. In 1667, Bruce became first Earl of Kincardine. The seventh Earl was adviser to Charles Edward Stewart. In 1714, the Honourable Thomas Bruce, son of the Earl of Kincardine, was made a member of the Royal Company of Archers of Edinburgh and, in 1853, the Hon. Thomas Charles Bruce was made a member. At a much later date, in 1965, the Earl of Elgin and Kincardine is noted as having been Grand Master Mason of Scotland 1951–1965. Although the last fact cannot be held to have much direct bearing on the earlier Bruces, the general pattern of the membership, over many years, of the Royal Company of Archers suggests that the Bruces, as a family, were Freemasons of long standing.

Edward Bruce, Lord of Kinross, was Ambassador to England in Queen Elizabeth's reign and died in London in 1611. His son, Edward Bruce, Lord Kinloss, was a Gentleman of the Bedchamber to James I, and his brother, Thomas, was in attendance on James I for many years. He married in London in 1622 and was created Earl of Elgin in 1633.

## James Cheape of Sauchie

The origins of the Cheape family are not easy to establish because the name Cheape is a common one in Scotland and it is difficult to distinguish between the various branches of the family.

James Cheape who signed the petition in 1754 was elected a member of the Royal Company of Archers in 1725, though he is described there as of 'Rossie'. At a later date, before 1821, the Cheapes acquired Strathtyrum, a property just across the road from the Old Course. In 1821, James Cheape of Strathtyrum owned an area of the links which he had purchased from the town; Cheape was a well-known and skilful golfer.

By 1848 the town had sold the whole links to George Cheape of Strathtyrum, a prominent member of the Society of Golfers at St Andrews. A condition of this sale was that the people of the town were to be allowed to continue their prescriptive right to play on the links, free of charge.

In 1893, the Laird of Strathtyrum was persuaded by the R&A to sell them the links for £5,000. Feelings ran high in the town: it seemed that the townspeople did not mind Strathtyrum owning the links but objected strongly to the R&A owning it. There was a Parliamentary appeal. Eventually, the R&A diplomatically withdrew its offer and the town regained possession of the links.

# The antecedents of some of those who signed the petition for the Silver Club of the Gentlemen Golfers at Edinburgh in 1744

## The Dalrymple Family

David Dalrymple was an Edinburgh advocate. He was made a Member of the Royal Company of Archers in about 1700 (exact date uncertain). Later, he became a Lord of Session, when he took the title of Lord Westhall.

Sir Hew, or Hugh, Dalrymple was also an advocate in Edinburgh. He became a Lord of Session and then took the title of Lord Drummore. He was the second son of the first Baronet of North Berwick; he was elected to the Royal Company of Archers in 1710.

Sir Hugh was a notable golfer in his day and was the 'unmatched Dalrymple' of Thomas Mathison's poem 'The Goff'. It is not surprising that David Dalrymple was Captain of the Gentlemen Golfers in 1749 and that Lord Drummore was Captain in 1752.

## The Rattray Family

John Rattray was a signatory of the petition in 1744. His family, of the same name, originated in Flanders and his forebears built a great fortress or 'motte' at Rattray Head, on the coast of Aberdeenshire, near the Moray Firth, in the time of David I. The Rattrays bear the same arms as Barclay and thus must be of the same family, so it is not surprising that the Barclays also built a fortress nearby.

John Rattray was a surgeon in Edinburgh and was elected a Fellow of the College of Surgeons of Edinburgh in 1740. He was a Freemason, having been elected to the Royal Company of Archers and, what is more, having won the Silver Arrow of that company in 1735 and 1744 and the Silver Bowl in 1732, 1735, 1737, 1740, 1741, and 1742. He was also a Jacobite.

He won the first competition for the Silver Club in 1744 and won it again in 1745, and was thus the Captain of the Golf two years in a row. Following his win in 1745, he had a very frightening experience. On the night before Culloden, Rattray had taken part in the tiring march of Jacobite troops toward Nairn, the intention being to surprise the Duke of Cumberland's army while they were recovering from celebrating his birthday (sic). The attack was a fiasco. When the tired and hungry troops returned to Culloden, Rattray went on to Inverness, where, in a state of exhaustion, he threw himself on a bed and fell asleep. Even the cannonade at the Battle of Culloden did not wake him and he was, eventually, awakened by the people in the house. He hastened to the battlefield but, on the way, he met Sir John Macdonald, who told him that all was lost and advised him that, as he was Doctor to the Army, he was a non-combatant and his best plan was to surrender. He did so and, when under arrest, heard remarks by Cumberland's officers that, being Prince Charles's doctor, he would certainly be hanged. He and a friend were put into the church at Inverness which was filled with wounded prisoners, but, as their instruments had been taken from them, they were helpless and could do nothing for the wounded who were moaning in pain all around them.

A few days later, his friend, and Masonic brother, Duncan Forbes, came to Inverness. Forbes, being an anti-Jacobite, interceded with Cumberland and got them both released. Their freedom was short-lived for, ten days later, they were rearrested and taken to London where they were confined in a house until January 1747. Pressure was put on them to appear as 'evidences' against the other rebels but, as they could not be persuaded to do this, they were discharged from custody. This last part sounds somewhat unlikely; it was much more likely, knowing Cumberland's reputation, that they would have been tortured and then, as they were not 'persuaded', killed. It seems much more feasible that Forbes again interceded on their behalf and got them released.

There is no further record of Rattray winning anything; this may have been because, after his great ordeal, he had no stomach for it, but it seems more likely that Forbes advised him to lie low, partly for his own safety and partly because Rattray's participation in golf or archery competitions might cause the authorities to reconsider their ideas about the Company of Archers and about the innocent Gentlemen quietly enjoying their healthful pastime of golf.

Rattray died on 5 July 1771. As a direct result of winning the first competition for the Silver Club, Rattray has gained undying fame as the signatory to the first, official, Rules of Golf.

In Thomas Mathison's poem 'The Goff', written in 1743, he writes: 'Rattray for skill and Corse for strength renowned' . . . . In the published edition of 1743, Mathison left out the names, and one can understand why.

## William St Clair of Roslyn

The St Clairs did not sign the petition for the Silver Club but they were instrumental in winning it and one, at least, St Clair of Roslyn, was winner on several occasions and a President of the Honourable Company.

We have already come across Lieutenant-General James St Clair who signed the petition for the Silver Club at St Andrews. The origins of the Sinclairs or St Clairs are not easy to elucidate and the author has Mrs Platts, in a personal communication, to thank for making some sense of it.

The name is fairly common in France and is mainly a territorial name, that is, a name taken from a parish called after a popular saint. The St Clairs who went to Scotland came from St Clair-sur-Elle in the Cotentin peninsula and were Morvilles. A representative of this family, Hugh de Morville, was responsible, in 1140, for the founding of the Abbey of Kilwinning, a curious institution which has connections with the Knights Templars.

At the outset, the St Clairs were not a family of great significance but they became more important as they poured money into the family Chapel at Rosslyn and became Hereditary Grand Master Masons in 1424.

The St Clairs became related to the Earls of Orkney and there is evidence that Orkney was a golfer when, in 1585, his 'servitor' sent a letter from Kirkwall asking for golf balls. The St Clairs were associated with golf from an early time.

The man with whom we are concerned is William St Clair of Rosslyn, born in 1700 and Hereditary Grand Master Mason of Scotland. Sir Walter Scott, when a boy, worshipped St Clair as his hero; as a result we have a good description of him, and of his athletic prowess, from the hand of a master of the writing craft (who was, incidentally, a member of the Royal Company of Archers). He says of St Clair 'a man considerably above six feet, with dark grey locks, a form upright, but gracefully so, thin flanked and broad shouldered, built, it would seem, for the business of war, or the chase, a noble eye of chastened pride and undoubted authority, features handsome and striking in their general effect, though somewhat hard and exaggerated, when considered in detail. His complexion was hard and grizzled and we, as schoolboys, crowded to see him perform feats of strength and skill in the old Scottish games of Golf and Archery . . . .'

George Pottinger is somewhat briefer on this matter and described St Clair as having 'a melancholy, almond-shaped face . . . and an unbelievable method of addressing the ball'.

Whatever Pottinger may have thought of St Clair's method of addressing the ball, he was a great golfer. Being an athletic sort of man, it is likely that he did not concentrate on golf until he had indulged in those sports which are for the youthful. At all events, his recorded golfing triumphs all happened when he was over sixty. One has to say 'recorded' because all records from before that time have been destroyed or lost; it is possible that St Clair won many more trophies and matches in the earlier years. He won the Silver Club of the Town of Edinburgh in 1761, 1766, 1770 and 1771, and the Silver Club of the Gentlemen of St Andrews in 1764, 1766 and 1768.

St Clair's score in 1764, at St Andrews, was quite remarkable; it was the last time that the competition was played over 22 holes. The score was 121, an average of 5.5 strokes per hole and equivalent, over 18 holes, to a score of 99. In those days, with a rough, narrow links, greens that did not see a mower or a roller, clumsy clubs and feather balls, it was an outstanding feat – especially at sixty-four years of age!

An indication of how remarkable it was is shown by the fact that a score of 94, in 1767, stood as a record for 86 years, until Captain Stewart, in 1859, playing with a gutta ball and on a links which had, by now, been improved out of all recognition, returned a score of 90.

St Clair, with his imposing presence and great golfing skill, was destined for high golfing office and it comes, therefore, as no surprise that he was President of the Honourable Golfers, and Captain, in 1761. He was Captain of the Society of St Andrews Golfers in 1764, 1766 and 1768.

His prowess as an archer was no less impressive. His record, as a member of the Royal Company of Archers, shows that he won the Musselburgh Silver Arrow in 1723, 1751, 1756, 1768, and 1769. He won the Silver Arrow of the Company in 1731, 1741, and 1761. He was President of the Royal Company of Archers from 1768 until he died in 1778.

The Honourable Company of Golfers of Edinburgh had his portrait painted but, when, many years later, they got into financial difficulties, they sold the portrait to their Masonic brothers, the Royal Company of Archers. This was a fitting action because St Clair had been President of that Company as well but, as a result, the picture that hangs in the Clubhouse at Muirfield is a copy and the original hangs in Archers Hall, Edinburgh.

St Clair having, as President, laid the Foundation Stone of the Golf House at Leith in 1744, carried the same idea on to the Royal Company of Archers and, as President of that Company, laid the Foundation Stone of Archers Hall in Edinburgh in 1777. He must, behind the scenes, have had much to do with both the idea of the Gentlemen Golfers becoming a Company and with the idea of a Silver Club, to be presented, as the Silver Arrow had been, by the City Council of Edinburgh, as a means of indicating the non-political and non-secretive nature of the Honourable Gentlemen who exercised their skill in the 'antient' art of golf in 1744.

## Duncan Forbes

The antecedents of the Forbes family have not been researched. Forbes was elected a member of the Royal Company of Archers in 1710. He was then an advocate, but by 1740 he was a Lord of Session and, shortly after, Lord President of the Court of Session, with the title of Lord Forbes of Culloden. He was an anti-Jacobite and a

man of great influence – he was also an obsessive golfer, but, as far as can be judged, not a particularly skilful one.

In Mathison's poem, 'The Goff' he is referred to as '. . . the great Forbes, patron of the just, the dread of villains and the poor man's trust'. He tried strenuously to stop the uprising in 1745 and, when it happened and ended disastrously at Culloden, he did his best to bring mercy to the defeated; his saving of Rattray is a typical example. As a member of the Royal Company of Archers, a mason and a man of great influence and wisdom, he must have had a hand in the idea of the Silver Club and have been of great help to the Jacobite members of both the archers and the golfers in their efforts to avoid arrest and imprisonment.

His passion for golf was such that, if the ground was covered with snow, he would play on the beach at Leith. In describing a game of golf against his son he writes: 'This day, after a hard pull, I got the better of my son at the gouf. If he was as good at any other thing as he is at that, there might be some hopes of him.' Pottinger thought that this was an example of 'restrained parental pride' but it sounds much more like the despair of a golfing father that his son appears to be useless!

By his efforts, Forbes played a big, but discreet, part in saving his fellow Masons and in keeping golf in existence at a time when to be a golfing Freemason was a dangerous diversion.

He did not play in the first competition for the Silver Club, but played in the second. He died in 1747 and was described at that time as 'a patriot without ostentation or pretense, a true Scotsman with no prejudices, an accomplished and erudite scholar and a man of genuine piety'.

## The Seton Family

Although the Setons were not signatories to the Petition at Leith nor at St Andrews, they were active in both the Gentlemen Golfers at Leith, where Sir Henry Seton was Captain in 1753 and 1756, and at St Andrews, where Sir Harry Seton (presumably the same man) was Captain in 1763.

Curiously, the Setons do not figure in the lists of the Royal Company of Archers but, as Paul admits in his book, the lists may not be complete (and the pages from 1679 to 1703 have been left blank 'as if for the purpose of being filled up at leisure').

The Seton family, from the arms that they bear, were of the Flemish family of de Lens in Boulogne. After the Battle of Hastings, Domesday records them as having been given a manor in Bedfordshire, at Wahull. By the twelfth century they owned land in Rutland and Walter de Lens was now known as Walter the Fleming. The manor in Rutland was called Seaton. They also acquired lands in Durham and Northumberland – there are five places in Durham called Seaton and eight in Northumberland.

The Setons were deep into Freemasonry, and Alexander de Seton, in 1306, was Master of the Hospitallers. When the Setons went north to Scotland, after Maud's marriage to David I, they settled on the shore of the Firth of Forth, in the neighbourhood of Cockenzie, an area on the southern shore which was strategically important in the defence of Edinburgh and Leith from the sea. There they built a house. The Sier de Seton was Queen Maud's uncle and thus a man of great importance; they were visited by the Royal Family quite frequently and added to their house until it became Seton Palace.

Understandably, they were most loyal and dedicated supporters of King David and, later, of the House of Stewart. Christopher Seton was a participant in the murder of John Comyn in 1306, a murder which successfully removed a potential rival to Robert the Bruce for the Throne of Scotland. This passionate support for the Stewarts was, in the end, their undoing. Lord George Seton, by now the Earl of Winton, was strongly and openly Jacobite and joined in the uprisings of 1715 and 1745; after Culloden, his palace and lands were confiscated. Nothing now remains of the palace. Although the Setons continued to exist, the Winton title was taken over by the Earl of Eglinton; the Eglintons were Montgomeries and one of that family had married into the Setons.

It is not surprising that Mary Stewart spent so much time at Seton Palace where she would have felt secure and at home. It is possible that the Setons, conscious of their open and well-known support of the Stewarts, decided to keep such matters as membership of the Royal Company of Archers to themselves in the early eighteenth century, and that their name was expunged from the records, not only for their own ends, but because the Seton name on the Archers' list might have meant the implication of the Archers as a secret Jacobite Society.

Henry Seton was one of the members of the Gentlemen Golfers at Edinburgh who was on the Committee which was appointed to communicate with the Gentlemen Golfers at St Andrews on the question of when the Gentlemen of Leith might enter for the Silver Club at St Andrews.

# The London Connection

## The Innes Family

Berowald, referred to in twelfth-century documents as Berowaldo Flandrensis – Berowald the Fleming –

possessed land at Berowald's-toun-ness or, as it is called today, Bo'ness. This town, on the south shore of the Firth of Forth in West Lothian was, at one time, the third largest port in Scotland.

Berowald was a relative of Freskin, a Fleming of the House of Boulogne who held land near him in Flanders. He also held lands in Moray (as did Freskin) being one of the Flemish families selected by David I to defend that dangerous area on his then northern border against the raids of the Norsemen. The principal family seat for several hundred years being at Bo'ness, it was natural for the Innes family to belong to Edinburgh Society and if they were interested in golf, Leith was very handy for that purpose. This neat solution to the family's golfing start is not borne out in the Honourable Company's records, or such of the Company's records as were allowed to continue in existence. No Innes was Captain, nor has one found evidence that any Innes won any of their important medals.

William Innes (1719–95) was a Captain of the Blackheath Goffers in 1778; he must have been both a golfer and a well thought of member of the Society for not only did they make him Captain but they had his portrait painted. Innes was a very rich man and a Director of the East India Company; he was the son of Alexander Innes of Cathlowm in West Lothian. Alexander Innes was made a member of the Royal Company of Archers in 1734. A William Innes, Writer to the Signet (lawyer), was elected to the Company in 1821 but whether this was the same Innes who appears among the golfers at Blackheath as a rich merchant venturer has not been established, and it is possible that the William Innes of London, far from Edinburgh, decided that a local masonic Golfing Society was adequate for his purpose.

## The Maule Family

This family came from a small town of that name in Flanders. Arnold de Maule had a son, Guarin de Maule, who fought at Hastings and was rewarded, according to Domesday, with the manor of Hatton in Cleveland. Guarin's son, Robert, travelled to Scotland when Maud married David I and was given lands at Fowlis, near Monifieth, not far from Dundee.

Robert's son, Peter, became Sir Peter de Maule; he married the daughter of William de Velognes of Panmure, another Fleming, who lived close to what is now Carnoustie. The descendants of this family became Lords of Panmure and owned lands at Monifieth, Barry Links and Carnoustie.

In the golf world, the first reference to a golfer by name is to Sir Robert Maule (1497–1560) who is described as '... ane man of comlie behaviour, of hie stature, sanguine in collure, both of hyd and haire, colarique of nature and subject to suddane anger . . . He had gryt delyght in hawkine and honntine . . . . Lykewakes he exercisit at the gowf, and oftimes past to Barry Links, quhan the wadsie [wager, *Author*] was for drink. This was the yeer of God 1527, or there abouts . . . .'

Patrick Maule was created Lord Panmure in 1646. He was a boyhood friend of James VI of Scotland (James I of England) and accompanied the King when he went south to England; he was Gentleman of the Bedchamber to James I and Charles I. He was appointed Keeper of Eltham Park, very close to the original site of the Blackheath golf course and on the site of the present course.

In 1847, the Hon. Patrick Fox Maule was a member of the Blackheath Golf Club and won the Gold Medal on the first occasion on which it was competed for. He was Captain of Blackheath in 1844 and 1845. In 1832 he is listed as a Founder Member of the North Berwick Golf Club. He returned to Scotland and, when he did so, took over the Panmure and Carnoustie Golf Clubs. He married into the Dalhousie family and took the title Lord Dalhousie. In 1866, both Clubs had Lord Dalhousie as Patron.

The Earl of Panmure was an early member of the Royal Company of Archers – some time between 1676 and 1704. In 1791, William Ramsay Maule of Panmure was elected to the Royal Company and, in 1803, Lord Dalhousie was elected.

One cannot leave the 'London Connection' without emphasising the importance of the retinue of Scottish noblemen, many of Flemish descent, who accompanied James I to England.

A complete list has not been prepared by the author, but a random selection of about fifty courtiers is enough to make the point.

Among the fifty who came south with James were: the two sons of the king, two Hamiltons, three Erskines, one Maule, a Lindsay, two Stewarts, a Graham, three Hays, a Bothwell and a Douglas. One can imagine that, once installed at Greenwich, they lost no time in finding a good piece of land on the Black Heath on which to practise their favourite pastime!

## Other Families of Flemish origin connected with Early Golf

THAT James IV played golf with the Earl of Bothwell has already been mentioned – but who was the Earl?

### The Bothwell Family

The Bothwell family name was Oliphant. Mrs Platts identifies them from their armorial bearings as descen-

dants of Roger de Torpel who lived in the Boulogne area; Torpel was a descendant of the de Lens family of Flanders.

The first Holyford, Olifard or Oliphant is noted as having lands at Lilford in Northamptonshire at the time of Domesday. Lilford is probably a corruption of Holy Ford hence the family name.

David Oliphant was a godson of Queen Maud and went north to Scotland in 1142; he remained in Scotland and served David I all his life.

At one time, the Oliphants, connected to the Setons by marriage, inherited the Palace of Seton on the Firth of Forth. They became Earls of Bothwell and, as mentioned, one of them is recorded as playing golf with James IV in 1503. Although, in the seventeenth and eighteenth centuries, not much is heard of them in connection with golf, in the nineteenth century they achieved some fame. William Oliphant won the Gold Medal of the R&A in 1808.

James Stuart Oliphant of Rossie became Captain of the R&A and won the Golf Medal in 1834, scoring 97, the first time that 100 had been broken in that competition.

In a poem, written by Carnegie in 1833 and entitled 'Golfiana', which is largely about the great golfers of his day, he declaims:

> And swiped – like Oliphant and Wood below –
> Smack over Hell in one immortal blow.

[Hell being an exceptionally large bunker on the Old Course at St Andrews. *Author*]. And again, in a poem entitled 'First Hole at St Andrews' of similar date and by the same author he writes:

> The tip top that to the Club belong,
> And Oliphant, the rival of the last
> Whose play, at times, cannot be surpassed.

In 1854, in another poem by an unknown author, entitled 'St Andrews to the Play', we read:

> Its unco' long since we have seen
> Bob Oliphant upon the Green.

The Oliphants will be mentioned again. Their name appears six times in the membership lists of the Royal Company of Archers, between 1676 and 1776.

### The Hay Family

The ancestor of this family was William de la Haie. He held lands in Normandy but he was not a Norman; his roots were at La Haie, near Loos, in west Flanders. He served a family who were castellans – castle holders – at nearby Lille. This family was called 'de Insula' and two members of the family fought at Hastings.

One of the grandsons of one of these men married a 'de Wavrin', another old Flemish family. The arms of the lord of La Haie are the same as those of the de Wavrins and it is very likely that William de la Haie was the second son of that marriage. William de la Haie appeared in Scotland in the time of David I and became a 'butler', or head of household, to Malcolm IV and, after, to William the Lion. He had married a de Senlis, and the family held lands near him in Normandy; they also held lands at Great Doddington in Northamptonshire. The de la Haie family became, in Scotland, the Hay family.

In 1527, Elizabeth Hay married George Seton and their eldest son became Lord Seton, close friend of Mary Stuart.

Of the golfing Hays: Major George Hay was Captain of the R&A in 1785; Thomas Hay was Captain in 1798; in the nineteenth century several Hays held golf Captaincies and one, at least, became a famous golfer – they will reappear later in the story. Numerous Hays appear in the lists of members of the Royal Company of Archers, starting with Thomas Hay, at some time between 1676 and 1704.

## The Montgomerie Family

As a result of their good services at the Battle of Hastings the Montgomeries were granted a number of manors in England, but the most important was the Earldom of Shrewsbury. Roger de Montgomerie (1025–1094) was wont to boast that he was completely Norman but he may have had Flemish family connections, which is, perhaps, why he was an important liaison officer between the Norman and Flemish forces at the Battle of Hastings.

A Flemish connection of importance is certain in the next generation when his son, Robert, Earl of Shrewsbury, married Agnes, daughter of Guy, Count of Ponthieu. This meant that the offspring of this family would have important Flemish blood in their veins, and also suggests that the father of Robert had some important Flemish relatives because marriages were most carefully arranged and the Count of Ponthieu would have been sure to select, for his daughter, a husband with the right credentials.

The Montgomeries had a number of quarrels with Henry I and lost all their lands and titles at Shrewsbury. It was probably for this reason that Robert de Montgomerie (no doubt, urged on by his Flemish wife) decided to go to Scotland and join Queen Maud. Montgomerie was welcomed and given lands in Renfrewshire. At some later stage in Scottish history they became Earls of Eglinton and held lands in southwest Scotland and at Tranent in East Lothian. In 1600, Alexander Seton became the first Earl of Winton, and he married a Montgomerie. When Lord George Seton, as Earl of Winton, publicly took a Jacobite stance and joined the uprising in 1745, he subsequently lost all his lands and title; the Montgomerie/Seton marriage connection allowed the Montgomerie family to take over the vacant title and the family then became Earls of Eglinton and Winton.

The Montgomerie family encouraged junior members of the family to join the Scots Guard in France in the seventeenth century. In 1606, the Montgomeries and the Hamiltons set up the Ulster Plantations in Northern Ireland; included in that scheme was a golf links, which was the start of Irish golf.

The Montgomeries were early members of the Royal Company of Archers, as Earls of Eglinton, and their name occurs frequently throughout the members list for over a hundred years.

The part played by the family in golf is considerable but occurred mainly in the nineteenth century (apart from the Ulster connection) and this will be discussed later.

## The Hamilton Family

The exact origins of the Hamilton family are somewhat obscure but Mrs Platts is of the opinion that they were, originally, Umfravilles and had their origins in Flanders. They were related to the Beaumonts, Earls of Leicester.

Umfraville is recorded in Domesday as holding land at Hambleton in Rutland; an alternative (recorded) name for Hambleton was Hamilton. That the Umfravilles came over with the Conqueror seems certain but what part they played is not known. In 1296, Umfraville was involved in a serious quarrel with one of the Ministers of Edward I; either he was in the wrong or his opponent had great influence, because he was forced to flee to Scotland. He had been a friend of David before he became King, when he lived in England, so it was understandable that he should be made welcome. The welcome, however, was somewhat muted by the fact that he had married a Comyn, from the family who, at a later date, became serious contenders for the throne of Scotland, a contention which was only resolved when a Seton murdered Comyn.

Nevertheless, the Hamiltons were given the Royal Castle of Cadzow in Lanarkshire and suitable areas of land around it. The Hamiltons subsequently became the Dukes of Hamilton. The family are not prominent in golf in the seventeenth and eighteenth centuries, except for their part in the Ulster Plantations in 1606, but made contributions in the nineteenth century which will be discussed later. It is interesting that Archbishop Hamilton, in 1552, gave the right to the Town of St Andrews to play golf on the links there 'for ever'.

The Hamiltons were strong supporters of the Scots Guard in France, so it is not surprising that the Hamilton name is frequently to be found in the lists of the Royal Company of Archers, both the Duke, in 1716, and his brothers, at other dates; how many Hamiltons were members before 1676 will never be known. In 1640 General Alexander Hamilton was inducted into Freemasonry at St Mary's Lodge in Edinburgh.

### The Moncrieff and Moncrieffe Family

I am indebted to Mrs Platts, in a personal communication, for information about the origins of this family. The name is a territorial one and stems from Perthshire.

Their original name was Mortimer or Mortemere and they were the holders of a castle of Mortemer-sur-Eaulne in Seine Inferieur. That castle belonged to the de Warenne family who were a famous family of Flemish origin. A daughter of William de Warenne married David I's son, Prince Henry; a number of de Warenne knights accompanied her and it is probable that a Moncrieff was in that number. From the golfing point of view, the Moncrieff and Moncrieffe (the latter a cadet branch of the family) appear at a much later date.

That the Moncrieffs were strong supporters of the Stuarts is undoubted. In 1248, Sir Matthew Moncrieff was put in charge of the armour of James II. Moncrieffs were recruited into the Scots Guard in the seventeenth century. A Moncrieff, in 1700, was listed as a 'suspected person' i.e., suspected of being a Jacobite.

Scattered throughout the list of members of the Royal Company of Archers, between 1676 and 1890, are ten Moncrieffs; how many more are unrecorded we do not know. The Moncrieffs, and the important part that they played in golf in the nineteenth century, will be discussed later.

It was the late Sir Ian Moncrieff of that Ilk who, talking about golf and Freemasonry, said: 'Anybody who was anybody in Scotland, in the nineteenth century, was a Freemason'.

## Summary

IT would be naive to think that all the families in Scotland, of Flemish origin, were, for 500 years, keen and skilful golfers, nor is it likely that they were all interested in archery. By the same token, there must have been large numbers of men of purely Scottish lineage who, from the start, became keenly interested in golf.

It must also be true that, despite the careful selection of family marriages to promote landed interests and political influence, marriages took place between families that were predominantly Flemish and families that were Celtic.

Yet, despite the diluting effect on blood lineage, there is a remarkable connecting thread between golf, the Scots families of Flemish origin and Freemasonry.

The families presented in this Chapter should be regarded as typical 'samples'. There are other families, such as the Grahams and the Lindsays, who could provide further evidence if space permitted, but enough has been said to indicate the general pattern, which is inescapable.

# The Formation of Golf Clubs

THE exact nature of the game which was banned in 1457 is not known but there are some pointers. In 1574, Andrew Melvill, while a student at St Andrews, was not discouraged by his father from playing golf and from practising archery; he was allowed one club for golf and some balls. Perhaps he was playing a form of jeu de mail, if only one club was necessary.

In 1587, in Glasgow, there was a Council ban on 'Golf, carrick and shinnie (Shinty) in the High. . .'. This ban is noted by David Hamilton who considers that 'the High' means either the High Street or the area around the Town's Cathedral and that the measure was designed to protect the townsfolk from the dangers of flying sticks and balls. Shades of Holland and Flanders! It seems unlikely that there would have been a hole in the ground to play into, in the High Street. There is evidence of playing golf at a kirk door in 1613 in Aberdeen and the death of a man in Kelso in 1632 while playing golf in a churchyard. By this time Thomas Kincaid is 'holling the ball' so, it seems, two forms of the game existed at the same time, golf and a type of colf, the latter being the sort of game that the Dutch might have brought to Scotland.

There is, by this time, some positive evidence of golf-like games, not merely, as in Holland and Flanders, negative evidence of banning the game. In 1502, the Treaty of Glasgow gave peace between England and Scotland and consequently the practice of archery was no longer as important as it had been before. Some control was still

exerted over the playing of golf on the Sabbath and laws were passed to forbid play on that day. Gradually even this ban was modified and golf was only banned 'at tyme of sermonis'.

The keenness of the Royal House of Stewart for golf was soon evident for, in the same year that the Treaty of Glasgow was signed, the Lord High Treasurer for Scotland paid out for clubs for James IV, bought from a Perth bowmaker. In 1503 the same man was buying 'clubbes and ballis to the King that he playeth with' and, later, paying His Highness' debt to the Earl of Bothwell after a match between them.

As the direct result of Royal enthusiasm for the game of golf, members of the Royal Court took up the game. As a fashionable game played by the great landowners, nobles and courtiers, it became expensive and changed from the simple village game played by the locals on links in their area. Van Hengel considered that golf in the fifteenth, six-teenth and seventeenth centuries in Scotland was played, almost entirely, on the eastern side and that this was because it was the region of Scotland which faced Holland. His observation was correct, but the deduction is wrong.

If one considers a simple area of pastureland in Scotland as a potential site for golf, in the days when there was no such thing as a mower and the only way to cut grass was with a scythe, it becomes evident that it was not in fact at all suitable. In winter the ground would be wet and muddy, except for the times when it was either frozen, or covered in snow. The one thing that ruined a feather ball was water. If the ball got really wet, it became a useless, soggy mass of feathers and play would have to be abandoned. Play in the snow would have been equally disastrous for the same reason. Play when the ground was frozen would have been possible because the ball would have bounced along the frozen ground, instead of burying itself in the mud, and would not have got wet. It was probably for this reason that, in the poem 'Glotta' written by James Arbuckle in 1721, about golf on the Green at Glasgow, he says the young men played golf upon the green 'when hoary Frosts o'erspread the verdant turf'. In the summer, golf in a pasture would have been equally impossible because the long grass would have caused a multitude of balls to be lost and would have made shot-making very difficult. Additionally, the grass was a very valuable crop for the farmer, as hay for winter feed, and golfers trampling the grass flat would have made it impossible to cut with a scythe. So golf could only be played, at all regularly, in spring or autumn and, even then, only if the weather was dry. Conditions on the east coast of Scotland were much better because here there was 'links' land. This was situated near the sea and was, in general, flat, but had many ''umps and 'ollers'. It had very short grass, and water drained through it very quickly. As the grass was short it was only suitable for grazing sheep – who kept the grass even shorter. The reason for this was because it consisted of very thin turf overlaying sand. On this sort of terrain golf could be played all year round; after rain, the turf would dry quickly. Apart from the penalty of sheep droppings everywhere, it was ideal. Further advantages were that, being at sea level, heavy snow was unlikely and that the eastern side of Scotland is appreciably dryer than the western side. At places where the sheep tended to lie down, the turf became easily broken, exposing the sand beneath; the fierce winds of winter rapidly enlarged and deepened these areas until they became pits of sand – or natural bunkers.

Many coastal villages had links land close to them and this enabled the locals to play on a natural area, where no upkeep was required, other than, occasionally, to cut new holes. Apart from the cost of clubs and balls, golf was free and much played. The form of the game was, always, foursomes matchplay. The playing of alternate shots by two players followed the tradition of the players of croisse or jeu de mail. The number of holes on a links must have varied considerably and depended entirely on the area of the links. No doubt the rules for any particular match were agreed by the participants before they started out – and before the bets were laid! Even today, in a match, the participants may make their own rules for play, provided none of the rules is at variance with the basic rules of the game. In the sixteenth, seventeenth and eighteenth centuries local fishing villages were isolated and communication between one village and the next could be difficult. Because matchplay golf was played, the rules which were used may have differed considerably from one village to the next, without any harm to the game; it was when scoreplay was introduced that it became necessary to have a uniform set of rules, so that all the participants in any competition were bound by the same rules.

There were, of course, no professional club- and ballmakers; each village had a variety of trades and skills and men would make the various implements for golf as an amateur sideline of their breadwinning trade. Such trades as bowmaker, fletcher, shipwright, carpenter, sailor, etc all had skills which could be put to use in the making of clubs and balls (and it is likely that some of the balls were made of wood).

When men of money and power started to play, things changed; such men had no skills of their own, so they needed skilled men who could make clubs and balls; they could afford labour to improve the golf links and caddies to carry their clubs. Groups of men played together on nearby land and, as these groups got larger and as, in the eighteenth century, Clubs and Societies became popular, it was not long before these groups began to form Golf Societies and to build Clubhouses where, with the employment of yet more servants, they could change their clothes, store their clubs, and wine and dine after the exertions of the game.

Before the golfers formed Societies they had been in the habit of dining together after golf and this usually took place at a local tavern. They wined and dined and discussed the games that they had played that day and also considered their next day's play and what wagers should be made. Because there were a number of them, they usually reserved a room for their entertainment, and at the end of the evening they all subscribed to the cost.

The earliest golfing groups in Scotland and England were all designated as Societies, with the exception of one, and it was only at a later date that they became, in many cases, Golf Clubs. The one exception to this was, and still is, the Company of Edinburgh Golfers, who changed their name over the years but have always retained the title of 'Company'.

There are small differences between a Society and a Club but they are not easy to define. Both are considered to be groups of individuals of a like mind meeting for the purpose of social intercourse and entertainment. However, a Club is noted as meeting at a tavern with the members jointly paying the expenses. There is also a general suggestion that, if all are interested in the same pursuit, all may join but, in a Society, there is talk of it 'meeting under certain regulations' and 'admission is usually guarded by ballot'. This suggests that not everybody who is interested in the same game or pursuit may become a member of the Society. The significant feature of a Society was not who it admitted, but who it kept out.

Perhaps it was because golf became a Court game that Societies were formed, rather than Clubs, and they exercised care in the selection of members. It is interesting, as we shall see later, that so many Societies eventually changed their name to 'Club'. Sir Hugh Lyon Playfair, a great benefactor of St Andrews Town, and Captain of the Royal and Ancient Golf Club, writing in 1856 of the days of his youth observes: 'The national and gentlemanly game of golf was, at that time, confined to the "Upper Ten" and was looked upon by the common people, who could not afford to pay for clubs and the stout leather case stuffed with feathers, called a golf ball, as a pastime fitted only for those whom they considered to have "mair siller than sense".'

Although the Societies were careful about whom they allowed to become members, on the golf links they would play their favourite matchplay foursomes with anyone who was a golfer and there seem to have been few class distinctions there; the links, owned by the Town, were there for the benefit of the townspeople; many of the members of the select Society did not live locally and thus, technically, had no right to use the links.

Perhaps the willingness to play with anybody on the links had its practical side, as it may have made the exclusiveness of the Society less obvious. That being said, there is no doubt that golf is a great leveller; on the course, the ability to play golf is more important than social status and always has been.

# Early Golf Societies in Scotland and England

### The Honourable Company of Edinburgh Golfers
The first Minutes are dated 1744.

### The Society of St Andrews Golfers
The play for the Silver Club was instituted in 1754. In 1834 this Society became 'The Royal and Ancient Golf Club of St Andrews'.

### The Edinburgh Burgess Golfing Society
The first Minutes are dated 1770.

### The Musselburgh Golf Club
The first minutes are dated 1784.

### The Bruntsfield Links Golfing Society
This was renamed the Bruntsfield Links Golf Club in a Minute of 1797.

### The Society of Goffers at Blackheath
This is the dedication of Lemuel Abbott in 1790 for a portrait of William Innes, who was Captain. In 1766, the Society is also referred to as The Blackheath Golf Club. Within the Blackheath Golf Club was a subsidiary Club called the Knuckle Club which was formed in 1791 and later disbanded itself.

### The Society of Golfers of Aberdeen
Believed founded in 1790, in 1815 it became the Aberdeen Golf Club.

THE reader will notice that a definite foundation date for each Society is not given, only the date of the first Minutes or, 'believed founded'; this is because, astonishingly, none of these ancient and historic Societies, with the possible exception of the Society of Golfers at St Andrews, know the exact date of their foundation. From the time that they had official Minutes, these Minutes have been kept most assiduously and everything is in order, but many have evidence of earlier beginnings in the shape of cups, medals, etc. Earlier Minutes have been lost, or were destroyed. At Blackheath, the Minutes were said to have been destroyed in a disastrous fire, but, in a detailed study of the Club records, there is no mention of a fire. Why should Clubs, or Societies, which kept excellent records for more than a hundred years, have lost their earlier records? This apparent destruction of valuable records occurring in nearly all of the most historic Societies cannot be a coincidental misfortune. Before turning attention to the details concerning each Society and their subsequent development, the possible significance of the loss of all the early Minutes merits some investigation. This investigation must start at a much earlier date.

In a most interesting and assiduously researched book, *The Temple and the Lodge*, by Michael Baigent and Richard Leigh, published in 1989, the possible origins of Freemasonry, its subsequent development and the influence of the Craft on events in both Britain and America are assessed. There is also much in this book which is grist to the mill of the golf historian.

The authors discovered, at Kilmartin, at the southern end of Loch Awe in the district of Argyll, about eighty old and weathered tombstones. While the stones had no dates or names on them they bore carved representations of Templar swords; all the evidence indicated that this was a Templar graveyard. The earliest stone was believed to date from the thirteenth century. Despite no indication of the status of the people buried there, the carving of the Templar swords suggested that those buried were men of substance and importance. Who were the Knights Templar and what were they doing in southwest Scotland?

The authors make the point that Templar tombs in the Holy Land, dated as early as 1218, had similar swords carved on them, but some also had a mason's square and plumbstone on them as well – the earliest evidence of a connection between Knights Templars and Freemasonry.

When Acre fell in 1291, the Crusaders (or Knights Templars) had lost the final opportunity to create a Christian Middle East; there had been three Crusades and, as might have been expected, none played a greater part in the Crusades than the Knights of Flanders, many of whom died in the Holy Land.

When the last Crusade failed, the Knights Templars had no raison d'être – and no real home. Many must have returned to their own homeland but a substantial number attempted to create a home of their own in France, only to be thwarted by the French King. The last straw in this sad series of events came when the Pope, in 1312, officially dissolved the Order. The Order of the Temple, which was the designation of the Knights Templars, had fought three Crusades in the name of Christianity; they must have felt their disbandment a poor reward. The Papal ban meant that no country of Christian Faith and owing allegiance to the Pope could offer them help.

Robert the Bruce, whom Mrs Platts has shown was of Flemish descent, must have had some sympathy with the Order, which included so many brave Flemish Knights; additionally, Robert had been excommunicated by the Pope, so the Papal ban did not affect him. Scotland must have seemed a natural haven for those members of the Order who could escape from Europe.

The Knights Templar, originally known as 'The Poor Knights of the Temple of Solomon' were formed in 1118. Their avowed purpose was to protect pilgrims to the Holy Land but, with hindsight, it is evident that, from the start, they had other purposes which they did not divulge. They became involved with the powerful Cistercian Order of Monks. In 1228, four years after David became King and invited the nobles of Flanders to take up residence in Scotland, the Council of Troyes granted the Templars 'monastic rule', thus giving them a formal constitution as Warrior monks.

After this, the Order rapidly expanded and acquired much wealth from donations. By 1138, they had acquired lands in Austria, Constantinople, England, France, Germany, Hungary, Italy, Portugal, Scotland and Spain.

In England, King Stephen, was a great supporter between 1135 and 1161 and, during this time, the Order set up a number of preceptories in England and built an important Temple in London. In 1161, they built a new Temple in London – now Temple Bar.

They flourished, even more, under the patronage of Richard Coeur de Lion, himself a member of the Order; later King John stayed at their preceptories. In 1214, the Grand Master of the Order, a close adviser to King John, played a part in persuading him to sign Magna Carta.

The Templars were exempt from taxes and had their own fleet which operated from London and Bristol. They are known to have had preceptories in Ireland and a Manor at Temple House, Sligo. Information about their Scottish activities is, according to Baigent and Leigh, patchy and unreliable, partly because of the turmoil in thirteenth-century Scotland, partly because 'much appears to have been deliberately concealed'. There was a main centre just outside Edinburgh, Balantrodoc, now called Temple.

By reason of wealth, land ownership, military expertise and considerable administrative ability, the Templars exerted great power and influence – but they had no kingdom of their own. They are credited, by some, as having been the earliest founders of a banking system; they lent money at high interest rates and more than one English and French King was chronically in debt to them. The Crown Jewels of England were, at one time, kept in a Templars' Tower; the Templars became virtually the Treasurers of both England and France. They maintained an integrity in financial affairs but, otherwise, they were ruthless and greedy for power; their behaviour was dissolute and often immoral.

Perhaps because of their wealth and power and because of their close secretive behaviour, even Kings were afraid of them.

It was when Philip of France, heavily in debt to them, found that they were secretly trying to form a Kingdom of their own in France that, on Friday, May the thirteenth 1307, he ordered their arrest and imprisonment.

The Templars' excellent system of communication and good network of informants, at all levels of society, meant that they had some advance warning of what was coming. As a result, all their treasure and documents in France were spirited away. The main fleet escaped and eighteen galleys, laden, no doubt, with a vast quantity of treasure and all their most secret documents, sailed for an unknown destination and were never seen again – they simply disappeared.

Philip, who had considerable influence with the Pope, would have had little difficulty in persuading him, in 1312, to dissolve the Order; they had, after all, been guilty of extensive usury, to name but one indictment. Many Templars were arrested and handed over the the Inquisition for torture and death; as they were believed to have many secrets, the torture was prolonged. So dreadful a time was it that Friday the thirteenth has become an unlucky day in the popular mind ever since that time.

The Order could have escaped to the Middle East or North Africa but, had they done so, such a large number of ships and so much wealth would, surely, have been recorded and the Templars themselves would have had to start trade, commerce and usury in whatever area they settled in, so that their presence could not have gone unnoticed.

Some Templars may well have escaped via Flanders. Despite the Papal ban, the noble families of Flanders would have felt in duty bound to help their erstwhile comrades in arms and it would not have been difficult to send them on to Scotland, as there was constant traffic in cloth and wool between the Port of Leith and Flanders.

Not only would the Templars have felt secure in Scotland because the Papal ban did not operate there but they would also have found a welcome from the many Flemish families who had much influence in Scotland and many of whose relatives had been to the Crusades. Moreover, Robert the Bruce, at war with the English, and himself with Flemish family connections, would have been glad of the help of these highly professional soldiers.

In England the persecution of the Templars was a weak affair and was not pursued with any vigour; most of those arrested were elderly and the young who escaped could, undoubtedly, have made their way to Scotland, taking all their money and arms with them. In Ireland things were the same and the round up of Templars was so slow that, when they finally made an effort, they found that only a few remained and they captured no treasure and few arms. The journey from Ireland to Scotland was not difficult.

There is no record of the fate of the fleet with its treasure and documents but it is very likely that it made its way up the west coast of Ireland and thence across to the west coast of Scotland, the area of Kilmory and Kilmartin being the nearest landfall that the fleet would make. On this relatively isolated coast, aided by well-disposed Celtic Scots of the old Kingdom of Dalriada, it would have been possible to dispose of the ships, and move the treasure and documents to a safe Templar holding; many of the Templar lands in Scotland had been left intact and even in 1596 there were 579 Templar holdings listed in Scotland. The Flemish holders of those formidable fortresses, built to a design from Flanders – the motte, would have been easily capable of keeping secure treasure and documents on behalf of the new arrivals.

In Scotland, family blood lines and a strong sympathy with fellow Crusaders saw to it that the Templars' lands were not broken up but, as Baigent and Leigh suggest, seemed almost to have been held in trust for the future. Influential families, closely interlocked by marriage, closed ranks and quietly directed attention away from these matters; this was why, in 1596, so many Templar land-holdings were still intact. That these lands

were preserved and not broken up by reason of cover up and secrecy and not by a bold and public declaration not to do so, was well in accordance with the secretive nature of the Templars and later of the Freemasons.

In 1314, when the Papal ban on the Templars was still in force, an institution was allowed to appear in Scotland which was definitely military and neo-Templar. The sons of the Flemish and Templar families were proud to be members of it and were readily recruited; this was the Scots Guard. Further recruitment came from France, Boulogne and, probably, Flanders because, although called the Scots Guard, it existed in France; the organisation, which had strong mythological elements in it relating to stonemasons and architecture, had much to do with the beginnings of Freemasonry in Scotland. The Setons were very prominent in its support and the St Clair family joined it in numbers; many of the old families of Flemish origin strongly supported it.

In 1445 the Scots Guard was the most prestigious and honoured part of the French army. This was because they had particularly distinguished themselves at the Battle of Vermeuil; their Commander was John Stewart, and Alexander Lindsay, Sir William Seton and the Earls of Douglas, Murray and Mar were all prominent officers – the Flemish families were well represented! Unfortunately, by 1610, they had lost much of their prestige and were in decline; this was because they had allowed themselves to be drawn into the bloody dispute between the House of Valois and the Houses of Guise and Lorraine; they began to support both sides, and this was their undoing. Nevertheless, during the period in which they existed, the Scots Guard had provided a most useful proving and training ground for the young men from Scotland's noble families. Today the Scots Guard has been replaced by the Royal Company of Archers, a quasi-military organisation whose other name is the Queen's Bodyguard in Scotland. They are most proud of their lineage, and certain ancient and noble Scottish families are able to make their male offspring members of the Company as of right, since within the Company there is a private order, semi-masonic and semi-religious, which admits them. As might be imagined, most of the noble families who are represented in the Company are of Flemish origin.

From the start the Templars had secrets; facts about their activities not being available, fiction and mythology grew up around them. They did nothing to dispel this; on the contrary, they did much to propagate it.

They allowed their name to become associated with the Grail Romances, the Knights of Charlemagne, the Knights of the Round Table and the Red Branch of Ulster. The more the Templars went into decline the more vigorously they propagated an air of mystery and romance. One such romantic effort resulted in the concept of Freemasonry. As the Templars went into decline, so the Masonic Brotherhood arose, like a Phoenix, from its ashes.

## The Grail Romances

THESE mythological tales are of importance in an understanding of some of the rituals that occur in Freemasonry. Written in the twelfth century, the Grail Romances were a series of legends of knights in shining armour, the Holy Grail which they guarded, and the romantic concept of chivalry. These romances contain Judeo-Christian material on to which has been grafted ancient and pagan Celtic tales of a similar nature. One such tale concerned the Celtic 'cult of the head'; the Celts believed that the soul was in the head and therefore decreed that the heads of vanquished foes should be cut off and preserved.

Other Celtic beliefs include the 'Green Man', a mythological God of vegetation and fertility, depicted as the head of a God with vegetation coming out of his mouth. In a poem written about the Holy Grail in the twelfth century, there is mention of the 'Son of the Widow'. The precise meaning of this phrase is not now known (except, perhaps to Freemasons) but it is a constantly recurring phrase in Freemasonry.

### The St Clairs of Roslyn

Although the Setons were, for three hundred years, the prop and mainstay of the Scottish Monarchs, the St Clairs wre only just behind them. They were very prominent in the Scots Guard and active supporters of Robert the Bruce; in particular, they were very active in the rise of Freemasonry.

In 1446, William St Clair started the building of a Chapel at Rosslyn (later Roslyn). He seems to have had some knowledge of architecture for he appointed himself the Master Architect for the project. No expense was spared and the Chapel, though large, was originally meant to be quite a small part of a large collegiate and church complex. It took forty years to build, and the rest of the building was never completed, due to lack of funds.

The Chapel is full of decorations of a decidedly Masonic character. The Green Man is there and the sculptured head of an apprentice, mysteriously slain in the building of the Chapel; there is the head (the Freemasons attached great importance to heads, which is probably a throwback to pagan Celtic beliefs) of the 'Widowed Mother'; it seems that the two heads signify the 'Son of the Widow'.

In 1441, James II designated William St Clair 'Patron and Protector of the Masons'; the title was hereditary and remained in the family until it died out. Baigent and Leigh point out that the term 'mason' at this time did not mean Freemason but referred to the Guild of Stone-masons. Whatever it may have meant originally, by the time of the last St Clair, in the eighteenth century, he is referred to as the 'Hereditary Grand Master Mason of Scotland'. The fact that, in 1722, all the family's papers were destroyed in a fire and that, at that time, the St Clair of Roslyn was the last of his line, is a further indication of the tendency of Masons, when faced with death, and of Masonic institutions, faced with dissolution, to ensure secrecy at all costs.

There is no need to elaborate further, suffice to say that many, if not all, the Scottish families of Flemish descent were involved in Freemasonry in later years. The Stuart dynasty was no exception and, in 1658, at Scone, James VI was admitted to the Brotherhood.

Because of the survival of the Templars in Scotland and because of the influence of the Grail Romances, dear to the Celts, the subsequent rise of Freemasonry was enthusiastically supported by all classes in Scotland. If the higher echelons of that society, the Royal Court, whose King was also a Freemason, were enthusiastic in playing golf, which they had brought to Scotland from Flanders, what was more likely than that they should have decided to form societies for the playing of golf as a prelude to a hearty dinner and social evening at a Masonic Lodge?

With this background in mind, one may now consider the history of the earliest Golfing Societies in Britain.

## The Royal Blackheath Golf Club

THIS Club is examined first because when the late Ian Henderson and the author were asked to write a history of the Club we uncovered, to our surprise, clear evidence of a Club within a Club – the Knuckle Club.

Although the Royal Blackheath Golf Club has been officially 'Royal' only since 1901, it was, unofficially, 'Royal' long before that. At the time at which we are considering it, however, it was simply the Blackheath Golf Club. Yet, when Samuel Abbott painted a picture of William Innes, one of the Captains of Blackheath, in 1797, he dedicated the picture to 'The Society of Goffers at Blackheath'. A description by a local newspaper of play on one of the Blackheath Medal days in 1787 states that 'the players were upwards of thirty gentlemen of the London Scots Society'. In 1785, a notice of an Anniversary Celebration began: 'The Anniversary of the Society. . .'. By whatever name it was known, there seems to be evidence that, before 1800, Blackheath was known to many as a 'Society'.

Hughes, in his *Chronicles of Blackheath*, remarks that all the Minutes of the Club, prior to 1800, were lost 'in an ever lamented fire at the end of the last century'; no evidence of a fire has been found and, although the Minutes have disappeared, many valuable trophies and objects belonging to the Club before 1800 have survived.

### The Knuckle Club

It is no coincidence that the Knuckle Club was founded in 1798, just before the mythical fire. The Club was also called the Winter Club and an impression was given that, as no one else played in the Winter, the Knuckle Club, or Winter Club would pioneer the effort; in fact, there is evidence that members of Blackheath Golf Club played golf in the winter.

The Knuckle Club was also known as the 'Green Man Knuckle' and one of its purposes was to 'discuss a dish of knuckles on Saturdays'. Their meetings took place at a local tavern called 'The Green Man' (whether it had always been called the Green Man, or whether it was given that name by the Knuckle Club, is not known). They played for a Gold Medal that was decorated with human knuckles and it was obligatory for any member wishing to speak at the dinner to be holding a knuckle bone in his hand. No one was allowed to take the knuckle out of the dining room. The Knuckle Club, formed in 1798, was wound up in 1825. The Gold Medal that they played for is still in existence and is played for by the Royal Blackheath Golf Club; it is one of the oldest golf medals in the world. It was obviously the intention of the Knuckle Club, true to the Masonic tradition, to destroy all evidence of their activities; on this occasion there was a slip-up and only four pages of records were torn out of a record book; the remaining twenty-two pages have much to tell of the doings of the Club.

New members went through an initiation ceremony and there are comments in the records such as: 'after a severe examination . . . passed the ordeal bravely . . .'; 'was initiated and passed the Sign in style . . .'. There was a well-kept and quite voluminous record of wagers. The wining and dining was stupendous; the fine for a breach of the rules was often a gallon of claret, to be drunk on the

**The Knuckle Club medal, 1789**

premises. The Knuckle Club drank many toasts. The standard ones, laid down in the rules, were: 'The King. The Knuckle. The Butcher's Wife'. The significance of the Knuckle is that bones and skulls were very important in Freemasonry and, indeed, feature in Templar traditions; many Templar graves feature crossed shin bones immediately beneath the skull.

The significance of the last we do not know; it was possibly a variation of the toast to The Widow, a classic Masonic toast. Many other toasts were drunk, especially on the occasion of one of the members marrying, or having a child. 'The Lady and the Younkers' health was drunk in a brimmer (a brimmer was a toast in which all glasses were filled to the brim and were then emptied).

In its heyday, it must have been a very jolly Club, with much wining, dining, betting on matches, toasts and speeches.

In 1910, Henry Leach, a knowledgeable golfer and writer on golf, published *Letters of a Modern Golfer to his Grandfather*. The letters were said to be the letters of Richard Allingham to his grandfather, assembled and edited by Henry Leach. Generally, these letters have been regarded as a series of fairy tales based on a few facts. Nevertheless, the letters talk much about the old Knuckle Club at Blackheath and the grandson appears to be slightly bewildered, but definitely intrigued, by the tales of good fellowship and jollity accompanied by certain secret rites and rituals.

If Henry Leach invented some of this, he nevertheless must have amassed a lot of facts, most of which occur in the old Knuckle Club book, which the late Ian Henderson and the author found in the Royal Blackheath Club archives; despite the suggestion that the tales told are fanciful, there is much fact in evidence.

Further research shows that John Leach was Captain of Blackheath in 1815. As Captain he must have been a senior member of the Club and a Freemason. It is believed that Henry Leach was John Leach's grandson. It seems very probable that Henry Leach had heard these tales from his grandfather and sought to pass on to the general public information about the Knuckle Club activities and about the good fellowship of golf in past times while making it appear, in the interests of secrecy, that the stories were apocryphal.

The Club did not end abruptly, while in full spate. It dwindled and died slowly. Apparently fewer and fewer members attended the dinners until the day came when the members agreed to disband the Club . . . 'The members, in future, to meet merely as golfers'. At the end there were only eight members.

The whole tenor of the Club and the way it attempted to destroy all evidence of its past activities when it disbanded makes it quite certain that this was a Masonic Club, not the ordinary sort of Lodge, but one which was specifically adapted to combine golf with Masonic ceremonies.

One interpretation of what occurred could be that, when the original, Masonic, Blackheath Golf Club destroyed its earlier records and decided to become a Golf Club, open to non-masons, the more ardent Masons decided to continue their secret Club and their initiation ceremonies, toasts, bets, and wining and dining and, while continuing to play golf on the Heath as ordinary members, took themselves off to The Green Man for their private festivities. Eventually, enthusiasm waned, and the Knuckle Club faded away.

Another interpretation will be discussed later.

That the Blackheath Club was in existence before 1766 (when Mr Foot gave the Silver Club) is probable; that they were in existence, as a Golf Club or Society, in 1608, is very improbable.

There is evidence of the Masonic nature of the Blackheath Golf Club from another source, in the founding of Golf Clubs overseas by charter or diploma.

In 1829, the Calcutta Golf Club was instituted at Dum Dum in Calcutta. The membership was mainly Scotch and Blackheath immediately showed a close interest by toasting the Club at one of their dinners. In 1873 they sent a gold medal to the Calcutta Club. The Calcutta Club followed the rules of Blackheath to the letter, including the habit of wearing uniforms and having dinners at which matches were arranged and bets were laid on the outcome. Regularly, the annual Minutes of the Calcutta Club were (and still are) sent to the parent Club at Blackheath.

As Blackheath was close to London, it had a (Masonic) membership derived from that City; many of its members were employed by, or were Directors of, the East India Company.

When Company employees were sent to India, they kept close links with their Masonic brothers at Blackheath Golf Club. It is certain that the Blackheath Golf Club gave a charter to the Calcutta Masons to form a Lodge in Calcutta and the Calcutta Lodge decided that it should take the form of a Golf Club similar in constitution to the parent Club at Blackheath; the Minutes of the

Blackheath Golf Club having been lost 'in an ever to be lamented fire', there is no documentary proof. It would have been useful to see the Minutes of the Calcutta Club and find the details of their charter from these, but the *History of the Royal Calcutta Golf Club* states 'the Club's records do not go further back than 1876. . .'. Similar close associations were made with the Bombay Golf Club, founded in 1842. When they announced that they had formed a Club in that year, the Captain of Blackheath sent them a copy of the rules of the Blackheath Club and made their first Captain an honorary member of Blackheath. The Blackheath Golf Club sent the Bombay Golf Club a gold medal to play for, in the same year.

The Blackheath Club had a very close association with the Blackheath Golf Club, of New South Wales. When, in 1841, the Captain of the NSW Blackheath Golf Club Alex Brodie Spark, announced to the parent Club the birth of a son and sent them a gallon of claret to celebrate the event, they responded by making the Captain an honorary member of the Blackheath Golf Club. Afterwards, they made donations of golf trophies to the NSW Club. This close association between the two Blackheaths still exists, although the original Golf Club and its records have long disappeared. It is known that Alex Brodie Spark was a Master Mason.

The reader will realise that, had there not been a slip-up in the destruction of the Knuckle Club records, none of the Masonic elements of both the Blackheath Golf Club and the Knuckle Club would have been suspected or uncovered; but they were found and an 'index of suspicion' was followed up. As there is not going to be any such concrete evidence in other Clubs, in which destruction of evidence was much more thorough, it is as well to recapitulate the indications, in an early Golf Club, that suggest that it was either, as in the case of the Knuckle Club, a Masonic Lodge, or at the very least, a Club in which there was a preponderance of Freemasons who controlled the Club's affairs.

The hints are:

1. The mysterious destruction, or loss, of the early Minute books.

2. The granting of charters or diplomas to overseas Clubs.

3. Wining and dining, speeches, wager books and the insistence on the wearing of uniforms, and of following definite regulations in all matters, even at a trivial level.

4. The use of the word 'Society', implying selectivity, as against 'Club', implying greater willingness to elect any one who is interested in golf.

5. Unusual toasts at dinner.

In the light of this, one may consider further some of the other early Golf Clubs or Societies.

# The Royal Burgess Golfing Society

THE first Minute of the Society is dated 8 April 1773 but the Society believes that it was founded in 1735. The Minute of 1773 states: 'We, Daniel Ker, Alexander Milne and Charles Rhind, three of the members of the Society of Golfers in and about Edinburgh, taking into our consideration the present state of the Society and that most of the old members thereof are either dead or have neglected meetings of the same, so that it is in danger of becoming extinct, and we being inclined that the said Society should be continued, have, therefore, resolved to admit and receive the persons after named to be members, and who are to be subject and liable to the rules of the said Society and to such other rules and regulations hereafter in place of the old rules of the said Society, and to such other rules as may be regularly enacted in time coming.' These were old gentlemen at that time, so it is reasonable to believe that the Society (in a different form, because the rules and regulations for these new members in 1773 were as stated, different from the 'old rules') was in existence well before 1773. Cameron Robbie, the chronicler of the Royal Burgess Golfing Society, writing in 1936, bewails in his Preface: 'It will always be a source of regret to the earnest and critical historian of golf that so much of the early material in the shape of old Minute Books, etc, has either been lost or destroyed'. Robbie then goes through considerable contortions in order to prove that the Society existed in 1735, thereby making it older than any other Golf Club or Society. The proof of exact date is not really important because we do not know the exact date of the foundation of any of the other early Golfing Societies.

Robbie goes on to say that 'the character and formation of the early associations of golfers needed no formal record, so written evidence contemporaneous with the year of institution is not to be expected'. The one thing that the Freemasons insisted on was the keeping of accurate records; this statement cannot be accepted and the truth must be that well-kept records were deliberately destroyed in order to preserve secrecy. It is clear from the sad statement of 1773 that the old order was about to change and that new blood was to be allowed into the Society; they were not Freemasons, so they were not to know what had gone on before and were not subject to the initiation ceremony to which earlier members would certainly have been subjected. They were simply instructed to obey the regulations as set down in 1773.

It must have been a deliberate and most useful arrangement that the Secretary in 1773 and 1774 was Daniel Kerr and that the Treasurer was Charles Rhind in 1773. Thus two out of the three signatories to the declaration in 1773 would have been well equipped to see that the secrets of the older Society were kept hidden, no doubt by a thorough destruction of all the old Minutes, etc. They would also have been in a good position to fend off inquisitive people who wanted to know what had gone before, no doubt, with pleasantly vague replies of 'old traditions', etc, when, asked.

The Burgess Golfing Society was not, as one might have thought, composed only of people who were Burgesses of the City of Edinburgh. Indeed, in 1791 a motion that 'no gentleman shall be admitted a member of the Club [interesting that it should be referred to as a Club in this Minute] unless he first becomes a Burgess and Freeman of Edinburgh' was rejected by a large majority. Probably, the motion was put to the Society, in all innocence, by a non-Masonic member. The fact that a large majority rejected it was because there must have been many Masons within the Society who were not Burgesses and therefore would have had to cease being members if the motion had been carried.

The fact that the members of the Burgess were not necessarily Burgesses of Edinburgh did not prevent the Society from entering into a close relationship with the Edinburgh Town Council. A Minute of July 1800 points out that 'the Magistrates of Edinburgh, from Lord Provosts to Convenors of Trades received honorary membership of the Burgess Society and frequently joined the members at their convivial dinners . . . .'. Robbie points out in regard to this subtle move that 'These events were but a natural prelude to Magisterial favours . . .'. It is likely that, unknown to the non-Masonic members, many members of the Council were also Freemasons. One of these favours was that the Magistrates all signed a 'Seal of Cause', which gave the Burgess legal status as a corporation; this move was to be very useful to the Burgess in later years.

So the Burgess decided to 'change with the times' and 'go public' – but not quite public, for they continued to behave in what might be termed a 'Masonic manner'. They issued diplomas or charters to Golf Clubs overseas in the same way as did Blackheath. They thus gave these overseas Clubs official status, which was a device used, particularly by 'Grand Lodge', on a much wider scale.

In 1810 the Society granted a Charter and Diploma to Charles MacKenzie of the Island of Barbados to found a golfing society there; for reasons which are not apparent, but may be explained later, there was a delay in implementing the Charter which was not confirmed until 1817.

In 1814, a similar charter was granted to Charles MacDowell of St Vincent. Robbie observes that 'the governing body of the Burgess Society considered it quite

# The Honourable Company of Edinburgh Golfers

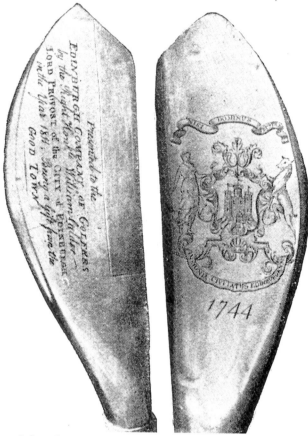

Sole and upper surface of the head of the first Silver Club belonging to the Honourable Company of Edinburgh Golfers – the oldest golf trophy in the world

CLARKE, in his *Golf: A Royal and Ancient Game* remarks of 'The Honourable the Edinburgh Company of Golfers' that the date of their institution is lost in antiquity, but the first regular series of Minutes signed by President Forbes of Culloden bears the date 1744.

They played on the 'links at Leith', though this land was not true links land, any more than Bruntsfield, where the Burgess Golfing Society and the Bruntsfield Links Golf Club were based, was links land. Both sites were convenient to Edinburgh and were therefore acceptable for that reason only.

There are plenty of records of golf being played on the links of Leith from 1672 onwards. By all accounts, the game was played by all classes and both nobles and commoners seem to have played happily together; as the links was common land, owned by Edinburgh Council, this is not surprising. After the golf the Gentlemen who golfed entertained themselves at a particular tavern and this does not seem to have included anybody else.

The principal tavern was Luckie Clephan's, although they did use other taverns at various times. At this point, there are no records of any attempt to form a Club or Society – but this may have been because they had destroyed all records of a Society at a later date.

In 1744, the City of Edinburgh offered the Gentlemen at Leith a Silver Club to play for. The full account of this presentation is as follows:

*Act of Council and Regulations to be observed by those who play for the City of Edinburgh's Silver Club.*

At Edinburgh, the seventh day of March 1744 years, The Lord Provost, Magistrates, and Council, with the Deacons Ordinary and Extraordinary of the City of Edinburgh, being in Council assembled – and it being represented to them That several Gentlemen of Honour, skilful in the ancient and healthful exercise of the Golf, had from time to time applied to several members of the Council for a Silver Club to be annually played for on the Links of Leith at such time and upon such conditions as the Magistrates and Council should think proper; And it being reported

within their prerogative to follow the example of the Grand Lodge of Freemasons, so these Charters were granted to their prospective offshoots of Barbados and St Vincent . . .'. Mr MacDowell was so grateful that he sent to the Society 54½ gallons of rum, which proved a great expense to the Society, who had to find £43 to defray the duty and expenses.

The Burgess had a great social life with much wining and dining, toasts, speechmaking, singing of songs, etc. They also had stringent rules about uniforms (and penalties for those who did not wear them) and a thriving Bets Book.

In 1807 the Burgess was split by a fierce dispute about the play for the Gold Medal; true to their tradition, they destroyed all Minutes relating to this internicine strife.

There can be no doubt that the Burgess Golfing Society was the same sort of organisation as Blackheath.

that the Gentlemen Golfers had drawn up a Scroll, at the desire of the Magistrates, of such Articles and Conditions as to them seem most expedient, as proper Regulations to be observed by the Gentlemen who should yearly offer to play for the said Silver Club, which were produced and read in Council. . . .

There followed regulations submitted to the Council by the Gentlemen Golfers and approved by the Council. Points from these Regulations worth emphasising are:

1. As many Noblemen, or Gentlemen, or other Golfers from any part of Great Britain or Ireland may play.

2. They have to pay a fee and enter eight days before the date of the Competition (which the Magistrates and Council will decide).

3. The entry book shall be kept at Luckie Clephan's, or such other house as shall be appointed from year to year.

4. Every winner shal be responsible for returning the Silver Club to the Council one month before it is to be played for again and shall give a surety of Fifty pounds.

5. The Club is always to remain the property of the 'Good Town'.

6. The winner shall be called the Captain of the Golf and, with the help of any two or three Subscribers, shall settle all disputes concerning the Golf and the Golfers.

By 2 April 1744, the Silver Club was first played for.

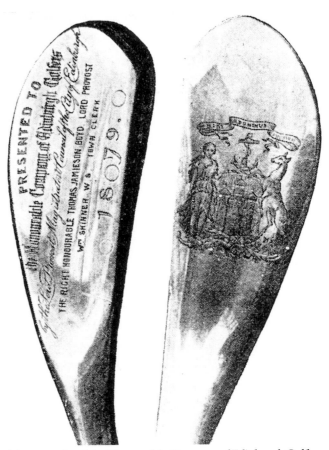

**A later trophy of the Honourable Company of Edinburgh Golfers**

What should one make of this document and its regulations? First, the Silver Club was not the property of any group of golfers.

The Council acknowledges that several members of the Council have been approached more than once by several Gentlemen of Honour. The impression that one gets is that a number of Gentlemen have made individual approaches to members of the Council. The capital letters in Gentlemen and Golfers does not imply a Company of Gentlemen Golfers – the general tenor suggests a casual approach by some gentlemen who liked playing golf.

That a valuable Silver Club would have been bought by the Council to please a few golfers – even if they were gentlemen – is surely very unlikely. The document at no time suggests that they were a corporate body of responsible golfers who had well-defined rules of golf which would be used as the rules of the competition on the links.

The Minutes of the Council state that they approve of the regulations (which the golfing gentlemen concerned seem to have drawn up) and give authority for the Silver Club to be bought. They appear to know nothing of the rules of the game which were going to be applied in the competition; the very fact that these rules existed suggests that there was some organisation already in existence and the fact that the council did not ask about them implies that they knew that rules for the playing of golf existed.

The book for entering was to be kept at Luckie Clephan's, the tavern that was frequented by the gentlemen and noblemen after golf.

The rules of the competition state that 'other golfers in Great Britain and Ireland' may play and the winner is to be the Captain of the Golf. One wonders how they would have managed if the Silver Club had been won by a carpenter from Glasgow! The truth is that they knew that one of their Company was going to win because it was not intended that anyone else should compete. This becomes evident in a change in the rules for the Silver Club in 1764. The regulations were considered to be 'too broad', for by it 'persons of bad fame or such as are not fitt company for Gentlemen, may play for and winn the Silver Club and if that should happen upon being declared Captain he must of course take the Chair and preside in all the Golf meetings which are purposely intended to be played for and won by Noblemen and Gentlemen only'. The Edinburgh Town Council, persuaded, no doubt, by several Gentlemen skilful in the ancient and healthy exercise of the Golf, had ejected the other golfers and openly made the Company of Gentlemen Golfers the only competitors, which is what the Company had always meant to happen. The noblemen and gentlemen who played golf were men of wealth and owners of land; many were lawyers or doctors and more than one was a Lord of Session; nearly all, if not all, were Freemasons and there must have been many on the Council that they could influence, either by reason of their own importance, or because of the Masonic bond.

John Kerr, himself a Mason, and one who had been awarded a Masonic jewel, writing in *The Golf Book of East Lothian* 1896, observes: 'A careful study of the subject brings us to the conclusion that, in the early part of the century, gentlemen of "independent means", Lords of Session, town dignitaries and wealthy merchants were associated together, without any written constitution or defined organisation, for the enjoyment of golf and for social fellowship. This competition, as we have suggested, implied that a company of golfers did exist in Edinburgh, whose object it was to foster the games. The competition brought them into evidence. It marked the opening of their written records.'

In 1768, the Company built a Club House for themselves at Leith. The Foundation Stone was laid in that year and the event is recorded as follows:

> This day Wm St Clair of Roslyn Esq, the undoubted representative of the Honourable and Hereditable G.M.M. [Grand Master Mason. Author] of Scotland. In the presence of Alexander Keith, Esq. Captain of the Honourable Company of Goffers, and other worthy members of the Goffing Company, all Masons, the G.M., now in his Grand Climax of Goffing, laid the Foundation of the Goffing House in the S.E. corner thereof, by Three Strokes of the Mallet.

This ends all supposition about the Masonic nature of the Honourable Company of Edinburgh Golfers; it is a fact the Company followed all the traditional habits of Golfing Societies of Masonic origins. It had an extensive and detailed Wager Book and dined and wined together in great conviviality. The wearing of a uniform was obligatory and there were fines for failing to wear it at a dinner and fines for other breaches of discipline. Speechmaking and the singing of songs were a part of all their evenings.

# Bruntsfield Links Golf Club

CLARKE, in *Golf: A Royal and Ancient Game*, writes of Bruntsfield: 'The names of the founders of the Bruntsfield Links Golf Club have not been handed down to us and there is reason to fear that they are irrevocably lost, nor is there any positive evidence when the Club was established. No records of its earlier years can be found. The first Minute Book dates from 1787, in which year the Club changed from a Society. . . .'

In 1790, the Club states that it has been established for thirty years and this gives it a founding date of 1760. No documents appear to have substantiated this claim but, nevertheless, the Club celebrated its Centenary in 1861 at the Freemasons Hall in Edinburgh.

In 1787 the Club Minutes state: 'The Society, having been formerly instituted as a Club, of this date agreed to. . .'. This suggests that the Club has become a Society but this must be an error in the Minute because it is referred to as a Club in all the Minutes thereafter.

In 1801, a Minute states that 'the Meeting, as usual, cracked their jocks (sic) over a glass and enjoyed the evening harmoniously with a song'.

In October 1801 a Minute states: 'It was recommended to the Treasurer to purchase a dozen caps and aprons . . .'

While not much has been said in the Minutes about uniforms, in 1815 it is recommended that the Captain's caddie should wear a uniform when carrying for the Captain; it almost certainly follows that the members have been wearing a uniform before this date.

Later Minutes show, on numerous occasions, a close friendship with the Burgess: dinners, matches, and competitions were often joint affairs.

In 1842 mention is made of matches arranged at the dinner. In 1861, at the Centenary dinner, the Lord Provost of Edinburgh was a guest of honour.

The Bruntsfield Links Golf Club followed the same pattern of behaviour as the Burgess. The loss of the early Minute books is typical and the statement that they are thirty years old in 1790 is unsupported by any documents; it was probably a matter that was in the memory of the Oldest Member. They may well have been founded before 1760, but we shall never know.

It is interesting, in view of the events described in Chapter 1, that both the Burgess and the Bruntsfield Club played over the area known as Bruntsfield Links. This area of land, adjacent to the City of Edinburgh, became open land after the destruction of the Forest of Drumselch; it was given to the City of Edinburgh, for the use and enjoyment of its citizens, it is believed, by David I, in the twelfth century.

## The Royal Aberdeen Golf Club

GOLF had been played at Aberdeen from at least the seventeenth century, if not before. The Club was instituted in 1815.

*The Golfing Annual* of 1888–90 states: 'The Aberdeen Golf Club appears to have come after a Club called "The Society of Golfers at Aberdeen", instituted 9 May 1783, a printed copy of whose Regulations, with a list of original members and the "Laws of Golf", is still extant; but this "Society of Golfers" had become dissolved before the institution of the present Club. A Golf Club [or Society. *Author*] must have existed even before 1783, as the Ballot Box, still in the possession of the Club, bears the inscription "The Aberdeen Golf Club 1780".'

The Club certainly had uniforms and no doubt wined and dined and laid bets on the games. But nothing of this is known prior to 1815 because there are no written records. The pattern is familiar.

## The Royal Musselburgh Golf Club

THIS was instituted in 1774. According to Clarke, 'The Minutes for the first ten years of its existence are unfortunately missing.'

The earlier date is known because of the dates on the old Musselburgh Cup, still in the possession of the Club, which go back to 1774; what this really means is that the Club goes back to at least 1774, since it may have existed for some years before it acquired a Cup.

The first Minute, in 1784, refers to them as a 'Company of Golfers' and, in several Minutes later on, they refer to themselves by the same title; it is not until 1786 that they regularly refer to themselves as a Club.

They dined and wined well; in 1788, the Minutes record '. . . that the Preses shall only allow Port Wine and Sherry, Rum, Brandy, Gin and Small Beer at dinner, and everyone must pay his share'.

In 1810 there is a surprising Minute that 'The Club resolve to present, by subscription, a new Creel and Shawl to the best female golfer who plays on the annual occasion on the 1st of January next, to be intimated to the Fish Ladies by the Officer of the Club. Two of the best Barcelona silk handkerchiefs to be added to the above premium of a Creel.'

The procession of the Silver Club at Leith

It seems that the all-male Club was prepared to encourage the Fish Ladies and, furthermore, had been encouraging them for some unspecified time before 1810. This must, easily, be the first Ladies' competition in the world.

From these Minutes we know that the Club had a Captain, President (Preses) and an Officer; no doubt, they also had a uniform.

## The Royal and Ancient Golf Club of St Andrews

IT is of interest, and may have some significance, that the first Magistrate of St Andrews was from Flanders and was appointed, in 1120, by David I.

A notice of 1754 states: 'The Noblemen and Gentlemen above named [there is a list of 22 people at the head. *Author*] being admirers of the antient and healthful Exercise of the Golf, and at the same time having the interest and prosperity of the Antient City of St Andrews at heart, being the Alma Mater of Golf, did in the year of our Lord 1754, contribute for a Silver Club weighing [...] Pounds and [...] ounces and having a St Andrew's Cross on the head thereof, to be played for on the Links of St Andrews upon the 14th day of May said year, and yearly in time coming, subject to the Conditions and Regulations following viz:- . . .'. The conditions which follow are almost identical with those laid down by the Honourable Company at Edinburgh ten years previously, for the Edinburgh Council's Silver Club.

There is, again, the curious use of capitals, the same reference to the 'antient and healthful' game and the same suggestion that a few gentlemen (not, apparently, belonging to any Club or Society) are presenting a Silver Club. The major difference is that, here, the gentlemen are buying the club and not persuading the local Council to do so. The reference to St Andrews as the 'Alma Mater' of golf served to give rise to the idea that St Andrews was the 'Home of Golf', which still persists today.

There is nothing to make one believe that this is the first Minute of the Society of Golfers at St Andrews. The title is not even mentioned; indeed, if it did exist then, one might almost say that the avoidance of the use of the title was deliberate.

In the same year that this Silver Club was given for play, the Gentlemen Golfers at Edinburgh asked the 'Gentlemen of Fife' [not the Society of Golfers at St Andrews. *Author*] if they might play for their Silver Club.

The term Gentlemen Golfers, with capital letters, today would indicate some sort of Club or Society but, at that time, the use of capitals occurred in a rather haphazard fashion and had no such meaning; the whole emphasis, as in the case of the Gentlemen Golfers at Edinburgh, seems to have been to promote the idea that they were definitely not an organised Society or Club. The first use of the term Society of Golfers in the Minutes was in 1770.

The play for the Silver Club was to be open to 'all golfers', but the fact that the Gentlemen Golfers of Edinburgh sought permission to play in the first Silver Club competition suggests that entry was not totally free to any golfer. In 1773, 'because of a poor entry,' the Society of St Andrews Golfers agreed that, in future, the competition should be open only to members of their Society and the Gentlemen Golfers of Edinburgh.

The Society of St Andrews Golfers followed the usual traditions of all the other societies and early clubs and engaged in wining and dining of heroic proportions. They had fines for non-attendance and wore uniforms. The uniforms are not mentioned much in the Minutes, but in 1780 there is mention that their uniforms are in a bad condition and they agreed to new ones, to a different pattern, so uniforms had existed long before the first mention of them.

The Society had minor differences from the others; the Wager Book was not such a prominent feature as it was in the other Societies and the Society was much more prominent in the organisation of balls and entertainments generally.

In 1834, they became the Royal and Ancient Golf Club of St Andrews. In 1853, the Committee asked the Captain of the Royal and Ancient to lay the Foundation Stone of the new Clubhouse but it was laid, in 1854, by Major Belshes, Secretary of the Club, 'with full Masonic honours'. This change, by which the Captain, Whyte-Melville, was deprived of the honour, was probably made because Belshes was a more senior Mason and therefore considered, by the Masons in the Club, as being a more suitable person to perform such an historic act.

Salmond, in *The Story of the R&A*, gives a description of the first Minute Book: 'It is a marble-sided, leather-backed volume of 22 sheets (12 x 8 in.), the paper is not all of a kind, and there are several different watermarks. The first page is blank, the second contains the rules, and pages 3–5 the names of the founders and conditions of play for the Silver Club.'

On 4 May 1766, the members decided to open an additional Minute Book, known as the 'Book of Records'. So there were now two Minute Books. The ostensible use of the second book was to record the attendance at dinners and at the fortnightly meeting, at eleven am at the Golf House, to play a round of golf and dine afterwards. One wonders why this required a second Minute Book? The Book of Records also details the many balls organised by the Society.

Salmon concludes: 'On 7 June 1800, the Secretary was ordered to purchase a new Book of Records. The last entry (which is written on the end paper) is dated 6 September 1800. It is much to be regretted that, when the Book of Records was rebound, at some unknown date, the binder trimmed the leaves and cut into certain of the entries.'

Thus we have an original Minute Book, in which the paper differs throughout, and a mutilated Book of Records.

There are two other pointers to the Masonic nature of the Society of St Andrews Golfers, later to become the Royal and Ancient Golf Club of St Andrews. The first is that Alexander Duncan, a known Master Mason, was, at one time or another, Captain of the Honourable Company of Edinburgh Golfers, Captain of the Royal and Ancient Golf Club of St Andrews, and Captain of Blackheath Golf Club.

**Two of the Silver Clubs belonging to the Royal and Ancient Golf Club of St Andrews. A silver ball for each Captain is attached. When a member of the Royal Family was Captain a gold ball was attached instead**

The second is that the *Fifeshire Journal* of Thursday, 14 July 1853 records that, in a cavity in the wall of the old Union Parlour, discovered when the Royal and Ancient Clubhouse was being built, there was found a bottle containing two golf balls, copies of *The Times*, the *Fifeshire Journal* and the *Fife Herald*, together with various Masonic items.

The general form and behaviour of the Society of St Andrews Golfers, subsequently rechristened The Royal and Ancient Golf Club of St Andrews, is the same as that of all the other early golfing Societies and the Honourable Company, with whom it had many members in common. In the case of the St Andrews Society, they have been more thorough and more subtle in destroying their records.

The cumulative evidence concerning the nature and formation of these early golfing organisations points to their origins as Masonic Lodges. They seem to have represented a less 'serious' type of Lodge, in which the amount of ceremonial and ritual was less than that which obtained in other Lodges; the main objective was to play golf in order to work up a good appetite for wining and dining, speeches, and a generally convivial and harmonious evening.

At first, the wining and dining were more important than the golf, as is shown in the Minutes of various Clubs and Societies, in which there are a few lines about the golf and a page or more about the menu for the next dinner and who is going to supply the drink. Later, the golf bug bit them and the golfing side of things became more important; the play for the Silver Clubs is evidence of this.

In the festive evenings of drinking, speechmaking and betting, there was some discipline and formality and the Captain, as President of the gathering, was the man who saw to it that the Meeting was kept in order and that uniforms were worn, etc. Even after the Societies became Clubs and admitted non-Masons, they continued to make a number of very 'Masonic' decisions, such as the licensing of overseas Clubs; how did they manage to do this?

In the early days, the Captains of all the Clubs, Societies and the Honourable Company would have been Freemasons. The idea of election 'by combat', as has been suggested by several golf historians, never really happened. The winner of the Silver Club was 'Captain of the Golf', and as far as further competitions for the Club were concerned, he was the man who made decisions; he was never designated as the Captain of the Society or Club. By the time that associations, such as the Honourable Company and the Society of Golfers at St Andrews, began to consider the winner as their Captain, they had taken steps to ensure that the only competitors were Masons. Dr Grierson in his *History of St Andrews* (1807) states that, although the competition for the Silver Club was played every year, the 'Captain of the Company' was elected, having been fixed before the players went out on the links.

It is probable that many Masons, being, in the early days, the most senior and experienced members of the Club, served on the Committee and were able to make resolutions by majority vote but, as time went by, more and more non-Masons became senior and experienced members and obtained places on the Committee.

One way in which the Masons tried to keep control of events and decisions was to ensure that at least the Captain was always a Freemason. This they achieved by having the Captain elected by the past Captains, not by the Committee. When, in 1764, the Gentlemen Golfers at Edinburgh, petitioned the Edinburgh Council only to allow those golfers who were 'fitt company for Gentlemen' to play for the Silver Club, the petition was signed by the Captain and the past Captains, not, as one might have expected, by the Committee.

By 1836, the Honourable Company had given a Gold Medal for the winner of the Silver Club, and the Silver Club, now apparently in their possession, became a Wand of Office for the Captain of the Company. Each Captain fixed (and still fixes) a silver ball to the Club to signify his year of Office. The Captain was elected by the past Captains, and the Committee were, traditionally, in duty bound to ratify that decision.

The Society of Golfers at St Andrews went about things in a different way. In 1837, William IV, as Patron of the Royal and Ancient Golf Club of St Andrews, gave them a Gold Medal to play for. In March 1838, the Dowager Queen Adelaide (the King having died) gave the Royal and Ancient a Gold Medal to be worn by the Captain on all formal occasions. In 1841 the Club decided to return to the regulations, 'formerly recognised', which gave the past Captains the right to nominate the Captain.

The Queen Adelaide Medal, as it was now called, was to be advertised as being played for at the Autumn Meeting, but there was only going to be one competitor, the newly-elected Captain; the moment that he drove off he became, automatically, the Captain – and so it has been ever since.

The Burgess elected their Captain through their Council in 1773, and afterwards. By what means a Captain was elected between 1735 and 1773 we do not know; the suggestion made by Cameron Robbie in his *Chronicle*, that such early Clubs did not need officers, is not tenable. The Masons were much too well organised for that; they would have had Captains, officers and uniforms from the start (which could well have been before 1735) but their

efficiency was such, in 1773, that no record remains. No doubt the early Councils, carefully and gently led by Rhind, the first Secretary, and Daniel Kerr, the first Treasurer, both members of the old brigade who knew all about the original Society, were Masons or certainly contained a majority of Masons; thus, at the start in 1773, the Captain would have been a fellow Mason. They seem to have taken no definite steps, like the other associations, to ensure that subsequent Captains all belonged to the craft, but they did make another move; the Captain had the privilege of electing three members during his year of office, 'by the shake of a hand'. These new members did not have to go through the process of being proposed and seconded. If the Captain wanted to introduce more Masons to the Society, he was able to elect three during his year of office.

The great majority of the Captains of these early golf associations were elected by the past Captains and this 'tradition' was followed by many Clubs after that time, though it is certain that few, if any, realised how the tradition had arisen, nor was the method used to promote Masonic control.

There was a further advantage in the past Captains electing the Captain; the past Captains became a sort of unofficial Committee. Though unofficial, they wielded great power because they were all very experienced members of the Club and it is likely that a number of them, at any one time, were also on the Club Committee. Their accumulated wealth of experience in the affairs of the Club was such that it would be a bold (or foolhardy) Club Committee that ignored their advice.

It was not too difficult for the past Captains of the early Societies and Clubs to ensure that the Committee made decisions favourable to the Masons.

## The Effect of the 1745 Uprising

IN 1745, Prince Charles Edward Stuart, 'Bonnie Prince Charlie', made an abortive attempt to gain the Throne. This was not the first attempt, a minor effort in 1715 having rapidly fizzled out. A strong uprising, which included a rally of the Clans (or some of them) occurred thirty years later, when Charles landed in the west of Scotland. He mustered an army and marched south.

At Derby, his situation became increasingly difficult. He began a retreat, which became a rout after a serious defeat at the Battle of Culloden. His army was crushed and scattered and the Duke of Cumberland, who was George II's General, exacted a fierce revenge.

The dramatic arrival in Scotland of a Stuart Pretender to the throne of a Hanoverian King aroused all the romantic, passionate and tendentious character of the

Celts, yet one of the reasons that the uprising failed was that not all Scots supported it.

The Scottish social and political fabric was torn in two; it was not possible to be neutral in Scotland, either you were a Jacobite or an anti-Jacobite. Families became divided, friends became enemies, passionate rancour and bitterness were rife.

In a climate such as this, the Freemasons, as divided as the general public in their political opinions, were in an extremely difficult situation during the time of the rising, and in a highly dangerous situation after the Battle of Culloden.

Cumberland was totally ruthless in his determination to eliminate all Jacobites and his soubriquet of 'Butcher' Cumberland was well merited; the breath of suspicion was enough to lead to imprisonment, torture (which would reveal further information on which to act) and death. The recognition of the presence of a secret society, most of whose members were Jacobites, would have been enough to ensure imprisonment or death for all its members.

The immediate reaction of the Masons was to destroy all records. This was done with great efficiency and, no doubt, speed, which is why all records and Minutes of the early golfing Societies prior to 1745, are lost. Speculation as to the date of origins of these early associations from ballot boxes, medals, cups, etc is as fruitless as it is inaccurate. Clubs or Societies could well have been in existence long before they aspired to such things – and probably were.

The only Company which has written evidence before 1745 is the Gentlemen Golfers in 1744. This is the announcement, by the Edinburgh Town Council, of the gift of a Silver Club to 'several Gentlemen of Honour, skillful in the antient and healthful exercise of Golf'. The Club is not being donated to a Society or Company, it is being given to a few Gentlemen who find golf a healthy exercise. The winner is to be 'Captain of the Golf', not the Captain of any organisation; he is to be concerned solely with the next competition for the Silver Club, which is to be open to any golfer.

Although this statement is in the archives of the Company it is certainly not a Minute of the Company and has nothing to do with its beginnings. Indeed, it goes out of its way to suggest that it is for the pleasure of some gentlemen who like playing golf but are not, in any way, organised. In the context of the times this was a very wise decision.

It is possible that the Silver Club was sought for the opposite reason. Duncan Forbes was a Mason, a powerful man, being Lord President of the Court of Session, a well-recognised anti-Jacobite and fanatical golfer. He, of all people, in 1744, would have been aware of what was likely to happen in 1745. There were Masons on the Edinburgh Town Council. Having ensured that all traces of the previous Society were destroyed, and being most anxious to continue playing golf, he arranged for the 'several Gentlemen of Honour' to make an application, as private individuals, for the gift of a Silver Club to play for. He might well have ensured, through the Masonic members of the Council, and by using his great office, to influence others so that the Council would agree. The Edinburgh Council, in the ensuing year, had quickly handed over the keys of the City to Cumberland when he and his army appeared at the gates, so they would have, ostensibly, been in the anti-Jacobite camp; Forbes may have known that, if pressed, they would do it. If the anti-Jacobite Council, openly supported by the anti-Jacobite Lord President of the Court of Session, gave a Silver Club to a few Honourable Gentlemen whose sole interest was playing golf, this would establish these gentlemen as anti-Jacobite, or, at least, totally non-political. The fact that Forbes was listed as a competitor in the first competition, though in fact he did not play, was additional support for the idea.

On this basis, the Silver Club was a device for diverting attention from a possible earlier secret society by implying that this play for a Silver Club was the bright idea of a few golfers, and allowed the continuance of golf at Leith.

As has been said earlier, the curious use of capital letters in the document was a feature of the times and does not have the implication that subsequent historians have given to it.

The Gentlemen who golfed lay low but, ten years later, arranged, with the permission of the Edinburgh Council, that only like Gentlemen could play for the Silver Club. It was not until twenty years after they had been given the Silver Club and when the Jacobite problem was almost forgotten, that they came out into the open and proudly declared, when laying the Foundation Stone for the new Clubhouse, that the President of the Honourable Company was the 'Honourable and Heretable Grand Master Mason of Scotland' and that all members of the Committee were Masons.

In 1743, two years before the Rising, Thomas Mathison wrote 'The Goff, an Heroi-Comic Poem in three Cantos'. The poem concerned the golfing virtues and failures of various well-known golfers on the links at Leith. The first edition was published anonymously, price 4 pence; the names of all the golfers in this edition were left blank. It was not until the second edition in 1763 that the author admitted his name – and inserted the names of the golfers.

## The Society of Golfers at St Andrews

THIS Society, clearly, took its lead from the Honourable Company and issued, ten years after them, an announcement which was almost the same as theirs, which was sent to the Town Council of St Andrews.

They are twenty-two Honourable Gentlemen, only interested in playing golf; private, non-political individuals, who seek permission from the Council to play golf for a Silver Club. The difference, after that, is that they have bought the Silver Club themselves – they do not seek a Club but only permission to play for it. The head of the Club will be decorated with a St Andrew [not the insignia of a Society. *Author*]. The Council agreed.

Although the competition was, originally, open to 'all golfers', it was soon designated as only for the St Andrews Gentlemen and the Gentlemen at Leith. It thus became, as at Edinburgh, a closed competition.

It was not until 1770, twenty-five years after the second Jacobite uprising, that the Gentlemen who golfed at St Andrews finally allowed themselves to be referred to, in a Minute, as The Society of Golfers at St Andrews.

The City of St Andrews had shown some Jacobite tendencies; for the City to have offered these Gentlemen a Silver Club might have branded them as Jacobite sympathisers and they did not have the open support of a powerful man who was also a recognised anti-Jacobite, like Duncan Forbes. The effect of this gift of a Silver Club was the same as the effect at Leith; it helped to dispel any idea that a secret society was involved in golf.

The necessity to destroy all evidence of a secret society and keep a low profile was even more important at Blackheath. Here, the Scottish Masonic golfers were in the middle of an English population which supported the Hanoverian regime; rapid and thorough destruction of all possible evidence was essential. In 1789, the Knuckle Club was formed, but was careful to meet secretly at a pub and not to involve the parent Club, which, probably, by that time, had a number of non-Mason members, blissfully unaware of the Masonic element.

The troubles of the '45 must have left their mark and the Knuckle Club only survived twenty-eight years before dwindling to a shadow of its early self and disappearing. Perhaps, so long after the troubles, they were a little careless in the destruction of their records – much to the benefit of later historians.

How many 'Clubs within a Club' continued to exist in the Scottish Golfing Societies and Clubs we do not know; if they did exist (and they probably did) they destroyed their records completely at the time of dissolution and all traces have disappeared.

While an account of the early Golf Clubs and Societies must, because of the careful destruction of so many records and Minutes, involve supposition, the general pattern, clearly revealed, indicates a heavy involvement of Freemasons in the organisation of early golf, and the events described in Chapters 1 and 2 show that this involvement was inevitable, rather than surprising.

Golf owes a great debt to the Freemasons, who kept it going when it might have disappeared and, moreover, initiated a feeling for the 'spirit of the game', which stemmed from the sense of chivalry and gentlemanly behaviour, which they had inherited from the Knights Templar and the noble Knights of Flanders. This code of behaviour was such that only a few, simple rules were required (and these were supplied by the Freemasons). The rest of the game was governed by a sense of fair play and a determination not to take unfair advantage of one's opponent, which were so fundamental that they did not require writing down. This was understood by all the 'Gentlemen Golfers' who played the 'antient' game for their health and enjoyment and who loved and honoured it.

That this debt is only acknowledged two hundred and fifty years later is due to the Freemasons' obsession with secrecy and the thoroughness with which they carried out their policy of concealment.

## Historical Connections between Golf and Archery

WHEN, in 1457, golf was banned, so, too, was 'futeball'. Both sports took place on the links land around villages. There was no obvious connection between football and the other sport, but there were affinities between archery and golf, both in the making of bows and golf clubs and in the organisation of both sports.

In an isolated village community on the east coast of Scotland in the fifteenth and sixteenth centuries the making of golf clubs was a local trade; indeed, much of it was probably not a trade at all, but was a hobby, practised by individual golfers who made the clubs themselves. Most of these villages were home for a number of trades: fishermen, shipwrights, bowmakers, blacksmiths, carpenters, and so on. The trades were not highly specialised and all artisans living in communities as small as these were something of a 'jack of all trades' and well accustomed to the policy of 'help thy neighbour'.

The spliced joint which connected the head of a wooden club to the shaft was a type of joint which had been used by shipwrights since Roman times; carpenters, cabinet-makers and shipwrights all had tools which could be used to shape wooden clubheads and the blacksmith was well able to shape the few iron clubheads needed. The whipping used in the early clubs was tarred fisherman's twine. The most specialised expert was the bow-maker, who had a specific knowledge of the elastic properties of various woods and was thus well placed not only to know the 'springiness' of different woods but, also, knew how to fine down a piece of wood so that the spring was in the right place; he would have been a very necessary expert in making wooden shafts.

The first intimation we have of the involvement of bowyers in making golf clubs was when, in 1502, James IV's Lord High Treasurer paid a bill of thirteen shillings to a 'bowar' of Saint Johnstoun (Perth) for 'clubbs'. Some have construed this as meaning that the King learnt to play at Perth, but this is probably wishful thinking by those who wanted to make Perth important.

At all events, the King ordered 'clubbs', the association of the Stuarts with golf had begun, and a bowmaker had made them. One hundred and one years later, in 1603, a bowmaker, William Mayne, a bowyer burgess of Edinburgh, became a Royal Warrant Holder for making clubs for James VI of Scotland (James I of England). If these two men were the only evidence available that bowmakers also made golf clubs, the evidence would be weak; there is other evidence, however, in the history of the Royal Company of Archers, which considerably strengthens this supposition; it will be discussed later.

One of the connections between archery and golf was that they both used the same ground. In the area of Dornoch, in northeast Scotland, there is evidence that the links land was very suitable for golf, archery and other sports.

At Leith, Musselburgh and Bruntsfield the evidence is even more revealing. Just as golf became a Court game, so did archery; as the Court was in Edinburgh, it was easiest to practise archery nearby. As with golf, when the Court began to indulge in archery, members of the Court required artisans to make bows and arrows for them.

At Leith, there were butts on the same land over which the golfers played. At Musselburgh, the Silver Arrow had been shot for since 1603 – at least, that is the supposition, because the earliest medal on it is dated 1603. All written records have been lost. The Royal Company of Archers shot their arrows on Bruntsfield, as well as Leith.

## Archery at St Andrews

At St Andrews it was reported that in 1582 one Patrick Learmonth, son of a Provost of St Andrews, fired an arrow at Archbishop Hamilton, who was playing golf during church hours.

Just as many students and members of the University of St Andrews were golfers, many were also archers.

There is no record of the start of the student archery competition for the Silver Arrow of the University of St Andrews, because all records have been lost, but the earliest medal on the Arrow is dated 1618, and the last 1754, the year that the Silver Club was first played for.

Throughout the eighteenth century, university men, well known as golfers a little later, had, earlier, when students, been winners of the Silver Arrow; of the twenty-two Gentlemen who signed the petition for a Silver Club in 1754, ten had been winners of the Silver Arrow. It could well have been that it was their familiarity with the Silver Arrow competition that gave them the idea for a Silver Club for the golfers.

The Union Club of St Andrews was originally opened for the use of members of the Archery Club. Its first Minutes are dated 1835. In 1853, being in funds, the Union Club, with the permission of the Town Council, decided to build a new Clubhouse. The sketch plans for the house in that year include 'Proposed Plans for Accommodation for the Golfers and Archers'. A large room, the 'Union Club Parlour' was to be used by both, and places in it were allowed for their 'Bows and Boxes' [Golf boxes. *Author*].

Although housed under the same roof, the two Clubs remained separate – the Union Club (archers) and the Royal and Ancient Golf Club. The Foundation stone of the Club was laid by the Secretary 'with full Masonic honours'. Not long after the Golf House was built, it was agreed that the two Clubs should merge, any member of one being, automatically, a member of the other.

By 1877, the golfing membership had increased dramatically while the number of archers had declined considerably. In May 1877, it was agreed that the two Clubs should merge completely and that the Club should be known as the Royal and Ancient Golf Club of St Andrews. This merger succeeded in submerging the archers completely. This demonstrates a longstanding affinity between archers and golfers; the bond was probably Masonic.

The important organisation of archers in Scotland was the Royal Company of Archers, otherwise known as The Queen's Bodyguard in Scotland. A history of this organisation was written by James Balfour Paul in 1875; his preamble to it refers to it as the 'Sovereign's Archer-Guard of Scotland'.

He starts by stating that The Royal Company of Archers is 'involved in considerable obscurity' because 'the ancient records of the Company were destroyed by fire in the sixteenth century'. The date is a mistake because he then goes on to say that the earliest records remaining are dated 1676. He continues: 'The Minutes of that date appear to have been copied in the year 1714 into the volume that now contains them'. The apparent destruction of the early Minutes and the clear evidence of tampering with some of the remaining ones must, as before, raise a high index of suspicion.

The first Minute (copied in) states: 'The Noble and useful Recreation of Archery, being for many years much neglected, several Noblemen and Gentlemen did associate themselves in a Company . . .'. The whole wording and tenor of this statement – and the use of the word Company – clearly indicate where the Gentlemen Golfers of Leith got their idea from in 1744.

The Privy Council, to whom they had applied in 1677 to be recognised as a Company, not only approved the idea but gave them twenty pounds towards the first prize. The fact that the first Captain of the Company was the Marquess of Atholl and that he had been made a Privy Councillor in 1660 and an Extra-Ordinary Lord of Session in 1663, may have had a bearing on the matter, in much the same way as Duncan Forbes had influence in 1744.

The Royal Company of Archers, however, was from the start very much a Company for the noblest in the land and its membership in 1703 was, in effect, a list of the Scottish nobility and, particularly, those of Flemish origin. All the Flemish families are there: Seton, Erskine, Stuart, Annandale, Eglinton, Montgomerie, St Clair, etc – the families who had supplied the Scots Guard with officers in earlier times in France. The Scots Guard, that neo-Templar organisation which was the forerunner of Freemasonry in Scotland, supplied the most élite section of the 9,000 Scottish troops who joined the French in their Hundred Year's War against the English.

Another feature of the Royal Company of Archers, which was almost certainly a direct successor to the Scots Guard, finally disbanded in France in 1662, was its quasi-military stance and obsession with uniforms. The Company had many ranks within it, Lieutenant, Captain, Captain-General, Brigadier, etc (at one time there were 53 Brigadiers) and spent much time organising semi-military parades and ceremonies. The Company dined at various taverns around Leith and Bruntsfield. As Paul records, in 1805, the Mess table always 'saw around it, more faces than the targets had seen earlier in the day'. The truth was that the Royal Company was a slightly 'snob' organisation in which, by the nineteenth century, few members took much interest in archery. It was a considerable social plum for those who could get in.

Throughout Paul's account of the Company there are constant references to a much earlier and obscure foundation. Curiously, they seem to have had little to do with the Honourable Company – except to buy the portrait of William St Clair from them when the latter were in dire financial straits; they wanted the portrait because St Clair was, at one time, their President, as well as, of

course, as being President of the Honourable Company. Rattray was a member and, like St Clair, had won the Silver Arrow. Thomas Kincaid, whose golfing diary is famous, was a member.

In 1703, feeling that it would be better if they had a licence to exist from a body more important than the Privy Council, they petitioned Queen Anne to grant them a Charter. The idea was put forward for Her Majesty's consideration by Lord Cromarty, past President of the Company and, at that time, Principal Secretary of State for Scotland. The Queen graciously consented; the Royal Charter so granted, among many other privileges, gives them the right 'freely, quietly, well and in peace' to fire their arrows and 'Prohibiting, by these presents all Magistrates, Sheriffs, Justices of the Peace . . . to cause any obstacle or impediment to the said Company. . .'.

Being strongly Jacobite, and guessing what might happen in the future, they must have felt somewhat relieved when they were granted such a Charter. However, they then went a step further and persuaded the Magistrates of Edinburgh to give them a Silver Arrow to shoot for, in 1709. Paul's account tells us that 'The Arrow is to be awarded to the winner. The only competitors allowed to enter were those who were of the Royal Company of Archers and, although the winner is awarded the Arrow, he is to return it to the "Dean of Gild" of Edinburgh until the next competition.'

Paul points out that in 1715, the year of the first Jacobite uprising, 'Probably wishing to show what a strong Jacobite body the Royal Company was, no less than one hundred and eleven members took part . . .'. He remarks that this seems to have caused the Magistrates some fright, for they refused to have a competition in the following year and in fact the competition is not mentioned again until 1726 when the Council of Edinburgh asked the Royal Company when they should deliver the Arrow to the Royal Company for the annual shoot; they received a haughty reply that, unless the Company could have the Arrow to shoot for when they chose to do it, it had better stay where it was! A Meeting took place and the Arrow was duly shot for.

We are not given, in Paul's account of the Company, the details of the petition to the Edinburgh Council for an Arrow but it is safe to assume that it talked of the healthy and ancient exercise, etc just as the Gentlemen of Leith did thirty-five years later.

Nevertheless, the Silver Arrow and the Charter from Queen Anne enabled the Royal Company of Archers, as a Company, to survive the '45 intact, despite the fact that all its members were strongly, and openly, Jacobite; some of its members were implicated and charged, but the Company itself was never disbanded or accused of being a secret society. It kept a low profile for several years and arranged no parades or ceremonials. Professor Bruce Leman in *The Jacobite Risings in Britain. 1689–1746* refers to the Royal Company of Archers as being, at the time of the '45 uprising, 'that hot bed of sedition'.

The curious separation of the Royal Company of Archers and the Honourable Company has meant that, unless an account of members, bowmakers and club-makers is culled from both sets of Minutes, the common features of both are lost. As an example, Thomas Kincaid was an Archer and wrote the Latin verses on the plinth of the Edinburgh Arrow; he is written of, in the Archers' archives, as an Archer but no mention is ever made of him as a golfer; in the Honourable Company his prowess as a golfer is shown but no one would know that he was an Archer. David Drummond, Rattray and St Clair of Roslyn are treated in exactly the same way.

When it comes to the bowmakers and clubmakers, reading the two accounts shows conclusively that the Royal Company's bowmakers and the Leith clubmakers were, often, one man. An early bowmaker, Donaldson, left the Company in 1783 because the Company did not think much of him as a bowmaker; in 1787, Donaldson appears as a clubmaker at Blackheath. No initial is given but it appears likely to be the same man who, apparently, was a better clubmaker than a bowmaker.

In 1760 George Neilson, the Company's Officer and bowmaker, found himself, after fifty-three years' service to the Company, too ill to make a living; assuming that he had joined the Company as a lad of 17, he must have been born in about 1690. He died in 1763. There is no record of him as a clubmaker but a Robert Neilson (1719–1767) was a clubmaker at Leith and his son, Alexander, born 1752, was also a clubmaker at Leith. It seems very likely that George Neilson may have been the father of Robert and that he was a clubmaker as well as a bowmaker. George Neilson was succeeded by Thomas Comb who, we know, was a clubmaker and who had been apprenticed to Neilson. This makes it even more likely that George Neilson was a clubmaker and bowmaker and that he taught Thomas Comb both trades. So, although neither the golfers nor the archers recorded bowmakers and clubmakers in common, there is no doubt that the two trades were frequently carried on by one man.

The importance of archery in general, and of the Royal Company of Archers in particular, in the history of golf is that the two have always marched side by side and that their later organisations had a common Masonic background. The archers and the golfers used the same ground at Leith, Bruntsfield and Musselburgh and, cer-tainly, at other sites as well.

When they formed Societies, Companies or Clubs there were all, basically, Masonic lodges and all concen-trated on good fellowship, uniforms, wining and dining, and bets and, to keep all this under reasonable control, rules and regulations.

At St Andrews the two occupied the same Club-house; it was only at Leith and Bruntsfield that the Royal Company of Archers and the Honourable Company and the Golfing Society at Bruntsfield seem to have kept their distance.

Even so, the Royal Company of Archers had many members in common with the golfers and the Company certainly showed the way for the golfers to avoid expo-sure as a secret society in the mid eighteenth century. Finally, the archers and the golfers used bowmakers and clubmakers, respectively, and usually one man fulfilled both roles.

One would have liked to learn more names of bow-makers to the Royal Company to see if they matched with known clubmakers, as it seems possible that Paul's account was incomplete; however, when the author wrote to the Royal Company of Archers for further infor-mation – or for permission to see the original archives and Minutes – he received a courteous reply from the Secretary that he was part-time and would not know where to look for what was required, and that, in any event, it was a rule of the Company that no member of the public was allowed to see the Company's archives, so, regretfully, he was unable to help. He offered that he would ask some of the older members for information. There was no further communication. While it would be inaccurate to say that the Royal Company of Archers in the seventeenth and eighteenth centuries was a Jacobite organisation, it would be true to say that the great major-ity of its members were Jacobite and even truer to say that, following its heritage from the Scots Guard, it was a totally Masonic institution and that the list of members is a list of Scottish Freemasons.

In 1734, when the Duke of Hamilton was the Captain-General, a poem was written, in French, in praise of one of the many parades that the Royal Company of Archers staged. One or two lines are interesting. About the Earl of Wigton, who brought up the rear of the procession: 'L'arrier garde est faite, par Fleming le valliant . . .'.

The last line in one of the end stanzas reads: 'Des Archers Ecossois, le garde du Corps du Roi. . .'.

The last line surely indicates that the writer believes that there is a direct connection between the Royal Company of Archers of Edinburgh and the Scots Guard, who were the personal Bodyguard of the Kings of France many years before.

Robert Forgan in his workshop, c.1895.
Behind him stands his son and partner Thomas

# Wooden Clubs and their Makers

## 1790–1930

## Forms of Wooden Clubs

Surviving examples of wooden clubs date from the late eighteenth century. The oldest known and authenticated wooden clubs are, therefore, not more than 200 years old. Prior to that time, one has to rely on a very few illustrations and on descriptions given by Thomas Kincaid in 1687. From such sources, however, it seems that there was very little difference in general form and shape of clubs from 1600 (or before) until 1840.

The reason that there are no older examples is that a broken or badly damaged wooden club is of little value and one which is infested with woodworm is positively dangerous to other wooden clubs. Wood being easily burned, this was the simplest method of disposal; apart from some slight delay, during which time the club might be cut down for use by children, the bonfire was the usual fate of early wooden clubs.

The earliest wooden clubheads are long and narrow and have a markedly hooked face. The faces are shallow – seldom more than 1 inch deep. The leading edge of the face has a horn insert and lead is positioned in a cavity at the back of the clubhead.

A generalisation is often made that such clubs are 'banana-shaped' but this is not strictly true. They are 'curved on flat', that is, the heel of the club is not curved – or only very slightly. It is possible that the concavity of the face may be more pronounced in old clubs than when

they were newly made because the centre of the face has been driven back by use and this may account for the slight curve of the heel in some clubs. Usually, it is only at about the centre of the face that the hook begins. The head is a graceful series of curves; a gentle curve between shaft and head; a hooked curve to the toe end of the face; a definite cambering of the top of the head – both at the back and the front and, in particular, at the toe, where it is often most marked. The back of the head makes a sweeping curve from a short toe back to the neck, where it joins the shaft. The old clubmakers used to insist that a wooden club, when soled, must look as if it clings to the ground; a very apt description.

It is curious that, despite the fact that clubmakers were very individual in their work and were working in isolated communities, the difference between clubs made by one clubmaker and another is minimal. The presence in the late eighteenth and early nineteenth centuries of a large number of clubmakers at Musselburgh and a smaller number at St Andrews might explain how a certain general shape was common to each centre but does not explain why clubs produced by individual clubmakers at each centre were so similar. In these days of easy travel the two centres may not be considered very far apart but in the early nineteenth century it was difficult, expensive and time-consuming to travel from one to the other. McEwan of Musselburgh found the journey to St Andrews so tedious that he only went once a year and appointed David Robertson, Allan Robertson's father, to act as his agent at St Andrews.

There were isolated craftsmen, such as Jackson of Perth and Munro of Aberdeen, who must have had few, if any, fellow craftsmen with whom to compare notes, and yet they produced clubs that, in general shape, were the same as those produced at St Andrews and Musselburgh. The author, over many years, has weighed and measured between 700 and 1000 old clubs and it has been found impossible, from the shape of clubheads, to ascribe them to any one maker.

There are two points to be made in this matter. Firstly, although the clubmakers had neither time nor money to make these journeys, the gentlemen golfers did. Many of the founder-members of the Gentlemen Golfers at Leith were also founder-members of the Society of Golfers at St Andrews. In later times, many members of Leith played a lot of their golf at Musselburgh, even before the move was made from Leith to Musselburgh. Golf clubs were 'bespoke' in those days. The customer had a lot of say about what sort of club he wanted; having played golf with members from other centres of golf and, no doubt, discussed the merits of various types of club, both in the clubhouse or tavern and at Masonic lodge meetings, he was in a position to ask the clubmaker at his own Club to make the same pattern.

Secondly, as we all know today, the appearance of a golf club is only a small part of what makes it the right club for a particular golfer; there are questions of weight, type of shaft, feel and, ultimately, whether the buyer can hit a ball well with it. Of two clubs which look the same, one may be definitely better than another. Thus, although one may not be able, by shape, to see much difference in these early clubs, clubs made by different clubmakers may have had very different qualities for the user; unfortunately, one cannot try out these clubs with a feather ball.

## Change in the Shape of Wooden Clubheads

ALTHOUGH there was no great change over the years, small changes did occur and are worth noting because they help to establish the approximate date at which the club was made.

### The face

In clubs from the earlier period, that is, before 1860, almost no wooden examples will be found which have a face deeper than 1 inch; it is only in the more lofted clubs, such as the baffing spoon, that, occasionally, the face may be 1¼ inches deep.

### The degree of hook

The hooking at the toe – or lack of it – can be deceiving. In general terms, the more the face is hooked, the earlier the date of the club, but some wooden clubs which were used over many years were 'updated' by their owners to conform with the later shape, that is, they had less hook. While an uncommon feature in drivers, it is much more common in wooden putters. There are Philp putters which cannot have been made later than 1856 but which have straight faces. They were not made so by Philp but had the toe filed back at a later date; the reason for this will be discussed in the section on putters; the filing can be detected by examining the sole of the club. The horn in the leading edge will not have parallel edges, but will narrow at the toe. The same will be found in some McEwan putters and, occasionally, in both Philp and McEwan drivers.

### Angle of head to shaft

Kincaid observed, in 1687: 'Your club must be allmost straight that is, the head of the club must make a verie

Typical shallow face and flat lie of a wooden club, *c.*1840

obtuse angle with the shaft'. He is describing an extremely 'flat lie' club as his idea of a good club. Over many years, mainly because of the changes in the type of wood used for shafts, and changes in the ball, the lie of wooden clubs became more upright, that is, the angle became less obtuse until, by the end of the nineteenth century, clubs were of approximately the same lie as they are today, though there were, as today, individual variations to suit the different physical build of the players. One can say, therefore, in general terms, that the flatter the lie of the club, the older it is likely to be.

## Wood used for Clubheads

THE earliest wood that we know was used in clubheads, was 'thorncut'; this was the wood of the blackthorn tree. What particular properties this wood had that made it most suitable for clubheads we do not know.

In his *History of Golf in Britain*, Sir Guy Campbell writes that the thorns were planted on sloping banks, with the result that the stem of the tree grew at an angle to the root, giving a piece of wood with a natural bend. The separation of the piece was done with wedges, rather than with a saw, thus giving a stronger piece of wood.

This rather dubious story is probably not true and is, in any event, not necessary as an explanation because the roots and branches of blackthorns grow at sharp angles to one another, quite naturally. That the wood was best cut with wedges to give a stronger clubhead was certainly likely.

The important thing about the clubhead was to have the grain running up the neck of the club, which would make it much less liable to split when the great strain of hitting a golf ball occurred, and the best way to achieve this was by having a natural bend in the wood.

In any event, up to about 1820 blackthorn was the preferred wood for clubheads. Philp used it exclusively; the author has not seen an authentic Philp clubhead made of any other wood. Many of the early McEwan clubheads, likewise, are of thorncut.

McEwan also used beech and this was the most popular wood for clubheads until 1900 and was used by all the other makers, who used thorncut only occasionally. The beech needed careful selection and the most suitable wood came from a tree that had grown on a hill, rather than in a valley, the latter being too soft. Cann, one of the most experienced clubmakers of the late nineteenth and early twentieth centuries, said that good beech from a tree at the top of a hill was the best wood for golf clubheads. Other woods were tried: applewood, hornbeam, holly, dogwood, etc, but beech remained the most popular. An advertisement in about 1900 suggests

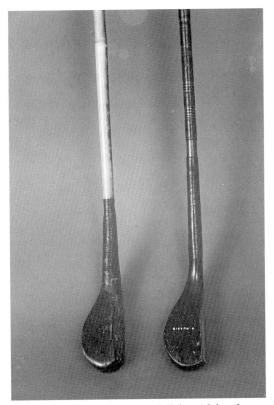

Two scared head long-nosed clubs with bamboo shafts, *c.*1876; the club on the right is stamped J. Morris and has a lot of whipping on the shaft, possibly to make it stiffer

that copper beech is a very special wood for the job, but there is no other information about this.

## Golf club Shafts, 1600–1900

KINCAID, in 1687, was definite that 'the shaft of your club most be of hazell'. This would have been a very whippy shaft as Kincaid himself confirms a little later when he remarks 'it most [must] bend as much at the handle as at the whopping [whipping at the lower end. *Author*] being both very supple and long'.

The next material that is mentioned is ash but when the changeover took place is not known. An ash shaft would have been a stiffer shaft than hazel. Some of the early wooden clubs that exist still have ash shafts (and most of the early iron clubs) but, in the case of wooden clubs, because there were no great changes in the form of the head for many years, many golfers would have had their clubs reshafted with the new hickory shaft, when hickory arrived in about 1820–25. This wood came from the southern States of America and, especially, from Tennessee. The quality that made it peculiarly suitable for golf club shafts was that it had a steely spring which was far superior to that of any other wood. Originally, it had been imported for axe handles, handles of hammers and for pit props for the mines.

Other woods were tried such as lancewood and, in particular, greenheart but, although the latter had a good spring in it, it was much heavier than hickory and was, moreover, brittle. A few earlier play clubs have greenheart shafts but it was used more commonly for putters; the reason for this is discussed in the section on putters.

The old clubmakers were willing to experiment and tried bamboo shafts. Drivers with bamboo shafts exist that were made by such well-known makers as Tom Morris and 'Watty' MacDonald but they are excessively rare; it must, apart from any other problems, have been difficult to make a scared joint, when one part of the scare was a hollow bamboo.

Even hickory varied in its suitability. The best shafts were of red hickory and, in all types of hickory tree, a shaft from the centre of the tree was the best. Being at the centre of the tree, the grain had a circular appearance and was called 'ring' hickory. Apart from the different varieties of hickory tree, it was important that it should come

Plate inserted into sole;
the owner has added the name of the club

from the right area. Hickory from low-lying areas was soft, lacking in steely spring, and was called swamp hickory; that from the higher hills had a good spring but was brittle. The best hickory came from the middle ground – neither too high up the hill, nor down in the valley.

Hickory was an instant success and became the preferred shaft for all clubs. It continued to be successful until, when the golf explosion came at the end of the century, so many shafts were required that properly seasoned hickory became increasingly difficult to find and clubmakers began to look for a substitute.

## Horn

Probably from the earliest times, and certainly during the latter part of the eighteenth and the whole of the nineteenth centuries, it was the custom to put a horn plate in the leading edge of the face of all wooden clubs. The plate was usually ram's horn but occasionally cow's horn. In the latter part of the nineteenth century, even the brassie, which had a brass sole, still had a horn plate beneath it. The clubmakers were quite certain that it was necessary; only Horace Hutchinson, Amateur Champion and Captain of the R&A, had the temerity to suggest that, in the presence of a brass plate, a horn plate was unnecesary. Probably, the clubmakers derived some comfort from the fact that, despite his exalted status, he was an Englishman.

The plate was made by cutting the horn in half longitudinally and then softening both pieces of horn by boiling them in water; the softened

**Hugh Philp club, showing face and horn insert
(depth of face and horn one inch)**

horn was then squashed flat by putting it between two pieces of metal in a vice. The plate was used to prevent the leading edge from becoming rounded and chipped when the club struck the ground; it was successful in this and could be easily replaced when worn. The horn plate was as long as the leading edge of the club face and was about ½ inch wide and ⅛ inch thick. It was rectangular in shape but the toe end was usually rounded to fit the curve of the club face there.

## Lead

Lead was heated until it was molten and was then poured into a cavity previously prepared in the back of the head. The cavity was undercut and there were four drill holes at angles in the bottom. When the lead had flowed down the holes and become solid, the angle of the holes would prevent it coming out again.

It was generally agreed that the lead should be soft lead, i.e., pure lead, particularly in putters, because, it was said, 'a hard lead will not unite itself to the wood in a satisfactory manner'.

In the great majority of wooden clubs the lead was ovoid in shape and was placed equidistant from heel and toe, but although to outward appearances the leads were the same, the cavity within might be quite different. The size and shape of the cavity was decided upon by the clubmaker and was done by eye; a club could be made toe-heavy or heel-heavy by the shape of the cavity. This is one of the reasons why, although most of the old clubs look alike, their swinging characteristics may have been quite different. The weight of the head had an effect on the shaft; as Horace Hutchinson observed: 'Essentially bound up in this question of weight of clubs is the question of their suppleness or flexibility. For each of the two depends greatly on the other. A heavy head may bring just the right amount of life – of what Tom Morris calls "music" – out of a very stiff shaft, while on a flexible shaft it would waggle it to pieces and be utterly useless.' It was this intuitive skill of the club-

**Early grip showing a) thread whipping in the edges of the wound grip, b) grooves where the diagonal whipping used to be**

maker – in which no measurement would help – which allowed him to make beautifully balanced clubs, although he had never heard of 'swing weight', and it was this mystical balance between head and shaft which meant that a change of shaft might ruin a club, because the chances of finding a new shaft which had exactly the same steely whip as the old one were nil.

The one point on which all the old clubmakers were agreed was that the lead must be behind the ball; the idea of putting lead in the sole of a club was anathema.

## The Grip

Some very early clubs did not have a grip; the upper shaft was of very large diameter and either the clubmaker had decided that a grip on this was not necessary – or the buyer had made the decision not to have a grip. Pictures of golfers in the eighteenth and early nineteenth centuries show that they all wore gloves to play and it may well have been that a thick hickory shaft, allied to playing in gloves, made a grip unnecessary.

The earlier grips were of white sheepskin or cowhide; whatever the leather used, the grip was obtained from a sheet of leather laid out on a piece of board and cut with a chisel. The grip was approximately 1–1¼ inches in width but was not of the same width throughout, as it tapered slightly from top to bottom. Before the grip was put on, an undergrip of coarse cloth, known as 'listings', was applied; when the leather grip was put on over this the result was a very thick grip. As the player was wearing leather gloves, there was a trememdous thickness in the hands. The club was gripped in the palms of the hands, not in the fingers as we do today; there must have been little sense of touch but at least this arrangement made it easier to follow Kincaid's dictum 'you most [must] grip verie fast'. The 'verie fast' grip was further aided by having a spiral of thread down the grip, crossing the spiral edges of the leather in the grip at about 45°, as is commonly found in clubs of that time.

Driver made in about 1892. Competitors would have used this type of wooden club, the head of which is quite like a modern club. It is attached to the hickory shaft by a long spliced joint held by thread whipping. Thickness of the joint can be seen above the head

## The Joining of the Shaft to the Head

DESCRIPTIONS of the form of wooden clubs and of the materials from which they were made do not consider the very important question of the way in which the head was attached to the shaft. Such a joint had to be strong but must not be clumsy and thick; the neatest joint, which was also strong, was a joint used since Roman times by shipwrights for mending the spars and masts of ships. The neatness of the joint stemmed from the fact that, when completed, the area of the join was of roughly the same diameter as the rest of the spar or mast; it consisted of two oblique, flat surfaces, the far end of each tapering to infinity. When glued together and held by whipping, it was only the thickness of the whipping that gave the spar or mast an appearance of being thicker in the area of the join.

The shipwrights who used this spliced joint called it a 'scarffed' joint; when the clubmakers took to using it they called it a 'scared' joint; clubs made with this type of join are commonly referred to as 'scared head clubs' to

Left: Rare socket joint; shaft is screwed into the socket with a left-hand thread. Right: Sole of a socket-head club. The end of the shaft can be seen. 'Vulcanite' has been used instead of horn in the leading edge, c.1910.

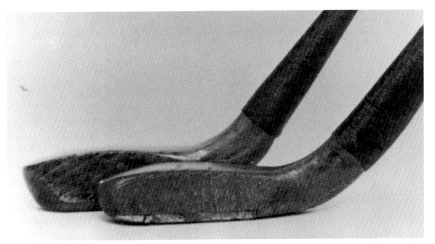

**Two scared head clubs: the one in the foreground has a shallower face and flatter lie, and is older than the one behind it**

distinguish them from the 'socket head' clubs which were made after 1900.

In the making of this joint, the clubhead had a long 'neck', up which ran the grain of the wood. This neck was given a flat surface at the back which came to infinity; this was the lower scare. The upper part of the joint was a similar flat surface, made as a counterpart to the lower scare, at the lower end of the shaft. The effect of this join was to give a long surface contact between the shaft and the head, which was very desirable.

This joint was very satisfactory, but craftsmen are always trying to do better and, at different times, a form of tenon joint was tried. Towards the end of the nineteenth century, A.H. Scott of Elie, using machinery, made a whole series of such tenon-jointed clubs which were quite successful and were claimed by him to be unbreakable. He was the most successful at using this joint, but he was not the first. The great Philp, in the 1850s, devised a joint which was a combination of a tenon joint and a scared joint. It was a complicated joint and nobody tried to copy it. Few were made because Philp died shortly after this; as a result, such clubs are very rare. At one time, in the mid nineteenth century, efforts were made to make a short 'vee' splice. How many of these were made is not known, and only a very few have come to light, but this may be because the joint is only to be discovered if the whipping is missing, thus uncovering the

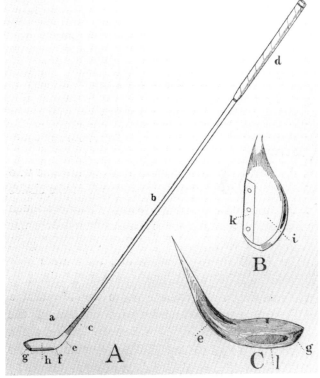

**Parts of a scared head wooden club**
*A – the whole club; B – the 'sole'; C – back view of the head;
a – the head; b – the shaft; c – the 'scare', or part where the
head and shaft are fastened and bound together;
d – the leather grip or handle; e – the neck; g – the heel;
g – the toe or nose; h – the face; i – the sole;
k – the bone; l – the lead*

**Somewhat exaggerated bulger shape. The head is almost round and the short face is flat and well in advance of the shaft. Such clubs were sometimes called 'baps' due to their resemblance to the round Scottish bun of that name**

joint; the external appearance of the joint is very like that of the usual scared joint, though close inspection will reveal that it is shorter.

The Dunn family tried to go a step further and made clubs in one piece, so that there was no join. As with the clubs made by Scott of Elie, they were said to be unbreakable. They did not state of what wood the clubs were made but, if beech was the best wood for clubheads and hickory was the best for shafts, it is difficult to see how a single piece of wood was going to be suitable for a golf club. At the time of this invention, which had a British patent, the Dunns were doing a good trade with the United States; it is likely that there were more one-piece clubs in America than in Britain. This general account of the form and make of the earlier wooden clubs is only a brief survey of the subject. Those who want more detailed information about how clubs were made, and with what tools, will find it in *The Great Club Makers, Golf in the Making*, and *Collecting Old Golf Clubs*.

## The Bulger

In 1885 there came a marked change in the shape of wooden clubheads; gone was the long, narrow type of head with the face curved in at the toe, and in came a shorter, wider and slightly deeper-faced clubhead.

The general construction of scared joint, horn in the leading edge and lead in the back of the clubhead, was the same; the change was principally in the shape of the face, which was convex, and in the position of the face relative to the shaft. In the new club, the face was definitely in front of the shaft, whereas in the long-nosed club the face was in line with the front edge of the shaft. Although the face bulged forward when new, Horace Hutchinson, an eminent golfer during the changeover period, said that it was soon driven back to a flat face when used. The forward shift of the face relative to the shaft was probably of greater importance, though what the effect of this change was is difficult to assess.

Why this sudden change? We do not know. Two people claimed to have thought up the idea: one was an inventive professional, Willie Park Junior, the other was Mr Henry Lamb, who originated in Scotland and was Secretary of Royal Wimbledon Golf Club. Mr Lamb, be it noted, was a very accomplished golfer and the winner of many important medals. Whoever conceived the idea we shall never know; despite a spate of letters to the newspapers of the time, no conclusion was ever reached, but conceived it was and it certainly owed something to the writings of a mathematician, R.A. Proctor, who stated that a ball struck from a convex surface with hook or slice, would hook or slice less than if it were struck from a concave surface.

This may have been a self-evident proposition to a mathematician, but golfing enthusiasts understood little of the theoretical side, what they wanted to know was – did it work? It did, and, as Robert Harris, an international golfer at the time, pointed out: 'At once it became the prince of drivers . . . Everybody wanted it.' The long, narrow driver head with the hooked face was finished.

But tradition dies hard and the craftsmen clubmakers, trained from boyhood to make the long, narrow shape, tried to make the best of both worlds. Some driver heads were produced which, while having a long narrow shape, had a convex face in line with the front of the shaft; the golfing public would have none of it and, as it did not sell, this type of club was soon abandoned, which is why clubs of this shape are now rare and very collectable.

Further compromise ensued and some clubheads were produced which, while shorter in the head and slightly wider than the old type, had a flat, or slightly convex, face in the line of the front of the shaft; there was

**Compromise between the long narrow-head club and the bulger. This clubhead has a straight face in line with the front edge of the shaft. The head is less long than the old shape of head and marginally wider. Made *c.*1885**

some sale for these but this did not last long and they, too, were abandoned. Later, some clubmakers, anxious to please their customers, made clubs in which the convex face was even further in advance of the shaft and the clubhead was almost completely round. Such clubs were called 'Baps', because of a resemblance to a type of round Scottish bun.

# The Clubmakers

### The Dickson Family of Leith

This family was active in both ballmaking and clubmaking but there is no coherent account of them, only sporadic references.

In 1629, Willam and Thomas Dickson, 'makers of golf balls in Leith', were involved in a legal action against Melville, who considered that he had a monopoly of ballmaking by Royal Consent. Melville had threatened the lives of the Dicksons and had forcibly removed 19 golf balls from them.

1637. John Dickson married Barbara Kennedie, and the husband is described as a ballmaker and clubmaker.

1642. Aberdeen Town Council licensed John Dickson to make golf balls.

1643. Andrew Dickson, 'ballmaker', signed a Solemn League and Covenant at St Andrews.

1681. Andrew Dickson, from indirect evidence, was said to have acted as forecaddie in the poorly substantiated match between the Duke of York, John Patersone and two Englishmen. John Dickson (1678–1729) was a bowmaker to the Royal Company of Archers. It is highly probable that both he and his brother, James Dickson (1713–1740) were clubmakers as well.

In Thomas Mathison's poem, written in 1743, he describes '. . . the work of Dickson who in Letha dwells and in the art of making clubs excels'. The clubmaker referred to here is probably John Dickson (1710–1755). Another John Dickson (1735–1787) is also recorded as a clubmaker.

It is sad that there is no further information on this family and what exists is somewhat disjointed. Dickson is a common name in Scotland and the first name 'John' occurs so frequently in the family that it is not possible to distinguish all the relationships, but it does seem certain that the family, starting as ballmakers, became clubmakers as well, and were active in the Leith area for 150 years.

### Simon Cossar (1766–1811)

Cossar is first recorded as a clubmaker in 1794, but this does not mean that he was not making clubs long before that. He seems to have been born and bred a Leith man and it is very probable that he learnt his craft from that other Leith family, the Dicksons, but there is no evidence in writing of this.

We are on firm ground in saying that Cossar was a clubmaker because three of his clubs exist at the R&A. His clubs seem well made and are characterised by having the name written along the top leading edge of the club. That clubs known to have been made by him are only to be found at the R&A does not mean that members of the R&A ordered them from Cossar at Leith; many members of the Honourable Company were also members of the Society of Golfers at St Andrews; they would have brought their clubs from Leith when they travelled to St Andrews.

### David Cossar (1788–1816)

Simon Cossar's son. He is listed as a clubmaker but no clubs with his name on have been seen.

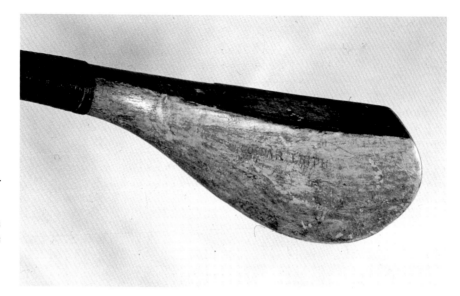

Scared head long-nosed driver by Simon Cossar of Leith. The club is unique in that the name is stamped along the line of the face

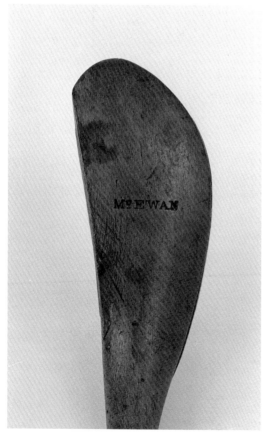

J Mc EWAN.

*The McEwan Family*

This is the most eminent family in clubmaking.

James McEwan (1747–1800) came from Stirling to Edinburgh in 1770 and took up residence in Wright's Houses, close to the links of Bruntsfield.

Whether he knew anything about the making of golf clubs before he moved is not known but it is unlikely.

At Wright's Houses he would certainly have met Thomas Comb, who lived in the area in about 1770 and is referred to in the *Chronicles* of the Royal Burgess Golfing Society in 1773 as 'Thomas Comb, Clubmaker, Bruntsfield Links or Wright's Houses'. Unfortunately, no clubs of Thomas Comb have survived and it is only by references to him as a clubmaker, such as in the Chronicles, that we know of his existence. It is very probable that James McEwan became an apprentice to Comb and took over his business when he died.

McEwan driver, *c.*1870. Note the McEwan stamp contains no initial. Head is of beech

Wright's Houses were a great centre for the golf trades, because the Gourlay family of famous ballmakers lived there as well – in fact the Houses could well have been rechristened 'Golf Wright's Houses' – the term 'wright' meaning one who practises a craft.

When James McEwan made clubs he stamped them 'J. McEwan' and put a thistle mark on them as well; unfortunately, he was the only one of the family who did so; for the rest of the time during which his talented family made wooden clubs, they only stamped 'McEwan' on the clubhead, so it is not now possible to say which of his sons made which clubs.

The family continued in clubmaking from 1770 until the end of the nineteenth century. Peter McEwan (1781–1836), Douglas McEwan (1809–1886) and Peter McEwan (1834–1895) made clubs to the very highest standard and at one time supplied the St Andrews golfers with clubs, but this trade dwindled when Hugh Philp became clubmaker there.

There is not much to choose between Philp and the McEwans in the matter of clubmaking. Philp, being a St Andrews man, has always had the edge in the matter of publicity. Douglas McEwan was regarded as the best clubmaker of all that highly skilled family. Dalrymple, a good amateur golfer who lived in the time of Douglas and who played both at St Andrews and Musselburgh (and therefore may be considered relatively unbiased) writes: 'Undoubtedly he [Douglas McEwan. *Author*] was the best clubmaker who ever lived and his clubs were models of symmetry and shape.

'Undoubtedly McEwan clubs show that the much praised elegance which is associated with Philp clubs is not missing in these McEwan clubs and, viewed impartially, there is little to choose between these two makers, with possibly a preference to McEwan in the matter of putters.'

**Hugh Philp, 1782–1856**

*Hugh Philp, St Andrews*

Philp (1782–1856) was born at Cameron in Fife. The St Andrews Census in 1831 and 1841 describes him as a 'wright', meaning that he was a skilled man who had served an apprenticeship to a trade. It is said that he only took to repairing clubs in 1812, when he was thirty, and only became a maker of clubs in 1819, at which time he was appointed clubmaker to the Society of Golfers at St Andrews.

**Scared head long-nosed Philp clubhead, *c.* 1840**

Philp clubhead: the horn is missing but the pegs that would hold it in place are there and can be seen to be slanted slightly forward – this tends to drive them in on impact

Philp was a quiet man and a good golfer but he never had any pretensions to being good enough to make a living at it. His characteristic was great workmanship and attention to fine detail, such that he would spend hours polishing a club. He made fine clubs – in both senses – for they were of fine workmanship and fine and delicate in construction. Some regarded his clubs as almost too fine, ie, not robust enough to cope with rough work, but, in his defence, his clubs were made for hitting the feather ball. It is, nevertheless, interesting that, of some 20 clubs reputed to have been used by Allan Robertson, a next-door-neighbour of Philp, only two are made by Philp – and one of those is not properly authenticated as having been used by Robertson. Towards the end of his life he railed against the new gutta ball which he said was like a

stone and it is certainly true that his clubs suffered severely when used with a gutta.

The members at St Andrews became his devoted admirers and, never at a loss for praising their heroes, dubbed him 'the Chippendale of clubmaking'. Such a value was put on his clubs that they were forged in his own lifetime by one or more clubmakers who had managed to acquire a 'Philp' stamp. A good number of his clubs survive.

### The Forgan Family, St Andrews

In 1852, Philp took Robert Forgan (1835–1900) into partnership with him. Robert was Philp's nephew. Presumably Forgan had served an apprenticeship to Philp for some years before that.

He was an apt pupil and became as good as Philp at clubmaking. He was, additionally, a good organiser and surrounded himself with a staff of really good workmen, many of whom he had taught the trade. To be able to say that you had worked for Mr Forgan and had a reference from him, would ensure a clubmaker a good job, and many left to set up on their own, but there was always a good nucleus of fine clubmakers in his shop; some of them were clubmakers who had tried on their own but had found life easier and more secure in Forgan's shop.

Forgan was a particularly good judge of wood for shafts; when he went to select wood from

**Brass blade putter made by Robert Forgan, c. 1890**

View of Forgan's workshop, taken soon after Robert's death, *c.* 1901. Note the substantial work-force and the Prince of Wales crest on the wall of the building which also appeared on the clubs

the timber yard he took with him a small hammer which had an 'R' stamped on the business end. When he selected a lath of hickory he rapped it with his hammer and by so doing he ensured that he only received the timber that he had selected, when he took delivery. Even over a century later, the beautiful, straight shafts of Forgan's clubs are witness to his skill.

As clubs for collectors, Forgan's clubs do not make the prices that Philp clubs make. This is not because they are inferior but because the name Philp on a club assumed an almost mystical significance at St Andrews and because Forgan, at a slightly later date, produced many more clubs than Philp.

### Andrew Forgan (1846–1926)

One of Robert Forgan's brothers, Andrew, made his living as a clubmaker, but left his brother's firm and set up in Glasgow on his own.

### Thomas Forgan (1853–1906)

Forgan's son, Thomas, carried on the firm when his father died.

### Peter Lawrence Forgan (1885–1942)

One of Forgan's grandsons, Peter, remained in the Forgan firm until they were taken over by Spaldings in the 1930s.

Forgan's other two grandsons went to America and became successful bankers.

Head of long spoon by Robert Forgan, *c.* 1875. The toe has been damaged and mended with a vulcanite insert. Note the Prince of Wales crest and the horn insert

Peter Forgan showed his organising abilities by leading his firm into the twentieth century, using machinery to make golf clubs, while keeping a high standard of hand finishing; in the early part of the twentieth century his firm was the largest makers of golf clubs in the world.

The old Forgan shop, opposite the 18th green at St Andrews, was on the site of the present 'St Andrews Woollen Mill' and a plaque at the entrance commemorates this fact.

### The Dunn Family

Jamie Dunn (1821–1871) and Willie Dunn (1821–1878) were twins and were born at Musselburgh. As teenagers they were apprenticed to the ballmaker, Gourlay, but what they really liked doing was playing golf. In 1851, Willie was appointed Keeper of the Green at Blackheath; his brother joined him a few years later. Although they stayed for 14 years, they were not an unqualified success and both must have pined for some good golfers against whom to try their skills. At that time, Blackheath was the only course in England, except for a rather poor course at Manchester.

Their principal claim to fame was not in ballmaking nor in clubmaking but in a series of famous matches that they played against other well-known professionals of the time. Their forte was matchplay foursomes and they beat

Head of a bulger driver by Robert Forgan. The crown indicates that he is By Appointment, Clubmaker to King Edward VII

many notable players at this. They seldom played singles and, in their few attempts at medal play, never did themselves justice.

In 1865, Willie moved back to Scotland and became Keeper of the Green at Leith Thistle Club. James never married but Willie did – and had two sons Willie Dunn (Junior) (1865–1952) and Thomas (1849–1902).

Willie Junior took after his father and uncle and was at his best when playing matchplay golf. He was a bit of a wanderer and took a job at Biarritz where he met W.E. Vanderbilt who persuaded him to go to the United States. There he laid out some courses, won the first (unofficial) Open Championship of America in 1894, and was runner-up in the first official one, in the following year.

Tom Dunn, Willie Dunn Junior's brother, stayed in Britain but moved from Musselburgh to be Keeper of the Green at Wimbledon. He was a good clubmaker and started to lay out some courses. In 1878, he went to North Berwick as Keeper of the Green but, finding that he was not making much of a living, he again returned to England and laid out a course at Bournemouth. He continued in business at Bournemouth, partly as a golf architect and partly in clubmaking. By the time he died, he had laid out 137 courses and had a good clubmaking business, exporting to the United States, in particular, aided by his brother and two sons, who had also settled over there.

### The Patrick Family

John Patrick (1820–1866) is listed as a cabinetmaker and golf clubmaker in Leven, Fife. When he died, Alexander Patrick (1845–1932) carried on the business but, by this time, the business was exclusively devoted to golf clubmaking.

Alexander had three brothers, John (1851–1916), Nichol (1853–?) and David (1858–1948). In the mid-1800s the business flourished and the brothers produced many clubs to a good standard. Subsequent generations, notably John Patrick's sons, continued in the business but failed to keep going and the family business had come to an end by the time of the First World War. They were willing to produce handmade clubs but were not prepared to attempt mass production.

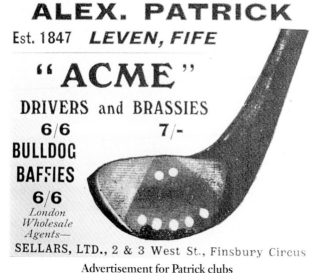

**ALEX. PATRICK**

Est. 1847 LEVEN, FIFE

"ACME"

DRIVERS and BRASSIES
6/6            7/-

BULLDOG BAFFIES
6/6

London Wholesale Agents—

SELLARS, LTD., 2 & 3 West St., Finsbury Circus

**Advertisement for Patrick clubs**

## The Anderson Family

David Anderson – 'Old Da' (1821–1901) was the founder of the St Andrews golfing dynasty. He was a 'cady', feather ballmaker and assistant greenkeeper at St Andrews and, very likely, made golf clubs as well, although he is not listed anywhere as such. In his old age, he ran a ginger-beer stall at the 4th hole and this hole has been known as the Ginger Beer Hole ever since.

Old Da's son, David Anderson (1847–1912), started the clubmaking business. David had a brother James Anderson (1842–1905) of whom, more later. David had five sons, who all went into the business, so he had a readymade work force. At one time they occupied premises, which were later used as engine sheds by the railway, and over which it was necessary to drive if one wanted the best line to the 17th hole.

By the turn of the century Andersons had a workforce of twelve men and were flourishing. They went out of business at the time of the First World War.

Not all clubmaking businesses were family affairs, there were also 'single' clubmakers such as David Denholm (d.1820), clubmaker to the Royal Burgess Golfing Society 1809–1820, who has already been mentioned, Munro of Aberdeen, who also made fishing tackle and was succeeded by Sandison. No clubs made by Denholm are known to exist and it is doubtful if any club, authenticated as made by Munro, exists either. One or two clubs by Sandison (stamped with his name) have been seen.

Among the 'single' clubmakers the following Perth makers are noteworthy: John Jackson, Bennett Lang and 'Watty' MacDonald.

## John Jackson (1805–1878)

Jackson was in the top class of clubmakers, alongside McEwan, Philp and Forgan. His clubs are beautifully made and of excellent balance. That they were good clubs for playing is evident from the fact that Robertson, despite fierce allegiance to St Andrews, used them. It is not known whether Jackson was apprenticed or whether he taught himself. Many clubs made by him have been seen and are highly valued by collectors.

# Noted Club-Making Family.

JAMES ANDERSON.   JOHN ANDERSON.   ANDREW ANDERSON.

WALTER ANDERSON.   DAVID ANDERSON.   DAVID ANDERSON, JUN

**'Old Da' with his five clubmaking sons, c.1906**

## Bennett Lang (1849–1913)

Lang was trained in Robert Forgan's shop and was said, by Robert Forgan, to be one of the best craftsmen that he ever produced. He was not suited to be his own master and subsequently worked for Tom Morris, Douglas McEwan, the Andersons and others. Many of the clubs that he made were not stamped with his name because he was an employee of others. The wooden clubs with which James Anderson won his third Open Championship were made for him by Lang. He finally settled in Perth, as his own master, and produced fine clubs stamped 'B. Lang'. A few of his clubs, stamped with his name, exist.

## Walter MacDonald (1836–)

'Watty' MacDonald was trained in Forgan's shop in the 1860s. By 1867, he is listed as a clubmaker, living in

Perth. He was Keeper of the Green at Perth and was a good golfer. He made fine clubs and some of them have been seen.

## James Anderson (1842–1905)

Anderson was the eldest son of 'Old Da', and David was his younger brother. He was the golfer of the family and won the Open Championship in 1877, 1878 and 1879. Although he lived at the same address as his brother, he does not seem to have joined in the family business. He certainly made long-nose clubs to a high standard of excellence and the R&A have more than one example of his work; his clubs are stamped 'J. Anderson'. It is said, by his contemporaries, that he was particularly skilled at making wooden putters.

## James Anderson (1878–)

He was the son of James Senior who was the Open Champion. It is interesting that he was apprenticed to Robert Forgan and not to the other Andersons. After training he went into partnership with David Blyth and they formed Anderson and Blyth, a clubmaking firm at St Andrews; this firm operated principally in the twentieth century.

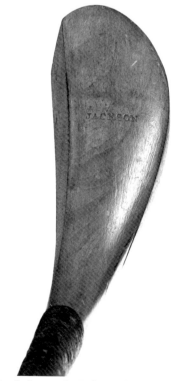

**Head of spoon by Jackson of Perth, c. 1840**

## The Park Family, Musselburgh

William Park Senior (1834–1903)
Mungo Park (1839–1904)
William Park Junior (1864–1925)
David Park (–?) William Park Senior's brother.

James Park, father of William Park Senior, is listed as a farmer but Willie Park Junior, in his book on the art of putting, says that he belonged to a breed of Scottish professionals who played golf for big money stakes; he goes on to point out that he was a believer in the old spirit of the challenge match 'which inspired my grandfather, my father, and my uncle'. It is clear that James Park was a golfer as well as a farmer and, presumably, a good one.

As has been said, the Parks, both Senior and Junior, were never Keepers of the Green but preserved their independence. Although both of them played challenge matches and made part of their living from them, they also had a thriving golf clubmaking business at Musselburgh. Willie Senior is listed as a club (and ball) maker in 1870 but he must have been making clubs for ten years before that. Willie Junior was apprenticed to him and joined the firm, as a partner, in the 1880s, after which the firm was known as 'W. Park and Son'. Willie Junior was also apprenticed to his uncle, Mungo, at Ryton in Northumberland from 1880 to 1884. Willie Park Senior made fine long-nose clubs and was as skilled as most of his contemporaries; his clubs exist in small numbers and prove this. His son, Willie Junior, probably never made long-nose clubs but, he fiercely contended, he 'invented' the bulger style of driver; as has been mentioned, Mr Henry Lamb also claimed to have thought of it and the matter has never been resolved.

Willie Park Senior was a clubmaker, but Willie Park Junior was unique because he was also a cleekmaker and his irons were of a high standard. He was a man of considerable invention and, using his experience as a ball-maker, he produced gutty balls, one of which he patented.

As part of his cleekmaking skills, he introduced, and patented, the wry-necked putter. A splendid tale exists that he hit upon the idea because, as he was driving in a trap to the links, his metal putter fell off and the wheel of the cart went over it and bent the neck; he found that he putted better with this shape of putter and thereafter made them that shape. Park, himself, gives a much more prosaic (and logical) explanation; he says that he had an old blade putter in which the shaft had warped in such a way that the shaft was in front of the clubhead. When he putted with it, he found it a good club; he then produced a putter in which the shaft was straight but there was a bend in the neck of the putter so that the blade was

Jack Morris in his shop at Hoylake, *c.*1911. With him, wearing a trilby hat, is Charles Hunter of Prestwick.
Note the 'one-leg' vices and the hickory laths in the rafters, slowly seasoning

behind the shaft. This putter was a great success and he sold many; others attempted to produce a similar club but, perhaps because of the patent, the bend at the neck was not the same as that on the Park putter.

Willie Junior became a good and popular golf architect and laid out many courses both in Britain and abroad; he also was prepared to construct golf courses. One which he designed and constructed was Sunningdale Old Course and he played a big part in the design and construction of Worplesdon.

Mungo Park was a very good golfer and won the Open in 1874. He was also a good club- and ballmaker as well and at one time was the Keeper of the Green at Alnmouth. While having great talent, he was a bit of a wanderer and spent a lot of his time at sea. His clubs are stamped 'M. Park'.

David and Willie Junior were very good golfers too. Davie in particular won a number of tough challenge matches and made a good showing in the Open on more than one occasion. They both worked in the family business at Musselburgh.

The golfing prowess of Willie Park Senior and Junior will be considered later.

The Parks were a remarkable family of professional golfers, and the history of the family has been written by John Adams in a well-researched book entitled *The Parks of Musselburgh.* The reader who wishes to know more about this family and their achievements is recommended to consult it.

*The Morris Family*

> Thomas Morris (1821–1908)
> Thomas Morris Junior (1851–1875)
> J.O.F. Morris (1856–1906)
> George Morris (–1888)
> Jack Morris

This family was from St Andrews. Tom Morris was apprenticed to Allan Robertson as a feather ballmaker. Keeper of the Green at Prestwick for fifteen years, Tom showed himself to be a splendid Keeper and was, in addition, a fine clubmaker and, of course, a very good golfer. He was a man of character and something of a philosopher; he had the ability to be at ease with his workmen and with the highest social stratum among the members and was loved by all.

He enjoyed being a Keeper of the Green and looking after the needs of his members. Unlike Robertson and Old Willie Park, he was not one who challenged any of the leading players to play against him but, if challenged, he was more than willing to accept. Robertson had much to do with teaching him to play golf and the two men were the best foursome combination of their time, as they proved on many occasions.

Young Tommy learnt his golf at Prestwick, as did his brother James Ogilvie Fairlie, known as 'Jof', who was named after a notable amateur and senior member of both the R&A and Prestwick who had befriended Tom when he and Allan broke up and was responsible for Tom going to Prestwick. Jof was a good golfer but never as good as his father or Young Tommy.

When Robertson died, Tom returned to St Andrews and became Keeper of the Green there for almost all the rest of his life. He did as good a job there as he had done at Prestwick and many R&A Captains paid tribute to the improvements that he made to the old links. Always diplomatic, but hard-headed and practical, he endeared himself to those of both high and low estate and became, in his later years, recognised for the great man that he was. He made good, practical-looking clubs and many of them still exist and are much prized.

Tom was in demand as a golf architect. Although he did not design new golf courses, he was particularly adept at making alterations to existing links to make them more interesting and a better test of golf. More will be said later of Old Tom's golfing feats, and those of Young Tom.

Old Tom's brother, George, was a good professional but seems to have done very little clubmaking, since no clubs of his have survived. For 25 years he was in the employment of Dr Robert Chambers as personal professional, servant and occasional foursome partner.

While working for Dr Chambers he went to Hoylake and designed and laid out the first links there. His son, Jack, accompanied him and stayed at Hoylake for many years; his great services to that Golf Club have already been mentioned.

Further information on the family, and on Old and Young Tom in particular, can be found in *The Life of Tom Morris*, *Golf in the Making*, and *The Great Club Makers*.

This general review of the clubmakers of the eighteenth and nineteenth centuries is, in the main, concerned with the makers of long-nose clubs.

Towards the end of the century, the golf 'explosion' meant that there was a demand for a greatly increased number of clubs and by 1885 the shorter, bulger clubs were in fashion. The more traditional of the craftsmen who made the long-nosed clubs were not enthusiastic about these less graceful clubs and one gets an impression that they made them simply because the customers wanted them and they, the clubmakers, had to make a living. The older craftsmen responded by taking on more workmen and continuing to make clubs by hand in larger premises;

others, of which the Forgans were the best example, made efforts at mass production, using machinery. Forgan, in a private letter in 1895, says that it is really only the finish of the clubs which is done by hand, and all the rest of the construction is done by machinery.

## A.H. Scott (1875–?)

An example of the 'new' school of clubmakers, Scott was clubmaker at Elie and Earlsferry and was a good craftsman. He probably never made a long-nose club and thus was not hampered by tradition. He realised that it was necessary, if one was to survive as a clubmaker, to use machinery to produce more clubs.

An excellent description of the methods and materials that he employed is to be found in *The Golf House Club, Elie*. The description was taken from an account in *Golf Illustrated* in 1904; by that time, it was a well-established method of manufacture that had been begun before 1900. In brief, Scott had abandoned beech for heads and was using hardwoods, such as dogwood and persimmon from the United States. The wood for heads was cut in planks and stored for over a year to season it.

Using a 10 hp motor to drive a copying lathe, up to 40 heads per hour could be turned, each exactly the same as the metal template which was the pattern. From this machine the heads were taken to a band saw which cut off the point at the toe and cut the scare; the heads then went to a lead-cutting machine, which cut the cavity for the lead, while another machine drilled three holes in the bottom of the cavity to the required depth and a tap screw was inserted into each which left an impression of a screw thread. The lead was poured by hand and the horn was fixed in by hand also. After that, the heads went to a sandpapering machine and were then varnished. The next step was to fix the head to the shaft, the latter being hickory which was seasoned. Then the lath was turned in a wood-turning machine to achieve the required shape and the splice on the shaft was also cut by machine. When the scare was complete, the club was finished by hand and this included taking down the lower end of the shaft to get the right 'whip'. By this means, Scott was able to produce 'thousands of clubs a year'. He also used machinery to produce his patent tenon-jointed clubs.

Traditional, handcrafting of clubs could not compete with this and the clubmakers either had to adopt Forgan and Scott methods, or go out of business.

This general review of the craft of clubmaking from 1650 to 1900 leaves out much detail. Those who have a particular interest in the subject are referred to books such as *The Great Club Makers*, *Golf in the Making*, *The Encyclopaedia of Golf Collectibles*, *Collecting Old Golfing Clubs* and *Golf in Britain*.

Early mechanisation, *c.*1910, showing, in the foreground a copying lathe

## Types of Wooden Club

WHAT sorts of wooden clubs did players use in the seventeenth and eighteenth centuries? Of very early times, there is no exact record. An early account occurs in a letter dated 20 June 1735 in which the writer desires clubs from Andrew Bailey, clubmaker at Bruntsfield. The writer wants 'nine clubs, viz, three play clubs, three scrapers, one of which a half scraper or spoon and three putting clubs and two dozen best St Andrews balls'.

The play club was used off the tee and its other (and later) name was a driver. We have no knowledge of 'scrapers'; the name is very 'ungolflike' and sounds as if it might be an iron club, but the fact that the half scraper is a spoon means that the scraper was a wooden club because a spoon was a wooden club, akin to today's No.3 or No.4 wood. The scrapers were, probably, other forms of woods used through the green, of less loft than the spoon. The three putting clubs would have been wooden putters.

There are other straws in the wind which give some information about the types of clubs used. Between 1627 and 1663, the Duke of Montrose, a keen golfer, was sent a bill: 'Bonker clubis, a iron club and twa clubis of my awin. For mending bonker club 1s 6d . . .'. It is safe to assume that the bonker club was some form of iron club, probably a rut iron.

When Professor Munro of the University of St Andrews sent a gift of clubs and balls to his friend John MacKenzie in 1691, the clubs were: 'Ane play club, ane scraper and ane tin fac'd club'.

So, there were play clubs, scrapers, half-scrapers, bonker clubs, putters, tin fac'd clubs and iron clubs.

In the early nineteenth century there are better records of such matters. The clubs that golfers used were driver or play club, grassed driver, long spoon, middle spoon, short spoon, baffing spoon, track iron, rut iron, wooden niblick and putter. Not everyone carried a wooden niblick and not everyone had two irons, often only one was carried. On the other hand, it was quite usual to carry two play clubs because they were prone to break. That, with one or two exceptions, the clubs were all wooden clubs was deliberate. While it was not a good thing to top a feather ball with a wooden club because it might burst, to top it with an iron club meant certain destruction. Iron clubs were only used in the most desperate situations, in sand (when the explosion shot was used), in areas of stones and hard mud, on roads and, later in the century, on railway lines; in such places a wooden-headed club could easily be broken – hence the word used in the Rules of Golf at a later stage – 'breakclub'.

## The Wooden Niblick

This club is worthy of special mention for a number of reasons. Firstly, because no one has found, as yet, the derivation of the word 'niblick'. It appears in no dictionary, yet it is clearly an old word, for wooden niblicks were used from the 1830s. Secondly, because it was unique among wooden clubs in those early days as being the only wooden club which was not long-nosed. Thirdly, because it is seldom recognised, being usually considered to be a wooden club of the 'bulger' era and thus not very old.

The club has a hooked face but, because the head is short, this is not as evident as it is in the longer-headed clubs. Its use was confined to 'cuppy' lies, where its shorter head could be soled behind the ball – a long-headed club would not have allowed this. The wooden niblick was, in fact, the 'rut iron' of the wooden clubs.

The wooden niblick was quite a popular club; when the Royal Calcutta Golf Club was ordering from Britain in 1877, they asked for: 'Twenty-four drivers, twenty-four long spoons and twenty-four driving niblicks, with wooden heads and brass bottoms'. The wooden niblick was often given a brass sole because it needed protection when digging the ball out of a cuppy lie. Horace Hutchinson states that the wooden niblick developed into the 'brassie' (No.2 wood with a brass sole) later in the century, when the bulger shape came in.

## The Baffing Spoon

This, too, was a special club and not to be confused with a club of later date called a 'Baffy'. It was the pitching club of its day and was given its name because the ground was 'baffed' behind the ball; as the club struck the ground immediately behind the ball it bounced off the ground and carried the ball into the air. It was said to be a very pretty shot but it was very difficult to judge the distance that the ball would travel. It would not have given much backspin but then, in early times, backspin was seldom needed as the approach to the greens was not obstructed by many bunkers. If there was a bunker in the way, the player might well have to play around it – unless he was a genius, like Young Tom Morris, who would play a pitch shot with his rut iron! The result of using such clubs was that the feather ball was not damaged – and neither was the golf links; there was no such thing as a divot!

Once the gutta ball arrived, iron club play became popular, the baffing spoon disappeared very quickly, and divots began to appear with equal speed.

## The Grassed Driver

This was a driver, or play club, with a little extra loft, which became incorporated into the later brassie.

Clubs made by Forgan for use in 1865 (after the gutty was well entrenched) were: driver, brassie, long and short spoon (Today's No.3/4 wood. *Author*), wooden putter; in the irons, a cleek (straight-faced iron), a general iron, a lofting iron and a rut iron. The lofting iron was a general iron for playing approach shots; it came in several lofts and had a long face.

By 1895, the golfer would have carried a driver, brassie, spoon (equivalent to today's No.3/4 wood), a wooden putter (or an iron blade putter might have been carried). In irons, a cleek, a lofter, a mashie (equivalent to today's No.5 iron), a mashie niblick (No.7/8 iron) and a niblick (wedge/sand wedge). Additional irons would have been available for those who wanted them: mashie iron, driving iron, deep-faced mashie, jigger or sammy (shallow-faced approaching irons), a putting cleek (blade putter with a little loft), etc.

**Belt-driven copying lathe in which a clubhead could be cut to exact size and shape of an iron model**

# Iron Clubs

## 1750–1910

THE clubmakers, experts in wood, knew nothing of working metal. When an iron clubhead was required, they turned to the blacksmith. The blacksmith was busy shoeing horses, making farm machinery, gates, etc; the demand for iron clubheads was very small compared with his other work, so he made clubheads as a part-time occupation.

Surprisingly few tools were used by blacksmiths for the making of iron heads. All that was required was an anvil, a furnace, a 2½ lb hammer, some rasps and files, and a cutter to slice off red hot iron and fashion the general shape. The only specialist tool used was a mandril or spike. This was a tapered rod of iron which was used to shape the hosel.

The process began with a flat piece of iron about 2 inches wide and 10 inches long. After heating, one half of this piece was flattened until it was about double its original width and therefore half the thickness. The thin portion was wrapped around the mandril to make the hosel and was so hammered that the line of join going down the hosel was not visible; the face was, at this time, in line with the hosel. It was then hammered to give it the necessary loft and lie and the face was also hammered so that it was dished and hooked; the term 'dishing' meant giving the face a concave shape. The face was left plain, i.e., there were no markings on it. Once completed, the clubhead was handed over to the clubmaker for shafting and the addition of a grip.

While some of the blacksmiths may well have played golf, generally speaking they did not know much about the proper dimensions and weight of the clubhead required by the clubmaker. Because of this, the clubmaker was present when the clubhead was being made, and indeed he often acted as the blacksmith's 'mate'. By this means he was able to influence the smith to make the clubhead to suit his ideas about shape and weight.

The result of this combined operation was a crude, heavy but serviceable iron clubhead. No great refinement or elegance was required because the club was going to be used for pretty rough work among stones, pieces of driftwood, hard, dry, caked mud and all manner of débris; 'play the ball where it lies' was the watchword and there were no local rules to allow the player to lift out.

The clubhead was made heavy because it had to be able to crash through all obstacles to hit the ball, which is why old clubs still in existence show considerable 'denting' due to previous use. To carry such a heavy head, a stout ash shaft was required and, because of the weight and the great force used in the shot, a proportionately thick grip was needed to make sure, as Kincaid advised, that 'your grip be verie fast'.

Iron is able to survive much longer than wood; as a result, iron heads exist that were probably made in the seventeenth and eighteenth centuries. In these very early clubs, the shaft was held into the hosel of the head by coarse serrated 'knopping' at the top of the hosel. By

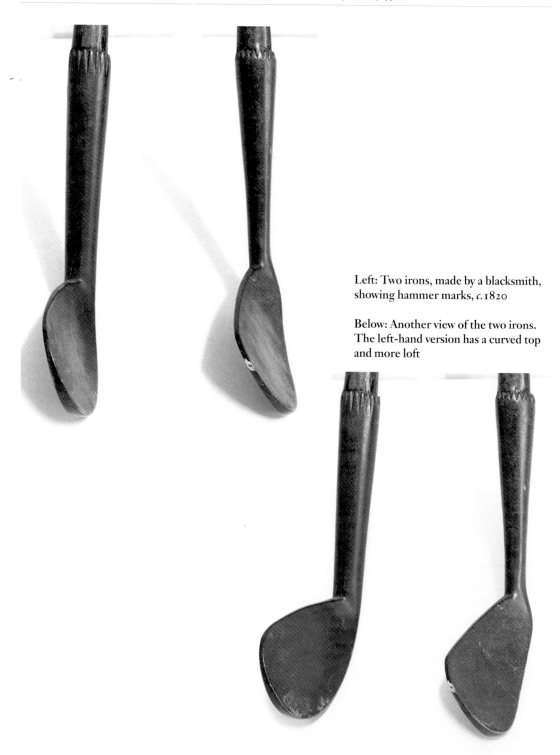

Left: Two irons, made by a blacksmith, showing hammer marks, *c.*1820

Below: Another view of the two irons. The left-hand version has a curved top and more loft

**Blacksmith's shop**

about the 1830s, rivets began to appear to hold the shaft in place and the knopping, while helpful, was no longer essential to the security of the shaft in the hosel. The serrated teeth in the knopping became smaller and, by the end of the nineteenth-century knopping was a tradition and more for decoration than purpose.

Both the head and the weight of these early iron clubs was very unusual when compared with today's clubs. The face was seldom less than 3 inches in length and showed a definite 'hook'. This no doubt was at the request of the clubmaker who was accustomed to making wooden heads with a distinct hook. The face of the iron was also well 'dished' (concave), to assist in getting the ball into the air. The face of the club was smooth.

The shape of the toe of the club varied. In many cases the toe was a vertical line, giving the appearance that the toe had been cut off (although it is doubtful if this is what actually happened); in others, the toe was rounded.

It has been suggested that the shape of the head, in the early clubs, gives a clue as to the era in which it was made, but this really has no validity; the shape of the club was dictated by the individual preference of the clubmaker and he was, in turn, influenced by the wishes and

ideas of the customer. Why some of the irons had a cut-off nose we do not know – it may have been to lessen the chances of the toe catching in obstacles in its path. The hosel of these clubs is massive because the hosel had to accommodate a very thick ash shaft. The clubs are heavy, too, weighing 18–28 ounces – the weight of a modern iron is about 13 ounces. Yet, despite their weight and crudeness, the old clubs have a good balance and an impression of great power.

The big irons of this shape are best called 'track irons' or 'general purpose irons' in order to distinguish them from certain specialist iron clubs designed, specifically, for getting the ball out of the narrow cart ruts that abounded on the old golf links. Carts were used to take seaweed from the shore to the farms to act as fertiliser; the cart wheels were narrow and, as the load was heavy, they made deep and narrow tracks – often only 2 inches in width. Any club with a face longer than 2 inches would bridge across such a track and could not be soled behind the ball. To overcome this, the blacksmith and the club-maker devised a special iron with a head sufficiently small that it could be soled behind the ball. Such clubs had a face only about 1½–2 inches long; the face was well-hooked and dished. In spite of the smallness of the head this club was still very heavy, deriving its weight from the thickness of the hosel and the thickness of the face, particularly at the sole of the club. These clubs are called 'rutters' or 'rut irons'; they were devised because the understood rule of golf was that the ball must be played 'where it lies'. The golfer, instead of writing indignant letters to the Secretary demanding a free drop, went to the professional and asked him to make a club with which he could play the ball out.

The rutter was used for bunker shots as well. The head of the club was so small that, unless kept well in line by playing out of a narrow cart-rut, it was all too easy to hit the ball off the shank. On the other hand, in a sand bunker it was easy to hit behind the ball, thus avoiding direct contact, since the small heavy head of the club would go through the sand easily. The explosion shot out of sand was an early shot in golf and one of the reasons for this was that by playing into the sand behind the ball one avoided topping it, which was the complete ruination of a feather ball.

Because of the disastrous effect of the topped shot on a feather ball, the iron club was used as little as possible. Consequently there was no great demand for iron clubs, as players carried, at the most, two irons and often only one.

As the clubmaker had much to do with the shape of the clubhead and as he then had to put a shaft in the hosel which had to be suitable for the weight of the head – and then put a suitable grip on the shaft – he was very much the dominant craftsman while the blacksmith worked under the clubmaker's direction.

When the gutta ball arrived in 1848, golf became cheaper and thus more golfers took up the game. Moreover, an iron club did not destroy a gutta ball, so there was an increase in the number of iron clubs used by each golfer. Because of this greatly increased demand, blacksmiths who were skilled at making iron clubheads found it more profitable to become iron clubhead makers and give up their other activities. When they became specialists in this work they were known as 'cleekmakers'.

They thus became experts in their own right and began to make many different types of iron clubs; they no longer required the clubmaker to stand over them and dictate the shape and, in any event, the clubmaker was now too busy to spend the time. The cleekmakers were

**Left: Rut iron with a very small head, specially made to play out of narrow cart ruts, c.1875**
**Right: Eighteenth-century rut iron with a 'cut-off' toe**

now making iron heads for more than one clubmaker; they took on more apprentices and more workmen.

As they achieved recognition, the cleekmakers began to put their names on the heads that they produced or, sometimes, to put a mark on the head which was peculiar to them. These marks, rather like pottery marks, were an early form of trade mark and, in later years, many of the cleekmakers registered them as trade marks.

Towards the end of the nineteenth century the cleekmakers were well organised, some employing 12–30 men and using a number of furnaces and anvils. Some degree of specialisation began: there were strong men who became 'hammer men' and did the heavy work; others, using dies, and with the aid of the hammer men, stamped a pattern on the face of irons so that the club would get a better grip on the ball and thus improve the backspin.

An important part of the clubmakers' work was to ensure that the tapered wood of the shaft fitted exactly into the hosel, since any looseness or 'play' could ruin the club. Some cleekmakers took to extending the taper in the hosel down to the heel of the club so that there was a hole right through to the sole at the heel. This allowed the clubmaker to take the tapered wood shaft right down to the sole of the club until it appeared on the surface. When the shaft had been driven right through and the fit was perfectly tight, the excess wood at the heel was cut off, flush with the surface, and a rivet inserted at the upper end. Using this method, it was possible for the cleekmaker to make the hosel shorter; this saved weight

**Typical shape of a cleek head: the upper and lower edges are almost parallel**

in the hosel which was then made up by increasing the weight of the head, thus giving more weight behind the ball and a longer shot.

There was a general opinion that many approach shots were easier to play with an iron club than with the old baffing spoon; at the same time, there was some relaxation of the rules of the game. The idea of the 'unplayable lie' came into being, and the spirit of 'play the ball where it lies' began to wane. By the end of the nineteenth century, rutters were no longer essential equipment, but many other clubs came into use. The rutter head became larger so that lofted shots to the green could be played with less fear of shanking, and the club, called a 'niblick', could be used out of bunkers as well.

In the longer game, the cleek supplanted the long spoon. The cleek had a characteristic shape, being long in the face and almost rectangular; the earlier cleeks had faces that were hooked and dished but, later, the faces were straight.

In the longer approach shots to the green, or for getting out of grassy lies and hollows, where the ball had to rise more quickly than was possible with a cleek, the 'lofter' was used. It had more loft than a cleek, the face was narrower at the heel and broader at the toe. Lofters were made with varying degrees of loft.

**Lofter: the face is lofted and fairly long, and the toe is wider than the heel**

Socket-head spoon 6 with a steel face, made by Jack Randall, *c.*1920

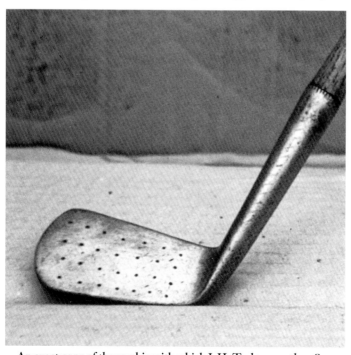

An exact copy of the mashie with which J. H. Taylor won the 1894
Open Championship at Sandwich

## The mashie

By 1880, the main iron clubs were: the cleek, the lofter, and the niblick. In 1882–5 a specific club for playing approach shots was devised – the mashie. This club was much shorter in the face than the lofter and was comparable to today's No.5 iron. While it had merit for approach play, it achieved fame because it was used by J.H. Taylor with consummate skill. With the assistance of the mashie, he perfected the art of stopping the ball on the green near the hole. The face was straight and not dished, and in shape was almost square, being deeper than the lofter.

After this date, the proliferation of iron clubs knew no bounds. The cleek gave rise to putting cleeks, approaching cleeks, 'jiggers', 'sammys', etc. The mashie gave rise to the driving mashie, the deep-faced mashie and the mashie-niblick. The niblick remained a niblick but had many different shapes of head which for the most part became larger. Iron clubs, by the end of the century, had the cleekmaker's mark, or his name, stamped on them and the professional's name and the Golf Club to which he was attached as well.

The professional would order ten or more clubheads at a time, based on an illustration in a catalogue produced by the cleekmaker, and would then proceed to shaft them and put on a grip.

As a result of the great increase in iron clubs, more divots than ever before were flying through the air (and not being put back!) and the problems of greenkeepers steadily increased.

For those with a special interest, more detail about cleekmakers and lists of cleekmakers, together with descriptions of the many iron clubs, will be found in books such as *Golf in the Making*, *Golf Collectibles*, *Collecting Old Golfing Clubs* and *Golf Curios and the Like*.

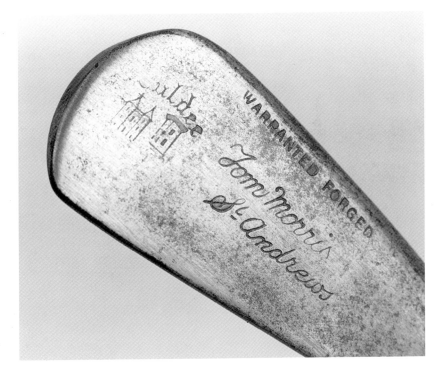

Unusual cleek mark on back of an iron. The club shafted and sold by the Tom Morris shop in St Andrews, *c.*1880

## Some Notable Cleekmakers

Those blacksmiths who, working singly, did not put their names on the clubheads that they made and who were not considered worthy of mention by the clubmakers for whom they worked, remain unknown. There are, however, some well-known cleekmakers.

### The Carrick Family of Musselburgh

The founder of this cleekmaking family was Alex Carrick; all that we know of him is that he was a blacksmith and was married in July 1785. He had two sons, Francis (1787–1855) and Archibald (1789–1817) and a daughter, Margaret.

In 1840, the two sons formed a Company, F.&A. Carrick, Edged Tool Makers, Musselburgh. As a toolmaking company, they were kept busy, but made iron clubheads as a sideline. It is very likely that they had learned how to do this from their father, but there is no proof of this.

Alex Carrick (1820–1901), son of Francis Carrick, and Archibald Carrick (*b.*1830–?) son of Archibald Senior, carried on the business after the death of their respective fathers and continued, still as a sideline, to make iron clubheads. The clubheads produced by this family were of a very high standard and they became famous cleekmakers, their clubheads being much in demand. Despite the fact that cleekmaking was said to be a sideline and that they continued to produce edged tools, it seems likely that the cleekmaking side became more important as the years went by and their fame as pioneer cleekmakers grew. The firm ceased to exist in 1904. Their mark was a rough cross.

In the 1800s the Carricks were the only family listed as cleekmakers in the Musselburgh area and they must have made most of the iron heads for the busy and important golf manufacturing town of Musselburgh, which was a much larger centre for such work than any other town in Scotland. It is likely that many of their apprentices, while carrying on their trade as blacksmiths after the completion of their apprenticeship, also used the skills that they had acquired in cleekmaking and made iron clubheads as a sideline, and their total output may have been considerable.

### W. Park Junior (1864–1925), Musselburgh

There is no proof that his father made iron clubs but Park Junior certainly did; possibly he acquired the expertise from the Carricks, not, perhaps, as a formal apprentice but because the Carricks and the Parks were in close proximity in a small town. Park made very fine irons and, of course, did all the shafting and gripping himself. He put his name on his irons usually as W.Park, Musselburgh or as Wm Park, Musselburgh. Being a cleekmaker (as

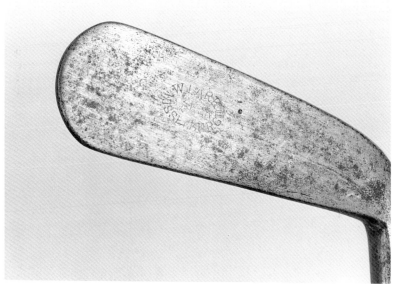

**Back of a cleek, *c.*1885, showing stamp often used by Willie Park Junior**

well as a clubmaker) he was in an excellent position to forge the wry-neck irons which were so successful and which he patented.

## The Anderson Family

James Anderson (1845–1895) was listed as a blacksmith and cleekmaker at Anstruther in Fife. He and his son, Alex Anderson (1879–1952), formed Anderson and Son. The company was successful and, by the end of the nineteenth century, was turning out 40,000 iron clubheads per year, employing 14 forgers to make the heads by hand but using machines to do the polishing and grinding. They made clubheads for Scott of Elie, cleeks for Forrester of Elie and they made the patent Carruthers Cleek – a club with a short hosel in which the shaft was taken right through the hosel into the sole, thus ensuring a good fit.

One of their advertisements states that they were founded in 1850. If this is correct, James Anderson's father must have been a blacksmith cleekmaker also. On the early clubs they stamped their name but later adopted the 'Arrow' as their trademark. The firm ceased to exist some years before Alex died.

## Robert Wilson (1845–1906), St Andrews

Robert was the son of a blacksmith, Alex Wilson, who was likely to have been a part-time cleekmaker, although there is no record of this. Robert Wilson is one of the 'classic' cleekmakers and is well recognised as a maker of very fine irons.

## Robert White, St Andrews

White was an Englishman, born in 1857. He was one of the blacksmiths who turned cleekmaker and is recognised as one of the best. One of his apprentices was Thomas Stewart of St Andrews, who was also to become a great cleekmaker and took over White's business when the latter went to the United States in 1894. In the United States, White joined the firm of Crawford, McGregor and Canby, one of the earliest American manufacturers of golf clubs.

## Robert Condie (1862–1923), St Andrews

Condie seems to have been one of the newer generation of cleekmakers, in that he was solely a cleekmaker and did not trade as a blacksmith. He produced many thousands of iron clubs, mainly by machinery. His mark was a rose.

## Stewart Senior (No dates known), Carnoustie

He was believed to have made iron heads for George Morris, who was professional at Carnoustie and Tom Morris's brother.

His son, Thomas Stewart Junior (1861–1931) has already been mentioned as Robert White's apprentice who took over his business. He was working mainly in this century and gained a great reputation as a cleekmaker. He used a pipe as his trade mark. His sons carried on the business until the Second World War. Stewart is known to have made sets of irons for famous golfers, such as Bobby Jones.

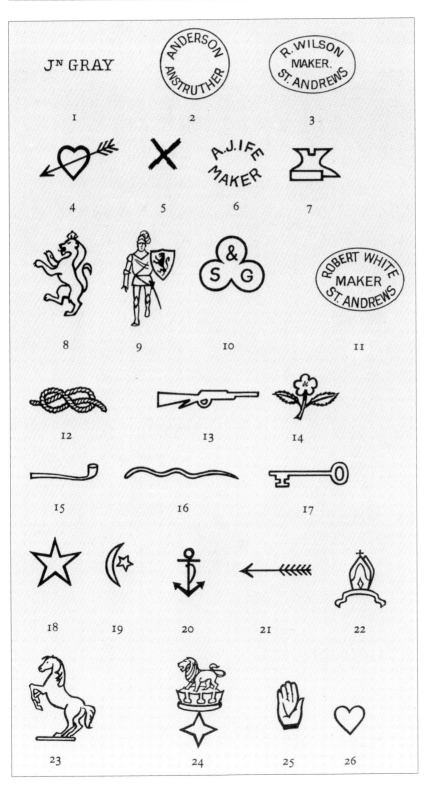

A selection of cleek-makers' marks. When the cleek-makers became more important they would put their own mark on the iron clubs they made.

1 John Gray, Prestwick
2 Anderson of Anstruther, Fife (early)
3 R. Wilson, St Andrews
4 Hewitt, Carnoustie
5 Carrick, Musselburgh
6 A. J. Ife, The Hague
7 Spalding, Britain and USA
8 C. Brand, Carnoustie
9 Cochrane, Edinburgh; 'false' cleek mark
10 Spence and Gourlay, St Andrews
11 Robert White, St Andrews
12 Cochrane, Carnoustie
13 J. and W. Craigie, Carnoustie
14 Condie, St Andrews
15 Stewart, St Andrews
16 Stewart, St Andrews (Ladies club)
17 Johnson, London
18 Gibson, Kinghorn, Fife
19 Gourlay, Carnoustie
20 Gourlay, Carnoustie
21 Anderson of Anstruther (late)
22 Bishop & Hendry, Leith
23 Gibson, Westward Ho!; 'false' cleek mark
24 Scott of Elie; 'false' cleek mark
25 Nicoll of Leven
26 T. Harrower, Carnoustie

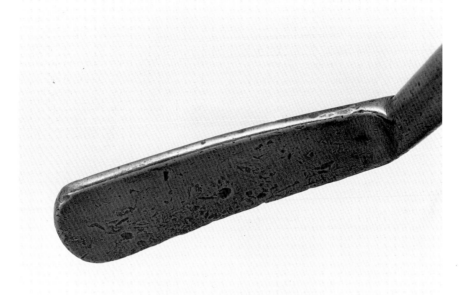

**Bronze cleek by R. Wilson, 1870, showing long narrow face, well hooked,
and upper and lower surfaces nearly parallel**

### George Nicoll (1861–1945), Leven

Another of the later cleekmakers, Nicoll was originally a blacksmith and did not start cleekmaking until 1881. He remained principally a blacksmith and started making bicycles as well.

Nicoll did not become a full-time cleekmaker until after the First World War. Then he produced irons of a good standard mainly by the use of machinery. In 1925 his firm started making wooden clubs and, for many years, under the management of Robert Nicoll, George's son, it became renowned throughout the world as makers of outstanding golf clubs. In the 1980s they were taken over by the Swilcan Company of St Andrews. Their mark was 'the hand of friendship'.

### John Gray (1824–1904), Prestwick

Originally a blacksmith, he was a keen golfer and turned to cleekmaking in 1851. For many years he was the only cleekmaker in southwest Scotland. He worked on his own and made all his clubheads by hand.

Although not one of the earliest cleekmakers, he was highly skilled and his irons were of a very high quality. His early career as a cleekmaker coincides with the period when Tom Morris Senior was Keeper of the Green at Prestwick (1851–1864). It cannot be a coincidence that Gray turned to cleekmaking as a full-time occupation at this time; Tom breathed life into Prestwick, improving the links, organising the caddies and labourers on the links, making clubs and giving lessons. He would need someone to make iron clubheads and Gray was the only man in the area who was expert at it; furthermore, by this time the gutta ball had arrived and Gray must have quickly become aware that many more iron clubs were going to be required.

John Gray married Charles Hunter's daughter. When Charles Hunter became Keeper of the Green in 1865, he would have worked closely with Gray and almost certainly put all the cleekmaking work his way.

The quality of John Gray's work is such that his clubs are very collectable. He put his name on the back of his irons in various forms.

### Walter Hewitt (1862–1940), Carnoustie

Hewitt was a blacksmith but appears to have turned cleekmaker at an early stage. He worked single-handed and all his iron clubheads were hand-forged; consequently, his output was small in quantity, but it was high in quality. His mark was a heart with an arrow through it. However, he also made many irons for the Simpsons of Carnoustie, the main clubmakers in that area, and these clubs had a Simpson mark and Hewitt's mark was omitted. There must be many irons made by Hewitt for Simpson which cannot be identified as such.

## Gourlay, Carnoustie

The dates of James Gourlay Senior are not known, nor is he listed as a cleekmaker, but a member of the Simpson family stated that Gourlay Senior was making iron club-heads 'before his time', fashioning them in a shed in which he also shoed horses.

When James Gourlay Senior died, his son, James Gourlay Junior, carried on the work but, after a few years, emigrated to Canada. The small firm survived, as his sister and an uncle carried on the work. The Gourlays used two cleek marks, a crescent moon and star, and an anchor. The anchor seems more in evidence on the clubs that they made for Simpson. Between them, for about half a century, the Gourlays and Hewitt supplied all the iron heads for the clubmaking family of Simpson.

## Some General Comments

The craftsmen clubmakers were to suffer from two disadvantages: competition from machinery, and emigration from among their numbers.

The emigration of hundreds of Scottish, and some English, professionals to the United States and Canada is clear, although a full account has yet to be documented. They were mostly young men who soon adapted to the American or Canadian way of life and remained there; the older ones also managed although some returned to Britain after a few years.

In the British Empire and in the rest of the world those Clubs that could afford a professional were forced to employ British nationals because there were no other nationalities, at that time, who knew anything about golf. The principal difference that the immigrant professional found, when he arrived, was that he was also expected to be an expert greenkeeper; Davis, who was the first professional at Montreal, complained to the Club Captain that he had not expected this and that, in Britain, a green-keeper was employed to do that sort of work. He was told, in no uncertain terms, that Clubs in Canada could not afford to do this and that he must undertake both jobs. The professionals' clubmaking skills were not put to the test because it was the habit to import such items from Britain and, in any event, by 1895 the United States was well into the mass production of golf balls and golf clubs. All the professional was required to do was to repair and refurbish golf clubs. The newcomer did not have to be a fully trained professional, but he needed an ability to play golf and to teach, an ability to carry out simple repairs, and an elementary knowledge of greenkeeping. Any young, half-trained apprentice could manage this; he would have learned to play as a young boy and had been around the professional's shop long enough to know how to repair clubs. Having been brought up on a links course, he would have had a rudimentary knowledge of how to look after one; unfortunately for him the courses that he would be required to look after would not be links courses. But in his favour was the fact that the members of the Club that he worked for would be beginners and in no position to criticise his efforts.

By 1895, the United States was exporting 100,000 hickory shafts per year to Britain; they were shafts and not laths, so little work was needed to shape them for the club. By 1901 the same number of rough-shaped heads, attached to the shafts, were exported. Because of mass production, this club was cheaper than a club which had been totally handmade. The wood used in such mass-production clubs was probably not as good as that which had been handpicked by Forgan at the docks at Glasgow, years before, but as the club had been finished by hand and had the professional's name on it, the customer was none the wiser as to quality.

The craftsmen clubmakers could only increase production by increasing the number of assistants but those who might have filled this role had emigrated to make more money and to be their own masters. As a result, the craftsmen clubmakers were forced out of business and whether they scorned mass production (as they probably did) or not was academic.

A few of the more enterprising, and some of the younger professionals, started using machinery and, by so doing, increased their production without increasing their staff; Forgan is the best example of the older generation changing their style and his business continued until the Second World War. Of the younger generation, Simpson of Carnoustie started using more modern methods: A.H. Scott of Elie used machinery and Ben Sayers of North Berwick did the same (the Sayers factory in North Berwick is still making clubs).

A factor which militated against the manufacturers in Britain was that the producers in the United States made sure that they got all the best hickory and persimmon; at the start of the century, persimmon had only very recently begun to be used for clubheads and was plentiful, but hickory was becoming scarce, particularly hickory that was properly seasoned. The best hickory stayed in the United States. A further difficulty that the British manufacturers had to face was cost – by the time that the somewhat inferior hickory had been transported to Britain it was more expensive than that used by the American manufacturers. Nevertheless, some British manufacturers, as opposed to professionals, began entering the trade of clubmaker, one of the most notable being the Army and Navy Stores in London; James Braid worked for them at one time.

The cleekmakers responded more rapidly to the American mass production threat. For them the change-over was easier; their workmen were not necessarily golfers, so there was no mass exodus of cleekmakers to the United States and to the world generally. They were able to increase their staff and were quite willing to use machines to help production. The raw material for their production could readily be obtained in Britain. The cleekmakers took on some clubmakers and used them to put shafts in their iron heads and thus produced complete clubs. The casting of iron by pouring it into moulds of many shapes was commonplace at the end of the nineteenth century and the cleekmakers took full advantage of this, producing clubheads by this method. In theory some iron heads were still forged by hand and this was a good selling point, so virtually all iron heads were so stamped. No iron heads were stamped 'cast iron' although Spalding, when they started using drop forging for irons, used a 'hammer head' trade mark to indicate that these clubs were not hand-forged.

The author had a rude awakening when he sent an iron head of about 1903 to a metallurgist friend to have the metal analysed. The report came back that the head was of cast iron. The head was made by a manufacturer considered as reputable and was stamped 'Warranted Hand Forged'. This must cast considerable doubt on the provenance of all iron clubheads, even if stamped 'Warranted Hand Forged', which were made after about 1885.

It is the increasing use of machinery in all club- and cleekmaking after about 1885 which has led to the greatly decreased value of antique golf clubs after that date compared with those before. Prior to 1885 one can be reasonably certain that 'Warranted Hand Forged' means what it says and that the maker's name on a wooden clubhead means that the club was made throughout in his workshop and at least under his direction.

Above: Dutch game on ice
(*Winter Pleasures* by Jan van
Goyen)

Left: Net for carrying croisse
balls, balls of varying sizes,
and the club. The game is
played using one club only

Far left top: William Innes, Captain of the Blackheath Golfers in 1778

Far left bottom: From a Book of Hours in the British Museum, *c.*1500, depicting a game of golf in Flanders

Left: William St Clair of Roslyn, *c.*1743. First President of the Edinburgh Company of Golfers at Leith. This is not the costume in which he would actually have played golf

Below: This painting, believed to date from about 1700, is the oldest painting of golf in Scotland. Note the form of wooden clubs at that time

'Alick', the old holecutter at Royal Blackheath Golf Club: note the windmills and red coats in the background

Below: Golf on the Old Course at St Andrews, *c.*1870. The interest of this illustration, in particular, is that the course is being played backwards, starting from the first tee and playing to the 17th green. This method of playing the course is practised once a year at St Andrews and goes back to the traditional way of playing it when there was only one fairway for each hole, both out and back. Tom Morris, on the right, is playing in a foursome and they are near the Swilcan Bridge (Painting by Bill Waugh)

'Daft' Willie Gunn, caddie
at Bruntsfield, *c.*1820

Below: General view of golf
on the Old Course at St Andrews,
with the old town in the
background, *c.*1880
(Painting by Bill Waugh)

Modern golf ball in front of a Philp driver, which demonstrates the
shallowness of the face of old wooden clubs

Rear view of a tenon-jointed club made by
A.H. Scott of Elie, Fife, *c.*1890

Usual shape of a bulger club: the head is wide
and short and the convex face is well in front of
the shaft. This is a socket-head club

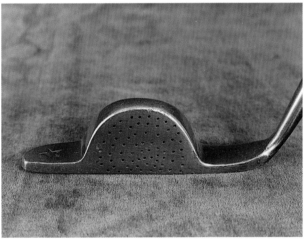

Top: General view of tools used in the making of a scared head club

Above: 'Jonko' putter by Gibson of Kinghorn, c.1910

Left: Scared head long-nosed Philp clubhead, c.1840. This shows the long, graceful neck, the convex back and the slightly concave face

Right: The Mills aluminium head mid-iron

Below: Eighteenth-century track iron

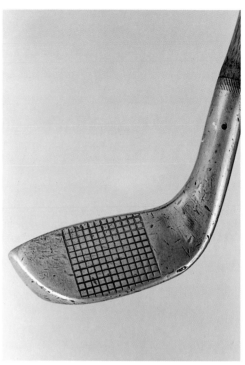

Above: Lofting iron, *c.*1840, with a well 'dished' face

Right: Patent putter, *c.*1900

# 6

# *Putters*
# *The Special Clubs*

THESE clubs have been given a section to themselves, partly because putters can be both wood and iron clubs, but mainly because putters and putting form a very special, and rather separate, form of golf.

Putting is both a science and an art. In this form of golf there is no 'grooved swing' and no generally accepted form of club. The grip in which the putter is held shows a large variation and there is an equally great variation in the stance of the player. As time goes by, putting is becoming more difficult. One hundred and fifty years ago the hole varied in size on different courses. The only feature that the old links course greens had in common was that they were very rough; the golfer was able to accept, fairly philosophically, that, if a putt missed, it might be pure bad luck, in that the ball had had to cross a particularly rough piece of green which deflected it from its course; the golfer might even be able to put his failure down to the fact that he had had a bad lie – even in 1921, Willie Park Junior, who wrote a book on putting, devoted a small section to how to putt out of a 'cupped' lie. The golfer had a good alibi in being able to blame the green; golfers still do this today, but usually the fault lies in the player rather than in the green.

Many years ago putting was less important. It was possible to achieve a good score, whilst having 'no luck on the greens' because the long game was difficult and it was thus possible to make up for errors on and around the green by playing the long game particularly well. Today, when a 500-yard hole is a drive and a short iron to the great professionals, it is not possible to gain many strokes from one's rivals in the long game and winning depends more and more on chipping and putting.

In the very early days of golf, putting was a more extensive game than now and a putter was often used from 100 yards, or more, from the green. There was a special form of putter which had a very stiff shaft and was used off the tee in order to hit the ball low into the wind; it was called a 'driving putter'.

Because of this, the old wooden putters were very similar to drivers, even to the extent of having a hooked face; the differences were that they tended to be heavier, shorter in the shaft and more upright in lie. This upright lie was often accentuated by 'bowing' the shaft – that is, the shaft was bent, just below the grip, so that the convexity was towards the toe of the putter. The effect was that, when one looked down the shaft, the line of the shaft passed through the junction of the inner ⅓ and the outer ⅔ of the putter face; such a bend in the shaft was considered important in the early putters and a putter with a bowed shaft was the hallmark of all the best clubmakers such as Philp and McEwan.

In the summer, when most golf was played, the unwatered greens and fairways were dry, dusty and brown; it was not possible to stop the ball, and golf architecture of the time, such as it was, allowed for the run of the ball

97

Above: Gassiat putter, showing
the built up top of the grip which
was an essential feature of the
club

Right: Three bow-shafted
wooden putters. 'Bowing' was
considered important for swing.
Raw linseed oil was allowed to
soak into the middle of the
hickory shaft, which was then
heated with an open flame and
bent

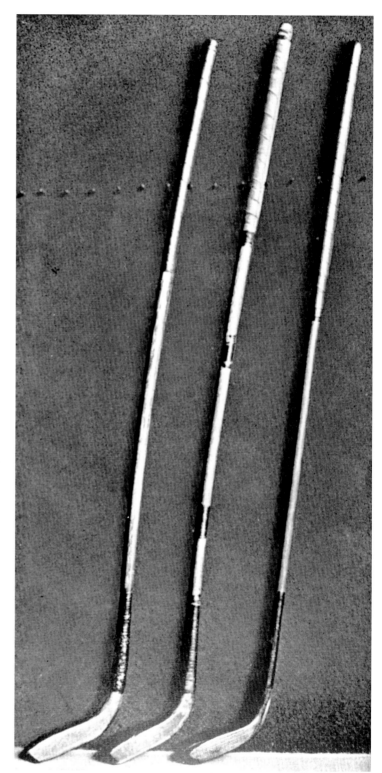

**Willie Park's original bent neck putter (otherwise known as a wry-necked putter)**

by keeping the hazards and difficulties to the side of the greens and leaving the ground in front of the green open. As a result, if the drive, or second or third shot, depending on the length of the hole, were straight there was a way into the green by playing a running shot, either with a little loft, using a baffing spoon, or all along the ground using a wooden putter.

The fact that early lady golfers used only a putter did not imply, as it would today, that they were only putting on a green, for they could be playing a hole of 120–180 yards.

With the arrival of the gutta ball and the golf explosion, iron shots became common, some backspin could be put on the ball, and the greens were occasionally watered; bunkering became tighter and the long run up with the old wooden putter – known as 'the long steal' – began to disappear.

Because iron clubs were easier to play with through the green, the idea grew that they might also be easier to putt with, and the iron blade putter began to appear. Some found that, on rough greens, a little loft on the putter was useful and 'putting cleeks' enjoyed some popularity.

By about 1885, the wooden putter was much less used and the majority of putters were iron blade putters. Nevertheless, wooden putters did not disappear entirely and there are still a few in use today.

At about this time, Willie Park Junior invented and patented the 'Bent neck putter', also known as the wry-necked putter; this putter had a bend in the hosel which brought the blade of the putter behind the line of the shaft. As a result, when the putter blade was placed behind the ball, the ball was in the line of the shaft. This type of putter became very popular and putters of this general type are used today.

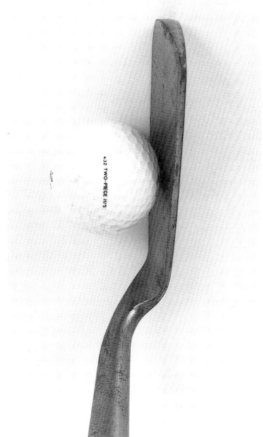

**Park's Putter, looking down on to the ball. The bend in the neck is just sufficient to bring the 'equator' of the ball in line with the shaft**

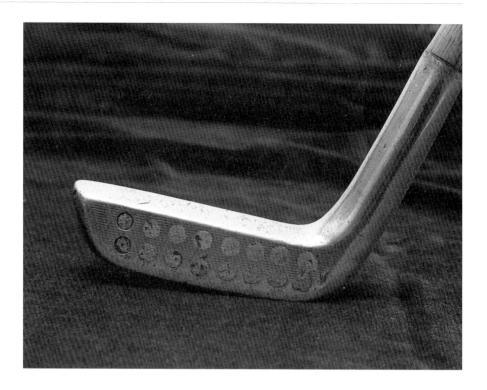

Above: Face of the 'Duralite'
putter by Jack Randall, showing
the discs of lead in the face

Right: Putter with lead face to
give a softer touch

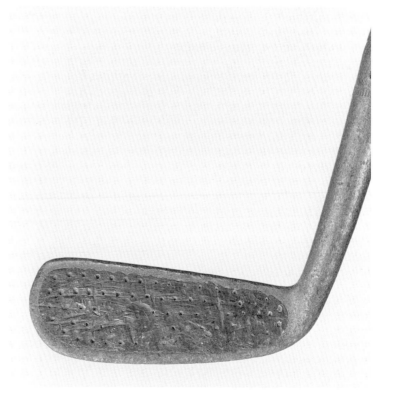

Left: Head of a scared head putter by Jack Randall, *c.*1925, subsequently copied in 'Duralite'.
Right: Walter Travis practising putting with a centre-shafted 'Schenectady' putter, made in the USA (1904)

In 1895, Mills of the Standard Golf Company of Sunderland, produced an aluminium clubhead frame which was filled in with wood; by 1900 he had produced a clubhead made entirely of aluminium. Some of these were copies of old wooden head clubs but the majority were aluminium putters. They were all shapes; some were copies of the old long-headed wooden putters, others were more akin to the shorter, bulger shape. They became popular, especially after James Braid, who had not been a good putter in his early days, started winning Open Championships using one. Aluminium-headed putters have continued to be popular and are still used today.

In 1896, a putter was invented with the shaft inserted in the centre of the face, but the R&A banned it. A little later, another type of centre-shafted putter was invented in the United States. This was the ill-fated club which sour old Walter Travis used to win the British Amateur Championship in 1904. The club was permitted in the United States but banned in Britain, and it remained banned until 1952. Before the First World War, a blade putter was invented in which there was an acute bend in the hosel such that, on looking down the line of the shaft, the shaft appeared to be inserted into the centre of the club face – this, too, was banned by the R&A. Since then the R&A has been called upon to ban large numbers of putters which can only be described as weird!

Top: 'Simplex' club, *c.*1910

Above: Cross-head club as used by Sir George Alexander, golfer and famous actor, *c.*1910

Right: Patent putter, showing blade set back and shaft coming through to sole, ensuring a good fit, *c.*1900

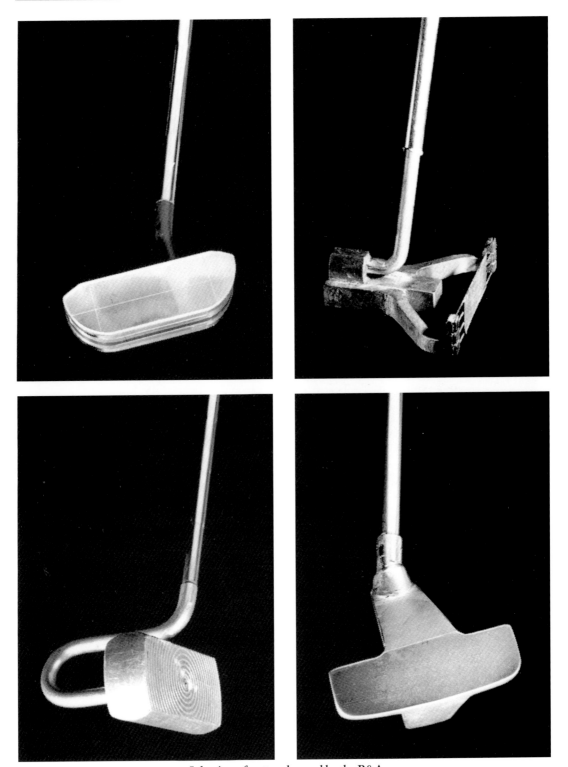

Selection of putters banned by the R&A

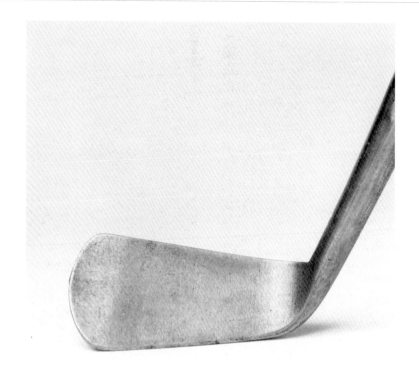

Iron clubs from the Robertson Collection
at The Royal Sydney Golf Club

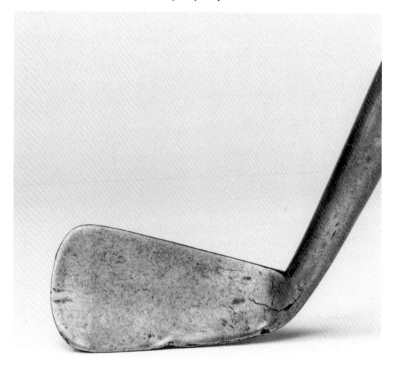

Feather balls from the Robertson Collection at the Royal Sydney Golf Club
Left: One made by George Robertson who is recorded as a feather-ball maker
at Wright's Houses at Bruntsfield Links, 1825–26, subsequently listed in Musselburgh in 1831
Centre: A feather ball made by Tom Morris. Right: A ball likely to have been made by Allan's father David

## The Robertson Collection, Royal Sydney Golf Club

CURIOUSLY, for a great winner of challenge matches, Allan Robertson, who (very unusually among the early professionals) neither drank alcohol nor smoked, left only £91 in his will. He had no issue.

Allan was the son of David Robertson and he had an older brother who was called David after their father.

David Robertson Junior never took part in the feather ballmaking craft and emigrated to Australia in 1848 – at the same time as the gutta ball first came into use. David took a job in a milliner's establishment in Sydney.

He may not have been a ballmaker but, living in St Andrews, he certainly played golf, and was responsible for introducing the game to Australia. Unfortunately, although there was some initial enthusiasm for golf in Sydney, it soon waned and died and only came into popularity later in the century.

David Robertson of Sydney had a son; he named him Allan after his famous brother. In 1916 the son, Allan, went to the Royal Sydney Golf Club and left with them some clubs and balls that had belonged to his uncle Allan and his grandfather, David. The Club accepted the gift but did not make much comment in their Club Minutes.

The Collection is composed of feather balls, wooden clubs and iron clubs.

### Feather Balls

There are twenty-six and while most of them are signed Allan, there are a number made by David Robertson, his father, and other contemporary feather ballmakers, both at St Andrews and at Musselburgh. It is one of the largest collections of feather balls in the world and some of the balls in it are unique.

## The Wooden Clubs

There are ten long-nosed, scared-head wooden clubs, some of which have the 'nick' on the shaft which meant that this was a club which Allan prized and used.

## Iron Clubs

There are eight clubs of great age and more than one has the Robertson 'nick'. One of these clubs has the name of both Allan and his father (David) stamped on the head; historically, this is important because it has always been believed that Allan was the first man to start using iron clubs for playing approach shots – the existence of this club suggests that his father played such shots before him.

Allan Robertson of St Andrews was so famous in his lifetime that clubs known to have been used by him sold for a good price and, because of this, there were those who 'forged' his clubs by placing the Robertson 'nick' on the shaft of an old club and selling it as a genuine Robertson club. This piece of cheating makes it very difficult to be sure that a club which claims to be a genuine Robertson club really is so. In the case of the clubs (and balls) in the Royal Sydney Collection, one can be sure because it is extremely unlikely that Allan would have left his only nephew clubs which were not genuine, and ones that he had not used and prized. Because of this, the Royal Sydney Collection is the largest authenticated collection of clubs and balls used by the great Allan Robertson in existence and is a collection of the greatest historical importance.

**A James Wilson long-nosed club, showing the shape of the club seen from above**

# The Golf Ball

## 1800–1910

HAVING considered, at some length and in some detail, the origins of the game and its subsequent development in organised Golf Clubs and Societies, it is time now to consider balls which they used.

## The Golf Ball

THERE is now much information about the development of the golf ball which is well set out in a number of excellent books; it is, therefore, only necessary to consider the general outline and certain aspects which have not been fully researched, leaving the reader who is particularly interested to find more detail in those books which specialise in the subject. Generally speaking, golf historians suggest that very early golf – before 1600 – was played with a wooden ball, but there is no hard evidence. From the descriptions of jeu de mail and croisse given earlier it is easy to see how the idea came about. If the very early forms of golf, gowf, golve, goff, etc, played in Scotland were derived from these games, as I believe, it is very likely to be true, but no wooden balls have survived to confirm it. A letter of 1585 in which a servant of the Master of Orkney asks for 'one doz: of common ballis' is evidence that there were two, or more, qualities of golf ball; it may be that the common ball was made of wood – or of a leather case stuffed with flock or hair, as we shall see later.

## The Feather Ball

THIS ball was certainly in use from the early seventeenth century. In 1687, Thomas Kincaid states in his diary: 'Your ball must be of middle size, neither too big or too little, and then the heavier it is in respect to its bigness, it is still the better. It must be of thick and hard leather not with pores or grains or that will let a pin easily passe through it, especially at the soft end.' He is clearly writing of a feather ball. Even earlier than that there is documentary evidence that the Dickson family of Leith were making balls in 1629. The Paterson family, whose principal trade was that of shoemakers, made golf balls in the sixteenth and seventeenth centuries but the main bulk of authenticated evidence is in the eighteenth century, with the well-recorded Robertson family at St Andrews and the equally well-recorded family of Gourlay at Edinburgh and Musselburgh.

In 1600 there is evidence of the importation of feather balls from Holland (and probably Flanders) when James Melvill and William Berwick were granted a Royal monopoly of feather ballmaking, thus saving money being sent out of Britain to Holland to buy balls. Melvill and Berwick were not ballmakers but sought to control the feather-ball market in Scotland; they soon had trouble with some ballmakers and the monopoly never came into force.

Van Hengel, in *Early Golf*, a history of the Dutch game, has documentary evidence of feather ballmaking in

Holland in the sixteenth century. It was a cottage industry and some ballmakers formed themselves into Guilds.

Although they stuffed leather cases to make balls, it is not clear whether they stuffed them with feathers or hair or flock. All three types of balls were made; the main trade of ballmakers who used cowhair was button-making because, at that time, buttons were stuffed with hair. In 1586, the ballmakers at Delft were forbidden to wash the hair for balls in the river, because this led to infestation of the water.

Van Hengel does not say what percentage of balls were made with feathers and what percentage were made with hair or flock, nor are we told what sizes the balls were; some may have been footballs or tennis balls. There was a well-documented trade in balls for 'Katsen', a game in which the ball was struck with the hand – it is still a popular game in Holland – but balls for katsen would not have needed to be as tight or robust as a ball which was struck with a golf club. It is possible that the 'common ballis' sought by the servant of the Master of Orkney in 1585 were made of flock or hair and not wood.

Van Hengel reports as many as 40,000 balls being sold in one deal at Bergen-op-Zoom in 1502 and says that, in 1631, three ballmakers in Goirle sent a consignment of 17,700 balls to Maastricht. Van Hengel believed that the latter consignment was due to go to Paris. These staggeringly large numbers of balls were, surely, many more than the relatively small numbers of colf players required and those sent to Paris would not have been for golf or colf because the game was unknown in Paris at that time; if the balls had been for jeu de mail they would have been made of wood. The Dutch were great ballmakers but the balls that they made were not all for golf, and the balls sent to Paris may have been footballs or tennis balls.

There is another reason for believing that only a few of the balls made by the Dutch were for golf. At St Andrews, in 1844, at a time of maximum demand, Allan Robertson, aided by Tom Morris and 'Lang Wullie', produced 2,456 balls in one year, and the *Statistical Account of Scotland* (Vol: IX, pp.476–477), reporting on the Parish of St Andrews, records that St Andrews Parish produced about 6,000 in one year. It was said by the old feather ballmakers that a good ballmaker could make three balls in a day but a poor ballmaker could make six in a day. This was because the poor ballmaker would not bother to stitch the ball as well, nor would he stuff as many feathers in, as his better counterpart. James Grierson, in *Delineation of St Andrews* (1807), writes that in his youth 10–12 ballmakers lived in the town and estimates that a total of 3,600 balls were used locally and the rest sent to Glasgow, Edinburgh, Perth, and Aberdeen. If three Dutch ball-

**Feather ball made by Gourlay**

makers could produce 17,700 balls for one deal, they could not have been making more than a few to the standard required by golfers and it is quite likely that most of the balls were for other purposes.

## The Making of a Feather Ball

THERE are descriptions of the way to make a feather ball in several books. These set out the basic procedures such as: using the breast feathers of a goose or chicken, boiling the feathers, cutting a sheet of tough, thick, leather into three parts, stitching the leather pieces together inside out, leaving a small hole through which to turn it outside in, and then stuffing the feathers into the casing, at first by using a hand 'stuffer' and after, stuffing in feathers much more tightly, using a long awl-like stuffer, held against the chest, or under the arm; finally, closing the small hole with a single stitch tied on the outside and painting the ball with several layers of white lead paint. A special refinement was that the leather should be soaked in alum which would cause the leather to shrink as it dried, thus making the ball even harder.

All this was an accurate description of the 'bare bones' but left out all the detail. This was quite understandable because, at the time when feather balls were in use, there was no such thing as a patent; the ballmaker taught his apprentice how to do it, in detail, but the apprentice was in duty bound not to reveal to others exactly how it was done until such time as he became a fully-fledged feather ballmaker and taught his own apprentices.

As the fine details are not available, the author decided to make a few feather balls in order to find out the snags

**Feather ball made by Sandy Pirie, *c.*1830**

and some of the tricks of the trade. The process was one of trial and error over many weeks, during the course of which many sub-standard balls were discarded but, in the end, a few feather balls were produced which, in appearance, looked quite good. There is no doubt that, during this time, both Allan Robertson and Gourlay were spinning in their respective graves! The experiment was not carried out to its ultimate conclusion because no full shots were played, but the balls behaved reasonably well during some chipping and putting. The following points came to light:

### Breast Feathers of Chicken or Goose

From whichever bird they are plucked they must be really fine breast feathers. Any feather with a spine that is thick or stiff is unusable. When the ball is really tightly finished, even a small spine will cause small lumps on the surface.

### Boiling the Feathers

This will soften any spines and will make the feathery part take up less room as the fine down clings together when wet but, as soon as the feathers cool, the small spines resume their stiffness.

### Stitching

Stitching the casing inside out is not too difficult; it is necessary to use very strong and thick thread because the stitches become very tight when the stuffing is complete.

A round-bodied needle is better than a cutting needle because the small cut made by the latter will readily lengthen under pressure. The stitching is of the 'under and over' variety; this allows one to have a deep free edge which can then be trimmed with knife or scissors – with an 'over and over' stitch trimming would not be possible.

The final hole must be about little finger size; if it is any larger the final stitch cannot be tied without causing some distortion; if too small, the various 'stuffers' cannot be used effectively.

The weight of the ball is due to the weight of the leather. An early effort with thinner skin (which made it easier to turn inside out) resulted in a ball which seemed like a table tennis ball.

If the leather is of the right thickness and toughness it is impossible to turn outside in through a hole the diameter of a little finger. On the advice of a shoemaker, the leather was wrapped in wet newspaper overnight and this made it much softer – but not soft enough. If the leather were boiled it was, initially, even softer, but still would not allow turning the leather outside in. The final answer was to stitch the casing and have the tied ends about half an inch apart. The ends were left long and, on each side, about two stitches were put in position but not tied; it was then possible to turn even thick leather (well-soaked) through the half-inch hole, making sure that the free ends of each 'two stitch' line did not pull out. Once turned outside in, it was possible to pull each 'two stitch' line tight and tie it on the inside, thus leaving the casing outside in and a hole about the size of a little finger through which to do the stuffing.

### Stuffing in the Feathers

A quantity of feathers much more than would fill a top hat could be stuffed into the casing. It is very difficult to stuff dry feathers into the casing because the fine feathers float all over the room – and up the operator's nose! Boiling the feathers is no great help but having them wet is a definite advantage; if they are totally wet, then, as they dry out, the tension in the ball becomes markedly less, as the water is lost. It is best to have the feathers well damped. The initial stuffing is done with a small wooden stuffer. This is a tedious process and it is essential to insert the maximum quantity of feathers that is possible; if this is not done, then, when real pressure is applied using a long awl, the tip of the awl can easily be pushed right through the contents and impinge in the casing on the opposite side.

When a maximum quantity of feathers has been inserted, using the stuffer, further feathers can then be inserted, using the long awl and pressure from the chest; this process must be continued until the operator feels sure that the stitches are going to burst from the pressure – and then he must force a lot more in. When it is absolutely as tight as a drum the ball must be left to dry out, either naturally or on a radiator.

As the leather dries it shrinks – and can be made to shrink more if the wet leather is treated with alum. Even so, when the ball is completely dry, it will be found that it is less tight, as the feathers have lost water. To combat this, further feathers, only slightly damped, must be forced in, using the awl. Despite the great pressure, there is no tendency for the feathers to come out through the stuffing hole when it is left open.

At the end of all this time (and even after stuffing yet more feathers in, if necessary) the stuffing hole can be closed with a single 'mattress' stitch. Great care needs to be taken when tying this stitch. If pulled tight, there will be a slightly flattened area at the site of the stitch which will affect the ball when it is rolling; if not tight enough, the turned in edges will not be completely closed and feathers will escape when it is hit.

The resulting ball is completely tight and bounces well. It is definitely not round, being slightly egg-shaped. Many of the minor marks will be obliterated by two or three layers of white paint but the stitch lines will always be apparent and this is what makes a feather ball fly well. It was the failure to recognise this that led the early gutta ballmakers to make the gutta round and smooth, only to find that it would not fly until it had been cut by a golf club a few times.

In conclusion it must be admitted that, as no leather cup was available (such as would have been used by the feather ballmakers) the author used a smooth gutta mould as the 'former' during the stuffing process; a half-mould was used for most of the time, the second half being added to the first from time to time to keep the ball at about the right shape. Despite this, the end result was still slightly egg-shaped.

The late Laurie Auchterlonie once said to the author that the idea of a feather ball containing enough feathers to fill a large top hat was 'a load of rubbish'. He would not enlarge on this statement and one did not know whether he meant that it was more than could be contained in a feather ball – or less. The reader now can be assured that it *is* a 'load of rubbish', because a feather ball contains a much greater quantity of feathers than would fill an old top hat!

**Feather ball (size 28-30). The date was probably added later as no feather balls were made after 1850**

This account of the difficulties of feather ball-making makes the statement of the old feather ballmakers that a good maker could make three balls in a day and a poor maker could make six, understandable, and reinforces the opinion that, if three ballmakers in Goirle made 17,700 in a year in 1631, they cannot all have been well-made, tightly-stuffed, golf balls.

## Value and Size of Feather Balls

IN 1672, feather balls cost 15 Scots shillings each, equivalent then to about one shilling and threepence in English money; the cost of a club at that time was about 4 Scots shillings; not only did the ball cost more than a club but a feather ball would seldom last for more than one round, even if not mishit. Feather balls wore out quite quickly and the stitching gave way; it was common for golfers, starting on a round, to have 4–6 feather balls in their pockets. The value of the fore caddie was not only to mark the ball, so that the player did not lose it, but, also, to remove it quickly from water because a wet feather ball rapidly became a soggy mass of feathers.

A poem written after the gutta ball had come into being, entitled 'In Praise of Gutta Percha', runs:

> Now what do you say to these balls of feather
> Which burst in the wet or frosty weather
> And if a man hit them but twice on the head
> The stuffing came out like a feather bed?

Small wonder that golf was expensive in the days of the feather ball and that, when the much cheaper and more durable 'gutta' appeared, so many more golfers were able to take up the game.

## Size of Golf Balls

IN the matter of the best size of a ball the customer was influenced by the suggestions of the ballmaker, particularly if the maker happened to be a champion golfer, such as Allan Robertson, but there was a rugged individualism in men in the Victorian era, so it is unlikely that they would slavishly follow the advice of the maker on all occasions. An article about Allan Robertson in *Golf Illustrated* (1907) mentions a man at St Andrews who had a fine collection of feather balls made by Allan. The owner of the collection is reported to have said that the disparity in size of the balls was so astonishing that it would be difficult to believe it unless one saw it. At this time there were no regulations about ball size. The commonest sizes (or weights) were between 27 and 29 pennyweights but 25s and 26s were made and Tom Alexander of Musselburgh made larger balls – some up to size 34. As has been said, the weight of a feather ball depended on the thickness of the leather – the quantity of feathers had no effect. Consequently, a larger ball with a thinner cover would weigh the same as a smaller ball with a thicker cover. The thicker the cover, the more difficult the turning inside out process but a smaller ball which was heavy would travel further than a larger ball which was light, as Kincaid had pointed out in 1687. It is probable that it was the ability of master makers like Gourlay to make a ball with a thicker cover, which, of course, would not only fly further but would withstand wear and tear better, that made Gourlay's balls superior to those of other makers. At the same time, the sizing of feather balls on the basis of weight cannot have been of much use.

A manufacturer of golf balls, writing in *Golf Monthly* in February 1914, states that he examined a number of gutty balls made in the last few years of the gutty era and found that none of them weighed even as much as 26 pennyweights; he felt that to make a feather ball of 26 pennyweights would have meant that it would have been larger than any of the gutties that he had weighed, which, we know, not to be true.

He measured the diameter of the gutty balls and some (later) Haskell balls and found that the diameter varied from 1·65 in. to 1·94 in., with an average of 1·68 in. He pointed that, if these measurements are converted into 16ths of an inch, the sizes are 27½, 27 and 26½, respectively. He concludes that golf balls were sized in 16ths of an inch and not by weight. This seems to be a much more likely – and accurate – means of measuring the size of a golf ball and it may be that the idea of sizing by pennyweights is an erroneous one, but has been so constantly repeated that it has been accepted as true.

William Gourlay (1788–1836) of Musselburgh was the most renowned maker of feather balls and charged a little more for his balls than the other makers. Following close on Gourlay's heels for fame was David Robertson of St Andrews, Allan Robertson's father, who is mentioned in Mathison's poem, 'The Goff' (1743):

. . . two balls with careful eye
That with Clarinda's breasts for colour vye.
The work of Bobson who, with matchless art
Shapes the firm hide, connecting ev'ry part

Then in a socket sets the well stitched void
And thro' the eyelets drives the downy tide
Crowds upon crowds the forceful brogue impels
The feathers harden and the leather swells.
He crams and sweats yet crams and urges more
Till scarce the turgid globe contains its store.

Gourlay's feather balls were often given as prizes and became so famous that reference to a 'Gourlay' meant a feather ball and 'ball' after Gourlay became unnecessary.

The reader will find the names of many feather ballmakers recorded but there were many who made feather balls whose names are not recorded. Clubmakers, in the feather ball era, made balls and, in greater numbers, so did 'cadies'. 'Lang Willie', famous as a caddie, who helped Allan and Tom to make feather balls in Allan Robertson's kitchen. It was a useful occupation in the spring and summer and would help to save him from starvation in the winter, but he is not in the records as a ballmaker.

When Tom Alexander (1803–1841) was Keeper of the Green at Musselburgh and William Gourlay (1813–1844) occupied the same position at the Honourable Company of Edinburgh Golfers (then playing at Musselburgh), they both must have had apprentices to whom they taught the trade of ballmaking. William Gourlay (1788–1836) of Musselburgh was also a ballmaker and no doubt his son, William, was apprenticed to him. There were other ballmakers in Musselburgh, men such as Alex Cosgrove (1821–67), David Gressick (1821–71) and John Ramsay (1822–?). It is likely that all these men were apprenticed to the elder Gourlay or to Alexander, but we have no exact record.

Grierson, writing in 1807, says that, at Musselburgh, Tom Geddes was making feather balls before Tom Alexander. No records of Geddes as a ballmaker have been found, nor have any balls made by him been found.

## Musselburgh as a Golf Centre

MENTION has been made of the ballmakers of Musselburgh. Gressick lived at Mrs Taylor's lodging-house which was in the Mill Hill area of Musselburgh, as did another ballmaker, Thomas Stewart (1816–?). It is probable that some of the ballmakers of Leith moved to the Musselburgh area when the Honourable Company moved there because there were then three Clubs or Societies playing at Musselburgh, Musselburgh Golf Club, the Honourable Company and Bruntsfield (whose clubmaker McEwan, and ballmaker Gourlay, had also moved to Musselburgh).

There were many clubmakers at Musselburgh. Not only had the McEwans moved there, but the Dunns,

Willie and Jamie, lived there, as did the Parks. William Ballantyne (1793–1845), originally of Leith, moved to Musselburgh in 1834 (and his son, William, also to become a clubmaker, moved there with him, when the latter was eight years old), and continued as a clubmaker until he died in 1844. From a slightly later era, there were Bob Ferguson (1846–1914), a clubmaker and professional golfer who won the Open Championship in 1880, 1881, and 1882 and tied, but lost the playoff, in 1883, and Thomas Hood (1843–1907) and W.D. Day (1837–?) who all lived at Musselburgh.

All these ball and clubmakers lived near the golf links, either at Mill Hill or in Links Road. All would have had sons or apprentices – or both – who were working there as well. It is clear that the area of Musselburgh must have contained the largest concentration of men skilled in the trades of club- and ballmaking of any area of Scotland, and, therefore, of the world.

## Life Expectancy of Feather Ballmakers

It has always been suggested that to make feather balls led to a short life because of chest disease, variously attributed either to inhalation of feathers or to the constant pressure against the chest of the large awl known as a brogue. The general figures do not bear this out, since the average age at death of eight ballmakers working in the early nineteenth century is 47; in a comparable period the average life expectancy of fourteen clubmakers was 52 years. The figures are small for statistical purposes but the difference is not great and around fifty years of age was about the average life expectancy of the general population in the early nineteenth century.

The killing disease of the time was tuberculosis. This was a chest disease and was encouraged by malnutrition and damp and poorly ventilated houses. It was natural that when a ballmaker, who had spent much of his life in a small room full of feathers, died, his death would be attributed to this cause but it is more likely that the chesty cough was a symptom of the pulmonary tuberculosis which killed him.

## The Gutta Percha Golf Ball

The use of sap from certain trees in tropical forests was first practised by forest dwellers. The Western world used these natural substances for various purposes.

### Rubber

Sap from a tree in the forests of Brazil, after exuding from the tree, became an elastic substance, impervious to wet. First discovered by Charles de la Condamine. he brought it back to France in 1736 and called it 'caoutchouc'. Joseph Priestley, the chemist, became interested in the substance in 1744 and found that, among other properties, it would rub out pencil marks.

As the British had difficulty in pronouncing 'caoutchouc' they called it rubber and, sometimes Indiarubber, not because it came from India (which it did not) but because the Indians of the forest of Brazil first drew attention to it. By the 1820s it was being used in Britain to waterproof garments; by 1838 it was found that it could be made much harder by adding sulphur and this was called 'Vulcanite'. However its most important property was insulation against electricity. Sixty-two years after it was discovered, rubber was used for making golf balls.

The second of the trees that produced a sap which flowed from the tree and subsequently hardened was the gutta percha tree in the forests of Malaya. Mr William Montgomerie (1797–1856), a surgeon to the East India Company in Malaya, noticed that the forest people used the sap from this tree to make knife and dagger handles; the sap flowed from the tree and then set hard, but could be softened in hot water. He recommended its use in making medical vessels. He sent specimens to London and was awarded the Gold Medal of the Society for the Encouragement of Arts, Manufactures and Commerce in June 1845. Some of the specimens were shown at the Great Exhibition in London in 1851. At some time between 1845 and 1848 the possible use of this material in the making of golf balls was discovered.

Who conceived the idea? A number of people suggest themselves.

### St Andrews

In 1900, Dalrymple of Leven in Fife suggested that a certain Reverend Doctor Paterson of St Andrews had thought up the idea and had made some balls of gutta percha in about 1845.

In 1902, the Reverend J.G. MacPherson, claiming to have been corresponding with Paterson, gave a highly romantic account of how Paterson did it. He said that Paterson was sent a statue of a Hindu god by his brother, who was a missionary in India; the statue was packed with chips of gutta percha and it was from these chips that Paterson made his first golf ball, painted it white and played with it. There were no witnesses to this experiment, nor has any correspondence survived between MacPherson and Paterson. Paterson emigrated to the United States and, according to MacPherson, wrote a couplet: 'I quit St Andrews for a louder call and left to golfers all I had – a ball'.

From the start, this story had little credence with authorities on golf at that time; it is curious that it was 50

**Bronze gutty mould with steel lining and mesh mark, c.1880.
Probably used with hydraulic pressure**

years after the alleged event that the first claim was actually made.

Paterson was of an Edinburgh family and did not come from St Andrews. He was born in 1829, so he would have been 15 years old in 1845. The term 'Reverend Doctor' is not a recognised title. James Paterson was a missionary in India and he sent the statue; the gutta percha tree does not exist in India.

*The Golfer* of 22 November 1995 specifically states that 'Dr Paterson's brother was the inventor of the gutta ball'. No evidence has been found to show that Paterson was educated at either Edinburgh or St Andrews Universities. Evidence of his career is very scanty. The date of his death is not known.

The Reverend MacPherson was a St Andrews man of some golfing skill. He appears to have accepted all the tales about Paterson without attempting to substantiate any of them, including the statement that Paterson was a St Andrews man, which he was not.

MacPherson produced a highly romantic account of Allan Robertson which was, in some respects, not factual. MacPherson was, in fact, a man who believed passionately that St Andrews was the only golfing centre in the world and that St Andrews was pre-eminent in everything connected with golf; he allowed his wish for a St Andrews man to have made the invention to cloud his judgement.

The statement that Paterson made the ball and then painted it white and played with it cannot be true; the great feature of gutta percha was that it would not take paint, which is why all the early gutta balls had no paint on them. It was later found that it was necessary to leave the gutta ball to 'mature' for a month or more before it would take paint.

*Blackheath*

James Balfour, in 1887, refers to his experience of the gutta ball as follows: 'About the beginning of the year 1848 balls were made of gutta percha. I remember the commencement perfectly. My brother-in-law, Admiral Maitland Dougal, played a doubles match at Blackheath with the late Sir Ralph Anstruther and William Blair of Blair Adam and another friend, with gutta percha golf balls, on a wet day. They afterwards dined together at Sir Charles Adams at Greenwich Hospital and Sir Ralph said, after dinner, "a most curious thing, here is a ball of gutta percha, Maitland and I have played with it in the rain and it flies better at the end of the day than it did at the beginning". Maitland came to Edinburgh immediately after and told me of this. We at once wrote to London for some of these balls. . . .'

These men played with gutta balls – they did not make them themselves – so somebody in the London area made them. Blackheath Golf Club whose members had interests in the Far East would have been aware of Montgomerie's discovery sooner than the general public. At Woolwich, not far from Blackheath, was the rubber works of S.W. Silver, a tropical outfitter. They were a fast-developing company who, in 1858, set up large premises on the bank of the Thames which they called 'Silvertown'. Later, they started producing gutty golf balls. It is unlikely that they commercially produced the first gutta ball – if they had, they would have been the first to make this claim, if only for advertising purposes – but it is possible that one or more of the merchants with access to gutta percha made a few balls as an experiment. There is no firm evidence of this. As Sir Ralph and Maitland Dougal were both from St Andrews (and members of the

R&A) it must be significant that they immediately wrote to London for balls; had such balls been available in St Andrews, they would certainly have got them from there.

## Musselburgh and Mr William Smith (1814–1903)

Mr William Smith was a clockmaker of an inventive turn of mind; in an interview with *Golf Illustrated* in 1901 he said that he had made golf balls from sheet gutta percha at Musselburgh in 1846, using wooden moulds, and that he and his friends had used them on the links. He afterwards left for Glasgow and he passed on the moulds to a Mr Goodsir, a grocer and spirit dealer of Newbiggin, who made and sold balls until his death in 1853. Research has shown that Mr Goodsir of Newbiggin did exist (1798–1853).

So far, we have then, Mr Paterson with very dubious claims, an anonymous person, or persons, at Blackheath, and a definite name, Mr William Smith, then of Musselburgh. But another man now enters the list of claimants, for Mr Hall Blyth, a well-known golfer in East Lothian who played golf between 1840 and 1890, reports, in giving his reminiscences to the indefatigable Mr Kerr, author of *The Golf Book of East Lothian*, that he remembers that the invention of the gutta ball was made by a 'poor man, who lived in the third storey of a house some way down a close in the Lawnmarket, either the first or second close west of the George IV Bridge and on the South side of the street'.

We shall never know who made the first gutta golf ball. Whoever invented it, by 1848 the gutta ball had arrived and changed the whole face of golf.

## The Effects of the Arrival of the Gutta Percha Golf Ball

For the purposes of this account, balls made of pure gutta percha will be called 'guttas' and those made (later) from gutta with added chemicals to make them harder and better will be referred to as 'gutties'.

The gutta ball was unaffected by wet, was cheaper to make and was more durable than the feather ball; as a result golf became much cheaper and people who previously had not been able to afford to play could now do so. Many more golfers appeared on the scene.

The gutta ball did not burst and lose feathers if it was topped with an iron club, and a player did not need to carry three or four balls, as was necessary in the feather ball era. A gutta ball was a perfect sphere and not egg-shaped, like the feather ball.

When gutta percha came into use as a material for making golf balls there was a rapid demise of the feather ball. This caused the utmost dismay to the feather ball-makers who were faced with a total loss of livelihood. The reaction of Allan Robertson and William Gourlay to the change represented two different attitudes to this calamity. Allan was very angry and proceeded to buy up

Gutta mould in
hand-operated
press

all the guttas he could find and burned them. He was told by his friends that the feather ball was finished but he refused to believe it.

According to H. Thomas Peters, a contemporary of Allan's, he, Peters, persuaded Allan to hit one of the new balls. It seems that Allan did so, deliberately topping the ball and then announcing that it would never fly properly. Allan made Tom Morris promise never to use the gutta ball but, on one occasion, Tom was out on the links when he ran out of balls, and he was lent a gutta ball and played a few holes with it. Allan got to hear of this and was furious and he and Tom Morris parted company.

Gourlay, at Musselburgh, having seen a player use one, was immediately aware that this new ball was here to stay. He promptly fulfilled an order from Sir David Baird of North Berwick, sending him six dozen feather balls! As a result of this astute piece of salesmanship, Sir David Baird was probably still playing with featheries long after his contemporaries were using the gutta ball.

Allan Robertson's attitude, similar to that of King Canute and the tide, soon softened and he took to making gutta balls and within a few years used a gutta to hole St Andrews in 79, the first time that the links had been holed in less than 80.

The feather ball could be hit further than a gutta, provided it was brand new and well made. The longest recorded drive with a feathery was 361 yards by Monsieur Samuel Messieux, a French master at Madras College at St Andrews in 1836, and there are records from the Glasgow Club of one, John Gibson, in 1786, making a series of drives of which the longest was 227 yards.

Using a gutta ball, F.G. Tait hit a record drive of 341 yards on the same hole at St Andrews at which Messieux had performed his feat – and under the same (frosty) conditions, but this was 57 years after Messieux had hit his drive and Tait was using a gutty ball much improved and modified since it had first appeared in 1848; it is almost certain, also, that the shaft of Tait's driver was a better one than that used by Messieux and that ground conditions had greatly improved on the links since 1836. Whoever invented it, by 1848 the gutta golf ball had arrived. It brought a new, cheaper, more durable, golf ball. It also brought a boom in golf.

## The Making of Gutta Golf Balls

THE very first guttas were made by rolling sheet gutta percha, softened by immersion in boiling water, in the hands, to make a rough sphere. It must have been a painful process because the gutta percha had to be almost at boiling temperature to be easily malleable; one elderly professional, whom the author knew when he, the author, was a child, could readily remember the painful process of taking the gutta percha out of the boiling water! The resulting ball was smooth and brown – because it would not take paint. Being smooth, it would not fly until it had been cut a few times.

In a very short time balls were made using a smooth metal mould, the two halves being compressed together, either by hand or by being put in a vice. This still left a smooth ball; instead of deliberately cutting it with a golf club, indentations were made on it by using the sharpened end of a tack hammer. At first, a few balls were made by making random indentations but, in a short time, hammerers began to use a pattern and the marking of the balls assumed a regular pattern. Because so few balls remained smooth and because the random marking quickly gave way to a regular pattern, smooth guttas and random-marked guttas are highly collectable and rare. Some makers marked the balls that they made by incising them with a knife; such balls are very rare and are not always recognised by collectors.

**Random hammered gutta ball made by Allan Robertson, c.1848**

The ball hammerers became very adept and could pattern a complete ball in about 1½ minutes. Although the gutta ball was very durable compared with the feather ball, the early ones occasionally split and there was a rule of golf, at that time, which, when this happened, allowed the player, without penalty, to put a new ball down at the spot where the largest piece of the broken ball was found. Horace Hutchinson, who played in those times, remarked wryly that the largest piece was invariably found on the fairway!

Hall Blyth, in his reminiscences to the Revd Kerr in *The Golf Book of East Lothian*, states that balls made of sheet gutta tended to split; when they were made from 'rope', a form of solid gutta percha, they did not split.

The greatest problem of gutta percha was that it would not take paint – at least, when new. Many different 'patent' paints were produced to overcome this but none was a total success.

The answer seemed to be to keep the gutta ball exposed to air for four to six months, a process known as 'seasoning' or 'maturing'; at the end of that time, paint could be applied with a reasonable chance that it would remain on the ball and the ball itself seemed to be improved. Advertisements of the time offered 'well-seasoned' gutta balls for sale. Because this seasoning was important, some golfers considered that 're-made' balls (that is, the reshaping of a ball which had been used and cut, by putting it in hot water and remaking it in a mould) were better than the originals.

**Hand-hammered gutta ball, Forgan pattern, c. 1860**

When the soft gutta was compressed in a mould some excess gutta percha exuded at the joins; the resulting ball thus had a ring of gutta around its equator so that, as Farrar described it in his excellent *History of the Royal Liverpool Golf Club*, the ball looked like Saturn with its rings. The balls were then left on a rack for the necessary seasoning time; during this time various chemical changes took place in the gutta percha which made it easier to paint and improved its quality as a golf ball.

The projecting 'fin' of gutta percha around the equator of the ball was pared down flat with a knife but there were special tools on the market which could make the job easier. Some years later, when golf ball manufacturers were producing large numbers of balls to keep the growing number of golfers supplied, moulds were produced which had a patterned lining; such moulds were not suitable for home use and were operated by an hydraulic press.

The pattern produced by this process was much deeper and sharper than any pattern which a 'home' press could produce, a feature which helps the collector to distinguish between the two.

By this time, golf ball manufacturers were experimenting in producing a harder and better gutta ball; balls made this way were quite unsuitable for 'home' presses and all the individual methods, used by golfers, and professionals in the shop, came to an end.

Hand hammering gutta golf balls, *c.* 1865. The man on the right is painting a ball by rolling it in the palms of his paint-covered hands

The darker ball in the illustration is a pure gutta ball with the pattern incised not hammered

We have now entered the time of the 'gutty' ball, a phase during which very hard gutty balls were produced; they were very durable and went further than the older gutta ball but their hardness had some unfortunate side effects, the most important of which was that the faces of wooden clubs began to break up.

They were repaired with inserts in the face of the club but eventually the damage was so frequent that some club manufacturers put an insert in the club face when it was made.

Another, indirect, problem caused by the gutta, but much more so by the gutty, was the ever-growing number of divots; this was because, as the gutty was not ruined by topping with an iron club, there was a great increase in the number and variety of iron clubs. More will be said of this later.

One of the earliest patents for a 'composite golf ball', i.e. a gutty, was taken out by Captain Duncan Stewart RN of St Andrews. Stewart was a keen golfer and

of an inventive turn of mind. He made a composite ball out of cork, gutta percha and metal filings. This ball was much more durable than the old gutta; it went off the club with a good, sharp, 'click' (which was the hallmark of the gutta ball) but it was a trifle heavy. Nevertheless, it was popular and Captain Stewart sold some and gave many away to his golfing friends, and took out a patent.

His inventive mind took him even further and he made, played with, and gave to his friends, a ball of his design which was made by winding rubber thread around a central core, this fully 30 years before the Haskell ball appeared. More will be said of this later but it is interesting that he did not proceed with the new type of ball because it had no 'click' off the club, which his friends thought was a drawback, although Stewart always maintained that this new ball was the better one.

A variety of composite gutty balls were patented between 1870 and 1890, all with varying success but, in 1877, William Currie patented a gutty ball made of vul-

**Gutties from the Robertson Collection, Royal Sydney Golf Club**

canised rubber, ground cork and leather. This was the 'Eclipse' golf ball. It sold fairly well – even though it did not have a 'click' like the other gutties – but, when Horace Hutchinson won two of the first three Amateur Championships using one, it became really popular. It was quite different from the other gutties because it was softer (which was why it did not 'click') and could be compressed between a finger and thumb. Because it was so soft and resilient it was virtually indestructible and even a topped iron shot did not mark it; it was lighter than the other gutties but suffered from the defect that it could not be made to carry far and was difficult to stop when pitching to the green. It more than made up for these defects by being easy to putt with and because, when cut or hooked, it did not veer as much to the right or left as other gutties. A further bonus was that it did not damage club faces like the hard gutties. It was still regarded as a bit of a joke and was given the nickname of the 'putty', but came to be regarded with greater respect when Hutchinson showed what could be done with it. The pros did not like it – and said so. The manufacturers then began to make alterations, which gave it a slight 'click' but which destroyed many of its good qualities so that, eventually, even Hutchinson gave it up and the ball vanished into obscurity.

By the end of the nineteenth century, the hard, composite gutty was the favoured golf ball; it was not until 1900 that a new type of golf ball appeared in Britain.

**Above:** Hand-operated machine for making gutta golf balls. The heavily weighted top half was drawn up to the top and then released by pulling the lever with a knob on it. It fell with considerable force on to the bottom half

**Right:** Machine for marking gutta golf balls, hand-operated

# The Golfing Scene in the 18th Century

**8**

THE links land on the east coast of Scotland lay between the sandy beach and the heavier farmland soil inland. It was thus very close to the fishing villages; even today this closeness is evident at Leven in Fife, at Musselburgh, North Berwick, Kilspindie, Gullane and Dunbar in Lothian, and in many other coastal areas too numerous to mention. At St Andrews the first tee and the eighteenth green are, virtually, in the town.

Because of this, the problem of getting to golf was very simple for the villagers and townspeople. For the landed gentry, living on their estates inland, the journey to golf was a short ride on horseback.

Bruntsfield, not a links course, was close to Edinburgh (which was the main reason that it was popular) and getting to it was quite easy.

Leith, near the sea and with some 'linkslike' qualities, was the port of Edinburgh but somewhat further from Edinburgh than was Bruntsfield. Nevertheless, it was not too difficult to get to Leith from Edinburgh as there was a regular coach service between the two; the fare was 12 Scots shillings single and 18 shillings return. This was no great burden for the wealthy but meant that the poorer people of Edinburgh did not play at Leith, which was a local golf links for Leith citizens only.

In 1672, when Foulis, one of the landed gentry who lived at Ravelston, near Edinburgh, played golf at Leith, it is believed that he travelled from Ravelston to Edinburgh on horseback and thence to Leith by coach; on his return journey, he returned to Edinburgh by coach and then stayed the night in Edinburgh, where he had a house. This enabled him to dine in Edinburgh with his golfing friends after the game.

Musselburgh, the nearest true links course to Edinburgh, was much further away and the roads were poor; there was no coach and the journey therefore had to be made on horseback, a trip that was not without risk, owing to the prevalence of thieves and highwaymen. The journey was sometimes made by boat from Leith.

To get to St Andrews from Edinburgh it was necessary to take ship at Leith and sail to one of the fishing ports such as Anstruther or Crail on the south coast of Fife, and then take a coach. There was no question of a day out at golf at St Andrews, starting from Edinburgh and returning on the same day.

The scene at Leith was one of social equality on the golf course but separation of the classes took place after golf, as the gentlemen took themselves off to their favourite tavern where they drank and dined among their own kind while the local Leith citizens returned to their humble cottages. This was later in the eighteenth century, when, golf being so popular among the gentry, taverns in Leith improved their standards to accommodate them, thus avoiding the journey back to Edinburgh to dine. By 1768, the gentlemen who golfed at Leith had built their own clubhouse, where they changed their clothes after the game and dined on their own premises.

## The Upkeep of Golf Links in the Eighteenth Century

THE layout of a golf links was dictated by the natural conditions of the terrain. The bunkers were already in place; these were areas where the sheep, for reasons known only to sheep, chose to lie. By repeatedly lying in the same place, they broke through the thin topsoil, exposing the sand underneath; as this hollow made an even better shelter, more sheep used it. The fierce winds of winter blew more sand out of the hollow and this resulted in a deep sand pit, or natural bunker. It was only necessary for a discerning eye to site a hole near to the bunker – or to arrange a teeing area so that the drive had to carry the bunker or be played to one side of it, for a golf links to exist. The number of holes depended on the area of links land available and the length of the holes decided upon.

The links required little or no upkeep; the grass was naturally short, and was kept even shorter by the sheep. There was no such thing as a mower, so a green was merely a rather flatter area; there was no tee, and the next drive was taken a few paces from the hole, the sand for teeing the ball being taken from the bottom of the hole. There were no flags or tee boxes, and the site of the hole was often indicated by a seagull feather stuck in the ground nearby. The bunkers were not raked. All that was needed was, occasionally, to cut a new hole; this was usually done using a pocket knife.

As the links consisted of a thin layer of soil on sand, rain soaked through very quickly so that, even after heavy rain, the links rapidly dried.

When golf became a game for kings and courtiers the popular areas for play were Bruntsfield and Leith. These courses were not links courses, especially Bruntsfield. Consequently, because the wealthy sought a course in good condition and on which they could play regularly, they were willing to pay for some upkeep and drainage. They started by having a levy at Leith of 5 shillings to get the links in good condition for the play for the Silver Club.

At Bruntsfield, which was heathland and could become waterlogged, a boy was employed, known as 'our Cady' or 'our Officer' whose job was to carry messages to members, serve as a waiter at dinner, carry the Captain's clubs and to alter and repair the golf holes. For this, he was given a uniform and 6 Scots shillings a quarter. In 1784 he was given a pair of shoes. At the Burgess Golfing Society no regular, designated greenkeeper was employed until well into the nineteenth century.

The old caddies had acquired a good knowledge of how to play golf and had a sound experience of the links on which they carried clubs; for a small fee or some clothes or food they were always willing to offer advice or do a little work on the course.

The great Allan Robertson, famous ballmaker and golfer, was born in 1815; his grandfather and father, plus a number of uncles and great uncles, all had a close association with St Andrews, being feather ballmakers, caddies and part-time greenkeepers from the early part of the eighteenth century.

At Blackheath a different system was adopted. Blackheath was a heathland and very stony; from the earliest records it appears to have required some upkeep and drainage and there was a further difficulty about cutting holes, because, instead of sand underlying the turf, there were stones. To keep things in good order, Blackheath employed one man to look after each hole. These employees were paid a shilling each for an afternoon's work. One of the men was a holecutter; eventually, they employed a specialist holecutter, 'Old Alick' (1756–1840), who came from Leith and had spent much of his life at sea. He must have been much liked because Blackheath had his portrait painted, probably the earliest portrait ever of a labourer on the golf course. Blackheath was fortunate in that it had, nearby, a source of manpower at the Greenwich Hospital, home of the Greenwich Pensioners.

## Golf Trades

CLUBMAKERS' names occur from the earliest times and, as has been stated, many were bowmakers as well. In the case of feather ballmakers the trade was far more specialised; any bowmaker, carpenter, shipwright or furniture-maker could have learned the clubmaking trade but making feather balls was a different matter. Probably because the craft was so specialised it tended to be taught by father to son and, as a result, several generations of the same family were involved in ballmaking. The Robertson family's involvement is well known but this is because one of them, Allan Robertson (1815–1859), became, in the first half of the nineteenth century, a famous golfer, as well as ballmaker; as a result of this, his family history became known to all. There must have been many ballmakers whose names are not known – and never will be – unlike the clubmaking profession.

The Dicksons of Leith are a typical example of a ballmaking family. William and Thomas Dickson were ballmakers in 1629. John Dickson of Leith was licensed to make golf balls by Aberdeen Town Council in 1642. An Andrew Dickson of Leith (1665–1729) was a ballmaker. They were probably all of the same family but their exact relationship has not been traced. A son and grandson of Andrew Dickson were clubmakers at Leith. It is likely that, in order to make a living, the Dicksons also carried clubs and there is a tale that Andrew Dickson was a fore caddie to the Duke of York in 1682 when the latter lived in Edinburgh. They probably helped out on the links at Leith, but this must be supposition; if only one or more of them had become as famous as Allan Robertson we would have a better record of the family.

## Caddies

THESE men are a constant thread of continuity in the tapestry of golf from its very earliest recorded beginnings. They helped the golfer find his ball, teed it up, advised on the line of putts, gave their master an occasional and impromptu golf lesson if, in their opinion, it was needed, bullied or cajoled him into taking the right club, and regularly backed him with such small amounts of money as they could spare. They regularly drank their winnings and, when times were hard, starved, or found another job (but always a temporary job because they intended to return to caddying as soon as they could).

## Golfing Traditions

IN the eighteenth century the day of professional golfers earning a living by playing golf had not arrived; likewise, an organised clubhouse with permanent club servants was yet to come.

Notices regarding a future golfing event would suggest that play should begin at about 12 noon but were quite peremptory that 'Dinner is at three sharp'. As dinner went on until about nine o'clock there was plenty of time to consume vast quantities of food and drink before returning home.

Withal, although there was great merriment and huge consumption of alcohol, there was also some Masonic discipline; members had to be properly dressed in the club uniform, and anyone failing to do this was customarily fined a gallon of claret ('to be drunk on the premises'). Similar fines could be levied for non-attendance and for speaking out of turn at dinner.

The dinners took place at local taverns approved by the gentlemen and where they had a room reserved for the purpose. There was much speechmaking, recitations of poems, singing of songs, while consuming vast quantities of food and drink. At the Aberdeen Golf Club they took simple pride in the fact that it was usual for each member to consume more than three bottles of wine per man. Smollett, writing of the golfers at Leith, in his novel *Humphry Clinker*, states that 'they never went to bed without each having the best part of a gallon of claret in his belly'.

At Leith, in 1776, Lieutenant James Dalrymple of the 43rd Regiment, having appeared at dinner five times not wearing his (Club) uniform, was fined six pints of claret and, at his own request, was fined three pints more.

Food and drink were cheap, gargantuan dinners of the type described cost about six shillings. During the course of such dinners, bets were laid on the outcome of golf matches, and on other matters as well. Despite the alcoholic haze, the bets were carefully noted and the Recorder had to have his wits about him. A gentleman always paid his debts; even those rash bets made in his cups had to be settled, so a true record was essential.

In 1778 there was a match for '100 marks and dinner for the Company'. 'Mr R. Allan bets a guinea that he will drive a ball from the Castle Hill without the gate of the pallisade into the Half Moon Battery over the parapet wall.' It is not recorded how many took this wager but, fortunately for him, Mr Allan won.

In straight matches, handicaps were not used because handicaps, as we know them today, did not exist. On occasions, some sort of physical handicap was used to put the better player at a disadvantage; as an example, 'Mr Armstrong played Mr Dunbar, Mr Armstrong to play with one hand'. Another match is recorded in which one prototagonist played standing on one leg; in another match the better golfer played using only one iron and a putter. On an even more bizarre level the better player struck the ball with a bottle; as he won, his opponent must have been a poor golfer! 'Mr Rose played Mr Mitchell, giving him a stroke a hole, for a gallon of malt whisky'; it would have been customary for this to have been consumed on the premises after the game.

All these matches were private affairs; only a few matches came to public notice. In 1724, Alexander Elphinstone played Captain Porteous of the Edinburgh City Guard, for twenty guineas a side. The match attracted many side bets and many spectators.

To cheat was to be ostracised by society for ever. To attempt to take an unfair advantage of an opponent was unforgivable and to fail to pay one's debts promptly meant loss of membership of the club.

This was all very well for the wealthy and the noble but it did nothing for the less wealthy citizens for whom golf had virtually ceased to exist, as clubs and balls were too expensive; those villagers who lived near a links played, but had to make do with second-hand featheries – or, even, wooden balls – and cast-off clubs that the wealthy no longer bothered to use.

On the one hand, golf could have disappeared altogether if it had not been for the support of wealthy Freemasons and the Royal Court but, on the other hand, if they had not taken it over, the game might have survived as a simple, cheap pastime which the poorer classes could have enjoyed in what little spare time that they had. The rich have always supported the arts and the finer crafts; if golf had remained a poor man's game the development of golf to its present state would not have been affected but the poor man's game would never have given the great clubmakers, cleekmakers and ballmakers the opportunities to specialise and thus develop their expertise. We would not now be admiring the elegant long-nosed clubs made by such as McEwan, Philp and Jackson, nor the heavy but beautifully balanced iron clubs by Wilson, Gray and Carrick, nor the neat stitching and exquisite form of the feather balls of Gourlay, Robertson and Alexander.

The picture was to change dramatically by the middle of the next century.

## Development of Organised Golf

THE nineteenth century in England was a time of triumph and momentous development. Even before Wellington had crushed Napoleon at Waterloo, the British Empire was expanding.

The British navy controlled the seas and this had largely contributed to the defeat of France. After Waterloo, Britain was the dominant power, not only in Europe, but in the world, and controlled, through its Empire, more than a fifth of it.

British invention, initiative and commercial instinct had set her on the path of industrialisation; in the grime of the Black Country, so-called because of the smoke from factory chimneys, all types of good were manufactured which were sold both in Britain and abroad.

The British aristocracy, already the possessors of large areas of land and much inherited wealth, became even richer and more powerful as they supported commercial developments at home and overseas trade abroad.

The aristocracy did much to help the lower classes, as they were called, but the huge profits that could be made using cheap labour meant that the British machinist in the factory and the British miner in the coal pits worked long, hard hours for little money and, to escape from poverty, made their children work long, hard hours as well. The mortality from tuberculosis was high and malnutrition among children was common.

Gradually, during the century, the middle class grew in importance and wealth, and their merchant venturer ideas brought imports from the Empire and exports in the other direction.

In the 1840s came the railways; travel became quicker, more reliable and cheaper. At first there were only main lines but, in time, many small branch lines came into

being and it became possible to get to a golf links by rail. Golf was particularly favoured in this respect because the railways had to get permission – and buy land – from the big landowners in order to get to the places that they wished to serve. The landowners were willing to accommodate them but usually expected favours, as well as money, in return for their co-operation; many of them played golf and, as part of the deal, they demanded, and got, small 'halts' near Golf Clubs where the train could be stopped on demand. Prestwick is an example of this. The Earl of Eglinton owned large areas of land between Prestwick and Glasgow and there is little doubt that, as the first Captain of Prestwick, he ensured that there was a station near the Golf Club. There were many Golf Club halts all over Britain until the Second World War left some of them in disuse, and Dr Beeching, who 'rationalised' the railways in a desperate (and unavailing) effort to make them profitable, some years later, put paid to the remainder.

In 1867 the passing of an Act of Parliament which gave every man and woman who paid rates, a vote, began to give power to the numerically superior workers, and the steady development of the Trade Union movement brought about a cohesion which enabled them to make changes in working hours and conditions and pay.

It is against this background of national development, with better transport, improved pay and more leisure, that one must consider the development of Golf Clubs but one has to consider, too, those technical developments which affected golf – the arrival of better wood for shafts, the discovery that, in 1848, gutta percha was a material from which golf balls could be made, golf balls which were cheaper and impervious to wet.

The invention, in the 1850s, of a machine that would mow grass was of the greatest importance; it allowed golf to be played on grassland which previously grew such lush and long grass that play from May to September was impossible (because balls would have been lost) and was equally impossible in the winter (because the land was so wet and muddy). With use of a mower and proper drainage of the ground, inland golf was now a possibility.

There were no dramatic developments until the middle of the nineteenth century.

Up to that time there was no great increase in the number of Golf Clubs in Britain – between 1800 and 1850 the number increased from 7 to 17 – but those pioneer Clubs did start to improve their Clubhouse facilities and their links. Regular subscriptions were levied and the money was put to good purpose. The arrival of a horse-drawn mower meant more efficient cutting of the grass and the occasional use of a horse-drawn roller, such as was used on cricket pitches, made the greens a little smoother; there was some attention to rather wet areas that required drainage but, generally speaking, golf links continued to be natural areas.

At some time the notion of a hole of 4¼ inches in diameter came into being; on links where such a luxury as a holecutter did not exist, the hole was cut with a pocket knife, using a small pot of the right diameter as a guide. Surprisingly, in those days of robust individualism, no one seems to have queried this, or, at least, there is no documentary evidence that the size of the hole was ever questioned.

The subscription money was also used to build better Clubhouses and to furbish them for greater comfort; Club servants, paid a regular wage, began to appear in the 1840s. Food and drink were rising in price and, although dinners saw the consumption of very large quantities of food and, particularly, drink, these orgies were less frequent than in the past.

The type of Club member showed little change. Although the members were mainly landed gentry and noblemen, some of the professions were accepted and it is reasonable to believe that they were all Freemasons. Clerics, regular service officers, doctors and lawyers were all allowed to join but anyone 'in trade' was beyond the pale and had no hope of becoming a member.

At Blackheath, close to the City of London, the commercial heart of a great Empire, there was a slightly different state of affairs. Many members were merchants from the City and they had many clerks and under-managers who were well paid and many of whom were Freemasons; those who could afford it and were attracted to golf, belonged to the Club. Many were exiled Scots; as a result, even as late as 1880 Blackheath was incorrectly referred to in magazines and newspaper articles as the 'London Scots Society', so strong was the impression of Londoners that they were all Scotsmen. When such men were posted overseas to India or the West Indies they took their passion for golf with them.

At the Burgess Golfing Society in Edinburgh there was a state of affairs similar to Blackheath; although one did not have to be a Burgess of the City of Edinburgh to be a member, many members of the Burgess were wealthy merchants of the City. This contrasted with the Honourable Company of Edinburgh Golfers who were all of a class of society not be prepared to recognise 'trade'.

## Clubhouses and Club Entertainment

THE Burgess Golfing Society of Edinburgh, for many years from the apparent date of their inception, ate and drank at various taverns in Edinburgh after golf, in the same way as did the Honourable Company, but not at the same taverns. At St Andrews, the Society also had their dinners at taverns in the town.

In 1773, the Burgess began to use a single site and had regular meetings at Thomas Comb's premises at Wright's Houses near Bruntsfield links. Thomas Comb was a clubmaker, so he was the right man, as his premises were the best place to leave your clubs (and, perhaps, get them cleaned and repaired) until the next time you were due to play.

In 1785, Alexander Fraser was the proprietor of the house which was then known as Golf House or Foxtoun; it was becoming very close to being a Clubhouse but, as the membership expanded, it became too small and, for some years members once more met in various taverns in Edinburgh. In 1826 Golf House still existed and meetings were held there.

By 1838 the Bruntsfield links were becoming grossly overcrowded and most of the competitions were played on the Musselburgh links. In 1878, the Burgess moved to Musselburgh and set up a Clubhouse in conjunction with the Musselburgh New Golf Club.

### Course upkeep at the Burgess

In 1809 David Denholm was appointed general factotum at a wage of 3 guineas per annum and was supplied with a uniform. By 1866, the Burgess were paying a person 'to make the holes, look after the flags, and mind the turf'.

### The Clubhouse of the Honourable Company of Edinburgh Golfers

As has been said, the Honourable Company erected a purpose-built Clubhouse in 1768 at Leith, close to the links. They used these premises for changing their clothes and keeping their golf boxes and for their regular dinners.

In 1836 the Leith links became, like Bruntsfield, grossly overcrowded and the Honourable Company moved to Musselburgh. At first, they were accommodated in part of the Grandstand of the Musselburgh Racecourse, in the centre of which was the Musselburgh links. There was, at this time, no annual subscription, and the cost of dining was shared equally among those dining – and some of those who failed to appear for no good reason! Nevertheless, they began to get things organised and, in 1840, they appointed Thomas Alexander, a well-known feather ballmaker and a golfer of repute, to be the 'Club Officer' at a wage of 4 guineas per annum.

In 1850, John Gourlay, an even more famous feather ballmaker, was paid £10 per annum for 'making the new course', though exactly what this meant is not known.

In 1865, the Honourable Company decided to build a Clubhouse at the west end of the links, and at the same time levied an annual subscription and an entrance fee of

6 guineas per annum. By this time there were no less than four Golf Clubs using the nine-hole links course at Musselburgh; it must have been very crowded and subject to much wear. Although it is not specifically recorded, there must have been some arrangement between the various Clubs to provide funds to maintain the links.

## Blackheath Golf Club

By 1807–9 the Club employed a clubmaker, who was also, a holecutter. In 1851 they employed Willie and Jamie Dunn from North Berwick as Keepers of the Green.

In 1843, Blackheath acquired a house adjacent to the course for a Clubhouse and installed a Club servant 'to make and mend clubs and look after the golfers' boxes'. At this stage, as we have seen in the Clubs in Scotland, the members did not dine in the Clubhouse, but by 1855 they were employing a stewardess and a Club gardener. This standard of staffing the Clubhouse was somewhat in advance of the arrangements at other Clubs, but

then Blackheath was a Club composed of wealthy members. There was a need for attention to the course which was more pressing than that which was required on the Scottish courses because Blackheath was not a links course. Bruntsfield was also not a links course and suffered from the same problems; in the case of Bruntsfield the problem was solved by moving to a true links course at Musselburgh but there was nowhere to move to from Blackheath. From the earliest times Blackheath employed a holecutter, because cutting holes on a stony heath was much more difficult than cutting them on a links, which required no great skill.

Because of the problems of the stony terrain and of drainage of wet areas, Blackheath, with typical Masonic organisation, developed a unique system of course maintenance. They used pensioners from the nearby Greenwich Hospital; these men were paid a shilling on Medal Days to look after a hole – one man to each hole – which meant the employment of seven men at Blackheath, which had seven holes. Their job was to look after the entire hole and take the flag. It was the habit to remove

Weeding a green in 1893. The light wood-and-canvas shelter was easily moved
as the weeders progressed across the green

the flags when there was no play because, Blackheath being a public common, they had a habit of disappearing! The men from the Greenwich Hospital were in addition to other men, also from the Hospital, who acted as caddies and fore caddies. The Club, in fact, were responsible for some 'nice little earners' for the pensioners.

Much of the dining and wining at Blackheath took place at The Green Man tavern and the reasons for this have been explained.

*St Andrews*

The Society of Golfers at St Andrews wined and dined at various taverns in the town of which the most used appears to have been the 'Cross Keys'; this tavern was particularly suited to them because it housed a ballroom and the Society was much given to holding balls.

In 1835, under the auspices of Sir Hugh Lyon Playfair, a great benefactor both of the town and of the Golf Club, a Golf House was proposed. Its site was where the present Hamilton Hall now stands and it was designed to accommodate both archers and golfers and was called the Union Club. The main parlour was designed with wood panelling up to a height of 6 feet, specifically so that club boxes could be arranged vertically around the room. By 1877, the Club had become the Royal and Ancient Golf Club of St Andrews.

*Course Upkeep at St Andrews*

For 25 years, up to 1805, Charles Robertson, ballmaker and caddie, had 'walked the links' on the day before the Medal and cut the holes. He, and such predecessors as we know of, were called 'Keepers of the Green'. Robertson was paid £1 a year for his services. When Charles Robertson retired, Thomas Robertson took over but was unsatisfactory and was dismissed after a short while, being succeeded by Robert Morris – a local man who played golf. He was given a salary of £2 a year. Predecessors to Charles Robertson may have been George Mill and Peter Robertson both of whom were paid 5 shillings a year.

In 1855 David Anderson resigned as Keeper of the Green. He was the well-known caddie and feather ball-

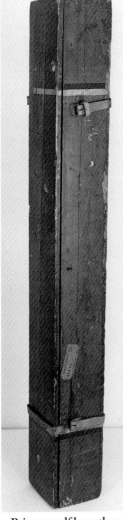

Prior to golf bags there were golf boxes, such as this, for carrying clubs from place to place. This one dates from *c.*1880

maker 'Old Da'. David had five sons who all went into the clubmaking business, starting with David Anderson (1847–1915). When David Anderson retired his place was taken by Alexander Herd and Walter MacDonald. In 1856, Allan Robertson was called upon to superintend some work on the greens but this is the only time that his name appears in the Minutes of the R&A and he never seems to have been a Keeper of the Green.

In 1865 Tom Morris, on the death of Allan Robertson, returned to St Andrews from Prestwick and was appointed Keeper of the Green at St Andrews; he was paid £50 a year on condition that he took 'entire charge of the golf course' and would be responsible for the proper upkeep of the links. He was allowed one man's labour on two days a week, to do the heavy work and, when he started his job, was given the tools of his trade – a wheelbarrow, a shovel and a spade.

## Golf Club staffing

From the foregoing account it is clear that from early in the nineteenth century the older Golf Clubs in Scotland and the only Golf Club outside Scotland – Blackheath – had begun to develop an organisation to maintain their courses and to provide some service in the Clubhouse.

*The Outdoor Staff*

This consisted of: The Keeper of the Green; caddies and professionals; labourers and apprentices.

*Keeper of the Green*

The term 'Green' meant the whole golf links, so the Keeper was in charge of all the course, and was not, as in today's terminology, a Greenkeeper. He was responsible to the Secretary of the Club for the proper maintenance of the links and was in charge of the caddies and professionals. He was, on the links, king of all he surveyed.

In particular, he looked after the links and superintended all the work that had to be done by the labourers; he cut the holes before competitions – or superintended and directed the work; he made and repaired clubs; taught the apprentices in his shop; gave lessons and

**Above: 'In February, horse boots are essential.' The horse does not seem too keen on the idea**

**Left: The upper part of a horse 'over shoe', 1900**

played with members, if they requested it. Some made feather balls and, later, many made gutta golf balls. Because he was an important man he was paid a regular salary and could supplement this by making and repairing golf clubs, giving lessons and playing with the members. Because of the multiplicity of his duties, he might, by personal inclination, become more expert in one aspect than another. When Tom Alexander and John Gourlay were, at different times, Keepers to the Honourable Company at Musselburgh, they continued their trade of ballmaker and it is likely that the apprentices in the shop at that time would have been ballmakers too, much of the club repairing and making being passed to local clubmakers. If the Keeper was an expert and keen golfer, he would probably want to get on the course and play; if he was a good clubmaker and no great golfer, he would spend as much time as he could in the shop, allowing the professionals to play and give lessons.

As a result of this state of affairs there developed, in general terms, two kinds of Keeper of the Green:
a) The Keeper who wanted, primarily, to be a good and true club servant and to look after his Club members.
b) The Keeper who was an expert golfer and who, while looking after his members well, seized every opportunity to play golf and to compete with his fellow experts.
All Keepers of the Green had, at one time, been caddies or apprentices. Two examples of Keepers of the Green as Club servants are given but it must be clear that these are only examples drawn from a large band of men who devoted their lives to looking after their members and who were, in turn, beloved and respected by the Club. The examples given are of men who were Keepers at well-known Clubs and thus are well known themselves; in the latter half of the nineteenth century, when there were many Clubs, men of equal worth and loyalty were rarely heard of outside their own locality.

# Keepers of the Green as Club servants

## *Jack Morris (1847–1929)*

In 1869 George Morris of St Andrews, brother of the famous Tom Morris, was invited to go to Hoylake in Cheshire and lay out a nine-hole course. He brought his young son Jack with him. George advised Jack to stay and become professional to the new Club and Jack took his father's advice but made the proviso that, if he did not like it there, he could come back to St Andrews.

The start was not promising as Jack's shop was in a loose box at the back of the Royal Hotel. The owner of the hotel was John Ball Senior (though he was not then Senior) who rented a room in the hotel to the Club, who used it as a Clubhouse. At an early stage Jack wrote to his father and said that he thought he would return home, but his father advised him to stay a little longer before making a final decision. In fact, Jack stayed 60 years and became a life member of the Royal Liverpool Golf Club on his retirement.

Jack was a good, steady player but never great. He played in the Open Championship of 1873 and was 16th out of a field of 21, being 21 shots behind the winner over three rounds. In 1878 he played in the Open at Prestwick and was 16th out of 22 players, 22 shots behind the winner. These were his only two appearances.

By all accounts, he was a competent but not great clubmaker. He was a good organiser and supervisor of the green (meaning the whole course) and was much in demand to play with the members.

In 1871 'Young Tommy', son of Tom Morris and by now a legendary figure in professional golf, who had won the Open Championship three times, thereby making the Belt his own property, came down to Hoylake to play in a small tournament designed to promote the new course. He won the tournament with a score of 87; Uncle Jack was second with a score of 93. Jack may not have been a great golfer but he was difficult to beat on his own links.

Few have written about Jack Morris as a teacher but he must have been good; he was there from the beginning and must have taught, at one time or another, all those youngsters who won the under-fifteen boys medal, Harold Hilton, Jack Graham, John Ball Junior, to name but three. He must also have had a hand in teaching John Ball Junior's father, proprietor of the Royal Hotel, who, taking up golf in his forties, brought his handicap down from 18 to scratch in one year.

Jack was frequently involved in challenge matches between John Ball Senior and Captain Molesworth of Westward Ho! Molesworth, who always came to the

**Jack Morris, son of George Morris and nephew of Tom Morris Senior. He was a professional at Hoylake from 1869 to 1929**

Hoylake meetings, used to bring the Keeper of the Green from Royal North Devon Golf Club (Westward Ho!), Johnny Allan, and, regularly, these two would challenge John Ball and Jack Morris to a match – and usually more than one.

Above all, Jack Morris enjoyed looking after his members. He acted as Starter to every big Medal Tournament and all the great championships played at Hoylake for over half a century.

When acting as Starter he was always immaculately dressed, with beautifully pressed trousers, shoes, as Leslie Edwards remarks in *Golf at Hoylake*, with 'a polish worthy of a Guardsman', and a smart cap. His command to the player was, simply 'Play away, Sir!' when each player's turn came.

He had all the courtesy and gentle manners of his renowned Uncle, Tom. Bernard Darwin wrote of him that he was one of the most entirely charming gentlemen that ever lived.

In his retirement, he was made an Honorary Life member of the Club to which he had devoted his life and, when he died, he was mourned by all. It is sad, and some-how rather typical, that his name is not mentioned in the 1912 *Golfer's Handbook* under 'Who's Who in Golf'.

### Charles Hunter (1836–1921)

Charles Hunter was a Prestwick man who in his early days had no thoughts of being a golf professional. It was Tom Morris, who came to Prestwick in 1851 as the first Keeper of the Green, who persuaded him to give it a try and took him on as his apprentice in the shop.

When Morris went back to St Andrews as Keeper of the Green in 1865, Charles Hunter was offered the job at Prestwick and accepted it but, within a year, he announced his resignation as he had been offered a better-paid appointment at Blackheath. His place was taken at Prestwick by Andrew Strath but, within a few months, Strath was stricken with the scourge of the time, tuberculosis, and died. The alacrity with which Hunter reapplied for the appointment at Prestwick suggests that, despite the money, he was ill at ease at Blackheath. He returned in 1868 and remained there for the rest of his life.

Trained in the shop by Tom Morris, Hunter was a competent clubmaker. He was a good golfer who, as a whole, did not do himself justice on big occasions, but this was due to the fact that he was not greatly interested in winning championships, rather than any lack of nerve. It is said that, when playing in a tournament at Prestwick, he was told that Lord Ailsa was in his shop, looking to buy golf clubs. He immediately picked up his ball and walked back to the shop; looking after his members' needs was much more important than winning tournaments!

When the Open Championship, then known as the Championship Belt, was first played at Prestwick in 1860, Hunter was a competitor. As he was playing on his home course, in front of a crowd of Prestwick supporters, he might have been expected to do well but he took 195 for 36 holes, 21 shots behind the winner. Although the Championship Belt was played at Prestwick for the next 10 years, Hunter failed to enter on a number of occasions, notably when he was at Blackheath. The best position that he attained was 3rd in 1862, but this was no great feat because the entry was only eight and, of that number, four were amateurs; he was 15 shots behind the winner. As a teacher, he developed a sound, if rather unimaginative method. His advice was, invariably, 'slow back' and 'keep your eye on the ball'. He usually suggested to those he taught that they should count to three – one at the start of the backswing, two at the top of the backswing and three on the downswing. He played in many foursomes matches with the members and became a shrewd assessor of their abilities. As a result he was much in demand to decide on handicaps for matches; on

one occasion, some Prestwick members, playing at Macrihanish, telegraphed Hunter to decide what the handicaps should be in their game.

He took his duties as Caddiemaster seriously and when, at one time, members complained to the Secretary that the caddies were extremely dirty and poorly dressed, he paraded the caddies each morning and personally examined their state of dress and general cleanliness before allowing them on the course. He acted as Starter in Club competitions and was in charge of the Club flag.

He was said to be a shrewd man of polished manners and able to cope with all the eccentricities and foibles of his members; small wonder that the Club had his portrait painted in oils, a portrait which hangs in the dining room. He was an Elder of the Kirk and was made a Freeman of Prestwick in 1904. As with Jack Morris, Charles Hunter was not considered important enough to be entered in the 'Who's Who in Golf' section of the *Golfer's Handbook* of 1912.

## Keepers of the Green as Golfers

### Thomas Morris (1821–1908)

Born in St Andrews, according to the 1841 Census, he was the son of a hand-loom weaver. In early life he was apprenticed to Allan Robertson in the craft of feather ballmaking. Having been born and brought up in St Andrews, he was surrounded by golf and golfers, so it was natural for him to play; he once said that he was unable to remember a time when he did not play golf.

After some years, he and Robertson broke up. Robertson, to whom feather ballmaking was a very large part of his livelihood, had a fanatical hatred of the gutta ball when it appeared in 1848. He made Tom promise never to play with one; unfortunately, on an occasion when Tom was playing in a foursome, he was persuaded to try a gutta ball. Allan got to hear of it and their friendship ended.

After this break up Tom Morris set up in St Andrews as a club- and ballmaker, making gutta balls; this must have been an uncomfortable time for him and, when he was befriended by Mr James Ogilvie Fairlie of Coodham, which was a few miles from Prestwick, where, largely through the efforts of Fairlie, a primitive golf links was in being, he was easily persuaded to take on the job of Keeper of the Green at Prestwick. He set up a links of 12 holes and looked after it with wisdom and zeal. He also started up all the other activities of a Keeper of the Green, including a shop in which he installed apprentices, one of these being Charles Hunter.

Tom was a good clubmaker, although exactly who taught him is not known; Allan Robertson was a specialist

**Charles Hunter with Jack Morris
from Hoylake, c.1905**

ballmaker who did not make clubs. No doubt, St Andrews being a hive of activity in the matter of clubs and balls, he could easily have picked up a good knowledge of the craft of clubmaking but there is no record of his apprenticeship to a recognised clubmaker.

Despite working in the shop, making clubs and gutta balls, teaching and steadily improving a new golf course, Tom always found time to play, because playing was what he really enjoyed, and not only playing but competing against his contemporaries. He undoubtedly played with the members and he became involved in a number of big matches against other skilled professionals. The matches that he played will be discussed later.

He organised Prestwick and its links so well that, when he left 13 years later to return to St Andrews as Keeper of the Green there, when Allan Robertson died, he left Charles Hunter with a well-ordered shop and links, together with a fund of goodwill among the members, for Tom was a very likeable man, always amiable and not given to voicing stern criticism. Invariably courteous,

he was a true gentleman and something of a philosopher. The equally courteous Charles Hunter may well have learnt from him.

Tom returned to his beloved St Andrews in 1864 and was appointed Keeper of the Green there. His qualities remained with him and his knowledge of greenkeeping became greater with the years. He was appointed at a salary of £50 per annum and was allowed a man two days a week to do the heavy labour. On his appointment he was given the instruments of his office – a wheelbarrow, a spade and a shovel! He was always a good friend to all who played golf at St Andrews. He served the St Andrews links well and faithfully all his days and was a fine clubmaker but he continued to be what he had always wanted to be – a highly skilful and competitive golfer.

Tom Morris was not a particularly elegant golfer, being rather stiff in his action, but he played well, using rather whippy clubs and a slow swing. His only weakness was a difficulty with short putts and this became more pronounced as he grew older. Like many pros after him, he tried many different methods of putting, including, at one time, putting the right forefinger down the shaft, a form of putting grip which is still in vogue and has become known as the 'over forties grip'. On one occasion, when using this grip, he putted so badly that his partner advised him that the best way to improve, in his opinion, was to have the finger amputated! Tom abandoned that grip.

He won the Championship Belt four times, in 1861, 1862, 1864 and 1867.

### The Dunn Brothers

The Dunns were born in Musselburgh and were twins, Jamie (1821–71) and Willie (1821–78). Their father was a plasterer. Both the boys were apprenticed to John Gourlay, a famous feather ballmaker; Gourlay, when at Bruntsfield, had lived in Wright's Houses close to the course and next door to the McEwan family, who were clubmakers. The two families intermarried and members of both families learned something of one another's craft. When Bruntsfield became overcrowded in about 1877, both the McEwans and the Gourlays moved to Musselburgh, whence had gone the Bruntsfield golfers. Before 1877, both the Gourlays and the McEwans had started shops at Musselburgh.

It was at Musselburgh that the Dunns were apprenticed to Gourlay as ballmakers but there is no doubt that they also learned all about clubmaking as well, probably from the McEwans.

Although the Dunns were very competent ball- and clubmakers their real forte was playing golf. Willie was a tall man and a powerful and graceful striker of the ball. James was not quite so large and was the poorer golfer. Nevertheless, particularly when playing together in a foursome, they were a most formidable partnership and played – and won – many money matches, of which more will be heard later.

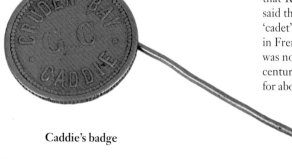

**Caddie's badge**

James remained a bachelor but Willie married and had two boys, both of whom became golf professionals and clubmakers.

In 1851 Willie Dunn was appointed Keeper of the Green at Blackheath. He took up the post and, two years later, brother James joined him. Although the Dunns may have made a good living at Blackheath, where the members were rich, they must have been frustrated at the few possibilities of top-class competitive golf because, at that time, Blackheath was the only Golf Club in England. Moreover, there began to be troubles at Blackheath, in which alcohol played a part; the Dunns (including Mrs Dunn) were accused, from time to time, of being rude to members.

In 1865 the Dunns returned to Scotland and Willie moved to Leith, where he became Keeper of the Green to the Leith Thistle Club. From there he later moved to Musselburgh, where he set up a clubmaking business with his brother; ultimately, they moved to North Berwick where the two sons, Tom and Willie Junior, were trained as clubmakers.

James Dunn entered for the Championship Belt at Prestwick in 1861 but could do no better than 10th. Willie played at Prestwick in 1866, by which time he was living at Leith which was a much shorter journey than from Blackheath, but could do no better than 10th. He played again in 1868 when he came last, and again in 1878 when he was well down the list. The two brothers were best suited to matchplay and, particularly to matchplay (two ball) foursomes, in which form of golf they played many challenge games with some success.

These three men represent Keepers of the Green who, while carrying out their duties, were more interested in playing competitive golf than most of their contemporaries in the same posts.

## The Caddies and Professionals

CADDIES were in existence before Keepers of the Green. Indeed, it was from the ranks of the caddies that Keepers of the Green were recruited. Some have said that the name 'caddie' came from the French word 'cadet' but this is very unlikely, not only because the word in French has a very different meaning but because golf was not played in France until well into the nineteenth century, by which time caddies had been carrying clubs for about 200 years in Scotland.

Although caddies is now the name for those who carry clubs, such carriers have had a variety of names over the years. When Sir John Foulis and Thomas Kincaid employed people to carry their clubs in the seventeenth century, they referred to them as 'boys'; these boys were paid about 3 shillings for a round. Today, this might seem a meagre wage but in those days it was a reasonable sum of money, being about half the cost of a golf club. If one considers the cost of a golf club today, a caddie who was paid half that amount would feel that he had been very well paid.

In the early eighteenth century there were carriers in Edinburgh called 'cadys' or 'cawdies'; by all accounts they were a rough lot, rather dirty and poorly dressed, but they were trusted carriers of parcels in Edinburgh. It seems very likely that they extended their activities to carrying golf clubs for golfers and that this is where the name caddie came from. The reader should note, in passing, that, although there are 'caddies' there is no verb 'to caddie'; caddies 'carry' clubs; it was also a feature of the caddie trade that, up to the end of the nineteenth century, caddies carried 'to' the master who employed them; the term carrying 'for' a master is a twentieth-century innovation.

At times, the name was shortened to 'cads'. At Blackheath, as has been mentioned, they were recruited from the ranks of the Naval pensioners at the Greenwich Hospital.

Although the general impression is that they were boys, they were of all ages and conditions; the common factor was that they were poor.

Golf, in the eighteenth and in the first half of the nineteenth century, was a summer game for reasons that do not need repeating. A caddie could only be certain of a living in the summer; in the winter, he must find another job or starve.

Many of those who carried were boys of school age; they carried in the summer when they did not have to attend school, or even, it has to be said, during school hours, by playing truant. Things became so bad at one time that Golf Clubs were forced to make rules and regulations to ensure, through the Keeper of the Green, that any boys who offered their services were not playing truant from school. The great majority of these boys carried either to provide spending money for themselves or in the poorer families to supplement the family budget.

They varied much in their abilities, depending on whether they developed an interest in the game, or were simply in it to make a little money. Their job was to carry the clubs, usually under the arm, with the heads of the clubs lower than the grips; they were also required to see where the ball went and to make a sand tee for their master's drive. Unless they were exceptionally good, they were seldom asked for advice about shots.

Sir Walter Simpson, a keen but not highly skilled golfer in East Lothian, in 1892 wrote a book based on a

'Fiery' Crawford, so called, not because he was bad tempered, but because he had a skin condition which gave him a very red face. He was Willie Park Junior's regular caddie, and carried for him at the Open at Sandwich in 1894

lifetime of golf called *The Art of Golf*; it contains a chapter devoted to caddies. He points out that a bad caddie is better than none at all. He lists caddies as 'boys, ragamuffins just out of prison and professional carriers'. He recommends that it is best to employ only professional carriers, and goes on to observe: 'A good boy to carry is not a bad thing. From him too much must not be expected. If the tees he makes are not over two inches in diameter, if each time a club is required he is not further than three minutes walk from his master, if he knows the names of the clubs, he is a good boy.'

This amusing description makes a number of points with which the modern golfer may not be familiar. The sand tee was best made with wet sand, since dry sand

# TO MY CADDIE.

"Persicos odi, puer, apparatus."—*Horat. Carm. i. 38.*

"I HATE GREAT SHOW OF APPARATUS."

I will not overload thee, boy !
I hate great show of apparatus :
Whilst I'm at 10 I'll still enjoy
My lowly status.

My brassie, iron, mashie, cleek,
For present wants I find sufficient :
Some small additions I may seek
When more proficient.

Some day, perhaps, when I'm at scratch,
You'll find my choice far more specific :
Ten clubs at least for every match—
A weight terrific !

Meanwhile, I do not care to spoil
Our tempers yet by turning faddy :
A game shall not be made a toil
For self or caddie.

P.S.W.

**Above: A verse which appeared in *Golf International*, 5 April 1901**

**Left: Caricature of the rather sloppy, casual type of Scots caddie**

would require a wide pyramid of sand to build it up to the required height. The sand in the tee boxes was usually dry, so it was the custom for a (good) caddie to carry a small pouch, slung round his neck by some string, which contained wet sand. Clubs in those far-off days had names and were not numbered. The schoolboy caddie was usually regarded as a 'second-class' caddie and was paid about sixpence a round. He wore any old clothes that the family could spare and was often barefoot. In order to encourage keenness in the boy caddie it was quite common for the master to deduct threepence from the caddie fee, if the caddie failed to find a ball. An old lady of the author's acquaintance told him that, when she carried in the early 1900s, the man that she usually carried for adopted this system; she found that the professional would pay ninepence for a good second-hand ball. As a result, she would lose a ball in the course of the round, by pushing the ball into the ground while looking for it in the rough, a system known as 'dumping', and then go back and find it afterwards and sell it to the professional. By so doing she lost threepence and gained ninepence! The same lady told the author that the coming of the motor-car made a great difference to her life as a caddie; before the car, she used to carry barefoot but, when the car appeared, she was able to tie short lengths of motor tyre on to each foot and so protect her feet.

## The Adult Caddie

Grown-up caddies were in a different category and, broadly speaking, were of two types. The first type were men who either could not get work, or did not try to get work; most of them had, in common, a considerable thirst for alcohol. They were adequate as caddies but did not take any great interest in the job and invariably drank their earnings. They were a motley collection who were poorly dressed in any old clothes that they could scrounge, and were strangers to soap and water.

The second type was the professional caddie. These were men who had known golf all their lives. Many were boy caddies who developed an interest in the game and continued in the job after they left school. Most of them were golfers, playing on the common land on which the links were situated, with clubs and balls that they had bought out of their earnings, or had been given at one time or another. The ambition of a professional caddie was to become a Keeper of the Green but this was not easy as there were not many jobs available.

If, from the start, a schoolboy showed an aptitude and keenness for golf he might well be taken on in the shop as an apprentice; there, it would soon become clear whether he was good with his hands and likely to become a good club- or ballmaker. He was allowed to develop his talent at golf by playing an occasional game with the members.

If he developed the necessary skills and became a responsible and likeable person he would be encouraged to apply for the post of Keeper of the Green, if one became vacant; before 1850, when there were only seventeen Golf Clubs in existence in Britain, his chances were few and far between. By 1870, there were double that number, and 387 by 1890, so the opportunity to become a Keeper of the Green was steadily becoming easier throughout the nineteenth century; unfortunately, by 1890 the position of Keeper of the Green was becoming extinct.

Many professional caddies failed to gain promotion and remained as carrying caddies who earned a little extra money by using their skills in occasional work in the shop, or in ballmaking. Some had to take a different job in the winter to avoid starvation.

When the Championship Belt was started by Prestwick in 1860, a condition of entry was that all competitors must be 'known and respectable cadies'. By making this stipulation Prestwick ensured that only those whose Clubs vouched for them could enter, thus eliminating the rougher and more alcoholic caddies who had no real ability or interest.

The regular professional caddie studied the golfer for whom he habitually carried and knew his golfing weaknesses and strengths; as a result, he became a valued and important factor in his master's game and helped him to play his best golf. He became, in fact, a member of a two-man team and his advice was frequently sought.

The caddie usually had one or more 'regulars' for whom he carried; on occasions he carried for one master only and a considerable camaraderie existed between caddie and golfer. It was characteristic of this type of caddie that, in talking of the game to others, 'we' was the usual prefix – 'we holed a good putt on the third', 'we missed our drive to the fourth', etc.

Master and caddie became inseparable and the golfer would look after his caddie off the course as well as on it. Regular caddies often wore the cast-off clothing of their master and thus became easily recognisable to other members. They were also helped in other ways by their master, with gifts of food and drink, visits when they were ill, advice on family matters and even, in some cases, a job in the winter, such as general handyman, gardener, bootblack, etc. Those who were not so fortunate as this had to find employment in the winter, many as general labourers, slaters, painters or weavers; some, who had been taught skills in the golf shop, occupied themselves in jobs that were associated with golf. Lang Willie, a tall, thin caddie at St Andrews, used to help Allan Robertson and

**The 'Maiden' (6th) hole at Royal St George's, *c*.1893.**
At that time it was a 'blind' short hole over a high sand dune, and the caddie on the top is there to signal to those on the tee when the players in front have cleared the green

Tom Morris Senior make feather balls, and two other caddies at St Andrews, Sandy and Willie Pirie, made feather balls as well as carrying clubs, and had a further job as weavers for the winter.

Not all caddies carried clubs; during most of the nineteenth century, and before that, it was the custom of most golfers to employ a fore caddie whose job was to go forward and mark each shot; this saved the ball from being lost and, also, meant that the ball could be quickly lifted out of ditches and ponds, for if a feather ball got wet it was ruined.

The fore caddie would walk forward to where, he judged, his master's shot would finish and would then look back to see the shot made; if he misjudged the distance, or had the sun in his eyes, he could be hit. A description of a game in about 1870 says that one pair in a foursome were driving exceptionally well 'and the fore caddies rubbing their stomachs'. An anecdote is told of one Lullah, who was acting as fore caddie to Lord D. and was standing on the edge of a sandpit at Blackheath. 'The sun, which was shining very bright at the time, prevented Lullah from seeing the flight of the ball, which struck him. Lullah threw up his arms and dropped as if he were shot, tumbling to the bottom of the pit. His Lordship,

much alarmed, ran to the aid of his caddie. He found Lullah with the whites of his eyes turned up and gasping for breath. His Lordship at once despatched caddies in all directions to find a doctor. Lullah, by this time, was apparently getting worse. 'Good gracious,' said his Lordship, taking a half crown out of his pocket, 'I may have killed the fellow, will no one run and get some brandy?' Lullah, upon hearing this and having, at the same time, spied the half crown and seeing that there was no one likely to go for the restorative, gradually got up and said 'Please, my Lord, I'll go myself!'

If it seemed likely that the fore caddie might be hit the player would shout a warning, 'Fore caddie!'. In time, this warning became shortened to 'Fore!', fore caddie being a bit of a mouthful to shout when you are in a hurry! This is the origin of the time-honoured shout of 'Fore!' used by golfers to warn others that they are in danger of being hit.

The fore caddie was something of a trainee caddie and was not paid as much as a carrying caddie. A further extension of the fore caddie idea was that of a stationary caddie who was placed on a prominent hill or sand dune where there was a blind shot, on competition days. Because the shot was blind, the people waiting to play could not see whether those in front were safely out of the way, and needed guidance from the caddie stationed on the hill, who had them in view. The caddie would be armed with a red flag, which would be held up to stop play and dropped when it was safe to play. Such caddies were paid by the Club.

For more details about the caddie and his history the reader is referred to *Carry Your Bag, Sir* a book on the subject by the author.

## The Club Secretary

As the Freemasons had organised golf, they had to have office bearers such as Secretaries and Treasurers.

Treasurers were men of figures and accounts, worthy and honest men who were members of the committee and spent much time considering budgets and expenditure in Committee Meetings and in offices but whose job did not necessitate regular contact with the members.

Secretaries, on the other hand, while being members of their respective Clubs, were not members of the Committee but were the servants of the Committee and responsible to the Committee for carrying out Committee decisions, however unpopular. They were forced to listen to the many complaints and grouses of the members and to decide whether action was justified; because they were always available they were the recipients of large amounts of criticism and were usually considered to be to blame for everything that went wrong, including the weather. A Secretary's lot was not a happy one and they were seldom the recipients of praise. The Secretary's job also included dealing with the Keeper of the Green, as representative of the outdoor staff, and of dealing with the Steward of the Club and the indoor staff. Little, in fact, has changed since those times, except that the job is now more complicated.

It was only when a Secretary retired that the Club, faced with finding a man of equal worth and dedication, realised what a good man they were losing.

It is certain that, in the eighteenth century, the Secretary was a Freemason, since there was no way that Masonic secrets could be kept from a non-Masonic Secretary. The post of Secretary was unpaid.

There were some notable Secretaries in the eighteenth century; four are considered here.

### Stuart Grace and his family

Stuart Grace was Honorary Secretary to the Society of Golfers of St Andrews from 1782 to 1812. By all accounts, he was an admirable Secretary. He was succeeded by his son, Charles, who continued as Secretary until his death in 1838; the Secretaryship was continued by Grace's part-

ner in the Grace business, but he died in the same year and Charles Grace's son, Stuart Grace, became Secretary. Stuart Grace, Secundus continued in his job until 1884, when he retired. On his retirement, he was given by the Club (as it was, by now) a piece of silver plate 'value 100 guineas' as a token of the gratitude of the Club, and mention was made of his hard work and of his kindness and courteousness to all. Mention was also made that the Grace family had served the Club, as Secretaries, for over 100 years, with the exception of a few months. Stuart and his successors must hold the record for long service as Secretaries to a Golf Club. What changes they must have seen and with what tact and firmness they must have guided the affairs of the Royal and Ancient Club. In 1956, Charles Grace Secundus' grandson was Treasurer to the Royal and Ancient Club of St Andrews.

### Charles Rhind. Secretary to the Royal Burgess Golfing Society 1773

Rhind has already been mentioned. He was Secretary for only one year but that year was a time of great change and, furthermore, secret change. This was the year in which the Burgess, almost extinct through lack of members, resurrected itself by admitting non-Masons. What a difficult time Rhind must have had and how ably he, and the Treasurer, Kerr, carried things through, so that it is over 200 years later that the full extent of the change that took place has been recognised!

### Henry Callendar. Secretary of Blackheath 1788–9. Captain of Blackheath 1790 and 1807.

Callendar was a Freemason which was why, when the Knuckle Club was formed in about 1797, he did not have to go through the initiation ceremony. He was, however, a poor attender at the Knuckle and, as a result, he and another member were thrown out of the Club for non-attendance in 1790. Despite this, Callendar was a popular and well thought of Secretary and Captain of the Blackheath Club, for, during the time that he was Captain in 1807, they had his portrait painted and he was given the curious rank within the Club of 'Captain General'.

A portrait (see p.140) shows Callendar in full uniform standing with a club in one hand and another leaning against a wall. The latter club appears to be a putter and this is easily confirmed by examining the club in the Club's collection, for this club has been preserved and still exists; for this reason, if for no other, Callendar deserves to be remembered. The existence of this club is additionally of interest because it is, as a general rule, accepted that all putters were made of wood, until about 1865; this putter may have been exceptionally rare in its time but, nevertheless, it is clearly an iron-blade putter.

*James Balfour: Secretary and Treasurer of the Honourable Company of Edinburgh Golfers c.1780*

Balfour is notable because he was a 'character' as well as being a good and loyal Secretary. He was a man of many parts, having been an athlete in his time, but it was his geniality and ability to sing a song and make jokes that endeared him to his fellow members. He was a great man at a party and was affectionately known as 'Singing Jamie'. He was the life and soul of the Club Dinners and was a well-known drinker and raconteur in Edinburgh. A staunch Jacobite, he was fond of singing Jacobite songs at a time when Jacobite songs were viewed with considerable disfavour.

His usual drink was claret and he was in the habit of drinking freely of it at many of the Edinburgh taverns after leaving dinner parties in the town. He usually finished up by drinking a very potent 'cappie ale', a mixture of ale laced with brandy. It is said that, on one occasion, a man walking home along an Edinburgh road at night heard a cry for help coming from a deep roadside ditch; he peered into the ditch and saw Jamie lying at the bottom of it. Jamie asked the man to help him out, but the man said that there was no point as Jamie was so drunk that he would, obviously, only fall in again. Jamie pleaded with him and said that, if the man would help him out, he, Jamie, would race him to the next tavern, the last one there to buy the drinks. The man helped Jamie out and Jamie ran at great speed to the next tavern, easily arriving first. The man bought the drinks and Jamie then said that, if the man would help him to the door, he would race him to the next tavern, on the same conditions; as soon as he got to the door, Jamie set off at great speed to the next pub, arriving comfortably first. The man again bought the drinks. Jamie's account then continued 'Clearly, the poor fellow was the worse for wear by now, so I hired a sedan chair, sent him home and continued on my way!'

He died in November 1795; twenty-seven members attended his funeral and were led by the Provost of Edinburgh. At a dinner afterwards, toasts were drunk: 'To Mr James Balfour, whose benevolent and cheerful disposition and happy social powers, while they captivated all, particularly endeared him to his numerous friends.' 'That the offices in the Society held by Mr James Balfour be generally supplied and attended to with that accuracy and precision for which he was generally distinguished.' His portrait, for which he paid Mr Henry Raeburn 30 guineas, graced the walls of the Clubhouse at Leith.

Selection of golf balls, including rubber cores, early Haskells, machine-made gutties, and hand-hammered gutta balls, with, at the bottom, one feathery sandwiched between a hand-hammered gutta ball (above) and a wooden ball

Old brown gutta ball, *c.*1855, on which the pattern has been incised with a knife

Gutta ball just out of the press mould. The ring of excess gutta was pared down with a knife

Tradition has it that a feather ball was stuffed with as many breast feathers as would 'fill a top hat'. This illustration shows how many feathers (in the tray) were stuffed into the right-hand casing by the author, to fill the feather ball shown in the centre

Hand-operated machine for making gutta balls

Old brown gutta ball with a pattern made by using a
hand-held type of press mould

Gutty golf ball, *c.*1890

Left: Golfer at Blackheath, with a caddie drawn from the Greenwich Pensioners
Right: Henry Callendar wearing the formal red coat and satin breeches, with epaulettes indicating that he was Field Marshal of Royal Blackheath Golf Club. Holding metal putter (*c.*1800) still in possession of the Club. Portrait dated *c.*1807

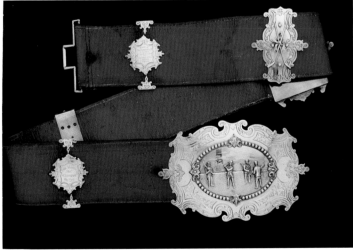

Top: George Glennie putting at Royal Blackheath, *c.* 1870

Left: Championship Belt, played for in 1860

Far left: The 'Maiden' (6th) hole at Sandwich in 1894. Because the hole is 'blind', there are two caddies on top to signal to the players on the tee when the game in front has cleared the green. On this occasion the players following have played before those in front are off the green and the player in the red coat is urgently signalling to the caddies on the hill to stop those behind hitting another shot

Bobby Jones completes a second shot. In the group watching him are Gene Sarazan and Walter Hagen
(Painting by Bill Waugh)

The Buccleuch Gold Medal of the Royal Perth Golfing Society.
left: obverse   right: reverse

Overmantel at the Royal Perth Golfing Society. The silver club with balls has a screwtop.
When a new member was elected the screwtop was removed and the club shaft filled with claret – to be drunk
by the new member without pause

Silver cover for small notebook

Top of claret jug belonging to the
Royal Liverpool Golf Club,
Hoylake

Matchholder, *c.*1880

Left: John Whyte Melville,
Captain of the Royal and
Ancient Golf Club of St
Andrews. He is wearing a
'playing' coat, typical of the
period, 1823

Below: Golf at Royal
Blackheath, c.1870

# Notable Golfers in the 18th and 19th Centuries

9

## Some Notable Golfers in the Eighteenth Century

Undoubtedly, Rattray, William St Clair of Roslyn and Duncan Forbes come into this category. The first two have already been discussed in some detail but Duncan Forbes requires further attention.

### Duncan Forbes, Lord President of the Court of Session

Forbes was not noted for his prowess at golf but he made up for this by his fanatical devotion to the game. It was as a result of his actions and advice that the Golfing Gentlemen of Leith procured for themselves, at the City of Edinburgh's expense, a Silver Club to play for, and were able to survive the Jacobite purge of 1745, becoming, subsequently, a Company which was at the very heart of the start of organised golf and which gave to golf its first Rules. The Rules were signed by Rattray, who owed Forbes his life. Forbes had such a passion for golf that, when snow and frost prevented play, he would play along the beach. He wrote, in his diary, of his son: 'This day, after a long hard pull, I got the better of my son at the gouf. If he was as good at any other thing as he is at that, there might be some hope of him.'

### James Durham of Largo

Durham was another notable golfer, by reason of his prowess. He became a member of the Society of Golfers at St Andrews in 1756, but does not seem to have bothered much with golf until 1767, when, at the age of 35, he showed himself to be a serious and proficient golfer. In that year he won the Silver Club with a score of 94 strokes, the first time that 100 had been beaten at St Andrews. Today, this does not sound a great feat but, at St Andrews, at that time, it was magnificent golf. The links were very narrow and rough, the fairways being full of ruts and sandpits; greens, as we know such things today, were non-existent. There was a large area of whins (gorse) – much more extensive than today. To emphasise the excellence of the score, it stood as a record for 86 years, during which time there had been a steady improvement in the condition of the course and, during the final six years, after 1853, a better golf ball – the gutta.

Having become a golfer of note, Durham developed a real enthusiasm and continued to play golf regularly, every week, for the next 25 years.

### Alexander Duncan

The third notable was a man of golfing skill who was, at one time or another, Captain of the Honourable Company, Captain of The Society of Golfers at St Andrews, and Captain of the Society of Goffers at Blackheath.

He was the son of James Duncan, Professor of Philosophy at St Andrews University, and became an advocate, being admitted to the Faculty of Advocates in 1755. Whether he practised as an advocate must be open to question for he was a skilful and much travelled golfer.

We know that he was a Master Mason because he is listed as such when he attended the laying of the foundation stone of the Clubhouse at Leith, on that occasion representing the Blackheath Club, of which he was Captain in 1766 and 1767, having won the Silver Club at Blackheath in both these years. He won the Silver Club of the Society of Golfers at St Andrews in 1756, 1761 and 1791 and thus was Captain of the Society of Golfers at St Andrews in those years. In 1781, he won the Silver Club of the Honourable Company of Edinburgh Golfers and became Captain of the Company in that year. In his win of 1791 at St Andrews he holed the links in 99 strokes, only one of four men to have bettered 100 before 1800 at St Andrews.

The second half of the eighteenth century and the first half of the nineteenth were the golden age of match-play golf. Scoreplay was only a small part of the golfing picture though it may appear to the reader today as important because the scores for the competitions for the Silver Club were recorded whereas there was little or no record of the matchplay in the great wager battles of that time.

Play in those games was carried on in a spirit of sportsmanship. There were few written rules but some very important unwritten rules, well understood by the players.

Handicaps, as we now know them, did not exist and the Bets Books of the old Golf Societies give evidence of how the matches were arranged so as to be fair to both opponents; if the company at dinner decided that the conditions were not fair to both parties, the bet was not allowed.

One accepted method was to offer the weaker pair, or opponent, odds against winning; another was to give an opponent some holes 'start'. Occasionally, strokes were given, a 'half' or 'half a stroke a hole' meaning 9 strokes, and a 'third' meaning 6 strokes. The holes at which these strokes were to be taken probably were decided by the competitors, and would have been announced at the time of the betting, so that those at dinner could assess the fairness of the match.

In most of the matches, the question of handicaps or odds were not necessary, because they were nearly all foursomes, and partners were so arranged as to make it an even contest.

All sorts of handicaps were devised in singles matches in order to make it a fair game; the Bets Books of the time show that the sense of fun was ever present:

> July 1803. 'Mr Mitchell to play Mr Rose next Saturday giving him one stroke each hole for a gallon [5 litres. Author] of whisky.'

> January 1791. 'Mr Turner bets Mr Walker one gallon of claret that he beats him three holes in four rounds. Mr Walker giving him a stroke a hole.'
> April 1824. 'Mr Robertson challenges Mr Black Senr for a gallon of whisky. Mr Black giving Mr Robertson 2 strokes a hole, which R accepts solely for the good of the Club and on account of it being whisky.'
> December 1822. 'Mr Black Senior bets Mr Lindsay a gallon of claret. Mr Black playing with a heavy iron and a putter and receiving a half a stroke a hole.'
> April 1825. 'James Stein v Sim. Playing him with one hand and getting one stroke each hole.'
> April 1824. 'Mr Black offers to play Mr Hastie one round, with a quart bottle, to tee his ball every stroke behind where it may lie and to have two strokes for one.'

In December 1803, there was a match between the married men and the bachelors for a claret dinner, each individual in the party on either side to play the ball in strict rotation.

> February 1828. 'A match between two golfers, each in striking to stand on one foot, in the month of May.'

Sometimes the bet was on a golfing feat and did not involve an opponent:

> May 1815 (At Bruntsfield). 'Mr Scott bets one guinea with Mr McDowall that he would drive a ball from the Golf House, over (King) Arthur's Seat, at 45 strokes.' (At this time there were no houses in the vicinity; later, this contest became quite popular and parties of people played over the hill, each trying to do the 'course' in the fewest strokes.)
> June 1813. 'Mr Laing offers a bet of a gallon (of claret) that he will drive a ball 500 feet, giving him a chance of 10 strokes to accomplish the feat and the choice of grounds.' It is clear that it was quite possible to drive a feather ball over 170 yards.

Many bets in Bets Books were not about golf at all. In the seventeenth century there are two matches which have a written record.

The first is an apocryphal, but withal, pleasant story about the Duke of York being challenged, in 1682, to a foursome match by two Englishmen. He found a partner with whom to play, one John Patersone, a cobbler. Patersone was not too keen to play but was persuaded and the Duke and the cobbler beat the two Englishmen handsomely. The stake for which they played was so large that a generous portion of it, given by the delighted Duke to the cobbler, enabled the latter to build a house in Edinburgh. There is little to substantiate this story, but it shows the Duke in a good light, as being willing and happy to play with a lowly commoner, and also shows that any two Scotsmen can easily beat any two Englishmen!

A much more authentic match was a 'solemn match at golf' played in 1724 between Alexander Elphinstone, a younger son of Lord Balmerino, and Captain John Porteous of the Edinburgh City Guard for a stake of twenty guineas (probably, today, £400 – or more). For some reason, the match was publicised in the press – probably the first golf match ever reported. Many Noblemen and ordinary citizens came to see the game, and, no doubt, indulged in some betting. Elphinstone won. This is a well-recorded match, but there must have been a large number of a similar type and for a similar stake, which remain unrecorded.

The Reverend John Kerr, a golf and curling enthusiast, a Freemason, and the author of *The Golf Book of East Lothian*, one of the classic books on the history of golf, published in 1896, observes of these matches arranged at Club or Society Dinners, that he found that matchplay brought out all the best in golfers. The parties engaged had not only themselves but also their supporters to vindicate, and not only their opponents but their opponents' friends to overthrow. They therefore played for all they were worth, determined to win. Kerr was referring to that most difficult form of matchplay – foursome golf.

In this era, which could be said to be the finest age of amateur foursome golf, the happy and carefree members of the old Clubs and Societies wined and dined in heroic style and laid bets on all manner of golf games, but principally on matchplay foursomes. The very nature of the bets shows a refreshing suggestion that golf is fun and that the matchplay foursome is its most exciting and enjoyable form. Despite the determination not to let one's partner down and to win the game, this was not a 'win at all costs' attitude; to lose was unfortunate but not a disgrace; to take an unfair advantage of opponents *was* a disgrace and no company of gentlemen would tolerate it. Sportsmanlike behaviour, fair play and an immediate settlement of any bet was expected of gentlemen.

## Notable Amateur Golfers of the first part of the Nineteenth Century

The Championship Belt was not the first scoreplay tournament for professionals, for there had been one at Perth in 1857, but it was the first real attempt at tournament golf.

The golf world, in the first 70 years of the nineteenth century, was still dominated by amateur golfers who considered that matchplay, and preferably foursomes matchplay, was the proper form of golf. At St Andrews, in 1857, a great amateur foursome tournament was staged by the R&A. One pair was to enter from each of a small number of carefully selected Golf Clubs and Societies. Many of the Scottish clubs were excluded and only one English club was invited – Blackheath – even though the Old Manchester Golf Club had been in existence for 20 years or more. The result was a win for Blackheath; the surprise and irritation of the Scots was lessened by the fact that the Blackheath representatives were both Scotsmen who had learnt their golf at St Andrews and, in the case of Captain Stewart, Prestwick as well.

In the following year, the R&A again staged a tournament, this time singles matchplay and open to members of all 'recognised Golf Clubs'. The entry was 28 and a number of notable names were absent; it was won by Mr Robert Chambers. In 1859 a third attempt was made but this, too, was a poor affair and the R&A then dropped the tournament.

It could be said that this was the first attempt at a national tournament. If it was, it was a very poor one and it seems as if the amateur game was not yet ready for the serious and relentless pursuit of championships which is such a prominent feature of the game today.

The first contest for the Challenge Belt took place on 17 October 1860 at Prestwick; apart from the local golfers, there was a good sprinkling of amateurs from further afield who came to watch. The reason that some came from afar was not because the Challenge Belt was considered to be important – it was not – but the following day was Prestwick Medal Day and they had come to play in that. During the Medal, on the following day, many of the contestants in the Challenge Belt would revert to earning a living as caddies; this would be quite important to them as there was no prize money to be won in the Challenge Belt – only the Belt itself.

In the amateur world, matchplay foursomes continued but, because the amateurs of the time were not as rich as their predecessors, the betting was not as heavy and the wining and dining less gross.

Nevertheless, the great amateurs were in the same position as the professionals were before the Championship Belt came into being. They had no tournament to decide who was the best golfer among them. For many, this was no loss, as this type of keen, dedicated golf, involving hours of practice and total commitment to golf did not accord with their idea of indulging in several sports and games, rather than concentrating on only one. They played golf for fun, among their friends, just as they went hunting, shooting and fishing with the same friends.

### Gilbert Mitchell Innes

Innes was another golfer in the same mould as Fairlie (and there were many such). On the Innes side of the family he was of that family of Bo'ness which originated in Flanders before 1066. He did not take up golf until he was 23 years old but became a great golfer when he could spare the time from deerstalking, shooting and fishing.

He won the important medals of St Andrews, North Berwick, the Honourable Company of Edinburgh Golfers and Prestwick. In one year he played in 22 major Medal competitions at the important Golf Clubs in Scotland and finished either first or second in all of them.

He won the North Berwick Gold Medal six times between 1873 and 1879 and won the Spring Medal at Musselburgh with a score of 76 for 16 holes, a record for that Medal.

On one occasion, he and Young Tom Morris (then playing at his very best) played Jamie Anderson, a man later to win the Open three times in succession, and Andrew Strath, who won the Championship Belt in 1865, in a foursome match over 600 holes. At the end Strath and Anderson were two matches up – and 8 holes behind – because, at one links, Young Tom and Gilbert Mitchell Innes won 11 up in 36 holes.

Mitchell Innes and Jamie Anderson challenged any pair in Scotland, laying £100 to £80, but there were no takers. Young Tommy used to complain that, no sooner had Mitchell Innes got into good form than he was away, hunting 'stinking beasts' on the moors. Here was a golfer, contemporary with Fairlie, who might also have been dubbed 'Amateur Champion of Scotland'.

### Captain John C. Stewart of Fasnacloich

Stewart was born at Fasnacloich, a few miles from Oban, in 1832. In 1852, he joined the 51st Highlanders and the R&A, though history does not relate in which order. He must have been a golfer before that time, but we do not know where he learned to play. He opened his account at the R&A by winning the Gold Medal in 1853. He joined Prestwick in 1854 and won the Spring Medal in that year. His regiment was then posted to the Crimea and he did not return to England until 1857, at which time he became a member of Blackheath. Although he must have lacked practice, he was invited to represent Blackheath at the great Tournament of 1857, which he and Glennis won. He was then sent to India at the time of the Mutiny and did not return home until the following year. He won the Prestwick Spring Medals of 1866 and 1867.

He was said to have played Allan Robertson and halved the match after being three down and four to play.

Tom Morris said that he did not know of any man who hit the ball harder and both Willie Park Senior and Tom Morris agreed that he had a real professional style. He was in the habit, when playing a tee shot, of throwing the ball on the ground and playing it from where it lay. His long absences on military duty prevented him from winning many more golfing laurels and he is not as well

known as his contemporaries – but, as a true amateur, this would not have worried him unduly.

### Captain Maitland Dougall

Dougall was a great golfer at St Andrews in the middle of the nineteenth century. He could play Tom Morris Senior and only require 2 or 3 strokes. He won the Silver Cross of the R&A in 1852 and 1855 and the Gold Medal in 1856, 1860, 1863 and 1865.

In 1848 he played at Blackheath in a foursome and used a gutta ball. Realising its potential, he brought some balls to Scotland, much to Allan Robertson's disgust, as he made a living out of feather balls.

Perhaps his most dramatic achievement was the winning of the 1860 Gold Medal at St Andrews. A great storm was raging, with much rain; a vessel was in distress in the bay and the lifeboat had been launched at the mouth of the Swilcan Burn, but there was difficulty in manning it. Maitland Dougall abandoned golf for the time being, and took the stroke oar. The lifeboat was five hours at sea and rescued the crew. When it returned, Maitland Dougall played his Medal round, after having taken the precaution of boring a hole in his gutta and inserting some lead, to keep the ball down in the wind – and won.

There were many more amateurs of the time deserving of mention but these examples underline the great part played by amateurs in continuing golf in the true spirit of the game, regarding it as fun and as part only of a wider spectrum of other sports and activities. They had both leisure and money, though some had less leisure than others, and they used their leisure, not only to play golf but to help in its organisation and administration. They were men of importance who used their position to foster golf and to give the lead, by example, in the proper etiquette of the game.

The fact that, as communications improved, these men came south to England was of great benefit to the English, who were not only instructed in how to swing a club but in how to behave on a golf course.

## Clubhouses and Trophies

In approximate terms, the number of Golf Clubs and Societies in Britain increased tenfold between 1860 and 1890. Apart from the increase in the number of Clubs, which was greatest in England, there was an increase in the number of golfers at each Club. Clubs levied subscriptions and entrance fees and used the money to improve both the Clubhouses and the links or course; the term course is necessary now, because mowers (horsedrawn) became more efficient and inland golf became possible. Greens improved and there were properly defined teeing grounds. Clubhouses became more commodious and provided such additional amenities as billiard rooms. The Clubhouse improvements were particularly noticeable in the older Scottish Clubs and at Blackheath; these had been in existence for about a century and their Clubhouses were already partially developed. In England, except at Blackheath and the Old Manchester Golf Club (the latter had been in existence since 1830 and, like Blackheath, had rich members from a nearby great City) the newly-formed Golf Clubs had to start from scratch and their amenities were as poor as those of the Scottish Clubs had been 70 or 80 years before.

When Westward Ho! started in 1864 they had to make do with a tent and, after that, a small tin hut; it was not until 1890 that they graduated to a 'commodious pavilion'. At Hoylake, in 1869, the 'Clubhouse' was a single room in the Royal Hotel and the professional's shop was in a loose box at the back. The term 'pavilion' for a Clubhouse was no misnomer for later in the nineteenth century there had come into being a form of prefabricated pavilion which was used by cricketers, and these also made useful, if primitive, clubhouses for golf. Failing a prefabricated pavilion, some Golf Clubs took over a suitable house near the course and made that into a Clubhouse. As the size and style of clubhouses improved, so did the internal decoration and so, also, did the splendour and number of trophies to be played for.

## Silver Clubs

EDINBURGH and St Andrews having set a fashion in 1744 and 1754 respectively, a number of other Golf Clubs and Societies, in later years, decided that they would follow suit, both in England and Scotland.

The Silver Clubs at St Andrews and the Honourable Company of Edinburgh Golfers, initially played for, became the Captain's staff of office. Balls were attached to the clubs annually, with the name of the winner who became the Captain for that year. When the club ceased to be played for the custom was continued by the Captain adding a ball to mark his term of office.

The clubs belonging to the Honourable Company and to the R&A are excellent, and full-size replicas of play clubs of the time, being about 45 inches in length. It must be speculation as to whether the silver balls of the early days actually contain a feather ball.

As time went on, the shafts of the clubs became so laden with silver balls that it was necessary to have another club; as a result, older Clubs and Societies have more than one Silver Club – some as many as four. As far as personal research is concerned, over 25 have been identified and located, not all in Britain.

**George Fraser, President of the North Manchester Golf Club, 1818. Note the handsome, decorated, uniform coat and that, as was common practice then, George Fraser plays in gloves**

Most of the Silver Clubs are play clubs or drivers but a few are modelled on the old wooden putter. At least one is a model of an iron club. Some are not all silver but have silver heads and ebony shafts.

At Royal St Georges Golf Club one of the balls is of gold; this is the one presented by the Prince of Wales when he was Captain of the Club in 1927–28.

There are, or were, ceremonies associated with various Silver Clubs. At the Royal Perth Golfing Society one of the Silver Clubs has a detachable top to the shaft. It was the custom to remove the top and fill the club with claret, when a new member was elected, the new member then being required to drain the club.

At St Andrews, the Silver Club is carried in procession to the dinner table at the Autumn Meeting. It is the custom for any member who is attending the dinner for the first time since his election to come up to the high table at the appropriate time and kiss one of the balls on the Silver Club, the club being held out by the new Captain, who has driven himself into office that morning.

At Royal Wimbledon Golf Club, a Silver Club is the Captain's wand of office; it was presented to the Club in 1882. Each Captain adds a ball to the shaft to commemorate his year as Captain. This tradition was carried on until 1939, when, presumably the club could not take any more balls, or because the silver balls were getting too expensive to continue. The Club decreed that the club should not be carried in procession and that there should be no ceremony associated with it at the Annual Dinner.

Royal Wimbledon have a second Silver Club, or, to be more exact, a club with a silver head and an ebony shaft, which was given by a member of the Club specifically for matchplay foursomes, in 1882. The donor, Mr Porteous, stated that it should be for foursome play to relieve the pressure on the green and to encourage foursome golf. The competition was played on handicap and, at the start, the handicap formula was that the number of strokes should be ⅔ of the handicap difference; experience found that this weighed against the high handicap partnerships so, in 1888, it was decided that ⅜ of the difference was fairer and this method was adopted. From that decision stemmed the now universal formula that, in foursomes, the strokes taken shall be ⅜ of the difference in handicap.

In 1886, also at Wimbledon, a Shield was given for a singles matchplay handicap competition. The formula was to be ⅔ of the difference in handicap but, just as with the foursomes, it was found that this formula favoured the lower handicap player and the formula was changed, in 1888, to ¾ of the difference; this, too, is now accepted as the correct method of stroke allowance in singles handicap matchplay.

A Silver Putter of the R&A has medals attached to it but no balls. This putter resulted from a macabre bet between John Whyte Melville and Sir David Moncrieffe as to which would live the longest. Whyte Melville won and duly honoured the bet. He stipulated, when he gave the club (which is a model of a wooden putter), that no balls should be attached to it. He said, at the presentation, that although he had great pleasure in proceeding to fulfil his duty to the Club which the bet imposed on him, he could not but regret the event which had led to it. Whyte Melville suggested that, as the Silver Club handed down to posterity the names of those who presided over its meetings, in a similar manner, the names of those who had distinguished themselves by the superiority of their play should be handed down to posterity on the Silver Putter. The Gold Medals should be attached to the Silver Putter, with the winner's name on each medal.

At Royal Lytham and St Annes there is a Silver Club which looks like a mashie. It was presented in 1892, and is still played for today, by 36-hole Medal round; it is the premier competition of the Club.

Not all the silver clubs are in Britain. A Silver Club – the Drummond Trophy – was presented to the Royal Montreal Golf Club in 1890, for a handicap matchplay competition. It is still played for today.

In 1980, the Edinburgh Town Council decided to continue the Muirfield tradition by giving a Silver Club to the new Muirfield Village Club in Columbus, Ohio. The Silver Club was to be presented to Jack Nicklaus, who had laid out the course and had formed the Club, at an important tournament occasion at the Club, when all the leading professionals would be present and a number of other important people as well. The Club was taken to Muirfield Village Club by the Lord Provost of Edinburgh who, during the journey, hit the longest putt ever recorded. He putted a ball along the aisle in Concorde; the ball was estimated to have rolled for 4 seconds. As Concorde was travelling at 1,320 mph at the time, it was estimated that the putt was 1½ miles long.

There was considerable commotion, at the time, on the Edinburgh Council, when it was reported that a surprisingly large number of Councillors intended to accompany the Lord Provost on this trip, at the Council's expense. After a fevered debate, the number of passengers was reduced to one – the Lord Provost.

The concept of a special club, with balls hung on it, to commemorate the winner, is not confined to silver clubs; the Oxford and Cambridge Golfing Society have two fine old putters on which balls are hung, held by silver bands. Each band has a winner's name on it and the ball that it holds is the ball with which the winner played. The competition is a matchplay singles knockout, played off scratch; it is played at Rye Golf Club (which is the unofficial home of the OCGS) in the very unpropitious month of January. The clubs reside in the main lounge and the competition is called the 'President's Putter'. It is a gallant symbol of matchplay golf at its most difficult and is played in the true tradition of the game.

The Singapore Golf Club – or Royal Singapore Golf Club, as it then was – had a fine Philp putter which was competed for and which had a ball hung on it commemorating each winner. It was presented after the Second World War by William Day, a senior member of the Club who had been in internment at the Club during the Japanese occupation of the Island.

## Medals

W HEN the Silver Club was no longer played for at the R&A and the Honourable Company, the Captain being then elected by ballot rather than by golfing combat, a Gold Medal was given, at each links, for the (scoreplay) championship of that Club or Company. After that it became something of a tradition to have a medal as the prize for scoreplay while cups, shields and all manner of other trophies were given for matchplay events. For this reason, it has become common for a scoreplay event to be called a 'medal' round. Few competitors in the 'monthly medal' are aware of the origins of the term.

The tradition has not been slavishly followed and there are exceptions; probably the most notable exception is the Open Championship. Originally the prize was a Challenge Belt; when this was won outright by Young Tom Morris the new trophy was a claret jug. Possibly, as it was the first competition in which professionals were allowed to take part, the amateurs felt that they would prefer them to play for a prize other than the traditional medal. In 1872, Gilbert Mitchell Innes wrote to Whigham of Prestwick at the time when, the Belt having become Young Tom's property, they were looking for a new trophy: 'I like the idea of the old fighting Championship Belt better than a cup, but that is a matter to be arranged. . .'. Mitchell Innes, like many of the other gentlemen golfers, equated the Championship Belt with the Championship Lonsdale Belt for professional boxers, thus putting the professional golfers and professional prizefighters on the same social level; the medal was for gentlemen golfers, who were much more important and from a higher social stratum.

The many medals at the older Golf Clubs are beautifully engraved and designed and represent the highest standard in the medallist's art. The Buccleuch Medal of the Royal Perth Golfing Society won an award for medal design and execution.

The oldest medal was the Gold Medal of the R&A given in 1771; this medal was won outright in that year and it was not until 1806 that the next medal appeared. The Medal of the Honourable Company was first played for in 1790. This medal is still played for and has now been competed for on three different links, Leith, Musselburgh and Muirfield.

The third oldest medal is the medal of the Knuckle Club at Blackheath, first played for in 1792, and still being played for at Royal Blackheath Golf Club.

The trophies and medals of the Golf Clubs in Britain, being mostly Challenge Trophies which are played for annually, are not, for the most part, removed from the clubhouse by the winner – who may well get a replica, or other memento, of his or her win – but remain in the Clubhouse on display. They appear, beautifully polished, on the table at the Annual Dinner and are a source of pride to the members. The older Clubs, and the richer Clubs, naturally have a grand collection of such trophies.

In many Clubs, the names of the winners of the more important competitions are displayed on an Honours Board. Again, this forms an important part of the Clubhouse decoration; in the older Clubs these boards have the names carved on them and make an impressive decoration as well as an historical record. Unfortunately, in recent years, because of the expense of carving and of the difficulty of finding a carver, plus the marked increase in Club competitions, it has become a habit to record the names of the winners by using transfer lettering on a plywood panel, which is an adequate record but not such an impressive decoration.

By 1870, the older Golf Clubs and Societies, which means Blackheath (not yet Royal), the Old Manchester Club and the long-established Scottish clubs had quite well appointed Clubhouses, either purpose-built such as the R&A, or a private house converted to a Clubhouse, as in the case of Blackheath. There were special rooms for changing out of golf clothes and for the storage of golf boxes, those boxes in which clubs were carried from place to place in the days before golf bags; they had bathrooms and lavatories and a few even had a billiard room. The main room was quite spacious and large enough for many members to dine at one sitting. The walls of such rooms were decorated with portraits in oils of past Captains and Presidents.

On formal Dinner Nights they had their trophies and medals on display and wines, particularly claret, were served from fine cut glass and silver decanters. Club servants were in attendance and the napery and tableware were befitting a gentlemen's club. At such dinners, the gentlemen wore ceremonial red coats, there was plenty to eat and drink and, after the meal, there was much betting on the outcome of matches with speeches and songs galore – some Clubs and Societies had their own 'Poet Laureate'.

But this situation obtained in only a few Clubs; the majority of Golf Clubs were new institutions and had little money because no one expected to pay much for golf and the annual subscription was of the order of £1. Borrowing money was neither as easy, nor as fashionable, as it is today, so Clubs had to live within their means and none could afford a purpose-built Clubhouse when they were formed. At Troon (1878) the first Clubhouse was a disused railway carriage from which the wheels had been removed. In 1848, North Berwick Golf Club (1832) purchased a small tollhouse as a Clubhouse. During these years, there was a great wave of enthusiasm for the game, both in Scotland and in England. The game had never been the national game of Scotland, which was curling, but the arrival, in 1848, of a cheaper and more durable golf ball, improved road facilities and the development of a railway system, which gave much better access to golf courses, raised the popularity of the game, in both countries, to new heights. In Scotland, in particular, there was a large and, up to now, unused area of links land which made more golf links easy to provide and, in England, once Westward Ho! was discovered to be as good an area for golf as any in Scotland, there was energetic exploration which uncovered many other areas of links land in England, all of which were put to golfing use. At the same time, inland courses began to appear; the golf explosion had begun and still continues.

# Trophies

THE main excitement and purpose of early golf was the playing of a match for a stake or bet – preferably a foursome game. The earliest mention of scoreplay in golf did not occur until 1744.

The early stroke competitions for the Silver Clubs were not popular and, both at St Andrews and the Honourable Company, there were times when the entry was so small that they did not bother to play them. Things changed with the passage of time and, particularly perhaps, when the gutta ball appeared and the membership of the existing Golf Clubs greatly increased and many new Golf Clubs sprang up. As well as the great increase in the number of golfers there was also a change in the type of people who played golf. For a start, not all golfers were rich gentlemen of leisure; most of them had to do some work and could only conveniently play at weekends and few of them had the money of their predecessors. With limited time for golf and fewer chances for betting at dinners on individual games, the idea of all competing at the same time in a score competition was attractive, even though it would lead to a need for golf handicaps – something to which not much thought had hitherto been given. The great majority of the scoreplay competitions were played for a Gold Medal.

It is not easy to be certain which are the oldest Medals played for. Because of the destruction of minutes by the Freemasons when they covered up their activities, there are some Golf Clubs who hazard a guess at their date of origin, not from the minutes (which have been 'lost') but from the date on their earliest Gold Medal or Silver Cup, which still exist.

The Honourable Company of Edinburgh Golfers, in 1774, played for a Silver Cup, which was presented to the winner. By 1790, this was found to be too expensive and play was for a Gold Medal; the winner did not keep the Medal but his name was inscribed on it.

## St Andrews

The Society of Golfers at St Andrews were playing for a Gold Medal in 1770 and there was also a Silver Cup for medal play which was first played for in 1772.

## Royal Blackheath

The Society of Golfers at Blackheath played for a Gold Medal in 1792.

## Musselburgh

The Club or Society at Musselburgh played a score competition in 1760, according to a founder member, even though the Club minutes that exist only give a foundation date of 1774 for the Royal Musselburgh Golf Club (earlier minutes were 'lost').

The founder member says that they played for a Silver Cup which the winner kept for that year and which made him Captain. It would seem that this Silver Cup was an alternative to the (very expensive) Silver Clubs of the other Societies and served the same purpose.

Why, in general, when the Silver Clubs ceased to be trophies, the Societies decided to have a Gold Medal, rather than a Silver Cup, is not clear, but this was what happened; Silver Cups became the customary prize for matchplay events.

In time Gold Medals became even more expensive and it became the custom to give a Silver Cup for all competitions, the winner receiving a small replica Cup to keep.

By the beginning of the twentieth century there was a huge increase in the number of golfers and the number of Golf Clubs. The idea of scoreplay competitions was now popular and the number of competitions generally increased greatly. The monthly medal was regularly played and all the other competitions continued to increase; as a result, Silver Cups were becoming a serious matter of expense and, at any rate, as far as the monthly competitions were concerned, it became a habit to give a silver tea or coffee spoon. These spoons were less expensive and were quite attractive; they often had a representation of two golf clubs in the handle and the Club crest at the top; some of the bowls of the spoons were decorated with golfing figures. They also had some practical value as one could use them for tea or coffee and, if one did well in the monthly medal often enough, one would end up with a 'set' of spoons.

These were not the only prizes for golf. Some competitions were played for a Shield on which the winner's name was engraved and the Shield hung up in the Clubhouse; this type of prize was commoner in Scotland.

When the ladies took to golf, tea or coffee spoons

Some famous amateur golfers, players and clubmakers. It is virtually impossible to tell amateur from professional by their dress. Mr Glennie, with cap turned so that he can see the line to the hole better, is putting. With the ball near his right foot is Colonel J.O. Fairlie. The face between the two is that of Jamie Dunn. On the right, carrying clubs, is Tom Morris Senior, with Willie Dunn on the extreme left. In the centre with silk hat is Sir Hugh Lyon Playfair, and peering out from behind his right arm is Allan Robertson

were particularly suitable as prizes for them but they also had other prizes, such as silver or gold brooches and silver hatpins; the brooches were usually decorated with some sort of golfing motif and the hatpins took the form of a golf clubhead surmounting a long pin.

The idea was taken up by other Clubs and Societies, both at home and abroad. Usually the trophy takes the form of an antique putter which is hung; attached to it are the golf balls of the winner of each year, attached to the shaft by a silver band around the ball and a short silver chain which is used to hang the ball from the shaft.

But, when all is said and done, and despite the many wonderful trophies (some, indeed, so large and over-decorated as to be vulgar) it is recording one's name as a winner that is really important.

## Notable Secretaries of the second half of the Nineteenth Century

*George Glennie 1818–86.*

Glennie was a man of such golfing talent that it is difficult to decide whether he should be in the section which tells of the great amateur golfers or in that part of this book devoted to notable secretaries; the following account of him will, hopefully, cover both aspects of the life of a man who loved the game, played with great skill and was more than happy to help in organising it for the benefit of others.

Glennie was a civil engineer by training and his early career was as Manager of the Monkland Canal Co. of Montrose. He moved south to England and was made a member of Blackheath Golf Club. He immediately made his mark as a golfer, winning the Spring Medal of that Club in 1854, and again in 1855, 1863 and 1865. He won the Summer Medal six times in 1859, 1860, 1861, 1863, 1864 and 1865.

Like a true Blackheathen, as the members of the Blackheath Golf Club were called, affectionately, when they made their visits to other Clubs, he played and won major competitions at other Clubs, winning the Club Gold Medal at Westward Ho! in 1865, 1866, and 1867. He won the Dowie Silver Cup at Hoylake in 1871. That he did not win more gold medals at both Westward Ho! and Hoylake is probably because he had no time to play in those competitions since by 1868 he was a busy Secretary at Blackheath (see colour plate on p.141).

Glennie was a member of the Royal and Ancient Golf Club; in 1855 he won the Gold Medal of that Club with a score of 88, a record score at that time and not beaten until 1884, when Horace Hutchinson won with 87. In 1851 he won the Silver Cross. He was elected Captain of the R&A in 1884.

Undoubtedly Glennie's greatest moment was when, in 1857, partnered by Captain Stewart of Fasnagloich and representing Blackheath, they won the Great Golf Tournament, beating a number of top class Scottish Clubs including the R&A in the final.

There can be no doubt that Glennie was a great golfer, and had there been an Amateur Championship in his time he would probably have won it more than once.

## Glennie as a Secretary

In 1862 and 1863 Glennie was Captain of Blackheath; when Crosse, the Secretary, died in 1868, Glennie was unanimously elected Secretary and Treasurer; he continued in that Office until he died in 1886. He transferred all his energy into his job and seemed indefatigable in his efforts. Together with another member he set up a billiard room and installed a billiard table, putting £100 of his own money into the project. During his period of office considerable improvements were made both on the course and in the Clubhouse.

Glennie was not only a good administrator but was a man of force of character and, being such an outstanding golfer, his opinions carried due weight. In 1875, the Club started medal play under handicap (unusual at that time). There was no such thing as a standard scratch score so Glennie sat in the Clubhouse, while the competition was in progress, and calculated the handicap of all the competitors; no competitor knew his handicap until he came off the last hole. It says much for Glennie's strength of character and for the respect in which he was held as a golfer that no one ever seems to have queried this arrangement.

In 1881 the Club honoured Glennie for his services by having the George Glennie Medal struck. There were, in fact, two medals: one was presented to the R&A and one was kept by the Club and played for annually. The R&A medal is still competed for and is awarded to the competitor with the lowest score for the aggregate of the Spring and Autumn Medals. In the same year, the Club held a great dinner at the Ship Hotel at Greenwich at which a portrait of Glennie was presented to the Club showing him putting, with some of his friends and an old caddy. When he died, the Club had a portrait painted of him which still hangs in the Clubhouse today. The club also subscribed to a memorial stone to be placed over his grave.

## Thomas Owen Potter

Potter was Secretary of Royal Liverpool Golf Club, 1882–1894. Known to his friends as 'Tosper', he was the very model of what a Secretary should be. To be Secretary of a Golf Club is not easy, and certain attributes and qualities are of great use in performing this task. Firstly, it is useful to be an Honorary Secretary, if one can afford it; as a member of the Club and receiving no pay, a Secretary is in a position to influence events, express his opinions freely, and have those opinions seriously considered. Secondly, it is useful to be a good golfer, or at least a competent golfer. Thirdly, and very importantly, it is necessary to have a skin as thick as a rhinoceros and to have a very strong personality.

Tosper, if one may presume to call him so, was an Honorary Secretary and a competent golfer; he had a strong personality. At this distance in time one cannot make firm statements about the thickness of his skin – but it must have been very tough. He had another quality, according to his contemporaries, that of geniality. His welcome to those visiting the Club was said to more than compensate for the harassing journey by train, tram and steamer which was necessary in those days. But the geniality served only to conceal a strong will and a determination to do what was best for the Club, which was his whole life. He ruled Hoylake and the Committee and gave to the Club an unswerving loyalty and loving labour. He must have had another quality which his contemporaries do not mention but which is self-evident, that of good judgement, because he made good decisions. He was somewhat addicted to good claret and prawns and it was an unwritten rule that a newly-elected member should present him with a good sample of each as a token of his gratitude.

He could give most golfers a good game and usually beat visiting golfers when introducing them to his beloved links. He was a great man at a party; he lived in the Royal Hotel and took part in many evening sessions of singing in the back parlour, usually taking the lead role with an ivory wand with which he used to conduct the proceedings; the wand is now the Wand of Office of the Captain of the Royal Liverpool Golf Club.

Potter invariably played with John Ball Senior in the competitions at the Club and it was their habit to take a small picnic basket with them, containing, inevitably, claret and prawns; they would stop at the 9th and consume the contents, playing the second nine like giants refreshed.

At the big Meetings of the Club, as Horace Hutchinson (who had known him since he was a young man, visiting from Westward Ho!) remarks: 'Tom Potter is always present to work the machinery with his unremitting attention and to lubricate its wheels with his unfailing courtesy'. In 1884, practically single-handed, Tosper conceived the idea of an Amateur Championship and organised it at Royal Liverpool in 1885.

His sense of history showed itself in his scrapbooks, for he kept newspaper and magazine cuttings on everything concerning Hoylake golf for all the time that he was Secretary, pasting them into a series of large scrapbooks and making notes in beautiful copperplate handwriting. His successors carried on the habit and, as a result, the Royal Liverpool Golf Club has a very complete and unique record of its history. This record is of such value that the R&A has photocopied the scrapbooks in their entirety as a vital contribution to golf history.

When he retired Hutchinson observed: 'What the club will do without his services one cannot think nor yet what Mr Potter will do without his duties'.

### Henry Lamb. Secretary and Captain of Royal Wimbledon Golf Club

Lamb was a Scot; it is not clear why he came to live in the area of Wimbledon but he joined the Club in 1869. In 1877 he was elected Honorary Secretary of Royal Wimbledon Golf Club and remained in his post until 1890. He was elected Captain of Royal Wimbledon in 1891.

During the time that he was Secretary, the Golf Club at Wimbledon went through momentous changes and Lamb's great firmness and unfailing courtesy saw them through this very difficult time; by the time that he became Captain, Royal Wimbledon had become an established Club in its own right.

A brief account of the difficulties that had to be overcome during his period of office as Secretary will serve to show his qualities; for a full account the Reader is referred to the excellent history of the Club written by Charles Cruickshank in 1986.

The London Scottish Rifle Volunteers had their practice shoots on Wimbledon Common; in 1864 they decided to set up a Golf Club. This idea was sanctioned by Lord Elcho, the Colonel of the Volunteers, and a Club was duly formed in 1865. By 1869 the Golf Club was in financial difficulties, mainly because it had so few members; it was decided to allow officers of any of the Armed Forces to join and the Club was christened 'The London Scottish Golf Club'. Some local civilians were also allowed to join but, whereas any member of the Armed Forces could join as of right, civilians had to be elected by ballot.

Because the London Scottish Golf Club was still short of funds, in 1872 the subscriptions of the civilian

**Henry Lamb**

members was doubled and, in 1874, doubled again. At this time there were 50 Forces members and 250 civilian members. Despite this high levy on the civilian members, the rules of the Club decreed that only Forces members could sit on the Committee and, in any event, the Colonel of the Volunteers had power of veto – Elcho was a total dicator. This was the situation which Lamb inherited as Secretary. Lamb and the Committee asked Elcho if they could have the power to elect more civilian members – Elcho refused. Lamb objected and Elcho then forbade civilians to use the Clubhouse. The civilian members then decided to build their own Clubhouse; as can be imagined there were interminable bad-tempered Committee meetings. After a long period of wrangling, the civilian members built themselves a Clubhouse and the Club separated itself from the London Scottish Golf Club and became Royal Wimbledon Golf Club.

Lamb's troubles were not yet over for the Conservators of Wimbledon Common then raised doubts as to whether common land was a suitable place to play golf. The golfers had already agreed to wear red coats to warn the public of danger but they themselves were getting tired of the public picnicking on the greens and damaging the bunkers. In the end Royal Wimbledon Golf Club bought an adjoining farm and laid out their own course. Henry Lamb saw the Club through all these difficult times, battling with courtesy but firm resolution. He well deserved to be made Captain in 1891.

Lamb was a good golfer. He entered the first official Amateur Championship in 1886 and was beaten in the final by Horace Hutchinson, but he covered himself with glory by beating John Ball Junior, the supreme amateur of his time, on Ball's home links, in the semifinal. Horace Hutchinson gives him full credit for this feat and, having beaten Lamb by 7 and 6 in the final, courteously states that he thinks that Lamb may have been tired by his exertions against Ball in the semifinal; he then spoils his remarks: 'What Johnnie can have been doing (in the semifinal) I cannot think. That he must have been playing some game widely different from his real one is certain.'

Despite the slightly derogatory remarks, Lamb proved himself a good golfer by winning the Gold Medal of the R&A in 1873 and 1878, and the Silver Cross of that Club in 1871 and 1873. He also won the Gold Medal of the Royal North Devon Golf Club in 1872 and won more than 20 medals at Wimbledon; he also won medals at Royal St Georges.

Lamb played in the Open Championship in 1873 and was 8th, being leading amateur; he entered from Royal Blackheath. In 1876 he was 7th, and, again leading amateur, entering this time from 'London'. He showed individuality in his style which is described by Hutchinson. He said of him that he was a fine and graceful golfer and possessed of a serene and friendly temperament which was an asset to his golf and made him a charming companion on the course. He addressed the ball as if playing at least 45 degrees to the right and then hit it splendidly straight to square leg; according to Hutchinson the whole stroke was nothing more than a cricketer's pull shot. His stance was so peculiar that, on more than one course, caddies who had not seen him play before, stopped him when he was addressing the ball and told him that he was playing the wrong hole. Perhaps it was this unorthodox style which caused Hutchinson to doubt his ability as a golfer and it must be significant that Hutchinson, in *The Book of Golf and Golfers*, in which he described and illustrated the swings and methods of all the great amateurs and professionals of his day, did not include Henry Lamb.

Lamb showed an inventiveness in golf club design for it was he who had a driver made with a convex face,

whereas, up to then, the traditional club face had been concave. This break with tradition was a distinct advance in club design and this shape has been used ever since.

In about 1890, Lamb and Dr Laidlaw Purves were asked to prospect the coast of southeast England to find suitable links-type land for a golf course. After some searching they found some land at Sandwich, and Lamb was the main instigator and organiser of a links course at Sandwich which became Royal St George's Golf Club. Lamb deserves to be remembered as a man of golfing invention, a very good golfer and a Secretary of distinction. He died in 1893.

The reader may be surprised that, in the lists of Secretaries who were what might be termed 'characters', that is to say, men who dominated Golf Club Committees and imposed their own ideas upon the Clubs, there is no mention of Secretaries in Scottish Golf Clubs, except those already mentioned in the late eighteenth and early nineteenth centuries. This is no accident, nor is it meant to suggest that there were not, in Scotland, many able Secretaries in the second half of the nineteenth century. Conditions in Scotland were different from those obtaining in England and were not conducive to secretarial domination.

In the first place, the Committees of all Scottish Clubs had a large number of expert golfers on them; thus, it would have to be a very exceptional golfer to have attempted to dominate them. Secondly, there was a strong Masonic element in the Scottish Clubs and, if the Committee had highly placed Masons sitting on it, a secretary who was a Mason of a lower grade would have had difficulty in asserting himself. In the Scottish system, the Captain was all important; he could, and often did, dominate the Committee proceedings. The secretary, however diligent and thorough, was the servant of the Committee and his job was to keep the Minutes correctly and see to it that the Committee's recommendations were carried out.

In the histories of the old Scottish Clubs, not a great deal is written about the various Secretaries – there is little about them in the histories of the Royal Burgess, the Honourable Company, or the R&A, though there is much said about Captains and Recorders. The Secretary, Mr Hart, is mentioned in the Prestwick history as being a bit of a character but then he is referred to as 'peppery', and by Bernard Darwin as 'fierce little Mr Hart'. It was in England, in particular, that a Secretary who was a good golfer and a strong personality could dominate a Committee which did not have the golfing expertise to argue with him.

A good example of this domination in England is that of the New Zezland Golf Club in Surrey; here, in 1895,

S. Mure Fergusson was appointed 'Hon Sec: pro tem'; but he had spent the preceding 18 months in designing and laying out the course; this was probably because he was a member of the staff of Mr Locke King's estate, which owned the land.

Fergusson was a very great golfer who had been the leading amateur in the Open of 1891 and was twice runner up in the Amateur Championship. Furthermore he was a Scot and had won some important medals at the R&A. No Committee of Englishmen, largely unversed in golf, could stand up to a man who was physically large and inclined to bully; as Emblem says in his excellent history of the Club. 'There was no Committee – he was the Committee'. Fortunately for posterity, he had good judgement about golf and his layout of the course was very good.

There were plenty of worthy Secretaries in England, apart from those already mentioned, but few had the golfing expertise to dominate a Golf Club Committee. The R&A was, in any event, in a different category from all other Golf Clubs in Britain because it had become the lawgiver of the game and had taken control of the design of golf clubs and balls as well; it had – and still has – a large number of Committees, on all of which there are men who are experts in their own field and it would be impossible for any Secretary to dominate all of them.

## Some Notable Golfers in the second half of the Nineteenth Century

### Amateurs

As the number of golfers grew rapidly in the second half of the century, this automatically produced an increasing number of good golfers, even though the proportion of good golfers to poor remained the same.

It is not possible to describe in detail the skills and successes of all the good amateur golfers of this era but an attempt will be made to discuss in detail the careers of a number of amateurs who, by their skill, were head and shoulders above their contemporaries.

### Horatio Gordon Hutchinson (1859–1932)

Hutchinson was the son of General Hutchinson who, at the time of Horace's birth, was General in Command of Western District with headquarters at Plymouth; although christened Horatio, Hutchinson Junior was always known as Horace.

When Horace was five the family moved to North Devon, where his uncle, Colonel Fred Hutchinson, often visited them and talked of golf, a game that he had learned to play when he was stationed in Scotland, not far from St Andrews. As a result, Horace, encouraged by his uncle Fred, who was a good golfer, became a keen golfer in the early days of golf at Westward Ho!, a Club which had been formed in 1864 and which was only about three miles from the family home.

As a child he was sickly and often absent from school; as a result he was not sent away to boarding school when older but educated locally at the United Services College at Westward Ho! When he was thirteen he found that 'the ball consented to allow itself to be hit cleanly'.

In 1875, he 'committed the blazing indiscretion of winning the scratch medal of the Club'; as a result he should have been the Captain, as of right. As the Club was not going to have a sixteen-year-old boy as Captain, they altered the rules and made the Captaincy a matter of election.

Horace went to Oxford, where he played cricket, rugby and football to a good standard. He also rowed in the 'Torpids' and won the University Billiards Championship – and, of course, he played golf. At that time, although there was a University Golf Club, there were very few members and they had no golf course; few of his undergraduate friends understood what the game was. Horace showed them what golf involved by teeing the ball up on a hairbrush and lofting it out of the Corpus Christi quadrangle into Christchurch Meadows; unfortunately, when his friends tried, the number of broken windows that resulted soon caused the authorities to ban any further efforts! While Hutchinson was up at Oxford, the first Inter-University match was played at Royal Wimbledon.

Although Horace did not get much golf at Oxford, the long University vacations gave him plenty of time at Westward Ho! and he rapidly developed into a formidable golfer. Of Oxford he remarked 'An Oxford education is all very well, but it does considerably interfere with the whole souled attention that a man ought to apply to golf'.

After University, he certainly applied himself and, moreover, he began to try many courses other than Westward Ho!, in particular, Hoylake, where, at the golf meetings, he met many good golfers from Scotland who came down each year to the Hoylake meetings.

It was at Hoylake that he also met and played with John Ball, father and son. In 1883, Hutchinson made his first visit to St Andrews; he also made the acquaintance of Old Tom Morris and he and Old Tom became firm friends. This was partly because Old Tom found in Horace someone akin to his son Young Tom who had died so tragically a few years before. In 1884, Hutchinson was elected a member of the R&A and played in his first Amateur Championship – at least, as Horace says (and he had a hand in planning it): 'It was considered best not to entitle it a Championship, seeing that it was the installation of one Club [Hoylake, *Author*] and had no official recognition'. They did not organise it very well because Macfie, Horace's opponent in the final, had a bye in the semifinal whereas Hutchinson had had a very hard struggle with John Ball Junior, finishing on the last green. The tournament was won by Macfie.

A number of years later the R&A, who had taken little interest in the first tournament but subsequently took it over and made it the official Amateur Championship, decided to make the first tournament official and thus Macfie became, in retrospect, the first Amateur Champion, or, as Darwin observed 'he was canonised after the event'. Horace won the next two Amateur Championships and played many times for England in the Amateur Internationals.

He was a very individual golfer and had a style that was peculiarly his own. His 'waggle' when addressing the ball was vigorous, and he followed this with a very loose swing with a big shoulder turn and his knees very slack; both elbows were well bent at the top of the swing. Despite this unorthodox style, he was a great golfer, being a fine long driver and a great iron player, hitting the ball with a very small divot. He was a good putter, especially under pressure, and used an iron-blade putter long before they had come into general use.

Bernard Darwin played a lot with Horace when they were both at Ashdown for a summer. Horace was then in his forties but Darwin recalls that although he had not the repetitive accuracy of John Ball Junior, his ability to recover from situations that seemed impossible was little short of miraculous. Darwin goes on: 'If the ball were at the bottom of a drain pipe or at the top of a tree, I would unhesitatingly send for Mr Hutchinson to get it out for me'.

Darwin also writes that, in the matter of varied skill, he had never seen a greater golfer, except, possibly, Harold Hilton, and that few people had taken into account that Mr Hutchinson suffered from much ill health, so that he could seldom play at his best for very long. Hutchinson always seemed quite imperturbable on the links, smoking his pipe throughout the game and showing no great emotion, whether things were going well or ill, but Darwin points out that he was a real

**Horace Hutchinson at the Starter's Box at St Andrews, *c.*1898. Note his abnormally long driver**

fighter: 'It was delightfully evident that he did not mean to be beaten and he could play with a kind of cold, sustained anger which was delightful to see'.

An example of this determination to win occurred in the semifinal of the Amateur Championship in 1887. Hutchinson recalls that he was playing John Ball Senior and was one down and two to play. The other semifinal was between John Ball Junior and Jack Tait and Ball Junior had already won that; the tale continues: 'Then he said to me, as we walked after our second shots to the seventeenth hole . . . "It would be a funny thing if father and son had to play it off together". It was an innocent enough remark and yet it nettled me and I said in answer, "Wait a bit, Mr Ball; you haven't done with me yet". Hutchinson then won the last two holes – and beat John Ball Junior in the final.

A good example of Hutchinson's unorthodoxy and of his ability to vary his swing is that, as he grew older, he found that some of the younger men could outdrive him. He decided, after considerable thought, that the best way to drive the ball further was to lengthen the shaft of his driver while, at the same time, decreasing its weight, because, as he said, if one did not do that 'the club would swing you'. He found that using this club he could hit the ball further without losing any accuracy. One of these clubs still exists, at Royal St Georges Golf Club. It is eight inches longer than any contemporary driver and, having gently handled it, the author is firmly of the opinion that only a golfing genius could have made it work!

Having become a member of the R&A in 1884, in 1908 Horace was elected Captain, the first non-Scot and the first Englishman to be so honoured since the founding of the Club. It was fitting that Hutchinson should be the first to break the mould of ethnic discrimination because, throughout his golfing lifetime, he was at the centre of things and always diplomatically trying to bring Scottish and English golf into harmony. He had a difficult task; when John Ball won the Open Championship, the first amateur to do so, Hutchinson noted that the professionals did not resent the fact that an amateur had won but what did cause them some irritation was the fact that an Englishman had won.

**John Ball Junior, 1892**

In the summer of 1913 his long periods of ill-health culminated in a serious operation, as a result of which he was never able to play golf again; he bore this tragedy with great cheerfulness and fortitude but his whole life took a different turn. He died in 1932 under curious circumstances – by falling out of a window in Sloane Square – probably deliberately.

More will be said of him in his capacity as an administrator and promoter of golf in England; enough has been said to help the reader to recognise him as a great golfer.

### John Ball (1861–1940)

Ball was a contemporary of Horace Hutchinson. During his great golfing years he was known as John Ball Junior, to distinguish him from his father, also John Ball, who was the owner of the Royal Hotel at Hoylake, in the Wirral area of Cheshire.

It was in the grounds adjacent to the Royal Hotel that the Liverpool Golf Club had its links golf course. Ball was born in the Hotel and eight years old when the Club was first formed; the Club had its changing rooms in the Royal Hotel and the hotel was in fact the first Clubhouse.

John Ball Senior was a man of athletic ability and played cricket to County standard; he became a keen golfer and lowered his handicap from 18 to scratch in the first year that he took up the game. John Ball Junior was therefore in an excellent position to become a golfer and he did so with a vengeance.

At an early age he became a stylish and powerful player and by the time he was twelve he had won the Boys' Medal, open to any boy under the age of fifteen. After that he played in many Club matches and was soon able to play against most of the members on level terms. In 1878, aged sixteen, he played in the Open at Prestwick and was fourth.

At this time in his life he was playing his best golf and was unbeatable round Hoylake. In an effort to stop him winning everything, he was, at one time, given a handicap of +11 but this did not stop him. He then went through a spell when he could not do himself justice in important events and there were those (outside Hoylake) who began to wonder whether he ever would. In 1884 the first Amateur Championship was played at Hoylake, who had

**John Ball Senior with his son, John Ball Junior**

In the following year, the same pattern was repeated: he played badly in the final and Hutchinson beat him. In 1888, John Ball finally laid his 'bogey' to rest and won the Amateur Championship at Prestwick, beating John Laidlay in the final.

From that year, John Ball came into his own and won, in all, eight Amateur Championships and one Open Championship, in 1890. He won open tournaments in many parts of Britain and he won the Irish Open Amateur Championship in 1893, 1894 and 1899.

What sort of golfer was John Ball? He had a fine full swing and was long off the tee but he was particularly long with a cleek, in spite of the fact that he was not a large man physically. He was a very straight hitter and a remarkably accurate iron player. His only weakness was on the green, particularly in the matter of short putts. Hutchinson wrote of him: 'The short game was where he gave you your chances. If you could live with him at all through the green and up to the hole you need not despair of stealing a shot or two back from him, now and then, on and from just off, the putting green.'

Hutchinson also remarks that Ball was the only man who could cut a ball out of a tight lie and then make it hook at the end of its flight; Ball got some of his extra length from the tee by hitting a slight hook which made the ball run 'till it made you tired watching it'.

Ball, in spite of a rather ugly palm grip with the right hand, had a most elegant swing; Hutchinson commented: 'Mr Ball's driving was the prettiest sight that golf had to give a man. I have never seen a player whose hitting was such a pleasure to watch, such a beautiful exhibition of grace and power, such an ability to concentrate, in a moment and on the spot, all the muscular power that a human frame was master of. It was a beautiful sight.'

Bernard Darwin observes: 'Let men talk as much as they like about beautiful swings but do not let them question which was the most beautiful swing of all, since there, for me, all argument ceases.' Ball had an ability to shape his shots for the conditions of the day and he delighted in playing on windy days; on one occasion, on being congratulated on winning one of the big Hoylake medals on a windy day, he simply said: 'I happened to be hitting it the right height for the day'.

Another feature of his play was his ability to hit high shots with a relatively straight-faced iron; he used an iron for his approach work and seldom could be persuaded to use a mashie; [equivalent to today's No.5 iron. *Author*] he

organised it; because it was under their auspices it was regarded as an unofficial championship and it was only in the following year that the R&A took it upon themselves to run it, thus making it official. Unfortunately, Hoylake ran it on the same lines as a rather poor attempt made by the R&A in 1859 to stage a Championship, an attempt which was so disastrous that the whole contest died a natural death shortly after.

Ball played well and strode confidently toward the semifinal where he was called upon to play Horace Hutchinson; Hutchinson beat him, but only by 2 holes, making a birdie at the 18th. Ball had lost but he had played well, except for some poor putting, and it seemed likely that he had finally begun to do himself justice in the big tournaments; as events showed, he had not quite arrived but he devoted more time to playing in major competitions outside Hoylake and became a better golfer for it.

In 1886, he played in the Amateur at St Andrews and reached the final by beating John Laidlay, one of the greatest of the Scottish players of the time. Ball was expected to beat Henry Lamb with some ease in the final but his 'bogey' returned, he played very badly, and Lamb won easily.

had no use for the niblick [today's wedge or sand iron, *Author*] and played his bunker shots with the iron, opening the face widely and hitting the sand about one inch behind the ball. Robert Harris, in his golfing reminiscences, states that he played once in a four at Princes Golf Club near Sandwich which included John Ball; at a short hole Ball cut his tee shot into a bunker beside the green; Harris and his two companions talked John into trying a niblick, much against his will, saying that there was no one nearby to see him do it and none of them would ever tell. Ball borrowed a niblick, with much protesting and many misgivings; he played the shot and holed it! He was much ashamed at having used such an unnatural implement and made his companions swear that they would never tell anyone. They remained true to their promise and Harris only revealed the secret after Ball had died.

What of Ball, the man? He was a local boy and did not go to public school or University. At the start he must have been slightly out of the social stratum which contained such men as Horace Hutchinson and many of the senior members of Hoylake but he became such a golfing

**John Ball Junior at the top of the backswing. He has pivoted on the inner edge of his left foot; there is a big shoulder turn, and the club has 'crossed the line'. The club is held in the palms of the hands**

hero and was such a quiet, likeable person that he soon became a close friend and social equal of all the members at Hoylake. Although he was much liked and admired he never went out of his way to court attention. On one occasion, when he had been away and had won one of his many Championships, the local village – and, particularly the local fishermen, to whom he was 'our Johnny' – decided to welcome the hero back in proper style; the local station was decorated with bunting and the fishermen had removed the horse from the station 'taxi' and were going to pull it in triumph to the Royal Hotel. The train arrived but Johnny was not on it; perhaps he guessed what was planned; whether he did or not, he had got out of the train at the previous station before walked home along the beach. At times his silence could be unnerving and Darwin remarks that he could appear almost sinister in his reserve but had a good sense of humour and, with close friends, could joke and banter with the best of them.

Ball was a match player. He could win medals, and frequently did, but he was at his best in matchplay golf – and was at his very best when 2 or 3 down on a windy day. He seemed to enjoy coming from behind; on one occasion, he was playing a good golfer who went off with a rush and was 4 up at the 4th; after that Ball demolished him comfortably. At the end of the game, when Ball's opponent made suitable remarks to him on his good golf, Ball said: 'Pity, I thought we were going to have a good game'. He meant no harm by this remark, he genuinely believed that he would have had more fun if his opponent had made a tighter game of it. His local supporters, when Ball was 2 or 3 down and with about 6 to play, would say 'Now let's see John win his half crown'. He loved 'hunting his man' and demonstrated this in many Championships.

Ball always remained a Hoylake man and seldom played elsewhere unless he had to do so in a Championship. He was made an Honorary Member of the R&A in 1902 but he never played in any of the R&A Medals; he had many friends who were members of Westward Ho! but he never played in a competition there, even though many of his Hoylake friends went to Westward Ho! every year. He seems to have had an affinity for Sandwich and played in that area on a number of occasions.

He won a large number of medals at Hoylake but they all disappeared, as did all his Championship Medals, and have never been found; Harris says that he once asked John Ball if he could borrow all the medals that he had won and put them on exhibition; Ball said that he was sorry but he did not know where they were and thought that he must have given them away to friends.

Needless to say, John Ball played for England in a large number of international matches; he played against

Scotland in the first encounter between the two countries in 1902, and for the next nine years.

Here, then, was one of the great men of golf; if he had had the doubtful advantage of present-day media hyperbole he would have been called 'the greatest golfer in the world'; how he would have hated it!

### Frederick Guthrie Tait (1870–1900)

Freddie Tait was from the next generation of great amateur golfers. He was the son of Professor Tait, a Senior Wrangler and Professor of Natural Philosophy at Edinburgh University.

Professor Tait was a keen golfer and the family used to travel to St Andrews to play golf in the University vacations. Thus Freddie was introduced to golf at an early age and, by the time he was twelve he was competing in local events. Freddie Tait was in the same mould as Hutchinson and Laidlay; he was educated at Sedbergh School and later went to Edinburgh University. At school, he was a good cricketer and rugby football player. His contemporaries were of the opinion later in life that he was very unlucky not to have been picked for Scotland at rugby. He was a first-class shot and an accomplished fisherman.

Freddie was a likeable and cheerful person and enjoyed being an all-round sportsman. At a very early age he became the sort of boy whose talents and exploits at school made him a hero to his schoolmates. He was not clever but always put maximum effort into everything that he did and, in consequence, did quite well academically and was, later, successful in his career in the Army. Being in the Army, he was able to indulge his many talents for sport and used that opportunity to the full, never concentrating purely on golf.

Like many young golfers, in his early days he was a noted long driver – but not a very accurate one. In 1893 he hit a drive of 341 yards (with a 'gutty') and the carry was 250 yards; this shot was the cause of some embarrassment to his father because he accomplished this drive on the same day that his father published a paper, based on the laws of physics, which proved that it was not possible to hit a golf ball further than 250 yards. It subsequently transpired that his father had failed to take into account the effects of underspin!

Later in life, Tait became a golfer of great accuracy who had, up his sleeve, as it were, a great reserve of power which he only used when necessary. He was always a fine putter and had a remarkable ability to play shots out of apparently impossible positions, which earned the admiration of Horace Hutchinson, who was also a master of difficult situations.

From the age of fifteen, Freddie kept a diary in which, among other things, he kept records of his golf

**F.G. Tait (artist: Thomas Hodge)**

matches and better scores. These records are reproduced in John Low's *F.G. Tait. A Record*; the records indicate a remarkable golfing talent and, also, the fact that Tait was just as interested in the singles and foursomes in which he played as he was in winning Championships and medals. In fact, he used to refer contemptuously to those golfers who set much store by such things as 'pot hunters'.

His swing was orthodox but appeared short in photos taken at the time; as he was six feet tall and a muscular man, he was still longer than most of his contemporaries off the tee. Posed pictures of his backswing at the time show what appears to be a rather cramped backswing, but Hutchinson stated that such pictures were deceptive and that, to a spectator, his swing appeared long and very powerful. It is possible that Freddie had discovered the 'wider arc' that modern golfers use but that did not show up in posed photographs. Tait was a good putter, using a blade putter and, according to his contemporaries, such as Horace Hutchinson, had a remarkable ability to hole long putts when they mattered, putts which, according to Hutchinson, were so long as to be considered lucky.

**Left: J.E. Laidlay about to play an approach shot. The ball is just inside his left foot; left elbow is well bent. The right little finger is overlapping and the grip is in the fingers and appears to be light. Right: The shot has been played and there is an unusually long follow through for what was a short shot. The club has been held well down the shaft and the weight is well forward on the left foot**

Some of his outstanding successes among a large number of competitions are as follows:

### Amateur Championship

He won the Amateur Championship in 1896 and 1898 and was runner up in 1899, being beaten at the 37th by John Ball. He was beaten in the semifinal in 1894 and 1895.

### Open Championship

| 1894 | 9th (Leading Amateur) |
|------|------------------------|
| 1895 | 14th |
| 1896 | 3rd (Leading Amateur) |
| 1897 | 3rd |
| 1898 | 5th (Leading Amateur) |
| 1899 | 7th |

In 1894, he holed the Old Course at St Andrews in 72, breaking all previous records. In 1897, playing in a four ball, he holed the course in 69.

In 1896 he established a record for Muirfield with a 73 and in 1894 he broke the record at Carnoustie with 72.

He won the Autumn Medal of the R&A five times and the Glennie Medal (for the best aggregate of the Spring and Autumn medals at St Andrews) three times.

All this he achieved before he was 30, playing with

a gutty ball for, in 1900, he was killed in action in the Boer War. Naturally he was – and is – a great Scottish golfing hero and his portrait, together with that of his beloved dog 'Nails', hangs in the Big Room at the R&A.

## J.E. Laidlay

Born in 1860 in Haddington, East Lothian, Laidlay was educated at Loretto School at Musselburgh; he came from a wealthy, landowning family and seems not to have had to earn a living. From his earliest days at school he showed a considerable athletic ability, becoming a very good cricketer and, in later life, playing for the Gentlemen of Scotland against Yorkshire. Hutchinson says that, at school, he was the only boy who could pull himself up on to the horizontal bar using only one hand. *The Golfer's Handbook* of 1912 lists his hobbies as fishing and shooting; he was a keen and expert photographer and more than one of his photographs was used by the Reverend Kerr in *The Golf Book of East Lothian*. He was also an expert cabinet-maker and, in his later years, when he had won 139 medals at golf, he made a fine cabinet in which to house them. Laidlay's background was more akin to that of Hutchinson than that of Ball and he found pleasure in many sports other than golf.

Nevertheless, being brought up close to Musselburgh and educated at Loretto which was a few minutes walk from the links, he had plenty of opportunity to learn to play golf. The great professional at Musselburgh in Laidlay's time was Bob Ferguson; whether Laidlay had any lessons from him is not known but he would certainly have been influenced by him.

After his school days, he played mainly at North Berwick and it was there that he developed his golfing skills. North Berwick was not a long course but had tricky, sloping greens; there were a large number of shortish iron shots to be played to these sloping greens. As a result of this golfing upbringing, Laidlay became very expert at pitching to greens and a more than useful putter. While Laidlay may have been influenced in his style of play by Bob Ferguson, he gives the impression, in his golf, of having been self-taught, for he had a most individual style which at that time was unorthodox. For a start, he used the overlapping grip at least thirty years before Vardon popularised it, thus making it the 'Vardon' grip; his style was rather ungainly as he played all his shots off the left foot. He was unusual, also, in that he had very thin grips on his clubs – and this at a time when everybody played with thick grips – and held the club very lightly at a time when most players, including such great professionals as J. H. Taylor, believed in holding the club firmly. In the address, he kept his left elbow well bent and, even for short shots, he had an exceptionally long follow through. The weakness in his play was in driving and wooden club shots through the green; the nearer he got to the green, the better he played.

Laidlay did not believe in practising and often played in matches and competitions when he had not played golf for some time; he had a curious idiosyncrasy that he liked to play with a new brassie on important occasions. Hutchinson remarked of him: 'He would go into Forgan's or Tom's [Morris. *Author*] shop and come out with a brand new club that he had never seen before'.

Laidlay's other valuable asset in golf was his magnificent temperament. He always played his best shots when under great pressure and this made him a very formidable match player. Although he won many medals, it was as a match player that he was most feared.

Laidlay's records speaks for itself:

### Open Championship
| | |
|---|---|
| 1886 | (Leading amateur) |
| 1887 | 4th |
| 1888 | 10th |
| 1889 | 4th (Leading amateur) |
| 1890 | 8th |

In 1893, he was runner-up, ahead of such players as John Ball, J.H. Taylor, Willie Park, etc.

### Amateur Championship
| | |
|---|---|
| 1888 | Runner-up, beaten by John Ball |
| 1889 | Winner, beating John Ball in the final |
| 1890 | Runner-up, beaten by John Ball |
| 1891 | Winner |
| 1892 | Semifinalist |
| 1893 | Runner-up |
| 1894 | Semifinalist |

At one time or another he won all the most important medals of the R&A, Hoylake, North Berwick and Muirfield.

Here was a man, golfingly speaking, in the Corinthian mould. Yet golf was only one of the many sports that he enjoyed and he never bothered to practise; his success on the golf links was entirely due to his natural talent and he enjoyed playing a match with his friends quite as much as (or even more than) trying to win important trophies. His many medals and prizes are now in the keeping of the British Golf Museum.

## H.H. Hilton (1896–1946)

Harold Hilton was another of the famous Hoylake golfers. As a small boy he was good at games – cricket, football, swimming and running, etc – but, at an early age, he showed that golf was what he preferred to all other games and he rapidly became proficient at it. He was educated at a local school and did not go to University, and he had plenty of opportunities to play golf out of school hours.

Perhaps he was fortunate, given his natural ability for the game, that, from the start, Hoylake was a links which was a Mecca for all good golfers and was accessible from both Scotland and England. The leading golfers from Scotland came to play in the Hoylake Meetings as did the great golfers from Westward Ho! and Blackheath; additionally, the professional from Blackheath, Bob Kirk, and the professional from Westward Ho!, Johnnie Allan, usually accompanied the members from their respective Clubs and were involved in matches. On one occasion, Young Tom Morris came to Hoylake and played in a tournament, together with other professionals. Finally, and very importantly, Harold Hilton had the example before him of the great John Ball.

As a result of this golfing environment Hilton developed into a great golfer himself. He stood only 5 foot 7 inches but was a muscular man who had a free swing and was as long as most of his contemporaries. As a lad, he used to play in one of his father's hats; as the hat was much too large it usually fell off at the end of the swing and this characteristic continued even when he was a grown man and wore a well-fitting cap.

His successes in important tournaments and Championships were phenomenal:

### Open Championship

He won his first Open in 1892, at Muirfield, when he was 23; he beat such golfers as John Ball (runner-up, together with Alex Herd and Hugh Kirkaldy) by 3 shots.

| | |
|---|---|
| 1893 | 8th |
| 1894 | Did not play |
| 1895 | Did not play |
| 1896 | Did not play |

No reason is given for these absences; it may well have been that he could not afford the trip. Even when he played in the 1892 Open his father baulked at the expense and he only entered when he was offered accommodation with a friend at Muirfield; Hilton did not come from a wealthy family, unlike many of his contemporaries.

| | |
|---|---|
| 1897 | Winner (at Hoylake). |

This win, in particular, established him as one of the very greatest golfers as, by this time, the Great Triumvirate of Vardon, Braid and Taylor were in full swing and dominating professional golf.

| | |
|---|---|
| 1898 | 3rd |
| 1899 | 8th |
| 1900 | 15th |
| 1901 | 4th |

Thereafter he was not highly placed in the Open, except in 1911 when he was 3rd at Royal St Georges.

### Amateur Championship

Hilton first played in the Amateur Championship in 1890 (at Hoylake) and was beaten in the 4th round by John Ball.

| | |
|---|---|
| 1891 | Runner-up, beaten by John Laidlay at the 37th |
| 1892 | Runner-up, beaten by John Ball |
| 1893 | Did not play |
| 1894 | Beaten by Freddie Tait in the 4th round |
| 1895 | Beaten by William Greig in the 3rd round |
| 1896 | Runner-up, beaten by Tait |
| 1897 | Beaten by Maxwell in the 4th round |
| 1898 | Beaten by Tait in the 4th round |
| 1899 | Beaten by Tait in the 5th round |
| 1900 | Winner |
| 1901 | Winner |
| 1902 | Beaten by S.H. Fry in the 5th round |

Hilton made no great showing in the Amateur thereafter, until 1907, when he was beaten in the 6th round.

| | |
|---|---|
| 1910 | Semifinalist |
| 1911 | Winner |
| 1912 | Beaten in the 5th round |
| 1913 | Winner |
| 1922 | Beaten in the 6th round |

### Championships outside Britain

| | |
|---|---|
| 1911 | American Open Amateur Championship |
| 1900, 1901 | Irish Open Championship |
| 1900, 1901, 1902 | Irish Open Amateur Championship |

**Horace Harold Hilton**

Hilton was a good golfer in all departments of the game. He was noted, in particular, for several types of shot; he was very deadly in his 'pitch and run' approach shots with a mashie and he was a great putter, rolling the ball up to the hole with top spin. Perhaps his most obvious skill was his ability to 'fade' or hook the ball with any club and to play half shots; he took great delight in playing these strokes, and it made him a particularly formidable competitor on windy days (and there were plenty of them at Hoylake).

Farrar, who saw him play, says that his address to the ball was very careful and exact but 'the impression of extreme care was swallowed up in the stupendous energy of the swing itself. It certainly did not give the impression of great accuracy, and yet no one had more control or delicacy of touch. He looked like a schoolboy having a real good smack at the ball . . .'.

If he had a weakness it was his delight in playing a great variety of strokes, so that he could never bring himself to play the simple stroke but must invent a stroke to suit each individual shot: 'there was something impish in his nature', as Farrar observes.

Unlike Ball, Hilton loved the crowds and excitement at the big Championships. He was a cheerful, extrovert character who was never without a cigarette in his mouth and, Hutchinson wrote, '. . . with smoke trailing from his cigarette, even when he was playing the ball, so that it seemed impossible that he could see through it to hit the ball correctly'.

There were those good golfers of his time who considered that he was a scoreplayer rather than a matchplayer; possibly this was because he had greater success in his early golfing life at scoreplay but, with hindsight, he was just as good at matchplay. In the early attempts at the Amateur, he was beaten in the final by both Ball and Laidlay, but he was then a young man and there was no shame in being beaten by those two experienced campaigners. Later, he was beaten by Tait on a great number of occasions and there seems no doubt that Tait established a psychological ascendency over him (which is what makes matchplay golf a more interesting form of golf than scoreplay), although Hilton was showing signs of overcoming this at the time that Tait came to his sad end. Nevertheless a man who wins four Amateur Championships in Britain and is runner-up in three others and who wins the American Amateur Championship, and the Irish Open Amateur Championship in three successive years, must be a great matchplayer, and the truth about Hilton is that he was a very great golfer indeed, with no weaknesses in any part of his game.

Accounts of Hilton make no mention of how he earned his living but he was, for some years, Editor of *Golf Monthly*.

What is not generally recognised about Hilton is that he was the first of the British amateurs to practise assiduously. Unlike the Corinthians, he devoted himself entirely to being a good golfer. There are stories of Hoylake which tell of a green looking as if struck by a snowstorm because Mr Hilton was out practising and the green was covered with white golf balls.

## Further Development of Golf Clubs

Dᴜʀɪɴɢ the second half of the nineteenth century there was a change from the secretive, Masonic, Golf Club to a private Club whose members were solely interested in playing golf. In the old Clubs the change was very gradual and, as we have seen, efforts were made to try to ensure that Masons kept some control of affairs, but covertly.

The long-established Golf Clubs had fine Clubhouses, long traditions in golf, and a comfortable way of

**Ballot Box**

life, with Dinners, Bet Books, etc. Non-Masons were allowed to join and were only subjected to the usual formalities of proposer and seconder, followed by submission of the proposal to the Committee. In most Clubs the Ballot Box was retained and a single 'black ball' was sufficient to refuse an application for membership, the Club being under no obligation to give a reason.

The concept of a Club arose in the eighteenth century and there were many Clubs for all sorts of purposes, political, literary, intellectual and sporting; there was even a club called the Lunar Club which met only at the time of the full moon, so that members could walk home by the light of it.

These Clubs flourished and multiplied in London and, to a lesser extent, in Edinburgh. In London, at least, they were a development of the social meetings at the Coffee Houses, such as Lloyds. One can detect a pattern of Freemasonry in them; the Athenaeum Club, for example, was originally called a Society.

Bernard Darwin, writes of 'British Clubs': 'Of the final stages of transition from a band of friends meeting in a coffee house to a formally constituted club we know much less than we would like. Records were few and casual and moreover there seems to be no club of venerable antiquity that has not at some time or another had a fire. A fire almost amounts to a patent of respectability . . .'. Needless to say, the fires destroyed all the earlier Minutes of these Clubs, hence the lack of information.

It was not surprising that associations of golfers should follow the general pattern and call themselves Golf Clubs, except for a few who preferred to continue to call themselves Societies, and the Honourable Company of Edinburgh Golfers.

'Boswell', said Dr Johnson, 'is a clubbable man'. This was a compliment. A perfectly honourable and sensible man could be elected a member of a Club but he might lack certain essential qualities which made him 'clubbable'; a clubbable man not only considered what he could get out of belonging to a Club but, also, what he could put in.

A Club did not necessarily have to have its own premises, though most did, especially in England; by the same token it was not necessary for a Golf Club to own, and have for its sole use, a golf links. In England most Clubs bought land for a golf course as well as land for a Clubhouse but in Scotland it was (and still is) common for a links, on common land owned by the local Town Council, to be shared by several Clubs; St Andrews is a good example of this.

A member of a Club was able to use the Club as a second home; he had a pleasant feeling of ownership, even though it was only a shared ownership. He had to share it equally with other members and not try to make himself important, create trouble, or gain any undue advantage for himself. A member had to conduct himself in a manner that did not cause offence or disturbance to other members and, most of all, a member had to be prepared to do a service to the Club, if he was in a position to do so, without expecting any reward.

As an example of equality within the Club of all members, it was not considered good manners for a member to tip club servants for services rendered because, by so doing, he was trying to secure better service from the staff for himself at the expense of fellow members; it was, however, expected that the member would, at the end of the year, subscribe to a fund which would provide a sum for all the staff to share as a recognition of the good work done by them during the year.

The early Golf Clubs did their best to emulate the codes of behaviour of the Clubs in London and Edinburgh. There were, however, great differences between those Clubs which had just started and those that, in the mid-nineteenth century, were almost a century old. Despite their ambitions to become, in time, as prestigious and rich as the earlier Clubs, these newer Clubs had to live within their means – and the means were pretty poor to start with.

Westward Ho!, starting in 1864, had to use a tent as their first Clubhouse; this did not stop them, on Christmas Day 1866, having their Christmas Dinner in the tent, at midday and, 'under the influence of cold turkey and plum pudding, drink the health of golfers everywhere'.

Despite their humble beginnings they stuck to the principle of Club membership and, as the years went by and they became larger, richer and more famous they used their money to find better premises, increase staff and improve the golf course.

However small the Golf Club, it required to have someone to look after the course and make golf clubs, and one or more people in the Clubhouse to provide meals and keep it clean and tidy. There was need for a Secretary to oversee all the staff, keep the accounts and write up the Minutes of the Committee meetings. The Secretary of the Club, true to Club principles, was unpaid and gave his time and services free; few were appreciated, until it became time to find a new one who could do the job as well as his predecessor. Of all the 'clubbable' members of the Club, the Secretary was the one who earned the compliment of that title best. There were dedicated and honourable men who became Honorary Secretaries and they had much to do with the further development of Golf Clubs and, therefore, of golf. In the last quarter of the nineteenth century there was a golf 'explosion' – in 1860, according to John Adams in *The Parks of Musselburgh*, there were 25 Golf Clubs in Britain. In 1890 there were 381 and, in 1900, 2,330.

The increasing demand for Clubhouses was met by building firms who had developed a system for making prefabricated cricket pavilions. These Clubhouses were relatively cheap and easy to erect, and as a result many of the smaller Golf Clubs of this period have Clubhouses which look like cricket pavilions.

The amateurs were not as good as the professionals in scoreplay but were able to give them a good game in matchplay, particularly in foursomes, when the amateur was a good partner for the professional.

Challenge matches were played for high stakes and the professional was granted a share when his side won, while not having to pay up if he lost; by this means, the professional earned some money and the amateurs became better golfers.

These foursomes matches, in Scotland, produced a camaraderie between the professionals and the best amateurs. On the links, remarks were allowed between a professional and his amateur partner which would not have been tolerated off the links. Even caddies, who were often better players than their masters, and who regularly carried for them and knew their play, were allowed to make somewhat caustic comments or, if necessary, offer words of encouragement, in order that 'we' should win the match. When it is realised that the caddies, on occasions, might be men who had won one or more Open Championships, this seems quite reasonable! In some of the group photographs which include both amateurs and professionals it is quite difficult to distinguish between them. This is due to the fact that the caddies and professionals are often wearing their master's cast-off clothing! A further reason for equality on the 'common land' links was that the land belonged to the local citizens, of whom the caddie or professional was one, while the amateur, if he came from another area, had less right to be playing on the common land than his caddie.

Things were not the same in England where most, though not all, the courses, were on private land and few of the caddies, at that time, were as expert as those for whom they carried.

One of the problems in assessing the golfing merits of the amateurs in the 1870s and 1880s was that there was no Amateur Championship until 1885. Most of the good amateurs played one another, mostly at foursomes.

By about 1865, rail travel was well established and the railway had built up an extensive network. It therefore became possible to travel from one golf course to another with relative ease. Wealthy amateurs, who could play on any day of the week, used the railway to travel to other courses and play against better players from other clubs.

In 1864, Blackheath travelled to North Devon to play in the August Meeting, open to all, and were able to match their skills against golfers at Westward Ho! Characteristically, although they played in the Medal competitions, the most fun was found in foursomes matches for a good bet. In these matches, the professionals from each club were frequent competitors, usually as partners for amateurs but, on occasions, they were matched against one another. The Blackheath amateurs, accompanied by Bob Kirk, their professional, were made very welcome at Westward Ho! and were known as the 'Blackheathens'; there was much jollity and a number of keenly fought matchplay foursomes over several days.

In 1869, a new Golf Club opened at Hoylake: it was also a links course by the sea. This allowed the Blackheathens, accompanied by members of Westward Ho! (which, by now, had become the Royal North Devon Golf Club) to travel to Hoylake and take part in the Open Meeting there, where they met groups of golfers from Scotland who had come down from Prestwick, St Andrews and the Honourable Company. As a result, the tournaments at Hoylake began to assume an almost national importance, due to the influx of golfing talent from a wide area both in Scotland and England.

When the Meeting at Hoylake was finished the combined operation proceeded to St Andrews for the R&A Autumn Meeting. The dates of these Meetings were all carefully arranged so that they did not clash. Horace Hutchinson writes with great affection of these annual pilgrimages.

Apart from the general jollity and excitement of such Meetings, it gave the leading amateurs an opportunity to test their skills against amateurs from other Clubs and it was probably the great Meetings at Hoylake which gave that Club the idea of suggesting to the R&A that there should be an Amateur Championship; the R&A agreed and the first Amateur Championship was played at Hoylake, under the auspices of the R&A, in 1885.

There were, in the second quarter of the nineteenth century, three 'grades' of Golf Club. The first was the long-established Golf Club with a prestigious membership, a fine clubhouse decorated with silver cups, gold medals, silver clubs, and portraits in oils of the more famous members, where the members dined and wined in style. The second grade consisted of Clubs which had beginnings in about the middle of the century and which, while not rich or prestigious at this stage in their development, meant to become so, and were careful only to accept the 'right' members. The third grade were all those newly founded clubs which had cricket-style pavilions as clubhouses, little fine silver, a minimum of staff both inside and outside the clubhouse and a mortgage at the bank. The third grade could not afford to be as discriminating as the higher grades in their choice of members, and usually arranged that those in the higher echelons of society should be on the Committee while the humble members, who were local businessmen and teachers, etc, learned about the codes of behaviour both on and off the course, as well as how to play golf.

The first grade of Club had a good number of expert amateur golfers, the second grade, a few, and the third grade, very few. Any who were good golfers set their sights on becoming a member of the top grade of club, even if only as country members.

In general, handicap competitions were looked upon with disdain and the ambition of all golfers was to become sufficiently good at golf as to be able to play against the best on level terms. The 'scratch' (handicap 0) man was all-important and the poorer golfers were there on sufferance, though their subscriptions were welcome.

There was, in fact, a good deal of snobbery, and the author can remember well, from the late 1920s, a prestigious club where all the members were lawyers, doctors, members of the armed forces, clergymen, members of parliament or gentlemen of 'private means', and anyone 'in trade' i.e. schoolmasters, businessmen and shopkeepers were either not proposed, or were blackballed if their names came before the Committee.

In fairness to the better golfers, they wanted to join the first grade of Golf Club because, in general, the first grade played on the better golf links, which they kept in good condition: good golfers were happy to join the second grade if they had a good course. For the most part, the third grade played on poor land for golf, could not afford an architect for the course, and were unable to keep it in good condition.

## Notable Men and Families in Golf in the Nineteenth Century

### James Ogilvy Fairlie (1810–70)

Fairlie, described by a contemporary as 'A handsome man, skilled at all manly exercises', lived at Coodham, about five miles from Prestwick. He was a Regular Army officer.

At what other 'manly exercises' he was skilled we do not know but, as a true blue landed gentleman of his time, he was no doubt a good shot, a good fisherman and a sound rider to hounds.

There is no question that he was a very good golfer; he lived in the times before there was an Amateur Championship but Lord Dalhousie, in a dedication to the 1866 *Golf Yearbook*, acclaims him as the Champion of Scotland as he had, in the same season, won the Gold Medals of the R&A, North Berwick and Prestwick, which suggests that Lord Dalhousie was probably right in his assessment.

He won the Gold Medal of the R&A in 1857 and 1862 and the Silver Cross in 1849, 1854, and 1860. At Prestwick, he won the Spring Medal in 1852, 1855 and 1859, and the Autumn Medal in 1862. He won the main medals at North Berwick on more than one occasion and George Carnegie, the North Berwick poet, in some doggerel verse wrote:

> Great Captain Fairlie! When he drives a ball,
> One of his best, for he don't hit them all.
> It then requires no common stretch of sight
> To watch it's progress and to see it light.

But Fairlie was much more than a great golfer; he was also a considerable administrator, in the best sense of the word. He was Captain of Prestwick in 1852, having been the prime mover in setting up the Club in 1851 and per-suading his friend, the Earl of Eglinton, to be the first Captain. It was Fairlie who persuaded Tom Morris to move from St Andrews to Prestwick and made him Keeper of the Green there. He was a friend and adviser to Tom who named his first son after his benefactor: James Ogilvie Fairlie Morris, later known to all his friends as 'JOF' Morris. Fairlie also introduced old Tom to the pleasures of smoking a pipe. He and Eglinton were great friends and Fairlie had taken part in the Great Tourna-ment in 1834. This was not a golf tournament but was the

**Colonel J.O. Fairlie**

last staging of a medieval jousting tournament in Britain. It was organised by Eglinton in the grounds of his house and was not a great success. Fairlie was Captain of the R&A in 1850 and of North Berwick in 1843. His brother-in-law was Campbell of Saddell, another great figure in early golf, who took part in the Great Match, as depicted by Charles Lees, and was a notable man for a wager on golf. Fairlie invariably stayed with him when in St Andrews, at his house, The Priory, in South Street.

Fairlie was an innovator in what might be termed the development of golf as a sport and tried to initiate a Golf Championship. His first effort was to suggest a foursome Championship in 1857 between teams from Golf Clubs; the reader may be surprised that this should be, at that time, the preferred form of Championship, but this was because, to golfers at the time, foursomes were the most important form of the game, bringing a team element into an exercise which was otherwise somewhat self-cen-tred. The scheme was put to both Prestwick and St Andrews and it was the latter who staged the first compe-tition, Fairlie being, quite properly, an important figure on the Committee which ran it. Mistakes were made. In the first place, it seems the R&A issued invitations to Clubs to enter, and invited, in all, thirteen Clubs of which one was Blackheath. While the implication is that all Clubs were invited, there were, at that time, thirty-three Clubs in existence and several of those such as the North

Manchester and Panmure which had not been invited were annoyed.

The second mistake was to call the tournament a Championship. Twenty clubs did not have a chance of playing; the Honourable Company, although invited, declined to play, and North Berwick, who did accept, arrived a day late and were granted a bye so that they could compete in the second round.

The foursome Championship was discontinued but Fairlie was not to be denied and he conceived the idea of a Championship for professionals, the majority of whom were what we would today call caddies.

Now Fairlie, who had put the idea to the R&A some years before and received little support, decided to run the tournament at Prestwick. Prestwick handled all the organisation and purchased a Championship Belt to be played for. Thanks to the vigour of Fairlie the first Open Championship was played for in 1860, and it continued to be competed for at Prestwick until 1870. It was fitting that, in the 1861 Championship, Fairlie was the leading amateur.

The invitations for this Championship were sent out by Tom Morris, Keeper of the Green at Prestwick, and the links were prepared for the Championship by him.

In 1897, J.O.R. Fairlie, J.O. Fairlie's son, was on a Committee at the R&A which was set up to consider the whole position of the R&A in relation to the Rules of Golf; it was on the recommendations of this Committee that the R&A ultimately became the governing body for the Rules of Golf in the United Kingdom and much of the world.

Fairlie deserves to be remembered and respected by today's golfers because he was an outstanding golfer of his time and, even more, because his foresight and administrative skills did much to develop the game along the right lines.

Fairlie had six sons, and all of them, according to Horace Hutchinson, were good golfers.

J.O.R. Fairlie was the Captain of Prestwick in 1891 and Captain of the R&A in 1893. W.E. Fairlie was Captain of the R&A in 1912. Of the other sons, Frank Fairlie was not only a very good golfer but was, also, of an inventive turn of mind and produced the series of 'Fairlie Irons'; these clubs had no shank, thus eliminating those distressing shots to which some of us are prone. He must have been a great benefactor to many golfers in the early twentieth century. That his invention is no longer of help to today's golfers is probably because the R&A have made such clubs illegal.

The Fairlies have been good golfers and played their part in about a century of golf and are entitled to be considered as a notable golfing family.

Finally, Mr David Fairlie, in the last few years has allowed the British Golf Museum to acquire a number of old and valuable golf clubs and balls used by the original James Ogilvie Fairlie and his sons, thus preserving a further link in the historical chain that bound the family of Fairlie to golf.

### Sir Hugh Lyon Playfair (1786–1861)

Before he was knighted, Sir Hugh was Major Playfair, a Regular Army officer. He was not born in St Andrews but at Meigle. His later education was at the University of St Andrews. He had served with distinction in the Army in India.

He retired from the Army in about 1848 and returned to St Andrews. He was a good and keen golfer and is the player putting in the painting by Charles Lees, 'The Great Match'. He was a man of decided views and great energy and he was soon bustling about St Andrews and being a very active member of the Town Council. He was also an eccentric, and designed and placed his tombstone several years before his death; his umbrella had 'Stolen from Major Playfair' engraved on the handle.

He devoted his energies not only to the R&A (then known as the Union Club because the archers and the golfers belonged to it) but also to the Town. As far as the Town was concerned he had to correct years of neglect and was responsible for removing dilapidated buildings, improving the sewage system and repairing the pavements, and it was for his work in these areas that he was knighted. He was Mayor of St Andrews in 1850 and was Captain of the R&A in 1856. As far as the links was concerned he did a lot of work on the area of the 18th fairway, which had been eroded by the sea and was very narrow. The 18th fairway was, at that time, also the first fairway and the 17th and first greens were the usual St Andrews arrangement of double greens. By building up the sea defences on the outer side he widened the fairway considerably and gained so much land in the area of the first that it became possible to have separate first and eighteenth fairways and to construct a new green for the first on the sea side, and separate from the 17th green. This move started the whole idea of separate fairways for each of the holes in the first and second nine and led to the general layout of the Old Course as it is today.

To Playfair, also, goes the credit for the R&A Clubhouse. The golfers of St Andrews had met and held their dinners in the Cross Keys Hotel for many years; Playfair was the prime mover in securing a site, not far from the present site of the R&A Clubhouse, and erecting there a purpose-built Clubhouse with lockers for the clothes of both golfers and archers, and a dining area. At a later stage they added a billiard room. All these ideas were largely those of Playfair and he did not allow matters to remain static for long for, in 1853, plans were laid for a new and larger Clubhouse on a site nearby and the foundation stone was laid in the following year 'with full Masonic honours'. It was in this year that Playfair resigned as Secretary of the R&A; nevertheless, he had seen the start of the new Clubhouse and had been one of those who promoted it. This Clubhouse, with some later additions, is the one which exists today.

When Playfair died, both the R&A and the town of St Andrews mourned the loss of a great benefactor. Playfair's portrait in oils hangs in the great room of the R&A Clubhouse.

## A.J. Balfour (1848–1930)

Balfour was an MP who became Secretary for Scottish Affairs and Secretary for Ireland in about 1886 and was Prime Minister from 1902 to 1905.

In his youth Balfour was a good tennis player while at Cambridge and was an exceptionally fine shot. His prowess at shooting stags was such that the Scottish ghillies regarded him with veneration and he held the remarkable record of having shot 28 stags without a miss on one occasion. Later in life he became a keen cyclist and did much to promote that sport also; in 1896 he became President of the Cyclist's Union of Great Britain.

Balfour did not come of an ancient Scottish family but his father had made a fortune in the Far East and, when he came home in 1817, he bought a house called Whittinghame, with land around it, in East Lothian, not far from North Berwick.

Balfour took to golf rather too late in life ever to become a great golfer but he set about learning the game with characteristic thoroughness. He had lessons from Tom Dunn at North Berwick and was a most competent handicap golfer, at his best when under pressure. In a speech he said that he was conscious of having thrown away, in his youth, a chance to take to golf which, had he taken it, would have made him a better player 'of the most difficult game that perhaps exists'.

He took on the two Secretaryships at a time when the affairs of Ireland were in a brutal and violent state; he tackled matters with calm, courage and decisiveness, and as a result was a popular figure and much in the public eye.

**A.J. Balfour, 1907**

As he was a keen golfer he took every opportunity to play, accompanied, invariably, by two detectives; he lost no opportunity, when circumstances permitted, to praise golf and extol its virtues. Horace Hutchinson, himself an important ambassador for the game, was of the opinion that Balfour's influence as a popular figure who played golf enthusiastically had much to do with the development of golf in Britain generally and in Ireland in particular.

At North Berwick, where he played a great deal of his golf, he was taken under the wing of a local caddie of some fame, a very large man, known locally as 'Big' Crawford, who had spent much of his carrying life as a caddie for wee Ben Sayers. Crawford directed operations on the golf links for Balfour and the two formed an inseparable partnership. When Crawford retired he took a small tent at the end of the links at North Berwick from which he sold drinks and things to eat. On competition days he would enquire whether 'Arthur' was playing; if he was, Crawford would run up a small Union Jack. On one occasion, Grand Duke Michael of Russia was playing at North Berwick in a competition; seeing the Union Jack he asked Crawford for whom it was flying, and was told, in no uncertain terms 'A better mon than you!'

In 1894, when Balfour was elected Captain of the R&A, he had a handicap of 13 but, shortly after, he brought his handicap down to 8. He was a golfing Scot and made no bones about it; in a speech at Chislehurst Golf Club in Kent he observed 'and I may be permitted to say without an undue exhibition of national vanity that I watch with satisfaction the gradual Scotification of England' and, later, 'the English have deliberately deprived themselves of what they are now beginning to discover is one of the greatest solaces of life'.

He made statements such as: 'A tolerable green, a tolerable day, a tolerable opponent, ought to supply all that any reasonably constituted human being should require in the way of entertainment'. He many times stressed the fact that people could go on playing satisfactory golf at a time when they would have had to give up most other games. On another occasion he said that if he had a choice he would choose literature before a political career and golf before both.

Such public statements, made by one who was a great public figure and who was not a notably good golfer, suggested to any who were considering taking up the game that it was well worth playing and that you did not have to be very expert to enjoy playing it. A golf boom in England was about to happen and Balfour was the man who triggered it off.

### The Earls of Wemyss

In 1896 the then Earl remarked to the Reverend John Kerr: 'The whole history of Gosford is golf'.

Gosford was the seat of the Earls of Wemyss but this had not always been so. In the sixteenth century it had been owned by the family of St Clair or Sinclair. St Clair has already been discussed in the history of early golf though the St Clairs of that time were living at Roslyn.

In the seventeenth century Sir Peter Wedderburn bought the Gosford estate and the Wemyss family acquired the property from him. It is often the habit to refer to a family by the property that it owns, and when Sir John Foulis refers, in his diary, in 1670, to 'playing golf with Gosfoord' he is referring to Wedderburn. As St Clair, Wedderburn and Wemyss were all golfers, it is true to say that Gosford was associated with golf from, at the latest, the 1500s, to the present day, and the Earl's remark to John Kerr was apposite.

There is documented evidence that James V of Scotland (1513–1542) visited Gosford frequently in order to play golf, although it must be said that he was much interested in three ladies who lived in the area of Gosford and it is not certain if he only played golf there. James would have felt safe there, for St Clair was a Scottish nobleman of Flemish origins, and next to his land was the property of Sir James Lindsay (now represented by the Earldom of Crawford and Balcarres), another Scot whose family originated in Flanders and who was a golfer. Not far away was Seton Palace, home of the Setons, again, of Flemish origins and golfers. They subsequently gave shelter to Mary, Queen of Scots who played golf there prior to her trial.

The Wemyss who is particularly associated with golf is of much later origins. He was born in 1817 and died in 1913. Before he inherited the title of Wemyss he was Lord Elcho. In his youth he was a great sportsman and a fine rider to hounds; later in life he became addicted to golf and played an important part in the development of the game in the vicinity of Gosford. Aberlady, Old Luffness and Gullane owe much of their origin to him and he was a regular player at Archerfield and North Berwick.

He objected strongly to the use of iron clubs, because they cut up the turf, and devised a club which would obviate the need for iron clubs; it was a wooden club with a

**The Earl of Wemyss**

brass sole. It had the loft of a modern No. 7 wood and was christened a 'Unionist' because it 'did not wear the green' – an allusion to Northern Ireland, where the Unionists were Orangemen and the Catholics' colours were green. The club did not gain favour and was used most at Luffness where Wemyss owned the land on which the Club played. In an after-dinner speech, Elcho spoke scathingly of 'a person called Mr Horace Hutchinson who presumed to write books on golf and advised beginners, when using an iron club, to take a bit of turf and was thus responsible for the terrible state of golf courses which now looked as if they all had bad smallpox'.

In a moment of poetic zeal Elcho wrote a poem about sport generally; about golf he had this to say:

Nor yet of golf, that gadfly game
That maddens even the most tame
I need not speak. For it is not –
Such the strange end of mortal lot –
The A-1 game King Jamie brought
To have the annexed English taught

A manly sport, a pastime true;
One that, if learned, they'd never rue?
Yet such the English want of sense
Or rather prejudice intense
That centuries have come and past
Until, by some strange chance at last
They've saved their race eternal shame
Through taking to the royal game.

Elcho, when he became Earl of Wemyss, in spite of his temperament and eccentricities, did much good for golf, encouraging, by example, the playing of it in the right spirit and, as a landlord, helping his local Golf Clubs, both financially and in the granting of land for their use. He continued to play golf until the year he died and, when he was over 90, played in a foursome with Harry Vardon and two others. When walking became a problem he used to ride a pony round the course, dismounting to play his shot. His efforts on behalf of golf deserve our respect and respect is due also to the only man who played golf with a feather ball, a gutty and a Haskell.

## The Balfour Family of Edinburgh

This family were not related to the Balfours of Whittinghame. The first golfing member of the family was John Balfour of Balburnie who was Captain of the R&A in 1842. His son, James Balfour, was playing golf in the early part of the nineteenth century; he seems to have been a better golfer than his father for he won several medals at the Club, including the Gold Medal on three occasions. Although he was never Captain of the R&A he has other claims to fame for in 1887 he wrote *Reminiscences of Golf on St Andrews Links*. In this charming little book he records what the links were like in 1842 and, among other interesting reminiscences, he describes the first occasion on which the gutta ball was played with. He became a member of the R&A in 1846, and when he died in 1898 had been a member for 53 years.

In 1893 he took the name Balfour Melville; John Whyte Melville, his cousin, had the misfortune to lose his only son during his lifetime. When Whyte Melville died the family possessions and the title went to James Balfour's brother, John. When John died, James come into the property and added Melville to his name.

James Balfour Melville had a son, Leslie, born in 1854, who, although he continued to use the name Melville, never seemed sure whether to put the 'Melville' before or after his other name and both spellings are recorded. He was a great sportsman and athlete and in later years became a great golfer. He had learnt to play when he was a boy but, having so many other sports to interest him, did not return to golf until later in life. His excellence at sports other than golf were considerable; he

played rugby for Scotland against England in 1872 and played cricket for Scotland from 1870 to 1910. He won the Lawn Tennis Championship of Scotland.

As might be imagined, he was a muscular man and he used his muscles on the golf links, being a very long and accurate driver; he was not a wild golfer, despite being a long driver but was, in fact, a very painstaking and deliberate golfer with great powers of concentration. Horace Hutchinson said of him that he bridged the gap between Hutchinson's generation of golfers and the younger men, so that he was a promising and dangerous opponent to the older generation and a well-established and equally dangerous opponent to the younger men.

Hutchinson is kind to him in his *Book of Golf and Golfers*. He was much taken with his driving abilities, to the extent of including an illustration of his position at the top of the backswing and observing that this is the proper position which everyone should copy. However Hutchinson is equally definite in stating that Balfour Melville's short game was weak; he also writes so much about his painstaking methods that one gets an impression that Hutchinson thought him a very slow and uninspiring golfer.

He was a successful golfer in the company of the best golfers in Britain. He was very much a St Andrews golfer and played nearly all his golf there. Between 1874 and 1892 he won 31 medals of the R&A, including all the more important ones; although he joined the Honourable Company of Edinburgh Golfers and won a number of their major medals, he did not play there much. In 1895 he won the Amateur Championship and in 1889 was runner-up. He represented Scotland against England in the International Matches in 1902 and 1903. In 1910 he was runner-up in the French Amateur Championship. In the Open Championship he was 16th in 1895 and 5th in 1888, being, on that occasion, leading amateur.

Not only did he play a lot of successful golf at the highest level, he also played an important role in the administration of the game. He was Captain of the Honourable Company in 1902 and 1903 and was Captain of the R&A in 1907; when Captain of the R&A he sat on the first Rules of Golf Committee.

It is evident that this Balfour family were influential golfers for about 100 years; it is such families as these which did so much for golf, in general, and by their example set standards of excellence; more importantly, it was they and their like who gave a lead to others in a sportsmanlike attitude to the proper playing of the game.

## Campbell of Saddell

Campbell was at the centre of golfing circles in the early part of the nineteenth century. He was no great golfer but was very keen. He was an eccentric, as so many landed gentry were at that time, and, with his fellow golfers, had a great influence on the manner in which golf was played.

Like many of his fellow golfers, he was, at least in his early days, a fashionable sporting man of his time and a noted and respected rider to hounds, even though above average height and well built. Like many of his contemporaries he was irascible and quick-tempered and somewhat pompous; as befitted a big man he had a fine resonant voice and was noted for the variety of his oaths on the golf course.

Saddell was a family holding and had been in the Campbell family for several generations. Campbell was a friend and close associate of J.O. Fairlie, who lived at Coodham in the Prestwick area, and in later years he became Fairlie's brother-in-law; as Campbell lived for many years at a house called The Priory, at St Andrews, his brother-in-law would stay with him there when he came over from Prestwick to play golf at St Andrews or North Berwick.

Both Campbell and Fairlie were close friends of the Earl of Eglinton, who also golfed at Prestwick, near where he lived. Eglinton also played at St Andrews and was a frequent golfer at North Berwick. At one time and another, Eglinton was President of Prestwick and North Berwick and a Captain of the R&A. These three men, and their many friends such as Whyte Melville and Playfair, must have played a lot of golf together and formed part of the close association of landed gentry who exerted such a great influence on the playing of golf and the formation of the early Golf Clubs.

At a time when ballooning was a dangerous experiment, Campbell achieved some fame by ballooning across the Firth of Forth from near Edinburgh to Fife.

During the time that he lived at The Priory he gave up most of his sporting pursuits and adventures and became a fanatical golfer of no great skill. He was a contestant in the Grand Match depicted by Charles Lees.

On one occasion, when playing a match against a rather slow golfer, he lost his temper when his opponent fussed about on the tee and tried several different places to tee up the ball, pulling up bits of grass and smoothing the area; after all that he skied his drive a short distance. Campbell exploded with rage: 'He takes more time to tee the ball than any three men, pulls up as much grass as would summer a hunter and, after all that he ends in an abortive puff!' One shudders to think what he would have said to the modern four to five hour round.

With Eglinton and Fairlie, he was a founder member of North Berwick Golf Club. In 1832, Campbell's contribution to the annual dinner was six bottles of whisky, and at a subsequent dinner he contributed twelve bottles of

whisky; Sir David Baird contributed thirty-six bottles of champagne. In 1842, Saddell lent the Club a portable kitchen for the dinner.

In later years Carnegie, a self-styled poet on the golfing scene, wrote of Campbell of Saddell:

> Still Saddell walks superb, improved in play.
> Still plays all matches – still is often beat.
> Still in iced punch drowns each defeat!

Campbell was the type of golfer who viewed medal play with contempt. For him a game of golf was a match, preferably a two-ball foursome, played for high stakes with a large number of side bets. As one was a sporting gentleman one played in that manner, and there was no need for complicated rules.

## John Whyte Melville (c.1790–1883)
### (See colour plate on p.144)

Whyte Melville was an important figure in the R&A. He was elected a member of the Club in October 1816 and was made Captain in 1823. It is known that a portrait of him was painted by Sir Francis Grant a few years later which shows him in the full-dress uniform of the R&A.

He was a very regular golfer and played three days a week, two rounds a day, until he was well over 80, whatever the weather. An example of his keenness and energy in playing golf is recounted by H.S.C. Everard. It seems that Whyte Melville had arranged a match with three other men at St Andrews; on the appointed day there was a gale of wind and a lot of driven snow. The three looked out from their respective houses and decided, independently, that this was no day for golf. As a result none of them went to the Club. Not so Whyte Melville: he drove down from his house in a dogcart, smoking his usual cigar and, not finding any of his partners in the Club, drove round to their respective houses and brought all of them to the Club to play the match that had been arranged. There is a nice sketch of him in the R&A, drinking a glass of beer. The picture is entitled 'Golf Extraordinary on December 10th 1880. 2 rounds in a gale of wind at 82!!'

In his later years, becoming tired of the long walk around the links at St Andrews, he took to riding a horse, dismounting to play each shot.

In 1820, Whyte Melville and Sir David Moncrieff made a bet on who would die first, the winner to present the Club with a silver putter on behalf of them both; Melville was the winner and duly presented the silver putter. When he presented it he said that, while he was sad to have won, he took some pleasure in honouring the bet.

He did a lot for the administration of the R&A and, because of this work, plus the fact that he lived to a great age, he was often referred to as the 'father of the Club'. He was one of the few men who were elected Captain of the R&A on more than one occasion. The second occasion was in 1883 but he died before he could take office; out of respect for him, the office remained vacant in that year.

## The Whigham Family of Prestwick

The Whigham family's first connection with golf occurred when David Dundas Whigham was elected a member of Prestwick in 1860. Whigham was originally a lawyer but later set up a successful wine business in Ayr, and he continued in that until he died.

He won the Autumn Medal of the Club in 1872 and was Captain in that year. He did not confine his golf to Prestwick and in 1884–5 he was Captain of the Honourable Company of Edinburgh Golfers. A beautifully detailed account of the family has been written by Mr D.C. Smail in *Prestwick. The Birthplace of the Open.* The author is happy to acknowledge that his details of the family is gained from this account.

David Whigham had five sons. All were golfers and distinguished themselves in different walks of life such as the Army, the Empire and, in the case of Henry James Whigham, as a journalist and writer in the USA. All the brothers were good golfers but Henry was certainly the best. Horace Hutchinson substantiates this in his *Book of Golf and Golfers.* Henry married the daughter of C.B. Macdonald. Macdonald was an ebullient and domineering golfer who figured largely in American golf after it restarted in 1888 at Yonkers. Macdonald was the first official US Amateur Champion and laid out the 'National' golf course on Long Island.

Probably because of his marriage, Henry Whigham lived much of his life in the United States and died there. He won the US Amateur Championship in 1896 and 1897; had he stayed in this country he would certainly have been a leading amateur here.

Another brother, George Whigham, won the Amateur Championship of India when working in that country.

The distaff side of the Whigham family were good golfers as well: Molly and Sybil Whigham were very important figures in early ladies' golf – both had a beautiful style. Molly was a noted long driver, having hit a gutty ball at Westward Ho! over 200 yards at successive holes.

This is only a sketchy outline of a family which

**David Dundas Whigham,**
*c.*1880

played an important part in the development of golf in the later nineteenth century, both in Britain and the United States, and is part of that nucleus of golfing enthusiasts in Britain which not only raised the general standard of golf in this country – and, in this case, in the United States – but also did much to maintain standards of behaviour and sportsmanship on the golf course which had been set by earlier generations.

## The Molesworths of Westward Ho!
### Captain George Frederick Molesworth RN (1824–1913)

Molesworth was the son of the Rector of Rochdale and came to live in North Devon when he took retirement from the Navy. He was a founder member of Westward Ho! and its third President. He had not played golf until he came to Westward Ho!

He was an eccentric and played golf with only three clubs and, usually, a dirty old golf ball. He and his three sons usually drove to the links at Westward Ho! in a horse and trap; Horace Hutchinson writes that the old Mole handled the reins in the same way that a sailor handles the rudder lines. The trap travelled at full speed over the bumps and ruts and only the luck of a sailor ever brought them to the old Iron Hut (which was then the Clubhouse) safely. The three clubs he called Faith, Hope, and Charity; Charity was the driver and Hope the (wooden) putter. The only iron club was a rather mongrel club, a cross between a rutter and a niblick which was called Faith because, as its owner was wont to point out, 'Faith can move mountains'.

He was affectionately called the Mole, partly because of his name and partly because a peculiarity of his golf was that he was incapable of hitting the ball to any real height; he was in fact a pretty poor golfer, until he got to the green, but he was a magnificent putter. He had another quality which stood him in good stead and which made up for his lack of skill through the green – he was a fierce competitor and always ready to back himself for £50 against anybody who was willing to accept the stake. He played many matches at Westward Ho! and many at Hoylake, to which he travelled regularly with other members of the Royal North Devon Club; he also played a number of matches at Wimbledon and Blackheath.

Molesworth did not only play ordinary golf matches.

As a great man for a bet, on one occasion, in 1877, he backed himself to walk three miles to the links and then play six rounds in under 660 shots, carrying his own clubs, afterwards walking home, all before dark. He attempted this feat in September, so he did not even try to do it on the longest day. He completed six rounds well within the allotted time but his total was over 660; nothing daunted, he played a further round which he did in 114. He then discarded the first round and was able to score under 660 while still getting home before dark!

Molesworth had three sons, Arthur, Reginald and George. George and Reginald were quite steady golfers but Arthur was a very good golfer and, at one time, had a handicap of +5 at Wimbledon (he was then employed in a London architect's office). He won many medals at Wimbledon and a number at Westward Ho! At Hoylake he won one of the more important medals when still a schoolboy.

Molesworth Senior issued a challenge to Mr Houldsworth, a member of Prestwick and the R&A (and a frequent visitor to Westward Ho!) that he and his three sons would play Houldsworth and any three players that he cared to choose a match at St Andrews and at Prestwick. The stake for the match is not mentioned but, knowing the old Mole, it would have been a large one.

The first match took place at St Andrews and Houldsworth picked a good team – Fairlie, Argyll Robertson, a doctor who was a renowned golfer and had won scratch medals at the R&A, North Berwick and many other courses, and Balfour Melville, also a great golfer, who was to win the Amateur Championship in later years. The match was played as four singles and was decided on total holes, each match being played to a finish. The Molesworths won, largely because of Molesworth Senior, who beat Houldsworth by 9 holes. In the return match, at Prestwick, the Molesworths again won and, again, it was largely because of Molesworth Senior, who beat Houldsworth by 10 holes.

They found no other takers for their wagers so, father being pleased with the way Arthur was playing, he backed him to beat Young Tommy Morris over six rounds at St Andrews, Tommy to give Arthur six strokes a round. In the first three rounds Tommy led Arthur by a comfortable margin but in the next three rounds Tommy romped away. The final three rounds were played in terrible weather, the course being deep in snow, so that only a small circle of snow could be cleared around each hole; one of the reasons for Tommy's easy win was that he could play pitch shots into the small circles around the holes (using his rut iron, no doubt) but Arthur Molesworth could not stop the ball. It must be said that Young Tom was really ill at the time and was only persuaded to continue playing in such weather because he did not want to let his backers down. A month later he was dead and it is possible that the last match that he played against Arthur Molesworth may have hastened his end.

The old Mole must be given great credit for continuing the traditions of matchplay golf and for travelling all over England and Scotland to do it.

These details of the part played both by distinguished and skilled amateurs, and by men of distinction who played golf, in shaping and developing golf in the second half of the nineteenth century, are only a part of the whole picture; the players mentioned are only some of the many who contributed. Among other notables are the following: Colonel Hegan Kennard, a gentleman who played over all the better known courses and was a member of all the more important golf clubs. Always well dressed – to such an extent that he was affectionately known as 'the dandy' – he was a good golfer and his name can be found on most of the honours boards of Clubs such as Royal Blackheath which was his home Club and of which he became Field Marshal, Royal North Devon, Hoylake, and St Andrews. He was a regular golfer from 1856 to 1910 and was a key figure in obtaining the prefix 'Royal' for Blackheath, Westward Ho! and Hoylake.

Admiral Thrupp was mainly a Westward Ho! golfer but travelled to Hoylake as well; as Captain Thrupp, he commanded a Royal Naval survey ship and, at one time, was surveying the waters off the coast of Western Australia. His ship went aground and had to wait for the next tide; during this time Thrupp found a golf ball in his cabin and immediately sent for the ship's carpenter and instructed him in the making of a driver. The driver completed, he had himself rowed ashore and played golf

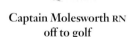

**Captain Molesworth RN
off to golf**

along the beach, claiming to be the first man to have hit a golf ball in Australia. It is not certain that he was right but, be that as it may, it showed the spirit of a true golfer. He liked the driver so much that he took it back to Britain and used it for some years at Westward Ho!

The families of Moncrieff and Moncrieffe were great supporters of golf both in Scotland and in England for several generations. They captained several of the more famous Clubs and played an important part in the administrative side, but were not distinguished for their skill.

Hall Blyth was a keen and very competent golfer in the early 1800s and once won a famous cross-country game against Willie Campbell (a professional) in the North Berwick area, which was where he golfed.

The Reverend John Kerr was a dedicated golfer and a man of some skill; he was the Minister at Dirleton for many years and was a golfer who played at most of the East Lothian links in his time. He deserves to be remembered, in particular, because he wrote *The Golf Book of East Lothian*, a most comprehensive and detailed book on all the East Lothian Golf Clubs and their history, which is one of the great history books of golf.

'Pendulum' Brown was one of the stalwarts of Hoylake and noted as a singer of songs in the back parlour of the Royal Hotel, a room which served as the Royal Liverpool Golf Club's Clubhouse in the early days. He was a fairly good golfer and was called 'Pendulum' because of a rather clockwork-like swing. On a moonlit night he made a bet that he would play the five holes around the 'Field' at Hoylake at an average of 5 a hole; his only stipulation was that the gallery should be absolutely silent after he had hit the shot so that he could hear where it fell. He accomplished the feat with a stroke or two to spare; on the next day, playing in the Medal, he took several more strokes at those holes than he had taken in the dark!

The list is endless but the foregoing examples serve to show that the early golfers had a good sense of fun, fair play and sportsmanship and were always willing to bet on the outcome of a match.

Scoreplay was not exciting enough and was viewed as a poor version of the real thing, a two-ball foursome was the proper form of golf and no one had heard of 'fourballs' – or wanted to.

These men developed a pattern of play and behaviour on the links, and they also had definite ideas about the 'nineteenth' hole and about all dining together after the day's golf.

One of the predominant features of golf in the early part of the nineteenth century was that the game was not only loved for itself, but was venerated and respected as was no other game, except perhaps cricket.

A good example of this respect is illustrated by what was written of Kennard after he died: 'He was renowned for playing the game for the game's sake; the best of golfing partners and the most courteous of opponents; always proud to be a winner, nevertheless, he did not consider this to be important and was wont to deplore, in later life, the loss of due reverence for the game that he had known in his youth'.

It is now time to leave the amateurs and turn to the development of professional golf in the latter half of the nineteenth century, in the course of which it will be seen how much the amateurs extended their sportsmanslike influence into the professional ranks.

Molesworth, determined not to lose his T. Dunn Driver, had his name stamped on the top of the club (as well as on the lead)

Clubhouse and members of the Royal Bangkok Golf Club, 1901

The eighteenth green at the Constant Spring Links, Jamaica, with Clubhouse in the background.
The 'green' is a very rough piece of grassland

# 10

# The Spread of Golf outside Britain

How did golf spread beyond Britain in the nineteenth century? Clearly, those parts of the world which constituted the British Empire were the areas in which, by reason of the Scots who went out, either as soldiers, to conquer and defend, as civil administrators, to establish law and order, or as businessmen, to trade and make money, one might expect golf enthusiasts to start playing.

That they did so, despite terrain and climates which were highly unsuitable, the fact that there were no club- or ballmakers within thousands of miles, and that the local inhabitants must have considered them mad, is a tribute to their enthusiasm and tenacity. Fortunately for these fanatics, the governing class in the Empire, while they might not be golfers, came from an island where golf was a recognised pastime, so that they indulged those who wanted to play. As most of the golfers were Freemasons, and a high percentage of Army officers, leading merchants and senior civil servants belonged to the same overseas lodge and were fellow Scots, they made no difficulties for them.

## The Start of Golf in the United States

Golf actually started in America in the eighteenth century, when America was a part of the British Empire. The terrain was not unlike that of Britain and the climate was good all the year round in Carolina, which is where it all began. In the northern part of America the winters were too cold for golf and in the extreme south the climate was too hot.

In 1743, the year before The Honourable Company of Edinburgh Golfers, the earliest Golf Club in Britain, was officially formed, David Deas of Charleston, South Carolina ordered from his brother, then in Leith, 96 golf clubs and 432 feather balls. The bill of lading for this shipment still exists, giving the name of the ship, the name of the consignee and the date of shipment. Unfortunately, the bill of lading does not give the destination of the ship, nor do we know the date of its arrival in America.

There will be those who will say that Blackheath predated the Honourable Company; this may be so but there is no proof of the existence of Blackheath, as a Golf Club, before 1766.

The Deas family came from Leith; it is clear that they were golfers and that David was pining to play and had found the local conditions suitable. Keen though he was, it seems in the highest degree unlikely that he would have required such a large quantity of expensive clubs and balls solely for his own use. The fact that David Deas was one of the earliest Provincial Grand Master Masons in America, and what we know of the connection between Freemasons and golf in Britain, makes it clear that the clubs and balls were going to be used by a Masonic lodge in the Charleston area. As similar Clubs in Scotland started in exactly the same way, it could be said that golf

**Clubhouse at Shinnecock Hills Golf Club, Long Island, New York, one of the oldest golf clubs in the United States, founded in 1891. The outside of the Clubhouse remains almost unchanged to this day**

at Charleston was the first organised golf in the world; unfortunately, because of Masonic secrecy and the destruction of all written records, such a statement would only lead to claim and counterclaim based on guesswork.

It must not be thought that this is the only bill of lading which suggests golf was played in America in the eighteenth century. In 1750 another bill shows that 72 golf clubs and 576 feather balls were sent from Glasgow to Virginia and, in 1765, 18 golf clubs and 144 feather balls were sent from Glasgow to Maryland. As with the Charleston shipment, it is safe to assume that such quantities were not for the use of one individual.

It is not possible to speculate further on the question of Masonic lodge Golf Clubs in Virginia and Maryland because, despite many enquiries from historical sources in the United States, the author has been unable to track down the name of the consignee nor the exact destination of the shipment within those States. In the matter of Charleston, although the Deas family have been contacted, they have been unable to shed any further light on the activities of David Deas in the field of golf; all that is known is that a later member of the Deas family, Colonel Deas, was proud of the fact that the family introduced golf into the United States. Research continues.

Clubhouse at Santa Catalina Golf Club, California, c.1902. This was a nine-hole course with a modest Clubhouse

**The Midlothian Country Club, Blue Island, Chicago, 1901. This Club had its own train which brought members to the Club from the city**

American evidence of early golf in the United States comes on 21 April 1799 from *Rivington's Royal Gazette* which advertises that a sporting goods shop has 'veritable Caledonian balls' for sale. There is also a notice in the *Charleston City Gazette* of 1788 reminding members of Golf Club anniversaries. An invitation to Miss Eliza Johnston to a Ball to be given by 'the Golf Club in this City' in 1811, has, fortunately, been preserved by the family.

In his admirable book *The Story of American Golf* Herbert Warren Wind mentions these indicators of early golf but dismisses the South Carolina claim 'because there is no further evidence and none of the implements have been found'. He concludes that the Charleston and Savannah Golf Clubs (which were known to have an early existence) were 'purely social'.

Evidence of Caledonian golf balls and of a Golf Club holding a Ball surely suggest that golf was actually played and the golf club and ball shipments now revealed, not only to Charleston but to Virginia and Maryland as well, strongly suggest that golf was being played, in an organised form, in the Southern States of America in the eighteenth century. The connection between Freemasonry and golf, with the secrecy of the Freemasons, is the reason why there are no records extant, and the fact that, by 1812, there was a War, during which all thoughts of golf would have disappeared and the Clubs been disbanded, is the reason why all the clubs and balls have disappeared as well.

The evidence that the Dutch played colf in the New York area is factual, but then colf is not golf and the reason that the Dutch played it is because colf was commonly played on ice in the winter in Holland and they were thus able to play in both winter and summer.

After a long gap, golf was resurrected at Yonkers in 1888. From the start at Yonkers, golf developed and

spread with great speed; the 'disease' had arrived and assumed epidemic proportions.

When Horace Hutchinson visited the United States in 1887, he reported that 'at that date there was no golf in the States'. He returned to America in 1888 and it was suggested to him that he should bring his golf clubs on that visit and show his host – and his friends – what sort of a game golf was. Hutchinson duly demonstrated, on Long Island, what golf was, having cut some holes with a carving knife. He played some shots and allowed his American friends to try, but he felt that his demonstration fell rather flat and said that 'the most favourable criticism that I can recall was that it might be a good game for Sundays'. Despite this cool reaction, his host did ask for some clubs and balls to be sent from England, and Hutchinson duly sent them.

As the United States had been sending hickory for golf shafts (and other purposes) to Britain for 50 years, it must have come as a pleasant surprise to Americans to find that some of the materials for golf clubs were actually on their doorstep, but they still did not know how to make such things and for some years relied on British imports of clubs and balls. The arrival of some Scottish professionals, together with American ingenuity and 'know how', soon solved that question. Indeed, within twelve years of the formation of the first Golf Club in America they had discovered a new and better wood for clubheads, a revolutionary and much better way of making golf balls, a different way of fixing the wooden head to the shaft of a club, and were exporting about 100,000 mass-produced clubs 'in the rough' to Britain annually.

They were no less vigorous in learning to play the game; the new Golf Clubs which were springing up all over the States required professionals to advise them about laying out and maintaining golf courses and then

Pittsburgh Golf Club, 1901.
Easily reached by trolley tram from the city and with a membership of 300

Quincy Golf Club, Illinois, 1901. A big brother of the 'cricket pavilion' style Clubhouses
which were common in Britain

Chicago Golf Club, Wheaton, Illinois, c.1903

**Clubhouse and caddies at the Kingston and St Andrews Golf Club, Jamaica, 1902**

teaching them to play. They lost no time in offering a good salary to British professionals to emigrate; this the professionals did in large numbers and many good golfers and apprentices from St Andrews, Musselburgh, North Berwick, Carnoustie, Westward Ho!, Dornoch and many other golfing centres in Britain, made the journey across the Atlantic.

On the golfing side, the immigrant professionals dominated the American Open and such other tournaments and challenge matches as were played, but the American golfers were determined and quick to learn and were rapidly getting themselves into a position where they could play the best in the world and win.

The tour that Vardon made in 1900 had a great effect on their progress in golf and was a remarkable success. He was recognised by them as the best golfer in the world

**Two Jamaicans, one a caddie and one a professional, playing the sixth hole at the Kingston and St Andrews Golf Course, Jamaica, 1902**

and they were going to get all the benefit they could from his visit. He travelled thousands of miles by train, playing matches and giving exhibitions and the Americans were so keen to see him that many shops in towns were closed for the day when he paid them a visit, so that everybody could watch; when he played in the vicinity of New York, the New York Stock Exchange was closed for the day.

## Start of Golf in India and the Far East

### India

When golf began in India 'India' included what is now Pakistan and India; in this account 'India' will include both countries.

Calcutta saw the first beginnings of golf in India. In the early 1800s India had become the jewel in the crown of the Empire; it was a huge country with considerable natural resources. After conquest, during the eighteenth century, Britain lost no time in despatching large numbers of civil administrators to establish law and order and these were quickly followed by businessmen, traders and plantation managers. A high proportion of the latter were employed by the East India Company which had its head offices in London. Although the Company was based in London, many of those who ventured overseas on its behalf were Scots. Inevitably, many of the Scots played golf and those who lived in London must have played at Blackheath – the only course in England until 1829.

If they played at Blackheath – and were members of the Blackheath Club – they would have been Freemasons. Many of the senior executives and major shareholders in the East India Company were members of Blackheath, and William Innes who is the figure in the famous 'Blackheath Goffers' print, as Captain of the Club, was a prominent figure in the Company and made his fortune from it.

**Top & above: Making the present Royal Calcutta Golf Course from very difficult terrain, 1911**

As the principal offices of the East India Company in India were in Calcutta, it followed that a high proportion of the clerical staff were employed in Calcutta, and traders and planters who were employed by the Company had, from time to time, to travel to Calcutta on business.

Those who wanted to start golf in Calcutta, coming, as many of them did, from London and Blackheath, even though they may have originated north of the Border, would have had the blessing of the Company and of Blackheath Golf Club and one would have expected that help and encouragement would come from there; in addition, as many of them were Freemasons, it was to be expected that the Golf Club in Calcutta would have been yet another Masonic Golf Club. The Masonic nature of the Club is revealed when, in the history of the Club, it is

**Golf at Calcutta, 1901. This shows the opening day of the golf season in November, with the Clubhouse in the background and the tent in which lunch was taken**

stated that all the Minutes before 1876 have been lost. The only indication that the club was formed in 1830 is a public announcement in the paper, which includes a list of the members. Among the original members – 29 in number – are many Scottish names, including that of Major H.L. Playfair, a member of that family, already discussed, who were the founders of Prestwick and had much to do with the start of the Open Championship Belt in 1860. Of the 29 members, 20 have military ranks, so it is clear that the army provided the major part of the membership at this stage.

The Minutes of the Blackheath Club confirm the newspaper announcement, stating that a Golf Club has been formed in Calcutta on 12 June 1830. Blackheath sent its very best wishes to the new Club and also sent them a copy of the Rules of Golf, as practised at Blackheath. In October 1833, the Blackheath Minutes record a visit from Major H.L. Playfair, whom Blackheath regarded as the founder of golf in the 'East Indies'. Since the early days, a copy of the Annual Minutes of the Royal Calcutta Golf Club have always been sent to the Royal Blackheath Golf Club. Blackheath Golf Club (for it was not Royal then) sent a fine Gold Medal to Calcutta and, a few years later, Calcutta Golf Club sent a magnificent Silver Cup to Blackheath. The Calcutta Golf Club, once having started, never looked back, although, as in other parts of the world, they had to move the course twice in order to remain outside the ever-enlarging city. The site of the original course was where Calcutta International Airport is now.

In 1876, it is recorded in the Calcutta Golf Club Minutes, that a Mr Letter is supplying 300 golf clubs and 'Mr Allan' is using his well-known talent to produce golf balls. There are two comments to be made on this state-

ment, firstly, that the 'Mr Allan' is not Allan Robertson (who had died in 1859) and, secondly, that the number of clubs to be sent to a well-established Golf Club which is increasing its membership, makes an interesting comparison with the numbers of clubs and balls sent to Charleston for David Deas over a hundred years before.

On the other side of India, a Golf Club was started in 1842 at Bombay. The foundation of this club is recorded in the Blackheath Minutes and the health of the new Club was drunk; Blackheath also sent a copy of their Rules of Golf to the Golf Club at Bombay.

In October of the same year Blackheath record that the Bombay Golf Club will play for the handsome Blackheath Gold Medal on St Andrew's Day. The Captain of the Bombay Golf Club was made an honorary ex-officio member of the R&A.

The Bombay Golf Club had a chequered career. At the start, the course was in a public park, consequently, they could not have permanent bunkers, and canvas bunkers were set up each day and taken down at the end of play. As with other clubs in the Empire, their land was constantly being encroached upon by town developments and there were times when the Club temporarily ceased to exist. It finally gave up the ghost, as a Golf Club with a course to play on, in 1947.

These two courses were the earliest courses in India but they were soon followed by many others. A course was started in Barrackpore in the mid 1880s and, in time, there were courses in the vicinity of many of the major Indian cities; they were, for the most part, laid out on unpromising land and were played on in a climate which at certain times of the year made them unplayable – nothing, however, can stop a true golfer from playing his game.

A sad little tale which illustrates the passionate devotion to the game of a keen golfer appears in a golf magazine in the early 1900s. A tea planter was a keen golfer but, living on an isolated tea plantation, with his nearest neighbour about 40 miles away across forest tracks, and there being no golf course within a hundred miles or more, he decided to make his own course. He set his workers to clear some forest in order to make a 3-hole course. He also wanted someone to play with, so he started teaching his houseboy to swing a golf club. The time came when the little course was finished and the houseboy knew something of the rudiments of the game; the following day was to be the great day. During the night there was an earthquake and most of the course disappeared. This disaster was discouraging, but not enough to stop a golfing enthusiast; the planter set the men to remaking the 3-hole course and, eventually, all was done. The next day was to be the great day. During the night the planter died of a heart attack (perhaps he got too excited?!); his faithful houseboy saw to it that he was buried beside the 3rd green.

The spread of golf in India proceeded at a great pace and, by 1912 there were 39 Golf Clubs listed in the *Golfer's Handbook*. There were Golf Clubs in most of the larger towns and near those towns which had a permanent garrison. There were many more than 39 in all; many were never listed in the *Golfer's Handbook* because they were very small. The author had experience of one at a small town in the United Provinces in 1943. The course was visited during the weeks before the hot weather really got started. The Clubhouse was a tin hut which provided one room in which to change and have a drink; as there was no ice-box the drinks were warm to hot. The course was laid out among sand and rocks, and there was no grass to be seen. The greens were sand greens and by no means smooth. There were no bunkers. It was necessary to have both a caddie and a fore caddie; the latter was of great importance, firstly because he could mark the ball; if the ball struck the side of a substantial rock it could ricochet off at an acute angle, and for a considerable distance and the bright glare of the sun would have made it impossible for the driver to follow it. The second reason for the fore caddie was that, when the ball landed on the ground, the local kitehawks would swoop down and make off with it; the fore caddie therefore had to leap after the ball and then cover it with, usually, one of the round tins which used, in those days, to contain 50 cigarettes. The fore caddie also carried the flag forward to the next hole; there was no question of leaving the flags in the holes for they would have been immediately stolen. On one occasion in the round (of 9 holes) when the author's opponent hit a drive, the ball struck a rock head on and it rebounded back over his head. Needless to say, the ball lasted about three holes, after which it was so damaged that it had to be abandoned and was gleefully received by the caddies as a present. How many members belonged to the Club remained a mystery. There was, of course, a war on at the time and no doubt all the usual members were otherwise occupied. Nevertheless, it seems highly unlikely that this little Club ever gained entry into the lists in the *Golfer's Handbook*. There must have been many like it which can be called monuments to brave and intrepid golfing enthusiasts, or examples of 'mad dogs and Englishmen', although, to be accurate, they were probably Scotsmen.

Illustration, dated 1845, showing the area in which the Royal Colombo Golf Club started in 1879

During the hot season, a passable climate and a reasonable terrain could be found in areas known as 'hill stations'. They were, for the most part, 5–7,000 feet above sea level and were more numerous in the Himalayan foothills but there were areas of upland in southern India which were equally pleasant. The most important area in the south was Ootacamund; in the north, Simla, Darjeeling, Mussoorie, Kashmir were well known and much used. In general, during the very hot weather, the British wives and families moved up to the hills while their husbands remained in the plains and continued their work. Nevertheless, when it became very hot indeed, the menfolk would move up to the hills and join their wives and families for a holiday. Naturally, many of them demanded golf; although the terrain was nothing like home, it was passable for a sort of inland golf and the trees and the cool air were a blessed relief from the heat of the arid plains.

The move to the hills was given official recognition by the Government of India and it was the habit of the Governor-General, senior civil servants, senior members of the Services, etc to remove to the hills in the hot weather, and govern India from there. As this exodus of the British Raj only lasted for about four months of the year, the Golf Clubs were temporary affairs. One course, in particular, a good 18-hole course, was at Gulmarg in Kashmir; at nearly 10,000 feet, it was one of the highest golf courses in the world.

## Ceylon

Known today as the Republic of Sri Lanka, Ceylon was previously a part of the British Empire. It was, and is, a beautiful island and many British lived there, the majority being involved in the tea industry. A Golf Club was started in Colombo, the capital, in 1879.

The site was a great 'maidan' called Galle Face Green – a large and relatively flat area outside the great fort. Unfortunately for the golfers, the area was used by many other sports as well and this led to difficulties. The initial support for golf came from the Scottish Regiments stationed there and they continued to play there in the early 1880s. Cricket, polo, rugger and tennis took up much of the area and a lot of ground was needed by the soldiers for marching, parades, etc. With the blessing of the Governor, Sir West Ridgeways, himself a golfer, they moved to some land known as the Model Farm, and laid out a golf course there. The first Committee contained F.A. Fairlie – Major Frank Fairlie – a member of the famous Fairlie family of Prestwick and a very good golfer.

Things were pretty primitive; there were flags in the holes but the greens were poor and as there was no real tee; it was customary to use a fairly level piece of ground near the green and then kick up a bit of turf to make a tee.

Although primitive, the course could provide exciting golf; there was a short hole at which a slice could land you in the lush grass of a cemetery, an area known to be infested with a large number of cobras. The greens were kept flat by using a roller; there were no bunkers because the military would not permit them. Many years later, a golfer who had known the old course was asked about the general layout. He could remember much of it but could not remember the exact position of the 18th green, but as when coming to the 18th he could remember how thirsty he was, he assumed that it must have been near the Clubhouse.

Fairlie was given a handicap of +15 at Colombo; he was a great sportsman and, in the true Corinthian tradition, played cricket and tennis; in the latter sport he became Ceylon Champion. In time, he set up another local golf course nearby.

The climate of Ceylon was more conducive to golf than the climate of India and there was no shortage of grass; many more courses grew around Colombo and a very fine course was developed at Nuwara Eliya in the mountains; the terrain was good and the climate pleasantly cool. The course became one of the best courses in the Far East and is still justly famous today.

The Hon. Michael Scott, in 1899, was a tea planter in Ceylon and won the Gold Medal at Nuwara Eliya; in 1900, he left Ceylon for Australia, where he became both Open and Amateur Champion of Australia more than once. He returned home and won the British Amateur Championship in 1933, at the age of 56, the oldest winner.

## Malaya

In the 1890s, British Malaya (including Singapore) was known as the Straits Settlements. Since independence it has been known as the Republic of Malaysia and this includes what used to be called British North Borneo but no longer includes the island of Singapore which is now an independent Republic.

A Golf Club was started in Singapore in 1891 and in Malaya in 1893, at Kuala Lumpur. It is generally believed that a Club started in Penang at about the same time as the Club in Kuala Lumpur but no records have been found. The Singapore Golf Club was in an area known as the Sepoy Lines; there was not much room and there were a number of Chinese cemeteries around which players had to steer a course; the site of the course is where part of the General Hospital of Singapore now stands and it continued to be used until the Second World War, even though the main course of the Royal Singapore Golf Club had long been in existence. As in other parts of the Empire, as the town encroached on the course and the golfers had to move further out. A fine

The Royal Hong Kong Golf Club, 1903. The Clubhouse is an adaptation of an existing building. The course was inside the race track in Happy Valley

course was made in the area around the McRitchie Reservoir; two other courses were also laid out. When the Second World War started there were three Golf Clubs on Singapore Island. The same pattern occurred in Malaya. The course at Kuala Lumpur had to be moved but in this case the move did not have to be made until 1920 and the new course was not far from the town. Today it is a fine course within the suburbs of Kuala Lumpur.

As in other countries, Golf Clubs sprang up near most of the major centres of population in the country and in 1912 the Straits Settlements boasted seven Golf Clubs. Many more were to follow and, as in India, there was a popular Club at a hill station – Fraser's Hill.

At the time of the Second World War the Japanese

were not golfers and they wrecked the course at Kuala Lumpur, planting tapioca, maize, etc on the fairways. The author was told by one of the many civilians captured at Singapore that after it fell, the civil prisoners were, in the early days, kept in the servants' quarters of the Club. At one early morning parade a Japanese officer said: 'Step forward all those people who were members of the Golf Club'. Nobody moved; after the parade there was much discussion among them as to what could be the Japanese motive in giving such an order. The prisoners finally came to the conclusion that the Japanese might wish to be taught to play golf and that, if they did this, the prisoners might get better conditions.

Accordingly, at the next parade, when the same request was made, all those who had been members of

The Shanghai Golf Club, 1902, showing a group of members with two caddies on the Clubhouse steps. The Chinese caddies were encouraged to play golf and there are pictures of a Caddies' Championship

the Golf Club stepped forward. They were all issued with digging tools and made to dig up the whole of the first fairway (420 yards) and plant tapioca.

## Hong Kong

In 1889 a Golf Club was started at Happy Valley, on the Island. The situation here was much the same as that which obtained in Ceylon. The Valley was a pleasant area of grass and was much used by other sports and by the services as an area in which to drill. Golf in Happy Valley became increasingly difficult and the Club acquired a new area for a course at Deepwater Bay, but this was only able to provide 9 holes and could only be visited by boat. The two courses continued until the Second World War; after the war, Happy Valley became even more congested due to the construction of a fine racecourse with corresponding buildings and the course at Happy Valley ceased to exist. The Club at Deepwater Bay still exists, but the centre of Hong Kong golf is now on the mainland about 20 miles from Kowloon, at Fanling. The course was first laid out in 1911 but has developed into three fine courses since then.

## Assam and Burma

Other golf clubs existed in Assam, at Shillong and Gorhat, and in Burma, at Rangoon. Many more were too small to be listed in the *Golfer's Handbook* and have long ceased to exist.

# Golf in the British Empire in Africa

## South Africa

After 1911, South Africa became the Union of South Africa and, later the Republic of South Africa. The start of golf in the area occurred while South Africa was a part of the British Empire.

It is fitting that the game first started in an organised form in Cape Province, in the vicinity of Cape Town; a Club was founded there in 1885. That it started at all was due to the golfing enthusiasm of General Sir Henry Torrens, Commander of the British troops at the Cape; he was so keen that he formed a Golf Club within ten days of his arrival. The terrain was poor and the greens were of gravel but that was no real deterrent. As the town grew in the area, the course had to be moved and eventually, in 1906, it moved to the site which it now occupies and where there is now a course (of grass) of the highest quality.

A Club started at Johannesburg in 1896; the rapid development of a prosperous mining town and the Boer War between them caused constant resiting of various

The Clubhouse, Deep Water Bay Golf Club, Hong Kong, 1901. This Clubhouse is described as a 'comfortable little Clubhouse where the best of luncheons can be obtained'

courses and there were ten moves before it arrived at the course which it now occupies.

Royal Durban Golf Club started in 1892 and was sited within the perimeter of the racecourse; it is still in that vicinity. A development, 25 years later, was the Durban Golf and Country Club which is some miles away and has a magnificent course, on which, many years ago, the author had the privilege of playing.

Golf Clubs were formed at East London, Adelaide, Rondebosch and Bedford between 1892 and 1896; by 1906 South Africa could boast many good golf courses.

## Rhodesia

Now the Republic of Zimbabwe; a Golf Club was formed at Salisbury (now Harare), in what was then Southern Rhodesia, in 1898; even earlier, a club was formed in Bulawayo in 1893.

## East Africa

A Club was formed in Nairobi in 1896, where the course was carved out of jungle. As in other parts of the world, the steady enlargement of Nairobi meant that a new course had to be found within a few years of the start of the Club.

A writer in 1929, who knew golf in East Africa in 1915, observed that when he arrived there were two courses of 9 holes in or near Nairobi, one at Muthiaga and one at Meru on the other side of Mount Kenya. He also mentioned that when the British moved into Dar-es-Salaam, in what was then German East Africa, in 1916, they found that the Germans had a golf course there. It was in good condition and he played on it but found it very peculiar because it had concrete greens. He remarked: 'A perfect approach shot which on an ordinary course would drop like a poached egg would keep on bouncing long enough for you to sit and smoke a pipe and one bright lad of my acquaintance got so fed up with the jumping of his ball that he drew his revolver and shot it on its forty-seventh bounce.' The British forces made some of the concrete greens into tennis courts.

## West Africa

In 1912, there were Clubs at Accra (Gold Coast, now Ghana), Assaba (Nigeria), Benin (Nigeria), Bonny (Nigeria), Sierra Leone (Sierra Leone) while, off the coast of Africa, St Helena where, nearly one hundred years before, Napoleon had been incarcerated, had a Golf Club with a membership of 40; it had 9 holes and a bogey (par) of 40. Temporary members were asked to pay 2s 6d (12½p) per month.

# Australia

THE earliest references in Australia to organised golf can be traced to the late 1840s – and the information is very sketchy. Reference to the Minute Books at Blackheath gives earlier information.

In October 1841 the Minutes record that a son had been born to the Captain of the New South Wales Golf Club, Alex Brodie Spark. That Spark took the trouble to inform Blackheath of the event can only mean that he had been a member of the Club or was well acquainted with many of the members, or was informing the Masons at Blackheath that he, a brother Freemason at the New South Wales Golf Club lodge, was blessed with a son. The latter is the most likely explanation, especially in view of the fact that Blackheath were so overjoyed at the news that they made Spark an Honorary Member of Blackheath on the spot.

On 15 May 1815, the Governor of New South Wales, Lachlan MacQuarie, had named a small settlement in New South Wales Blackheath. The area of Blackheath, in Australia, was described by MacQuarie's Major of Brigade, Captain H.C. Antill as 'a kind of heath but very wild scenery'. Antill was a golfer and had been stationed at Woolwich in Britain. Woolwich is close to Blackheath and it is likely that Antill would have played golf there.

Evidence is circumstantial but it is possible that it was Antill's idea to call the settlement Blackheath and that the New South Wales Golf Club was situated there; the fact that there are no records of this is not evidence that the Club did not exist. In 1909, an Australian Blackheath Golf Club was started at Blackheath village. That there was a New South Wales Golf Club and that its Captain in 1841 was Spark cannot be denied and this was probably the earliest Golf Club in Australia.

Apart from the New South Wales Golf Club, some of the earliest records of golf come from Tasmania. It is suggested that some golf was being played there as early as 1830 but the evidence is not definitive and, in any event, there is no evidence of an organised Golf Club there until 1900.

## Melbourne

There is evidence that there was a Golf Club there in 1847 – only twelve years after the town came into being. Founder members were Scottish immigrants from Fife and there were also several Scots from a Scottish Regiment stationed nearby. There are records enough to name the President, Secretary and Treasurer but no detailed Minutes of the activities exist, and any information about golf there can only be gleaned from the local newspapers. What is known is that the President was the Grand Master Mason of the Colony. There is no record of the existence of a Clubhouse but it is known that the members of the Club dined at a local hotel. Shades of the early Scots Golf Clubs and of Blackheath in England!

## Sydney

The origins of golf in Sydney are of a different nature and the start of golf there has been dealt with elsewhere in this book with reference to Allan Robertson and David, his brother, and the famous Royal Sydney Golf Club Collection. It was not until 1893 that the Royal Sydney Golf Club was formed; the Australian Golf Club, as a fully organised Golf Club seems to have started in 1895 but there are records of an Australian Golf Club which started and became dormant, going back to 1881 – or even before – but this is a matter of such concern locally that it would be highly inadvisable for an outsider to become involved!

## Adelaide

Here, the formal foundation of the Golf Club was in 1892 but, it is well known that a Club had existed in the 1870s. The members of this Club played in red coats and were regarded as snobs; there were flags in the holes but, generally speaking, it was no more than a pitch and putt course, like the St Andrew's course at Yonkers in America. The excellent history of Royal Adelaide tells us that: 'No formal records of the Club's affairs appear to have survived . . .'. All that remains is a record of the names of the President and the founder members and some of the Rules. The Club used the Mason's device for the election of members, the secret ballot box – one black ball among any five white ones meaning that the candidate was excluded from the Club. This was a useful device for excluding anyone who might, innocently, have been proposed for membership but who was not a Freemason. Instead of having to admit publicly that a non-Mason could not be a member, the candidate's name went forward but, provided a black ball had been dropped into the ballot box, he would not be elected and no one would know why.

There is the same pattern of events in Australia as in Britain and the older parts of the British Empire. First, attempts by the local Masonic lodge to emulate what they knew had happened in Britain, followed by later and better organised Golf Clubs. The difference between Australia and the other places discussed is that, whereas in Britain and India, clubs which were Masonic gradually gave way to clubs which had more non-Masonic members than Masons, in Australia, the old Masonic clubs disappeared and there was then a gap in golfing activity of up to thirty years before golf was resumed. This happened in America but that is easily explained by the War of Independence, followed by the Civil War, but there was no such state of affairs in Australia and, in that country, it is difficult to explain. Some in Australia consider that it was due to the great difficulty of getting clubs and balls (it took six months for such items to travel from Britain to Australia) but this cannot be the whole answer. Perhaps the explanation is that given in the fine *Centenary History of the Royal Melbourne Golf Club* where it is pointed out that: 'the discovery of gold in the 1850s caused a massive dislocation of the colonial society of the day – golf was merely one of the many activities pushed aside in the helter skelter'. In more prosaic language, and more to the point, the author states: 'There are few things that will drag a dedicated Scotsman away from the links – the fact that nuggets of gold are lying on the ground in paddocks not far away is one of them'.

## The Beginnings of Golf in New Zealand

Some individual golfers started to play where they could in the Otago/Dunedin area in the 1860s but there was, at that time, no progress toward a Golf Club. In 1863 gold was found in the Dunedin area and this put paid to any golfing activity. Once the fever had subsided, men from Scotland began to think about golf again.

One of the most active in this respect was Charles Ritchie Howden, born in Edinburgh in 1838. He had arrived in New Zealand in 1861 and worked in sheep runs in Otago. By 1870 he was a successful businessman in the whisky-distilling business.

Largely due to his energy and initiative some formal golf was started at Caversham near Otago; a Club was formed and Howden was the first Captain.

Originally, all clubs and balls were imported from Britain but there were two men in Dunedin who knew how to make clubs; both were Scots and they were soon in business.

Despite a promising start things did not go well and the course at Caversham disappeared; the City Council allowed the golfers to play at Mornington and there the Clubhouse was in Fogarty's Hotel, thus following, perhaps unwittingly, the pattern of so many of the early Masonic Golf Clubs. The golfers also followed the time-honoured habit of playing in red coats; unfortunately, play at Mornington became very difficult when the cows, which kept the grass short, were removed and the grass became so long that golf for much of the year was impossible.

An even more disastrous situation arose when, without any warning, Fogarty's Hotel went bankrupt and, in the ensuing sale of the Hotel contents the members' clubs, bundled together with string, were sold, without their knowledge, to a local man, for £1. By the time that they were retrieved they were useless.

At about the time of the Dunedin disaster, a Club was founded at Christchurch; it led a precarious existence and, at times, little or no golf was played there – but it still retained a name and an entity. It was finally resuscitated in 1891 by George Gossett, a local doctor who had come from England, where his father had been one of the founder members of Westward Ho! Gossett had learned to play golf there as a boy and was a competent golfer, representing Oxford in the first Oxford and Cambridge Golf Match. He was a boyhood friend of Horace Hutchinson, also of Westward Ho!

In his reminiscences, Hutchinson tells a story of George Gossett. He says that he went to play in a competition at a Club at Crookham, near Newbury in Berkshire; he had won the competition twice and was hoping to win it a third time as, under the rules of the competition, he could then have won the Cup outright and taken it home. He duly won and returned in triumph to Oxford. He travelled by train and had to change trains at a rail junction. When he got out of the train he saw George Gossett standing on the platform with his golf clubs; he asked Gossett where he was going and George said that he was going to Crookham to play next day in a competition because he had, in the past, won it twice and hoped to win it a third time, in which case he would be able to keep it. Hutchinson continues: 'Oh dear, I had to reply, I'm sorry but I am afraid that you must have made a mistake in the day. It's today it was played for and I have won it for the third time, so it is now mine, I'm afraid . . . I opened the case and showed it to him. I was obliged to tell him because it would have been worse still for him if he had gone all the way to Crookham to find he was a day behind the fair. As it was, it was a cruel tragedy for him but a comedy for me. No man ever took a knock more pleasantly; he was the first to start a laugh against himself and to give me congratulations and express gratitude for being saved the journey to Crookham. So he took train to Abingdon and I to Oxford, and shortly after, whether as to the effect or no of this blow, he went out to New Zealand, where he won the Championship of that country more than once.'

In 1893 the first New Zealand Amateur Championship was played at Otago. Gossett won the Championship in 1895, but it was his only win, so Hutchinson was not correct. New Zealand golf was now a well-established fact and has gone on thriving ever since.

Howden has been mentioned as the father figure, quite rightly, but, in later times, the Gillies family deserve mention. Judge Gillies had four sons; C.E.S. Gillies was a very good golfer from the Auckland area who acquitted himself well in New Zealand and won the Australasian Championship in 1899. One of his brothers, Harold, is not so well known in New Zealand because he spent much of his life in England. He was a great surgeon and is entitled to be called the father of plastic surgery; among his successors he trained Archibald MacIndoe who became famous for his skill in reconstructive surgery in the Second World War and after. He was also a considerable golfer – in 1912 he had a handicap of +3. He reached the sixth round of the Amateur championship in 1907

and the fifth in 1910. He represented England against Scotland in 1908 and was runner-up in the South of Ireland Championship in 1907. For a man who led a very busy life as a surgeon (with therefore little time for practice) this was no mean feat.

Harold was a considerable character with a great sense of fun and was well known among his contemporaries as a great practical joker. At one time, as a joke, he used an eighteen-inch hosepipe as a tee and on another he drove off the top of a beer bottle; he was such a good golfer that watchers thought that this would improve their play and the R&A and the US Golf Association, in the end, had to legislate against it. He was a member of the R&A and on one occasion played a practical joke on the night before the Autumn Medal when he persuaded people to play up the first and last holes in the dark and then loosed off rockets and whiz bangs all over the fairways to the great amusement and surprise of about 3,000 spectators, some of whom fell into the Swilcan Burn.

It was Harold who saw the possibilities of land at Hamilton and spent large sums of his own money in making a golf course there, which he then presented to the local community at a very low rental. The course was entirely designed by him and despite some alterations over the years has remained much as it was and is one of the best golf courses in New Zealand.

There is a fine painting of one of the St Andrews holes done by Harold Gillies in the 'back parlour' of the R&A Clubhouse.

Golf at Pau: those playing are *(left)* Sir Victor Brooke and *(right)* H.E. Kennard

The Clubhouse at the Paris Golf Club, La Boulie. The course was laid out in 1901 by Willie Park Junior

# The Beginnings of Golf in Europe and around the Mediterranean in the Nineteenth Century

## France

France was the first country in Europe to start organised golf and it was, as usual, the British who introduced it and played it. Pau Golf Club was formed in 1856; Pau is in southwest France, close to, and sheltered by, the Pyrenees. It has an excellent climate in winter and was one of the favoured spots for wealthy Britons who wanted to escape the British winter.

As far as the playing of golf in France is demonstrated by orders for golf clubs, as in the evidence for the start of golf in America, there is an interesting aside concerning the wine trade in France. A Mr Richards, wine merchant in Pall Mall, wrote to *Golf Illustrated* in August 1901 as follows: 'It may interest you to know that, in looking through an old account book of my firm in the eighteenth century, a few days ago, I found the following charge made by the then partners of the firm, Messrs Chalie & Dolignon, against their Bordeaux representative, with whom they had a cross account: 'June 30th 1767. By cost of golf balls and clubs. £1 11s 6d.' There may not have been a golf club in France at that time but, clearly, someone was playing golf.

The wine business between Britain and France was flourishing at that time and Golf Clubs must have been among the better customers, judging from the amount of claret that they regularly consumed. One is left to wonder whether someone from Britain, working at the Bordeaux end of the wine trade and a golfer, wanted to play in France and introduced the French to the delights of the game, or whether a French member of the firm who had travelled to Britain and seen golf at Blackheath or Leith, decided to play on his return to France.

There is a legend, which may be based on fact and is certainly plausible, that some golf was played there towards the end of the Peninsular Campaign, in about 1812. Pau was an area used for convalescence for sick and wounded and the legend says that some soldiers played golf there. While this may be true there is no suggestion that a Golf Club was formed at Pau at that time.

Once the British started wintering at Pau it was inevitable that they should wish to play golf, among other sports. The countryside was quite suitable for golf (and also for hunting, which flourished). One of the leading spirits, and a founder member, was Colonel Hutchinson, Horace Hutchinson's uncle, who was to be a strong supporter of Westward Ho! and was a competent golfer. In 1857, the Duke of Hamilton gave the new Golf Club a Gold Medal to play for.

As both ladies and gentlemen wintered in Pau, the ladies were introduced to golf as well (it was a young American lady, who had wintered in Pau and learnt to play golf there, who returned to Boston and introduced the Bostonians to golf); the exact date on which the ladies started to play golf at Pau is not known but it is quite possible that the earliest organised golf for ladies began at Pau and not at either St Andrews or Westward Ho! The Club at Pau was a purely British organisation; the Secretary was British, as was the professional, a man called Lloyd who came from Liverpool.

In 1888, a Golf Club was formed at Biarritz, inevitably by the British, and the course there is described in general terms by Horace Hutchinson, who played there within two years of its formation. He describes golf at

Biarritz thus: 'Some of the most curious and amusing golf to be played that a man could meet with – up and down immense cliffs, in lies that were unspeakably bad, and yet, withal, the whole making, by some extraordinary means, not only an interesting species of golf, but also a species that has produced some fine players'.

In 1894, Lord Kilmaine gave a Cup for an annual match between Biarritz and Pau which Hutchinson, who took part in it more than once, describes as a very joyful and happy social occasion.

Of the many fine players that Biarritz produced, none was more gifted than Arnaud Massy, who won the British Open Championship in 1907, the first player from the Continent of Europe to do so – and that at a time when the Great Triumvirate were in full flow.

Massy was the professional to a famous, and early, Golf Club in France, La Boulie near Versailles. This course was laid out by Willie Park Junior and was a good test of golf; it was the first entirely French Club and by 1912 had a membership of 830. By that year, there were 45 courses in France; four principal courses were to be found in places where the British wintered – Pau, Biarritz, Nice, and Cannes. Apart from La Boulie, the remainder were near the Channel coast – places such as Wimereux, Dinard, Le Touquet and Etretat, where many British liked to play in the summer and which were easy to get to from London. Special trains and channel crossings were available, so that it was possible get to Le Touquet in four hours from London. All these Channel coast courses were organised by the British and both Secretaries and professionals at these clubs were from Britain.

### Belgium

Six men from Britain formed a Golf Club at Antwerp in 1888. The club still exists as the Royal Antwerp Golf Club but the original course has long disappeared. By 1912, there were seven Golf Clubs in Belgium, those at Knocke and LeZoute being of a links character.

### Germany

Golf was brought to Germany by the British. The German health spas were famous and the British aristocracy took full advantage of them; they offered much for aches and pains, gout, and the result of over-eating, but they did not, initially, offer golf.

In 1891, General Duff of the Brigade of Guards, a Scot, decided that there were so many keen golfers visiting the Spa at Bad Homburg that it would be worth starting a Golf Club and he did so.

The Prince of Wales, though a very poor golfer himself, supported golf in Britain; both as Prince of Wales and, later, as Edward VII he was a regular visitor to Bad Homburg. As a result of such Royal Patronage, Bad Homburg became a resort par excellence for members of the British Royal Court and it became fashionable for both ladies and gentlemen to play a little genteel golf on a short and well-mown golf course with very few hazards. Two more Golf Clubs were formed in 1895 and, in 1899, a better course was laid out at Bad Homburg, which, by this time, had a large membership, most of whom were from Britain and played there only when they came to take the waters.

### Italy

Rome had a large international community and, at the end of the nineteenth century, the British representation was considerable. In 1903, a Golf Club was formed near Rome by the British. A second Club was formed by them at Menaggio and Cadenabbia on Lake Como, in 1907.

The Club at Rome was visited by J.H. Taylor on two occasions. He has this to say of the course: 'There is not a single obstruction on the whole course made by the hand

Golf at Le Touquet, *c.*1905

**Ostend Golf Club, 1903**

and the cunning of man. The problems that are to be solved are presented by the Lord of the Universe and are more intricate and more subtle than would be the puny efforts of men's minds.

'My knowledge of Roman history is not so sure that I can say what the ground was used for in bygone days but whatever took place there it does not need a very vivid imagination to conjecture that a golf course was its ultimate end. The ground is very rugged in places, undulating and inspiring. There is not a single hole of the nine that has its counterpart in the other eight. Every hole has

its own particular features and each one demands the players' undivided attention. To one who is a student of Roman history and a reverent admirer of things that will last to the end of all time, it is somewhat of a task to focus the mind when playing golf at Aqua Santa.

'At every turn of the eye one's mental vision is stimulated, and one is reminded that all around historical associations abound. Playing to the eighth hole it is quite an easy matter to slice one's drive on to the Appian Way that St Peter trod, as we are reminded in the Book of Holy Writ. Again, we see the remains of the noble aqueduct

**Golf at San Remo, Italy, 1907**

that was built to convey water into Rome from the Alban Mountains and we are given, as a direction for our stroke, the tomb of Cecilia Martella.'

Other accounts suggest that it was not a great course; it is clear that Taylor, who was a great reader and student of history, was somewhat carried away by the course's magnificent historical associations. How many golf professionals in 1913, rising from the ranks of the caddies, as Taylor did, would have shown such appreciation of the history surrounding a golf course and how many would have been capable of writing such fine English to describe it? Apart from golf, 'J.H.' was a cut above his contemporaries.

## Austria

A Golf Club was formed in Vienna in 1901. The course was laid out by Willie Park Junior; the Secretary and professional were British, as were most of the members.

## Denmark

There was a Golf Club in Copenhagen in 1898.

## Holland

A Golf Club was formed, by the British, at Utrecht in 1894 and at Rosendaelche in 1895.

## Portugal

A British Golf Club was formed in 1890.

## Spain

The first Golf Club in Spain was opened at Las Palmas in the Canary Islands in 1891. It was an entirely British institution and the course was much used by the British when they wintered there.

# The Start of Golf in the Mediterranean Region

## Gibraltar

The early golf here, in about 1885, was played in the area of Algeciras. As might be expected in a town which was mainly a naval base, the Royal Navy had a big hand in this. The Golf Club and course were at Campamento, which was most easily approached by sea from Gibraltar. Naval personnel were allowed to use small naval craft to get there; civilian members were allowed to use these little ships when the Fleet was in port but on all other occasions they had to hire local boats.

How long this Club remained in being is not clear but, by 1914, soldiers, sailors and civilians were playing on the Rock itself. The course was popular but golf there would have made those who played in Scotland recoil in horror. It was played on a very limited area of land which was mainly gravel with a little grass; the course was so constricted that a powerful drive would either land in the sea or in a part of the fortress from which it could not be retrieved. Part of the ground was occupied by a cemetery and the ubiquitous goat was prone to eat the golf balls. A third problem that the golfers faced was Spain, for a wayward drive could cross the Spanish border and the player would either have to go through official diplomatic channels to get his ball or bribe one of the sentries to look the other way. During hot weather play was confined to 6–8 a.m. or 7–8 p.m.

## Malta

That keen and energetic golfer General Torrens, who started the first Golf Club in South Africa within ten days

**Sand putting greens in the Sudan, c.1920**

of his arrival there, subsequently founded the first Golf Club in Malta when he became Governor-General in 1888. Golf here was played in conditions which were, if possible, worse than those in Gibraltar. Again, Malta being a naval base, the sailors had an important role among the members. The course was situated entirely within the ditches and moats around the island's fortifications. There were no putting greens because there was no grass, the greens were patches of concrete covered with a thin layer of sand and tees were also patches of concrete. The course was described by those who played it as very winding and there was much 'local knowledge'. Ladies were keen golfers on this course.

By 1912, there were two more Golf Clubs on the island; these, being near Army bases, were predominantly military; they approximated more to true golf courses and one of them had 18 holes.

There were plenty of Maltese caddies; their comments on the game were frank and basic as they had learnt all their English from the barrack-room soldier. Clubs and balls were procured from Britain and were expensive.

## Nice and Cannes

By the 1880s the Riviera was well established as the fashionable place for the British to winter; other nations soon followed, Russian and French 'society' being prominent. As far as practicable the British took their sports with them and one of these was naturally enough golf. However, as in Germany, the golf was of a genteel character; it was desirable to be seen on the course, elegantly dressed and in the right company. Golfing ability had a very low priority.

In 1901, Grand Duke Michael of Russia founded a Golf Club at Napoule. The Course could be reached by rail but the wealthy and fashionable usually made the journey by the newly invented motor-car. A condition of play was that golfers should wear scarlet coats.

## Egypt

The dates of origins of the various Golf Clubs in Egypt have not been discovered but it is probable that Golf Clubs started in about 1890. Often the golf course was part of a much larger Sporting Club which offered many other facilities.

In 1912, the Alexandria Sporting Club had 600 members and the Cairo Khedival Sporting Club 900. The Gezira Sporting Club had 750 members. The Secretaries and professionals were British and the membership was predominantly British too, many members being from the Armed Forces. A note about the club says that 'Rubber or rope-soled shoes are necessary as the course is on sand'.

A Golf Club existed at Suez in 1912 and is described as 'A typical sand course abroad'. Extracts from a description of the course are of interest in indicating what sort of golf a sand course provided. 'There are only nine holes but plenty of variety; not a blade of grass is to be seen from the first stroke to the last. . . . The rough is heart-breaking sandcups and ruts. . . . The third hole has a buttressed line of dried reeds, 10 feet high and 30 yards long to drive over. . . . There are several conditions detracting from good scoring to be taken into account – the clean "get away" necessary on sand, the punishing rough, the frequent heel-pits and the glare of the sun off the sand. . . . Also, the greens, though wonderful in their uniform goodness . . . require much judgement and knowing, especially on a breezy day, when the volition of the wind alone will roll a ball off the green.' Of a course further south, in the Sudan, it is simply stated that there is no professional and that the course is 'a 9-hole course in the desert'.

In 1931, the Port Said Golf Club stated that the professional and record holder was 'A. Goebbels'!

Accounts also exist of golf in Mesopotamia, Mauritius and other places.

## The Start of Golf in Canada

FROM the very beginning of its colonisation Canada had a high percentage of Scots. As with other parts of the British Empire, there were soldiers, civil service administrators and traders and business people; many of the Scots entered the fur trade but there were Scots in the Army and it is rumoured that some of them brought golf clubs and balls with them but, alas, there is no documentary evidence of this. There is documentary evidence of another kind; in 1824 a Montreal newspaper carried the following notice: 'To SCOTSMEN – A few true sons of Scotia, eager to perpetuate the remembrance of her customs have fixed upon Dec: 25 and Jan: 1 for going to the Priests Farm, to play at golf. Such of their countrymen who choose to join them will meet them before ten o'clock am at D.McArthur's Inn, Hay Market. Steps have been taken to have clubs provided.'

The first organised golf in Canada was at Montreal; this city was an important port and an important communications centre. There was no links land but the terrain was very suitable for an inland golf course.

By 1867 Canada was no longer a 'colony' but a Dominion. Nevertheless, it still had a Governor-General who hailed from Britain and Britain had a considerable say in its affairs. In 1873, eight men sat in a dockside area of Montreal and planned to set up a Golf Club there. One of the prime movers was Alexander Dennistoun, born in Edinburgh in 1821; he had played golf around Edinburgh in his youth and was familiar with the organisation of a Scottish Golf Club. He came of an ancient Scottish family and may well have been a Freemason. He was ably and actively supported by the two Sidey brothers, also Scots.

The Club got off to a good traditional Scottish start and played at Fletcher's Field, a park area at the time in Montreal. That they found this site was largely due to the Sidey brothers who had hit golf balls in that area for some years and knew the local farmer well. Aided by Dennistoun's ideas of a Scottish Golf Club the members were introduced early on to the idea of red coats for play and, by 1881, they were the proud possessors of a Silver Club to which balls were attached annually. Dennistoun gave them a Gold Medal to play for but made it known that he desired to be the first winner and he proposed that he should enter and be given a bye into the final in which he was to be the only competitor – he must have imbibed the idea of the Queen Adelaide Medal of the R&A, of which the winner, who is the only competitor, having driven off the first tee, then becomes the Captain for that year!

The Club suffered, as the old Scottish Clubs had suffered, by having to play on common land to which the non-golfing public had free access; this made the idea of red coats practical, as it had, years before, in Britain. Later, the club was forced to move further out of a rapidly growing city and, in 1959, had to move, yet again, to the site that they presently own on Ile Bizard.

From the point of view of climate, Canada had problems which the southern States of America did not have to face. The Canadian winter, at least east of the Rockies, is not conducive to golf. From November to April, generally speaking, golf is not possible because of snow and ice; these seasons, however, are not fixed and vary from year to year – there are even records of golf being played in January! When the author was playing at Mount Bruno, a fine golf course (laid out by Willie Park Junior) outside Montreal, he asked one of the members when play stopped for the winter. He was told that there was no fixed date – 'when the flags are so stiff that we cannot bend them, we reckon it is time to stop!'

Quebec was the next course after Montreal and at short intervals thereafter Golf Clubs sprang up close to most of the major cities in Canada. Curiously, considering the climatic advantages of the Vancouver area, the beautiful Golf Course at Capilano was not laid out until the 1930s.

Canada now has many fine golf courses and, thanks to easy air travel, if the courses have to close in winter, the members can, like migrating birds, wing their way south to Florida or California and exercise their passion there.

The enthusiasm for golf in Canada is exemplified by an account in *Golf Monthly* of 1924 which tells of one, Inspector Hall of the Canadian Mounted Police, who found himself stationed at Herschel Island, 200 miles inside the Arctic Circle. The course that he played on there was believed to be the most northerly golf course in the world – and the worst; it had the added distinction that it was only ever played on by two men, Inspector Hall and Bishop I.O. Stringer of the Yukon Territory. The Inspector was a great golf enthusiast and found it hard to believe that no one else would want to play but, sadly, his constables disillusioned him. Hall therefore played by himself but, on one occasion he persuaded the Bishop to play with him; the Inspector won easily but, as the Bishop said, Hall had had long practice on a course on which no Christian should play. Hall could not play all the year round because of the terrible weather, the area was subject to terrific winter storms during which no one could venture outside; the buildings had no windows and daylight entered through a glass panel in the roof; paper was pasted over all keyholes because the snow would, otherwise be driven through them. The supply ship came once a year; before it came, Hall's golf season had come to an end – not because of the weather but because he had run out of golf balls!

## Argentina

Mungo Park, Willie Park Senior's brother, was a seaman and a great golfer; he had a wanderlust and but for this he might have won more than one Open Championship. Some of this wanderlust must have been passed on to his son of the same name and, to a lesser degree, to his other son, Willie Park Junior, who certainly showed a willingness to travel in pursuit of his business as clubmaker, golf architect and golfer. Mungo Junior went to the Argentine as part of his travels. He did not start golf in Argentina because there were no less than six courses there when he arrived. It is possible that Mungo Senior had been there before him and had got things started, but there was a large business community in Buenos Aires, which included many Britons, and it may have been their enthusiasm which promoted the game. Mungo Junior arrived in Argentina in 1901 and completed the good work. He set up as a professional and was much helped in his work by his wife, who was a good golfer. Mungo won the Argentine Open Championship and his wife won the Ladies' Championship. The principal Golf Club in the Buenos Aires district was the Mar del Plata Golf Club. In 1900 it had a membership of 48; by 1903 there was a membership of 93. In 1907, the Club boasted 300 members, of whom 100 were ladies. The

**The Clubhouse at Kobe, 1905**

professional was Jack Park, yet another member of the Park family. The Club was highly organised and much had been done to improve the course. Jack Park had laid out a further nine holes and a fine watering system had been installed. The size of this Club is accounted for by the fact that the Argentines, both men and ladies, took to golf like the proverbial duck to water and an Argentine Golf Club in 1907 contained a high percentage of Argentines. The subsequent development of golf in the Argentine, during which it has produced a number of golfers of the very highest quality, seems to support the idea that they have a natural affinity for the game.

## Japan

THE first Golf Club in Japan was the Kobe Golf Club which was sited at the top of Mount Rokku near the great seaport of Kobe. The course was at about 3,000 feet and this made it pleasantly cool in the summer but meant that play could not continue during the winter.

It was formed mainly due to the efforts of three Britons – Mr A.H. Groom and two friends. Groom was a tea merchant who came to Kobe on a visit and decided to stay there. He married a Japanese girl and settled in Kobe for the rest of his life. He was a keen mountaineer and took to climbing Mount Rokku; he enjoyed the mountain greatly and, in the course of time, built a holiday bungalow there.

In 1901, Groom and two friends decided to build a golf course on the top of the mountain and, in 1903, a Golf Club was started. The course initially consisted of four holes, which became, two years later, nine holes. The greens were of sand and very difficult, especially in the very windy weather which was not infrequent there.

The enthusiasm of the British for golf was a puzzle for the Japanese and some of them thought that golf was a form of gambling. Getting to the Golf Club was not easy, since it involved a climb up the steep mountainside which took about one and a half hours. It was possible to get there by rickshaw and it took four strong rickshaw men to get one European up to the course; many of the rickshaw men, anxious to earn a little extra money while they were there, became caddies.

The Japanese did not have a natural affinity for golf, unlike the Argentines, and were a little hampered by their physical build, but in no time at all they were keen, if inexpert golfers, and their willingness to practise and work on their game suggested that, given time, some good golfers would emerge.

The rapid development of golf in Japan was difficult due to the facts that, in the early days, golf was a rich man's game (there was a very heavy tax on imported golf clubs) and that much of Japan is hilly. The flatter areas were heavily cultivated and it was difficult to acquire land for golf courses; nevertheless, Japanese men and ladies were playing golf by 1905.

Left: Caddie at the first golf
course built in Japan, Kobe
Golf Club (Rokkosan), 1903

Below: Sand green at Kobe,
1905

Royal Selangor Golf Club, Kuala Lumpur, 1992

Royal Colombo Golf Club, Sri Lanka

Golf at Pau. Oil painting by Allin C. Seeley, 1893

'Crossing Jordan': Pau Golf Club. Watercolour by Gordon Grant Smith, 1892

Philp putter used as a trophy at the
Royal Singapore Golf Club, *c.*1959

Golf at Biarritz, *c.*1880

Above: Golfing advertisement for a course in Tunis, 1920s

Below: Golfing advertisement for Le Coq sur Mer, 1898

Above: Clubhouse at Kobe, *c.*1905

Below: Interior of the Clubhouse at Kobe today

Ladies Golf at Westward Ho!, 1868

Ladies Golf at Westward Ho!, *c.*1875

Miss Joyce Wethered driving from the second tee at Royal Troon, watched by her opponent, Miss Glenna Collett, in the British Ladies Open Championship, 1925
(Painting by Bill Waugh)

Left: Book for birthday notes for a lady, decorated with silver cover depicting a lady golfer, c.1910
Right: Lady's brooch, c.1920

THE EAST COAST.
IDEAL FOR GOLFING.

Left: Poster

Below: Captain Molesworth RN driving his trap to golf at Westward Ho! Iron hut clubhouse glimpsed in the distance. From a painting by F.P. Hopkins

# 11

# Championships and Challenges

THE era of challenge matches for money among professionals was ushered in by Allan Robertson in about 1835. From the earliest times, the gentlemen Freemasons of the Royal Court had played games among themselves for large wagers, but these were entirely private games and were recorded only in many of the Bets Books of the early Golf Clubs. At St Andrews, Allan had, since his early youth, been in the habit of playing in foursome matches with the members; these games were played for a wager and, no doubt, Allan, while not taking part in the wager because he could not afford it, was given a portion of the money when he and his partner won. This was probably one of the reasons that Allan was such an admired figure at St Andrews. He had demonstrated his skill when playing with amateurs and was so good, compared with their standard of play, that he was regarded as a world beater. When he expressed a willingness to test his prowess against professionals from other areas the idea caught on and the gentry, no longer personally involved, were inclined to 'back their fancy' and make large wagers on their man. The challenge match was a serious affair on which, apart from the prize money, many large wagers depended, and many small wagers among the ordinary citizens; the matches were no longer private and were given some local publicity.

A challenge match had nothing to do with the 'exhibition match' which came later; as one elderly writer stated in 1903: 'One can imagine therefore the stamina, pluck and nerve required in playing a true challenge match as compared with the present-day exhibition matches where both the winner and the loser end on the safe side'. There was considerable passion and money involved in these challenge matches and the players not only had the pressure of playing for sums of £50 or £100 – large sums of money in those days – but, also, of knowing that much larger sums of money were riding on them as well. The analogy with wagering on prize fights is clear and is the reason why, in 1860, the first Open was for a Championship Belt which could be won outright if it was won three times in succession, in the same way as the Lonsdale Belt in boxing. It is necessary to point out as well that, until about 1875–80, medal play, or scoreplay was regarded as a mundane and characterless form of golf compared with the excitement and the ups and downs of matchplay golf.

H.S.C. Everard, an eminent member of the R&A, writing in 1901, and referring to the middle of the nineteenth century, observed: 'Medal playing in those days did not appeal to the fraternity as an altogether alluring pastime: it was regarded with tolerance, rather than enthusiasm, endured as a necessary evil. . . . The match was the thing; and the keenly contested foursome [two ball. *Author*] rather than the exclusive single.' The use of the word 'fraternity' has a typical Masonic ring!

J.G. McPherson, a good golfer from the time of Old Tom and Old Willie Dunn, who wrote so eulogistically about Allan, in 1894 bewailed the arrival of scoreplay and 'records' and was particularly scathing about those players who insisted on keeping their score in a match. He points out how much faster golf was in the old days when, if you lost your ball, you lost the hole and went on to the next. He concluded: 'Go into the clubhouse after the first round is over [the first round of a matchplay tournament. *Author*] and the talk is very much about the score. Not, as of old, "I beat him at the Burn" but "I am round in 81". It is a matter of moonshine what holes are lost or won, or what his opponent has been about. Is that Golf? It is unworthy of the name. The glorious prestige is waning. Individualism is possessing players. Now, in many cases a man does not play against another man but has another there only for company, while he is trying to beat his own or some other bodies' score ...'.

This feeling among the 'fraternity' explains why matchplay challenge matches were enthusiastically supported and why, on more than one occasion, there were no competitors in the Silver Club competitions.

## Allan Robertson (1815–59)

ROBERTSON was a smiling, bewhiskered man, somewhat rotund and of small stature. He was a neat and accurate golfer and was particularly good around the green. He used long, light, whippy clubs and played with considerable artistry. He was very hard to beat at St Andrews, partly because he knew the links so well and partly because the fine turf at St Andrews suited his style of play. On rougher links he did not do so well.

He was not only a fine striker of the ball but was a very canny player as well; he was adept at sparing shots – unrealised by his opponent, who would then misjudge the length of his own shot. He was even known to take a club from his caddie and give a hint as to what club it was,

**Allan Robertson's signature on the flyleaf of**
*Struan's Poems*

whereas he had a different club in his hand. He was not particularly long off the tee but was skilled at shaping his tee shots, hitting them low into the wind and hooking or slicing them to get around bunkers that he could not carry. He was a wonderful chipper and a good putter especially under pressure.

His air of imperturbability and cheerfulness made him a very good foursome player and the bad play of his partner neither worried him nor gave rise to any reproach. He was also clever at judging a game and would usually arrange to win at about the 16th thus taking the game while giving his opponent the idea that it was a close match and encouraging him to play again!

He used the clubs common to his time but, among his contemporary professionals, he was one of the first to use a cleek for play to the green. As mentioned in the account of the Robertson Collection at the Royal Sydney Golf Club, he was probably not the first to do this, and may have got the idea from his father. His outstanding skill with the cleek made it a popular club in a short time, much as the mashie was made popular by J.H. Taylor in later years.

### Single Matches of Allan Robertson

| 1840 | Tom Alexander (Musselburgh) | 18 holes. St Andrews | Won by Allan by 4 holes. |
|---|---|---|---|
| 1843 | Willie Dunn Senior | 360 holes. St Andrews | Allan won by 2 rounds up and 1 to play. |
| 1844 | Willie Dunn Senior | 54 holes. One round each at Musselburgh, St Andrews, N. Berwick. | Won by Dunn by 2 holes. |
| 1846 | Willie Dunn Senior | 54 holes. Leven | Won by Allan by 6 & 4. |
| 1846 | Willie Dunn Senior | 54 holes. One round each at St Andrews, Musselburgh, N. Berwick | Won by Allan by 2 holes. |
| 1858 &? | Tom Morris | 18 holes. St Andrews | Morris won both. |

**Willie Dunn Senior**

Allan would not play against Willie Park Senior.

The second match which Allan played against Tom Morris was for a red coat, presented by Mr Wolfe Murray. When Allan lost he said that he thought the coat fitted Tom better!

Allan was the first man to hole the Old Course at St

**Jamie Dunn**

Andrews in under 80 when he scored 79 in 1858, the year before his death.

The fact that Allan consistently refused to play against Willie Park Senior, despite a public challenge, added to the fact that he showed a marked reluctance to play against Old Tom Morris, and, when he did, was beaten each time, tarnishes his reputation as 'the champion of the world', bestowed on him by his devoted admirers at St Andrews. His other title of 'Feather Ball Champion of Scotland', whilst quite unofficial, is probably deserved because Willie Park Senior (*b*.1834) would have been only sixteen years of age when the gutta ball arrived.

## Willie Dunn Senior (1821–78) & Jamie Dunn (1821–71), Musselburgh

WILLIE's identical twin brother Jamie was a good golfer but played in very few single matches.

One of the reasons that the matches between Allan and Willie Dunn Senior were so interesting, dramatic and exciting was that the matches were invariably close and strongly supported by totally partisan crowds who had, in all, got a lot of money riding on the result, and that the two men were physically unalike and of a different style of play.

Willie Dunn was about 6 feet tall and of an athletic build. His style was powerful and majestic. He was a long and straight driver; when he had hit a drive and followed through it was his habit to hold his driver aloft and wave the ball forward, as it were, in the air and made the spectator wonder when it was going to stop. He was an excellent putter. He gave the appearance of being a very natural player who did not need much practice.

One Mr Peters, said to have been a neutral observer and who was a good judge of players and saw most of the matches between Dunn and Allan, said of them 'Allan is an artist and Dunny is a genius'. He considered that they were 'about equal' as golfers, though it appears from the record of Willie's matches with Allan, that Allan was rather the better.

Dunn does not seem to have played any important singles matches except those that he played against Allan – or, if he did, they are not recorded. Allan, of course, died before the institution of the Open Championship Belt; Willie and Jamie both played in it, though neither played in it in 1860.

In 1861, Willie Dunn played, and was 6th, 17 shots behind the winner. He played again in 1866 and was 10th, 20 shots behind the winner. He played four more times, the last time in 1882, but was never 'in the hunt'. James Dunn played once, in 1861, and was 11th, 25 shots behind the winner.

In fairness to the Dunns, they were both at Blackheath from 1854 to 1865. The journey to Prestwick was long and expensive and they may not have been able to afford it nor, in all probability, would they have had much practice against good golfers at Blackheath. They were very much matchplay golfers and it is likely that, as was the fashion at the time, medal play did not appeal to them – certainly they made a poor showing when they did appear in the Open Championship Belt.

## Thomas Morris Senior

Essentially a fine and conscientious Keeper of the Green and a good clubmaker. Tom was kept busy at Prestwick. He was a man who enjoyed competing against his brother professionals – and against the good amateurs. Like Allan Robertson, he must have been much in demand as a partner in foursomes among members of Prestwick. He seldom, if ever, challenged any of the professionals of his time but, if challenged, he was always ready to accept; as he was one of the best golfers of his time, there was a shortage of challengers and no shortage of backers for Tom.

He was just as willing to play scoreplay as matchplay and competed most successfully in all the competitions for the Championship Belt. Not only that, he had much to do with the promotion and organisation of the first Open Championship Belt, in conjunction with his friend and mentor Colonel Fairlie.

**Old Tom Morris, portrait by Thomas Hodge**

### *Tom Morris Senior's Singles Matches*

| 185??? | Willie Dunn | 18 holes. St Andrews | Dunn won by two holes |
|---|---|---|---|
| 1852 | Willie Park | 18 holes. St Andrews | Stake £100. Park won. |
| 1853 | Allan Robertson | 18 holes. St Andrews | Said to have been a lot of money on the match. Morris won by 3 holes |
| 1854 | Willie Park | 108 holes: six matches | Each for £100 over different links. Matches halved. |
| 1856 | Willie Park | 36 holes each green, over Musselburgh, Prestwick, St Andrews and North Berwick | Stake £100. Park won. |
| 1856 | Willie Park | Match over four greens, 36 holes each green | Stake £100. Park won. |
| 1860 | Tom challenged Willie Park, on the day after the Open Championship Belt, to a 36 hole match at Prestwick for £20. Morris won. | | |
| 1861 | Willie Park. | 48 holes. Prestwick | Willie was 7 down at one time but won. |
| 1862 | Willie Park | 18 holes. Prestwick | Stake £5. Park won. |
| 1862 | Willie Park | 72 holes over four different links | Stake £100. Morris won. |
| 1862 | Andrew Strath | 36 holes. St Andrews | Strath won by 6. |
| 1862 | Andrew Strath | 36 holes. St Andrews | Morris won by 6. |
| 1863 | W. Dow (Musselburgh) | 18 holes. Prestwick | Tom won by 1 hole. |
| 1866 | A. Strath | 24 holes. Prestwick | Tom won by 7 & 6. |
| 1868–69 | Bob Ferguson | Luffness, Musselburgh, North Berwick. Six matches played of one round each. | Ferguson won all six |
| 1872 | James Anderson | 36 holes at St Andrews | Tom won. |
| 1882 | Willie Park | 72 holes over four greens | Stake ? Morris won. |

## *1882. Tom plays Willie Park over four greens*

Tom had trained very hard for this match for six weeks and said that it had interfered with his business so much that he would never play a match over four greens again.

It was noticed at this time that Tom's short putting was very bad, otherwise he would have won by a much greater margin.

In 1869 Old Tom tied with his son, Young Tommy, and only lost because Tommy had a better score on the last 12 holes. He continued to play regularly in the Open, though as the years went by he began to miss out when the Open was held at a distant venue. His last Open was at St Andrews in 1895, when he was 74 years old, a competitor to the last!

This record of Singles and Tournament play is remarkable and sets Tom Morris Senior apart as a golfer of the very highest calibre. What sort of golfer was he?

He was a man who was not loose and supple, and as a result his swing was slow and looked rather laboured. He made up for his stiffness by using whippy clubs. He was a fine driver and sound in all departments of the game, until he came to short putts! This affliction

**Tom Morris Senior starting his downswing. His method stems from the feather-ball era. Note the flat plane of the swing**

must have attacked him in later life: he could not have won all that he did in his prime unless he putted well. Unfortunately (as happened to Vardon) his poor putting later in life was well remembered so that one gets an erroneous impression, from accounts of his golf, that he had always been a bad putter. The hallmark of his game was determination, tenacity, excellent powers of concentration and careful attention to playing the safe shot, rather than the risky one. Tom won not by making brilliant shots but by not making bad ones.

### Tom Morris and the Open Championship Belt

| | |
|---|---|
| 1860 | Runner-up to Willie Park. |
| 1861 | Winner. |
| 1862 | Winner. |
| 1863 | Runner-up. |
| 1864 | Winner. |
| 1867 | Winner. |
| 1869 | Runner-up. |

### Tom Morris Senior's Tournament Record

| | |
|---|---|
| 1864 | Perth. At an Open Tournament, Tom won, Willie Park 2nd. |
| 1865 | In a similar Tournament at Perth, Tom was 7th. |
| 1866 | Tom was 6th in an Open Tournament at Montrose. |

**Tom Morris Senior in old age**

**James Bruen's 'loop'. The club is at the start of its circle around the head and resembles the 'hurley' swing. Willie Park Senior had a similar loop in his swing**

**Willie Park Senior, from an oil painting in the possession of the R&A**

### Challenge Matches of Willie Park Senior

| 1856 | W. Dunn | 54 holes. St Andrews, Musselburgh, and Prestwick. | Park won. |
|---|---|---|---|
| 1861 | W. Dow | 18 holes. Prestwick. | Park won. |
| 1861 | W. Dow | 18 holes. Prestwick. | Park won. |
| 1862 | Andrew Strath | 36 holes. St Andrews. | ? Stake. Strath won 6 & 4. |
| 1865 | Andrew Strath | ?36 holes. St Andrews. | Park won. |
| 1866 | W. Dow | 18 holes. Prestwick. | Park won. |
| 1873 | David Strath | 18 holes. St Andrews. | Park won. |
| 1873 | David Strath | 18 holes. N. Berwick. | Park won. |
| 1873 | David Strath | 18 holes. Musselburgh. | Park won. |
| 1873 | Tom Morris Jr | 36 holes. Musselburgh. | Park won. |
| 1877 | Tom Morris Sr | 72 holes. Musselburgh. (four individual matches). | Park won 3 out of 4. |

This sort of play lacks drama and it is partly because of this that he has never been fully recognised for the great golfer that he was; another reason is because of the sheer brilliance of the play of his son, Young Tommy, who had all the flair for playing the superb stroke at the right moment.

Tom's bad putting in later life he accepted philosophically, although he tried any method that he thought would help and never gave up trying; towards the end of his career he became a reliable putter – but no one would believe it! At one time he adopted a method of putting which involved putting his right forefinger down the shaft of the putter, a method of gripping the putter which was 'invented' about 100 years later, as the 'over forties' grip – there is nothing new in golf!

A letter addressed to 'The Misser of Short Putts', St Andrews, was delivered to him without any delay. Horace

**Final round of 'Grand £100 Challenge Match', 1890. Willie Park *(centre)*, Bob Ferguson *(right)*, won by Andra Kirkaldy *(nearest Park)* by 8 and 7**

Hutchinson, who was a friend of Tom's, describes, sadly, how bad a putter he was for a great golfer and how he would rake a short putt back the moment it had missed the hole, in order to try it again and even, on occasion, hook it back before it reached the hole and when it might have gone in, so sure was he that he was going to miss!

## William Park Senior

A man of quite good physique but with a definite stoop and round shoulders, he was said never to have been a robust man. He had a fine rhythmic swing in which the club showed a well-marked 'crossing of the line' at the top, i.e., the club was pointing well to the right of the hole at the top; this was quite usual in his day and most of the good swingers did it, but his contemporaries say that, at the top of the swing, his club described a circle around his head. This is the sort of swing that hurley or shinty players have and was the sort of swing that James Bruen had a century later. Like Bruen, Willie was a very long driver – and accurate as well. A contemporary states that, when he hit a drive, the ball went off with a sound like

| The Open Championship Belt. Willie Park Senior's Results | |
| --- | --- |
| 1860 | Winner |
| 1861 | Runner-up |
| 1862 | Runner-up |
| 1863 | Winner |
| 1864 | 4th |
| 1865 | Runner-up |
| 1866 | Winner. His brother, David, was runner-up |
| 1875 | Winner |

a pistol shot. He was a fine cleek player and a brilliant putter; those who saw him putt, and later saw his son putt (and his son was regarded as the best putter of his time) say that Willie Senior was a better putter than his son. His weakness was in the shorter irons which he tended to sweep away rather than hit them crisply.

*Singles Challenge Matches and the Open Championship*

Allan once said of Willie, 'He frightens us all with his long driving'. The other feature of Willie's play was the fact that he never played a friendly game, however friendly the preliminaries, and even if he was playing his dearest friend, once they drove off Willie concentrated on winning. Unlike Tom, Willie was always willing to take a risk and would go for the dangerous line, so confident was he of success; this was the cause of his undoing on a number of occasions.

Willie, more than most of his contemporaries, reckoned to make a living out of his winnings, and he made a good one. He had an advertisement in *Bell's Life* for nine years offering to play any man for £100 in a 'home and home' match, i.e. one round on Willie's home links, Musselburgh, and one round on his opponent's home links, though he did not strictly adhere to this and would often be willing to play away from home. He was confident of his abilities almost to the point of arrogance.

The fact that he played to win did not mean that he had no sense of fun on the golf links; he made a substantial portion of his money from playing with local amateurs. Even when they were considered good golfers, Willie would devise physical handicaps for himself rather than give the usual strokes.

Willie used to play a local man, Mr Tait of Aberlady level, but Willie had to stand on one leg to play his shots.

**Willie Park Senior as an old man**

On another occasion he played when standing on one leg and playing with only one hand. No doubt his opponents, many of whom had played bizarre games against their fellow Masonic Club members, as can be seen in the club Bets Books, enjoyed this sort of contest and, possibly, thought that Willie had overestimated his ability but, one can be quite sure that Willie had shrewdly estimated the odds and, once on the tee, was playing very seriously to win – he had a living to make!

*Singles against other Professionals*

The games that he played against Old Tom have already been considered. In these, although the margin was close, Willie had the better record. In this connection, mention should be made of an unfortunate ending to Willie's last

match against Tom. The final round of this match was played at Musselburgh; Willie's local followers and backers were very vociferous in his support and had even gone to the unsportmanlike lengths of cheering when Tom missed a putt and getting in his way when he wanted to play. This sort of support was not unknown at St Andrews but, on this occasion, the referee considered that the intimidation of Tom was excessive and stopped play, intending to start again the next day when, he hoped, sportsmanlike feelings would prevail and when he could have a means of crowd control. Willie would have none of it and claimed that the referee had no authority to stop the match. The match had stopped at the 9th hole, close to Mrs Forman's pub, Willie and others went in for a drink and, thirty minutes later he came out, teed up and drove off, saying that, if Tom did not follow suit, the match was his. He then played the remaining holes by himself and declared himself the winner.

There was much partisan feeling about this and many said that the referee had made a wrong decision. The match was never replayed and feelings ran high at both St Andrews and Musselburgh for a long time; to the credit of both Willie and Tom, the event seems not to have left any ill feeling between them.

Park beat Willie Dunn so comprehensively in the three-round contest in 1856 that Dunn would never play him again.He last played in the Championship Belt in 1886.

When Willie was older he played a series of matches against Bob Ferguson, an 'up and coming' young professional at Musselburgh, for £25 a match. Bob Ferguson won all of them.

## The Great Foursome

Most of the singles matches were followed with enthusiasm and there were plenty of wagers on the result. For the Open Championship Belt there was much less enthusiasm. It was when it came to the (two ball) foursomes that enthusiasm knew no bounds. The dramatic ups and downs of foursome play, a form of golf in which no side is certain of victory until the last putt is in, fired up the spectators.

In a foursome, a player is playing only every other shot, so he needs his partner to support his ideas and play the same game; if his partner is not like-minded, he may find this difficult and begin to play badly. Things can rapidly go from bad to worse and result in a landslide of lost holes and this is especially likely to happen if one partner shows his disappointment or, worse, urges his partner to do better. The balance is delicate and each one in a foursome must understand the thinking of his partner.

**Group of golfers at Westward Ho!, *c.*1869. In the front row, recumbent, left to right: Young Tom Morris, Bob Kirk, John Allan**

As a result of such problems two players who, when playing their own game, are skilled and successful, may find that they do not win foursomes together, even against two players who, normally and individually, they would expect to beat.

As these games concern four players and two teams, it is neither desirable nor practical to attempt to classify the games according to the people involved. The matches are presented, as far as possible, according to dates and to venue. Even this is not always easy and there is no doubt that many exciting matches have never been recorded.

1849. Allan Robertson and Tom Morris played Willie and Jamie Dunn for £400 a side over three greens: Musselburgh, St Andrews and North Berwick, 36 holes played at each links and the result to depend on which pair won the most greens. This match has already been referred to in connection with Allan Robertson but it was such a fascinating struggle that it will bear further consideration. Allan had beaten Willie Dunn more often than he had lost and Tom had beaten him several times as well.

Jamie Dunn was reckoned to be the weakest of the four players, but Willie and Jamie were twins and thus had a good rapport, and as a result, they were known to be a very strong foursome pair.

The Dunns went off at a great pace and were 13 holes up on the first round at Musselburgh, so they were one green up. At St Andrews, where Allan and Tom were on home ground, they, as expected, got some holes back, and won the St Andrews leg by 3 holes, not a handsome victory but enough to make the tally of greens one all.

When they went to North Berwick the Dunns again started off at a rush and were 4 up at the halfway stage. After lunch, the St Andrews pair began to come back and the holes that the Dunns had gained began to slide away; at the 16th they were all square. The Dunns' supporters were less jubilant and the St Andrews supporters began to look cheerful.

At the 17th, Tom and Allan had played three more than the Dunns to reach a bunker short of the green, the Dunns had had a magnificent drive but their second shot was out to the right and was on a cart track, the ball lying against a large stone. The Dunns wanted the stone removed but the referee would not allow this because it was off the course and a fixture; the ball must be played where it lay. One of the Dunns attempted to hit it, but hit the stone, the other did the same and thus they had now to play the same score as the other pair. The Dunns began to regain some composure and played the ball with the back of an iron on to some grass on the other side of the track but they ultimately lost the hole; by now they were quite demoralised and lost the last hole easily – and the match. Had they kept their wits about them and played the shot first that they eventually played as the third of their efforts to get away from the stone, they would have won. They were a little unfortunate to get into such a bad lie and not be able to drop out and they were unfortunate in that, had the match been counted in holes rather than greens, they would have won easily, despite their misfortune at the 17th. Spectators at the match said that Allan played badly during the early part of the game and that it was the solid and reliable play of Tom that held their side together.

In scoreplay, there was nothing between them. In singles play, Willie had slightly the better record, in foursomes Tom was better. They were great golfers and the equal of one another.

Among distinguished foursomes players were: Andrew Strath, Young Tom Morris, Bob Kirk, Bob Ferguson and James Anderson; these were the rising

generation of young and talented professionals, and more will be heard of them later.

## The Championship Belt

The reader will not be surprised to learn that the early competitions for the Belt were low-key affairs. To the Prestwick Golf Club must go the credit for promoting, not only the Belt competition, but the whole idea of national, as opposed to local tournaments. In 1857 they proposed an Open National Foursomes tournament, two pairs from each Club to be allowed; they suggested that the competition should be staged, either at Prestwick, or at St Andrews. The R&A decided to take it on and Prestwick gave 15 guineas toward the prize. This tournament was only for amateurs and, when it was played, was only open to some of the Scottish Clubs and to Blackheath, which had a high proportion of Scottish members. The event was won by Blackheath who were represented by two Scottish golfers, George Glennie and Captain Stewart. As not all Golf Clubs had been invited it was not, strictly speaking, an open tournament.

Prestwick, since 1856, had been pressing for a National Professional Tournament. The R&A were very lukewarm in the matter and, as they were a prestigious

Tough golfers at Westward Ho! 1886. A variety of head gear, a mixture of trousers and breeches with canvas leggings. The huge stones of the Pebble Ridge are in the foreground. The wooden angled support is to stop the tin hut blowing over in the strong winds

Club with many influential members, their lack of enthusiasm meant that nothing happened.

In 1860, Prestwick decided to stage the tournament themselves and they had made a handsome Championship Belt of red leather with much silver decoration, at a cost of £25. One of the conditions that they made was that, if any man won the Belt for three years in succession, it should become his property. Major J.O. Fairlie, a senior member of Prestwick and also a member of the R&A was the main organiser and was ably assisted by Old Tom – in fact, it was Tom who wrote to invite professionals to play. The entrants were to be 'known and respectable cadies'. The competition was to be over 3 rounds of the 12 hole links. The terms of this competition meant that it was a Closed Professional Championship. The winner could take the Belt away with him, to be returned in one year on pain of a £25 fine, or he could leave it at Prestwick. Each competitor had to have a marker and there was an umpire to ensure that the 13 Rules of Golf were followed and, more importantly, 'in the spirit of the game' to make those difficult decisions which were not covered by the Rules.

Although the winner won a handsome Belt, he got no prize money – and, of course, had to pay his own expenses to get to Prestwick and back; it was not until 1863 that the winner won £10 as prize money.

Not surprisingly, there were only eight entrants. Willie Park Senior won and Tom Morris was runner-up. Citizens from Prestwick town turned up to watch and there was quite heavy betting; most money was on Morris, who was the local professional and had much to do with the layout of the links and was in charge of its upkeep. Willie Park had his backers but, coming from another part of Scotland, he was not well known to Prestwick; Morris coming from St Andrews had a reputation which preceded him.

An interesting statistic is that the competition started at 12 noon and all competitors had completed 3 rounds – 36 holes – before dark, in October! The local town provided the gallery and there were, also, some of the gentlemen golfers and their ladies; these golfers happened to be there because a much more important tournament was to be played next day, in which they were going to compete for the Gold Medal of Prestwick Golf Club.

The second, and all the other competitions for the Belt, could truly be called 'Open' because amateurs were allowed to compete. Even at this early stage of golf, the professional caddies outclassed the amateurs. An amusing sideline was that, when the amateurs played, they were not required to have markers; being gentlemen amateurs they were completely above suspicion of cheating and it was assumed that they would make a fair decision about all those problems in playing which needed to be decided 'in the spirit of the game'.

The leading positions of Morris and Park over the first seven years have already been discussed. Of the other entrants: Charles Hunter was the local boy and was, besides, Tom Morris's apprentice, but he was never really a serious contender. Bob Andrew, from Perth gave a good account of himself; David Park, Willie's brother, played and did well, on one occasion being runner-up to his brother, the only occasion, so far, in which a competitor has been runner-up to his own brother in the Open. Andrew Strath acquitted himself well and won in 1865. Willie Dow, of Musselburgh, said to be a great stylist, was a regular competitor and was usually in about the middle of the field. Bob Kirk, of St Andrews, was a regular competitor after 1865, when he was 20, and was runner-up to Tom Morris Junior in 1870 and to James Anderson in 1878.

The appearances of the Dunns in the Championship Belt have already been noted. James Anderson first appeared in the Open in 1869, aged 25.

Old hands such as Tom Morris Senior, Willie Park Senior and the Dunns, from time to time played against the youthful and talented professionals from the next generation and partnered them in foursomes as well.

In the first seven years of the Championship Belt, the event was dominated by Tom Morris Senior and Willie Park Senior. The amateurs were never in the hunt, though W. Doleman, from Musselburgh and then living in Glasgow, deserves credit for being leading amateur on eight occasions between 1862 and 1872. He was a very stylish golfer and was the only amateur, at that time, who could play on level terms with most of the professionals.

The younger generation of professionals was steadily improving, and in 1867 a young man reached the very first rank and set new standards of golf in winning the Championship four times in succession; this was Tom Morris Senior's son, 'Young Tom' or 'Young Tommy' as he was affectionately known to all.

## The Professionals in the second half of the Nineteenth Century

Not many, today, will recognise what a major upheaval it was for Tom Morris to go to Prestwick in 1851. The general attitude at St Andrews was that he was emigrating to another country; an extract from a local St Andrews paper helps to underline the point: 'Tom departs from St Andrews for Ayrshire in the end of this month, to a place in the vicinity of Ayr called Prestwick, where they have links and upon which Tom will likely soon astonish the natives of those parts; he will no doubt reign supreme as a golfer.' Such was the self-importance of St Andrews in the golf world. A St Andrews writer of golf history points out that Tom 'went to Prestwick, laid out the links and remained as custodian for 14 years'. The facts are that Tom made many improvements to the links which, however, were well in existence before he arrived. His principal functions were to get the course into better condition, to play and, by his example as a great golfer, to teach the game; these functions he achieved most admirably and he had much to do, on the practical side, with the formation and running of the first twelve Open Championships.

Virtually on arrival at Prestwick, Tom played a match against Willie Dunn of North Berwick, which Tom lost at the last hole. In the next year Tom and Allan played at St Andrews against Sir Robert Hay and Willie Dunn, Tom and Allan backed themselves for £100 to £50 and won.

It is an interesting commentary on foursome play that Tom and Willie Park Senior, clearly the two best golfers of their era, played together in one or two foursomes and never won; had they played a fourball they would, almost certainly, have won all their games.

Tom must have had a happy life at Prestwick. He brought up his children there and had a kindly benefactor in Colonel Fairlie. When Allan Robertson died, Tom was invited back to St Andrews as Keeper of the Green and there can be no doubt that he was glad to return to his native town; there was no doubt either in the mind of a St Andrews writer: 'It would therefore be with joy and gratitude he would return to take charge of the classic links on the invitation of the Royal and Ancient Club'. So Tom came back to St Andrews with his two sons, where he fulfilled a long and honourable career in charge of the links and played challenge matches until quite an advanced age.

One son, Jof Morris, became a more than competent professional who won many challenge matches but, in young Tommy, Tom Morris Senior brought a golfing star to St Andrews .

## Tom Morris Junior (1851–75)

Tommy Morris was born in St Andrews, but went, as a baby, to Prestwick with his family when they moved and it was at Prestwick that he developed his golf; by the time that he returned to St Andrews, as a boy of fifteen, he was already an accomplished golfer.

The fact that he learned to play at Prestwick had an influence on his style of play and accounted for certain shots that he played which were not commonly in use. Many of the greens at St Andrews were open and undu-

lating; such greens were approachable by using a wooden putter from quite long range, although Allan Robertson's father and Allan had begun to develop the art of using irons in approach play. At Prestwick, as Horace Hutchinson described, 'the course went dodging in and out among lofty sandhills. The holes were, for the most part, out of sight when one took the iron in hand for the approach, as they lay in deep dells . . .'. It was the layout of Prestwick which caused young Tom, as a lad, to develop the art of the pitch shot; the only club with enough loft to play a high pitch was the 'rutter', otherwise known as a rut iron. This club was designed specifically to play out of narrow ruts made by the wheels of the carts which crossed the course carrying seaweed to the farms, where it was used as fertiliser; because the clubhead had to fit into a rut it was very small – little larger than a golf ball – consequently, to use it for pitch shots from the fairway meant that the slightest error would result in a shank. It was part of the genius of young Tom that he had taught himself to play pitch shots to the green with this club, a shot which no one else dared to attempt.

At the same time, as Tommy returned to St Andrews at fifteen, he was still adaptable enough to learn other shots which were useful at St Andrews, rather than Prestwick, and thus became a more complete golfer for it.

Young Tom was a brilliant golfer: in his method of playing he was a law unto himself. His swing was one of great power and vigour and the preliminary 'waggle' was of the same order. At times, it was said, his 'waggle' was so vigorous that he actually snapped the shaft off below the grip. His swing was not as long and easy as was customary in those times but was definitely shorter and quicker and was accompanied by a strong hand action. The swing was so free and dashing that his 'Glengarry' cap invariably fell off in the follow through. When he wanted to hit a particularly long shot, he simply hit the ball harder – this despite the well-recognised principle that 'pressing' is not the way to hit the ball further but is a sure recipe for disaster. As has been said, he was also capable of playing pitch shots with a rutter which no one else would attempt but it was his putting which was outstanding. On 'good' putting greens he used a wooden putter, but on bad ones he used a blade putter. Before he hit the ball he made a small push forward (in the line of the putt) with the right knee; what exactly this achieved is not clear but it suited Tommy and, for very many years, especially among the professionals, it became a common practice to copy this. He hit his putts half way up the back of the ball, i.e., he topped them. The topspin that resulted made the long putts run right up to the hole and, as he hit the short putts firmly towards the back of the hole, they tended to dive in rather than jump over the back.

There were no chinks in his golfing armour and he had a great temperament for the game. One of the features of his play was his ability to concentrate on the ball throughout the swing; he would allow nothing to distract him and advised amateur golfers not to use shiny iron clubs, as even this shine might be enough to distract the player's eye from the ball. It is not surprising that this golfing prodigy carried all before him.

## Young Tommy in the Open Championships

At age seventeen, in 1868, he won the Championship with the lowest score that had ever been recorded – 154 for 36 holes, winning by 5 shots and beating the previous best score by 9 shots.

In 1869, he won with a score of 157, doing the last 9 holes in 49 and creating a new record for Prestwick and, in achieving that, he did the 8th hole in one, the first time that this had been done in an Open Championship. In this Championship he tied with his father but, as he was declared the winner, it can be assumed that he won by the virtue of his last 9 holes. It is impossible to believe that a father and son will ever tie for the Open again.

In 1870, he won the Championship Belt again, this time with the phenomenal score of 149, beating his previous best score by 5 shots and winning by 12 shots. He did the first 9 holes in 47 shots thus beating his record for the Prestwick course again. In the course of this he did the first hole in 3; the first hole at Prestwick was 537 yards long and he accomplished his three by holing a full iron shot. The reader will appreciate that he was playing with an early gutty ball and that, with that ball, a shot of 200 yards was very long. Young Tommy's score of 149 was never beaten between 1870 and the end of the 36 holes Championship in 1892, after which it was played over 72 holes. In the four round Open the record score for the first 36 holes was still held by Tommy until 1908. By this time the rubbercore ball had been in existence for seven years and the state of golf courses had greatly improved.

By winning the Belt three years in succession he won it outright and the organisers were left to acquire a new

trophy. This took them more than a year, so there was no Championship in 1871.

In 1872, the new trophy, a silver claret jug, with which we are all familiar today, was played for, and Tommy won that by 3 shots.

By this time the Open Championship was being organised by the R&A and was played over three venues, Prestwick, St Andrews and Musselburgh. The 1873 Championship was won at St Andrews by Tom Kidd, Tommy being 3rd.

In 1874 the Championship was at Musselburgh; it was won by Mungo Park, Willie Park Senior's brother, and Tommy was runner-up. Clearly, apart from his father, young Tom knew Prestwick better than any of the other competitors and, by the time that the first Open was played at St Andrews, he knew St Andrews well; at Musselburgh, he was at a slight disadvantage.

Tommy died in 1875 at the age of twenty-four.

Curiously, in Tulloch's *Life of Tom Morris* which includes information about Young Tom, the fact that Tommy did not win at St Andrews or Musselburgh is not mentioned!

Tommy played a number of challenge matches and won nearly all of them. His toughest opponent was David Strath, a St Andrews boy who was a friend of Tommy's. In some respects David was a slightly better golfer than Tommy but, when it came to putting, Tommy was always the better and it was this that made Tommy a frequent winner.

Young Tom played two matches against Old Willie Park (a much older man) and lost both but, in their best recorded encounter, 27 holes at North Berwick, Tommy won at the last hole.

Tommy played a number of foursomes with his father as partner and they won the large majority of them on many different courses.

As has happened since, the arrival on the golfing scene of a new golfing star had the effect of raising the golf standards of the other players, and, in particular, in raising the standard of golf in the professional ranks.

There were a number of good professional golfers in

**Mungo Park, brother of Willie Park Senior**

the era of Young Tommy but, generally speaking, he was so outstandingly good that they tend to appear in a minor role and their ability does not become apparent until after Tommy's tragic death only a year after his young bride's death in childbirth.

From St Andrews there were Tom Kidd and Bob Martin. Kidd won in 1873 and Martin in 1876 but, good golfers though they were, apart from these successes not a lot is heard of them. They were, essentially, talented caddie golfers, who returned to carrying after a brief time on centre stage.

## James Anderson (1842–1905)

Anderson was a much more formidable golfer and, moreover, one who had much more sustained success. He came from a clubmaking family of St Andrews; the family were three generations in clubmaking and James had four brothers who, with their father, were important clubmakers at St Andrews. At one time they used the sheds, which later became engine sheds for the railway, over which golfers had to drive at the 17th on the Old course.

James was a very good golfer and a good clubmaker. While he may not have achieved Tommy's standard he played well enough to win the Open three years in succession, 1877, 1878 and 1879; as he was runner-up in 1873 and 1881, he must clearly be recognised as a formidable competitor and a golfer of the highest skill. His principal attribute was consistency; he did not hit bad shots and was a very good putter. Horace Hutchinson, who knew him well and played with him often, said that he never put his full power into a shot but was astonishingly accurate and H.S.C. Everard remarks that the little man (he was not physically large) told him that he had once played 90 holes and had not, during them, played any shot that was not as he intended; he was known as a very quiet, modest man who was not given to boasting.

Although, generally, he won his tournaments and matches rather unexcitingly by virtue of relentless accu-

**James Anderson, from a portrait by Thomas Hodge in 1889**

racy, his win in the Open of 1878 produced high drama. Playing at Prestwick, he needed to do the last four holes in 17 strokes to win; the 'par' for the last four holes was 5, 4, 3, 5. When told what he had to do he said that he could do it. At the first of the holes he holed a full iron shot to make a 3, at the second of them he holed a putt right across the green for a 4. At the 17th he, by mistake, teed his ball up in front of the marker; a lady spectator remarked to her companion that he had done so, Anderson heard her and reteed his ball in the right place, whereupon he then holed his tee shot. This left him with a 9 at the last to win – and he did the 18th in 5!

A contemporary of Anderson's stated: 'It was sometimes quite extraordinary to see with what judgement he would pitch a ball up to within a few feet of the hole, perhaps 6 times in succession, and each time, hole the putt'. He was a particularly good player in bad weather which seemed not to affect his play at all. He was said to be a charming man to play with and always had his whole

---

### Ferguson's record in the Open Championship

| 1874 | 12th |
|------|------|
| 1875 | 4th |
| 1877 | 3rd |
| 1879 | 6th |
| 1880 | (Musselburgh) Winner |
| 1881 | (Prestwick) Winner |
| 1882 | (St Andrews) Winner |
| 1883 | (Musselburgh) Tied first with Willie Fernie and lost the play-off over 36 holes by one shot. In this Championship in the last round in order to tie with Fernie he had to do the last three holes in three each. |

He came of a very poor family and it is said that, until he won this tournament, he was unable to afford a full bag of clubs and therefore played with the few that he had and borrowed some from his friends for the day.

Having, to the surprise of St Andrews and to the pleasure of East Lothian, broken through to the front rank of professionals Ferguson was soon engaged in challenge matches. In 1868, he played Tom Morris Senior over 36 holes at St Andrews and was beaten 6 and 5. The following year he played a return with Morris at Musselburgh and won by 4 and 3. In the same year he played Young Tommy over 36 holes at Luffness. Tommy won by 8 and 7. In 1869, he again played Morris Senior at St Andrews over 36 holes. Bob won by 4 and 3. He played Young Tom at Musselburgh over 36 holes. They finished all square and their backers persuaded them to play 9 more holes; Bob won by one hole. Ferguson played a number of challenge matches with David Strath and each won an equal number. At Alnmouth, in 1879, he won a tournament from a field which included Tom Morris Senior, Mungo Park (the local professional), Willie Park Junior and James Anderson.

In 1883, he became chronically ill with a prolonged bout of fever. Although he recovered he was never the same again and reverted to being a caddie.

There are three contemporary opinions of him as a golfer. First Mr H.S.C. Everard: 'To see him address the ball was, in itself, a study; broad-backed and sturdy, it apeared as if nothing short of a volcanic upheaval or a dynamite cartridge would have the power to make him budge until the stroke was finished. His game was accurate and scientific at every point, while his physical power made him an efficient wielder of the cleek and iron.'

Ferguson was a great cleek player and used Carruther's Patent cleek to such effect that he achieved for it a fame that equalled the fame that J.H. Taylor later gave to the mashie. He played a match at Prestwick against Young Tommy in which each player used only a cleek, and Ferguson won by 4 holes.

Horace Hutchinson has this to say of him: 'Greatly to be admired is the swing of Bob Ferguson . . ., so square and solid he looks, his very stance expressive of the dogged resoluteness of his play, yet with great loose, free-working shoulders swinging as true as if the backbone were a pivot! And that forward dig with his iron which used to lay the ball up on the plateau-pitched greens of North Berwick as if by magic! His is a style which any golfer may, with advantage, study.'

A third contemporary writer has this to say: 'In his

**Willie Park Junior**

attention concentrated on the game. Unquestionably a great golfer one must, nevertheless, keep a sense of proportion – despite all his successes he never equalled the best scores of Young Tommy.

The reader may think that all the talents were concentrated in St Andrews, but this is far from the case.

## Bob Ferguson (1844–1924)

Ferguson was from Musselburgh; although many of the trade directories of the time class him as a clubmaker and ballmaker (he was certainly apprenticed as a clubmaker) his main claim to fame was as a golfer.

He first came to public notice when he won a tournament at Leith in 1867, at the age of twenty-three. Among the competitors were Tom Morris Senior, Willie Park Senior, James Anderson, Tom Morris Junior, and Bob Andrews, a good professional golfer from Perth. His win came as a shock and brought him immediate fame. A photograph of the competitors in the tournament was taken, but Ferguson was not included: presumably they did not reckon him as a competitor!

prime, which was after Young Tom had died, he was the best golfer. When it had to be done – he did it – by sheer downright tenacity of purpose and determination. Many of the golfers of the time did wonderful scores but, in anything worth winning, Bob Ferguson was pretty sure to be in front. He was never troubled with nerves and was one of the finest players in bad weather.'

He was in the habit of playing long approach putts with a putter, a habit which had, by then, gone out of fashion. Ferguson used an iron putter and the caddies at Musselburgh used to refer to this shot of his as 'the Musselburgh iron' – shades of the Texas wedge!

He is known to have taught at least two great golfers: J.E. Laidlay, amateur, already discussed, whose splendid approach shot to the green was no doubt acquired from Bob Ferguson, and Willie Campbell, who became a leading professional.

## Willie Park Junior (1864–1925)

After Willie Fernie had beaten Bob Ferguson in the play-off for the Open Championship in 1883, the Open was won in the following year by Jack Simpson and in 1885 by Bob Martin. David Brown won in 1886. Over the four years from 1883, Willie Park Junior steadily improved as a golfer, and he won the Open in 1887.

His putting practice was unusual, to say the least, as he used to putt on the pavement outside the shop into shallow holes scooped in the stones. Later he practised into shallow holes scooped out of the bricks in the workshop floor. From his earliest days he was surrounded by golf clubs and golfers and, outside the family, he had chums such as Willie Dunn Junior with whom he had many a tussle. Small wonder that he grew up to be a great golfer and, probably, one of the best putters of his time. An excellent and detailed account of the Park family of Musselburgh has been written by John Adams.

The Parks differed from the contemporary professionals in that they were men of some education and independence. Neither Willie Senior nor Willie Junior were ever professionals attached to a Golf Club. They were independent businessmen whose business was golf and the making of its implements; they were fine makers of clubs in their own workshops and employed several men. Willie Park Senior did some work as a golf course architect and Willie Junior became active and well known in that capacity, both in Britain and overseas.

They were confident of their golfing ability and willing to back themselves. Willie Senior was always willing to play any golfer, on any course, for a stake and, in fact, had a permanent advertisement in *Bell's Life* challenging allcomers. When his son became famous, he did the same.

Whereas his father was a great matchplayer and played many challenge foursomes with success, when his son became famous the pattern of matches had changed somewhat; by 1890 there had come to be more emphasis on scoreplay and the old matchplay games were fewer. Willie Junior did his best to maintain the tradition and played many matches but he was always a better scoreplayer than a matchplayer.

To complete Willie Junior's record in the Open Championship, he won again in 1889, after a tie with Andrew Kirkaldy, at Musselburgh. He was 4th in 1890, 6th in 1891, 7th in 1892; thereafter, he faded out of the picture in the Open except in 1898, when the Open was played at Prestwick and was won by Harry Vardon. Willie had done some practising and had hopes of doing well; he was runner-up, one shot behind Vardon, failing to hole a putt on the last green to tie.

In 1892 he had a big hand in organising a professional competition at Musselburgh which was a rival to the Open Championship, due to be played at Muirfield for the first time. The prize money was over £100 and it was timed to be played near the date of the Open; as a result, there was a big entry from most of the leading professionals. Willie won this tournament and at the same time set up a new record for the Musselburgh links.

## Willie Park Junior's play

Willie had a long, unhurried backswing in the drive but it was a very loose swing and he favoured a 'piccolo' grip, holding the club at the top of the backswing with the tips of the fingers; his shots through the green were adequate but, once he got on the green, he was the master.

His driving method led to inconsistency and he was prone to bad hooks; he constantly saved himself by putting and he coined the phrase 'The man who can putt is a match for anyone', proving the adage on many famous occasions. His method of hitting the long shots was that of the old school of Scottish golfers, with a marked 'crossing the line' position of the club at the top of the backswing; the newer players, accustomed to a better golf ball than that used in the earlier part of the century, had abandoned this type of swing in favour of a more compact and upright style with a firm grip of the club. This made them consistently straight drivers, without losing any length.

In putting, Willie was accustomed to cutting and hooking his putts against the borrow; he putted entirely with the wrists, the right hand predominating, and only used his arms when faced with a very long putt. He always hit the top half of the ball, thus imparting topspin, and advocated a complete concentration on the ball, banishing the hole from sight when making the stroke.

Willie Park Junior was a 'workaholic' and his business was making money out of golf. He adopted an entirely different attitude from the earlier caddie/professionals and did not regard prize money from playing as his principal income. He was a busy and successful maker of clubs and remained an important clubmaker all his life, but he realised that iron clubs were equally important and became an accomplished cleekmaker as well, thus extending the range of his business and becoming, at that time, the only manufacturer who combined both wooden and iron clubs in his repertoire.

Willie was of an inventive turn of mind and produced a very important model of a blade putter which had a bent neck – the 'wry-necked' putter; as he used the putter with conspicuous success, it became a very good 'seller'. The general principal of the bent neck putter has been a feature of many putters ever since. In later life he invented the 'unbreakable driver' in which the wood for the club-head was treated by oil compression; it was highly successful but, coming at the end of a long career, Willie did not live long enough to make much money out of it.

Willie was the first of the true golf architects; Tom Morris and Old Willie had laid out one or two links courses and had suggested improvements to many more but Willie Junior became a really accomplished golf architect and many of the courses that he constructed have stood the test of time and remain great courses despite all the changes in the golf ball and golf clubs. In England, he was responsible for many fine courses such as Sunningdale, (Old) Hollinwell, Worplesdon and Huntercombe. In Scotland he laid out the (new) Luffness course and other courses; in addition, he made extensive improvements to many Scottish courses.

Willie was a traveller and made two visits to the United States, during the course of which he played exhibition matches and laid out a number of courses. He travelled to Europe and laid out, or planned, courses such as Royal Antwerp in Belgium, Mont Agel at Monte Carlo and La Boulie in France. His work load was prodigious and it is not surprising that he had what is popularly known as a 'nervous breakdown'. It will be appreciated that all this travel was done without the benefit of either motor-car or air travel.

The catalogue of Willie's activities is of importance in assessing his abilities as a golfer, for there is little doubt that he played less competitive golf than his contemporaries and, on many occasions, he played in major tournaments or challenge matches having played very little golf beforehand and when exhausted by his business activities and travels.

In 1899 Willie played a challenge match when he was in good practice and well rested, against Harry Vardon.

For six weeks before the match, Willie practised and thus, for once, he was thoroughly prepared for the game which was to be played at North Berwick and Ganton, in Yorkshire, where Vardon was the professional at the time; it was said that Vardon would not agree to play at Musselburgh because he knew that there he would be faced with a highly partisan and vociferous crowd of Park supporters.

There was indeed a big crowd for the match; over the first 18 holes at North Berwick, Park was one up, the second 18 holes was won by Vardon by three holes; Vardon thus finished the North Berwick part of the contest two up.

On 22 July the second part was played at Ganton. Ganton was a relatively new course and a fine one but it was of a different character to North Berwick; at Ganton it was necessary to be a good driver and this Willie was not. He was humiliated, being beaten by 11 and 10. All Scotland was shocked.

Willie Park Junior was a remarkable man and a great golfer. He was also a pretty good businessman, although, it must be admitted, he made a bad misjudgement when he put virtually all his money into buying and designing Huntercombe.

After Willie Park Junior had won the Open in 1889 there was a brief period when the great amateurs came to the fore, as has been described. Willie Auchterlonie won the Open in 1893, the only Open that he won although, great golfer that he was, he might have won more had he not dropped out of tournament golf because he genuinely preferred to make golf clubs. The question of whether he would have won more is problematical because, in 1894, there appeared the first of a trio of great professional golfers who were to dominate the professional game for 16 years.

By this time there had come about a change in the pattern of professional golf. Challenge matches were still played but were becoming fewer and this, in particular, was true of (two ball) foursome matches which virtually disappeared. The new form of competition between individual professionals was the exhibition match, either single or four ball. For the professionals this was a pleasant, relaxed and easy way to earn a living; each received a fee according to his status and there was no great wager on the result. Many of these exhibition matches were played at the opening of new golf courses; as there were 387 Golf Clubs in existence in 1890 and about 2,130 by 1900, there was plenty of opportunity for them. The other form of professional competition was scoreplay over 36 or 72 holes. The competitions were, in the main, played between April and the end of October and were quite numerous.

Although there was an American Open Championship in 1894 (matchplay), the rewards for winning it were so small and the difficulties in travelling to the United States so great that, as far as British competitors were concerned, only those then resident in the United States competed.

There were, by now, sufficient tournaments and exhibition matches for a professional who wished only to play golf to make a living; as a result, the professional ranks were divided into Club professionals and Tournament professionals. The former were much more numerous; the latter were still officially attached to a Golf Club and derived some income from the professional's shop but they had to have assistants and clubmakers to repair clubs and give lessons because they were away so much.

Even the clubmakers in these professional shops were no longer really necessary because, by the turn of the century, mass production of clubs was a thriving business and the assistants sold the clubs and balls and carried out minor repairs for members. The craftsmen clubmakers were put out of business by mass production and it was only Forgan of St Andrews, who was prepared to change over to mass production methods, who survived.

**J.H. Taylor putting**

## John Henry Taylor (1871–1963)

Taylor was the first of the new breed of professional golfers. He was born at Northam, in North Devon, in 1871. The village was close to the links of the Royal North Devon Golf Club at Westward Ho!

As a lad, Taylor was a boot boy in the Hutchinson household and Horace Hutchinson was one of his boyhood heroes. He soon became attracted to golf and in his spare time worked as a caddie at the Club. There is evidence that as a teenager he did some work on the links as an assistant greenkeeper and he may have done some work in John Allan's workshop but it is doubtful if he ever became a full-time apprentice. He came of a poor family and his father died when he was still at school; carrying and doing odd jobs on the course were important in bringing some income into the family. Later in his life he gave much credit to the Allans, and James Allan in particular, for teaching him the rudiments of the golf swing.

By the time that Taylor was seventeen, Charles Gibson, the master clubmaker from North Berwick, was installed at Westward Ho! and had a team of apprentice clubmakers; Taylor was not one of them but many of his boyhood friends at Northam were.

In 1891, at the age of twenty, Taylor was given the appointment of professional to the new Golf Club at Burnham-on-Sea in Somerset. In 1893, Andrew Kirkaldy of St Andrews, a recognised and skilful professional, was the professional at Winchester Golf Club. A match was arranged, at Burnham, between Taylor and Kirkaldy which Taylor won. Shortly after, Kirkaldy went back to St Andrews and Taylor took his place at Winchester. Kirkaldy took back to St Andrews the news that there was a very good professional at Winchester but none of the other Scots professionals took much notice, even though Taylor had scored a 75, the lowest score of the Open at Prestwick, in the same year; he took 89 in the second round and finished 10th. In the following year 'JH,' as he became affectionately known, proved his worth by winning the Open at Sandwich.

| *J.H. Taylor's record in the Open Championship up to 1900* | |
|---|---|
| 1893 | 10th |
| 1894 | Winner |
| 1895 | Winner |
| 1896 | Tied for first place with Harry Vardon but lost the play off. |
| 1897 | 11th |
| 1898 | 4th |
| 1899 | 4th |
| 1900 | Winner. |

**J.H. Taylor in 1894, when he won his first Open Championship**

Taylor's four years at Winchester were of great importance to him, not so much because of the golf but because he was introduced to the world of learning. Thereafter he had a great reverence for learning and became a reader of books. He developed the habit of reading the Bible every day. From Winchester he went to Royal Mid-Surrey Golf Club and remained there until he retired, after which he returned to his beloved Devon.

He seems never to have become interested in golf architecture and laying out golf courses – though he effected many improvements at Royal Mid-Surrey Golf Club over the years. He was a shrewd businessman and, even as early as his time at Winchester, he took George Cann into partnership and together they set up a small factory for making golf clubs there. George Cann was one of 'JH's' boyhood friends at Northam and had been about the best of Charles Gibson's apprentices at Royal North Devon Golf Club. When Taylor moved to Royal Mid-Surrey, he and Cann moved the factory to nearby

Richmond, and the firm was registered as 'Cann and Taylor'. It ran successfully for many years and was a much respected firm of clubmakers. Cann did the clubmaking and Taylor showed how well the clubs could be used.

There will be more to say about Taylor, but 1900 is the era when the gutty ball gave way to the core-wound ball, such as we know today, and when the old beech head on wooden clubs gave way to the much harder and tougher persimmon. These were important changes in the game and merit discussion before we come to consider golf in the twentieth century. Before that, however, it is time to introduce the other two members of the trio of great golfers who, like Taylor, started their careers before the end of the nineteenth century and then, like him, changed their golfing techniques and methods to accommodate balls and implements in the twentieth.

### Harry Vardon (1870–1937)

Vardon was born in Grouville, Jersey, in the Channel Islands. In Jersey there was common land which offered fine quality links. Vardon was only one of the caddies on Jersey who became good golfers when they grew up and who became professionals. Harry's brother Tom was the professional at Royal St Georges and became a well-known and successful Tournament professional and another brother (there were five brothers, in all, including Harry), Fred, was the professional at a Club in the Isle of Man. Another Channel Islander was Phillip Gaudin, professional to one of the Manchester Golf Clubs in 1890. Of all the Channel Islanders who became professionals, however, Harry Vardon was, by far, the greatest golfer.

Harry Vardon's father was a gardener; there is no written record that he played golf, but there is a photograph showing Harry's father playing golf, c.1900. Vardon describes himself as a thin delicate boy who was never very strong; he was made an assistant gardener as a teenager and worked at it for a few years. During that time he was a keen cricketer and footballer; even, some years later, when he was the professional at Ganton, he was the captain of the local football team. During his time in Jersey as a gardener he continued to play golf in his spare time.

Tom Vardon was the first to leave for the mainland and became assistant professional to George Lowe at Lytham St Annes. He wrote enthusiastically to brother Harry about the prospects of being a professional in Britain and, when Lowe laid out a 9 hole course at Harrogate for Lord Ripon, Tom wrote to his brother and told him that the post of professional to the new club was available. Harry applied for the job and was duly appointed.

Unfortunately, there was little golf to be had at the new Club and, urged on by wellwishers, he applied for the same job at Bury Golf Club and was appointed there; in this post he got rather more golf and began to build up his game.

In 1893 he made his first entry for the Open but came 25th; shortly after, he played in a Tournament at Portrush and reached the final, beating both the Kirkaldy brothers in successive rounds.

---

### Vardon's record in the Open Championship up to 1900

| | |
|---|---|
| 1893 | 25th |
| 1894 | 5th |
| 1895 | 9th. He returned the lowest score in the first round. |
| 1896 | Winner. He tied with Taylor and won the play-off. |
| 1897 | 6th |
| 1898 | Winner. Beat Willie Park Junior by one shot at Prestwick. |
| 1899 | Winner. At Sandwich. |
| 1900 | Runner up to Taylor at St Andrews. |

---

In 1896, prior to the Open Championship, he had beaten Taylor in a challenge match.

Vardon was, essentially, a medal player and said that he believed this was the best way to find the best golfer. He was a man of slightly above average build but was gifted with huge hands (this was probably what made him adopt the overlapping grip which Laidlay had used nearly twenty years before). Many years later Walter Hagen met him; Hagen's most lasting recollection was that, when they shook hands, his hand disappeared into Vardon's!

His swing was the epitome of style and grace; he seldom seemed to hit the ball hard and yet he hit it further than most of his contemporaries – and was notably straight. At the top of the backswing, his left arm showed a slight, but definite, bend at the elbow. This was against the accepted best practice; when asked how he played so well, while bending his left elbow, he made no direct reply except to say that he liked playing against people with straight left arms!

Vardon was a fine iron player and a very good putter. He was a modest man of impeccable manners and was regarded by all as a true gentleman. He always played in a cap and was a regular player in knickerbockers, calf-length trousers, fastened just below the knee, which were the favourite wear for those who went shooting and were the predecessors of the more exaggerated form of trousers known as 'plus fours'.

In 1900 he made a tour of the United States; he played and behaved so well that he made a great impres-sion on American golfers and had a great influence in both popularising golf in the United States and in show-ing them how the game should be played. In his exhibi-tion matches he usually played the best ball of two American golfers and was almost never beaten. He won the US Open Championship in 1900 from a field which included John Henry Taylor.

Vardon was very impressed with the American desire to learn and willingness to practise and forecast that they would become a force to be reckoned with in golf – a forecast which, at the time, nobody took seriously.

### James Braid (1870–1950)

The third member of the illustrious trio of professionals was James Braid of Elie and Earlsferry, in Fife.

As in the case of Taylor, Braid's father was not a golfer but, unlike the other two, Braid's father was definitely opposed to golf for his son, regarding it as an occupation with little future. As a result, Braid was apprenticed to a joiner. Possibly, in the context of the time, it was com-mon sense on the part of his father because there were few golf courses in Scotland at the time and only about three in England and, in any event, not every Golf Club had a professional. It is possible that James Braid's train-ing as a joiner may have been quite useful to him when he became a clubmaker.

Braid had played golf, carried, and been among golfers, from his earliest days – he once said that he could not remember when he had not played golf – and he required no formal teaching to develop a golf swing, for the golf links in his area could boast a large number of golfers, many of whom became famous.

Whenever he could, Braid played golf and he played with good local players, developing a fine swing and a good game. Playing in a caddies competition against older boys when he was eight years old, over 9 holes, he won by 20 shots and he broke the record for the Elie links when he was sixteen.

At one time his job as a joiner took him to St Andrews; there he was able to indulge his passion for golf even more and, when he subsequently was moved to Edinburgh, he played much on the Braids course.

In 1893, a friend from his boyhood, Ralph Smith, went to London to work as a clubmaker in the Army and Navy Stores. James needed no encouragement to join him and worked at the Stores as a clubmaker from 1893 to 1895, becoming an expert. During this time, he played as much golf as he could in his spare time and the word went round that one of the clubmakers at the Army and Navy Stores was a good golfer.

He was a tall, thin, supple youth but one who had trouble with his eyes; at some time, when he was working as a joiner, he had accidentally got lime in his eyes and this badly affected his vision. From time to time, throughout his life, his eyes became particularly bad and his poor eyesight worsened with age. Braid had played a few rounds at West Drayton Golf Club and the members both liked him and admired his golf. In 1895, they arranged a match for him at West Drayton against the reigning Open Champion, John Henry Taylor. The game was tight and the golf was very good; it finished all square after 36 holes. Taylor had not known his opponent before the game; he was impressed by Braid and said so in a little speech after the game. Braid was now accepted as an up and coming golf professional.

James Braid, although a fine golfer as a youth, was, for his height and build, a short driver. The reason seems to have been that he stood close to the ball and had an unusually upright swing. When he acquired some better clubs to play with, he stood further away from the ball and very rapidly developed into a very long driver. He also became renowned for his immensely long cleek shots. His long putting was always good but his short putting was poor. Later in life he putted with an aluminium putter; his putting stroke became slow and rhythmic and he became a very fine long putter and a devastatingly good middle distance putter. Taylor said of him, in later life, that he could not think of anyone who was more likely to hole putts of this length than Braid. The short putts remained a problem, but never a severe one. He had a long, full swing with a great deal of knee action and was an obvious hard hitter; he was described as 'hitting the ball with a divine fury'.

He first entered the Open Championship in 1894 and was 10th, 15 shots behind Taylor, the winner.

Shortly after his match with Taylor he was offered, and accepted, the post of professional to the new Golf Club at Romford and remained their for six years. It was while there that he married and his two sons were born.

**James Braid**

He lost no time in setting up a clubmaker's shop and employed several of his old chums from Elie.

James Braid was a man of few words; when he spoke it was after thought. Although quiet, he was a very kindly man and possessed of a good sense of humour. He had a natural dignity and impeccable good manners. He allowed no facial expression to show his emotions on the golf course and always remained in total control of himself. As a boy he played no other game than golf and he had a passion and respect for the game which few have ever equalled. Although he played very widely in the United Kingdom, he did not play much outside and never visited the United States; the reason for this was that he had a morbid fear of the sea, and even the short passage to the island of Islay from the Scottish mainland caused him physical distress. Added to that was the perennial trouble with his eyes; he was always afraid that they would become worse in constant bright sunlight.

This takes the story of the Great Triumvirate, as they came to be known, up to 1900. Important changes took

### Braid in the Open Championship up to 1900

| 1894 | 10th |
| 1895 | Did not play. |
| 1896 | 6th |
| 1897 | Runner-up. |
| 1898 | 11th |
| 1899 | 5th |
| 1900 | 3rd |

# What the Players in the
# 1904 Open Championship Used.

## What do You Use?

| NAMES. | | | | Aggregate for first two rounds. | | Third Round. | | Fourth Round. | | Total. | What he Used. |
|---|---|---|---|---|---|---|---|---|---|---|---|
| 1. | J. White (Sunningdale) | .. | .. | .. | 155 | .. | 72 | .. | 69 | .. | 296 | HASKELL |
| 2. { | J. Braid (Walton Heath) | .. | .. | .. | 157 | .. | 69 | .. | 71 | .. | 297 | HASKELL |
| 2. { | J. H. Taylor (Mid-Surrey) | .. | .. | .. | 155 | .. | 74 | .. | 68 | .. | 297 | HASKELL |
| 4. | T. Vardon (Sandwich) | .. | .. | .. | 154 | .. | 75 | .. | 72 | .. | 301 | HASKELL |
| 5. | H. Vardon (Totteridge) | .. | .. | .. | 149 | .. | 79 | .. | 74 | .. | 302 | HASKELL |
| 6. | J. Sherlock (Oxford) | .. | .. | .. | 154 | .. | 78 | .. | 77 | .. | 309 | HASKELL |
| 7. { | A. Kirkaldy (St. Andrews) | .. | .. | .. | 157 | .. | 74 | .. | 79 | .. | 310 | HASKELL |
| 8. { | Mr. J. Graham, jun. (Royal Liverpool) | | .. | | 152 | .. | 78 | .. | 80 | .. | 310 | HASKELL |
| 9. | A. Herd (Huddersfield) | .. | .. | .. | 160 | .. | 76 | .. | 75 | .. | 311 | HASKELL |
| 10. { | B. Sayers (North Berwick) | .. | .. | .. | 160 | .. | 76 | .. | 77 | .. | 313 | HASKELL |
| 11. { | Mr. R. Maxwell (Tantallon) | .. | .. | .. | 160 | .. | 76 | .. | 77 | .. | 313 | HASKELL |
| 12. { | R. Thomson (Romford) | .. | .. | .. | 151 | .. | 80 | .. | 84 | .. | 315 | HASKELL |
| 13. { | W. Park (Huntercombe) | .. | .. | .. | 156 | .. | 81 | .. | 78 | .. | 315 | HASKELL |
| 14. { | A. H. Toogood (Chingford) | .. | .. | .. | 164 | .. | 74 | .. | 77 | .. | 315 | HASKELL |
| 15. { | E. Ray (Ganton) | .. | | .. | 162 | .. | 77 | .. | 76 | .. | 315 | HASKELL |
| 16. { | G. Coburn (Portmarnock) | .. | .. | .. | 161 | .. | 75 | .. | 80 | .. | 316 | HASKELL |
| 17. { | J. Rowe (Ashdown Forest) | .. | .. | .. | 168 | .. | 75 | .. | 73 | .. | 316 | HASKELL |
| 18. | Mr. J. Ball, jun. (Royal Liverpool) | | .. | | 161 | .. | 79 | .. | 78 | .. | 318 | HASKELL |
| 19. { | G. H. Cawsey (Malvern) | .. | .. | .. | 162 | .. | 78 | .. | 79 | .. | 319 | HASKELL |
| 20. { | F. Collins (Llandudno) | .. | .. | .. | 165 | .. | 75 | .. | 79 | .. | 319 | HASKELL |
| 21. { | E. Grey (Littlehampton) | .. | .. | .. | 161 | .. | 74 | .. | 84 | .. | 319 | HASKELL |
| 22. | Mr. J. S. Worthington (Mid-Surrey) | | .. | | 164 | .. | 78 | .. | 78 | .. | 320 | HASKELL |
| 23. | T. G. Renouf (Silloth) | .. | .. | .. | 161 | .. | 79 | .. | 81 | .. | 321 | HASKELL |
| 24. | P. J. Gaudin (Manchester) | .. | .. | .. | 162 | .. | 80 | .. | 80 | .. | 322 | HASKELL |
| 25. | A. Thompson (North Surrey) | .. | | .. | 167 | .. | 75 | .. | 81 | .. | 323 | HASKELL |
| 26. { | F. Cawkwell (Sandy Gate) | .. | .. | .. | 166 | .. | 79 | .. | 80 | .. | 325 | HASKELL |
| 27. { | Mr. Edward Blackwell (Royal and Ancient) | | .. | | 165 | .. | 81 | .. | 79 | .. | 325 | HASKELL |
| 28. { | R. Jones (Wimbledon Park) | .. | .. | | 166 | .. | 77 | .. | 82 | .. | 325 | HASKELL |
| 29. { | A. Bellworthy (Mitcham) | .. | .. | .. | 166 | .. | 83 | .. | 77 | .. | 326 | HASKELL |
| 30. { | J. Hepburn (Surbiton) | .. | .. | .. | 167 | .. | 79 | .. | 80 | .. | 326 | HASKELL |
| 31. { | P. Hills (North Manchester) | .. | .. | | 168 | .. | 80 | .. | 78 | .. | 326 | |
| 32. | G. Pannell (Littlehampton) | .. | .. | .. | 166 | .. | 81 | .. | 81 | .. | 328 | HASKELL |
| 33. | W. J. Leaver (Harlech) | .. | .. | .. | 165 | .. | 82 | .. | 81 | .. | 328 | HASKELL |
| 34. { | E. Risebro (Norwich) | .. | .. | .. | 166 | .. | 85 | .. | 78 | .. | 329 | HASKELL |
| 35. { | A. Denholm (Hove) | .. | .. | .. | 165 | .. | 84 | .. | 80 | .. | 329 | HASKELL |
| 36. { | P. Wyatt (Herne Bay) | .. | .. | .. | 165 | .. | 81 | .. | 83 | .. | 329 | HASKELL |
| 37. { | C. Neaves (Lossiemouth) | .. | .. | .. | 166 | .. | 80 | .. | 85 | .. | 331 | HASKELL |
| 38. { | C. Roberts (Woolton) | .. | .. | .. | 165 | .. | 86 | .. | 80 | .. | 331 | HASKELL |
| 39. { | H. A. Howlett (Puttenham) | .. | .. | .. | 167 | .. | 86 | .. | 79 | .. | 332 | HASKELL |
| 40. { | A. Matthews (Rhyl) | .. | .. | .. | 166 | .. | 78 | .. | 78 | .. | 332 | HASKELL |
| 41. { | W. C. Gaudin (Scarborough) | .. | .. | .. | 168 | .. | 79 | .. | 86 | .. | 333 | HASKELL |
| 42. { | H. Cawsey (Ashford Manor) | .. | .. | .. | 163 | .. | 88 | .. | 82 | .. | 333 | HASKELL |
| 43. | W. McEwan (Formby) | .. | .. | .. | 167 | .. | 83 | .. | 85 | .. | 335 | HASKELL |
| 44. | T. Yeoman (Seaford) | .. | .. | .. | 167 | .. | 86 | .. | 85 | .. | 338 | HASKELL |
| 45. | R. Gray (Berkhampsted) | .. | .. | .. | 168 | .. | 87 | .. | 89 | .. | 344 | HASKELL |

## The B. F. GOODRICH CO., 7, Snow Hill, London, E.C.

Advertisement demonstrating how quickly the Haskell ball had taken over from the gutty place in the golf ball and in golf clubs, almost exactly at this time, which affected the future development of golf and the style of play of these three great golfers.

## Golf clubs and Balls at the end of the Nineteenth Century

In about 1885 a change took place in the shape of wooden clubs as has already been described in the chapter on clubs. Previously the head of the club was still attached to the shaft by a long splice, glued and supported by whipping.

In 1900 clubs were made in which the shaft was inserted into a hole in the head and held by glue. Exactly why this method was adopted is not certain but in the many iron clubs which were, by now, coming on the market, the shaft was fitted into a cavity in the hosel in the traditional method for iron clubs and it may have become evident to the wooden clubmakers that perhaps a similar method was quite suitable for wooden clubs. In addition there was, by then, a rapid development of methods of mass-production to cope with the huge increase in demand; it was easier to devise machinery to make the 'socket head' type of club, as they were called, than the spliced head clubs.

The traditional wood from which club heads were made was beech. Toward the end of the nineteenth century gutty balls were made which flew better and were harder than the old gutta ball; while they flew better, the hardness did much damage to the club faces of wooden clubs and there needed to be inserts of bone or leather, or vulcanite, into the faces of the clubs to repair the damage.

A 'Tiger' rubbercore ball, with circular markings, made in the USA, c.1908

In the United States there was a very tough, hard wood called persimmon which was used extensively for making 'shoe trees', and this was found to be very suitable for the heads of wooden clubs and took over from beech. As a result of this, the heads of wooden clubs needed less repair. However, another factor entered into the equation; in the United States a new and revolutionary golf ball was developed. It consisted of a central core around which was wound miles of thin strip elastic, the whole being covered with a gutta percha skin. These balls were known as 'rubbercores' or 'Haskells', the latter after the man who was credited with the invention.

Advertisement for Kite rubbercore balls

The ball was very much livelier than the gutty ball and could be hit a lot further. Whereas it could be hit further off the tee with a wooden club, the effect on iron-play was even more dramatic as the ball flew off the iron club with great ease. Generally, when playing shots 'through the green', the use of the Haskell ball made life much easier and it was taken up by poor golfers with enthusiasm.

To those brought up on strict sportsmanship and a tradition of fair play, the ball made the game so much easier that it seemed to them that those who used the ball had an unfair advantage over those who still used the gutty.

The new ball was referred to as 'Bounding Billy' by the devotees of the gutty and those who used them were referred to, slightingly, as 'Bounders' – now an accepted expression for one who is willing to take an unfair advantage of others.

The new ball was used, not because it did not break up in play, because the new ones often did, nor, unlike the gutta ball when it took over from the feathery, because it was cheaper, because it was not. It was used because it made the game easier. It did not make all aspects of the game easier, however; it was much more difficult to stop on the green and it was very lively off the putter face. Being softer than the hard gutty, it did not damage wooden club faces.

So strongly did some of the older golfers feel about it that a golfer of about ninety years of age told the author that he had teed one up in a foursome with three old friends in about 1905 and one of them stepped forward, picked the ball off the tee, handed it back to him and demanded that he use a gutty!

The result of these changes in the golf ball on the play of skilful professionals such as Vardon, Braid and Taylor was significant and will become apparent as the story of these great golfers continues.

# 12

# Golf at the start of the 20th Century

Bᴇᴛᴡᴇᴇɴ 1900 and 1902 there were great changes in Britain in the implements of golf and the conditions under which golf was played. There was a huge increase in the number of golfers. To accommodate such an increase there needed to be a corresponding increase in the number of courses, most of which were inland courses. As a rough guide, there were about 34 golf courses in Britain in 1870 and about 3,000 by 1905. Rail travel and the motor-car made golf courses more accessible. Golf architecture, first put in proper perspective by Willie Park Junior, was steadily developing and a knowledge of land drainage and better machinery made it possible to make good golf courses on land which, thirty years before, would not have been considered suitable.

In golf clubs, the bulger wooden head was well established but the type of joint between the head and the shaft had changed. The shaft was now inserted into a hole in the head and held by adhesive and some external whipping – this type of club was referred to as a 'socket head' club. This type of joint was not, of course, new; caddies had been making clubs in this way for many years, as Vardon recalls in the reminiscences of his boyhood in Jersey. The joint was simple and effective although some of the old hands doubted if it was as good a job as the 'scared' method and even later professionals, such as Walter Hagen in 1912, expressed the same view. The important thing was that it was perfectly adequate and was a much easier joint for mass production.

In iron clubs, Spaldings, a firm of American origin, had perfected a method of using 'drop casting' as a means of making iron heads; this, too, was an effective method and easy for mass production, making the irons cheaper.

An additional benefit of the new ball was that unlike the gutty, it rose easily from the club face and it was thus much easier to play the ball from a bad lie. The tendency to rise meant that the good golfer had to devise means to keep it down. This gave rise to the 'push shot' in which the club was brought steeply down on the back of the ball, giving it back spin and a lower flight; unfortunately, the result of this was to produce deeper and longer divots.

A problem which also affected the better golfer was that the lively rubbercore was much more easily deflected from its line on the green by minor blemishes than was the gutty, which put the good putter at a disadvantage.

There was a lot of correspondence in golf magazines about the pros and cons of the new ball and, eventually, in 1902, *Golf Illustrated* decided to send a Questionnaire to all the leading amateurs and professionals. It posed the following questions:

1. Do you feel that the rubber-filled ball adds to your drive?
2. Do you find that you play a better all-round game with the rubber-filled ball?
3. Do you think that the rubber-filled ball improves the play of one class of golfer more than another?
4. In your opinion, does the rubber-filled ball spoil the present courses and, if so, in what particulars, and what remedies do you propose?

These were some of the answers:

*Charles Hutchings* (He had won the Amateur Championship in 1902, using the new ball):
1. It adds to the length of both wood and iron shots.
2. Driving through the green is made easier; on the green and with short iron shots the ball is more difficult to control.
3. It helps enormously the man who has a good short game but lacks distance off the tee.
4. I do not think courses are ruined. What you gain in length from the tee you are liable to lose in control around the green.

*Horace Hutchinson*:
1. Yes, I do, 10 yards with the drives and 30 yards with the irons.
2. Yes, I do.
3. Yes, I do. It improves the play of the accurate but not hard hitter the most. It adds much to the length of ladies' drives, etc.
4. Present courses are quite long enough and difficult for me, even with rubber-filled balls.
N.B. Your queries do not, in my opinion, touch the great point in which Haskells make the game easier – that is, in the greater ease with which they are able to get up and away from indifferent lies. . . .'

*J.E. Laidlay*:
1. I gain very considerable distance . . . especially off the iron clubs.
2. I have not much experience as yet . . . . they certainly make the game easier through the green.
3. The ball is of more benefit to the second-class player than to the first. Accuracy in hitting the ball through the green is not so necessary as with the gutty.
4. Not much experience as yet . . . They certainly make the courses easier . . . next year records will be lower all round the country.

*Mure Ferguson*:
1. I am quite certain that I can drive a Haskell ball 20 yards further, with both wood and iron clubs.
2. I have not much experience yet . . . . there is little doubt that, if one practised with it, it is superior to the gutty.
3. It is of most benefit to the short driver.
4. Present golf courses are spoilt by the new ball and, if further improvements are contemplated, it will ruin the game.

*Robert Maxwell* (Prominent Muirfield golfer who would be Amateur Champion in 1903 and 1909):
1. They go further [Paraphrase. *Author*].
2. They have made the game easier, some say that they are more difficult to putt with.
3. They certainly level up players . . . .
4. 'The ball has spoiled some courses more than others'. Maxwell thought that the golf ball should be standardised: 'One would hate to see courses like St Andrews, Hoylake and Prestwick altered out of all recognition'.

*S.H. Fry* (Runner-up in the Amateur Championship in 1902, using the new ball):
1. Adds 15 yards to my drive.
2. I play a much better game because I get more distance.
3. Thinks that it helps players with a handicap of 10 or over but also thinks that Braid, Vardon and Taylor will improve by one stroke per round.
4. Does not think that it spoils courses.

*H.H. Hilton* (Open and Amateur Champion at different times):
1. An average shot with a Haskell goes further. A poor shot with a Haskell goes *much* further.
2. Iron clubs show an even greater difference; it is much easier to play from a bad lie.
3. The Haskell helps the poor golfer.
4. 'You cannot spoil a really good links. The putting is more difficult. I think that it is a pity that the rubber-filled ball was ever introduced.'

*L. Balfour Melville* (Senior R&A member and Amateur Champion in 1895):
1. Adds considerably to all full shots through the green.
2. I think that it makes the game easier.
3 and 4. The game is much equalised between the poor and good golfers; the ball is apt to spoil the present courses. The golf ball should be regulated.

*Edward Blackwell* (A senior R&A member, international golfer and runner-up in the Amateur more than once. A noted long driver):
1. I drive the ball 15 yards further. It is better with irons out of a poor lie but the ball tends to soar.
2. The game is not made easier because it is more difficult to putt with.
3. Do not think that it helps any particular class of golfer.
4. Do not think that it spoils courses.

*John Low* (Senior R&A member, international golfer, a renowned putter. Member of the Rules of Golf Committee):
General statement: 'The ball is an evil to the game'. Unfortunately, the golfers who have profited by the invention are slow to admit that the credit belongs to the ball. The 4 handicap man of last year has been converted into a scratch player without acquiring any new skill.'

*A. MacFie* (First Amateur Champion in 1885, noted for accuracy rather than length):
1. 'It is more suitable for my feeble long game than the gutty. I gain considerably in driving and even more with the irons. On the other hand, they are more difficult to putt with; if you play firmly for the back of the hole in a short putt, the Haskell is liable to jump out.'

## The Professionals' view

*J.H. Taylor*, natural leader of the professionals and a man of integrity and conscience, stated that he had contacted nearly all the leading professionals on the subject of the new ball. 'Every one of them holds the view that the game should be kept as it is at present, at the high water-mark of pure skill; we contend that the rubbercore ball tends to discount this and puts a premium on the less skilful players.'

In later correspondence, John Low points out that, once courses are lengthened to accommodate the new ball, it will never be possible to go back to the gutty [Which was, at that time, the official golf ball. *Author*]. He goes on to say that the ball will be improved further 'and where is the lengthening process going to cease?'

MacFie had mentioned that the new ball could jump out of the hole. However, there was another hole over which the new ball could jump and a letter to *Golf Illustrated* in 1903 addresses the problem: 'The rubber core presents Green Committees with a problem. At greens where Nature has not given an adequate supply of properly placed bunkers around the green to stop the topped ball reaching it. Flat pot bunkers do not do this. The first duty of a bunker is to stop the topped ball and ensure that the topper loses a stroke. A bunker with a raised bank would be effective but ugly-looking, like rifle butts. Is there a middle way which will avoid the Irish bank type of bunker, so offensive to the eye?'

Well, there was no middle way to be found and so, today, all bunkers have a bank, except on one or two courses where some of the old-style, simple, pit-type bunkers still remain – such as at Westward Ho! What the overall cost of banking every bunker amounts to (plus upkeep) is incalculable.

Editorial comment on all this correspondence in *Golf Illustrated* is revealing: 'The ball is being steadily improved and the results on play are alarming.'

'There is little doubt that the R&A will have to legislate in the near future. They, undoubtedly do spoil holes that are of perfect length for the gutty. The Haskell's ability to bound along and jump hazards serves to place the second-class player on a par with the crack player.'

'The way to discount this advantage would be to lengthen golf courses – a very big undertaking and expensive, and which would be of little use if the ball were then further improved.'

The editorial then goes on to point out that action by the R&A to limit the ball would be difficult because, when a standard ball was mooted at the United States Golf Association, the idea had no supporters at all; as the editor rightly points out a 'standard' ball would have to be widely accepted.

What the editor did not point out was that by lengthening golf courses the whole character of such courses would be changed, and hazards and difficulties which, in the days of the gutty, were well designed and placed for the purpose would become redundant and, in some cases, hazards designed to catch the second shot would catch the drive.

The *Yorkshire Observer*, quoted in *Golf Illustrated* in September 1902, has this to say: 'The present state of affairs is inimical to the best interests of the game. Even men who benefit from it are heard to say that this ball should be banned. Vardon says that he can play with it

**Harry Vardon (left) with Archie Compston, *c.*1927**

better than with a gutty. He never plays with it in a match because he could not take a bit of credit for winning with such a ball. He says that he finds it better and easier to play with, all round [including putting. *Author*]. In spite of this, Vardon declares that he will stick to the gutty, if he loses every game that he plays.'

The fact that Vardon, with a living to make (and, perhaps, monetary inducements from the manufacturers of the new ball) did not keep to this principle, does not alter his feelings about the new ball, feelings which he, and the other leading professionals, communicated to J.H. Taylor.

Although the majority of golfers – that is, the poor players – enjoyed the new ball and supported it, not with letters to the editor but by buying it, the better golfers felt that it was spoiling (or going to spoil) the game and wanted it banned. Those who were considered to be the commercial golfing interests in the USA.

The other surprise is that there is almost no reference to the problems associated with the new ball in the textbooks written about golf and how to play it by Taylor, Vardon and Braid; in Taylor's case it is understandable because his book was published in 1902 and therefore must have been written months before the problem arose, but Vardon was writing in 1905 and Braid in 1908. In neither book is there any mention of the much changed conditions for golf in the early 1900s and the virtues, or otherwise, of the new ball.

## Harry Vardon (1870–1936)

An account of Vardon's early career and first trip to the United States is given on p.228. During his first American tour he made a short return to Britain to defend his Open Championship; this sudden change back to British-style golf and golf courses cannot have made it easy for him and he did very well to be runner-up to J.H. Taylor.

Vardon was very conscious of the need to win the American Open Championship to crown a successful tour. If he had had to beat only American competitors, the task, barring accidents should not have been beyond him but his old friend and rival, J.H. Taylor, entered and this made things much more difficult. He won the Championship from J.H. Taylor by two shots, Taylor being 8 shots ahead of the third man. Vardon thus achieved his ambition and secured his revenge for having been beaten by Taylor in the British Open. It is probable that Taylor was faced with the same difficulties that Vardon had faced when he crossed the Atlantic in the other direction to play in the British Open.

Harry Vardon always said that he played the best golf of his life in the United States in 1900 and that he left a little of his game there when he returned to Britain. He returned home in early 1901 and was, undoubtedly, a tired man. Nevertheless, he managed to be runner-up in the Open of that year. He was again runner-up in 1902, the year in which Sandy Herd won, playing with the new rubbercore ball. In 1903, Vardon won the Open again; it was a great victory because he was not a fit man.

Vardon was 4th in 1904, 7th in 1905, 3rd in 1906, 5th in 1907 and in 1908, 15th in 1909 and 9th in 1910.

In 1911 he won the Open again, beating Arnaud Massy in a play-off.

Harry Vardon at impact, c.1907. The excellent position shows why he was such a good golfer. His left arm may have been bent at the top of the swing – it is certainly straight now

leaders of the game and arbiters on the subject were, in the main, the better golfers; it thus seemed likely that the R&A would ban the ball. The Rules of Golf Committee, headed by the redoubtable John Low, a strong opponent of the ball, did so, observing 'The rubbercore balls are not calculated to test golf on our present courses to the same extent as gutta percha balls.' This firm decision by the Committee was not ratified by the R&A.

As the R&A had failed to ban the ball and the USGA were very much in favour of it, it was inevitable that the new ball would become generally accepted. The only surprise was that the Rules of Golf Committee did not immediately resign en masse.

The outcome must have been very pleasing to

In 1912 he was runner-up to Ted Ray by one shot. In 1913, he was 3rd and it was in that year that he made his second visit to the United States.

## Vardon's second visit to the United States

On this occasion Vardon was accompanied by Ted Ray. The details of the tour are not clear; what is clear is the dramatic result of the American Open Championship. It was generally conceded that either Ray or Vardon would win it. What no one expected was that a 20-year-old amateur American golfer, Francis Ouimet, would tie with them for first place and then beat them both in the play off.

One aspect of this tour, which has not been reported before, concerns the opening of a new course in Utah. About twenty years ago, a patient on holiday from the United States was taken ill and I attended him medically. He subsequently had an operation from which he made a slow recovery, mainly because he was 86 years old. I detected beneath his American accent a different accent. When asked about it he said that he originated from Prestwick and had gone to the United States in 1911. He said that he was a retired golf professional and had laid out a course in Utah in 1911–12 and was the professional there until he retired. In 1913, on hearing that Vardon and Ray were planning a tour of the United States, he asked if they would be willing to play an exhibition match to open his new course. They agreed and travelled overnight to a station near the town in which he lived. They arrived at about 7.30 in the morning and the professional went to meet them at the station in his 'Model T' Ford (which, in those days had hickory wheel-spokes). He took them back to his house and offered them breakfast but they declined, saying that they had breakfasted on the train. He then asked them if they would like a drink and they said that they would. He got out two tumblers and a whisky bottle and handing Ray a glass he tilted the bottle, telling him to 'say when'. Ray said 'Stop when you get to the top' and Vardon said 'and the same for me'.

After about ½ pint of neat whisky each, they then went to the course and gave a fine exhibition of golf. My patient was particularly struck with Vardon's driving and said that the sensible thing would have been to take Vardon's ball and place it in the middle of the fairway at 250 yards and ask him to play the second shot but that would have deprived one of the pleasure of seeing him hit it there with elegant ease off the tee!

In 1914 Vardon won the Open for the sixth and last time. There was no Open from 1914 to 1920. After the First World War he continued to compete but never recaptured his best form. Nevertheless, he remained a beautiful and elegant golfer for many years to come.

## Vardon's third American tour

In 1920, Vardon and Ray made a second joint trip to America and played in the US Open Championship. There was a large entry and two days of qualifying rounds. Vardon, with 151 for 36 holes, led the first-day qualifiers and Ray, with 148, led the second-day qualifiers.

At the end of the third round, Vardon led by one shot from Hutchison and Leo Diegel and by two from Ray. After 63 holes Vardon was going along very comfortably and had done the first 9 holes in 36; it was reckoned that he could take 41 for the second 9 and still win.

Vardon made par at the 10th and then birdied the 11th; on the 12th tee (522 yards), before they drove, a sudden and vicious storm blew up and they had to play the 12th into a howling gale. Vardon needed four wooden shots to reach the green and took 6. At the 13th he stood firm in the lashing wind but jabbed a 2 foot putt wide of the hole. Herbert Wind says that he was 50 years old and utterly weary; he 3 putted 15 and 16 and, at the 17th, he failed to carry the brook with his second and took yet more strokes. He dropped, in all, 7 strokes to par in the last 7 holes and was beaten by Ray (43 years old) by one stroke.

## Vardon's swing

Vardon's swing had nothing revolutionary about it. It was simply a fine elegant swing of which the most noticeable feature was a smooth rhythm, so that he never seemed to be hitting the ball hard. Bernard Darwin, who was a contemporary and saw him play in all the big events reports that, in his early days, he had a rather ungainly body lift in the backswing but, with the passage of time, this lift became imperceptible and was lost in the beautiful, slow, rhythmical swing.

A feature of his swing was a much more upright backswing than any of his contemporaries and he also allowed, at the top of the backswing, a definite bend in the left elbow. By the 1920s the gospel of golf demanded a straight left arm and Vardon was sometimes asked why he did not try it; his short reply, delivered with an amiable smile, was that he liked playing against men with straight left arms. Whatever happened to his left arm at the top of the swing, it was definitely straight at the moment of impact. Even when he had a lift in the backswing – normally a recipe for trouble – he continued to hit the ball very straight and long, much to the chagrin of the purists.

The result of this upright type of swing was that he hit a drive which was fairly high and had a long carry; this he attained with the gutty ball and he must have had to make adjustments to his swing to keep the rubbercore from soaring too high.

that he usually only grazed the turf or took a minimal divot. The author was fortunate enough to see him play on one occasion. Vardon was then past middle age (and the author was still in single figures!) and the occasion was the opening of Teignmouth Golf Club in 1924. One shot, in particular, comes immediately to mind; the 16th hole at Teignmouth, in South Devon, was a short hole of about 150–160 yards. The green was small and tilted slightly towards the tee; it was surrounded on three sides by a quarry, and it was only at the back of the green that it was connected to some heathery land. The weather was dry and, in 1924, as there was no regular watering of greens, the 16th green was very hard and bare. Vardon hit a low iron shot which floated up to the green and stopped in a few feet; neither of the other three professionals could stay on the green. A clergyman, who was obviously a Vardon fan, hurried across the tee as soon as Vardon and the others had left and picked up Vardon's divot. He had brought a tape measure with him and measured the divot, which was a fraction under six inches long and extremely thin.

Vardon was a good putter, for as Darwin points out, he could not have won all that he did unless he was. During the period 1901–08 he putted badly on occasions but, during that time, he was not playing the rest of his game well. This period in his career will be discussed later.

Darwin, who should know if anybody does, says that he was a genius on the golf course and head and shoulders above his contemporaries. An example of his versatility occurred at Totteridge, where he was the professional for many years. When he played with the members he usually played the best ball of three of them and gave them six strokes in addition. He always won and this became rather boring, so he decided to play left handed and got his clubmakers to make him a set of left-handed clubs. He continued to play the members left handed and, within two weeks, he was back to giving any three of them the same start and beating them.

**Harry Vardon at the top of the backswing. Note the buttoned-up coat, the bent left arm, and the club 'crossing the line'**

He used the overlapping grip; possibly this was after Taylor had taken to it but, in any case, long after Laidlay had used it 30 years before both of them. In Vardon's case the overlapping grip was particularly suitable because he had unusually large hands.

### Vardon's play

A feature of Vardon's play was that he was very consistent, making a large number of good shots and hardly ever a bad one. He was long off the tee – and always straight down the middle; his long woods to the green were in a class by themselves. Indeed, they were so good that the rest of his game was seldom mentioned. He was a great iron player and one of the pioneers of the push shot with the cleek. His ability to play the high cut up pitch shot was second only to Taylor's. A feature of his iron play was

### Vardon the man

Vardon was a man of serene temperament who himself said that, apart from a short period in his early youth, he was never bothered with nerves.

He always maintained that golf was better with a gutty ball than a rubbercore because, with a gutty, one could not get away with a bad shot.

He was a courteous and gentle man, possessed of natural good manners, but beneath that disarming exterior was a determined golfer. The absence of nerves made him a particularly formidable opponent in tight situations and he always coolly assessed shots before he played them, going for the big shot when he considered it necessary but always willing to play a safe one if logic so dictated. He had no enemies among his brother professionals and Taylor, who knew him very well, was a firm admirer and friend. He had little conceit in himself and preferred to stay in the background.

## Vardon's health

Vardon was said as a small boy to be delicate and to have a weak chest and his father was advised by the family doctor to get him a job in the open air. There is no doubt that Harry suffered from tuberculosis of the lung; it was a common disease in those days and was a chronic disease. From time to time sufferers had acute episodes which required hospital treatment but the disease was always with them and it was rare for them to feel really fit at any time.

The disease was commoner in the poorer classes because it tended to occur in large families who lived in small, overcrowded, damp, dark rooms and who existed on a poor diet which was short in vitamins. Because it was associated with poverty and poor housing, tuberculosis was regarded as a rather shameful disease and, as it was contagious as well, families who were infected tended to keep quiet about it because the neighbours might shun them if they knew.

**Harry Vardon, c.1905. He wears shoes, and the left heel is markedly raised with the whole foot turned to the right**

There was no specific treatment for tuberculosis. The only hope was to reverse the conditions which had promoted it and to ensure that the patient had plenty of fresh air and as much sunshine as could be had and to provide a really good diet with vitamins. The fact that the family doctor had advised that Vardon should get a job in the open air suggests that the doctor had made a diagnosis. Perhaps it was unfortunate that Vardon was a regular pipe smoker.

It is interesting that Vardon was very happy when he played golf in Florida, where it was warm and sunny and where, no doubt, he ate a lot of fruit. Nevertheless, the strain of such a long tour in the United States, involving many long train journeys and the constant pressure of public appearances, must have undermined his health and made it more likely that he would have an acute episode.

There is no hint that Vardon was unwell during 1902 but then there never is a hint from him about being unwell until he was so ill that he could not play golf. In his book *The Complete Golfer* he writes: 'How difficult is our task when sometimes we are not feeling as well as we might wish – as must occasionally happen – I shall leave the charitable reader to imagine. Has he ever felt like playing his best game when a little below par in mind or body?'

Vardon always considered that winning the Open in 1903 was one of his best performances: 'For some time I had been feeling exceedingly unwell; as it appeared shortly afterwards, there was serious trouble brewing. During the play for the Championship I was not at all myself and while I was making the last round I was repeatedly so faint that I thought it would be impossible for me to finish.' As has already been recorded, he won by 6 shots!

On 13 July 1903 he broke the record for the Totteridge course with a 66.

On 15 July 1903, he played in a competition of the Northern Section of the PGA; he led after the first round but was beaten into second place by Ted Ray at the end of 36 holes. The report states that 'rain fell without ceasing from start to finish'.

On 18 July 1903 Vardon made a flying visit to the Manchester District Club where he played a 36-hole match and broke the course record in the morning and then broke his new record in the afternoon.

A move to have his portrait painted on 22 August 1903 had to be abandoned because he was too ill and on 25 August 1903, Herd had to take his place in a match against Willie Fernie, again because Vardon was too ill.

When Vardon said that he had been 'exceedingly unwell for some time' prior to the Open of 1903 (which was in late June) he must, in view of the chronic nature of his disease, have been talking of a period of at least two months. He continued to be ill after that, but went on playing superb golf, as has been recorded. Less than a month after his great golfing spell, he was in a sanatorium having had a lung haemorrhage; he must have been feeling very unwell during the period between winning the Open and entering the sanatorium.

In August 1903, while Vardon was in the sanatorium in Norfolk, the Northern Section of the PGA sent him a letter of condolence, sympathy and best wishes for a speedy recovery. It happened that the President of the Northern Section was Phillip Gaudin, a Channel Islander and a longstanding friend of Vardon's. This was Vardon's reply:

> Sanatorium. Mundesley. Norfolk.
>
> Dear Gaudin,
> I have received the kind letter from the Northern Section and hardly know how to thank you for the kind wishes. I can assure you that I will always cherish the kind words. I may say that I am doing well here but I cannot say that I shall ever play golf again; if not, I shall never rest, as golf taken away from me would be as hard for me to give up smoking. The doctor here tells me that he thinks he can put a leather face in my body [this is a reference to the leather faces which were put into wooden clubs when the face began to break up and thus preserved them for future use. *Author*] but, if I have yet another haemorrhage, it may be all up with me. Again, thanking you for your kind wishes and wish you all a pleasant time at Huddersfield with my great friend A. Herd,
>
> Your bunkered friend,
> H. Vardon.

Here is a letter from a man of courage and humour. He is not sorry for himself and is prepared to face the outcome

**Golf in the Channel Islands, *c.*1905.**
**The two mounds are seaweed, drying out prior to use as fertiliser**

**Harry Vardon's father in play, Jersey 1898**

of his treatment philosophically – nor does he forget to wish his friends a happy time.

By 4 September 1903, *Golf Illustrated* is reporting that he is showing improvement and has put on weight [A good sign, *Author*]. The report goes on to say, that, of course, his cure must be slow.

His progress is not detailed in the magazine but it seems very likely that he left the sanatorium at about Christmas time and returned for convalescence to his home in Jersey. In April 1904 there is a brief report that he played a match against the local professional in Jersey and beat him easily.

Although on 7 August 1903, Vardon told *Golf Illustrated*: 'As a pro I find the game a great strain. We never get a rest and when you have got to keep up your reputation, every match has a wearing effect . . . I feel that the Championship match last month has aged me by at least 10 years and I do not think that I shall face such another 4½ hours again'; he played in the Open of 1904, and was a creditable 4th, 4 shots behind his old friends and rivals Braid and Taylor.

It seems that by July 1904 he had recovered from his illness, no doubt having put on weight and lost his cough, but his stamina would have been much affected and it would be months, or years, before he would cease to feel very tired at the end of a tournament. Moreover, it is likely that his regular golfing commitments would not have left him much energy for practising.

In fact, he had, even in 1905, not fully recovered from his illness for there was a great foursomes match over 144 holes, in 1905, in which Taylor and Vardon represented England and Braid and Herd represented Scotland. The match was played over St Andrews, Troon, Lytham and Deal; at St Andrews, the English pair were 2 down (the behaviour of the very partisan gallery was such that Vardon, the mildest of men, had to be persuaded to continue play); at Troon, the Englishmen had a great victory and were 12 up over all. At Lytham, the Scots pair put up a gallant fight and were only 7 down when they came to Deal. It was not possible for Braid and Herd to give their opponents 7 up over 18 holes and have any hope of winning.

On the night before play at Deal, Vardon had another haemorrhage and it was feared that he would be unable to play but he played very well and the Englishmen won easily.

*Golf Illustrated* of 3 August 1906 has a picture of him looking very well. The magazine observes: 'Although the unfortunate state of his health has prevented Vardon from maintaining the pre-eminent position which he occupied 2–3 years ago, he remains today, by universal consent, the most consummate golfing artist whom this generation has seen . . . It is good news for his countless admirers that his health seems to be at last on the mend . . .'.

Through all those long years of malaise and lack of stamina he continued to give an excellent account of himself, as his Open records show; when he failed to make the top he never once attributed his 'failure' (for he was always expected to be first) to ill-health.

In 1911 and 1914 he gave great pleasure to his faithful supporters by winning the Open twice more, thus achieving a record of six wins, which has never been equalled.

The First World War probably gave him a much-needed rest from competitive golf and aided a complete recovery from his lung troubles.

After the War, Vardon ceased to bother with the serious business of top-class competitive golf but remained a beautiful and elegant golfer; his only serious attempt at top honours was his effort to win the American Open in 1920. *Golf Monthly* has a picture of the great professional of the past standing beside Bobby Jones, the great amateur of the future, who was to set the golf world alight in the 1920s and 1930s. This is reproduced on p.231 of this volume.

Of this last great attempt Vardon said: 'I have not the stamina I once possessed. There is nothing I would have liked better than to return home from my last visit to America with the Open Championship, but I lost the best chance I ever had for a Championship I did not win.'

Vardon faded out of a top position in golf more rapidly than his contemporaries, Braid and Taylor, because he was content to continue to serve as Club professional to the Totteridge Golf Club which had so generously supported him in his great tournament career. Braid carried on his career by expanding his activities as a golf architect and Taylor continued, with Cann, to take a leading position in golf clubmaking and, in Taylor's case, also as a golf architect.

It is a curious irony that, brilliant golfer that he was, Vardon only did one hole in one in his lifetime; that was on the course at Mundesley in Norfolk, close to the sanatorium where he was treated in 1903. The circumstances are not clear but the hole was not done in a tournament and it is not difficult to imagine Vardon in the sanatorium feeling much better and fretting to hit a golf ball, being allowed on to the course to get some fresh air and exercise. To do a hole in one at such a time must have been good for morale! There are one or two comments about Vardon, made over the years, which serve to emphasise his greatness as a golfer.

**J.H. Taylor with Dr W.G. Grace**

In his old age, a caddie who had caddied for him in the United States during his second visit in 1920, said that Vardon had played 15 consecutive tournaments without ever playing a shot out of the rough.

Horace Hutchinson, writing a review of the year 1903, observed: 'Harry Vardon, after the Open Championship, broke down in health and did not play again in public . . . when we speak of him as being in the rank of all these others, we are doing them a trifle too much honour, for, really, he stands by himself above them all.'

Finally, Henry Cotton, that great golfer and student of the game writing, in 1937, about the golf swing, concluded: 'I must add that I have learnt a great deal of golf through talking with Harry Vardon, and that I have always felt that he knew more about the game than he ever put on paper.'

J.H. Taylor at the top of his backswing for a mashie shot, *c.*1907

J.H. Taylor putting in 1901. In a class-conscious society, Taylor was proud of being of the artisan class. Here he demonstrates, almost aggressively, by playing in an open-neck shirt with his sleeves rolled up and wearing a belt to support his trousers

## J.H. Taylor in the Twentieth Century

BY 1900, 'J.H.' as he was affectionately known, was one of the leading professionals and in constant competition with two other leading figures, Vardon and Braid. They dominated the golfing scene for the next fourteen years. As far as the Open is concerned, Taylor's record after 1900 is as follows:

| | | | |
|---|---|---|---|
| 1901 | Third. | 1914 | Second. |
| 1902 | Sixth. | 1920 | Twelfth. |
| 1903 | Tenth. | 1921 | Thirtythird. |
| 1904 | Second. | 1922 | Sixth. |
| 1905 | Third. | 1923 | Fortythird. |
| 1906 | Second. | 1924 | fifth (if the two |
| 1907 | Seventh. | (aged 53) | qualifying rounds |
| 1908 | Seventh. | | had counted he |
| 1909 | Winner. | | would have won). |
| 1910 | Fourteenth. | 1925 | Eighth. |
| 1911 | Seventh. | 1926 | Twelfth. |
| 1912 | Twelfth. | 1927 | Fortieth. |
| 1913 | Winner. | | |

In 1928, he ceased to play in the Open.

In other Championships, Taylor won the French Open in 1908 and 1909, the German Open in 1912 and was runner-up in the American Open of 1900.

### *Style of play*

Brought up at Westward Ho! where the Atlantic winds blow fiercely, Taylor developed a style particularly suited to playing in rough weather. He was a man of average height but was very muscular and had strong arms and legs. He was, at the same time, less supple than his taller colleagues. His backswing was on the short side compared with Vardon and Braid and, in consequence, he did not hit the ball quite as far, but then, both Vardon and Braid were notably long drivers. He believed in keeping both feet firmly on the ground ('Flat-footed golf, Sir! Flat-footed golf') and this necessarily shortened his backswing. In his swing he kept his elbows close to his side and, as a result, his follow through was shorter than those of the other two. In fact, he seemed to punch the ball away, a form of swing which was well suited to iron play.

Bernard Darwin, who saw much of his golf from 1896 onwards, wrote of Taylor many years later: 'None have seen him in his pomp; none have seen him, with his cap pulled well down, with his feet planted on the ground like two rocks defying the sea, hitting the ball with a venemous grunt into the teeth of a gale'.

**J.H. Taylor at the end of a drive, showing how well he kept his feet firmly on the ground and had his cap pulled well down when playing in the wind. His jacket is buttoned up, as was the usual fashion at the time, *c*.1906**

he was pre-eminent when playing in high winds. He won the Open Championship at Hoylake in 1913 when the winds were so strong that Bernard Darwin, who was present on all three occasions, remarked that, in his opinion, the wind was stronger than when Cotton won at Carnoustie in 1937 and when Whitcombe won at Sandwich in 1938. Darwin pronounced that his win at Hoylake was a triumph of man over nature and he described a second shot to the 6th hole, the Briars, as 'making a hole in the wind'.

### Taylor the man

Starting from very humble origins, J.H. made himself into a well-educated and articulate man and was a commanding speaker. Despite his fame as a professional golfer and his high standard of self-education, he was always a man of the people and proud of it.

He was of a nervous temperament and told the author that he never slept on the night before an Open championship. None of this showed on the course for he kept himself from displaying any emotion; he was a player of inspiration and capable of great concentration. He would doggedly and dourly work his way through a spell when things were not going right but, when he hit a good spell and really 'got going', there was no holding him.

He was ever thoughtful of the needs of his brother professionals and was a passionate and articulate promoter of their interests. This trait made him the prime mover – and first Chairman – of the Professional Golfers Association in 1900. He was an active Chairman who demanded – and got – from those in charge better amenities for the professionals at major tournaments and it was mainly due to him that a Benevolent Fund was set up to help retired professionals and those who became incapacitated while still working, a scheme which has been a conspicuous success.

In Scotland it was – and still is – possible to play golf cheaply but Taylor always considered it a disgrace that cheap golf was not available around London; he remembered with gratitude and affection the fact that in his native village he had been a member of the Northam Artisans Golf Club, founded in 1888, the first Artisans Club in England. Just before the First World War he had

Taylor more than made up for his slight lack of length by being exceptionally accurate. It was said of him when he won one of his Championships that his only problem when driving was to avoid hitting the guide posts. He was accurate with his brassie [equivalent to today's No.2 wood. *Author*] shots, hitting the ball boldly up to the hole, and his play with the mashie, equivalent to today's No.5 iron, was a revelation to his generation, since he was able to put cut on the ball and thus stop it quickly, even on the hard, unwatered greens.

Taylor was capable of winning a Championship under any conditions, and was the first English professional to win the Open at St Andrews although the Scots said that his high approach shots were not suited to that links. But

**James Braid, *c.*1906**

great pleasure in laying out, for the LCC, a public course at Hainault in Essex – the Hainault Forest Golf Club; in later life, when professional at Royal Mid Surrey Golf Club, he set about establishing a second public course at Richmond. After months of difficulties and setbacks he finally obtained the ground and then designed the course and superintended its construction – all without any payment – and was delighted when the 9-hole course was opened by the then Prince of Wales. He was even more pleased when he received permission to open a further 9 holes which was opened by the then Duke of York, later to become George VI.

J.H. was Chairman of the Council of the Artisan Golfers Association and Chairman of the Committee of the Public Golf Courses Association and remained active in the affairs of these two organisations, and the PGA, for many years. His fellow professionals and the general golfing public owe him a debt of gratitude.

Never afraid to express an opinion, he told St Andrews that the 17th hole was not a good golf hole because the penalties demanded by missing the green with the second shot were too severe and that most sensible players would lay up short with the second shot and play a run up, which he did not consider made for a good hole. As he made this remark just before he won the Open there it took some courage. He was so sure that he was right that, when invited to speak at an Open at St Andrews many years later, he reiterated it. Those who remember some recent Open Championships at St Andrews will appreciate J.H.'s advice to lay up short with the second shot!

When he returned to Northam, on his retirement, he was made President of the Royal North Devon Golf Club, the Club at which, many years before, he had been a humble caddie. It was an honour that he greatly appreciated. He resettled into village life at Northam with ease: he usually had some sweets in his pocket for the village children, who rapidly came to call him 'Uncle J.H.' and he sang in the choir of Northam Church until he was well over 80.

## James Braid in the Twentieth Century

It is now time to follow the fortunes of James Braid into the twentieth century.

Bernard Darwin, who saw most of Braid's great golf and understood much about his swing and methods of play, always felt that his swing was particularly suited to the gutty ball and that it was in the gutty era that Braid should have had his greatest triumphs. In fact, it was in the rubbercore era that Braid, for a few years, was almost unbeatable.

Braid, in his earlier days, was a very poor putter, especially in the matter of short putts – if you cannot putt you cannot score. Braid, however, is the classic example of putting being not a matter of inspiration but of diligent practice and attention to detail.

Braid played with apparent calm and assessed the shot that he was going to play with care, so that it always came as a slight surprise when this calm and careful man then attacked the ball as if he wanted to kill it.

### Braid in the Open Championship

1900  He was 3rd, 13 strokes behind the winner. An expert and experienced amateur golfer who followed him round said that his putting was enough to make the angels weep and that if he had been able to hole from 2 feet he would have won.

1901  The Championship was played at Muirfield. Braid was hitting the ball a very long way and was the only man in the field who could reach the 12th hole with a drive and an iron. He got comfortably in the lead at the end of the 3rd round but, when he started the 4th round, troubles began; he hit a number of timid putts, which he missed, and he was not helped by the highly partisan Scots crowd who, literally, continually slapped him on the back and told him that he was bound to win; he endured so much back slapping that when he came off the course he was very stiff and sore. Nevertheless, he held on to win and this was the start of a great series of successes over the next nine years.

1902  He was second in a tie with Vardon, both men using the gutty ball in this Championship, which was won by Sandy Herd, using the new rubbercore.

1903  5th. 10 shots behind Vardon.

1904  He was second, tied with J.H. Taylor, one shot behind the winner. In this Championship he became the first man to break 70 in the Open.

1905  Winner at St Andrews by 5 shots.

1906  Winner at Muirfield by 4 shots. In this Championship he came from behind to win, completing the last 9 holes in one under par.

1907  5th.

1908  Winner at Prestwick. He won by 8 shots; his winning score was 3 over 4's despite an 8 at the Cardinal hole in the 3rd round.

1909  Runner-up, tied with Tom Ball.

1910  Winner at St Andrews by 4 shots.

Thereafter, he slid down the lists somewhat but always gave a good account of himself.

It is interesting, and may be coincidental, that Braid never won an Open Championship in England. He was a Scot and, perhaps, although never showing it, he was inspired by playing in Scotland before a Scots crowd.

## Other triumphs

Braid suffered from sea sickness and also had, as has been said, much trouble with his eyes. The effect of these disabilities was to prevent him crossing the sea – even crossing the Channel on a calm day meant that he had to lie down throughout the crossing and was sick for some time afterwards – and it meant that he avoided, as far as possible, playing in bright sunlight. It is probably for these reasons that he never played in the United States. He made five trips to France, the first after Massy had won the Open in 1907, when he was accompanied by Taylor and Vardon.

In the French Open in 1907, he was 3rd, in 1909 he was 2nd and in 1910 he was the winner.

As with the other two members of the Triumvirate, Braid lived in the era of the challenge match and he played a large number of such games, winning a fair proportion of them. It could be said that he was more at home in matchplay than medal play and he certainly had a very good record in the *News of the World* Matchplay Championship; this Championship has, alas, now disappeared but, for many years, was the equivalent of the Open in matchplay form and was fiercely contested by all the better professionals. It was a 'knockout' competition

**James Braid at the top of his backswing, 1910**

over 18 holes and such a short sprint meant that there could easily be an upset in the form book and a lesser golfer could beat one of the great men. Braid won this event in 1903, 1905, 1907, and 1911 and was much more successful than his brother professionals in this form of golf.

## Braid the man

Braid was kindly and quiet. He seldom expressed an opinion unless he had given the matter some thought and he expressed his opinion in as few words as possible. He had a good sense of humour but it was always quiet – the loud laugh was not for Jimmy.

When the Professional Golfers Association, a form of trades union for professionals, came into being, J.H. Taylor became the first Chairman and James Braid the first Captain, being Captain four more times because he was Open Champion five times. He said little at these meetings but what he did say was to the point and worth listening to.

His reading was limited to 'Wild West' magazines. Of all the professionals, James Braid was probably the one who was most devoted to golf; a day in which he did not play was a wasted day – and he did not waste many. He played many games with the members of Walton Heath and was always courteous and kindly, so that the members regarded him with great affection and respect.

An example of the respect in which he was held was recounted to the author by a friend who had been a member at Walton Heath for many years and had, in fact, learned to play there as a boy. When he started to play regularly in about 1948, the question arose as to what was to be his handicap; he was asked by Braid to hit a few shots and Braid then pronounced that his handicap was 19 and this became his official Club handicap. The same friend told me of another member who joined Walton Heath in the 1950s and was already a good golfer with a handicap of 2 at other Clubs. In addition he had won a minor National Championship in Europe. He, too, was despatched to see Braid who, after seeing him hit one or two shots, announced that his handicap was 4!

Braid was the complete Club professional and often acted as Starter in competitions at Walton Heath; the author had the unnerving experience of driving from the first tee in one such competition, while the great man stood impassively by. It was noticeable that whether the tee shots of the competitors were very good or very bad, there was no comment from the Starter!

### Braid as an architect

Jimmy was much in demand in this capacity. He laid out a number of important and fine golf courses of which the most notable was Gleneagles, but he also did a great deal of work in improving existing courses. He had an excellent eye for country and a prodigious memory for what he had seen, being quite capable of walking over a course once and then being able, without further reference, to make a sketch of all the holes with suggested improvements.

The author had the pleasure of seeing Braid play, with other professionals, at the opening of two courses in Devon which Braid had laid out. The first was Tiverton Golf Course and the second a new golf course at Exeter –

both in the early 1930s. Although Braid was, by then, well over middle age, the magnificent attack on the ball was still there and he was able to hold his own with other professionals much younger than himself.

Personal experience allows one to offer anecdotes from both occasions. At Tiverton, four professionals played in the morning. In addition to Braid there were J.H. Taylor, E.W.H. Kenyon, at that time a Ryder Cup player, and the professional for the new course; they played a round in the morning and were due to play again in the afternoon at 2 o'clock. At 2.15 they had not appeared, and enquiry among the waiting spectators disclosed that, as it was raining slightly, Braid was asking for more money for all four of them for the afternoon round. It seemed that they were being paid £5 per round and Braid wanted the fee raised to £7 10s (£7.50) for the afternoon. This may well have been true and is an interesting comparison with the fees of modern professionals!

At Exeter, Braid was to play with the new course professional, J.H. Taylor and one of the Whitcombe brothers – probably C.A. While they were standing on the first tee, Whitcombe said to Braid 'Jimmy, why did you put that bunker on the right? It is the best line to the hole and will catch a good tee shot.' Braid said nothing and they all drove off; Braid drove into the bunker on the right. As they went off the tee, Whitcombe said: 'See what I mean?' Braid said nothing but his face became a little redder. When we came to the bunker, Braid's ball was lying well and well back from the bank; he took a spoon [No.3/4 wood. *Author*] and played a magnificent shot, cutting it up over the bank and reaching the green about 200 yards away, at which Whitcombe exclaimed: 'Not only is it in the wrong place but it isn't deep enough!' Braid made no reply.

### The Great Triumvirate

Why were these three men collectively famous? Probably because their great consistency and ability kept them at the top of the professional tree for such a long time – much longer than any of their successors have managed.

The golf boom was well developed and there were 60–70 competitors in each Open Championship, including players from France and the United States, but, for fourteen years, the three men dominated the game. In their time the challenge match was still popular so that, in addition to watching their prowess in major competitions, the public were able to see, frequently, each of them play against leading professionals of the day in matchplay, and those challengers were usually playing on their own home course. The result was invariably a win for one of the three. Sometimes two of them in a foursome partnership played much lengthier matches such as four rounds over four different courses against up and coming professionals; the result was always the same. When matched against one another, any of the three was liable to win but between 1900 and 1903 Vardon was the more likely to win.

It is curious that no one among the newer professionals or young amateurs attempted to copy the style of any of the three. Vardon popularised the overlapping grip (although he did not invent it and Taylor used it also) but nobody attempted to play with a bent left arm like Vardon, including Braid and Taylor. No one attempted to mimic their styles even though each wrote a book on how to do it.

An attempt was made by the press to associate Sandy Herd with the three and thus make it a grand foursome but it failed and there is no doubt that Herd was never really in the same class.

The opinion among not only the general public but those who were experienced golfers was that Vardon was the best of the three. Horace Hutchinson commented that Vardon 'stood head and shoulders above them all'. Ted Ray, who played a lot of golf with Vardon, reckoned that he was the best player that there had ever been and Darwin was a fervent believer in his greatness.

Why was this? True, Vardon had won six Open Championships to the five of the other two but, given the amount of luck that there is in golf, this was not sufficient in itself to make Vardon so obviously the best. One is forced to the conclusion that it was the sheer demonstration of style and elegance which made him appear to be head and shoulders above them; when one considers the constant nagging ill-health from which he suffered his dominance becomes all the more remarkable and deserving of praise. If it had not been for this ill-health Vardon would certainly have won more Championships and if it had not been for the First World War, the other two would have done the same.

J.H. Taylor did not like the title 'Great Triumvirate' because he thought it put the three of them on a pedestal and was, by inference, an unfair comment on the prowess of the other professionals. Taylor observed: 'From now on [1910] the fame of Vardon and Taylor became associated with that of Braid and, speaking for myself, as well as Harry Vardon, the association welded itself into a most happy companionship that carried no trace of envy with it'. It was, perhaps, this comradeship, combined with keen and fierce competition which made them so popular with the public.

So much has been written about the Great Triumvirate that there is a danger that one might overlook the other good professional golfers who made their mark at the same time.

# Alexander ('Sandy') Herd (1868–1944)

A native of St Andrews, Sandy Herd was a fine golfer; possibly, his temperament was against him, for Taylor remarks that he was to Vardon as the exuberance of a whirlwind to the soft caress of a summer breeze.

Herd was always sure that he was going to win. As a result, when in a difficult situation he always went for the big, risky, shot and this was his undoing. He put every ounce of his fiery nature into his play and consequently though an exciting player to watch was often the gallant loser. Despite his bold play through the green he was a rather timid putter and prone to leave his shorter putts short of the hole. One of the characteristics of his play was a large number of 'waggles' at the address – usually 32. His main career was as professional at Moor Park, where he became a much loved and respected Club servant.

### Herd in the Open Championship

| | | | |
|------|------|------|------|
| 1891 | 13th. | 1908 | 4th. |
| 1892 | 2nd. | 1909 | 7th. |
| 1893 | 3rd. | 1910 | 2nd. |
| 1894 | 6th. | 1911 | 2nd. |
| 1895 | 2nd. | 1912 | 5th. |
| 1896 | 3rd. | 1913 | 12th. |
| 1897 | 4th. | 1914 | 29th. |
| 1898 | 14th. | 1920 | 2nd. |
| 1899 | 12th. | 1921 | 10th. |
| 1900 | 9th. | 1922 | After this time he only |
| 1901 | 5th. | | played in the Open |
| 1902 | Winner. | | when it was at St |
| 1903 | 4th. | | Andrews and was |
| 1904 | 9th. | | never better than 10th. |
| 1905 | 15th. 20th. 12th. | | |

It has to be said that, when he won in 1902, the rubber-core ball had just been introduced into Britain, and Herd was one of the few who had managed to find one with which to play.

Nevertheless, this is a proud record and there seems little doubt that he would have been one of the very top golfers if he had not had the misfortune constantly to be competing against three quite outstanding golfers.

# Edward Ray (1877–1943)

R AY was from Jersey and was a very large, amiable man with a swing that was forceful rather than elegant. When he played, he invariably wore a 'trilby' hat (which occasionally fell off in the follow through) and he always smoked a pipe which remained in his mouth throughout. He said that, if you wanted to hit the ball a long way it was best to hit it hard. This method, combined with the fact

'The Great Triumvirate', c.1910, a picture by Clement Fowler of
Vardon (driving), Braid and Taylor (seated), who between them won 16 Open Championships
in 21 years

that he was a physically large man, meant that he was a notably long hitter. He was unorthodox in that he swayed back slightly in the backswing but, despite this, he was a fairly straight driver and very long, and he was a fine iron player and a very good putter. If he did drive into the rough, his great strength enabled him to get out better than most. It was noticeable in his play that he favoured the 'niblick' [about a No.9 iron. *Author*] for his approach shots; at that time Taylor, Vardon, etc were strong supporters of the mashie for approach shots, so the idea of using a niblick was, then, slightly unorthodox and it is probable that Ray was one of the first of the professionals to adopt the 'wedge shot' method of approach play.

### Ray in Championships

| 1899 | (His first entry, from | 1910 | 5th. |
| | Jersey) 17th. | 1911 | 3rd. |
| 1900 | 13th (entering from | 1912 | Winner. |
| | Churston Golf Club, | 1913 | 2nd. |
| | S. Devon). | 1914 | 8th. |
| 1901 | 13th. | 1920 | 3rd. |
| 1902 | 6th. | 1921 | 9th. |
| 1903 | 14th. | 1922, 1923, 1924 | Did not |
| 1904 | 9th. | | figure in the first 12. |
| 1905 | 8th. | 1925 | 2nd. Thereafter, |
| 1906 | 8th. | | although he continued |
| 1907 | 4th. | | to play until about |
| 1908 | 3rd. | | 1932, he was always |
| 1909 | 5th. | | well down the list. |

### French Championships

| 1907 | 4th. | 1914 | 3rd. |
| 1909 | 3rd. | 1912 | 4th. |
| 1911 | 3rd. | | |

### German and Belgian Championships

Tied for first place for both in 1912 but was beaten in the play-off.

### American Open Championship.

| 1913 | Tied for first but was beaten in the play-off. |
| 1920 | Winner. |

For much of his career he was the professional at Oxhey, north of London.

The author saw him on three occasions. The first was when he played at the opening of the Teignmouth Golf Club in 1924; the second was at the opening of the Stover Golf Club in 1930. At Teignmouth, his golf was somewhat overshadowed by that of Vardon but at Stover he was the main attraction and one can remember him demonstrating how to hook the tee shot by moving the head back in the backswing and then coming forward as the ball was struck. The third occasion was at Oxhey. The author had gone there to play with a friend, who turned

out to be an exceptionally bad golfer, having difficulty in hitting the ball past his left foot. It was suggested to him that, instead of struggling round, he could leave the author to play, and go and have a lesson from the professional. When playing the 17th, Ray could be seen giving the lesson; when near enough to hear, the pupil was heard to say, 'Did I move my head that time?' (he having just had an airshot). This was obviously not the first time, for Ray said 'Oh! for Gawd's sake Sir, just *hit* it!'

## Jack White (1873–1949)

A nephew of Ben Sayers and born in North Berwick. In his youth he became a friend of J.H. Taylor and often caddied for him.

The weak part of his game was his wooden club play which was not as reliable nor as long as many of his contemporaries. He was a sound iron player but his chief talent was in putting. He was a master putter, using a blade putter; he was of the school which, when faced with a small left-hand borrow on a putt, would hook the ball out of the toe of the putter and hit it straight – and vice versa for a small right-hand borrow. This school was initiated by Willie Park Senior, who was the accepted master of the technique. The excellence of his putting seems to have been unaffected by the change-over from gutty to rubbercore.

Jack White, in matchplay, was a difficult man to beat because he 'stuck' well and was aggressive. In his early professional life he was a great and persistent challenger of the leading professionals, often for quite large sums of money. He did not win much but he developed into a fine golfer who stood up well to pressure in his prime.

### White in the Open

| 1899 | 2nd. | 1903 | 3rd. |
| 1900 | 4th. | 1904 | Winner. |
| 1901 | 6th. | 1905 | 18th. |
| 1902 | 12th. | | |

Thereafter there are few records of White playing in the Open.

When White won the Open he was the first man to break 300; possibly, as a short driver, the new rubbercore ball had something to do with his win, but, in fairness, most of the field (except Vardon) were using the rubbercore ball by then.

He was a good clubmaker and at Deal in 1909 won a Silver Medal at the International Golf Exhibition for drivers and brassies.

He was a fine and much respected professional at Sunningdale Golf Club from 1901 to 1926.

# Arnaud Massy (1877–1958)

MASSY was a great golfer who was born in Biarritz and learnt his golf there. He deserves a niche in the Hall of Fame, if only because he was the first golfer from outside Britain to win the Open Championship.

When he started to play he played left-handed. His iron play and his putting were superb but, in his driving, he had a curious twirl at the top of the backswing which was said to be a relic from the time when he changed over from left-handed to right.

He was a Basque and was a big, athletic man with a good sense of humour and a lovable character.

He spent a year, as a young man, as apprentice to Ben Sayers at North Berwick and, while there, married a Scots girl.

### Massy in the Open

| | | | |
|---|---|---|---|
| 1902 | 7th. | 1912 | 7th. |
| 1903 | 13th. | 1913 | 5th. |
| 1904 | Not listed. | 1914 | 8th. |
| 1905 | 4th. | 1920 | 17th. |
| 1906 | 6th. | 1921 | 5th. |
| 1907 | Winner. | 1922 | Not listed. |
| 1908 | 8th. | | |
| 1909 | 18th. | | |
| 1910 | 11th. | | |
| 1911 | Tied first with Vardon but lost the play-off. | | |

### French Open Championship

Winner 1906, 1907, 1911, 1925.
Runner-up 1908, 1910, 1926.

**Arnaud Massy, the first Frenchman to win the Open (in 1907)**

Massy won the Belgian Open in 1910 and the Spanish Open in 1911, 1927, 1928.

For most of his golfing life he was professional at La Boulie. He was badly wounded at Verdun in the First World War.

As might be expected, when Massy won the Open in 1907, the British professionals went over to France in succeeding years to play in the French Open, but Massy gave as good as he got and won the French Open against men such as Vardon, Taylor and Braid (the latter braved severe sea sickness to play) in the same year that he won the Open.

It seems that he and his wife returned to Scotland during the Second World War and his address in 1947 was in Edinburgh.

## Men Amateurs between 1900 and 1920

WE have seen how the Great Triumvirate dominated professional golf up to the First World War; it is now time to consider men's amateur golf in the same period.

If one attempts to pick an amateur Triumvirate, it is certainly not as well defined as the professional one, but the names that come to mind are: John Ball, Harold Hilton and Robert Maxwell.

### John Ball

This great man has already been discussed in some detail and it is perhaps sufficient to record his triumphs in the period to show his dominant position. It must be remembered that Ball lost a full two years, 1900–1901, while serving in the Boer War.

***Amateur Championship.*** Winner. 1907, 1910, 1912.
***Open Championship.*** Leading amateur 1908 and 1910.

## Harold Hilton (1869–1942)

Hilton has also been discussed in some detail. His record in the period under review was:

**Amateur Championship.** Winner 1900, 1901, 1911, 1913.
**Open Championship.** Runner-up 1911. Leading amateur. 1901 and 1911.
**American Amateur Championship.** Winner 1911.

## Robert Maxwell (1876–1949)

By the early 1900s, Maxwell, essentially a Muirfield golfer, had become the leading Scottish player. Darwin describes him as a massive and powerful man. He had a method which was neither elegant nor orthodox; he adopted an open stance with a wide straddle and used a threequarter swing. His left hand was well turned over and he played with a shut face and a very stiff left wrist and arm. He was a very good chipper and putter.

**Open Championship.** In 1902 he was 4th in the Open at Hoylake and leading amateur; in 1903 he was again the leading amateur, this time at Prestwick which showed that he was not merely a Muirfield 'specialist'.
**Amateur Championship.** Winner 1903 and 1909.

These three amateurs dominated the Amateur Championship and were the amateur leaders in the Open between 1900 and the start of the First World War.

There were a number of other good amateurs during that time but time and space do not permit discussion of all of them. However, there are two men who are well worthy of a detailed account.

## John ('Jack') Graham of Hoylake (1877–1915)

All contemporary accounts agree that he was the best amateur golfer who never won a major Championship. He was a golfer possessed of a beautiful style and was so close, in accomplishment, to Ball and Hilton that he was, locally, designated one of the Hoylake 'Triumvirate' – and by no means the least of them.

Away from Hoylake he was not as good as the other two but he gave a very good account of himself in the Amateur Championship, reaching the semi-final five times. Darwin thought he was a golfing genius.

He was a rather better medal player than a match player; it seemed that the strain of playing a series of 18-hole matches was not to his liking. In the Open Championship, he was leading amateur on five occasions. There seemed to be no weakness in his game, except the occasional very short putt. His death at 38 was a sad loss to the game.

## The Honourable Michael Scott (1869–1939)

Lord Eldon, Scott's father, had a private course on his estate and young Scott certainly started there but, in golfing terms, he was brought up at Westward Ho! at the Royal North Devon Golf Club.

In about 1900 he had to go overseas and spent a year in Ceylon where he won several scratch medals; within a year he had moved to Australia, where he remained for about ten years.

### Australian Record

*Australian Open Championship.* Winner 1904 and 1907.
*Australian Amateur Championship.* Winner 1905, 1907, 1909, 1910. Runner-up 1904. He won both the Victorian and New South Wales Championships many times.

### British and European record

On his return to Britain, he was runner-up in the Irish Open Championship in 1911.
He won the French Amateur Championship in 1913 and 1922, and was runner-up in 1923.

### Amateur Championship.

He reached the semifinal in 1920 and was the winner in 1933, the oldest winner of the Amateur Championship.

### Open Championship.

Leading amateur in 1912 and 1922.

Scott was not physically a large man and the secret of his success was total accuracy and reliability. He was never a long hitter but was a fine iron player and a completely reliable putter.

Although not a big man he had very strong hands; on one occasion, at Westward Ho!, the author, playing near him, hit a shot with a cleek. Scott immediately asked what club had been used; when told 'A cleek' he nodded and said 'I thought so', adding, 'I gave up those when I could no longer tear a pack of cards!'

In 1935, the author watched Scott beat Cyril Tolley in the final of the West of England Amateur Championship at Burnham-on-Sea, Somerset. Scott was regularly outdriven by 40–50 yards but won comfortably by 4 and 3 over 36 holes.

This tribute to Michael Scott has taken us outside the time frame of 1900–1920 but it is justifiable, in order to pay tribute to one who is not as well known as he should be in Britain because so many of his notable wins were gained on the other side of the world.

## Walter J. Travis (1862–1927)

The account of men's amateur golf between 1900 and 1920 has, so far, omitted the Amateur Championship of 1904. This is not because it was not important but because it was of great significance and warrants special attention. It was the first year of an American invasion which was to develop, in the 1920s, into a rout of British golf.

In 1904 the birth – or, rather the rebirth – of American golf was only about ten years old. American golfers were regarded in Britain as keen, welcome, but inexpert, arrivals in the world of golf. The masterly triumphs of Harry Vardon in his American tour of 1900, coupled with the unstinting praise heaped upon him by an admiring American golfing public, had led British golfers into a belief that American golfers were not up to the standard of golf in Britain; they failed to realise that Vardon was such an exceptional and outstanding golfer that he would have dominated any golfing scene, whether in the United States or Britain.

This idea of American ineptitude at the game was reinforced by reports that Vardon was asked questions about his golf which showed clearly that the majority of those who followed him knew little or nothing about the game.

It should be mentioned that J.H. Taylor also visited the United States in that year, primarily to play in the American Open Championship (in which he was runner-up to Vardon).

Both Vardon and Taylor, separately, played with the leading American amateur Walter J. Travis, a man who came from Australia but had lived in the United States for many years and had taken up golf at the ripe age of 36. At the time that they played with him Travis had

**Walter Travis, c.1905**

been the American Amateur Champion in 1900 and 1901 (later, he was to win the Championship, for the third time, in 1903).

Both Vardon and Taylor expressed respect for his game and each considered that, when he came to play in the British Amateur Championship of 1904, he was a serious contender. To British golf, in general, he was classed as a golfing 'new boy' from the United States who would soon be eliminated from the Championship. This feeling was accentuated when it was found that he was not a long driver. Long driver he may not have been but his iron play was good and his putting superb.

His capture of the British Amateur Championship in 1904 came, therefore, as a shock, and was the more surprising because, in the final match, he was considerably

outdriven by his opponent, Ernest Blackwell, a noted long driver.

The win was well deserved, though British golfers found this hard to believe, but there were two factors which made it downright unpopular.

The first was the attitude of the winner, who proved himself to be both belligerent and sour. He had a huge chip on his shoulder and showed his resentment of British golf at every turn.

In 1910 he wrote an article for *The American Golfer* magazine on 'How I won the British Amateur Golf Championship' which was ten pages in length. His complaints, summarised, were as follows:

1. In the first round he claimed the hole when his opponent soled his club in a bunker which had grass patches in it. He said that his opponent was very annoyed and never stopped talking about it for the rest of the round, thereby putting him off his game.

2. He was given the world's worst caddie possible, the young man being 'a natural-born idiot and cross-eyed at that'. When, in succeeding rounds, he tried to get a better one, the caddie master could not find him another, even though the number of players was halved each day.

3. He was given a very frigid reception in the Clubhouse and could not get a locker.

4. He resented being classed as a short driver.

5. Mr Blackwell, in the final, did not talk to him.

6. He considered that, had Blackwell won, there would have been the usual celebratory dinner but because he won there was none.

It is not surprising that he was not a popular winner. For years afterwards he continued to be aggressively critical of British golf and expressed the greatest satisfaction when, some years later, Harold Hilton, who was defending his title as American Amateur Champion, was beaten in the first round.

Travis was investigated by the USGA three times for allegedly endangering his Amateur status by accepting expenses when playing in tournaments in the Southern States. The second factor that led to his unpopularity was that he used a 'Schenectady' putter. This was a putter

# The Open Championship
## 1920–30

Professionals from the United States, about 1924. Walter Hagen and Leo Diegel demonstrate the smart but casual American style of golfing dress

BEFORE the First World War only one American professional had taken the time and trouble to sail over from the USA and play in the Open: Jimmie McDermott was the first American Open Champion to be entirely native-born American; in 1913, he was a very creditable 4th at Hoylake. Amateurs such as Chick Evans and Francis Ouimet had played in the Open prior to that but no one from the professional ranks.

After the War, the idea of playing in the Open Championship became more popular in the United States. This was probably due to a number of factors: the American participation in the War, when many American members of the armed forces visited Britain and became conscious that it was the place from which many of their ancestors had come, that they had some fine and, to American eyes, unusual links golf courses and, finally, that there were good British golfers, so that, if you were an American and wanted to be known as the best golfer in the world you had to win, not only the American Open Championship but the British Open Championship as well.

In 1920, the Open was won by the mercurial George Duncan; Jim Barnes from the United States was 6th and an unknown American professional (who had no conception of British links golf), Walter Hagen, was well down the field.

From 1921 to 1930 the Open was won by an American professional except on one occasion. The bitter pill was less bitter when Jock Hutchison won in 1922 and Jim Barnes won in 1925, as both had been born and brought up as golfers in Britain. But the other winners, Jones and Hagen, between them won every year except 1923 when Arthur Havers was the British winner, and they were completely American and American-trained.

### Open Results

1921    Winner. Jock Hutchison. After a play-off, having tied with Roger Wethered, a great British amateur. On this occasion Walter Hagen had moved up the field and was 6th.

1922    The winner was Walter Hagen and there were two Americans in the first three.

1923    The gallant Arthur Havers was the winner but Hagen was second and MacDonald Smith of America (though

with an aluminium head in which the shaft was inserted into the near centre of the head and not into the heel. The USGA had not made such putters illegal but they were banned by the R&A and Travis should not, in a British Championship, have been allowed to use it. He had not used the putter until the day before the Championship. The R&A did not disqualify him yet the ban on such putters remained in Britain for a further 50 years.

The whole episode was made unpleasant by the ungracious behaviour of the winner but this did not alter the fact that he won well and gave the very first indication of what was to come, in professional golf, in succeeding years. Golfingly, the United States had 'come of age' in 1904 and, from then on, was a force to be reckoned with.

The Open Championship Cup, which is in reality a Silver Claret Jug

Harry Vardon and Bobby Jones at the US Open in 1920. Jones played with Vardon in the last two rounds

a golfer with origins in Carnoustie) was third; Joe Kirkwood, then entering from Australia, was 4th. The Open was beginning to be an important international event with entries from all over the world.

1924   Walter Hagen was again the winner, with MacDonald Smith 3rd and Aubrey Boomer from St Cloud, Paris 5th.

1925   Jim Barnes from the United States (but originally from Cornwall) won and MacDonald Smith of the United States was again 4th.

1926   Robert T. Jones of the United States was the winner and five out of the first seven places went to the United States.

1927   Bobby Jones was again the winner, Boomer from France was second and Joe Kirkwood, now from the United States, was third.

1928   Hagen won again. Gene Sarazen of the United States

was second and four of the first six places went to Americans. Boomer of France was 5th and Jose Jurado from Argentina was 6th.

1929   Hagen again won and the first three places went to the United States; there were 10 Americans in the first 12 places.

1930   Bobby Jones was the winner and MacDonald Smith runner-up, and there were five Americans in the first nine.

It was abundantly clear, by now, that the Americans were beginning to dominate the Open Championship. There were plenty of good British golfers, but with two exceptions no British professionals won during the decade.

Who then, were the British professionals who made good attempts to stem the tide?

Above left: Walter Hagen in about 1920

Above right: Walter Hagen and Gene Sarazen, 1922. What the smart American professionals were wearing

Right: Bobby Jones relaxing in 1921

Above left: An iron shot by Bobby
Jones in his Grand Slam year, 1930

Above right: Presentation ceremony
when Bobby Jones won the US
Amateur Championship in 1927.
The last round was played in a
deluge of rain

Right: Bobby Jones in 1930 when
he won all four Championships to
complete the Grand Slam

**Abe Mitchell plays out of a ditch at Westward Ho! during his final against John Ball in the Amateur Championship, 1912**

# The Old Guard

## J.H. Taylor

He was 13 shots behind George Duncan, the winner, in 1920, and was 6 shots behind the winner in 1924 – in fact, had the qualifying rounds counted as well, John Henry would have been the winner. In 1925 he was 10 shots behind the winner but anno domini took its toll and he was never in the hunt after that; neither were Braid nor Vardon.

The three important professionals in this era were Abe Mitchell, George Duncan and Arthur Havers.

## Abe Mitchell (1887–1947)

Originally from the Cantelupe Golf Club, the artisans Golf Club at Ashdown Forest, Mitchell was beaten in the Amateur Championship at Westward Ho! at the 37th hole, by John Ball. In the following year he turned professional.

## Mitchell's golf

He was a remarkably powerful and straight driver and the rest of his game was equally impressive. He won a lot of tournaments and challenge matches and, as far as the latter were concerned, he was probably the most successful match player of his time but he was to professional medal play golf what Jack Graham was to amateur golf, always the bridesmaid, never the bride.

**The Open.** 1914, 1920, 1925, 1926, 1929: 4th. 1923: 6th.

Accompanied by George Duncan, he made extensive tours of the United States in 1921, 1922, and 1924. Both he and Duncan had a lot of success in their matches but neither of them were a great success in the major tournaments; there was no doubt that the Americans were, by this time, successful and formidable score players but did not bother much with matchplay because there was little money in it compared with medal play.

J.H. Taylor's opinion of Mitchell: 'I remember play-

**Abe Mitchell, *c.*1920.
The curve of the club shaft
shows well the whippiness
of a hickory shaft**

ing Abe at Sonning in 1921 and I was astonished by the power and brilliance of his play and recollect my remarking in a spirit of bombast that, if I could drive as far and as straight and flip my iron shots up to the hole with such accuracy, I would win every Championship that I entered for and I believe, at that time, I surely would'.

In the 1922 Open, Mitchell led by six shots going into the last two rounds but collapsed to an extraordinary 84 in the third round and lost.

Again, John Henry remarked of Mitchell: 'He shuns publicity and I believe that if he found himself winning a Championship he would deliberately throw away the chance for fear of the publicity it would bring him'.

Bernard Darwin commented: 'His play was marked, above everything by immense power. The tautness of his body at the moment of hitting and the clipped follow through suggested strength and particularly strength of hands and wrists. He was not an especially good putter. Darwin thought that his failure to win the Open in 1922

had a most profound effect on his professional golfing career. Darwin expressed the view that Mitchell was the best match player in Britain but that he was too kind and retiring to do well in big golf. He had, said Darwin, never enjoyed the hum of the crowd and the clash of battle.

Finally, Henry Cotton said of Abe Mitchell that no one struck the ball harder and truer between 1910 and 1933 than he did. Cotton's only criticism was that Abe was too kindly and too gentlemanly. Cotton said that, before he became a professional, he would follow Mitchell whenever he could and said that, if the Open were awarded for skill and consistency, Mitchell would have been a multiple winner. Cotton concluded: 'Although he was an athletic type of man and very strong physically, a delicate nervous system affected, to some extent, Abe's career as a professional'.

In view of these remarks one can understand why Abe Mitchell played for some years as 'Unattached' being then the private professional to Mr Samuel Ryder. There can be no doubt that he had a considerable influence on Mr Ryder's decision to give a Cup for matchplay competition between Britain and America in 1927, a match which has become the most famous and prestigious event in the golfing calendar of matchplay golf.

Later Abe Mitchell became a loyal and much loved professional at the Verulam Golf Club at St Albans – how relieved he must have been to leave the battlegrounds of tournament golf!

The author had the pleasure of seeing Abe Mitchell play on a number of occasions and, from a much humbler sphere, can endorse Cotton's opinion of his ability to strike a golf ball. Mitchell never hit a particularly high ball off the tee but the ball simply looked as if it was never coming down again! The fact that he achieved all this in a tightly buttoned jacket makes his driving all the more remarkable.

## George Duncan (1883–1964)

Duncan was another remarkable golfer who was as different from Abe Mitchell as chalk and cheese.

He entered professional golf much earlier than Mitchell and was representing Scotland against England in 1906, when only 23.

By 1913, when Mitchell turned to being professional, Duncan had already won the French Open and the PGA Tournament.

Duncan was an entirely natural golfer and his golf swing was chameleon-like, because he was an expert at mimicking the style of any golfer he had seen and frequently played whole tournaments in the style of a golfer whose swing, at that time, he particularly admired.

He was an inspirational golfer and, like the little girl of the fairy tale, could be very very good or very very bad. Playing steady, safety-first shots was not to his liking.

After watching Vardon (who became his hero) he changed from being a double-handed golfer with a rather flat swing to a Vardon-type swinger, almost overnight. He drove with accuracy and power and followed the maestro's idea of hitting all his second shots through the air right up to the pin.

When in the mood he was a golfing genius up to the green and, if he putted well, no one could hold him – but he often putted badly. His method of putting was quick and rather 'stabby' and he did not believe in taking much time over the question of the line: his declared motto was 'Miss 'em quick'. When he putted well, the speed with which he did it made putting look easy but, when putting badly, he looked careless and as if he was not really trying. He played through the green very quickly too and this gave the same appearance, depending on whether he was playing well or badly.

Cotton commented that Duncan always appeared to be finding the most difficult way of playing any shot through the green; as a result of this, he was inconsistent and his tournament rounds, unlike Abe Mitchell's, were models of inconsistency, rounds of 82 followed by 68, were all too common. In the Open of 1922 he was second with rounds of 76, 76, 81, 69. In 1925 he was 5th with rounds of 79, 72, 83, 81.

---

### Duncan in the Open Championship

| | | | |
|---|---|---|---|
| 1906 | 8th. | 1921 | 4th. |
| 1907 | 5th. | 1922 | 2nd (76, 75, 81, 69). |
| 1908 | 10th. | 1923 | 6th. |
| 1909 | 14th. | 1924 | 5th. |
| 1910 | 3rd (73, 77, 71, 83). | 1925 | 13th. |
| 1911 | 4th. | 1926 | 11th. |
| 1912 | 4th. | | |
| 1913 | Not listed. | | |
| 1914 | 8th. | | |
| 1920 | Winner (he was 13 shots behind Herd with two rounds to play and finished 71, 72 to win by two shots). | | |

---

Thereafter, Duncan often did not play and when he did play was never in the first ten.

As has been remarked, he and Mitchell made three tours to the United States and were well received; they won most of their matches but never won a big tournament there.

Duncan won the Irish Open Championship in 1927 and the French Open in 1913 and 1927.

It was typical of Duncan that when he had a 7 at the second hole in the last round of the Open in 1927 he afterwards said: 'I tried a shot at the 2nd which only Ray can do'.

In the 1929 Ryder Cup match he beat Walter Hagen by 10 and 8.

## Arthur Havers (b.1898)

Havers was a very big man, over 6 ft 3 ins tall and big-boned. He deserves admiration because he was the only man to stem the flood of American success between 1921 and 1933 in the Open Championship.

Cotton says of him that he was so big that he had to narrow his downswing by swaying into the shot. He used an open stance and hit the ball with a slight fade but was, nevertheless, a long hitter. He hit hard and his left wrist tended to 'give way', so that he always played with an elastic wrist band. He always seemed to be fit and was prepared to travel; he had paid visits to various courses on the Continent of Europe and had visited Argentina and America.

As a tall, slim, youth of 16 he had qualified for the Open Championship in 1914.

### Havers in the Open Championship

| | | | |
|---|---|---|---|
| 1914 | Qualified (age 16) | 1927 | 5th. |
| 1920 | 7th. | 1928 | Not listed. |
| 1921 | 3rd. | 1929 | 9th. |
| 1922 | 10th. | 1930 | Not listed. |
| 1923 | Winner. | 1931 | 7th. |
| 1924 | 12th. | 1932 | 3rd. |
| 1925 | 10th. | 1933 | 6th. |
| 1926 | 14th. | 1934 | Not listed. |

For the ensuing years he was sometimes not listed and when he did play was never better than 10th.

He was a good match player and, during visits to the United States, he defeated R.T. Jones in 1924 in a 36-hole match and Gene Sarazen 5 and 4 in a 72-hole match.

He was a sound putter and a fine wooden club player but his short approaches sometimes let him down.

The author, who, in the mid 1930s, played a little at Sandy Lodge, can testify both to his geniality and size. He had a bull terrier in the shop at Sandy Lodge; Havers' 'party trick' in the shop was to throw a tennis ball to the bull terrier, which would immediately clamp its jaws on the ball and refuse to let it go. Havers would then take hold of the exposed piece of ball between a finger and thumb and then lift the bull terrier off the ground and swing it rapidly round and round for several complete revolutions!

### Archie Compston (1873–1962)

Born in Wolverhampton, Compston entered golf by caddying, and occasionally caddied for the author's father. At 16 he turned professional. He was, in his prime, a tall, lean, giant of a man whose face looked as if it had been carved out of granite. He did not say a lot on the course and his general appearance was one of grim determination.

### Compston in the Open

| | | | |
|---|---|---|---|
| 1920 | 8th. | 1928 | 3rd. |
| 1921 | 12th. | 1929 | 10th. |
| 1922 | 15th. | 1930 | 4th. |
| 1923 | 23rd. | 1931 | 14th. |
| 1924 | 10th. | 1932 | 7th. |
| 1925 | 2nd. | 1933 | 5th. |
| 1926 | Not listed. | 1934 | Not listed. |
| 1927 | 10th. | | |

Thereafter he did not play or was low down the list.

### French Open Championship.

| | |
|---|---|
| 1929 | Tied first. |
| 1925 | 2nd. |
| 1927 | 3rd. |

As befits an athletic man of over 6 ft, he was a long hitter and the rest of his game was sound. In 1928 Henry Leach, in his *Reflections on the Open*, remarked that 'Compston overweighted himself. . . by taking 7 at the second hole in the morning of the last day'.

Although Compston looked grim he was a very genial man and was always glad to meet people; he was very fond of a bet. When he was professional at Coombe Hill he was rather too familiar with the members and laid many bets on their scores, often going out to the 9th to lay differing odds on what they would do on the second nine. He made quite a lot of money at this but, in the end, the Club had to stop him. He also made a handy revenue by betting on the putting green at Coombe Hill.

He was a good matchplayer and, in 1928, he beat Walter Hagen 18 and 17 in a 72-hole match. However, it must be said that Hagen had only just come off the boat and was not in practice; when he was in practice he won the Open about two weeks later!

In 1932, Compston played Gene Sarazen over 36 holes at the Exeter Golf Club and won 13 and 12 over 36 holes. The author was fortunate enough to see this match; there was no doubt that Compston was a worthy winner (although, as in the Hagen match, Sarazen was not long off the boat and, a few weeks later, won the Open). The interesting feature of the match was that Compston hit the ball off the tee very hard and with a low trajectory, while Sarazen, relaxed and with his usual, slightly catlike smile, appeared to hit the ball quite easily and at about the height of the old elm trees; he regularly outdrove Compston throughout the match which, as Compston was 6 ft 3 ins and Sarazen was 5 ft 6 ins, was very surprising. Compston was, clearly, very unpleasantly surprised and used some language which was highly unprofessional. It was the first time that the virtue of hitting the ball slightly on the upswing was demonstrated so clearly.

An amusing incident occurred at Moortown in a big tournament in the early 1930s. Compston had missed a 5 foot putt on one green and one small boy in the gallery said to his friend 'Cor, what a bad putt!'. His young friend agreed, adding, 'I could have done better meself!' Compston upon hearing this, seized one of the boys by the scruff of the neck, dragged him on to the green, put a ball down 5 feet from the hole, gave him his putter and said 'Hole it!'. The boy was almost paralysed with fear and taking the putter with shaking hands waved it at the ball – which went in to the centre of the hole!

Compston did much for the status of the professional golfer in the 1930s; he was the golfing tutor and companion of the then Prince of Wales. The Prince took him round to many Golf Clubs and always insisted that

Compston should be allowed the full facilities of the Clubhouse like any other visitor. Before this time the professionals were not allowed into the Clubhouse to share the members' locker room or to use the changing facilities and some of the more self-important American professionals, such as Walter Hagen, were considerably annoyed by the social distinction.

There were many fine professional golfers in Britain during this period – Fred Robson, Jim Sherlock and the redoubtable trio of Whitcombe brothers from Burnham-on-Sea. All did well (E.R. Whitcombe was runner-up to Walter Hagen by one shot in 1924 and C.A. Whitcombe was 6th in 1923) but no one could stem the American invasion. R.A. Whitcombe's turn was to come later.

### T.H. Cotton (1907–87)

John Henry Taylor, in *Golf. My Life's Work* (1943) stated that Mr G. Cotton wrote to him in 1923 asking if he would be kind enough to evaluate the golfing abilities of his two sons, Henry and Leslie, because they wished to consider turning professional. J.H. played with both of them and told their father that, while both of them were good golfers, Henry, in particular, was capable of great concentration and would go far. Taylor was, later, proud of his opinion.

So, Henry Cotton became a professional. He had, from the start, a slight social advantage because he was educated at a Public School; when he came on to the golfing scene, the press were not slow to point this out, as it gave Henry 'snob' value. Cotton, to give him his due, never made any virtue out of this, but, by the time that the press had trumpeted this, his background became very public knowledge, which may have helped him in his relations with the golfing customers but was a disadvantage to him in his relations with his fellow professionals.

Cotton took several jobs as assistant professional and, during all that time, he practised assiduously for hours on end, sometimes even playing by moonlight.

In 1926, when 19½, he became professional at Langley Park Golf Club; in the winter before he took up the appointment he worked at the Mougins Golf Club at Cannes. He was always happy on the Continent of Europe and spoke French quite well (his mother was from Guernsey).

When he was employed at Langley Park Golf Club they were very kind and helpful to him; he was there for five years and, during that time, he won the Kent Professional Championship five years in a row. He continued to put in many hours of practice.

In the winter of 1928 he decided to visit the United States because he was impressed with the standard of play exhibited by the American professionals who visited Britain and wanted to find out how they managed it.

Langley Park Golf Club gave him leave of absence; he used £300 of his savings, and travelled first-class by sea. Once there, he had a pleasant time and was helped by American professionals, in particular, MacDonald Smith, and played in a few tournaments. He continued to do much practising and won enough money in tournaments that he was able to return to Britain with his £300 still intact. He gained much experience, not least, in the use of steel shafts – at that time legal in America but illegal in Britain – and also made some modifications to his golf swing which enabled him to hit the ball further.

He returned to Langley but, in the winter of 1929, he made a tour of the Argentine with Aubrey Boomer and while there won the Mar del Plata Argentine Open Championship.

In 1932 he left Langley and took up an appointment at the Waterloo Golf Club in Belgium. He made the move because he considered that the remuneration of professionals in Britain was but little better than that of a caddie. He won the Belgian Open Championship 1930–34.

---

### Cotton in the Open Championship up to 1932

| | |
|---|---|
| 1925 | His first entry, when the Assistant Professional at Rye. |
| 1926 | Entered but did not qualify. |
| 1927 | 6th. 13 shots behind the winner. |
| 1928 | 13th. |
| 1929 | 17th. |
| 1930 | 5th, 8 shots behind the winner. |
| 1931 | 7th. 6 shots behind the winner. |
| 1932 | 7th. 10 shots behind the winner. |

---

Young Henry was steadily working his way up the golfing ladder.

It is necessary now to make a small digression to discuss steel shafts and their effect on the game.

## Steel Shafts

MENTION has already been made in the chapters on golf clubs, of the historical background to the development of steel shafts, and, in the chapter on Patents which appears later in the book, there is an account of the difficulties experienced between the USGA and the R&A about legalisation. By 1929, the R&A had come into line with the USGA and had legalised them.

It is time to consider what effect steel shafts had on the playing of golf generally and on the technique called for in hitting a golf ball.

## Changes in the Playing of Golf

THE most significant change was in the huge increase in the amount of time that golfers could put in on the practice ground. When hickory shafts were in use long hours of practice would have ruined the shafts; most professionals kept a second set of clubs with which to play exhibition matches and for practice; a better set was kept for major tournaments and Championships. The situation was both difficult and delicate; two No.5 irons with exactly the same heads and hickory shafts would not feel the same. This was because no two hickory shafts were identical. If it became necessary to change the shaft in a favourite club it could never be perfectly matched and the newly shafted club would never feel the same. With the arrival of steel shafts, two No.5 iron heads with two exactly similar shafts would feel exactly the same.

Breaking a shaft was no longer a disaster, and since no amount of use would alter the steel shaft, unlimited practice became possible. As a result, there was a rise in the standard of golf by those who were willing to put in enough practice to achieve a 'grooved' swing. As the American golfers had had steel shafts legally in their own country since 1923, the ability to practise (in a good climate) for unlimited periods was a contributory factor in the 1920s which accounted for American supremacy over their British counterparts.

Apart from the deterioration of hickory shafts if over-used, constant maintenance was necessary to keep them in good condition. With the steel shaft, and especially when both steel shafts and iron heads were truly rustless, care required for clubs was minimal.

### Changes in golfing technique with steel shafts

Being thinner than hickory shafts, the wind resistance with steel shafts was much less in the downswing, and one of the magazines of the time advised that the celluloid covers which some shafts were given to protect them from the weather were best avoided because they thickened the shaft and made for more wind resistance. It is interesting that the covers were given a colour and pattern to suggest a 'wood effect'.

One of the reasons that practice was so valuable was because the steel shaft could be made with a degree of whip and the site of maximum whip could be exactly defined – something that was impossible with hickory shafts. It was possible to become more exactly attuned to one's club if it had a steel shaft.

Another advantage of steel shafts was the marked reduction in the amount of torque: this allowed for a later hit than could ever be achieved with hickory and professionals were quick to take advantage of it.

The golf swing became a trifle shorter and the hit much later, without any loss of length from the tee (in fact, rather more length was possible) and with an ability to put more backspin on the shots to the green.

As the reader can well imagine, there was considerable criticism of the R&A for continuing the ban, especially as they had lifted the ban on steel shafts in the British Empire. There was an illogicality in the stance of the R&A, not because they had banned steel shafts but because they did not make the ban absolute.

In June 1929, the Coombe Hill Golf Club staged a competition in which competitors were permitted to use steel shafts. Throughout 1929 golf magazines in Britain were advertising steel shafts and many golfers were using them. Editorials in many of the leading magazines criticised the R&A for its obstinacy in not rescinding the ban.

The PGA supported the R&A in their action and refused to allow Accles and Pollock to advertise steel shafts in their journal; unfortunately, their support of the R&A was based purely on the fact that they thought that steel shafts would be detrimental to sales in the professionals' shops and to the living that the professional made out of repairs.

In November, 13 Golf Clubs in England joined with the Irvine Golf Club in Scotland and sanctioned steel shafts in all their competitions.

Faced with a rising rebellion in Britain over the matter, the R&A capitulated and steel shafts were legalised at the end of 1929.

## The Amateurs (1920–32)

THE First World War had a significant impact on the fortunes of the leading amateur golfers of the early part of the century. A number of them died for their Country; of those that survived, some were injured and gave up the game and most of those who were not had had a five year gap in their golf and failed to regain any real form afterwards.

There were splendid exceptions in the latter group, the most notable being the Hon. Michael Scott – already mentioned – who was to win the British Amateur Championship in 1933, at the age of 54, and Robert Harris, who won the Amateur Championship of 1925 and who captained the Walker Cup side of 1922. But the most notable of all was Ernest (later Sir Ernest) Holderness.

### Sir Ernest Holderness (1890–1968)

Holderness was younger than Scott or Harris but, in 1914, was a good enough golfer to enter for the Amateur Championship, although without success. He had got a Blue at Oxford in the years 1910–1912.

After the War, he became a hardworking and distinguished civil servant and his opportunities to play regularly and to practise were few and far between.

He had a fine swing and, rather like Michael Scott, he won not by making superb and dramatic shots but by not making bad ones. He was of average build and not very strong; Bernard Darwin described him as an artist; another correspondent described him as a 'long and accurate driver with ripe judgement but never at the best of times in robust health'.

He won the British Amateur Championship in 1922 and 1924 and was selected to play in the Walker Cup side of 1922 but could not get away from work and had to refuse the invitation. He never entered for the Open Championship.

He played regularly in the Oxford and Cambridge Societies matchplay competition, at Rye, for the President's Putter; the competition started in 1920 and Holderness won it every year for the first four years and then again in 1929. While this was not a major competition, there played in it, in those years, such formidable golfers as Tolley and Wethered.

Holderness was a private person and enjoyed playing golf with his friends; because of this, added to the fact that he had no time (and, possibly, no inclination) to play in those golfing events that the press considered important and the fact that his golf was undramatic, meant that he was never as well known to the general golfing public as were his principal opponents, both of whom were undergraduates at Oxford immediately after the War. These two outstanding golfers were Cyril Tolley and Roger Wethered.

### Cyril James Hastings Tolley, MC (1895–1978)

Tolley was too young to have played in any major events before the War but was old enough to command a tank in the War, win a Military Cross and spend a long time as a prisoner-of-war in Germany.

**Cyril Tolley in the mid-1920s.**
**He had a cigarette or a pipe in his mouth when he played golf**

When he came home, he won the British Amateur Championship in 1920. Those who praised his fine victory also mentioned that he had been successful at tennis, cricket, long jumping and hurdling and had started to play golf when he was 12. He was praised, not only for his win, but for being lionhearted and a good sportsman. Although in his early days he was regarded as a good match player, he later was recognised as a great medal player. It was said of him that 'the man and his golf are built on majestic lines and, when playing his best, his game is one of genius and power'. His swing was one of beautiful roundness and rhythm and the power only became evident when one saw how far the ball went. His driving was immensely long and usually straight; as one correspondent said: 'On many courses the caddies can always tell you where Tolley's drive finished at the long holes'. The author had the good fortune to play against Tolley in the West of England Championship at Burnham and Berrow in 1935 (although, at the time, one felt that it was a misfortune!). Anxious to see the great man play, the author went to see him play some holes with his friends on the practice day. The second hole at Burnham and Berrow, from the special tees used for the West of England Championship, was approximately 430 yards long; Tolley was offered the (hickory-shafted) driver by his caddie but declined, saying that with it he would get to the narrowest part of the fairway. He took the spoon (No.3 wood) and his next shot was a putt from the front of the green – nor did the shot dislodge the pipe from his mouth!

Tolley won the French Open in 1924 and 1929, each time from a field which included players such as Hagen, Sarazen, and other leading American professionals and leading British professionals as well. In the German Open of 1929, he was the leading amateur, coming 9th in a field which included Horton Smith, Hagen, Farrell, Ed Dudley, Turnesa, Boomer and Percy Allis, who won.

That he did not win much more was due to his temperament. He was something of an inspirational golfer, when in the mood, unbeatable, but prone on other occasions to believe that nothing was going to go right – and to play like it. The final of the West of England Championship in 1935 gave the author an indication as to what could happen to Tolley on bad days; in the final he played Michael Scott. Scott was outdriven by 40–50 yards at every tee; as a result, he played the second shot first. When Tolley came to play his second shot, the second shot of Scott, a beautiful iron player, was already on the green; Tolley became obviously dispirited and Scott beat him comfortably by 4 and 3 over 36 holes.

Tolley had a great sense of humour and was courteous and lovable to a degree but was also capable of the thoughtless word that hurts, according to a writer of the time, who described him as 'the Peter Pan of golf'. The author can confirm some of this for, in the West of England Championship in 1935, he arrived on the first tee about one minute late for his tee-off time against Tolley, and the starter announced to Tolley that he was entitled to claim the match; Tolley immediately said 'No! No! let's play and may the best man win!' He then turned to his chauffeur, who was near the tee, and said: 'Bring the car round to the 12th'. (At Burnham, in those days, the 12th green was near the road). Although soundly and rightly beaten, the author had the slight satisfaction of getting to the 15th!

Later in the decade, a correspondent, picking a mythical Walker Cup side, felt that Tolley would come high in the list because 'He continues to play with that delightful abandon which is such a striking feature of his golf', adding, 'Mr Tolley is never out of form, he just has bad patches'.

Tolley won the 1929 Amateur Championship, fairly comfortably; in the Amateur of 1930, he was beaten in the semifinal by Bobby Jones, losing on the 19th hole because of a stymie.

When Tolley retired from golf he went to live at Eastbourne, the town from which he originated; it is said that he gave up golf for croquet and became a very proficient player – you cannot keep a natural talent unfulfilled!

Perhaps the final words on this great, colourful golfer should be left to Bernard Darwin, who saw him play most of his finest golf: 'There is no player in the world who can make the opponent feel how vain it is to struggle, and the spectator how futile it is ever to play again'.

## R.H. Wethered (1899–1983)

Wethered, together with Tolley and Holderness, formed the great British amateur golfing triumvirate of the 1920s. As with Tolley, he first came into prominence after the First World War, when he and Tolley were undergraduates at Oxford.

### Championship Records

Wethered won his Amateur Championship in 1923. He had played in 1920 and 1921, but on both occasions was beaten in an early round. In 1922 he was beaten in the 6th round. In 1924 and 1927 he was a semifinalist and in 1928 and 1930 he was runner-up.

### Open Championship

1921   Tied 1st with Hutchison but lost the play-off.
1922   17th. These are the only two occasions on which he is recorded as playing.

He won the Long Driving Championship in 1927.

Wethered won many of the medals of the R&A and was a winning competitor in many of the important medals of the major British Golf Clubs. He played a notable part in the Walker Cup matches.

On paper, this record clearly indicates that he was a great golfer but, in reality, he was a very great golfer indeed.

He was a great iron player and a very long driver; prior to 1923 he was a straight driver but, in later years, he became erratic off the tee. As he continued to hit the ball a very long way, his tee shots sometimes finished in some wild country.

He had a good style and played with quite a wide stance but his swing for tee shots was something of a downward strike, like his irons. With the irons Wethered achieved the downward stroke by turning the left hand well to the right, so that at least four knuckles were showing, when seen from above; this method worked well with the irons but, applied to the tee shot or fairway wooden shots, may have been the reason for an occasional wild stroke. He was such a fine iron player that he managed to overcome his occasional driving problems and continued to be a great golfer for many years.

*Wethered the man*

Wethered was essentially a sportsman who would try very hard on the course but did not regard winning as the most important thing. Like his sister Joyce Wethered (see page oo), he obtained much pleasure from hitting the ball properly and putting well, thus giving a good account of himself. If, as a result of good play, he won, then that was an added bonus but winning, of itself, was not all-important; taking part and playing well was what mattered.

In 1930, when he was beaten in the final of the amateur by Bobby Jones, in the year in which Jones made his Grand Slam of US Open and Amateur and the British Open and Amateur, a feat which will, almost certainly, never be repeated, this is what Jones said of his prospects in the final: 'I felt the utmost respect for my opponent, Roger Wethered. But I had to know all factors, both physical and psychological were on my side. I felt that I could wear Roger down over the long route [The final was over 36 holes. *Author*] simply by keeping up an unremitting pressure . . . I honestly felt that Roger himself had very little hope of winning. I am not even certain that he cared very much. Roger was a fine golfer and a wonderful sportsman who could be counted on to give his best at all times. But he was also a completely charming person without any semblance of aggressiveness on the golf course. I recall so well the evening in 1921 when he, an amateur, had surprised everyone by finishing in a tie for the Open Championship with Jock Hutchison. I had stood in a group of Roger's friends near the eighteenth green . . . and had joined in an effort to persuade him that

it was more important for him to remain over to participate in a play-off for the Open Championship than to return home for a neighbourhood amateur cricket match in which he had agreed to play the next day . . . that little session convinced me that Roger thought Championships were very nice things but it was plain that he did not want to win them as much as I did.'

Writing of him in 1929, Cockell, speaking of his contribution to golf, observed: 'Wethered has touched it and brightened it with the wand of his personality'. He went on: '. . . I met him and found him to be a quiet voiced and peculiarly shy individual . . . as one gets to know him better, one's initial impression that his shy modesty is utterly honest is confirmed . . . He is the beau ideal of a British sportsman – modest and sympathetic in victory, philosophical in defeat and quick to offer a genuine word of congratulation to his conqueror . . . Golf is but one interest in his life, he is not just a golf enthusiast and the fact that, at a time when his golfing abilities could be developed to the full, he should wholeheartedly espouse a commercial career, is typical of the spirit in which he has always aproached the playing of golf.'

The Open Championship in which Wethered tied for first place was not without incident. Wethered completed the last two rounds in 72 and 71 to come from behind and tie Hutchison; the last round was then a record score for the Old Course and yet it was accomplished despite a penalty of one shot when Wethered, walking back to his ball, after having walked forward to see the line, accidentally trod on it. One does not know whether anyone else saw the accident but Wethered immediately called a penalty on himself. The general feeling was that, without the penalty, Wethered would have won and this may well be so but J.H. Taylor, who was playing with him, with characteristic candour says that it was very careless to tread on his ball and that, in his opinion, Wethered lost because he failed to hole a shortish putt on the seventeenth!

After he had agreed to play in the play-off with Hutchison, Wethered then persuaded the R&A to allow him an earlier starting time than they had originally intended so that he could hurry back to play in the cricket match.

Nothing underlies the different approach to championships at that time, between the United States and Britain, than Wethered's and Jones' attitude to the Amateur Championship of 1930; it was this attitude which made Americans at the top put in so much time practising (aided by the fact that since 1923 they were playing with steel shafts) in their total determination to be first – was it not the Americans who coined the phrase 'Nobody remembers the runner-up'?

**A young Henry Cotton. He had at this time made a trip to the United States and had absorbed the idea that a professional should be smartly dressed when playing**

So we come to the end of the 1920s, a time during which the Americans dominated the Open Championship while the British kept their hold on the Amateur Championship, though it must be said that the greatest amateur of the time, Bobby Jones from the United States, was too busy winning American Open and Amateur Championships to bother to cross the Atlantic and win the British Amateur. He made two attempts, one early in that period, when he was defeated by Jack Graham, but on the other he was successful.

## The British Golf Scene 1932–39

THE 1920s were a depressing and confidence-sapping time for British golf; it seemed that the Americans had a number of players, apart from the great Bobby Jones, who could cross the Atlantic with every prospect of beating the best professionals in Britain.

In the early 1930s Jones retired from amateur golf and became a professional but did not play as a professional, preferring to continue a career outside golf.

Nevertheless, in 1931, 1932, and 1933 American golfers were still winning the Open, though there was a slight sop to British pride in that T.D. Armour, who won in 1931, was a Scottish-American who had learned his golf at Carnoustie. Gene Sarazen, who won in 1932, was an American and Densmore Shute, who won in 1933, although his origins were in Devon, had learnt all his golf in the United States. In 1934 things changed and British professionals, during the rest of that decade, were supreme in their own Open Championship. This change was, in large part, due to Henry Cotton.

### Sir Henry Cotton, CBE (1907–92)

Cotton's early career in the 1920s has already been noted; he worked very hard on his game and took the trouble to go to the United States, at his own expense, to gain experience of American-style golf.

He learned much and began intelligently to put what he had learned into practice, not only golfing technique but his attitude to the business side of golf, to the status of the professional in Britain, and to the conditions under which the British professional was called upon to play. In the last of these ideas he followed the good work that J.H. Taylor had so bravely started many years before, and Taylor was the first publicly to praise him for his efforts.

Henry Cotton, three times Open Champion, demonstrating the swing in the mid-1930s

The fact that Cotton was the first British professional to have been educated at a British Public School was helpful and Cotton was able to further the good work of Compston in securing permission for professionals to be allowed full use of Clubhouse facilities at tournaments. His trip to the United States had opened Cotton's eyes to the status of the American professional in that country, and he was determined to raise the status of the British professional to that level.

### Cotton's standard of golf

As has been shown, Cotton steadily improved his position in the Open in the 1920s and also won a number of lesser tournaments. In the 1930s, the arrival of steel shafts made long hours of practice possible and Cotton, of all the British professionals, took full advantage of this. His intelligent, analytical approach to the golf swing began to pay off. He had always made a study of other golfers' swings and analysed their faults and virtues. He not only was familiar with the swing techniques of all his contemporaries, both British and American, but he also studied the methods of the great men from a past generation, such as the Great Triumvirate and, in doing this, became firm friends with Taylor, Braid and Vardon.

He continued these studies throughout his career and became an expert analyst of the swings of many of the young men, both in the United States and Britain, who became champions after he had retired. He distilled all this knowledge into making a swing of his own, extracting all those bits that he considered good for him and discarding those parts which did not suit him.

The resulting swing was slightly artificial but long practise made it more natural in appearance as the years went by. It was an eminently repeatable swing, a little shorter than some of his contemporaries and characterised by a very firm straight left leg at impact and a fine follow through, hitting past a chin turned slightly to the right. He was a great believer in strong hands and exercised continuously to achieve hands that were so strong that he could hit a ball 200 yards whilst sitting in a chair; he also believed in being able to hit the ball with either hand alone and was notably successful when demonstrating this.

There was no weakness in his game but he was not one of the great putters – entirely adequate, but not a man who won by holing long and difficult putts. In his books, he shows a number of different putting styles that he adopted at different times and this seems to be the one part of his game in which he never arrived at a definitive method. He admitted that he was fortunate not to have acquired the 'yips' during his great tournament career.

There is much more to being a great champion than having a fine, repeatable, grooved swing and an adequate putting skill; Cotton's great attribute was a determination to win and great powers of concentration. The latter made him appear very grim on the course; not for Cotton the jokes with the gallery and the smiling relaxation between shots; in order to succeed he had to wrap himself in a cocoon of concentration throughout the period of the round. It took a lot out of him and he was prone to bouts of indigestion and stomach cramps throughout his life and had always to stick to a careful diet.

Cotton's win in 1934 was a great morale booster for British professionals. In 1930 Cotton had been 5th, in 1931 7th and in 1932 7th again. In 1933 he was 4th. He was steadily moving up the ladder but, in 1934 he reached the top rung by 5 clear shots, and this despite a rather poor last round of 79. The foundation of his success were his first two rounds – 67 and 65; the latter was a record for Royal St Georges and was also the lowest score ever recorded in the Open. At that time he was using Dunlop golf balls and on that day the 'Dunlop 65' was born.

Cotton's win in 1934 was all the more impressive in that he not only won from the best British professionals but also from American professionals such as Macdonald Smith, Densmore Shute, and Gene Sarazen. In the years before, although the Americans had taken the title, there had been relatively few of them competing. This was partly because the regular wins by them had somewhat reduced the prestige of winning the Open, partly because the money prize for the Open was still rather small by American standards, and because there was by now a thriving and busy American tournament schedule and travelling by sea to Britain to win the Open meant missing several lucrative tournaments at home.

Cotton says that, after his win in 1934, he went over to the Guildford Hotel near Sandwich, taking the Cup with him. Vardon was staying there; he had come over to see the play but was taken ill and had to stay in bed. Cotton gave him the Cup to hold; Vardon had won it six times and, Cotton says, the tears ran down his face and Cotton himself was also reduced to tears.

It was a great win and the effect on the British pro-

fessionals was such that in the next two years they beat the man who had restored their morale – but Cotton was not far off – 6th in 1935 and 3rd in 1936.

In 1937 Cotton won again and this was a victory as convincing and as prestigious as his win in 1934, for this was a Ryder Cup year in Britain and the best Americans stayed on to play in the Open; Cotton thus won from such great American professionals as Byron Nelson, Ed Dudley, Horton Smith, Sam Snead, Ralph Guldahl, Densmore Shute, Henry Picard and Walter Hagen. An additional heartening fact was that the runner-up was British and that there were six Britons in the first nine. The Open was at Carnoustie in that year and the weather in the later stages was atrocious. There was so much rain on the last day that there were ideas of calling off the last round – Cotton's last round of 71 was the best round of the day and, under the circumstances, little short of miraculous.

In 1938, Cotton was 3rd in the Open; this was the year of the great hurricane which blew all the press tents out to sea at Sandwich. Whitcombe's last round of 78 was regarded, quite rightly, as magnificent golf – and yet Cotton, in a great effort to catch him, holed Sandwich in 74!

In the Open of 1939, Cotton was 7th. After that, the Second World War interrupted golf as far as Britain was concerned. Seven years later Cotton was still giving a good account of himself. He was 5th in 1946 and, in 1947, won the Open again, this time from a younger generation of professionals, both British and overseas – but this is post-war golf and outside the scope of this book.

Here then, was one of the very great British professionals, who not only won major Championships but also used his position to benefit his fellow professionals and gave much time to charitable work. His CBE for services to golf he received in his lifetime but, his knighthood, alas, was posthumous.

Although Henry Cotton was the outstanding figure among the British professionals of the 1930s he was not the only pebble on the beach.

While taking nothing away from that beautiful swinger and golfer Percy Alliss, nor from the ebullient and wholehearted play of Alf Perry, winner of the Open in 1935, nor from Richard Burton, who won the Open in 1939, both Alfred Padgham and Reginald Whitcombe deserve special mention.

### A.H. Padgham (1906–66)

Padgham came from the Ashdown Forest, an area which had within it a very strong artisan golfing community and which produced such great golfers as Abe Mitchell. He was assistant to John Rowe, a well-respected and long-standing professional at Royal Ashdown Forest Golf Club.

He first began to make his presence felt in 1930 when he won a number of less important tournaments but was well down the list in the Open of that year and, also, in 1931.

In 1932 he did better in the Open and was 4th; in 1933 he was again 4th. In 1934 he was 3rd and in 1935 he was 2nd. During those years he continued to win important tournaments. His win in the Open of 1936 was no meteoric rise to fame but was the culmination of a steady progression and came as no surprise.

## Padgham's style and character

His style was orthodox and beautiful, his swing very easy and relatively short. Some of his contemporaries considered that, for rhythm and grace, it was a style reminiscent of Harry Vardon.

He had a good physique and, to outward appearances, had a very placid temperament, although Darwin said of him that 'no man could be as placid as he looks'. He had exceptionally large hands.

If Cotton was a player who won by ruthless efficiency up to the green and competence on it, Padgham was the opposite. When he won the Open he was not playing his long game as well as he could, but owed his success to outstanding putting.

He conceived the idea that a putt was no more than a small drive. On this theory, he stood comparatively upright and well away from the ball and his feet were well apart. He concentrated on a slow backswing and a good follow through, using a blade putter.

His putting in 1936 was phenomenal. He not only holed all the holeable ones but he holed a very large number of putts that were so long as to be indecent. He was an outstanding putter before 1936 and a very good putter after 1936 but in 1936 his putting was miraculous.

It is interesting that Darwin always considered Padgham's long game, with its sleepy rhythm and accuracy, to be the best feature of his play. He said of Padgham's putting in 1936 that such putting 'would have frightened a less placid nature into a belief that his ration was exhausted'. He did not care for Padgham's method of putting and was sure that it could not last – and he was right. Some time after 1939, the scales fell from Padgham's eyes about the infallibility of the 'small drive' and he descended into the ranks of the human putters who missed a few.

## Reginald Whitcombe (1898–1958)

The three Whitcombe brothers from Burnham-on-Sea, Somerset, have already been mentioned; they constituted a solid phalanx of three golfers who were constantly at the top of the golfing tree in the 1920s and 1930s. How-

ever, Reggie Whitcombe's record in the Open singles him out as the most outstanding golfer of the three:

| | |
|---|---|
| 1925. | 10th. |
| 1926 | 9th. |
| 1927 | His name does not appear. |
| 1928 | 15th. |
| 1929 | A long way down the list. |
| 1930 | 8th. |
| 1931 | 9th. |
| 1932 | 10th. |
| 1933 | 4th. |
| 1934 | 10th (there were three Whitcombes in the first 10). |
| 1935 | Well down the list. |
| 1936 | 5th. |
| 1937 | 2nd. |
| 1938 | Winner. |
| 1939 | 3rd. |

The enforced rest during the Second World War was a setback for his generation of golfers but, nine years later, at the age of 50, he was still giving a good account of himself. In golfing terms he was a 'late developer', winning his first Open at the age of 41.

## Whitcombe's style of play

Whitcombe was a burly man with strong hands. He used a three-quarter-length swing and attacked the ball crisply without delay. The tempo of his swing was on the fast side – no long and easy swing for him. He used the interlocking grip with the little finger of the right hand hooked into the index finger of the left – in fact, this was the grip used by all the brothers and, although there may have been those who had used it before, it was the Whitcombe brothers who made it famous.

Whitcombe was a fine driver and a great iron player; it goes without saying that he was a very good putter but this was not the outstanding feature of his game. Brought up in the fierce winds of Burnham, he was at his best on stormy days when his strong physique and three-quarter-length swing were well suited to the conditions.

When Cotton won at Carnoustie in 1937, Whitcombe was runner-up. The weather was so appallingly bad that there was talk of calling off the last round; the main feature of the weather was incessant and heavy rain. At the end of the first day (two rounds a day in those days) Whitcombe led Cotton by four strokes at the end of the first 36 holes. On the second day, in a great storm of wind and rain, Whitcome returned 74 and Cotton returned 73 to get one stroke back; in the afternoon, in terrible weather, Reggie returned a magnificent score of 76; Darwin recalls that at one hole, Whitcombe's club slipped clean out of his hands and he also recalls Whitcombe trying to dry his hands on a sopping wet towel before hitting a beautiful brassie shot to the last green over the burn. It was, says Darwin, a winning score – and yet Cotton returned a miraculous score of 71 to win!

In 1938, Reginald Whitcombe won at Sandwich. On the first day, calm and sunny, he returned 71, 71, to lead Cotton by 5 shots. During the night there was a hurricane and it blew all the next day; the press tents were blown out to sea and all the flags were in tatters. The wind continued to rise throughout the day, and at the 11th in the afternoon Padgham drove the green – 380 yards – and holed his putt for a two. Most of the leaders were blown off the scoreboard and the general opinion was that it was 'a Whitcombe day' – and so it proved to be. Darwin says that the wind was so strong that it was impossible to guess what the winning score would be and yet Whitcombe did the first eight holes in two under fours, but took four putts at the ninth. He finished in 75 and gained a further two shots on Cotton, giving him a lead of seven shots over Cotton, but he was only two shots ahead of Jimmy Adams of Liverpool.

In the afternoon the wind was still rising, the 16th hole (a short hole of approximately 160 yards) was a full brassie shot and the 17th, a medium length par four hole was, for Whitcombe, two drivers, a long run up and a good putt. He returned a 78 in the last round, which gave him a lead of two shots over Adams. Cotton, needing a 71 to win, finished with a magnificent 74.

The author, who knew Whitcombe, asked him a week or two after he had won, how he had managed it and was told: 'Against the wind I hit it off the tee with a driver and then hit the second shot with a driver, being very careful to hit neither shot more than 20 feet off the ground!'

So ends a great decade for British professionals; there is little doubt that, had it not been for the Second World War, the great British professionals of that decade would have continued to win for several years more.

## The Amateurs (1931–39)

The period was one of nostalgia and of British amateur success – with notable exceptions.

The Amateur Championships of 1931 and 1932 were won by British golfers, Eric Martin Smith and John de Forest, respectively. In 1931 the formidable George Voigt of America was defeated by Bernard Darwin in the fifth round and this disposed of the last American in that Championship.

It must be said that the American entry for the Amateur Championship in 1931, 1932 and 1933 was low, but this was probably accounted for by the economic depression in America.

The nostalgic part came in 1933 when the Honour-

THE POINT OF VIEW.

*The Sad One* – "But, young man, do you not at times feel that this Sunday golf is jeopardising your chances of heaven?"
*Golfer* – "Jeopardising! Why it *is* heaven!"

able Michael Scott won the Amateur Championship at the age of 54, the oldest man ever to win that event.

In 1934, the entry from overseas jumped. There were eleven entries from the United States and entries also from India, Australia, Argentina and South Africa. The strong American entry was headed by Lawson Little and he proceeded to devastate his opponents, winning the final by 14/13. He came back in 1935 to win again but, this time, only after a stern struggle with the redoubtable Dr Tweddell, who, outdriven by all of forty yards, made Little go all the way to the 36th hole. (Lawson Little was also the holder of the American Amateur Championship in 1934 and 1935, the only amateur to achieve the double twice. He turned professional and won the American Open Championship in 1940.)

In 1936 Hector Thomson of Scotland was the winner and in 1937 Robert Sweeney; it is difficult to decide whether this was a British or American win as Sweeney was American-born but played all his golf in Britain. In this Amateur Championship A.D. Locke of South Africa was beaten in the third round; as he had played in the Open Championship of 1936 and been easily the leading amateur, 5th overall, and was again leading amateur in the Open of 1937, being 13th overall, one may assume that either matchplay golf did not suit him, or that he did not try very hard! By 1938 he had turned professional and was 6th in the Open of that year.

## Dr William Tweddell (1897–1985)

Tweddell deserves special mention because not only did he win the Amateur Championship in 1927 but he gave Lawson Little the fright of his life in 1935 in the final of the same Championship. He was Captain of the Walker Cup side in 1928 and in the Open of 1927 he was 13th.

This record of success alone would make him a very good golfer but when set in the context of a busy professional life as a doctor, it is clear that his talent for golf was remarkable and he is the epitome of the dwindling band of 'true' amateurs who played golf as a sport when they could spare the time from a busy life. Hours of practice were not for such men and in Dr Tweddell's case he made valiant attempts to compete, with poor preparation, against those amateurs who were fortunate enough to play golf almost full time.

Tweddell was English-born but learned much of his golf when at Aberdeen University, where he was a medical student.

Tweddell was no stylist, having a curious stance and keeping his arms stiff and well away from the body. Darwin says that he 'aimed over long off and then hit the ball over the bowler's head'. Because he did not have an impressive style he was underrated by those who did not know his golf. He was a great match player and gained some notable scalps in a long playing career.

His greatest moment was when he played Lawson Little in the final of the Amateur in 1935. Darwin, who saw the game says: 'Never have I admired a golfer more than I admired Tweddell in the disastrous beginning of that match [he lost three of the first four holes. *Author*]. He was outdriven all the way round and was five down at the 11th. He hung on grimly and was three down at lunch. In the afternoon he was still three down at the 8th but then won 9, 11 and 12 to square the match. He had a putt to win 13 but missed it and Little then counter-attacked and won 14 and 15; Little then lost 17 to a gallant four out of a bunker but held on to halve the 18th in four.'

The Naval Lieutenant's way out of a difficulty.    Idea good, but result disastrous!

Sketched at the Xmas Meeting of the Royal Isle of Wight Golf Club

# 13

# The Ladies and their Game

HORACE HUTCHINSON, who wrote so charmingly and knowledgeably about golf in the late nineteenth and early twentieth centuries, pointed out that, when people try to write about the origins of golf, they will often find themselves in a thick fog because of the absence of valid records.

In the matter of ladies' golf, we are slightly better off because the earliest history of their game, apart from one or two very early records which are charming but do not provide much concrete evidence, is much more recent and is therefore recorded. The difficulties for the historian arise from the fact that, particularly in Scotland, the game was dominated by males, many of whom were Masons, who felt it their duty not to recognise that women played golf at all and did little or nothing to help them.

There are three early tales which show that women were, in some way, involved in the game at a time when ladies' golf, as we know it today, did not exist.

The first comes from England in 1513 and is in a letter from Katharine of Aragon, Henry VIII's wife at that time and therefore Queen of England, to Thomas Wolsey, then Almoner and Councillor to Henry, later to become Chancellor and Cardinal.

The letter is as follows: 'Master Almoner, from hence I have nothing to write you but that you may not be so busy in this way as we be encumbered with it. I mean that as touching my own concerns for going further, when I

shall not be so often here from the King [he was away at the French Wars. *Author*]. And all his subjects be very glad. I thank God to be busy with the Golf, for they take it for a pastime, my heart is very good to it and I am horribly busy making standards, banners and bagots.'

The implication here is not that Katharine played golf (though she may well have) but that she was involved with it.

The game does not sound like the golf that we know now, but then, as has been said earlier, the earliest games of golf in Scotland were probably not golf as we know it today. The game that Katharine refers to is probably a form of cambuca and the letter is further evidence of a golf-like game, mentioned earlier in this book as being very popular in England as early as 1323.

A more direct reference to a lady playing golf concerns Mary, Queen of Scots. She was a lady of intellect but doubtful morals. She was, ultimately, executed by order of Queen Elizabeth I in 1587. At her trial, a point was made that she played at golf and paille maille in Seton Fields [the grounds of Seton Castle in East Lothian. *Author*] only a few days after her husband, Lord Darnley, was murdered. This is direct evidence of golf played by a lady and, in addition, indicates that golf and paille maille were played over the same ground; as the only difference between golf and jeu de maille à la chicane was that the former was played into a hole in the ground and the latter to a stake, this must have been easy to arrange.

The third reference that we have concerning golf played by ladies is somewhat later, but still well before it became a recognised ladies' pastime; it concerns Musselburgh. On 14 December 1810, the Minutes of the Club state: 'The Club resolve to present, by subscription, a new Creel and Shawl to the best female golfer who plays on the annual occasion on Jan:1st, old style (12th Jan:new), to be intimated to the Fish Ladies by the Officer of the Club. Two of the best Barcelone silk handkerchiefs to be added to the above premium of the Creel.' The Minute is signed 'Alex.G.Hunter'. It is clear from the Minute that the competition had been played before but, unfortunately, no records have survived.

*The Statistical Account of Scotland*, Vol. 1 (Edinburgh 1791-9) makes comments about playing golf at Musselburgh and points out that children are brought up to play from an early age. It continues: 'As they [the women. *Author*] do the work of men and their strength and activity is equal to their work, their amusements are also of a masculine kind'. It goes on to say that the women played an annual football match. It would not be surprising, therefore, if another of their amusements was the playing of golf. The reference to 'the Fish Ladies' must mean those women who were employed in cleaning the fish catch.

These sporadic references to ladies playing golf are of interest because they show that women, from the earliest times, attempted to play. However, the first properly constituted Ladies' Golf Club did not appear at St Andrews until 1867. The course was a long putting course, the holes being from 20 to 40 yards long. There were 18 of them and the ladies played only with a putter but, it must be remembered, the wooden putter was often used for distances of up to 120 yards by men in the course of a game of golf. The ladies' game was played with the utmost decorum and it was more important not to show one's ankles than to hit a good shot. The costume of women at that time was not conducive to a free golf swing. Men were allowed to be Associate Members but confined their activities on the ladies' course to marking the cards of the competitors and taking the flags.

Within a year, the enterprising golfers of North Devon had followed suit and a Ladies' Club was started at the North Devon and West of England Golf Club (later to become the Royal North Devon Golf Club); its members played on a special links which was longer than the links for ladies at St Andrews the holes being 50 to 120 yards long; like the St Andrews ladies, they played only with a putter. Again, the men were allowed to be Associate Members, but did not play on competition days, helping the ladies in the same way as did the men at St Andrews on those occasions. The ladies were provided with a white silk tent, which was erected on the days that they played, to act as a refreshment tent; it was removed after play.

At Instow, a few miles from Westward Ho!, there was a small hamlet and nearby, a small area of links land. A course was started there, which must have been very short, as the area is constricted. The ladies played there, as well as the men. There are records of ladies playing there in 1868; is it just possible that Instow, in 1868, was the first links in the history of golf on which women and men played on the same course? I think this is reasonable. At St Andrews and Westward Ho! the ladies had a separate course but at Instow the small links was played on by both men and women. Alas, all records and Minutes of the Club, like the Club itself, have long since disappeared. The only documentary evidence for the playing of ladies' golf at Instow is recorded in a local newspaper which gives the results of a competition played there. The only other evidence of play at Instow was given to the author by a friend, now dead, who said that he caddied for his uncle when he played there.

To return to the ladies at St Andrews; there is evidence that as early as 1830 ladies played some golf on a small 4-hole course on the right of what is now the 17th on the Old Course. It was not a Club and the play was unofficial but it became a diversion for the townsfolk of St Andrews to watch the ladies at play. A course was set up and a Ladies' Club formed in 1867, in a quieter area 'between the Swilcan and the flagpole'. This area is still used as a putting green.

The Ladies' Club at St Andrews was no haphazard organisation; there were strict rules which had to be obeyed. The ladies were dismayed when, shortly after the course had been laid out, Mr Cheape of Strathtyrum, who owned the land, forbade them to play there, but as he stated that 'there was no excuse for taking another man's property and that they could not play there unless they paid an annual fee of £15', it was clear that it was only a matter of money; once they had paid up there was no further problem. Indeed when, in May 1873, Mr George Bruce, an eminent local citizen, protested that they should not be playing there, it was Mr Cheape who said that they could, and took the matter to the Sheriff and, after that, to the Court of Session in Edinburgh, winning them the right to play.

In 1868, not only did the ladies play at St Andrews but they organised a competition for youngsters who were at Mr Hodge's school nearby. Mr Hodge was a schoolmaster and artist; he was also a fine golfer who won several medals at the R&A, and not surprisingly he produced from his school a number of boys who were very fine golfers in later life.

By 1890, the ladies, irked by the restrictions of their course, tried, without success, to persuade Mr Cheape to let them have more land. A little later, they were somewhat grudgingly allowed to play on the Old Course, but the men soon claimed that they were taking so long to play a round that they were interfering with men's golf.

In 1899, it was noted in the local Press that 'Mr and Mrs Asquith were devoted to golf and spent much time on the links'. The fact that Mr Asquith was the Prime Minister may have had something to do with the fact that no further attempts were made to oust the ladies from the Old Course!

It is now necessary to turn attention to England because it was in England that decisive steps were taken to put Ladies' Golf on the map.

Between 1868 and about 1890 there developed in Scotland some 10 to 12 Ladies' Golf Clubs; in England about the same number were founded during the same period. The numbers are equal

**The earliest medal for Ladies' golf**

but there were many more Golf Clubs in Scotland than in England – in 1868 there were only three courses in England, whereas Scotland could boast about 31. When viewed on a percentage basis, it is clear that England was much more amenable to the idea of ladies' golf than Scotland; this difference was almost certainly due to the strong Masonic nature of the Scottish Clubs. In England, at Blackheath, a notably Masonic institution, the Captain of the Club, Christian Gray, was asked by his wife, a keen golfer, if she and other ladies could be allowed to play on the course. He was so disturbed by this idea that, rather than give a direct refusal, he bought land at nearby Barnhurst and gave it to the ladies for their own golf course, and this became the Blackheath Ladies' Golf Club.

Blackheath was so averse to women that when, in 1906, a member suggested that the ladies might be allowed into the Clubhouse in order to see the Club's trophies, the suggestion was refused.

Blackheath was an exception, mainly because it was exceptionally masonic; other English Clubs were less prejudiced.

In 1872, the London Scottish Golf Club helped in the formation of the Wimbledon Ladies' Golf Club. Male members of the London Scottish were to be Honorary Members of the Ladies' club, were to have control of

the upkeep of the course, and would settle all disputes. The Annual General Meeting was to be held 'as near St Andrew's Day as possible'. The men were very supportive and provided the ladies with a handsome trophy to play for; despite all this support, the Club died a natural death in 1879.

Several unsuccessful attempts were made, from time to time, to revive the Ladies' Club until, in 1890, a more determined attempt was made, very actively supported by Dr Laidlaw Purves. As a result, the Wimbledon Ladies' Golf Club was resurrected and recruited initially 145 members.

Three years later on, Dr Purves, appalled by the state of men's golf nationally which he saw as totally chaotic, decided, with the aid of other enthusiasts and the Wimbledon Ladies' Club, to form a Ladies' Golf Union; the object of such a Union was to standardise the rules of golf for ladies and the handicap systems and to prepare the way for national tournaments for ladies.

A meeting was held in London, which eleven Ladies' Clubs attended, under the chairmanship of Dr Purves. There was a fund of goodwill and encouragement from other Clubs and Associations and from such notable figures as J.H. Taylor, the then Open Champion. The meeting was conducted with great energy and decisiveness and, by the end, a Ladies' Golf Union had been set up which was to have a (lady) President and four (male) Vice-Presidents.

The Vice-Presidents were to be: Dr Laidlaw Purves of Wimbledon, Mr Talbot Fair of Lytham and St Annes, Mr H.S.C. Everard of the R&A and Mr T. Gilrow of Portrush. Miss Isette Pearson, a notable lady golfer and member of the Wimbledon Ladies' Club was the first Hon. Secretary and Miss Blanche Martin, the first Hon. Treasurer.

Curiously, their resolution failed when it came to electing a President and it was not until fourteen years later that Princess Victoria of Schleswig-Holstein was elected the First President.

Subscriptions were asked for, and received, for a handsome Championship Trophy. Within two weeks of the inaugural Committee Meeting a Constitution was drawn up and within two months the first Championship had been held on the ladies' course at Lytham St Annes; it was regarded as a great success.

In 1875, Mr R. Clark mentioned in his book *Golf. A Royal and Ancient Game* that ladies play golf! His actual words are: 'Of late years the ladies, as an improvement on such drivelling games as croquet and lawn billiards, have taken vigorously to Golf'. . . He goes on to observe that when they have a competition it is a gay scene and that the skill of the fair sex is not to be despised.

In 1890 *The Girls' Own Paper* made an effort to publicise the game as being quite suitable for young ladies and again in 1894 (the year after the first Ladies' Championship had been played) they published an article, this time by Garden Smith, a golfer and a journalist; he, too, describes a genteel game but, at least, there is a picture of a young lady making a full swing, whereas, in the earlier article the pictures show only a little putting.

While the founders of the Ladies' Golf Union (and many other Golf Clubs and golfers, both male and female) regarded the first Championship meeting as a great success, no Scottish lady golfer entered and there

**Lady Margaret Scott, Ladies' Champion 1893**

were some sour letters to various golf magazines saying that the Championship was really an English one and not an Open one because there were a number of Scottish lady golfers who were much better players but who had not played. The impression one gets from most of these communications is that the Scottish ladies were not allowed to enter. Despite these Scottish sour grapes, the meeting was a success and, in 1896, the first entry from Scotland was received.

The first Ladies' Championship was dominated by one woman – Lady Margaret Scott. Although lady golfers had a reputation at their own Golf Clubs, few of them had ever played against lady golfers from other Clubs, and consequently the relative merits of golfers from different Clubs was unknown – there was no 'form book'.

For the first Championship there was no Clubhouse, since the ladies' course at Lytham did not boast one; instead, a tent was erected at the ninth, or last, hole in the 9-hole course and the local hotel set aside its drawing room solely for use by the ladies.

There was a large crowd at the start of the first round in which only four competitors took part. Each round was played over 18 holes. The crowd became larger in the second round, in which 16 players took part. The costumes of the many ladies in the crowd were said, by the reporter, to be dazzling and to give 'a brilliant appearance to the gathering'. It was generally considered that Miss Pearson, Mrs Catterall and Lady Margaret Scott were the best players in the field. Lady Margaret Scott showed that she was the only one to be considered by winning decisively, no one being able to take her past the 15th hole. Her play was characterised by powerful and accurate shots allied to a remarkably cool temperament. Lady Margaret's father was Lord Eldon, who was a keen golfer and had a private golf course in his grounds. He had sons who all played golf: Osmond, who was a finalist in the Amateur Championship of 1905 and was an international golfer for many years; Michael, who was both Open and Amateur Champion of Australia and subsequently became, in 1933, the oldest man to win the British Amateur Championship; and Denys, who was a fine golfer and won Championships in Europe. Lady Margaret played with her brothers on the private course; it is not surprising, therefore, that she became an outstanding golfer.

Left: The first four ladies in the first championship *(left to right)*: Issette Pearson (2nd), Florence Carr (4th), Effie Terry (3rd), Lady Margaret Scott (champion)

Below: The Ladies' Championship Challenge Cup

## The Ladies' Championship

THE trophy won by Lady Margaret Scott at the first Ladies' Championship was a handsome silver Challenge Cup; this had been bought with money subscribed by Wimbledon, Lytham and St Annes and a number of other English Clubs; outside England there were subscriptions from St Andrews and Belfast.

The second Championship was played at Littlestone in Kent and was played on the men's course, the ladies having special forward tees. In spite of this concession, the course was still about 4,000 yards long – twice the length of the previous venue. It was again won easily by Lady Margaret Scott, who was said to be playing even better than she had done the previous year.

The third Championship took place at Portrush, in Northern Ireland. It was, yet again, won comfortably by Lady Margaret Scott; her only uncomfortable moment was in the first round, when a Miss Phillips took her to the last hole before losing. The records show that Miss Phillips was the only competitor to take Lady Margaret

Above: Miss Whigham and
Miss Adair at the 11th tee at
Westward Ho!

Above right: Group at the
first championship at
Lytham and St Annes

Right: Lady Margaret Scott:
top of backswing, c.1880

Far right: Draw for the
Ladies' Championship, 1893

## DRAW FOR THE LADIES' CHAMPIONSHIP, 1893.

| NAME OF CLUB FROM WHICH PLAYERS ENTER. | FIRST HEAT, 13TH JUNE. | SECOND HEAT, 13TH JUNE. | THIRD HEAT, 14TH JUNE. | FOURTH HEAT, 14TH JUNE. | FIFTH HEAT, 15TH JUNE. | SIXTH HEAT, 15TH JUNE. | |
|---|---|---|---|---|---|---|---|
| Minchinhampton, | Mrs. Davies ............ Bye | Mrs. Davies ............ „ | *Miss Terry* | *Terry* | | | |
| Lytham and St. Anne's, | Miss Effie Terry ...... „ | Miss Effie Terry ...... „ | | | *Terry* | | |
| Eastbourne, | Miss M. Starkie Bence ... „ | Miss M. Starkie Bence ... „ | *Miss Lythgoe* | | | | |
| Lytham and St. Anne's, | Miss M. Lythgoe ...... „ | Miss M. Lythgoe ...... „ | | | | | |
| Pau, | Miss Newall ............ „ | Miss Newall ............ „ | *Miss Newall* | *Hoare* | | | |
| Lytham and St. Anne's, | Miss Rosie Fair ...... „ | Miss Rosie Fair ...... „ | | | | *Scott* | |
| Minchinhampton, | Mrs. Wilson Hoare ...... „ | Mrs. Wilson Hoare ...... „ | *Mrs. Wilson Hoare* | | | | |
| Lytham and St. Anne's, | Mrs. Hermon ............ „ | Mrs. Hermon ............ „ | | | | | |
| Lytham and St. Anne's, | Mrs. Brown ............ „ | Mrs. Brown ............ „ | *Mrs. Brown* | *Brown* | | | |
| Lytham and St. Anne's, | Mrs. Miller ............ „ | Mrs. Miller ............ „ | | | | | |
| Formby, | Miss A. Welch ............ „ | Miss A. Welch ............ „ | *Miss Lythgoe* | | *Scott* | | |
| Lytham and St. Anne's, | Miss E. Lythgoe ...... „ | Miss E. Lythgoe ...... „ | | | | | |
| Lytham and St. Anne's, | Miss Maud Fair ...... „ | Miss Maud Fair ...... „ | *Miss Fair* | *Scott* | | | |
| Royal County Portrush, | Miss Alice Hamilton ...... „ | Miss Alice Hamilton ...... „ | | | | | Winner. |
| Pau, | Miss M. Newall ...... „ | Miss M. Newall ...... „ | *Lady M. Scott* | | | | *Scott* |
| Cotswold, | Lady Margaret Scott ...... „ | Lady Margaret Scott ...... „ | | | | | |
| Ilkley, | Miss K. Moeller ...... „ | Miss K. Moeller ...... „ | *Miss Moeller* | *Thompson* | | *Scott* | |
| Lytham an St. Anne's, | Miss A. H. Thompson ...... „ | Miss A. H. Thompson ...... „ | | | | | |
| Formby, | Mrs. Ainsworth ...... „ | Mrs. Ainsworth ...... „ | *Miss Welch* | | | | |
| Formby, | Miss B. Welch ............ „ | Miss B. Welch ............ „ | | | *Carr* | | |
| Formby, | Miss Florence Carr ...... „ | Miss Florence Carr ...... „ | *Miss Carr* | *Carr* | | | |
| Lytham and St. Anne's, | Miss Mugliston ...... „ | Miss Mugliston ...... „ | | | | | |
| Lytham and St. Anne's, | Mrs. Eason ............ „ | Mrs. Eason ............ „ | *Miss Fair* | | | | |
| Eastbourne, | Mrs. W. Ryder Richardson ... „ | Mrs. W. Ryder Richardson ... „ | *Miss Thomson* | | | *Pearson* | |
| Lytham and St. Anne's, | Miss Mary Cunliffe ...... „ | Miss Mary Cunliffe ...... „ | | | | | |
| Wimbledon, | Miss Lena Thompson ...... „ | Miss Lena Thomson ...... „ | | *Thomson* | | | |
| Formby, | Miss Wrigley ...... „ | *Miss Wrigley* | *Miss Stewart* | | | | |
| Wimbledon, | Mrs. Cameron ...... „ | | | | | | |
| Kenilworth, | Mrs. Smith-Turberville ...... „ | *Mrs. Stewart* | | | *Pearson* | | |
| Ashdown Forest, | Mrs. Stewart ............ „ | | | | | | |
| Lytham and St. Anne's, | Miss May Mugliston ...... „ | *Miss Drake* | *Miss Drake* | | | | |
| Eastbourne, | Miss A. L. Tyrwhitt Drake ... „ | | | | | | |
| Formby, | Miss Welch ............ „ | *Miss Cox* | | *Pearson* | | | |
| Royal County Portrush, | Miss Helen Cox ...... „ | | | | | | |
| Eastbourne, | Miss O. Hoare ...... „ | *Miss Isette Pearson* | *Miss Isette Pearson* | | | | |
| Wimbledon, | Miss Isette Pearson ...... „ | | | | | | |
| Lytham and St. Anne's, | Mrs. Ernest Catterall ...... „ | *Mrs. Catterall* | | | | | |
| Formby, | Miss D. Wrigley ...... „ | | | | | | |

Above: Group at 2nd
Ladies' Championship,
Littlestone 1894

Right: Miss E.A. Nevile in
the Ladies' Open
Championship, Westward
Ho! 1900

**Group at 3rd Championship, Portrush 1895**

Scott past the 16th hole in any of the three Championships that she won. In the following year Lady Margaret married and became Lady Margaret Russell Smith and never again competed in a major Championship.

By now, the ladies had the bit between their teeth and were determined that golf was not to be a genteel pastime but a vigorous and skilful game; the Ladies' Golf Union constantly strove to make the courses over which they played their Championships both longer and more difficult. In 1897, in a ladies' long-driving competition, the longest carry was 134 yards and at Westward Ho! in 1900 Miss M. Whigham of Prestwick drove over 200 yards at two holes in succession – and this when playing with a gutty ball. It was clear that the ladies had every right to want to play over longer and more difficult golf courses.

At the beginning of the twentieth century the Haskell ball made its appearance and this lively ball benefited the ladies considerably; at the same time, changes in fashion allowed them much more freedom to swing and, even more important, their keenness to excel at the game overcame all the earlier reluctance to appear too athletic and all their earlier shyness about appearing to be determined competitors – to be determined to win was now quite acceptable and gone was the genteel putting image.

## Dress for Lady Golfers

THE courses on which the ladies played were initially little more than long putting courses and there were few hazards. The ladies' course on which the first Ladies' Championship was played is described as 'not very sporting, being as flat as a pancake and with only one natural hazard, being a cop, or sod, wall which had to be crossed at the 1st and 9th holes'. Some hazards were constructed in front of a few of the tees.

By far the most difficult problem with which the ladies had to cope was their clothing; they must conform to fashion and decorum. Fashion decreed that they had to wear a stiff 'stand up' collar, and this caused many ladies to have a stiff, sore neck at the end of a round. It was essential to have a 'wasp' waist and all the skirts had stiff petersham belts; it was considered necessary to wear two petticoats which came to the bottom of the skirt – and the skirt came down to the boot. A fashion for very voluminous sleeves was in vogue at one time and these sleeves were so wide that they prevented the player seeing the ball at the top of the backswing; as a result, it was necessary to wear an elastic band on the left sleeve to keep it under control. Because the skirts were so long they

Top: Miss Elsie Grant Suttie. Golfing dress, *c.*1910. It was now permitted to show an ankle
but the tailored coat is buttoned up. No-one would play golf hatless
Above: Group at the 13th Championship, Cromer 1905

**Left: Summer golfing costume for ladies, *c.*1890. Note the straw hat, blouse, and long full black skirt**
**Right: Lady playing in the French Ladies' Championship, 1910. She wears an elastic band at knee level**
**to stop the skirt billowing in the wind and concealing the ball. It was known as a 'Miss Huggins'**
**after the lady who thought up the idea**

trailed in the mud and many ladies had a hem of leather put on the skirt so that the hem could be sponged off after playing on a wet day. Because the skirts were so voluminous they could be blown forward on a windy day, thus obscuring the ball; it was customary to wear an elastic band at the waist, which, on windy days, could be pulled down to about knee level to keep the skirt under control. To add to the discomfort and difficulty, it was customary to wear a bustle at the back of the skirt, at waist level, and it was obligatory to wear a hat. Some hats were very large and required a number of hat pins to keep them in position, supported, on windy days, by a scarf going over the hat and tied under the chin. Ladies usually played in gloves, not to get a better grip of the club, but in order to prevent their hands becoming calloused. The elastic

waistband was known as a 'Miss Huggins', after an American lady who first thought of the idea. The ensemble was completed by button-up boots which had nails in the soles with big heads – the same kind of 'tackety boots' as worn by the men.

Fortunately fashions change and they changed in a manner which helped lady golfers. By 1911, ladies were allowed to show their ankles, and the problem of the wet skirt hem was thus eased. It was further eased by 'spats' becoming fashionable in sport, thus protecting the ankles. The bustle disappeared and waists were not required to be quite so wasp-like. Most women still wore hats but a few daring spirits did not. While most women still wore boots, a few began to wear shoes, which were much lighter than boots.

**British Girls' Champion, 1922. She is wearing a cloche hat, a style with almost no brim**

## The Ladies Open Championship (continued)

Ladies' golf grew apace. The original number of Clubs in the Ladies' Golf Union was 19, by the end of the nineteenth century there were 41, and by 1914 there were 400.

By 1910, courses for ladies only had ceased to exist, with one or two notable exceptions, and it was accepted by the men that ladies played on the main course, but off special forward tees.

In 1897, the Ladies' Championship was played at Gullane and this gave the necessary fillip to the Scottish ladies. There were 102 competitors and, of these, 38 were Scots; the remainder were English with the exception of a Welsh lady and ten Irish ladies.

The final was contested by two Scottish sisters – the Misses Orr. From that date until 1908, no Scottish lady won the Ladies' Championship. This may have been due to the Scottish reluctance to play outside Scotland.

In 1899, an Irish lady came to the fore. Although the Irish had been enthusiastic supporters of ladies' golf from the start, there were not many Irish lady golfers until the Ladies' Championship was played at Portrush in 1895; this Championship opened their eyes to the possibilities of ladies' golf and there was a rush of enthusiastic lady golfers in Ireland. The lady who won was Miss May Hezlet; she had won the Irish Ladies' Championship in that year also and was to win the Ladies' Championship again in 1902 and 1907, as well as winning the Irish Ladies' Championship many times. In her win in 1907, May Hezlet beat her sister, Florence, in the final.

In 1904 the Ladies' Championship was won by Miss Lottie Dod of Cheshire, who had a remarkable athletic talent. She took up golf late in life having been, for many years, a tennis player of international reputation; she was also an international hockey player, an expert skater, and a champion at croquet. Not long after she had won Championship honours at golf, she turned her talents to archery and achieved great success there also, winning a Silver Medal in the 1908 Olympics.

There then appeared on the Championship scene two golfers of outstanding merit; the first was Miss Rhona Adair. Miss Adair won the Championship in 1900 and 1903. This makes her a very good golfer though not, perhaps, any better than several of her predecessors, but she was, by all accounts, the possessor of a strikingly beautiful style and her contemporaries much admired her.

After the First World War, the rapid emancipation of women and the dramatic changes in women's fashions made the playing of golf much easier for them and, throughout the 1920s, golfing dress became steadily more casual and practical. Nevertheless, however practical it had become, the practicality did not extend to wearing trousers and it was not until 1934, in the Ladies' Championship at Westward Ho!, that Miss Gloria Minoprio dared to wear trousers. She added to her notoriety by playing with only one club. Had she won, she would probably have become the most famous lady golfer in the world but, to the chagrin of the Press, she only survived one round. Despite this she got more lines in the Press than the eventual winner.

Ladies' Championship, Burnham, 1906. It was unladylike not to wear a hat – on windy days a scarf was tied over the hat and under the chin. It was also unladylike to show an ankle. Ladies were forced to play golf as best they could without breaking the rigid rules of fashion

Miss Peggy Leitch, the youngest of the Miss Leitches, playing out of a bunker, 1913

11th Championship, Portrush 1903

12th Championship, Troon 1904

**Left: Miss Rhona Adair, 1901**
**Right: Miss S. Whigham: Ladies' Open Championship, Westward Ho! 1900**

The second lady golfer of note was Miss Dorothy Campbell. This remarkable player is not as well known as she should be, though this may well be because of her innate modesty and the fact that she lived in the United States and Canada for over 25 years, and died in Canada. She came from North Berwick and learned her golf there. She won the Ladies' Championship in 1909 and 1911 and was runner-up in 1908; she won the Scottish Ladies' Championship in 1905, 1906 and 1908 and was runner up in 1907 and 1909.

Miss Campbell won the Canadian Ladies' Open Championship in 1910, 1911 and 1912; she won the United States Ladies' Open Championship in 1909 and 1910. In 1924, when she had not played competitive golf for some years, she decided to try again; she remodelled her swing to bring it 'up to date' and then won the United States Ladies' Championship again – a truly remarkable feat! In both the United States and Canada Miss Campbell won a great number of State and other major tournaments. Ultimately, she retired to Ontario; she is said to have endeared herself to all the golfers that she met by her sweet disposition. As the only lady (or man) who has ever won the Championships of the United States, Canada and Britain – and very nearly all in the same year – she well deserves to be honoured in the annals of ladies' golf.

In a golf magazine of 1911 there is an illustration showing Miss Campbell's swing and a description of her style of play. The illustration shows a swing of control rather than power and some idiosyncrancies which were uncommon at that time. For example, Miss Campbell plays with a shut, or 'square to square', face and has an unusual grip of the club, with the right thumb behind the shaft.

The writer in describing her golfing method and prowess says that he is not surprised that she was off her long game at Portrush in 1911, when she won her second Ladies' Open Championship. Despite being off her long game, she won the Championship and the writer pays tribute to her short game and to her excellent temperament.

**Miss Cecil Leitch**

Until the First World War, ladies' golf grew apace and the standard of play steadily improved. Possibly the best players were no better than their predecessors but the general standard of play of all lady golfers was rising.

In 1914 there appeared a lady who was to dominate ladies' golf for the next decade and raise the standards of ladies' golf yet further. Miss Charlotte Cecilia Pitcairn Leitch of Silloth in Cumberland was born in 1891 and known to all as Cecil Leitch. She had two sisters who were good golfers – Edith and May – but Cecil was the outstanding golfer of her era and won the French Ladies' Championship in 1912, 1914, 1920, 1921 and 1924. She won the Ladies' Open Championship in 1914, 1920, 1921 and 1926. Miss Leitch also won the Canadian Ladies' Championship in 1921. She never played in any United States Championship. As might be expected, she represented England in many international matches. While her general standard of play was high, it was her long shots which were outstanding and she hit the ball much further than any of her contemporaries. Allied to her skill was a dominating and forceful personality.

Miss Leitch was more than willing to take on men at golf and, given an appropriate number of strokes, she beat many of them, including Harold Hilton, at that time the Open Champion. Had the First World War not interrupted her career she must surely have won many more Championships.

After the First World War, Miss Leitch continued to win but not perhaps quite as frequently as before and she was no longer the only pebble on the beach, for another remarkable lady golfer had appeared on the scene, Miss Joyce Wethered.

### Miss Joyce Wethered (Lady Heathcote Amory)

Like Lady Margaret Scott, but unlike Cecil Leitch, Miss Wethered had an elder brother who was also a great golfer; she must have played a lot of golf with him when they were young and this would have influenced her golfing skill and developed her competitive spirit. It does not seem to have influenced her style for she had a most stylish swing, whereas her brother, great golfer that he was, had a swing that was very much his own.

Miss Wethered, born in 1901, first won public recognition as a golfer in 1920. She had been too young to play in the important events before 1914, but from 1920 onwards she quickly made up for lost time. The antithesis of Cecil Leitch, she was tall and slim and very feminine; her swing was unassuming and deceptively easy but she was a fine long hitter of a golf ball. It is said that Robert Jones, after seeing her play, stated that in his opinion she was the finest golfer that he had ever seen, man or woman.

Henry Cotton played with her and afterwards said that 'except perhaps for Harry Vardon I do not think a golf ball has ever been hit with such a straight flight'. She had come to see Cotton because, she said, she had not played much golf lately and wanted him to help her regain her form. Cotton remarks in his account that after a few shots on the practice ground 'I timidly suggested

**Young Miss Wethered at the height of her fame in the early 1920s**

holes of the match, but what could you do when your opponent played 4 pars and 6 birdies over 10 consecutive holes? You could congratulate yourself on having stood up as well as you did against the most correct and lovely swing golf has ever known and thank your lucky stars that there was only one Joyce Wethered and that she lived in England.' Miss Collett played against Joyce Wethered on only one other occasion, in the Ladies' Open at St Andrews in 1929. They played in the final and Miss Collett was at one time 5 up with 7 to play, but Joyce Wethered won 6 of the next 7 holes.

Miss Wethered won five consecutive English Ladies' Championships between 1920 and 1924. In the course of these wins she beat Miss Leitch in the final in 1920; after being 4 down to Miss Leitch at the end of the first round, and 6 down at one stage in the afternoon round, she then played superb golf to win 8 holes consecutively and take the match.

## Miss Joyce Wethered and Foursome Play

A slight digression is needed to explain some of the difficulties and niceties of foursome play. The playing of foursomes or, what the Americans call Scotch Foursomes, that form of golf in which two partners play alternate shots, is an art.

To be a good partner in a foursome, the most difficult form of golf, is a gift that not everyone has. While each partner in a foursome may be a great golfer, when put to play together they may not be a great foursome combination. A good example of this are the partnerships of Old Tom Morris and Willie Park Senior.

Of the first eight Open Championships, between them they won seven. Each was an outstanding challenge match player in singles and each was seldom beaten – but they never won a foursome playing together. On the other hand each was more than capable of winning big wager matches at foursomes with other partners. There is no rational or scientific explanation for this. It was simply that their temperaments were such that they did not perform well as a foursome couple.

Occasionally, two golfers, not obviously suited to one another, will form a great foursomes partnership and are much more successful as a foursomes partnership than either is when playing a single. To be a good foursomes partner you need to be receptive to the way that your partner's mind works; in some foursomes it may be necessary to play a dominant role, in others, a supportive

to her that her perfect swing of the old days was much narrower than usual. Lady Heathcoat Amory [Miss Wethered's married name] widened her swing a little and there followed a string of perfect golf shots which might have been poured out of a machine.' Impressed though he was with all her golf, Cotton thought that Wethered's best shot was the pitch and run with a mashie.

Herbert Warren Wind, describing the magnificent golf of Glenna Collett (who won six US National titles and was the dominating golfer of 1923–4 in the United States), recalls that she went to Europe and won the French Ladies' Championship in 1925. Miss Collett then played in the Ladies' Open in England; she and Miss Wethered met in the third round, and Wind's description is as follows: 'For nine holes Glenna managed to stay on even terms with the great English stylist. As a matter of fact, Glenna was only one over par in the wind for the 15 one. In foursomes it is often necessary to change your normal pattern of play at each hole because such a pattern is not the best one for your partner. All these considerations, and many others, must be observed if a foursomes partnership is to be successful and it is this that makes foursomes play the most difficult form of golf – sadly, it is now much neglected.

It was in this form of golf that Miss Wethered was at her finest; she demonstrated this quality, in particular, in that delightful and keenly contested event, the Worplesdon Mixed Foursomes. This is a scratch event and the entry is full of distinguished golfing names, both male and female. To play with Miss Wethered, or, as she later became, Lady Heathcoat Amory, meant a near certain win;

**Jean and Margaret Park, daughters of Willie Park, both of whom played for Scotland in 1902**

with seven different partners she won the Mixed Foursomes eight times, a record that has never been equalled. As Miss Wethered, she won the Ladies' Foursomes twice and, in the many international matches in which she played, her record in the foursomes speaks for itself.

By the time that Miss Wethered and Miss Leitch had come to the end of their careers they had raised the standard of ladies' golf considerably and there were many fine golfers competing in the national events, among them Miss Wanda Morgan, Miss Dorothy Park (daughter of Willie Park Junior), Miss Molly Griffiths and Miss Mollie Gourlay, but the outstanding golfer from this period was Miss Enid Wilson. She won the Ladies' Championship in 1931, 1932 and 1933 and the English Ladies' Championship in 1928 and 1930. She won many regional Championships and was a regular member of the team in all the international matches in the 1930s.

Miss Wilson was *the* lady golfer of the 1930s; she was a lady of some physical strength and hit the ball a long way, she was a fine long iron player and had a deft short game. Apart from her golfing ability, she was somewhat in the Cecil Leitch mould, having a strong and dominant personality and a keen sense of competition.

During the 1930s there also appeared on the ladies' golfing scene a young woman of great golfing skill and great competitive determination, Miss Pam Barton. She was born in 1917 and learnt her golf at Royal Mid Surrey Golf Club. At the age of 17 – in 1934 – she won the French Ladies' Open Championship and, in the same year, she was runner-up in the Ladies' Open Championship and was, again, runner-up in 1935. In 1936 she won the Ladies' Open Championship and, in the same year, won the American Ladies' Open Championship; she was runner-up in the French Ladies' Open Championship in 1936 and 1938.

When the Second World War started she was 22, already the winner of three major ladies' championships and an international golfer. There can be no doubt that she was at the start of a brilliant golfing career. Miss Barton joined the WAAF at the outbreak of War and was killed while on active service, thus depriving Britain of a great golfer.

Having reached the Second World War in the story of British ladies' golf; it is now time to retrace our steps and consider ladies' golf in other countries.

Ladies' golf in Perth, Western Australia, 1917

## Origins of Ladies' Golf in other countries

ONE would expect that the earliest ladies' golf played overseas would be in countries forming part of the British Empire and, generally speaking, this is so. However, it is surprising how long after men's golf had established itself that the ladies' game became established. In India, for example, golf was available for men at Calcutta in 1829 and at Bombay in 1842. In 1886, on a vote of 43 for and 16 against, the ladies were granted permission to play on the links at Calcutta in the mornings; a motion to allow them to play once a week in the evenings was defeated.

When the golf course was laid out at Dum Dum in 1892, a new site for the Royal Calcutta Golf Club, the first competition held was the Ladies' Challenge Cup which had been presented by the Ladies' Golf Club, described as having 'just come into existence'. In 1900 the ladies built themselves a Clubhouse (which still exists on the Calcutta maidan); it was not until 1906 that the first Ladies' Championship of India was played.

At Colombo in Ceylon (now Sri Lanka), a Golf Club was founded in 1879; a Minute of 1895 mentions 'the takeover of surplus golf balls by the Ladies' Club' ; we do not know when this Club started. In 1907 the Ladies had a Clubhouse and in 1920 the first Ceylon Ladies' Championship was played.

This general pattern of golfing facilities for ladies was repeated in many widely separated areas of the world, though with local variations. In the older Clubs women were not allowed because the men, quite simply, were not willing to consider it; the men who formed the Clubs were predominantly Scotsmen and they had had a good grounding from the Masonic Clubs in Scotland and, in particular, from Blackheath in England, about the importance of a Golf Club as a male institution.

At the start of the twentieth century, Edwardian attitudes had given women more say in the world; when the suffragette movement started in England it had repercussions all over the world and women were no longer willing to be lorded over by men. This attitude led women to demand that they be allowed to play golf on the men's course. The men reluctantly agreed and the next step was for the women to have a Clubhouse of their own, followed, quite quickly, by the formation of a Ladies' Golf Club; from there it was only a matter of time before there was a national or regional Ladies' Golf Association.

When they formed a Ladies' Golf Club, they began to play for silver cups among themselves, and when they formed national associations, they began to play national Ladies' Championships.

This emancipation of women golfers occurred primarily among the women of Britain and the United States and among expatriate British women living throughout the Empire.

## Australia

The old colonies of Britain were, generally, much less hampered by the 'male only' tradition than the Mother Country, which was a great help to the development of ladies' golf. It meant early entry of ladies to golf and it meant, also, that ladies were not asked, except in a few instances, to play on a separate course.

In Sydney, women were allowed to be Associate Members in 1896 – only three years after the founding of the Club. They were allowed to play on the (men's) course off forward tees but there were certain days on which they could not play.

In Melbourne, from 1892, women were allowed to play, again, as in the case of Sydney, as Associate Members, on the main course at certain times of the week.

In Adelaide, women were permitted to play in 1896 on the main course. The significance of making the ladies Associate Members was that, while it allowed them to play golf, it did not allow them to attend and vote at the Annual General Meeting; thus, the men controlled the regulations about times of play for women and made regulations about women's play generally.

The Australian Golf Club put up a token resistance, having been frightened by a posse of women cyclists in the previous year (cycling being 'all the rage' at that time, in Australia). In 1898, they granted Honorary Membership to eight ladies; this was the thin end of the wedge and, by the end of the century ladies were freely allowed to play.

The first Ladies' Championship of Australia was played in 1894 at Geelong.

## New Zealand

In Auckland, ladies were permitted to play – on their own course – in 1896. However, they soon abandoned their course and played on the men's. But women's golf in New Zealand started before that and probably the earliest instance was in 1892 at Otago. G.M. Kelley's book *Golf in New Zealand* states: 'From the foundation of the first Clubs, the ladies joined in. If the men made the courses, their women contributed moral support, morning tea and even manual labour.' Despite this statement, there is no mention of women playing golf in Otago, where the Dunedin Golf Club started a precarious existence in 1871. Once started, how-ever, the ladies were very active and the first New Zealand Ladies' Championship was played in 1893.

In 1872 a Golf Club was formed at Christchurch, but Kelley states: 'Profoundly English in its habits and sympathies, however, Christchurch remained aloof. Significantly, all the sponsors were of Scots background.' The Christchurch Club did not prosper and subsequently disappeared. One would suggest that 'profoundly English' should really have been 'profoundly Scotch'! What aloofness the Club showed we do not know but the aloofness would certainly have extended to women golfers! When the Christchurch Club was resurrected, in 1891, it flourished; by this time, one of their leading golfers was George Gosset; he was the son of the Reverend George Gosset who was a Founder member of the Royal North Devon Golf Club, at Westward Ho! in England, in 1864, and was the prime mover in setting up a Ladies' Golf Club at Westward Ho!, the first Ladies' Club in England. One can assume that his son would have been sure to include women in the revived Christchurch Golf Club.

## Canada

The Royal Montreal Golf Club is a good example of how women came to play golf in Canada. The Club was formed in 1873 but had much trouble with various courses for some years. In 1883, it started a habit of afternoon tea for ladies in the Clubhouse. This social feature rapidly developed and, in no time, there were important balls and soirées held in a hotel in the town.

By now the ladies, having seen the course, were insistent that they wanted to play and sought membership. Under some pressure, the Club decided to admit 'ladies and boys' as members in 1891. This was the thin end of the wedge and, by 1899, the ladies not only had full rights of play on the men's course but had their own Clubhouse.

By 1901, there was a Canadian Ladies' Championship which was won by Miss Young of the Ladies' Club at Montreal. The Championship was dominated after that by Miss M. Thomson, who won it 5 times in the next 7 years. After that date there was a period during which the Championship was won by lady golfers from outside Canada; the first was Miss Campbell, who, as already mentioned, won it three times in succession. Other winners over the years were Miss Muriel Dodd, sister of Miss Lottie Dodd, Miss Alexa Stirling, Miss Cecil Leitch and Miss Collett. The Canadian Championship became, in fact, a popular one for leading American lady golfers.

## Malaysia

The Selangor Golf Club in Kuala Lumpur, the capital of what was then Malaya, was formed in 1894; 'changing rooms for ladies' are recorded but there is no mention of ladies playing. However, by 1897 they played a competition for a Cup.

Argentina in 1904. When Mungo Park Junior went to Argentina in 1904, accompanied by his wife, who was a good golfer, she won the Ladies' Argentine Championship in 1905. She was not the first winner; it follows that women's golf in Argentina must have been in existence from well before 1904.

The foregoing is an incomplete record but, as far as present research is concerned, is all that has been gleaned so far. Although it has not been specifically stated, the reader will understand that, in all these examples, the initial moves to found Golf Clubs were made by expatriates from Britain, who had played golf there. The rise of golf in what were then the colonies is really an extension of British golf.

### The United States

The rebirth of golf in the United States occurred in 1888 and was a game for men. Women were not encouraged. Unlike their counterparts in Britain, those who started things up were not hampered by tradition, and although they revered all things Scottish in connection with golf, they went about things in a thoroughly American way.

The most noticeable feature of this was the opulence of the Clubhouses; the concept of a Country Club was entirely American. Unlike the rather austere Clubhouses of the early clubs in Britain, which at one extreme were designed to house gentlemen and their golf clubs as well as having a rather grand dining-room for formal dinners and, at the other, consisted of 'cricket pavilion'-type Clubhouses among the poorer clubs, the Americans had to have spacious and well-appointed Clubhouses so that their wives could use them as well. It was not that American males wanted their wives or girlfriends to play golf but they wanted the ladies to be suitably housed and amused in the Clubhouse while *they* played golf.

American women were much more emancipated than their British counterparts and it was socially acceptable for them to take part in many sports; the ladies could not see why they should not play golf, and it was not long before they were proving the point. As soon as it became plain that the ladies were not going to be denied their golf, efforts were made to give them a putting course on which to play but this would not do for the ladies. In New Jersey, in 1893, a course for ladies only was initiated and it was not long before they were playing on the men's courses from forward tees. In 1895, they played their first

**Golf at Le Touquet, France 1939. The ladies wear shoes and socks and have pleated skirts. One wears a hat**

### France

Mention must be made of the Golf Club at Pau, in south-west France. The Club was formed in 1856 and was the first Golf Club in Europe. Early pictures of Pau show both men and women playing together. We have no accurate records to show at what date ladies officially started golf but it is quite likely that the ladies played at Pau – on the men's course – before ladies started golf at St Andrews and were, in fact, the first ladies' Golf Club in the world.

### Belgium

The Royal Antwerp Golf Club was founded in 1888. Ladies were admitted to the Club in 1901 and played on the men's course.

### Argentina

Golf was flourishing in 1895 and there were six courses in

American Ladies' Championship; it was a medal event won by a Mrs Brown with a score of 132 for 18 holes.

Tradition in dress was also less evident and the restrictions imposed on the British ladies in order to appear 'ladylike' on the course did not apply to American ladies. Even as early as 1895, American ladies were accustomed to skirts for golf which definitely showed an ankle and they eschewed very frilly blouses and wasp waists. Some of them went so far as not to wear hats. Although the ladies were less hampered by tradition, they were not very good golfers but, with the steady flow of Scot immigrant professionals and the tour of Harry Vardon in 1900, they were coming along fast, working on their game with typical American enthusiasm and thoroughness.

Vardon says of the American lady golfer, after his tour in 1900: 'The American girls are adopting the game more wholeheartedly than their English sisters and their devotion to it will tell. The lady of the States who is a golfer dresses for golf and golf only . . . she tucks up her sleeves like a man . . . and does not look a tittle the worse for these things.'

## Notable American Lady Golfers

MISS BEATRIX HOYT was the first American lady golfer of great talent. In 1896, at the age of 16, she started a run of three successive wins in the American Ladies' Championship and during those three years she completely dominated ladies' golf in America. The ease with which she won her three Championships and the scores with which she won scoreplay tournaments strongly suggest that she was 6 shots per round better than any other American lady golfer of the time. At the age of 20 she gave up tournament golf and disappeared from the American golf scene.

The next lady of outstanding talent was Miss Alexa Stirling who, in 1916, at the age of 19, won the American Ladies' Open Championship; Miss Stirling came from Atlanta and was a friend of Bobby Jones. She won the American Ladies' Open Championship in 1916 and then, after a gap of three years, due to the First World War, won again in 1919 and 1920; she was runner up in 1921. She was also runner up in the Canadian Ladies' Championship in 1922 and 1923. In 1921 she travelled to Europe and played in the French Ladies' Open Championship and in the Ladies' Open Championship in Britain but was not particularly successful. Nevertheless, Miss Stirling was a great golfer and was the first American lady who could compete on level terms with golfers outside America and give a good account of herself; with Miss Stirling's arrival on the golfing scene, American ladies' golf had become a force to be reckoned with in international golf and it never looked back.

Following the era when Miss Stirling dominated American ladies' golf there were a number of good golfers, such as Marion Hollins and Edith Cummings, but they were quickly outshone by a new arrival, Miss Glenna Collett. She was born in 1903 and it was evident,

The Ladies' Course at Pau, in the days of the crinoline

**Left: Miss A. Pascoe at the finish of her swing**
**Right: Miss Glenna Collett (later Mrs Glenna Collett Vare).**
**She was one of the great US lady amateur golfers, *c.*1929**

in her early teens, that she was blessed with an athlete's timing and co-ordination, being a 'natural' at many other sports. She took seriously to golf after seeing Alexa Stirling play an exhibition match. Glenna was an assiduous practiser and her standard of play improved greatly. She still tended not to do herself justice in the tournaments but, following a victory over Cecil Leitch in 1921, in a tournament, she developed self-confidence and began to win. She won the American Ladies' Championship in 1922, 1925, 1928, 1929 and 1930 and won the Canadian Ladies' Championship in 1923 and 1924. She played in the British Ladies' Championship but could do no better than runner-up in 1929 and 1930. She later married and was known in golf as Mrs Glenna Collett Vare. She was well liked, not only because of her golfing ability but because she was a pleasant, good-looking, extrovert girl who played golf in a businesslike manner and was not given to displays of emotion. What, above all, made her the idol of America was that she was a winner.

Following the Collett Vare era, Virginia van Wie took three American Ladies' Amateur Championships in succession in 1931–33.

There then strode on to the ladies' amateur scene Miss Patty Berg. At 17 she was runner-up in the American Ladies' Amateur Championship. In 1938, when 21, she won the Championship. In 1940 she turned professional and continued as a professional when the Second World War ended, winning the first US Ladies' Open Championship – Open in this context meaning, for the first time, open to both amateurs and professionals.

## The Curtis Cup

In 1905, when the Ladies' Open Championship was played at Royal Cromer, an unofficial match was played between a group of American ladies and some of the British ladies.

Two of the American team were the sisters Harriet and Margaret Curtis. The Curtis ladies were very good golfers. Harriet won the American Ladies' Championship in 1906 and, in 1907, was beaten by her sister in the final. Margaret won in 1907, 1911 and 1912. Margaret was the better golfer of the two and was an athletic woman who won the American Tennis Doubles; she continued to play golf to a great age, competing in the American Ladies' Championship in 1947, 50 years after the first one had been staged.

The Curtis sisters were very pleased with the unofficial match at Royal Cromer in 1905 and suggested that an official match should be played 'involving women golfers of many lands'.

Despite their enthusiasm, nothing was arranged until 1932 when the first Curtis Cup match was played between the United States and Great Britain. The Curtis Cup matches have been a great success and are popular with both players and spectators.

## Lady Professionals

UNTIL about 1920, there was talk of the possibility of ladies becoming professional golfers but it never got further than that, with one exception. Willie Campbell of Scotland, a great amateur golfer, emigrated to America in the 1890s and became a professional at Boston. He died while in post and *Golf Illustrated* records in 1901 that his widow succeeded him as superintendent of the course in Boston and, with her daughter Mary, would be going South in the winter to give golf lessons.

The idea of a woman giving lessons to other women was quite acceptable and it was recognised that a lady professional would more readily appreciate the problems that women face in trying to play golf, than a man. There were two problems that, it was considered, women professional golfers faced. The first was that women did not have the physical strength to make golf clubs and the second was that it was not considered that they could be expected to work their way through 4–6 years of apprenticeship which would, of course, involve a period of time as a caddy.

By 1920 the professional, as a maker of golf clubs, was to all intents and purposes, finished, and only those professionals who were particularly skilled and keen bothered with manufacture. It was easier and simpler to buy the clubs ready made in sets. That part of the problem was thus solved and all that a lady professional would need to be able to do was to carry out a few repairs.

Nevertheless, it was not until the early 1930s that a full-time lady professional appeared; as might be expected the United States was the scene of this change. All credit must go to Mrs Campbell, who must have been, one imagines, a strong and formidable lady who had learnt the trade from her husband.

The first American woman golf professional is listed in the *Golfer's Handbook* of 1936. She was Miss Helen Hicks; the *Handbook* records that she won the Women's Canadian Open in 1929, the American Ladies' Championship in 1931 and was also runner up in that Championship in 1933. There were, in addition, several other important tournament wins. The *Handbook* reports that she 'Turned Business Woman Golfer in 1934'.

The professional golf circuit for women golfers and the American Women's Open Championship did not appear until 1946.

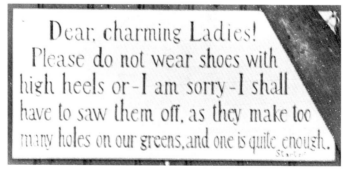

**An attempt by the Secretary at a French Golf Club to persuade the English ladies to behave properly**

# Getting to the Golf Course

By its nature, golf must be played in wide open spaces, which is one of the main attractions of the game but which means that the course is not usually on the players' doorstep.

In Scotland, golfers were more fortunate in the past, and, to a certain extent, are still fortunate today, for the links land on which so much of Scottish golf is played is very close to local towns or villages. This is the case at Musselburgh (the old links), North Berwick, Prestwick and Gullane, while at St Andrews the last green and the first tee are, virtually, in the town.

Because of this proximity, in Scotland the local townsfolk or villagers could easily get to golf without needing transport. The landed gentry were less fortunate because their properties were further inland and they needed a carriage or a horse to get to the links; mention has already been made of the problems of Sir John Foulis whose home was at Ravelston, about eight miles west of Edinburgh; he usually rode to golf at Leith on horseback, either directly, or on his horse to Edinburgh and then by coach to Leith. Much later, Colonel Hutchinson, Horace Hutchinson's uncle, who lived in Fife and played at St Andrews, was in the habit of riding to a friend's house nearby. After breakfasting with him, they would both mount their horses and proceed to golf. Some of the gentry, either as a result of old age or because of some infirmity, rode to golf and then used the pony as a sort of caddy, riding forward to each shot and dismounting to play the next one. Sir John Low, Captain of the R&A in 1856, who was still playing golf when he was over eighty, is recorded as doing this, and the Earl of Wemyss, who was still playing when he was ninety-six, rode a chestnut cob between shots.

In the days of the feather ball, the advantage that the local villagers had over the landed gentry was that they could go out and play between showers of rain, for playing in the rain was the total ruination of the feather ball. The gentry were not so lucky, as they had to make up their minds whether the day was going to be fine or wet before they started out from home; to those who live outside Britain this may seem a fairly easy choice but the weather in Britain is notoriously fickle and changeable and the fact that it is fine in the morning is no guarantee that the afternoon will not see it raining heavily!

## The Coming of the Railways

In the 1840s, two developments occurred which greatly facilitated the increasing popularity of golf. The first was the discovery that a golf ball could be made of gutta percha, and the second was the rapid development of the railway system.

The appearance of the gutta ball and how it was made have been described in the chapter on the golf ball. The impact of the new ball sprang from the fact that the ball was cheaper and that, using one, golf could be played in

Irish 'side-cars' on their way to golf at Portmarnock, *c.*1910

Ferry at Cannes Golf Club, *c.*1905

**The Campbelltown light railway that took passengers to Macrihanish, 1913**

the wet without the ball deteriorating in any way. This cheaper and long-lasting golf ball meant that golf ceased to be a game only for the rich.

The coming of the railways meant that it was easier, quicker and cheaper to get to the golf course and a horse or carriage was no longer needed to make the journey. The railway companies were determined to press ahead with all speed; they were committed to laying lines throughout the entire country because, if the system was to be effective and profit-making, it was vital to link all the major cities, and many towns and villages, by rail. To achieve this they had to buy land, or a right of way, across large tracts of Britain. The railways were in a hurry – and the landowners, mostly landed gentry, were well aware of it. They made the railway companies pay a good price but, in addition to money, the landed gentry, accustomed to privilege, sought more. Some managed to secure the right to stop any train in their area, whether an express train or not; they were also given free rail travel. These privileges were confirmed by the issue of a 'Gold

**Patent for carrying a golf bag on a bicycle, _c._1901**

Card' to the individual concerned. Those landowners who played golf (and there were many) also insisted that lines crossing their land should have a 'Halt' near the Golf Club. Those gentlemen who golfed and on whose land there was a 'Golf Club Halt' were thus very well catered for: they could stop any train at the station near their home, travel free and insist on even the most important express stopping at the Golf Club Halt.

Although the arrival of the railway was a great boon, there were still some areas which were less well served than others; one such area was St Andrews which had a station in the town but was difficult to get to because the Forth Bridge had not yet been constructed. As a result of this, to travel from Edinburgh to St Andrews meant taking a steam ferry from Leith to Burntisland, across the Firth of Forth on the coast of Fife, and then taking a train from Burntisland to St Andrews, via Leuchars Junction, where it was necessary to change trains. The journey was tedious and took all of four hours.

Golf Links Station on the Rye–Camber tramway

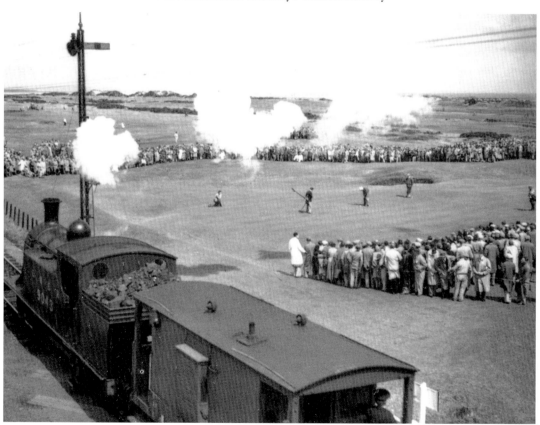

A good view of the 16th green at St Andrews
from the line between Leuchars junction and St Andrews. It was not unknown for the driver to stop
the train to watch the golf!

There were Golf Club Halts all over Britain and many of these remained in being until Dr Beeching instituted his railway 'cuts' in the 1960s. Many of the Halts were on small branch lines and thus it was usually necessary to change trains at a rail junction on the mainline and transfer to a local branch line. Bernard Darwin, when a youthful and promising golfer of limited means, developed a lasting affection for these junctions on the way to golf. This was not because the junctions were places of charm and beauty – far from it, for they were often drab, dirty, and positively depressing on a wet day. However, Darwin remembered them with affection because when you arrived at them you were within a few miles of a golf course and could anticipate being on the first tee in a short time. There was Leuchars, change for St Andrews; Minster, change for Sandwich; Drem, change for North Berwick (and Muirfield); Preston, change for Lytham and St Annes and, finally, for Darwin, Dovey Junction (in Wales), change for Aberdovey, a

**The Prince of Wales preparing to cycle to golf, 1912**

Station Hotel at Taunton (which, in those days, was owned by the Great Western Railway Company) and travelled free on the train; additionally, as the author can well remember, the Colonel would ring the mainline station at Exeter when he wanted to travel back to Taunton and order the next train to be stopped. It did not matter whether the next train was a local stopper or the English Riviera Express which would normally have hurtled through the station at Dawlish Warren at 60 mph.

There were variations on this saga of railway travel; at Macrihanish Golf Club on the Mull of Kintyre in southwest Scotland, there was a special railway which took passengers from Campbelltown to the links. It was the only narrow-gauge railway in Scotland. In the United States the Midlothian Golf Club of Chicago went one step further: it owned its own railway which took golfers from central Chicago to the Golf Club.

In the second half of the nineteenth century, the bicycle appeared and those golfers who

links course on which, as a boy, he had spent many happy hours playing golf in the school holidays. The ageing author has vivid memories of travelling to golf as a boy, the tram ride to the station, the train journey down to the seaside, where the station was little more than a Golf Club Halt and the platform was right beside the 18th green, separated from it by high wire netting to protect the passengers from over-hit second shots.

The author recalls from his youth Colonel Fox, a member of Dawlish Warren Golf Club. He was a retired Army officer and a bachelor, who lived in the Station Hotel, Taunton, some 50 miles up the line. The station at Dawlish Warren was very small – and 20 yards from the 18th green – and only a few local trains normally stopped there. Colonel Fox was more than just a retired Army officer, he was a member of the family firm of Fox which for over a hundred years had made 'Fox's Puttees', a standard form of leg protection for the lower legs of the British Army. It was because of the family connection as suppliers to the British Army that Colonel Fox had a 'Gold Card'; he would have got very cheap terms at the

only had a few miles to go to the course found this a useful and cheap method of travel; various ingenious additions could be made to the bicycle to make it easier to carry golf clubs but, for the most part, they were just slung across the back by the usual strap. At the beginning of the twentieth century the golf bag was nothing like the huge affair it is today, so it was not too difficult to transport it by bicycle.

A cycle ride from the junction to the Golf Club was sometimes useful but it was not a perfect solution. Sometimes junctions were distant from the Club, a good example being the junction at Drem, which was 3½ miles from Muirfield. When A.J.T. Allan won the Amateur Championship at Muirfield in 1897 he travelled each day from Edinburgh to the station at Drem and then cycled 3½ miles to the Golf Club. History does not relate whether he carried his golf clubs back to Edinburgh each night and brought them out again the next day nor whether he cycled to the station at Edinburgh each day and took his cycle on the train with him.

Another method of getting to the Golf Club from

**Off to golf in the United States, *c.*1910**

the local mainline junction was to use a tram; Sydney Golf Club, in New South Wales, had a tram that took golfers from the town of Sydney to the Club at Rose Bay, and at Rye, in Sussex, there was a local conveyance, something between a tram and a railway, which took golfers from Rye to Camber, where the Rye Golf Club was situated.

By 1905, the motor-car had appeared, at first in small numbers and not very reliable. It steadily improved and became a much commoner sight as the century progressed. As with the bicycle, gadgets were invented which could make the carrying of golf clubs easier. Golf Clubs had to think about parking spaces for the first time.

Before the car took over as the recognised form of transport there was a period when bicycles with small petrol-driven motors, fore-runners of the mopeds of today, were experimented with.

The motorcycle also made its appearance at the start of the century and those who could afford one travelled to the course some-what faster than the cyclists and without the need for pedalling.

By the eve of the First World War, the motor-car was the usual

means of getting to the golf course. Many golfers used their cars to travel long distances to golf on the now much improved roads and dispensed with rail travel alto-gether. Alternatively, golfers could travel from the local rail junction, either by taxi or by motor-coach. Even before the First World War, aeroplanes had been used to get to golf; in 1911 Gustave Hamel flew his plane from Hendon to Bushey Hall Golf Course, a journey which took five minutes, and had a golf lesson, flying back afterwards. The reporter who recounted this pointed out that Mr Hamel had previously flown the mail between Hendon and Windsor at 122 mph.

After the War, air travel became ever more popular but was still not used as a regular means of getting to golf, perhaps because of the absence of good landing areas near many golf courses, though a magazine of 1925 shows a Tiger Moth being used to get to golf.

Travel by air to golf has become more and more common of course, and in Japan it is now becoming popular to leave the office in Tokyo by helicopter from the top of the office block, thus avoiding the horrendous traffic jams in that enormous city, landing on a helicopter pad close to the Clubhouse.

**Flying to golf in a Tiger Moth, *c.*1925**

# Golf in Time of War

When war comes, golf, even for fanatical golfers, loses much importance – but not all; those who cannot take part in the war itself seek solace in hitting a golf ball, however decrepit, on a course which may be only partly playable and is in a very poor condition; those away on active service can only dream. Golf Clubs in wartime lose members to the Armed Forces and some of these never return – or return wounded and unable to play again, or unable to play for a period of time.

Some golf courses were suitable for agriculture in order to grow food, some in strategic areas and were virtually destroyed by barbed wire, minefields, training areas, shooting ranges, etc.

These circumstances meant that links courses and inland courses became subject to different penalties; the links courses, by their nature, deteriorated less than inland courses and were of little use for agriculture, but, unfortunately, many links courses, being on the coast, were frequently in strategically important areas, subject to possible invasion, whereas inland courses, while they deteriorated more rapidly without constant care and were much more likely to be put to agricultural use, were, in many cases, not in areas of strategic importance.

## The South African War (1899–1902)

This war was relatively short-lived, was largely fought by regular Armed Forces and was a long way from home. As a result, food remained in plentiful supply and few staff enlisted for service. The effect on Golf Clubs was that they had members who were at the War and thus suffered a slight loss of income. The effects were so minimal that Golf Clubs in Britain hardly found it worth mentioning in their Minutes. As Royal Wimbledon Golf Club state in their history: 'The effect of the South African War was slight'.

One sad outcome of the South African War was that F.G. Tait went to War and never came back and a happy outcome was that John Ball volunteered and went to War, mounted on a fine charger bought by devoted supporters, and came back to win more Championships.

## The First World War (1914–18)

This was a quite different war because it was large and bloody, and resulted in huge casualties.

In this war there was also, a shortage of golf balls. This was not because of a major shortage of rubber and gutta percha but because the factories were understaffed, as many of their workers had been called up for service with the Armed Forces.

### Effects on Golf Clubs

At Seaton Carew Golf Club, situated in a strategic coastal area, the entire course was taken over, including the Clubhouse.

At Walton Heath the course was not taken over and the Dormy House and the Clubhouse remained in use, although the green staff and the indoor staff were much reduced. All formal competitions ceased. A small amount of land near the Professional's shop was taken over; vegetables were grown there and some pig-styes were built. It is possible that the rather stony, heathery area was not suitable for agricultural purposes but one would have thought that it might have been of use for military training. Perhaps the fact that Lloyd George, the Prime Minister, was a keen golfer and played there frequently throughout the war, often with Winston Churchill and Mr Riddell, the Government Press Officer, who was a member of Walton Heath, may have had something to do with the fact that it was not turned over to the military.

Royal Wimbledon Golf Club suffered the usual penalties but the Clubhouse remained open and the course was not requisitioned. The Club owned nearby Warren Farm, having bought it in order to enlarge the golf course. This they were able to put to use, the farm growing vegetables and grazing cattle; the farmhouse was used as a dormitory for Belgian refugees and the Club raised funds to help the escaped Belgians. At a later date, the 2nd, 15th and 16th holes were used for food production; the Clubhouse was made available to convalescent

NCOs and privates on weekdays and they were allowed to play bowls and putt.

At South Staffordshire Golf Club cattle were grazed on the course as well as sheep; the soil was not suitable for ploughing. Gangs of boys invaded the course in search of lost golf balls which they sold to the professional.

One would have thought that North Berwick Golf Club was in an important strategic area but the only effect on the Club, apart from the usual wartime penalties, was that sheep were grazed on part of the links and the Secretary and two greenkeepers joined the Forces. All that could be done was 'to prevent it reverting to its wild and natural state'.

The lesser Portland course at Royal Troon was used for a grenade school but there was no great disturbance to the main Clubhouse and the old course, except that occasioned by staff shortages.

At Gullane Golf Club the Committee agreed to pay half wages to eight members of the green staff who had joined up but, as the war went on longer than expected, the decision was rescinded in 1915. Sheep were grazed 'earlier than usual and in larger numbers' in 1915. By 1915, there were only two green staff left. Formal competitions were discontinued but, it would seem, the local citizens could continue to play under somewhat primitive

South Africa, 1902. British people enjoying golf during the Boer War, with, in the background, a tented refugee village for those displaced during the War

**Exhibition match on Wimbledon Common, proceeds for the relief of Belgian refugees, 1914.**
**James Braid is driving**

conditions such as would have been in existence 100 years before.

On the East coast of England, Aldeburgh and Caister and Yarmouth Golf Clubs were virtually destroyed, as barbed wire and ditches were used profusely, and the respective Clubhouses were taken over by the military.

At Woking Golf Club the Officer Commanding the 1st London Division demanded the right to carry out manoeuvres on the course. The Club agreed and then made all the officers of the Division Honorary Members. The Division carried out no manoeuvres and the officers enjoyed golf on the course; some soldiers were accommodated in the Clubhouse. Later, the Club demanded that horses should not be ridden over the course – and were successful; they also refused to allow sheep to be grazed on the course and were, again, successful.

At The Honourable Company of Edinburgh Golfers, Muirfield, Club Dinners were abandoned and there were no competitions. There was the usual shortage of green staff and indoor staff, otherwise the Club does not seem to have been greatly affected.

'The War years dealt kindly with us,' reported Lytham and St Annes Golf Club. Club life appears to have continued as usual, except for the usual penalties of war. The Club was remarkable, as it made a profit! The Dormy House continued in operation, one room being set aside for convalescent officers. The Secretary helped to solve the ball shortage problem by buying, at the Club's expense, 15 dozen golf balls.

In 1919, to prepare for a good celebration to the end of the war, the Club bought 41 dozen bottles of Champagne, 15 dozen half bottles of Champagne, 2,000 Romeo and Juliet cigars and 110 dozen bottles of Vintage Port – clearly some had a better war than others!

Rye Golf Club seems to have had a very easy war and, like Lytham, made a profit. There was a shortage of Clubhouse staff but catering continued at a nearby pub. Seven out of thirteen of the green staff went to the war.

### Golf Overseas in the First World War

Perhaps Royal Calcutta Golf Club summarises the position in the Empire: 'The war years passed off uneventfully in this part of the world, as the various cockpits and battlefields were sufficiently far away not to make any impression. . .'.

In general terms, Clubs in Australia, New Zealand, South Africa and all the distant parts of the Empire were affected in the same way as the British Clubs had been affected in the South African War – members were lost, green fees were lost; there was no obvious shortage of golf balls. Much money was raised by playing golf competitions in which the entry fees were paid into funds for various charitable War funds.

### Golf for Prisoners-of-War

At the time of the outbreak of war there were a number of British professionals in Germany, France, Belgium and Austria; many of them made hair-raising escapes, leaving

Above: Professionals in Trafalgar
Square about to join the Niblick
Brigade. A number of well-known
professionals are in the group,
including George Duncan (who
survived the War and won the Open
in 1920)

Right: George Duncan in straw
boater at the Trafalgar Square rally in
London when he enlisted

Above: Golf professionals and
assistants who rallied at the foot of
Nelson's column in Trafalgar Square
before enlisting in 1914

Left: Charles Mayo, a well-known
professional, who thought up the
idea of the Niblick Brigade,
pins a sprig of white heather in
Wilfred Reid's buttonhole. The third
man is Arthur Grant who came from
North Berwick to London to join up
but was rejected for the Brigade as he
was not a bachelor!

all their possessions behind, but the German advance was very fast and not all escaped.

One of those who did not was Cuthbert Butchart, who had been professional in Berlin. He was interned and later was put in the prisoner-of-war camp at Ruhleben. Whether Butchart was instrumental in pushing the idea forward to the Germans we do not know but, in about 1916, prisoners were allowed to play golf. Butchart says: '. . .the holes are five in number and are laid out on waste ground inside the racecourse. A Club has been formed and there are 73 members. A number of firms have sent out clubs and balls, so that the Ruhleben course is quite busy between the hours of eight an d nine. . .'.

### Golfers in the Forces in the First World War

There was, of course, conscription, so many golfers were called up to the Services. Those who were not con-scripted were either unfit or were in special occupations; those in special occupations who played golf were glad of a game occasionally on what remained of their local golf course. Their problem was shortage of golf balls and they hoarded and repainted any golf balls that they happened to have. Another problem that they had to face – and it was a problem that even the unfit had to face, if they could manage to play – was the possibility of public con-demnation. This was sufficiently well-marked for *Golf Monthly* to point out in January 1915 that to take the atti-tude that a round of golf was somehow unrighteous was unreasonable as few men who still indulged in the game were eligible for the front.

*The Irish Times*, of January 1916, stated: 'No man feels exactly comfortable walking through the city [Dublin, *Author*] with a big bag of clubs slung across his shoulder. . .'.

### The Niblick Brigade

Albert Tingey was the professional at Fontainebleau when the war started. He had a perilous and difficult escape from France, managing to reach Dieppe, with the loss of almost all his possessions and sailing from there to England. After he got back he became professional at Woodcote Park Golf Club.

In October 1914, he, together with Charles Mayo, conceived the notion of the 'Niblick Brigade'. The idea was that young professionals should all join the Army in the same unit, the only other qualification being that every man should be a bachelor.

He was given full support in this project by the Professional Golfers Association. George Duncan, Wilfred Reid and W.R. Reith took a personal interest in

Some of the bachelor golf professionals who joined the Niblick Brigade in 1914

**The Secretary of Eltham Golf Club and representatives of golf manufacturers assembled in Trafalgar Square to see recruits to the Niblick Brigade join up, 1914**

the idea and wrote to many young professionals and assistant professionals. As a result of these efforts, 26 young bachelor professionals, having been found fit, were drafted into the King's Royal Rifles at Winchester in October 1914. They had a luncheon at Gatti's Restaurant in London and all assembled as a group in Trafalgar Square before their departure. More than one young professional was refused entry because he was found to be married. For a while after this Tingey wrote letters to *Golf Monthly* on behalf of the 'Brigade' (who, in fact, must have just about formed a platoon), giving news of their progress.

The magazines of the times record the various well-known golfers, both amateur and professional, who joined up and there is, as well, sad news from time to time of deaths in action. One contingent worth special mention is that from Coombe Hill Golf Club, where Sandy Herd was the professional; his son, Robert Herd, George Turner (winner of the Assistants Championship that year), George Bright and Phil Rodgers, both assistant professionals, and three groundsmen, two waiters, 18 caddies and the starter.

Among the older professionals who were either unfit or too old to join up, Vardon worked on a farm at Totteridge, Taylor worked in a Red Cross canteen, and Braid worked in a munitions factory. All worked part-time and spent much time and effort in playing exhibition matches in aid of various War Charities.

In 1917, the government decreed that imported hickory was not to be used for golf clubmaking; this had little effect on such golfers as were still playing because the professionals had a good stock of hickory. The shortage of rubber meant that new golf balls had disappeared by 1918.

Two Scots, Willie Park Junior and Thomas Winton, left for the United States on 1 April 1916; they announced that they had decided to reside permanently in the United States where they each expected to find plenty of opportunity to exercise their skill. 'Park is the first holder of the Open Championship to settle in America.'

Did any good for golf come out of the First World War? The answer is a little. With the men away at the war, the proportion of golfers that were women rose and Golf Clubs allowed them more days in the week on which to play, even to the extent of letting them play at weekends. Although there was no great increase in the number of women golfers, those that played got used to playing more often and at weekends and thus began to feel as if they were proper members of Golf Clubs instead of being merely 'Associates', restricted in their play and generally being made to feel second-class citizens. The new status that they achieved was one that they never relinquished after the war.

Another emancipating move was that, because so many green staff were away at the war, women had to be brought in to help maintain the courses. This educated Secretaries into realising that women were capable of doing such work quite as well as men had done and further accustomed members to seeing women regularly on the course.

A third benefit was that the old Scottish taboo against golf on Sundays was weakened; members played golf when they could and that might well include Sundays.

# Golf in the Second World War (1939–45)

Just as the First World War had changed the golfing scene dramatically so, in the Second World War, enemy action came even nearer home and the effects on golf were yet more dramatic. No longer was any part of Britain safe from attack, as bombers and fighters could cover the sky over Britain and the danger of airborne landings was added to the possibility of seaborne landings.

Nearly every golf course was in a strategic area and the desparate need for food meant that all land that could possibly yield crops or pasture animals was in use. Rubber and gutta percha were required for multiple uses and steel production was totally taken up for the making of aircraft, tanks, ships, landing craft, weapons, lorries, etc. The reader might well think that, under these conditions, golf would have disappeared altogether, but golfers are made of stern stuff and not easily to be deflected from their chosen sport!

## Effects on Golf Clubs

The same penalties existed as were created by the First World War but there were additional difficulties.

At Royal Liverpool Golf Club ground staff were greatly reduced. One hundred sheep were grazed on the links and wooden and concrete posts were placed on the links to prevent enemy landings. The Clubhouse was used by the Home Guard as their headquarters. Bathrooms were made available, between 7 and 9.30 am, for a local Searchlight Detachment. The Clubhouse staff were all women.

By 1940, at Rye Golf Club, there were gunsites, searchlights, minefields and pill boxes littered all over the first nine holes. A battle school occupied the nearby Coastguard cottages and the 5th and 6th holes were requisitioned. Three large concrete fuel tanks were sunk into the 18th fairway. The nearby pub was requisitioned

but the Professional's shop and the Clubhouse were not taken over. The Steward, and his wife and family, lived in the rear quarter of the Clubhouse; in 1944 the Clubhouse was hit by a flying bomb, but the Steward and his family survived unscathed.

At Lytham and St Annes Golf Club, fire-watchers were housed over the Professional's shop. The Clubhouse was left untouched because it was considered too small for use as an Officers' Mess and the Club was not asked to graze sheep on the course. Vegetables were grown in the Dormy House garden. The RAF played monthly competitions and there were exhibition matches played in aid of various charities. The Club history does not mention minefields, barbed wire, pill boxes, etc. A large US Airforce base was situated nearby and personnel from that base were made overseas honorary members; they played regularly at Lytham and expressed their gratitude to the Club for the benefit conferred on them.

Overseas guests in the Forces were offered two rooms in the Dormy House and a week's golf free of charge. An American reported: 'Fernie [the Professional. *Author*] would question us about our scores and proffer sets of first-class clubs to those he deemed worthy of them. These came from members overseas or even in POW camps.'

Published after the war, the Club's history states: 'Tournament golf was resumed immediately,' which further supports the view that no damage had been done to the course, neither by enemy action nor by barbed wire entanglements, concrete posts, minefields, etc.

At Royal Troon the Clubhouse was taken over by the military but the Portland Clubhouse was not required and the members used that. The side car park was dug up and planted with vegetables. Much of the Portland course was requisitioned but the main course appears to have been left unmolested. The Club complained that tanks exercised on the shore and were not supposed to go on to the course, but frequently did so.

At Aldeburgh Golf Club pits were dug all over the course and concrete pylons erected to prevent enemy landings. Barbed wire was everywhere and a big tank trap was dug by the 6th green.

The course at Caister and Yarmouth Golf Club was devastated, as most of it was used for military purposes. Tank traps were dug right across it. The Clubhouse was destroyed by a bomb and the 18th green was also destroyed.

According to the Club history, part of the Royal Wimbledon course was damaged by enemy action but the billiard room was converted to an air raid shelter for members (the table was moved into the ladies lounge).

Concrete blockhouses and gun emplacements were

constructed all over the course at Seaton Carew Golf Club and there were minefields and barbed wire at the 16th, 17th and 18th holes. Golf was played.

All formal golf ceased at Walton Heath Golf Club. 'Bridge could be played in the Clubhouse up till midnight, provided the players were staying in the Dormy House.' In 1940, the Dormy House was requisitioned for military use and, later, was used to accommodate homeless families. The Clubhouse was used by golfers.

In the Second World War, sheep were grazed on the course at Royal Blackheath Golf Club and the Clubhouse was taken over by the Fire Brigade and the ARP. Considerable structural damage was done to the beautiful and historic Clubhouse by a bomb which dropped on the putting green.

Neither the course nor the Clubhouse at St Andrews seem to have been affected in any way by the war and both were used by the members – although there was a period of time when, due to shortage of staff, the acting Secretary was a woman!

Sheep were grazed beyond the North Wall at North Berwick Golf Club. The Home Guard took over the caddie shed and the short course. In 1941, the 12th and 13th fairways were fenced off as a minefield. In 1943, the 9th and 10th holes were requisitioned as a range by the Air Ministry.

At the Honourable Company of Edinburgh Golfers, Muirfield, sheep grazed the links. In 1940, poles were placed on the course to prevent enemy landings and trenches were dug as tank traps. No part of the links was ploughed up and there were no minefields (the Club having strenuously opposed both, locally). Club dinners and all the competitions were cancelled. There were the usual shortages but the Clubhouse seems not to have been taken over.

### Effect of the Second World War on Overseas Golf Clubs

At first the war seemed very far away but when things began to go badly, Canada became more acutely involved. When the Japanese came into the war in 1942, the whole Pacific was at risk and this included Canada, Australia, New Zealand, Malaya, Singapore, Hong Kong, India, Ceylon and Burma; they faced the real possibility of invasion. When Burma, Singapore, Malaya and Hong Kong rapidly fell, the remaining countries were in even more imminent danger. What had, at first, seemed a situation similar to the First World War – Golf Club Members leaving for the war areas far away and the Golf Clubs holding competitions for war charities and otherwise being little disturbed – all changed in 1942 and India and the Commonwealth countries of the Pacific area found that they were close to the fighting and in danger of

invasion. Petrol rationing and an acute shortage of rubber and gutta percha meant that it was difficult to get to the golf course and that golf balls were hard to come by. There was no shortage of food.

At Royal Montreal Golf Club, Canada the ladies' active membership became larger than the men's. Competitions were played for war charities and for Saving Certificates. The petrol shortage and consequent difficulty in getting to golf was partially solved by hiring a private street car. Golf balls became very scarce. The ladies made the most strenuous efforts to raise funds and helped the Canadian Ladies Golf Union to save enough to buy a Spitfire.

Nothing is said about the conditions at Royal Sydney Golf Club, Australia in either war except to record the sad fact of members lost at the front and of the great efforts of the ladies to raise money in both Wars for the war effort. It is clear that, even in 1942–45, there was no real apprehension of physical invasion by the Japanese; as a result, there were no precautions against enemy landings such as obtained in Britain.

At Royal Adelaide Golf Club, Australia, there was not much disturbance to the tenor of life in the Club, except the usual problems of petrol and ball shortage.

All major competitions at Royal Melbourne Golf Club, Australia were cancelled and there were monthly medals for war charities. In 1940, when petrol rationing was introduced, a horse-drawn waggon was used for getting golfers from the tram stop to the Club. In 1942, recognising that golf balls were going to disappear, the Club bought 150 dozen new golf balls. Play continued on both courses throughout the war but the general condition of the courses deteriorated owing to shortage of green staff.

At Royal Colombo Golf Club, Ceylon (Sri Lanka) the whole course was taken over by the military.

The Royal Calcutta Golf Club contributed 50,000 rupees to the East India Fund, set up to buy an aircraft. It became necessary to take precautions against landings of enemy aircraft. A scheme was drawn up and slit trenches were dug to the left of the 11th fairway. Petrol rationing began to have an effect but there were plenty of golfers and caddies and much golf was played on both the New and Old courses. Golf ball rationing was introduced and the ration was only two balls at one time and not more than four in one calendar month. The 5th green of the New course was requisitioned for military purposes. Refugees began to pour in from Burma and those who played golf were offered temporary membership. Members of the Rangoon Golf Club were given honorary membership. Nevertheless, the daily activities of the Club were not unduly disturbed and a purchase was

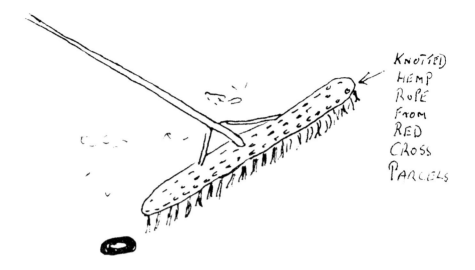

KNOTTED HEMP ROPE FROM RED CROSS PARCELS

made of 40 cases of White Label whisky. The rationing of golf balls became tighter and, by 1943, members were only allowed one new ball every two months.

## The effect of the Second World War on the individual golfer

The first problem was getting to golf. The wartime train service was unreliable and infrequent and, in any event, most golf courses were some way from a railway station – those Clubs that were near a station became very popular! Bicycles were much in use. Many of the Scottish courses did well because they were virtually in the small towns and it was easy to walk to the course.

The most dangerous item on a golf course was a minefield but there were always pathways through them so it was just a matter of rearranging the holes so that the minefield was not too much in play. There were a lot of 'out of bounds' where, due to minefields or barbed wire, it was not desirable to drive. The fairways were very rough and the rough was very deep, especially on the inland courses.

New golf balls disappeared completely after 1940; those that remained were scrubbed, cleaned and repainted time after time and seldom have golf balls been so well marked in play!

The author had a good example of this severe shortage when, on being warned for overseas service, he decided to try and have one last game. The nearest course to the camp was Pulborough in East Sussex. Having presented himself at the Secretary's Office, the author (in battledress) asked if he might play; the ensuing conversation went something like this: 'Of course you can play,

there will be no green fee. Have you got any clubs? Well, not to worry, you can borrow mine, but you will need my Wellington boots.' It transpired that the boots were needed in order to find a golf ball with which to play, in the pond at the 5th hole. When one arrived there, there were a number of elderly gentlemen in Wellington boots tramping in the mud in the pond; occasionally there was a cry of triumph and one man moved off to the first tee carrying a blackened object, as if it were made of gold.

Eventually, the author found one and played a round with it – a ball has never been marked as closely as that one was. Returning in triumph to the Secretary's Office with the ball helped considerably to repay his kindness.

## Wartime Rules of Golf

Playing golf during the Second World War meant that there had to be additional local rules:

> 'A ball moved, lost or destroyed by enemy action may be replaced without penalty.'
> 'A player whose shot is affected by the simultaneous explosion of a bomb may play a ball from the same place, penalty one shot.'
> 'If the player's ball enters a minefield, he is advised not to attempt to retrieve it; a ball may be dropped outside the minefield within two club lengths, not nearer the hole, without penalty.'
> 'If an enemy airplane or doodle bug [flying bomb. *Author*] is heard in the vicinity it is permissible to take shelter without being penalised for undue delay nor for taking shelter during a medal round.'
> 'A ball coming to rest in, or close to, a bomb crater may be dropped two club's length's away, not nearer the hole. No penalty.'

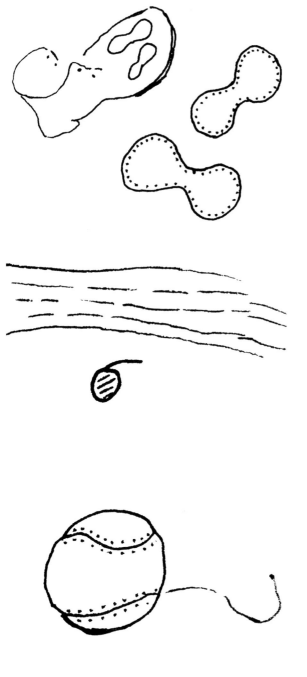

## Golf for Prisoners-of-War

The playing of golf in the First World War at Ruhleben Camp near Berlin, has already been mentioned. In the Second World War no such help was forthcoming. You cannot keep a golfer down, however, and many ingenious means of playing golf were invented. Clubs were made out of any old scrap that could be found, such as a stick and a tin plate, spoon or lump of wood; the whole was shaped laboriously into a parody of a club and then came the question of a ball. One camp solved the problem by using a glass marble as a centre and then cutting very thin strips from the rubber sole of a gym shoe. The strips were then glued around the marble and the outer ones were actually sewn with fine thread, being built up until the ball was about the same size as a golf ball. A golf course was then devised and the enthusiasts played fiercely competitive golf matches around it. It was curious that, in this camp, the Germans would let the inmates have baseball bats but not golf clubs which, they said, could be used as offensive weapons! The baseball bats could be shaved down to make a club shaft.

Conditions varied from camp to camp. Below is an interesting letter which Mr Wilfred Wise of Scarborough very kindly sent me, describing what happened in his POW Camp. The ball described is now in the possession of the British Golf Museum, St Andrews.

Dear David Stirk,
 At last, as promised, I enclose the Stalag Luft III Golf Ball. You will notice that one stitch has come loose, but I have not the skill to mend it. The ball was made by Lt. Idwal Evans (Taffy) of the Fleet Air Arm, who had the misfortune to be shot down by a wave whilst dropping mines in the Meuse Estuary, flying a 'Stringbag'.
 The only people I really remember as originating this golf course were Flt Lt 'Percy' Thomas and Flt Lt 'Paddy' O'Brien, but everyone interested took part in the construction. Being sand and pine needles, it was only necessary to dig a hole to make a bunker, but the Germans would not let us dig too deep, as a hollow of any depth might give cover against the searchlights, and also would make suitable places to dispose of sand excavated elsewhere.
 You will understand that each person could only find the materials to make himself one club, which had to serve every purpose. Usually it took the form of a No.5 iron, and the face had to be closed for putting.
 Once the ball hit the ground, there was really no 'run' available, so it was advisable to 'nip' the ball on impact, closing the face, to ensure as long a carry as possible. This inhibited the follow-through as the clubhead became embedded in the soft sand, and it was easy to develop a 'sledge-hammer' swing.

CUT

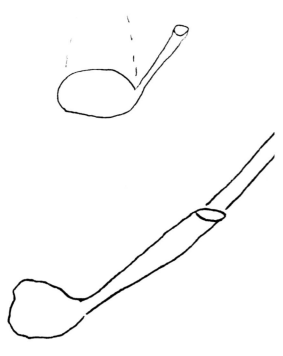

This must be why my golf has deteriorated !!!

Of course, the greens never wore out, but footprints etc., were not easy to smooth out, so several times a day, some person had to sweep them, by starting at the centre with the string broom illustrated overleaf, and walking round in circles radiating outwards. This left a quite satisfactory surface. It could then be watered if necessary. Grass would never have stood up to the constant use the course endured.

I have no doubt that there are many people who could supply further details, but I regret to say that I have not cultivated my old war-time friends, being immediately immersed on discharge in making a living amongst these mad civilians!

Two "Figure of eight" shaped strips of leather cut from the soft part of a RAF issue boot

Perforated around the edges to accept the twine

Very fine strips of rubber, obtained by finely slicing the rubber sole of the boot with a razor blade (this took *days*)

Wound carefully round a marble, rolling it all the time, to be certain it was perfectly round, and tucking in the ends to be sure it didn't unwind

Final stitching and tightening, using a semi-circular needle

A good shoe-shine with black polish after every game kept it in good condition!

Knotted hemp-rope from Red Cross parcels

Old water jug lead-based which became unsuitable for drinking water, which we were able to 'write off'

The base was of a heavy soft metal material, which melted down well so that by sawing off the jug handle, this made a good receptacle for the club shaft which was honed down from a broken Ice Hockey stick shaft

(I have often seen Ice Hockey Sticks used as weapons at Earls Ct or Harringay but presumably the Germans had not)

Then the problem was to shape a niblick out of a shapeless blob of metal. We had no tools, so mostly this was achieved by rubbing along the top of a wall.

The final effect was very good.

A good drive could be 150 yards.

Yours sincerely

Wilfred Wise

# 16

# Patents and Inventions

THERE was something about golf, and the difficulties of becoming an expert at it, which stimulated human inventiveness to help the golfer hit the ball straighter and further, while still allowing him or her to stop the ball quickly when such a shot was required. There was also a wish to make golf a pleasant game.

Inventions offered better ways of making golf clubs and balls so that more of these could be produced to keep the ever-increasing numbers of golfers happy; an easier way to make a sand golf tee and, when proper teeing grounds were introduced, boxes for sand from which to make the tee, or an entirely new form of readymade wooden tee on which to place the ball; better ways of painting golf balls and adding a pattern to the surface, and of marking balls for identification.

Other improvements included: waterproof clothing to keep the golfer dry in the rain without impeding the swing, nails in the shoe soles to help a firm stance, gloves to keep hands warm, and many types of hats; many features were derived from those experienced in making clothing for fishing and shooting.

There were ideas for carrying golf clubs in bags (the first of these golf bags was probably invented at Royal North Devon Golf Club in 1868, when the steward, an old sailmaker, made some canvas bags for the use of members).

Golf practice was not neglected and there were 'captive' golf balls for practice in the garden and, at Ranelagh, in 1890 there was an automatic golf ball delivery machine for golfers which dispensed new golf balls on the insertion of one shilling; the machine could also be adapted to produce remade balls for sixpence (half a shilling) for those who wanted to practise, or who were not prepared to spend a shilling on a new ball which they were very likely to lose while playing the first few holes.

Nor was the improvement of the golf swing neglected by the inventors and there were many gadgets, both clever and completely impractical, to give the enthusiastic beginner a 'grooved' swing.

Even more indirectly, much machinery was invented for use on the golf course which helped to improve the condition of the course and thus make a more appealing round for the golfer.

The bulk of these innovations were devised between the 1890s and 1914, because this was the period of enormous expansion in the numbers of golfers and golf courses and because this period also witnessed the meteoric rise of golf in the United States, particularly after Vardon's tour in 1900. The result was that there came into being a very large market for British golfing equipment of all kinds in the United States and, equally, a great stimulus to American golf inventors who not only produced new ideas for American golfers but, also, began exporting these ideas to Britain.

This sudden wealth of innovations was produced by golfers with imagination and also by non-golfers. Many of the ideas produced by the latter were either impractical for golf or were considered by the R&A to be illegal. Many inventions were patented but never saw the light of day. Some of the ideas put forward by the golfers were equally impractical or illegal.

So numerous were the inventions that it is impossible to attempt a detailed listing. A number of 'patents' have been listed in *Golf in the Making*, and Olman's *Collectibles*, while not having a patents list, has records of a large number of patented ideas.

Matters concerning the 'form and make' of golf clubs were dealt with, at the time, by the Rules of Golf Committee of the R&A (the main problems concerned clubs rather than balls). In 1894, the new American Golf Association was formed and they, too, gave consideration to the form and make of golf clubs and their views did not always coincide with the views of the R&A. Three important matters show the difficulties in reconciling the views of the R&A and the American Golf Association.

## 1. The Rubbercore Golf Ball

HERE was an invention, from the United States, which was specifically designed to make it easier to play golf. Coburn Haskell had, with other co-workers, discovered that a golf ball could be made by winding hundreds of yards of fine rubber thread around the central core and then covering the whole with a gutta percha cover. He took out a patent and started to manufacture the new ball. The rubbercore was more expensive than the gutty and, in its early days, more liable to break than a gutty, but it made golf much easier for the poorer player. If it were topped it bounded along for quite a distance whereas the gutty went, literally, nowhere; it was much easier for iron play and the ball went much further off an iron club than did the gutty; it was much easier to play out of a poor lie because of its tendency to rise easily compared with the gutty. For all these reasons, the less skilful golfers took to it with enthusiasm. Its drawbacks were that it was more difficult to stop on the green – something that did not affect the less skilful golfer greatly; it was Trevino who, many years later, said, in answer to a golfer who asked if he could learn to stop his iron shots on the green, 'how far do you hit a No.4 iron?' His questioner replied that he reckoned he hit one about 140 yards, to which Trevino replied 'What do you want to stop it for?'!

The other problem associated with the rubbercore was that it was lively on the green and putting became a more delicate business; this also affected the skilful golfer more than the less skilled.

In Britain, those who had played all their lives with the gutty considered that those who used the new ball gave themselves an unfair advantage over those who stuck to the gutty.

The professionals were not in favour of the new ball because they said it allowed an inferior golfer to compete successfully with a better one but, in the professionals' case, there was more to it than that. The professional could make and re-make gutties in his own shop, but he could not do that with a Haskell ball, and consequently he lost money. Furthermore, the mark up on a Haskell was not as high as with the gutty made in his own shop. Although he was ostensibly against the new ball, he used it in competition because if he did not he would be at a disadvantage. Sandy Herd won the Open Championship in 1902, using

Patent golf tee of 1892.
The cardboard could be folded flat when not in use

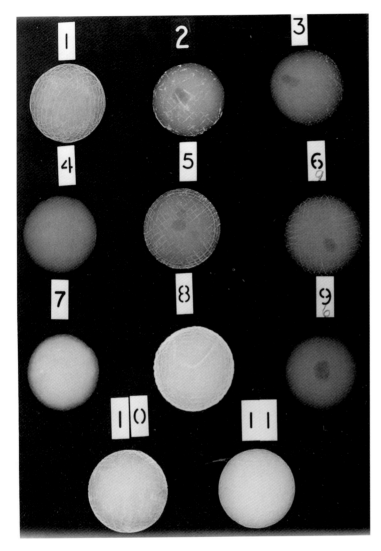

X-ray of gutta balls. It has always been rumoured that it was common to put lead in a gutta to keep it down in a high wind. Numbers 7, 8, 10, 11 are opaque because they have lead paint on them. 1 and 2 show vestiges of lead paint. The darker shadows near the centre of 2, 3, 5, 6 and 9 are caused by small air pockets. There is no evidence of lead having been inserted

one, and, in the following year, the British Amateur was won using a Haskell. The new ball had arrived and, unless the Rules of Golf Committee of the R&A made it illegal, it had come to stay. In the United States, the American Golf Association had permitted it from the start, so, as the R&A had taken no action up to 1903, by which time both the Open and the Amateur Championships of Britain, organised and run by the R&A, had been won using the new ball, they were in an impossible position and did not ban the ball, although a powerful minority of the Committee were in favour of a ban. For more detailed information the reader is recommended to consult an excellent and detailed treatise on the subject by Mr P.N. Lewis, Curator of the British Golf Museum at St Andrews, published in *Golfiana*, Volume 3, 1991.

This is the first of numerous examples of the failure of the R&A immediately to consider a problem and make a firm decision, as a result of which, by the time that they came to decide, they were so far behind events that they could only agree a decision already taken in the United States and by hundreds of golfers in Britain.

## 2. The Centre-Shafted Putter

A quite an early stage in its life the American Golf Association let it be known that it was not going slavishly to follow the traditional ideas of the Rules of Golf Committee of the R&A, and the foregoing account of the rubbercore ball is an example of this.

On the question of the form and manufacture of golf

Gassiat putter, *c.*1930, showing shallow face, and lower end of steel shaft, painted yellow to look like wood

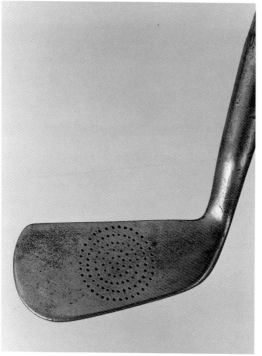

Smiths Patent anti-shank mashie, face on

clubs, the R&A Committee went a long way to accommodate the ideas of the American Golf Association but they jibbed at the question of springs to be inserted in the face of golf clubs and were insistent that the shaft of a club must be inserted into the heel of the head.

In 1909, when New Zealand pleaded that a croquet mallet was a suitable instrument for putting, the R&A was adamant that 'a croquet mallet is not a golf club'. Yet, in 1904, when Walter Travis played in – and won – the British Open Amateur Championship, he used a centre-shafted putter which, under R&A rules, was illegal. The American Golf Association had no ban on such clubs and they were very popular in the United States after Travis had demonstrated how well he could putt with such a putter. They were popular in Britain as well and, after 1904, thousands of them were sold in Britain and the owners regularly used them in competitions although, presumably they were not used in R&A national tournaments.

A centre-shafted putter had been invented in Britain in 1891, before the Travis-type putter – known as the 'Schenectady' – was born. This putter was superior to the Schenectady because it had a joint at the head so that the putter could have the lie adjusted from upright to flat lie to suit the player; this putter never seems to have gone into production, probably because it was banned by the R&A.

In 1910, the Rules Committee went even further and forbade the use of any club which was constructed on the mallet principle. The fact that they had allowed Travis (who was a member of the American Golf Association Rules of Golf Committee) to play with just such a club in one of the R&A National Championships in 1904 was blandly ignored and it was not until after the Second World War that the R&A allowed mallet-head putters, approximately 50 years after they had first banned them.

The divisions between the two Ruling bodies was not good for the game and the Americans attempted to get around the problem by invoking Section 10 of their Rules which allowed them to interpret the R&A Rules as they saw fit; had this not happened there might well have been such an open split between the two that there would have come into existence two differing sets of Rules of Golf. Both parties can thank Mr C.B. MacDonald of the American Golf Association for some masterly diplomacy which avoided this disastrous possibility. Had the Rules of Golf Committee of the R&A stuck to its guns and forbidden Travis to play with a centre-shafted putter – or disqualified him if he insisted on using it – they might have gained the day and the American Golf Association might have banned such clubs as well; as it was the R&A found themselves in a false position and were, perhaps, lucky that others did not use such putters in competition in Britain and make their position quite impossible.

## 3. Steel-shafted Clubs

THE idea of a steel shaft for a golf club was first seriously considered in 1894 when Thomas Horsburgh, a blacksmith in Edinburgh, made some clubs with solid steel shafts and then took out a patent. He was a good golfer and played so well with his steel shafts that his friends would not play with him. The original clubs with which he played are still on exhibition in the Clubhouse in Baberton Golf Club.

Although he took out a patent in Britain and, subsequently in the United States, he never made any money out of it because the R&A and the American Golf Association banned such shafts; apart from the official banning of the clubs, the professionals refused to use them because steel shafts would harm their business of selling and fitting hickory shafts to golf clubs.

In 1914, immediately before the First World War, Accles and Pollock demonstrated some tubular steel shafts at the Open at Sandwich; golfers were interested but, as the ban remained, the exhibition did not result in a sale of clubs.

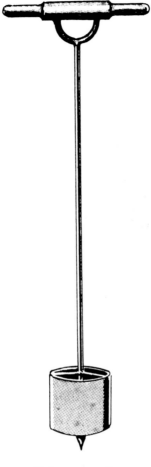

Holecutter, *c.*1823

Association in Britain supported the ban, because, in general, they thought that their members would lose money if steel shafts were made legal but, at the same time, they were selling steel-shafted clubs imported from America in large numbers.

By 1929, the pressure for the R&A to legalise the steel shaft was increasing. Steel shafts were widely advertised by golf manufacturing companies and Coombe Hill Golf Club staged a well-publicised competition in which competitors were encouraged to use steel-shafted clubs. The report of this competition in *Golf Illustrated* on 5 July 1929 was accompanied by a plea from the Editor for the R&A to 'read the writing on the wall' and make steel shafts legal.

In August 1929, the Vice-President of A.G. Spalding Brothers, golf club manufacturers based in the United States but with outlets in Britain, said that of one million hickory shafts passing through their factories, only 17–20 per cent were Grade 1. In September 1929, Accles and Pollock approached the PGA, but the latter refused to reconsider the matter, saying that they had already given their views to the R&A.

In November 1929, thirteen Golf Clubs in Britain announced that, despite the ban by the R&A, they were staging competitions in which they would permit steel shafts to be used.

After the War, in 1924, because of the shortage of good hickory, the American Golf Association removed the ban on steel shafts; the R&A did not, but allowed golfers in the tropics to use steel shafts because, it was recognised, hickory shafts were very difficult to keep in good condition in hot countries, whether humid or dry.

The golfers of the world were then faced with the curious situation that steel shafts were legal in America but illegal in Britain, but had been made legal by the R&A in 'hot' climates. Repeated attempts were made to get the R&A to legalise steel shafts. The Professional Golfers

Faced with open insurrection in Britain, the R&A succumbed and legalised steel shafts in 1930. The open difference of opinion between the two (self-appointed) law-givers of the game of golf was not good for the game. It was confusing for those who played it and made potential difficulties for those who had to organise major golf tournaments on both sides of the Atlantic. It had also given the American manufacturers a good head start in making and selling steel shafts.

# F. H. AYRES, L<sup>TD.,</sup>

## *Manufacturers of all Indoor and Outdoor Games and Sports.*

### 111, ALDERSGATE STREET, LONDON, E.C.

### The "CERT" Putter.

(Patent and Registered.)

The latest and most accurate putter introduced makes putting a "Cert.

## The "SUPREME" Rubber-cored Golf Ball . .

A first-class ball for match or practice play at a reasonable price.

## The "ION" Golf Trainer

(Patent).

PERFECT HOME PRACTICE FOR WINTER EVENINGS, &c.

The "Ion" Trainer, although a simple invention, has completely overcome the difficulty experienced in regard to "Indoor" driving.

At this date (1907) centre-shafted putters such as the one on the left were legal in America but not in Britain. Nevertheless many British golfers used them, in defiance of the R&A ruling

## *Special Light Worm-Cast Roller and* Brush. *Bradford's Patent.*

BRUSH IN USE.

This tool has been designed to meet the want of a very light roller and brush, by means of which worm-casts can be very quickly picked up from Putting Greens, with the minimum of labour in the process.

As will be seen from the wood-cut, a light roller is attached to the brush, so that when the Green has been lightly brushed by **drawing the brush over it** (thus scattering the worm-casts), the machine has only to be turned over to bring the roller into use to pick up the scattered casts and to give the finishing touch to the Green.

The machine is so light—the rollers being only 4 in. in diameter—that casts are not flattened out on the surface of the Green, but are really picked up and removed.

The Machines are made in three sizes, viz., 3, 4, and 5 feet long, and either size **can be quite easily taken from Green to Green as required.**

PRICES : 3 ft. long, **£2 0 0**    4 ft. long, **£2 5 0**    5 ft. long, **£2 10 0**

The Machines are made in a substantial manner, and the brushes and rollers are of the best quality.

Both brushes and rollers are made in 12-inch lengths, so that when a roller or a brush is worn out it can be replaced at a very moderate cost.

Mr. A. W. POWELL (Enfield Golf Club), writes :—"Your Roller Brushes are the best things I have ever seen for wormy greens, whether the casts are wet or dry ; they pick them up when wet and break them up when dry. They are a great saving in labour."

## *Worm-Casts.*

**A very cheap, simple, and effective method of dealing with Worm Casts** consists in sweeping the Greens with a long Bamboo Rod of Special Quality (about 16 feet) which tapers to a point, in place of the ordinary birch broom treatment. A long sweeping stroke, with more or less pressure, as required, **instantly breaks up the casts,** and sweeps them into any depressions or holes there may be, thus, in one operation, improving the surface of the Green, and supplying nature's own nourishment to the grass. An immense improvement in the Greens is said to be the result, while the labour of rolling is reduced to a minimum. As used at St. Andrews, &c., &c. These Rods are greatly liked where used. They cost practically nothing, as when worn out for Sweeping they can be used for Guide or Flag Poles of about 10 feet high each, or thin whippy bamboos about 5 feet long, can be supplied at a nominal price, to whip on the tops of the worn bamboos thus prolonging the 'life' of the originals considerably. A second quality can be supplied, but it is not recommended. The Railways will not carry less than 2 rods, owing to risk of breakage of single ones.

Ordinary Bamboos are almost useless for the purpose, owing to their sharp joints and brittleness, and lack of pliability.

Some greenkeeping aids for removing wormcasts in 1912. The long fine bamboo for removing wormcasts is still the best equipment for this purpose and is still used at some golf clubs

# Recent Golf Patents.

**Contributed by Mr. George Barker, Fellow of the Chartered Institute of Patent Agents, 77, Colmore Row, Birmingham**

**E. Burr, of Harpenden, Herts. No. 19,988, 1902.**

CLUB.—The striking face of this club is formed with a series of longitudinal grooves, the upper surfaces of which grooves are at right angles to the plane of the face, and the lower surfaces thereof

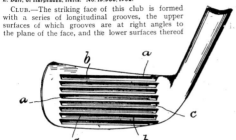

incline rearwardly and upwardly from the face. As the ball is struck an "under spin" is imparted to it which has the tendency to prevent rolling or running forward as the ball reaches the ground. The

iron, but the same may be employed to a wooden head in the form of a steel plate secured thereto by screws. *A* designates the longitudinal grooves bounded by upper surfaces *B*, which are at right angles to the striking face and lower surface *C*, which are inclined thereto.

**A. F. Wale, Elmdon, Birmingham. No. 19,702, 1902.**

The club handle described in this specification numbered as above is formed from fabric of helical coils of wire interwoven with one another longitudinally, transversely, or both in such a manner as to form a tube of the required diameter to fit the handle.

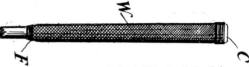

The tube of interwoven wire fabric *W* forming the handle is provided with a padding of solid flexible or resilient material and is finished off at the upper end with a cap *C*, and at the lower end

**The left-hand club face was not legal and was banned by the R&A Golf Club**

# Notice Tablets.

### (BEST MALLEABLE IRON.)

These Tablets are Well Galvanized, have Bold Raised Letters in black, and are fitted with strong Wrought Iron Spikes. They are very neat and effective, and are so strong as to be Unbreakable. They will last many years in perfect condition. They are stocked with the following wordings:—

TURF MUST BE REPLACED        PLEASE REPLACE TURF
GROUND UNDER REPAIR         LIFT AND DROP
OUT OF BOUNDS               PLEASE DO NOT SPEAK ON THE STROKE
PLEASE KEEP OFF THIS GREEN    PLEASE DO NOT WALK THROUGH THE BUNKERS

**PRICE 2/- EACH.**

Tablets without spikes for screwing to Boxes, Fences, etc., can also be supplied:—

TURF MUST BE REPLACED    PLEASE REPLACE TURF    OUT OF BOUNDS

**PRICE 1/9 EACH.**

Extra Large Malleable Tablets (spiked) are made with the wording:—

TURF MUST BE REPLACED    **PRICE 4/- EACH.**

## Cast-Iron Tablets.

The following Tablets, fitted with strong Wrought Iron Spikes, as per illustrations, are stocked:—

**PRICE 1/6 EACH.**

GROUND UNDER REPAIR    OUT OF BOUNDS        LIFT AND DROP
PLEASE REPLACE TURF     LIFT AND COUNT ONE
TURF MUST BE REPLACED   PLEASE KEEP OFF THIS GREEN
PLEASE REPLACE DIVOTS   PLEASE DO NOT WALK THROUGH THE BUNKERS

## Larger Tablets.

As illustrated at foot, but fitted with Heavy Spikes, are stocked in the following wordings:—

PLEASE REPLACE TURF    GROUND UNDER REPAIR
TURF MUST BE REPLACED   LIFT AND DROP

**PRICE 3/- EACH.**

## Extra Large Tablets.

As above, but Larger and Heavier, are stocked in the following wordings:—

**PRICE 4/- EACH.**

PLEASE REPLACE TURF    GROUND UNDER REPAIR
TURF MUST BE REPLACED   LIFT AND DROP
PLEASE DO NOT WALK THROUGH THE   PLEASE KEEP OFF THIS BANK
   BUNKERS           PLEASE DO NOT DAMAGE THE GORSE
PLEASE DO NOT WALK ACROSS THIS   PLAYERS CUTTING IN MUST ALLOW THOSE
   GREEN              DOING THE FULL ROUND TO PASS
PLEASE DO NOT STICK THE FLAG IN   THE PUBLIC ARE REQUESTED NOT TO
   THE TURF            WALK ACROSS THE GREENS
SILENCE IS REQUESTED WHILE PLAYERS   PLEASE DO NOT WALK UP THE FACE OF
   DRIVE FROM THIS TEE      THE BUNKERS

**SPECIAL TABLETS.**—These can be supplied in Cast Iron with any wording required. Quotations on receipt of particulars.

E. W. Mitchell, Esq. (Folkestone Golf Club), writes:—"The Notice Tablets are very satisfactory."

**Cast-iron notice tablets from 1912**

# Pattisson's Combined Roller and Cart.

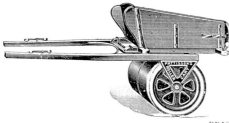

These Combined Rollers and Carts are extremely useful on Golf Courses as they not only do the work of ordinary Carts, but roll the Course at the same time, instead of cutting it up into ruts as the usual farm carts do. They can also be used as Rollers when not employed in carting material, **either with or without the cart,** the latter being very easily removed by the simple withdrawal of two bolts—this is a novel and very convenient fitting.

Pattisson's Roller Carts are built very substantially and are so constructed that the body of the cart does not overhang the roller and there is, therefore, no liability to turn over, as is the case where the cart is wider than the roller.

PRICES—

| | | | | |
|---|---|---|---|---|
| Rollers, 36 in. long by 30 in. diam., weight | | ... | ... | £15. |
| Rollers, 42 in. long by 30 in. diam., weight | | ... | ... | £16 10s. |

## Golf Course Cart. SPECIAL WIDE WHEELS.

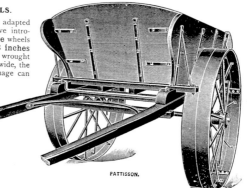

In response to numerous enquiries for Carts specially adapted to work on Golf Courses without damage to the turf, we have introduced the "Pattisson" Cart, with, as shown above, **very wide** wheels which prevent any marking of the turf. These wheels are **8 inches wide** and are of very great strength, being entirely made of wrought iron. As ordinary cart wheels are only 2½ to 3 inches wide, the **extra** width of 5 to 5½ inches makes it impossible that damage can be done in carting.

The cart is most substantially built, the body being made of Stout Pitch Pine, and the Frame and Shafts of Oak and Ash, all thoroughly well painted.

It is impossible to produce a cart of more substantial construction or one better suited to the special work of a Golf Course.

The "Pattisson" Cart is made in two sizes :—

No. 1. Holding about ¾ cubic yard of soil

No. 2 ,, ,, 1¼ ,, ,,

PRICES.—No. 1, with 3 ft. 9 in. diam. wheels, **£15.**

No. 2 ,, 4 ft. 6 in. ,, ,, **£17.**

PATTISSON.

---

E. J. Byrne, Erdington, 19,242, 1902.

The striking face of the golf club forming the subject of this invention is provided with an elastic packing between the striking plate and the head.

On the illustration, Fig. 2 shows a cross-section of the improved club head. Fig. 3 represents the elastic cushion before it is attached to the head ; and Fig. 4 shows the method of forming the elastic core for the said cushion.

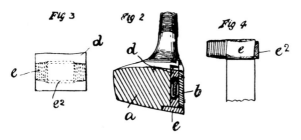

The head $A$ has the usual leather striking face of pad $B$ and sole plate $E$ of horn or like material. At the rear of the striking face is arranged the cushion $D$ composed of a pad of gutta percha in which is embedded an elastic pad or core $E$. The inner pad $E$ is made by winding thin strips of rubber upon a small piece of sheet steel $E_2$ which has been previously covered with canvas so as to present no sharp edges.

**Above: Rollers and carts advertised in 1912**

**Left: This shock-absorbing club was banned by the R&A**

# 17

# Some Comments on the Rules of Golf

THE first written Rules of Golf were those of the Honourable Company of Edinburgh Golfers in 1744.

**Articles and Laws in playing of Golf.**

1. You must tee your ball within a club's length of the hole.

2. Your tee must be upon the ground.

3. You are not to change the ball you strike off the tee.

4. You are not to remove any stones, bones or any breakclubs for the sake of playing your ball, except upon the fair green [fairway, *Author*] and that only within a club's length of your ball.

5. If your ball come among water, or any watery filth [sewage, *Author*], you are at liberty to take out your ball and bringing it out behind the hazard, and teeing it, you may play it with any club and allow your adversary a stroke for getting out your ball.

6. If your balls be found anywhere touching one another, you are to lift the first ball, till you play the last.

7. At holing, you are to play your ball honestly for the Hole, and not to play on your adversary's ball, not lying on your way to the Hole.

8. If you should lose your ball by its being taken up, or any other way, you are to go back to the spot where you struck last and drop another ball and allow your adversary a stroke for the misfortune.

9. No man, at holing his ball, is to be allowed to mark his way to the Hole with his club or anything else.

10. If a ball be stopped by any person, horse, dog, or anything else, the ball so stop'd must be played where it lyes.

11. If you draw your club back in order to strike, and proceed in the stroke as to be bringing down your club – if then your club shall break in any way, it is to be accounted a stroke.

12. He whose ball lyes farthest from the hole is obliged to play first.

13. Neither trench, ditch or dyke made for the preservation of the links, nor the Scholars' holes, or the Soldiers' lines, shall be accounted a hazard, but the ball is taken out, teed and played with any iron club.

These Rules were purely local rules and applied only to the Honourable Company with no application elsewhere.

When the first Rules of the Society of Golfers at St Andrews were written, ten years later they, also, were purely local rules which applied only to that Society.

In each set of rules there was at least one very local rule designed for one specific local condition. In the case of the Honourable Company it was Rule 13.

The rules did not remain static but were subject to change. In 1842, the Society of Golfers at St Andrews produced a very local rule which said: 'When a ball lies on clothes, or within a club's length of a washing tub, the clothes may be drawn up from under the ball and the tub may be removed'. It was the custom of the washerwomen of St Andrews to wash clothes in the Swilcan Burn; after washing, the clothes, on fine days, were laid out on the grass to dry. It will be noticed that the clothes are to be drawn up from under the ball and the tub removed. The ball is *not* lifted or touched because this would break a very fundamental, but unwritten, rule that the ball must not be touched by hand.

It is in this respect that the rules of the Honourable Company, surprisingly, break the old tradition for, in their rules, there are at least three occasions where the rules allow the ball to be picked up and dropped. This was a break with the fundamental rule that had, from very early times, always been faithfully adhered to and it was the thin end of the wedge. The principle that the ball may not be touched was broken and from that time rules that allow the ball to be lifted and dropped have become ever more frequent.

A rule which illustrates this change, or, as some would say, deterioration, appeared in about 1853. The early gutta golf ball was brittle and on occasions would disintegrate when hit; a rule was made that, in that event, a new ball could be dropped where the largest piece of the old ball was found. Horace Hutchinson comments wryly that it was surprising how often the largest piece found was on the fairway. It is probable that 100 years before that rule, if the gentlemen who played golf had had a ball which could burst (and feather balls could burst) when hit, the matter would have been discussed before they arrived at the first tee; they might have come to an agreement that a ball could be substituted but it would have been far more likely that the idea of doing this would have been distasteful to them and they would have agreed that it would constitute a 'rub of the green' and the player whose ball had burst would have forfeited the hole under rule 3 of the old rules. At the same time, there would probably have been a side bet on this possibility and the player whose ball had burst would stand to gain financially from his misfortune!

The similarity of the rules in force in widely separated Golf Clubs needs some comment. Apart from very local rules they showed a marked similarity; the reason for this is clear. Firstly, the two most important Clubs, the Honourable Company of Edinburgh Golfers and the Society of Golfers at St Andrews had many members in common. Secondly, both were Masonic Lodges and therefore had close ties. As an example of the close relationship between various Clubs, Alexander Duncan, Master Mason, was Captain of Blackheath in 1766, Captain of the Society of Golfers at St Andrews in 1756, 1761 and 1781 and Captain of the Honourable Company of Edinburgh Golfers in 1771.

At first, the rules of the Honourable Company were regarded as the important rules of golf and, if other Clubs

had problems, they referred to the Honourable Company. However, in the 1830s the Honourable Company fell on evil days and at one stage had neither golf course nor Clubhouse. It was five years before they returned to their former glory. In the meantime, the R&A had flourished and grown in importance and the whole idea of St Andrews, as the 'Home of Golf' and the R&A as the most important golf institution, was well to the fore; consequently, matters concerning rules were now referred to the R&A and this has been so ever since.

Golf matches had been played by gentlemen golfers for many years before the rules of 1744 were promulgated but we do not know what those rules were. This is either because they were so well understood by individual players that there was no need to write them down or, more probably, they were written rules elaborated by the Masons for the conduct of matches and were subsequently destroyed when Golf Clubs ceased to be solely Masonic institutions.

The rules of 1744 were written for the playing of the Silver Club, a score or medal competition. It is possible that the fundamental rules were altered to cope with this. Perhaps the concept of lifting and dropping was introduced so that there was a fair chance of most of the competitors completing the course and returning a score; even then, there were some errors for, quite clearly, Rules 5, 7 and 8 are matchplay rules and cannot be applied to medal play.

While it is clear that the concept of not touching the ball with the hand was being abandoned, the most surprising omission from these rule was that of 'play the ball where it lies', but perhaps that was because they had, in the rules, abandoned the concept by allowing players to lift out of certain areas – they were no longer playing the ball where it lay.

What rules did the older generation of Masonic gentlemen golfers use? We do not know, but there are two fundamentals which would have been included – 'play the ball where it lies' and 'do not touch the ball with the hand'. If those two fundamentals were observed, how would this affect the rules of 1744?

Rules 1, 2 and 3 would remain, but Rules 4, 5, 6, 8 and 13 would not be within the framework. This would leave only eight Rules of Golf which would be quite close to the ideal set by the late Henry Longhurst, who remarked that the Rules of Golf should be capable of being written on the side of a matchbox.

The introduction of medal play meant more rules for the game, and the start of tournament golf among professionals who were going to make their living out of golf and who had not been trained to recognise all the niceties of behaviour associated with being a 'gentleman' led to

**String measure from the Old Manchester Golf Club, about 1860. Text states:**

Balls may be removed if within six inches of each other

Balls must be tee'd within four club's lengths of the hole

The putting green extends six club's lengths from the hole

The measure is six inches in length

The first knot on the cord represents four club lengths

The extreme length of the card represents six club lengths

further detailed and complicated rules and regulations.

By 1912, the 330 or so words of the original Rules had been replaced by 9,000 words requiring 19 pages in the *Golfer's Handbook*. Many golfers did not know all the rules and were not in a position to make decisions on matters of rules in the light of past experience and a sense of fair play.

Many of the older amateurs objected to the elaboration of the Rules and voiced their protests. 'Some men are in mutual spirit with the game and, although they do not know all the rules by heart, they are able, instinctively, to make a proper judgement about any situation.' What the elders of the game failed to recognise was that the new generation had not been brought up in the true tradition and the ever-growing numbers of professionals had a living to make in tournaments; although they had no wish to cheat, they felt justified in taking advantage of loopholes in the letter of the law and were not concerned with the spirit of it. Being considered a good sportsman was fine but it must not interfere with winning tournaments and making a living.

The fact that the rules of the game were becoming more detailed and complex led to differences between the rules of us golf and British golf and this was a source of discomfort, not only between the two governing bodies but in the many countries which looked to the us or St Andrews for rules by which to play.

In 1952, the United States and St Andrews came to an agreement about the rules and published a unified 'Code of Rules' with which both agreed (including the problem of the centre-shafted putter which the us had long legalised and which St Andrews had not!). There was a general feeling of relief at a difficult job well done and a sense that the rules of golf were, at last, complete.

It was a job well done but it was not complete – and one wonders if it ever will be. In 1988 the Rules of Golf occupied 62 pages in the *Golfer's Handbook* and used 24,000 words. This did not include a wider section on the Government of the Game, which included such problems as the definition of an amateur golfer and the length of time that must elapse before a professional can become a reinstated amateur.

It is the sheer detail in which the rules have to be constructed so that they may cover all eventualities, that makes them so lengthy and complicated; golfers no longer know all the rules and are certainly not in a position to make decisions based on a sense of fair play and equity.

The need for detailed and accurate wording has led to the R&A electing a high percentage of men of the legal profession on to their Rules Committee; such men are not noted for their brevity and, in fairness to them, they are being asked to frame rules which may decide whether a top professional wins, or fails to win, about half a million pounds. The resulting rules are so complex that it is necessary for members of the Rules of Golf Committee to travel around the world to explain to golfers worldwide what the rules mean; it also means that in any major tournament it is necessary for experts on the rules to act as referees, since ordinary golfing citizens are no longer capable of interpreting the rules. In professional golf it is fait accompli, and the almost total dedication to scoreplay golf makes it impossible for the old game to return – and

yet golf spectators seem to find the Ryder Cup more exciting than most tournament golf involving scoreplay. Is it possible to return to matchplay golf in the amateur game and, at the same time, to make simpler rules?

## The Stymie or Stimie

THERE are two ways of spelling this word. Originally 'stimie', later, the alternative spelling becomes more common.

To anyone who only played golf after 1952, the word will have little or no meaning but, before that time, the state of affairs associated with the word 'stymie' was of great significance and had been since the very start of organised golf. It was so important that it crops up in the first Rules of Golf and, as there were only 13 of them altogether, the stymie must indeed have been of great importance.

A stymie occurs, in matchplay on the putting green, when one ball is in the line to the hole of the next player's putt; if the stymying ball is exactly in the line, it is said to be a 'dead stymie', if it is not exactly in the line it is said to be a 'half stymie'. Until 1952, the putter who was stymied could not ask his opponent to remove his or her ball but had to try and circumvent the obstructing ball as best he or she could. In the early eighteenth century the question of an obstructing ball applied to shots through the green also – you could be stymied on the fairway.

This early Rule of Golf stated: 'At holing, you are to play honestly for the hole, and not play upon your adversary's ball, not lying in your way to the hole'. If your opponent's ball was close to the hole and not in your way you could play, in billiard terms, a 'half ball in off'; the result of this shot would be that your ball would be in the hole and your opponent's ball would be much further away than it had originally been and the opponent would have to play the next putt from where the ball lay – he could not replace it. It will be noticed that this rule only applied if the opponent's ball was not in the way, i.e., there was no stymie. If there was a stymie, no shot was barred, one could hit one's ball very hard and 'follow through' into the hole while propelling the other ball right across the green into a bunker. These sorts of manoeuvres, however, also transgressed another fundamental Rule of Golf – that one must not interfere with the opponent's play, so there was an impasse.

J.H. Taylor lofting a stymie, 'the prettiest shot in golf'

It seems that in early golf (which was, of course, all matchplay) many were in the habit of 'playing on the opponent's ball' and considered that this was a perfectly proper stroke. In 1754 the R&A, as a local rule, decided not to allow it and introduced another rule, which stated that, if two balls were touching, the ball nearer to the hole should be lifted. This was a local rule and did not apply to the Honourable Company of Edinburgh Golfers, nor to others such as the Edinburgh Burgess; the latter retained the right to play on the opponent's ball until 1838.

In 1775, the Honourable Company amended their Rule to allow the obstructing ball to be lifted, if it were within 6 inches of the opponent's ball. This soon became a general Rule of Golf and remained in force until the stymie was abolished in 1952. The 'touching ball' Rule has also become a Rule of Golf.

Those who favoured the retention of the stymie reckoned that it was just a matter of luck and should be accepted as such, just as, in the same way, two good drives might finish in a good or a bad lie, a half-topped shot might bounce over a bunker, etc. Golf is full of bad luck and good luck and a stymie is in that category. For very many years now, it has been accepted that, if your opponent's ball knocked yours away, you could replace it, so, it was felt, the more objectionable results of a stymie had been removed. The supporters of the stymie also pointed out that, with a really large and ragged hole and a very rough green, it was not too difficult to circumvent a stymie and that, in any event, a stymie could give rise to a very pretty and skilful shot when the opponent could use a lofted club and chip over the obstructing ball into the hole.

The opponents of the stymie pointed out that it occasionally robbed the better player of a hole and that, as a fundamental rule of the game said that one could not interfere with the opponent's play and the stymie transgressed that rule, it should be abolished.

The battle raged – and became particularly furious when a stymie occurred in a big match and affected the result. In 1833, stymies were abolished for a year at the R&A; this was due to some very strong lobbying by Sir Hugh Lyon Playfair, a very senior and respected citizen of St Andrews and a senior member and great benefactor of the R&A. The ban only lasted a year and the stymie was then reinstated.

Towards the end of the nineteenth century the battle between those for and those against took a sharper edge, mainly because Freddie Tait, one of the great champion golfers and the idol of St Andrews, had been defeated in the semifinal of the Amateur Championship by reason of a stymie.

The golfing press decided to publish the opinions of all the great golfers, both amateur and professional, on the subject. Before reviewing the results of this survey one should mention the views on the subject, in 1883, of a University Professor who was a keen golfer. 'The fine old "stymie" can well be spared along with the fine old prizefight, and the fine old cottage, innocent of ventilation and balmy with fine old odours. It must not be granted the privilege of fine old port, fine old ladies, and fine old customs and institutions, which have some poetry, meaning and nobility about them. The "stimie" is distinctly ignoble.'

In 1890, the Committee of the R&A, after due deliberation, recommended to the Club that the stymie should be abolished; the members would have none of it and refused to support the Committee.

The questionnaire from the golfing press was issued

**Lofting a stymie: the ball is about to disappear down the hole**

in 1894; the following well-known golfers of the time made these replies:

**Amateurs:**
John Ball. Abolish in Championships only.
Mure Ferguson. Abolish in Championships only.
F. Tait. Do not abolish.
Balfour Melville. Abolish.
Arnold Blyth (old-time golfer). Abolish.
Hall Blyth (old-time golfer). Retain.
H.S. Everard (Good golfer and golf historian). Abolish.
John Low. Retain.
Harold Hilton. Abolish.
C. Hutchings. Abolish.
Dr Laidlaw Purves. Retain.

**Professionals:**
J.H. Taylor. Retain.
A. Kirkaldy. Retain.
W. Auchterlonie. Retain.
Ben Sayers. Retain.
Douglas Rolland, Retain.
Willie Fernie. Abolish.
Bob Simpson. Abolish.
Tom Morris. Abolish.
Peter Paxton. Abolish.

It can be seen that, in general, views were divided equally and the division went across the spectrum of all golfers, both amateurs and professionals.

One or two added a qualification to the effect that, if the player laid himself a stymie he should have to play it but, if the stymie was laid by an opponent, he should be made to lift the ball. To the author, the latter compromise seems a fair one, but this idea was never taken any further and the contentious stymie continued on its way until it was abolished in 1952.

When Golf Clubs began to print cards of the course, it became a general habit to produce cards of such a size that the card was 6 inches across and thus could be used to measure the distance between two balls on the green. If the balls were *less* than 6 inches apart the obstructing ball had to be removed.

The views of a later and very distinguished golfer are well worth recording; Robert Tyre Jones was one of the greatest golfers who ever lived. He was at the peak of his skill and fame from about 1921 to 1931 and had played in all the major Championships in Britain and America in that period. The reason that he was such a great golfer was not only because of his skill but because of his behaviour on the golf course; he was notably fair minded and a great upholder of all the best traditions of the game.

One of the most dramatic and famous stymies in the game of golf occurred in 1936 in the US Amateur Championship when, in the final, Johnny Fischer of America was playing Jack McLean of Britain. McLean was one up at the 34th hole; let Bobby Jones, who was a spectator, take up the story:

McLean's second shot to the thirty-fourth hole had stopped 10 feet past the hole. Fischer had been in the rough off the tee, been short of the green with his second and had chipped not too well so that, in three his ball lay short of the hole and only a little nearer than McLean's.

I was standing with Grantland Rice [golf writer, *Author*] in the gallery behind the green. I think that we both appreciated the possibilities in the situation. Obviously, it was a time for conservative play by McLean. The wise play here was to sneak his ball down as close as possible to the hole, leaving Fischer the job of holing his putt to avoid being two down with two to play. A good putt here would make a punishing stymie impossible [provided he was within 6 inches of the hole. *Author*]. I was horrified to see McLean going boldly for the putt on that keen green. The ball over-ran by more than a yard – and Fischer stymied him.

Still trying to win the hole, McLean attempted to pitch from a dangerous distance. I just knew that he was going to knock Fischer's ball in for the win that would have squared the match. Fortunately McLean made over certain that this would not happen, but he had to hole a four-footer to save a half. I have never experienced so many chills and thrills in so short a time. This hole cost McLean the Championship . . . The stymie had been the decisive factor but the blame lay squarely on McLean.

With the stymie in the game, matchplay golf becomes an exciting duel in which each player must be on guard against a sudden, often demoralising thrust . . .

In my observation the stymie has more often been the means of enforcing a decision in favour of the deserving player rather than the contrary. I think it merits a respected place in the game. I know a return to it would greatly enhance the interest and excitement of matchplay golf for player and spectator alike.

The stymie certainly provided interesting and difficult problems: the question of whether to chip over the ball was one; if the stymying ball was near the hole it was perfectly possible to hit the ball a little short, in which case one could hit the opponent's ball into the hole; the ball could not, under these circumstances, be replaced because it was now out of play, so the chipper would then be left with a putt for a half, instead of a win, or a lost hole, if he was chipping for a half.

When, in 1952, the stymie was abolished by the R&A there was no fierce reaction from the pro-stymie lobby, as there would have been in the past. One reason for this was due to the prevalence of scoreplay. Matchplay golf was on the way out and the pot hunters all played medal rounds; another, more important reason was the fact that foursome play had given way to the ubiquitous four ball.

In this form of golf, with four balls on the green, stymies were not practicable. As a result, no one felt very strongly about stymies and there was a general feeling that they were somehow unfair. The R&A decision was accepted, not so much with enthusiasm, as indifference.

A minor contributory factor to the desire to abolish the stymie may have been that, by 1952, the putting green had become a very carefully tended and smooth piece of turf and no one wished to see an inexpert golfer cut a divot out of the immaculate surface while trying to chip over a ball.

Perhaps the last word on the subject of stymies should be allowed to a golfer of the old school, Professor Tait, father of Freddie Tait; by 1890 he was an elderly golfer who had known golf 50 years before. His views are not necessarily absolutely correct but they do show, most clearly, the spirit in which the game was played in earlier times and the great respect, amounting almost to reverence, for the notion that the ball must never be lifted but must be always played 'as it lay'.

To the Editor of *Golf*, 26 September 1890.

Sir, Neither your Problem nor the vexed question of stimies, presents any real difficulty to a student of the old laws of Golf. For in them we find that the true game is essentially one of *holes*. The counting is by the 'odd', the 'like', 'two more', etc. The ball, once played off, must not touch or be touched by anything connected with either player; except a legitimate club, used in a legitimate manner by the owner of the ball. The penalty is, in every case, loss of the hole by the side touched – or wrongly touched. (Of course any person, other than the players and their caddies, is to be regarded merely as a chance obstacle on the links which, so far at least as the laws of Golf are concerned, may be struck with impunity.) In this true game, stimy or no stimy, the ball furthest from the hole must be played. The modern six-inch rule is an innovation altogether contrary to the true spirit of the game.

When two balls touch, the last player has of course (in the rigorous game) lost the hole. He has wrongly touched his adversary's ball. But few have been Spartan enough to enforce this penalty.

When the balls lie near one another, that furthest from the hole must be so played as not, *in any way*, to interfere with the other's position. Witness the Draconian severity of the rule against even *touching* sand in a bunker. If you must not improve your own lie, it follows, *a fortiori*, that you must do nothing which may, in any way, injure that of your adversary.

The counting by *strokes*, with its inevitable accompaniments (such as abolishing of stimies, lifting out of difficulties and losing one or more strokes, etc) is a mongrel game, introduced by competitions for medals or prizes, when the players are so numerous that an exhaustive carrying out of the true game is impossible.

Apart from emphasising the importance of never touching or lifting the ball, this letter from an old golfer suggests that 'playing upon your opponent's ball' is manifestly wrong (as the early Rule points out) but it suggests, too, that, in the old spirit in which the game was played, if the balls were touching you would have had to play the ball sideways, so as not to interfere in any way with the position of your opponent's ball and it would certainly not have allowed you, in the event of a stymie, to drive your opponent's ball off the green and play a 'follow through'; you would have had to try to hole the ball while being scrupulously careful not to touch the other ball because, if you did touch it, you would lose the hole.

The interesting point about this letter is that this was the way that Tait remembered playing Golf (note the capital 'G' used in his letter for a game which he clearly reveres); the point that he makes is not in the early Rules of Golf but it was one of the Rules that gentlemen honoured when they played (at least, at St Andrews), an example of the many unwritten Rules which they played to and which were scrupulously adhered to because, if you were not scrupulous in the observance, you might not be considered a gentleman and become a social outcast.

The contempt for golf as a scoring game was common to all Tait's generation of golfers.

## Golf Course Design and Upkeep

It would be nice to say, simplistically, 'in the beginning there were links' but, as far as Golf Clubs and Societies were concerned, this was not so.

Unorganised and casual golf was certainly played on links land which was entirely untended and left to the sheep; the only piece of equipment required was a knife for cutting a hole. The turf being on sand, it drained very rapidly and long, lush, grass did not survive. Fescue, a very fine grass, was natural to the links turf, it could survive long periods without rain and was not harmed by the salt spray which was blown across from the sea. The links were not subjected to much wear because they were only played over after working hours by a few enthusiasts, all of whom used wooden clubs so that the question of divots did not arise. A green, as such, did not exist; there was simply a flat piece of ground in which there was a hole and the next driving off point was about two paces from it. As has been described, natural bunkers were scattered over the links and interesting holes could be formed by arranging the 'green' area at a suitable position behind or to the side of, one of the bunkers – the bunkers were the fixed points and the course was arranged around them.

This pleasant, rather haphazard arrangement changed when the wealthy Masonic brethren took up the game.

Most of them were landed gentry and the rest were professional men, doctors and lawyers and members of the cloth. They were wealthy and not too tied down to a day's hard work. They enjoyed playing and liked to take full advantage of the weather; as travel over long distances was time-consuming they wished to have the chance to play golf near their homes, even though such courses would, usually, not be links courses. The majority of these men lived (or had a second home) in the Edinburgh area, where the Royal Court was situated, or in the vicinity of the larger towns, such as Glasgow, or in the towns where there was a University. There was a Golfing Society at Glasgow from early times and there were the well-known Societies at Bruntsfield and Leith. Those at St Andrews were much favoured because there was a beautiful links course right in the town. Indeed, it was such a fine links that the rich were willing to travel for several hours to get there, just as they were willing to travel to Musselburgh and North Berwick. The courses at Glasgow, Edinburgh and Leith, the latter the port of Edinburgh, were pleasantly close but had the drawback that they were not links courses. In England, the same conditions obtained. Blackheath was within five miles of St Paul's Cathedral and was thus quite suitable for Londoners but, until 1864, no links courses existed in England.

Because these courses were not natural links courses they required constant work to keep them in a passable condition; in the first place they required proper drainage and, secondly, they needed to be cleared of stones; there were no natural bunkers, so patches of heather or bog land had to make do instead. It was difficult to cut holes in such stony ground; a simple knife would not do the job and, certainly at Blackheath, a specialist hole cutter had to be employed. Apart from hole cutters, men were employed on the course to maintain it, the job of 'Keeper of the Green' with a staff of underlings became common and, by the middle of the century, this practice had spread to links courses as well, because, by now, the amount of golf played over the links had increased considerably and with it the added wear and tear occasioned by iron clubs cutting divots, due to the arrival of the gutta ball. Filling in divot holes was becoming a large part of the work on the links. The Keeper of the Green by now was supervising the upkeep of the course, but had a greenkeeper with a small staff working under him; he was becoming a professional and was well occupied in playing golf, giving lessons and making and repairing golf clubs. William Davis, an immigrant from Britain and the first professional to the oldest Golf Club in Canada, at Montreal, found that his appointment required also that he worked on the course as a greenkeeper; he complained to the Captain of the Club saying that, in England, greenkeepers did that sort of work. He was told, in no uncertain terms, that Clubs in Canada could not afford such luxuries and that he must do both jobs.

By the middle of the nineteenth century there was a machine called a mower which would cut grass and this allowed golf to be played over farmland; prior to that it was necessary for inland courses to be on stony heathland because on better land in the summer, the grass grew so long that golf would have been impossible.

**Royal St George's Golf Club, Clubhouse and first tee, _c._1894**

**Stone wall used as a hazard, *c.*1905; not a good architectural idea!**

By 1870 travel was much simpler and quicker, and the wealthy could travel outside their immediate locality with ease; links golf was still regarded as the only true golf, so the gentry in Edinburgh had no difficulty in getting to Musselburgh or North Berwick and the citizens of Glasgow could readily get to Prestwick or Troon. The inland courses at Bruntsfield and Leith were abandoned; Blackheath was not abandoned because links courses at Westward Ho! and Hoylake were far distant but Wimbledon Golf Club, playing on Wimbledon Common, was looking out for a links course near at hand and despatched Dr Laidlaw Purves and Mr Henry Lamb to examine the coastal areas of Kent and Sussex. They found some good links country in Kent at Sandwich, and Royal St Georges Golf Club was born – initially as a summer seaside links for Wimbledon members. By 1870, Blackheath members and, to a lesser extent Wimbledon members, who were determined to play links golf, had evolved a system which suited them very well. They made an annual tour, starting at Westward Ho! in the summer, where they played in the Summer Meeting and played many matches against their friends there; they usually took their professional with them – Bob Kirk – and he joined in the matches as well as playing a match against John Allan, the local professional. As can be imagined, Molesworth was in his element on these occasions and the betting was furious. When all had had their fun, the members of Westward Ho! accompanied their Blackheath friends (whom Westward Ho! members called, affectionately, 'the Blackheathens') to Hoylake where they had a further golfing jamboree and were joined there by various Scottish golfers, mostly from Prestwick and St Andrews. Much golf was played and

many bets were made; Jack Morris and the two professionals from Westward Ho! and Blackheath were in the party as well and the meeting of these golfers was a great social occasion.

At the end of the meeting at Hoylake, everybody went on to St Andrews and there joined in with the R&A members in yet further golfing excitement. It is worth mentioning that in all this golf, probably 90 per cent was matchplay and, although there were many foursomes, no one considered a fourball.

By 1875, travel was easy and the golf explosion was well under way. More and more golfers travelled to the seaside links in Scotland and England and the demand for golf was so great that it became necessary to construct many inland courses. Whereas the links courses required little reconstruction, the inland courses needed a great deal of reshaping, draining, making of obstacles and hazards; greens had to be sited and shaped and teeing areas constructed. But there was more to it than that, if a course was to be a proper golf course; as an example, on stony, heathery land it was vital to remove stones, establish drainage and make a humus on which grass would grow. The latter meant moving large quantities of earth – not difficult today but a considerable task when no earth-moving machinery was available.

A plan of the projected course had to be made and there had to be knowledge and experience to decide which areas could be made into good golfing land and which would not be suitable and therefore had to be left undisturbed. Decisions of this sort could not be made by the professional and the Committee of the Club, and as a result there came into being golf architects and specialists in golf course construction.

With the increased use of the links courses changes were needed there; at St Andrews, already, in 1830, one of the most popular golf links, there was such overcrowding that it became necessary to enlarge the greens. Before that time there were nine greens on the Old Course, the same greens were used going out and coming home, and the golfers, in each direction, played to the same hole; it was a matter of courtesy when both parties were playing to the same hole on the same green as to which gave way to the other. With the greatly increased numbers playing, the situation, with all the courtesy in the world, became impossible and there was a great slowing up of the game; it was decided to enlarge the greens, so that each green had two holes, well separated, one hole being used by those playing out and the other hole by those playing back. At varying times over a number of years the communal fairways were separated and this became easier at the first and last holes when more land was gained from the sea by making barriers on the outer side, a piece of work which was suggested by Sir Hugh Lyon Playfair. These changes did not need any great earth-moving and were brought about slowly. The later stages of such changes would have been very largely under the supervision of 'Old' Tom Morris and he would have been well suited to such work. From time to time one reads that 'Tom Morris laid out the course'. What really happened was that Tom visited a links where golf had been played for some time and made suggestions as to how the layout could be improved. Willie Park Senior was employed in the same way. Between them these men did much to improve the links courses, and ensure that they were a good test of golf during the period when improvement in the golf ball meant that courses needed to be constantly lengthened. It was the next generation of professionals who became involved in real golf architecture; they lived in the times when the golf explosion was at its height and the demand for inland courses was at its most urgent.

Many professionals became minor golf architects in their own area; a good example of this sort of work was that done by Charles Gibson of Westward Ho!. Gibson came from North Berwick and had been apprenticed to Tom Dunn. He came to Westward Ho! in 1888 and remained there for the rest of his life. He was responsible for laying out the first nine-hole course at Porthcawl, in South Wales, just across the Bristol Channel from North Devon, and also laid out the first nine-hole course of the Burnham and Berrow Golf Club in Somerset. Both these courses were links courses and, being situated in natural golf terrain, required only a shrewd eye and a good instinct to make them into golf courses.

Tom Dunn, Gibson's teacher at North Berwick, took the job of professional to the Royal Wimbledon Golf

**Charles Gibson at the door of his workshop, _c._ 1920**

Club and was in the London area when the demand for new golf courses was expanding. Tom Dunn became the fashionable golf architect and laid out 137 courses. He cannot, really, be given an important place among the company of golf architects because his approach to laying out a course was both dreary and totally predictable, as he used the same formula for all courses. A ditch or bank had to be carried from the tee and a similar obstacle had to be carried for the second shot. The green of each hole was, roughly square and flat. Judging from the number of courses that he laid out, his employers must have been quite satisfied with his work but only, one feels, because they lacked experience of other possibilities. Perhaps the fact that he was a Scot and came from a well-known golfing family made the English feel that they were not in a position to argue with him and, in any event, his designs had the advantage of being cheap.

Undoubtedly, the man who made golf architecture a science and who used imagination and sensitivity in constructing golf courses was Willie Park Junior. He designed, in all, 106 golf courses and constructed the majority of them himself. His courses have, with minor

**Princes Golf Club, Mitcham, Surrey, 1901**

alterations necessary due to changed conditions and the improvement in golf ball and golfing performance, remained as he laid them out, and they have stood the test of time – which must be the most important criterion when assessing the competence of a golf architect. Park, more than any of those who were responsible for designing and making golf courses, made as close a study of the actual construction of a golf course as he did of its design. He had a great eye for terrain and a great knowledge of turf and soil generally; as a result he was much in demand for constructing golf courses and was quite willing to work as constructor for another architect.

In Britain, he designed, among many, Sunningdale (Old), Huntercombe and Hollinwell. He certainly had a hand in the design of West Hill and he had an even greater hand in Worplesdon, although at the latter there is no doubt that Abercrombie did much of the planning and Park was, in the main, the constructor; it is difficult to believe that Park did not have a lot of influence in the design of courses even when he was technically only the constructor. His daughter told the author that the sixth green at Worplesdon is easily recognisable, to any who knew Musselburgh, as a copy of one of Musselburgh's greens. At Sunningdale – which Willie always regarded as his greatest golf course design – he showed his intuitive knowledge of soil and turf. He says in his account that the area was a mass of rough heather and dry sandy soil, and there was no grass; at the ninth hole, in particular, the men felt that it was impossible to take the manure up the

steep hill; Park told them that it must be taken up, even if they moved it in teaspoonfuls. Two horses were killed in doing this. His daughter recounted to the author that, in all, six horses died in the making of the course and that, at one stage, the Club Committee were so upset by this that they asked Park if it was really necessary; he was adamant that it was.

Park laid out courses in Austria, Belgium, Canada, France, Monte Carlo and the United States. The author has had the pleasure of playing on one of Park's courses in Canada – Mount Bruno – and on another of his courses in the United States – the Maidstone. Both are beautiful examples of well designed and interesting golf courses and are by no means 'dated', as a test of golf, by the passage of time.

Park was a remarkable man and capable of prodigious energy, and he became so involved in golfing business that he no longer had time to play top-class golf. He deserves to be remembered for plenty of reasons but one of them should be as the first of the golf architects. Those who want to learn more about this great man should read an excellent account of him written by John Adams, *The Parks of Musselburgh*, Park was succeeded in the sphere of golf architecture by men of great talent such as J.F. Abercrombie, H.S. Colt, Donald Ross, Hawtree (who went into partnership with J.H. Taylor), T.G. Simpson, W.H. Fowler, C.H. Alison, all of whom designed courses, both in Britain and abroad, well into the twentieth century – but the pioneering genius was Willie Park Junior.

Clubhouse of the Nairn Ladies' Club, Scotland, 1903. This is a typical cricket-pavilion style Clubhouse, many of which were prefabricated and advertised by building businesses around this date

Sidcup Golf Club, 1903

Royal St David's Golf Club, Harlech, North Wales, 1903

## The Size of a Golf Hole

ONE feature that distinguishes golf from all other stick and ball games is that the ball has to be played into a hole in the ground. Logically, one would expect that the exact size of the hole would be a matter of the greatest importance and that in the history of the game there would be clear indications as to what size of hole was considered the best and how this decision was arrived at. In fact it was not until 1892 that the R&A, in its wisdom, ordained that it should be 4¼ inches. This would tend to indicate that, before that, there had been no standard size. The Minute Books of the old Clubs contain little information about hole size and it was not until the size was fixed by the R&A in 1892 that some of the older golfers began writing about it.

In the days when golf was very much a local affair, each Club decided, empirically, on a size that the members considered adequate. Few Clubs had a hole cutter and the hole was cut using a gallipot or a small flower pot as a guide and a knife to do the cutting.

The exact size was not of the greatest importance because practically all golf was matchplay golf; whatever the size of the hole, it was the same for each player. Handicaps were invented for each match between old friends who knew one another's form exactly and who could always be relied upon to arrange a game so that it

was a good, keen contest; any strokes that were to be given were taken at the holes mutually agreed – there was no Club arrangement as to where strokes should be taken.

There was another reason why the size of the hole did not matter too much; after the hole had been cut it did not remain the same size for long. In early days there were no tins in the hole and it was the custom for the sand for making a tee for the next drive to be taken from the bottom of the hole; as a result, the hole became larger and deeper and developed ragged edges. If it were left in the same place long enough it could become markedly larger, extremely ragged and so deep that the player who holed out had some difficulty in removing his ball. Horace Hutchinson recalls that at Westward Ho! in the late 1860s a burrowing rabbit's hole joined up with the bottom of the hole on one of the greens. Players who holed out found that their balls completely disappeared. The matter was not reported to the Secretary for several days. Hutchinson said that he thought the rabbit had set up as a second-hand ball dealer and was selling the balls to the professional!

Grierson, in his *Delineations of St Andrews* (1858), states that the edges of the holes were neat when cut but as the caddies took sand from the bottom of the hole, they became larger and more ragged but that this enlargement was offset by the roughness of the green. It might be thought that, as taking the sand from the bottom of the hole was the cause of the trouble, Secretaries would instruct caddies to stop following this practice, but this was far from the case. In 1870 a Notice was placed in a conspicuous position in the Clubhouse of the Elie Club; it read as follows: 'The destruction caused to the green [meaning, in those days the whole course, *Author*] by the prevalent practice of taking sand from the course instead of from the Hole is becoming so serious that the Committee feel compelled in the interests of the game to request that all golfers will abstain from this pernicious practice and will positively prohibit their caddies from infringing this regulation.'

Hall Blyth, writing of 1856 comments: 'The introduction of tins in the holes had not then taken place; there were no teeing boxes, and the caddie obtained sand for tees from the holes, so they got deepened and worn at the sides becoming sometimes far too large.'

Ernest Lehman writing to *Golf Illustrated* in 1929 reported that he played at St Andrews in 1876 and that there were at that time no tin linings to the holes. Sand for tees was taken by the caddie from the bottom of the hole. He continues: 'The state of the hole towards the end of the week can well be imagined, and would have satisfied the most ardent advocate of the larger hole because the ball would trickle into the hole from all sides owing to their large size and dilapidated and ragged state.'

The fact that sand had to be taken from the bottom of the hole is a pointer as to the size of the hole. A man's hand, at its widest, is about 4 inches; it can be passed down a hole smaller than this but, if that hand has to hold a fistful of sand, as when a caddie takes enough sand to make four golf tees, it must definitely be at least that size. Holes must have been cut before there were gallipots or small flower pots to act as a guide and, in the absence of these, the simplest method was to put your fist on the ground and use it as a diameter to cut a circle; as one would not want to cut oneself, a small margin around the hand was necessary and this would give a hole of about 4¼–4½ inches diameter. Another reason for having a good margin around the fist was the fact that, as the hole got deep, not only the hand but a part of the sleeve of the jacket would need to go into the hole when reaching in for the sand. It was well known that the hole would get ragged edges and larger with use, so the canny men who cut the holes probably recognised that the hole would end up about 5 inches in diameter before another one was cut.

Such early hole cutters as exist do not suggest a standard hole; a very ancient hole cutter from Musselburgh (1823) has a cylinder of 4¼ inches; yet another, believed to have been used in the St Andrews area in about the mid 1800s, has a 4-inch cylinder and a wrought-iron hole cut-

ter of about 1850 has a diameter of 3¼ inches. It is recorded by the Royal Wimbledon Golf Club that, in 1875, the holes on their course were 3 inches in diameter.

In 1888, 4 years before the R&A made its pronouncement, a letter to *The Field*, signed 'A Fossil' – bemoans the size of the holes at Luffness Golf Club. The writer states: 'My desire is to see a rule determining the size of the golf hole on all links. On Luffness the holes are so large and the greens so good that a fair player will generally hole out from any distance short of three yards, while at Sandwich they are so small that they add at least 5 strokes to the round. . . I have found holes on different greens ranging from 3½ inches to 4½.'

Another player asks the Editor of *The Times* what is the proper size of a hole remarking that he has found them to vary, on different golf courses, between 4 and 4½ inches.

H.B. Farnie, writing in 1857, says that the size of a golf hole is 'about 4 inches in diameter'.

Robert Forgan, eminent clubmaker at St Andrews, in a glossary of terms in his *Golfers Handbook* (1888) writes of a '4-inch hole lined with tin'.

One of the reasons for standardisation was because of the growth of scoreplay at the expense of matchplay. The idea of handicaps was well to the fore and it was clearly difficult to equate the handicap of a player from a links which had, say, 4½ inch holes with that of one who came from a links where the size was 4 inches.

It became necessary for the R&A to come to a conclusion in this matter; when they decided upon 4¼ inches, this gave rise to yet further correspondence and differences of opinion.

A golfer wrote, after the Open Championship at Sandwich in 1894, that he had measured the holes with care and found that they were only 4 inches in diameter. (Could it have been that, despite the ruling of 1892, Royal St Georges had used the same hole cutter that they had used in earlier times and which 'Fossil' had said resulted in smaller holes?!)

This statement aroused John Low, an international golfer and renowned putter who, in later life, became Chairman of the Rules of Golf Committee of the R&A. In his letter to the Editor of *Golf* in 1894 he starts by doubting the truth of the assertion that the holes at Sandwich were only 4 inches in diameter. He then goes on: 'It would also be interesting if any of the Committee who framed the new Rules were to state why they fixed 4¼ inches instead of 4½ inches. I am strongly of the opinion that the latter was, before 1891, the usual size. At Carnoustie, in my memory, the holes used always to be slightly larger than at St Andrews but I think both were over 4¼ inches. At Perth, the holes are 4½ inches and probably have been so for the last two or three centuries. I know that on many links, the tins had to be made smaller to meet new Regulations.'.

Tins certainly existed in 1880 and those who wrote about hole sizes state that tins were not used in 1860. They may have been introduced gradually, according to local needs and finances, because, once the tins were there, the caddies could no longer take sand from the hole. If the 'pernicious habit' were not to be renewed the Club would have to provide sand boxes on the tees – a further expense! At Elie, in 1874, they gave authority for 'the getting of iron bands for the holes'; this was probably a useful device for protecting hole sides but leaving the bottom of the hole free for the caddies to take sand from it and was probably the start of the whole idea of lining the hole with a complete tin.

To complete the saga of hole size it is necessary to move forward into the twentieth century. The edict of the R&A in 1892 was not readily accepted and there were plenty who did not agree with it; when play became very slow in the 1920s, the idea of a larger hole was promulgated because, it was felt, it would speed up play.

The principal protagonist was Mr Maxwell-Lyte, who felt that the new ball had made the long game easier and that, to restore the balance, the short game should be made easier. He also felt that golf would become quicker and it would make negotiation of stymies a more practical proposition.

There were those for and those against and much correspondence in the golfing journals; in the end, the larger (5 inch) hole was put to the test and a competition was arranged in July 1929 at West Hill in which a field of eminent amateurs would try out the idea.

Before the great event took place, letters continued to fill pages in the golfing journals. An Editorial in *Golf Illustrated* in August 1929 contradicts Maxwell-Lyte's idea that all the undulations between the ball and the hole cannot be calculated with total accuracy suggesting that luck plays a big part in putting, which would partly be eliminated by a larger hole. Maxwell-Lyte gave his opinion that a really first-class player would put the ball within 3–4 yards of the hole when playing from 50 yards and that he would be properly rewarded for this by making his putt easier by the use of a larger hole.

**Outline of the hole has been cut using a pocket knife around a clenched fist. The piece of cardboard is exactly 4¼ inches long**

**Hole at Westward Ho! ten hours after it was cut. The cardboard is 4¼ inches long**

Maxwell-Lyte says that he does not criticise those who, in 1892, chose 4¼ inches as the best size because they could not have foreseen the great developments in improved golf courses and in the Haskell ball which would make the long game easier but that, as the long game was easier, then putting should also be made easier to maintain the balance. He speaks of the different sizes of hole in the past and points out that when Tom Morris was given the essential emblems of his trade he was given a spade, a wheelbarrow and a shovel – but no hole cutter. He continued to hold that the different grasses on the green, the many undulations and the fact that the ball was not perfectly balanced, made exact calculations about a putt impossible.

The latter idea was reinforced for the author about thirty years ago when he had the good fortune to sit next to the late Joe Davis at a dinner. When the greatest snooker player that the world has ever known said that he played golf, the author suggested that he must be a very good putter. The immediate and very positive response indicated that this had been said to Mr Davis many times before. He said that, if the author would place six balls in the centre of the top end of the table, he would guarantee to pot all of them into the bottom corner pocket; if, however, the author were to sprinkle cigarette ash on the line of the pots he could only guarantee to pot 5 out of 6. Davis then pointed out that if one considered the weight of a snooker ball and the influence on it of cigarette ash and then considered the weight of a golf ball and the obstacles in the line of a putt, such as grasses of different textures, tiny pieces of grit, old pitch marks and, on a wet day, different amounts of water droplets held by different grasses, the putt became so chancy that he wondered how anyone ever holed anything!

On 25 October 1929 the great experiment was tried at West Hill Golf Club; the day was wet, the holes were 5 inches in diameter and about 100 amateur golfers of varying handicaps took part. So popular was the idea that the entry lists were over-subscribed two weeks before the tournament took place.

The conclusions, in brief, were that most of those who took part preferred the smaller hole but a substantial

**Impressions at the larger hole competition at West Hill Golf Club**

minority preferred the larger hole. A number of competitors 3 putted and many said that the hole looked so large that the first putt was hit with reckless abandon but that, on sizing up the long return putt, the hole appeared to have contracted!

The premise that the good players' good approaches would benefit from an easier putt was by no means proved. That which suggested that play would be speeded up was completely disproved. The evidence for the idea that an accurately hit putt would always go in from up to 6 feet was not conclusive.

The notion that stymies would be easier to play was proved to be true.

A. Frostick, a professional, invented a machine for hitting putts. When he demonstrated his machine which hit the ball accurately and at the right strength, although he claimed that the machine proved the various points he had made about the 4¼ inch hole being satisfactory. No one seems to have taken much notice of it.

Those who favoured the larger hole said that putting was easier, mainly because of the psychological effect – the ball was hit firmly and well because the size of the hole gave the player confidence.

One player pointed out that putting might be easier with a larger hole but this did not mean that it was necessarily fairer. Several competitors suggested further trials but nothing ever came of the idea and the standard hole remains 4¼ inches to this day.

If the experiment and the arguments about it accomplished anything, they led to some research into the history of the game and this established the fact that there had never been, in the past, a standard hole; the decision of 1892 had been purely arbitrary.

During the controversy about whether the hole should be larger, a letter was written to one of the golf magazines, which stated that, whatever size the hole was originally cut, it would not remain the same because, the writer averred, the edge would contract and the hole become smaller; it was suggested that the hole would become smaller within two hours of being cut. No comment was made, in the subsequent numbers of the golf magazine, to contradict this statement, presumably because all attention was on the size of the hole when cut.

The statement was made so positively that the writer might well have been speaking from first-hand experience and it seemed that it might be worth investigating the matter. The author found that a golf hole, measured two days after it had been cut, was between ⅛ and ¼ inch smaller, i.e. it was 4⅛th inches down to 4 inches in diameter; a hole measured two hours after it had been cut was

4¼ inches in diameter; eight hours after it had been cut the hole was ⅛th inch smaller. This diminution in size was exaggerated because there was a tendency for the grass at the edges to grow in a little.

In matchplay the conditions would be the same for each party and the smaller hole would not affect the result of the game but in medal play those who went out 8 hours after the holes were cut would be at a disadvantage to the earlier competitors.

Why should this be? Perhaps it is because the pressure of the tin below the edge. Perhaps it is because of the pressure of many feet around the hole, because, when a ball is taken out of the hole, one foot, at least, with all the player's weight upon it, is placed near the hole. Possibly it is because the earth dries out above the tin and some contraction occurs. Most probably it is a combination of a number of factors – whatever the cause, a change occurs in the hole size 8 hours after it has been cut.

Quite recently, Mark McNulty, playing in a tournament when there had been a lot of rain, decided that the hole was smaller and demanded re-measurement; we are not told what the measurement was but the hole had to be recut; the newspaper correspondent decided that this diminution in the size of the hole was due to the pressure applied by those using a 'squeegee' to get the water off the greens. It seems possible, from this, that the diminution in hole size is more likely when the greens are wet and is therefore more likely in warmer climates when the greens are well watered. To assess the effect of climate and different terrain on hole contraction the author measured golf holes in Malaysia, Japan and Australia: everywhere the hole contracted to the same degree as it had done at Westward Ho!, St Andrews and other courses where measurements had been made.

A difference of ⅛th of an inch does not seem that great but, combined with a little ingrowth of the grass edges which makes the hole seem even smaller, the hole may appear to be only 4 inches in diameter and this will have an effect, in that, putts which lip the hole might, with a larger hole, have always gone in; the psychological effect on the player could be considerable.

Perhaps, if the hole were cut with a board in position and the greenkeeper's weight on the board, the cutting would take place with the earth around the hole already under compression and subsequent contraction of the hole would either be less or not occur at all; additionally, there would be no crowning of the hole. Efforts should be made to ensure that the tin is always sunk the same distance below the rim of the hole and it would be advantageous to have the tin as near the surface as is practicable.

# Bibliography

*Allan Robertson, Golfer*, A.B. Adamson, Worcester 1985

*The Bobby Jones Story*, O.B. Keeler and Grantland Rice, Cincinnati 1980 (reprint)

*Bobby Locke on Golf*, Bobby Locke, London 1953

*The Book of Golf and Golfers*, Horace G. Hutchinson, London 1899

*British Clubs*, Bernard Darwin, London 1943

*The Chronicles of the Royal Burgess Golfing Society, 1735–1935*, Vol.1, Edinburgh 1936

*The Complete Golfer*, Harry Vardon, London 1912

*Early Golf*, Steven J.H. van Hengel, Netherlands 1982

*Early Golf in Edinburgh and Leith*, David Hamilton, Glasgow 1988

*Early Irish Golf*, William H. Gibson, Dublin 1988

*The Encyclopædia of Golf Collectibles*, John M. and Morton W. Olman, Cincinnati 1985

*F. G. Tait: A Record*, J.L. Low, London 1900

*Fifty Years of Golf*, Horace G. Hutchinson, London 1914

*A Game of Golf*, Francis Ouimet, London 1932

*The Game of Golf*, Willie Park Jnr, London 1896

*Golf*, Horace G. Hutchinson, London (Badminton Library) 1892

*Golf*, Cecil Leitch, London 1922

*Golf: A Royal and Ancient Game*, R. Clarke, Edinburgh 1875

*Golf between the Wars*, Bernard Darwin, London 1944

*The Golf Book of East Lothian*, John Kerr, Haddington/Stevenage 1987 (reprint)

*Golf in New Zealand: A Centennial History*, G.M. Kelley, New Zealand Golf Association 1971

*Golf Illustrated*, various issues 1890–1943

*Golf in the Making*, Ian Henderson and David Stirk, Winchester 1979

*Golf is My Game*, Bobby Jones, London 1963

*Golf Monthly*, various issues 1890–1943

*Golf, My Life's Work*, J.H. Taylor, London 1943

*Golf: The Great Clubmakers*, David Stirk, London 1992

*The Great Yarmouth and Caister Golf Club 1882–1982*, M. Powlesland, published by the Club 1982

*Green Memories*, Bernard Darwin, London 1928

*The Guinness Book of Facts and Feats*, edited by Donald Steel, London 1980

*A History of Golf*, Robert Browning, London 1955

*A History of Golf in Britain*, Bernard Darwin et al., London 1952

*The History of the R&A*, J.B. Salmond, London 1956

*The History of the Royal Company of Archers*, John Balfour Paul, Edinburgh 1875

*The History of Royal Wimbledon Golf Club*, Charles Cruikshank, published by the Club 1986

*In the Wind's Eye: North Berwick Golf Club*, A.B. Adamson, Edinburgh 1980

*James Braid*, Bernard Darwin, London 1958

*John Ball of Hoylake*, John Behrend, Worcester 1989

*Ladies Golf*, May Hezlet, London 1907

*The Life of Tom Morris*, W.W. Tulloch, Bury St Edmunds 1982 (reprint)

*The Lytham Century 1886–1986*, E.A. Nickson, published by the author 1986

*Muirfield: The Home of the Honourable Company*, Norman Mair, Edinburgh 1994

*Muirfield and the Honourable Company*, George Pottinger, Edinburgh 1972

*My Golfing Album*, Henry Cotton, London 1959

*My Golfing Life*, Harry Vardon, London 1933

*The Norman Heritage 1066–1200*, Trevor Rowley, London 1983

*The Norman Kings*, James Chambers, London 1981

*The Old Manchester Golf Club 1818–1988*, Jean M. Russell, Kendal 1988

Old Minutes of Royal Wimbledon Golf Club, 1865–1929

*The Parks of Musselburgh*, John Adams, Worcester 1991

*Prestwick Golf Club, Birthplace of the Open*, edited by David Cameron Smail, Glasgow 1989

*Prestwick St Nicholas Golf Club*, William Galbraith, Alva 1950

*Royal Adelaide Golf Club 1892–1992*, Michael Cudmore, published by the Club 1992

*Royal and Ancient Championship Records*, edited by Peter Ryde, published by the Club 1981

*Royal Blackheath*, Ian Henderson and David Stirk, published by the Club 1995 (second edition)

*The Royal Calcutta Golf Club: 150th Anniversary 1829–1979*, Pearson Surita, Calcutta 1979

*Royal Colombo Golf Club: 100 Years 1879–1979*, Pam Fernando et al., Colombo 1979

*Royal Golf Club de Belgique 1906–1986*, Antwerp 1986

*The Royal Liverpool Golf Club*, Guy B. Farrar, Birkenhead 1933

*The Royal Melbourne Golf Club*, Joseph Johnson, Melbourne 1991

*The Royal Montreal Golf Club 1873–1973*, edited by Duncan C. Campbell, Montreal 1973

*The Royal North Devon Golf Club 1864–1989*, E.J. Davies and G.W. Brown, published by the Club 1989

*Royal Perth: A History of the Club*, Jack Lee, Perth (Western Australia) 1978

*The Royal Sydney Golf Club: The First Hundred Years*, Colin Tatz and Brian Stoddard, Sydney 1993

*Scottish Hazard*, Beryl Platts, Vol.1 London 1965; Vol. 2 London 1990

*The Second Crusade and the Cistercians*, Michael Gervers, New York 1922

*South Africa's Wonderful World of Golf*, Paddy O'Donnell, 1973

*St Andrews, Home of Golf*, James K. Robertson, Edinburgh 1984

*The Story of the Open Championship*, Charles G. Mortimer and Fred Pignon, London 1952

*The Sunley Book of Royal Golf Clubs*, Sir Peter Allen, London 1989

*A Swing through Time in Scotland*, Olive M. Geddes, Edinburgh 1992

*The Temple and the Lodge*, Michael Baigent and Richard Leigh, London 1990

*Thanks for the Game*, Henry Cotton, London 1980

*This Game of Golf*, Henry Cotton, London 1948

*The Walter Hagen Story*, Walter Hagen, London 1957

# Index of Names

Abercrombie, J.F. 333
Aberdeen 35, 37, 47, 65, 108, 120
Aberdeen Golf Club 121
Aberdovey 301
Aberlady 172
Adair, Rhona 278, 284, 287
Adams, Jimmy 271
Adams, Sir Charles 113
Adelaide 190, 292, 311
Aldeburgh Golf Club 305, 310
Alexander, Sir George 102
Alexander, Thomas 111, 122, 123, 126, 210
Alexandria Sporting Club, Egypt 197
Alison, C.H. 333
Allan, A.J.T. 301
Allan, John 127, 164, 217, 331
Allis, Percy 265, 269
Alnmouth Golf Club 73, 223
Anderson, David ('Old Da') 71, 125
Anderson, David junior 71, 125
Anderson, James senior 71, 72, 84, 218, 219, 222, 223
Anderson, James junior 72, 148
Anderson and Blyth 72
Andrew, Bob 219, 223
Anstruther, Fife 84, 119
Anstruther, Sir Ralph 113
Antill, Captain H.C. 190
Antwerp 16, 194
Arbuckle, James 36
Archerfield 172
Argentina 198, 260, 262, 293
Armour, T.D. 267
Asquith, Herbert 275
Assaba, Nigeria 190
Atholl, Marquess of 54
Auchterlonie, Laurie 110
Auchterlonie, W. 328
Australia 105, 187, 190, 192, 252, 292, 305
Austria 196

Baberton Golf Club 319
Bad Homburg 194
Bailey, Andrew 75
Baird, Sir David 115, 174
Balfour, A.J. 171
Balfour, James 113, 136, 172
Balfour, John 173, 176
Balfour, Leslie 173, 234, 328
Ball, John senior 127, 159
Ball, John junior 127, 156, 158–61, 164, 251, 258, 303, 328
Ballantyne, William 112
Bangkok Golf Club 178
Barnes, Jim 254
Barton, Pam 290
Belgium 14, 15, 194, 195, 262, 293, 333
Belshes, Major 48
Berg, Patty 295
Bergen-op-Zoom 108
Berwick, William 107
Bethune, Alexander 26
Bethune, Henry 25
Bethune, John (of Blebo) 25
Bethune, John (of Nydie) 26
Biarritz 70, 193, 194, 204, 249
Blackheath Goffers (see Society of Golfers at Blackheath)

Blackheath Golf Club (see Royal Blackheath Golf Club)
Blackheath Golf Club (New South Wales) 42, 190
Blackheath Ladies Golf Club 275
Blackwell, Edward 234, 253
Blair, William 113
Blyth, Arnold 328
Blyth, David 72
Blyth, Hall 114, 115, 328
Bombay Golf Club 42, 185, 291
Bonny, Nigeria 190
Boomer, Aubrey 255, 262, 265
Bothwell, Earl of 32, 35
Boulogne, Duc de 18, 25
Bournemouth 70
Braid, James 88, 101, 165, 228, 229, 241–3, 245–9, 251, 268, 305
Bright, George 309
British Golf Museum, St Andrews 170, 313, 317
Brown, David 224
Bruce family, 27, 28
Bruce, George 274
Bruen, James 214
Bruntsfield 53–5, 66, 75, 123, 130, 331
Bruntsfield Links Golfing Society 37, 46, 55, 111, 119, 120, 330
Bulawayo 189
Burnham-on-Sea Golf Club 226, 250, 262, 265, 332
Burton, Richard 269
Bury Golf Club 228
Bushey Hall Golf Club 302
Butchart, Cuthbert 308

Cadenabbia 194
Cairo Khedival Sporting Club 197
Caister and Yarmouth Golf Club 305, 310
Calcutta Golf Club (see Royal Calcutta Golf Club)
Callendar, Henry 135, 140
Campbell, Dorothy 287, 292
Campbell, Sir Guy 19
Campbell of Saddaw 169, 173, 174
Campbell, Willie 177, 224, 296
Canada 87, 287, 288, 328, 333
Cannes 194, 197, 262, 298
Cantelupe Golf Club, Ashdown Forest 258
Cape Town 189
Capilano Golf Course, Vancouver 198
Carnegie, George 169
Carnoustie 31, 86
Carnoustie Golf Club 32, 84, 163, 183, 244, 270, 336
Carr, Florence 277
Carrick, Alex 83
Carrick, Archibald 83
Carrick, F.&A. 83, 122
Carrick, Francis 83
Carrick, Margaret 83
Caversham, Otago 191
Ceylon (see Sri Lanka)
Chambers, Robert 74, 147
Channel Islands 227
Charles I 21, 24, 25, 32
Charteris, Hon. Francis (later Fifth Earl of Wemyss) 26
Cheape, George 28, 274

Cheape, James 28
Chicago Golf Club 182
Christchurch, New Zealand 191, 292
Churston Golf Club 250
Collett, Glenna 207, 289, 292, 294, 295
Colt, H.S. 333
Comb, Thomas 55, 66, 123
Compston, Archie 235, 261
Condamine, Charles de la 112
Condie, Robert 84
Constant Spring Links, Jamaica 178
Coombe Hill Golf Club 261, 263, 309
Cosgrove, Alex 111
Cossar, David 65
Cossar, Simon 65, 66
Cotton, Henry 242, 244, 259, 260, 262, 266–71, 288
Crawford, 'Fiery' 131, 171
Crawford, McGregor and Canby 84
Cromer 282, 295
Crookham Golf Club 191, 192
Culloden, Battle of 28, 30, 59
Cumberland, Duke of 28, 50
Cummings, Edith 294
Currie, William 117
Curtis, Harriet 295
Curtis, Margaret 295

Dalhousie, Lord 32, 169
Dalrymple, David 28
Dalrymple, Sir Hugh (later Lord Drummore) 28
Dalrymple, Lieut. James 121
Dalrymple of Leven 112
Darwin, Bernard 127, 158, 160, 237, 238, 243, 244, 252, 259, 264, 271, 272, 301
David I, King of Scotland 20, 22, 23, 25, 31–4, 38, 46, 47
David II, King of Scotland 23
Davis, William 330
Dawlish Warren Golf Club 301
Day, W.D. 112
Day, William 150
Deal 241, 250
Deas, David 179, 180
Deepwater Bay Golf Club, Hong Kong 189
Denholm, David 71, 123
Denmark 196
Dennistoun, Alexander 197, 198
Dickson, Andrew 120, 121
Dickson, John 65, 107, 120, 121
Dickson, William 120, 121
Dickson, W.&T. 65, 120, 121
Diegel, Leo 237, 254
Dinard 194
Dodd, Lottie 284, 292
Doleman, W. 219
Dornoch 53, 183
Dougal, Admiral Maitland 113
Dougall, Captain Maitland 148
Douglas, Earl of (Scots Guard) 39
Dow, Willie 212, 214, 219
Drummond, David 55
Dudley, Ed 265, 269
Duff, General 194
Duncan, Alexander 48, 145, 324
Duncan, George 258, 260, 306, 308
Dunedin 191

Dunn, Jamie 70, 111, 124, 130, 153, 211, 217, 219
Dunn, Thomas 70, 130, 171
Dunn, Willie senior 70, 111, 124, 130, 153, 209–212, 216–20
Dunn, Willie junior 70, 130
Durham, James 145

East Africa 189
East India Company 42, 112, 184
Edinburgh 28, 29, 31, 36, 38, 43–6, 53, 66, 107, 108, 113, 119, 121, 198, 301
Edinburgh Burgess Golfing Society 37, 43, 44, 66, 71, 120, 123, 135, 156
Eglinton, Earls of 31, 33, 122, 169
Egypt 197
Elcho, Lord (see also Wemyss, Earls of) 152, 172
Eldon, Lord 250, 276
Elgin, Earls of 27, 28
Elphinstone, Alexander 121, 147
Eltham Golf Club 309
Etretat 194
Evans, Chick 254
Everard, H.S.C. 209, 223, 275, 328
Exeter Golf Club 247, 261

Fair, Talbot 275
Fairlie, David 170
Fairlie, Frank 170, 187
Fairlie, James Ogilvie 128, 147, 148, 153, 169, 170, 174, 212, 220
Fairlie, J.O.R. 170, 219
Fairlie, W.E. 170
Farnie, H.B. 336
Ferguson, Bob 112, 164, 212, 216, 218, 223, 224
Ferguson, S. Mure 157, 234, 328
Fernie, Willie 222, 224, 328
Fischer, John 328
Flanders 13, 18, 21, 22, 35, 39, 90, 107
Forbes, Duncan 29, 30, 44, 51, 54, 145
Forgan, Andrew 69
Forgan, Peter Lawrence 69, 70
Forgan, Robert 56, 68, 69, 71, 72, 74, 76, 87, 116, 226, 336
Forgan, Thomas 56, 69
Foulis, Sir John 130, 172
Fowler, W.H. 333
France 10, 13, 14, 18, 21, 246, 247, 288, 293, 333
Fraser, Alexander 123
Fraser, George 149
Fraser's Hill Golf Club, Malaya 188
Frostick, A. 339
Fry, S.H. 165, 234

Ganton, Yorkshire 225, 227
Gaudin, Phillip 227, 240
Geddes, Tom 111
Gentleman Golfers at Edinburgh 28, 29, 31 (see also Honourable Company of Edinburgh Golfers)
Gentleman Golfers at Leith 30, 31, 44, 54, 58, 330
George II 50
Gibraltar 196
Gibson, Charles 226, 227, 332
Gibson, John 115
Gibson of Kinghorn 95
Gillies, C.E.S. 192
Gillies, Harold 192
Gilrow, T. 275
Glasgow 36, 108, 114, 115, 330
Glasgow, Treaty of (1501) 23, 35
Gleneagles 247
Glennie, George 141, 153, 154, 218
Gosford 24, 26, 172
Gossett, George 191, 292
Gourlay family 67, 107–9
Gourlay, James senior 87

Gourlay, James junior 87
Gourlay, John 123, 126, 130
Gourlay, Mollie 290
Gourlay, William senior 111, 114, 115, 122
Gourlay, William junior 111
Grace, Charles 135
Grace, Dr W.G. 242
Grace, Stuart primus 135
Grace, Stuart secundus 135
Graham, John ('Jack') 127, 252, 258, 267
Grant, Arthur 307
Gray, Christian 275
Gray, John 86, 122
Greenwich Hospital 113, 131, 140
Greig, William 165
Gressick, David 111
Griffiths, Molly 290
Groom, A.H. 199
Guldahl, Ralph 269
Gullane Golf Club 172, 297, 304
Gulmarg Golf Course, Kashmir 187
Gunn, 'Daft' Willie 93

Hagen, Walter 142, 233, 254–6, 260–2, 265, 269
Hainault Forest Golf Club 245
Hamel, Gustave 302
Hamilton, General Alexander 34
Hamilton, Archbishop 33, 53
Hamilton, David 22
Hamilton, Dukes of 33, 55
Harare 189
Harris, Robert 64, 263
Harrogate 227
Haskell balls 137, 230, 235, 281, 316, 317
Hastings, Battle of 19, 20, 27
Havers, Arthur 254, 258, 261
Hay, Major George 33
Hay, Sir Robert 220
Hay, Thomas 33
Henry I 33
Henry VIII 21
Henry Frederick, son of James I of England 24
Herd, Alexander ('Sandy') 125, 165, 236, 240, 241, 246, 248, 260, 309
Herd, Robert 309
Hewitt, Walter 86, 87
Hezlet, Florence 284
Hezlet, May 284
Hicks, Helen 296
Hillène, Henry J. 17
Hilton, Horace Harold 127, 164–6, 234, 251, 252, 288, 328
Holderness, Sir Ernest 263–5
Holland 11, 13, 18, 21, 35, 107, 108, 181, 196
Hollins, Marion 294
Hollinwell 225, 333
Hong Kong 188, 189
Honourable Company of Edinburgh Golfers 26, 30, 36, 37, 44–6, 48, 51, 55, 65, 91, 111, 123, 126, 137, 147, 149, 150, 156, 167, 168, 170, 173, 179, 305, 311, 324
Hood, Thomas 112
Horsburgh, Thomas 319
Howden, Charles Ritchie 191
Hoylake (see Royal Liverpool Golf Club)
Hoyt, Beatrix 294
Hunter, Charles 73, 86, 128, 129
Huntercombe 225, 333
Hutchings, Charles 234, 328
Hutchinson, Horace 60, 76, 115, 154, 156–64, 170, 172, 173, 175, 181, 191, 192, 194, 215, 223, 234, 242, 273, 335
Hutchison, Jock 254, 265, 266

India 184, 185, 186
Innes, Alexander 31

Innes, Gilbert Mitchell 143, 147, 148, 151
Innes, William 31, 40, 90
Italy 194

Jackson, John 58, 71, 72, 122
James I, King of Scotland 23
James II, King of Scotland 23, 34, 40
James III, King of Scotland 23
James IV, King of Scotland 23, 24, 32, 35, 53
James V, King of Scotland 172
James VI, King of Scotland (James I, King of England) 24, 28, 32, 40, 53
James II, King of England 24
Japan 199
Jones, Robert (Bobby) 84, 142, 255, 256, 257, 261, 266, 267, 328
Jurado, Jose 255

Katharine of Aragon 273
Kelso 35
Kennard, Colonel Hegan 176
Kenyon, E.W.H. 247
Ker, Daniel 43, 50
Kerr, Revd John 46, 135, 177
Kidd, Tom 222
Kilmaine, Lord 194
Kilmartin 37
Kincaid, Thomas 9, 22, 35, 54, 55, 58, 61, 107, 111, 130
Kingston and St Andrews Golf Club, Jamaica 183
Kirk, Bob 164, 168, 217–19, 331
Kirkaldy, Andrew 215, 224, 226, 228, 328
Kirkaldy, Hugh 165, 228
Kirkwood, Joe 255
Knights Templar 37, 38, 39, 52
Knocke 194
Knuckle Club (Blackheath) 40–2, 52, 135, 151
Kobe Golf Club 199, 200, 205
Kronenberg 11, 14
Kuala Lumpur 187, 188, 201

La Boulie Golf Club, France 193, 194, 225, 251
Laidlay, J.E. 160, 163–5, 224, 228, 234
Lamb, Henry 64, 72, 155, 156, 160, 331
Lang, Bennett 71
'Lang Willie' 108, 111, 133
Langley Park Golf Club 262
Las Palmas 196
Leach, Henry 41
Leach, John 41
Learmonth, Patrick 53
Le Coq sur Mer 204
Lehman, Ernest 336
Leitch, Cecile 288, 290, 292, 295
Leitch, Peggy 285
Leith 24–6, 31, 39, 44, 46, 47, 53–5, 58, 65, 66, 107, 111, 119–21, 123, 130, 136, 179, 193, 223, 331
Leith Thistle Club 70, 130, 136, 146
Leslie, James 27
Leslie, Hon. Thomas 27
Le Touquet 194, 293
Leven 86, 112, 119
Lewis, P.N. 317
Leyden 11
Lindsay, Alexander (Scots Guard) 39
Lindsay, Sir James 172
Little, Lawson 271, 272
Littlestone 277
Locke, A.D. 271
London Scottish Golf Club 155, 275
Lowe, George 227
Low, Sir John 234, 236, 297, 328, 336
Luffness Golf Club 27, 172, 212, 223, 225, 336

McDermott, Jimmie 254
Macdonald, C.B. 175, 318
Macdonald, Sir John 28
MacDonald, Walter ('Watty') 60, 71
MacDowell, Charles 43
McEwan, Douglas 67
McEwan, James 57–9, 71, 97, 111, 130
McEwan, Peter (1781–1836) 67
McEwan, Peter (1834–95) 67
MacFie, A. 234
MacKenzie, Charles 43
MacKenzie, John 75
McLean, Jack 328
McNulty, Mark 339
McPherson, J.G. 209
MacPherson, Revd J.G. 112
Macrihanish Golf Club 128, 299, 301
Maidstone Golf Course, USA 333
Malcolm IV, King of Scotland 33
Malta 196, 197
Mar, Earl of (Scots Guard) 39
Mar del Plata Golf Course, Argentina 198
Martin, Blanche 275
Martin, Bob 222, 224
Mary, Queen of Scots 24, 31, 172
Massy, Arnaud 194, 236, 246, 251
Mathison, Thomas 28, 29, 30, 51, 65, 111
Maud, Queen (of Scotland) 20, 22, 25, 31, 32, 33
Maule, Patrick (Lord Panmure) 32
Maule, Hon. Patrick Fox (Lord Dalhousie) 32
Maule, Sir Robert 31
Maule, William Ramsay 32
Mauritius 197
Maxwell, Robert 165, 234, 249, 251, 252
Maxwell-Lyte, Mr 337
Mayne, William 24, 53
Mayo, Charles 307, 308
Melbourne, Australia 190, 292, 311
Melvill, Andrew 35
Melville, James 107
Melville, James Balfour (see Balfour, James)
Menaggio 194
Meru, Kenya 189
Mesopotamia 197
Messieux, Samuel 115
Michael, Grand Duke 171, 197
Midlothian Golf Club, Chicago 181, 301
Mill, George 125
Mills aluminium head 96
Milne, Alexander 43
Minoprio, Gloria 2
Mitchell, Abe 258, 259, 260
Molesworth, Arthur 176
Molesworth, Captain George Frederick 127, 175, 208, 331
Molesworth, George 176
Molesworth, Reginald 176
Moncrieff, Sir Matthew 34
Moncrieff of that Ilk, Sir Ian 34
Moncrieffe, Sir David 150
Monte Carlo 225, 333
Montgomerie, William 112
Montreal 87, 197, 198
Montrose 213
Montrose, Duke of 75
Moortown 261
Morgan, Wanda 290
Morris, George 73, 84, 127
Morris, Jack 59, 73, 127, 129, 331
Morris, J.O.F. 73, 74, 220
Morris, Tom senior 60, 61, 73, 74, 83, 84, 86, 93, 108, 115, 125, 127–9, 134, 148, 153, 158, 169, 209, 211–17, 219, 220, 223, 328, 332
Morris, Tom junior 73, 74, 76, 127, 148, 151, 164, 176, 213, 214, 217–23, 225
Mount Bruno Golf Course, Montreal 198, 333

Muirfield 150, 163, 164, 224, 245, 246, 252, 301, 305, 311
Muirfield Village Club, Ohio 150
Munro of Aberdeen 58, 71, 121
Murray, Earl of (Scots Guard) 39
Murray, Wolfe 211
Musselburgh 53, 55, 57, 58, 70, 72, 83, 105, 111, 114, 115, 119, 123, 130, 164, 211
Musselburgh Golf Club (see Royal Musselburgh Golf Club)
Muthiago, Kenya 189

Nairn Ladies Club 334
Nairobi 189
Napoule 197
Neilson, Alexander 55
Neilson, George 55
Neilson, Robert 55
Nelson, Byron 269
Nevile, Miss E.A. 280
New South Wales Golf Club 190
New Zealand 191, 192, 292, 305, 318
New Zealand Golf Club 156
Niblick Brigade 306–309
Nice 107, 194
Nichol, George 86
Nichol, Robert 86
Nicklaus, Jack 150
North Berwick Golf Club 27, 32, 70, 87, 115, 130, 148, 151, 164, 170–2, 174, 176, 183, 210, 212, 217, 220, 223, 225, 226, 251, 287, 297, 301, 304, 311, 330–2
North Manchester Golf Club 149, 169
Northam Artisans Golf Club 244
Northam, Devon 226, 227
Nuwara Eliya, Ceylon 187

Old Manchester Golf Club 147, 149, 151, 325
Oliphant, James Stuart 32
Oliphant, William 32
Orkney, Earls of 29
Ostend Golf Club 195
Otago, New Zealand 191, 192, 292
Ouimet, Francis 237, 254
Oxford and Cambridge Golfing Society 150, 191, 264
Oxhey 250

Padgham, A.H. 269–71
Panmure Golf Club 32, 170
Panmure, Lord 32
Paris 108, 193
Paris Golf Club (La Boulie) 193, 194, 225, 251
Park, David 72, 73, 219
Park, Jack 199
Park, James 72
Park, Jean 290
Park, Margaret 290
Park, Mungo senior 72, 73, 198, 221, 223
Park, Mungo junior 198, 293
Park, William senior 72, 73, 112, 148, 198, 211–16, 219–21, 225, 250, 332
Park, William junior 46, 72, 73, 83, 99, 112, 131, 193, 198, 223–5, 228, 290, 309, 333
Park, W. & Son 72
Pascoe, Miss A. 295
Paterson, Revd Dr 112, 113
Patersone, John 24, 65, 107, 146
Patrick, Alexander 70
Patrick, David 70
Patrick, John 70
Patrick, Nichol 70
Pau Golf Club, France 193, 194, 201, 293
Paxton, Peter 328
Pearson, Isette 275–7
Penang 187

Perry, Alf 269
Perth, Scotland 108, 213, 223
Perth (W. Australia) 291
Peters, H. Thomas 115
Phillips, Miss 277
Philp, Hugh 58, 59, 63, 67, 68, 71, 94, 95, 97, 122, 142
Picard, Henry 269
Pirie, Sandy 109, 134
Pirie, Willie 134
Pittsburgh Golf Club 182
Playfair, Sir Hugh Lyon 37, 125, 153, 170, 171, 327, 332
Playfair, Major H.L. 185
Porteous, Captain John 121, 146
Porthcawl 332
Portmarnock 298
Portrush 228, 275, 277, 281, 286, 287
Port Said Golf Club 197
Portugal 196
Potter, Thomas Owen 154, 155
Pottinger, George 29
Prestwick Golf Club 73, 74, 86, 122, 125, 127, 128, 143, 147, 148, 150, 168–70, 176, 212, 214, 218–24, 226, 228, 252, 281, 297, 331
Priestley, Joseph 112
Princes Golf Club, Mitcham 333
Princes Golf Club, Sandwich 161
Purves, Dr Laidlaw 156, 275, 328, 331

Quincy Golf Club, Illinois 182

Rangoon Golf Club 311
Ramsay, John 118
Randall, Jack 82, 100, 101
Rattray, John 28, 29, 55, 145
Ray, Edward 237, 240, 248, 250, 260
Reid, Wilfred 307, 308
Reith, W. R. 308
Rhind, Charles 43, 50, 135
Ridgeways, Sir West 187
Ripon, Lord 227
Robbie, Cameron 43
Robert II, King of Scotland 23
Robert the Bruce 23, 31, 38, 40
Robertson, Allan 58, 68, 73, 74, 104–6, 108–11, 113–15, 117, 120, 122, 125, 128, 129, 133, 138, 148, 153, 190, 209, 210, 212, 215, 217, 220
Robertson, Argyll 176
Robertson, Charles 125
Robertson, David 58, 105, 106, 111
Robertson, David junior 105
Robertson, George 105
Robertson, Peter 125
Robertson, Thomas 125
Robson, Fred 262
Rolland, Douglas 328
Rosendaelche, Holland 196
Ross, Donald 333
Rothes, Earl of 27
Rowe, John 269
Royal Aberdeen Golf Club 47
Royal Adelaide Golf Club 190, 311
Royal & Ancient Golf Club of St Andrews 26, 28, 32, 33, 37, 47–50, 53, 60, 65, 74, 101, 103, 114, 125, 135, 144, 147, 148, 150, 151, 156, 157, 159, 160, 161, 164, 168, 170, 171, 173, 176, 192, 198, 218, 235, 236, 297, 317, 318, 327, 328, 335
Royal Antwerp Golf Club 194, 225, 293
Royal Ashdown Forest Golf Club 269
Royal Blackheath Golf Club 32, 40–2, 48, 52, 70, 92, 113, 114, 120, 124, 128, 130, 131, 138, 141, 144, 146–8, 151, 154, 156, 164, 168, 169, 175, 176, 179, 184, 185, 193, 212, 275, 291, 311, 324

Royal Burgess Golfing Society (*see* Edinburgh Burgess Golfing Society)
Royal Calcutta Golf Club 42, 76, 184, 185, 291, 305, 311
Royal Colombo Golf Club 186, 201
Royal Company of Archers 26–34, 39, 53, 54, 55, 65
Royal Durban Golf Club 189
Royal Hong Kong Golf Club 188
Royal Liverpool Golf Club, Hoylake 74, 116, 127, 129, 143, 149, 154, 155, 157, 159–61, 164, 165, 168, 175, 176, 244, 250, 254, 265, 310, 331
Royal Lytham and St Annes Golf Club 150, 227, 241, 275, 301, 305, 310
Royal Melbourne Golf Club 311
Royal Mid-Surrey Golf Club 227, 245
Royal Montreal Golf Club 150, 197, 292, 311, 330
Royal Musselburgh Golf Club 37, 47, 111, 123, 148, 152, 212, 214, 216, 217, 297, 328, 333
Royal North Devon Golf Club 127, 156, 168, 175–7, 226, 227, 245, 274, 292, 315, 331, 336,
Royal Perth Golfing Society 72, 142, 149, 151, 336
Royal Selangor Golf Club 201, 292
Royal Singapore Golf Club 150, 187, 203
Royal St David's Golf Club, Harlech 335
Royal St George's, Sandwich 131, 134, 149, 156, 159, 165, 227, 228, 244, 269, 319, 330, 331, 336
Royal Sydney Golf Club 104, 117, 190, 210, 302, 311
Royal Troon Golf Club 131, 241, 286, 304, 310, 331
Royal Wimbledon Golf Club 64, 70, 150, 155, 156, 175, 176, 304, 310, 332, 336
Ryder, Samuel 259, 260
Rye Golf Club 150, 262, 300, 302, 305, 310
Rymer 19
Ryton 72

St Andrews 21, 24, 28, 29, 31, 57, 58, 65, 67, 71–3, 84, 92, 93, 105, 106, 108, 112, 113, 115, 119, 125, 127–9, 134, 148, 149, 151, 158, 163, 167, 168, 171, 174, 176, 183, 193, 209–14, 217, 218, 219, 220, 221, 222, 223, 226, 228, 245, 246, 248, 274, 289, 297, 300, 311, 325, 327, 330–2, 336
St Andrew's Golf Club, Yonkers 190
St Clair, Lieut-General James 27, 29
St Clair, William (15th century) 40
St Clair, William (of Roslyn) 26, 27, 29, 30, 54, 55, 91, 145
St Helena 190
Santa Catalina Golf Club, California 180
San Remo 195
Sarazen, Gene 142, 255, 256, 261, 265, 267, 269
Sayers, Ben 87, 171, 250, 251, 328
Scott, A.H. 63, 64, 74, 84, 87, 94
Scott, Lady Margaret 276, 277, 288
Scott, Hon. Michael 187, 252, 263, 265, 276
Scott, Osmond 276
Seaton Carew Golf Club 303, 311
Seton, Alexander 31, 33
Seton, Christopher 31
Seton, Lord George (Scots Guard) 31, 33, 34, 39, 40, 54, 55
Seton, Sir Henry 30

Seton, Mary 24
Seton, William (Scots Guard) 39
Seton Palace 24, 31, 32, 172
Shanghai Golf Club 188
Sherlock, Jim 262
Shinnecock Hills Golf Club, Long Island 180
Shute, Densmore 267, 269
Sidcup Golf Club 334
Sierra Leone 190
Silver, S.W. 113
Simpson, Bob 328
Simpson, Jack 224
Simpson, Sir Walter 131
Simpsons, Carnoustie 86, 87
Smith, Eric Martin 271
Smith, MacDonald 255, 262, 269
Smith, Horton 265, 269
Smith, Ralph 228
Smith, William 114
Snead, Sam 269
Society of Golfers at Aberdeen 37
Society of Golfers at Blackheath 31, 37, 40, 41, 90, 137, 152
Society of Golfers at St Andrews 24, 28, 30, 31, 37, 49, 50, 52, 65, 125, 135, 137, 146, 152, 323, 324
South Africa 189, 305
South Staffordshire Golf Club 304
Spain 196
Spalding Brothers 69, 319
Spark, Alex George 42, 190
Spence, Lewis 10
Spens, Dr Nathaniel 27
Sri Lanka 187, 201, 252, 291, 311
Standard Golf Company 101
Stewart, Capt. Duncan 116, 154, 218
Stewart, John (Scots Guard) 39
Stewart, John C. 148
Stewart, Thomas senior 84
Stewart, Thomas junior 84, 111
Stirling 66
Stirling, Alexa 292, 294, 295
Stover Golf Club 250
Straits Settlements 188
Strath, Andrew 128, 148, 212, 214, 218, 219
Strath, David 214, 221, 223
Stuart, Charles Edward 24, 29, 50
Suez 197
Sunningdale Golf Club 73, 225, 250, 333
Suttie, Elsie Grant 282

Tait, F.G. 115, 159, 162, 207, 303, 328, 329
Tasmania 190
Taylor, John Henry 82, 164, 165, 194, 196, 210, 223, 226–9, 234–6, 238, 239, 241, 242, 244–51, 253, 258, 259, 262, 268, 275, 328, 333
Teignmouth Golf Club 250
Terry, Effie 275
Thomson, Hector 271
Thomson, Miss M. 292
Thrupp, Admiral 176
Tingey, Albert 308
Tiverton Golf Club 247
Tolley, Cyril 250, 264, 265
Torrens, General Sir Harry 189, 196
Totteridge 240
Travis, Walter 101, 252, 253, 254, 318
Troon Golf Club (*see* Royal Troon Golf Club)

Tunis 204
Turner, George 309

USA 60, 64, 70, 84, 87, 101, 175, 179–81, 192, 225, 228, 231, 236, 237, 239, 246, 247, 254, 255, 258, 260–2, 266, 268, 271, 287, 293, 302, 309, 315, 317–19, 325, 333
Utrecht 11, 196

Vancouver 198
Vanderbilt, W.E. 70
Van Wie, Virginia 295
Vardon, Harry 165, 173, 183, 224–8, 233, 235, 236, 238–42, 246, 248–51, 253, 255, 260, 268–70, 288, 294
Vardon, Tom 227
Veer, Gerrit de 12
Verulam Golf Club, St Albans 260
Victoria, Princess 275
Vienna 196
Voigt, George 271

Wales, Prince of (later Edward VII) 194
Wales, Prince of (later Edward VIII) 261
Walton Heath Golf Club 301, 311
Warlop, Dr Ernest 16
Waterloo Golf Club, Belgium 262
Wedderburn, Sir Peter 172
Wemyss, Fourth Earl of 26, 27
Wemyss, Fifth Earl of 26
West Africa 190
West Drayton Golf Club 229
West Hill Golf Club 333, 337, 338
Westward Ho! 127, 152, 154, 157, 161, 164, 167, 175–7, 183, 191, 193, 206, 217, 218, 226, 235, 243, 258, 274, 281, 284, 287, 292, 331, 335
Wethered, Joyce (Lady Heathcote Amery) 266, 288, 289, 290
Wethered, Roger 254, 264, 265, 266
Whigham, David Dundas 151, 175
Whigham, Henry James 175
Whigham, Molly 175, 278, 281
Whigham, Sybil 175, 287
Whitcombe, C.A. 247, 262
Whitcombe, E.R. 262
Whitcombe, R.A. 244, 262, 269, 270, 271
White, Jack 250
White, Robert 84
Whyte Melville, John 48, 144, 150, 173, 174
William the Conqueror 19, 20, 22
William, Robert 84, 122
Wilson, Enid 290
Wilson, James 106
Wimbledon Ladies' Golf Club 275
Wimereux 194
Winchester Golf Club 226, 227
Wind, Herbert 237, 289
Winton, Earl of 31, 33
Winton, Thomas 309
Wise, Wilfred 313
Woking Golf Club 305
Worplesdon Golf Club 73, 225, 333

Yonkers, USA 175, 181, 190
York, Duke of (later James II) 65, 121, 146
York, Duke of (later George VI) 245
Young, Miss 292

Zimbabwe 189

# Acknowledgment

The illustrations of the notebook cover on p.143 and the birthday book and brooch on p.207 are reproduced by kind permission of my wife, Joan Anne.